Homecomings

Homecomings

RETURNING POWs AND THE LEGACIES OF DEFEAT IN POSTWAR GERMANY

Frank Biess

PRINCETON UNIVERSITY PRESS

PRINCETON AND OXFORD

Copyright ©2006 by Princeton University Press
Published by Princeton University Press, 41 William Street, Princeton, New Jersey 08540
In the United Kingdom: Princeton University Press, 3 Market Place,
Woodstock, Oxfordshire OX20 1SY

Library of Congress Cataloging-in-Publication Data
Biess, Frank, 1966–
Homecomings : returning POWs and the legacies of defeat in
postwar Germany / Frank Biess.
p.   cm.
Includes bibliographical references and index.
ISBN-13: 978-0-691-12502-2 (cloth : alk. paper)
ISBN-10: 0-691-12502-3 (cloth : alk. paper)
1. Germany—History—1945–1955. 2. Ex-prisoners of war—Germany—
History—20th century. 3. World War, 1939–1945—Prisoners and prisons. I. Title.
DD257.B54 2006
940.54′72′092243—dc22   2005052162

British Library Cataloging-in-Publication Data is available

This book has been composed in Sabon

Printed on acid-free paper. ∞

pup.princeton.edu

Printed in the United States of America

10 9 8 7 6 5 4 3 2 1

For Uli, with love and gratitude

Contents

List of Illustrations   ix

Acknowledgments   xi

INTRODUCTION   1

PART ONE *From War to Postwar*   17

CHAPTER ONE
Impending Defeat: Military Losses, the Wehrmacht,
and Ordinary Germans   19

CHAPTER TWO
Confronting Defeat: Returning POWs and the
Politics of Victimization   43

CHAPTER THREE
Embodied Defeat: Medicine, Psychiatry, and
the Trauma of the Returned POW   70

PART TWO *Making Citizens*   95

CHAPTER FOUR
Survivors of Totalitarianism: Returning POWs and the
Making of West German Citizens   97

CHAPTER FIVE
Antifascist Conversions: Returning POWs and the
Making of East German Citizens   126

CHAPTER SIX
Parallel Exclusions: The West German POW Trials and the
East German Purges   153

PART THREE *Divergent Paths*   177

CHAPTER SEVEN
Absent Presence: Missing POWs and MIAs   179

CHAPTER EIGHT
Divided Reunion: The Return of the Last POWs   203

CONCLUSION
Histories of the Aftermath   227

Notes   233

Bibliography   307

Index   359

List of Illustrations

FIGURE 1. German POWs in Berlin being marched off into
Soviet captivity (April–May 1945)   20

FIGURE 2. A mother welcoming her son home from Soviet
captivity.   54

FIGURE 3. *Without Home, without Possessions*, taken by the
Berlin photographer Friedrich Seidenstücker   55

FIGURE 4. Female auxiliary forces after their capture by
the Red Army, 1945   61

FIGURE 5. A returnee in the Friedland transition camp   72

FIGURE 6. *The Crowned;* by K. Sieth   103

FIGURE 7. *The Crucified*, a bronze relief by Fritz Theilmann   104

FIGURE 8. Paul Merker, the SED's expert on POW issues,
addressing a group of returned POWs in October 1948   132

FIGURE 9. Returnees leaving the transition camp in Gronenfelde
in April 1949   137

FIGURE 10. Returnees in the Gronenfelde transition camp
reading a party advertisement for the SED, October 1948   138

FIGURE 11. A two-minute traffic stoppage in Berlin on the occasion
of the POW remembrance week in 1952   188

FIGURE 12. The wife of a still missing POW arrives in Berlin to hand
over the light for the memorial candle to be lit on the occasion
of the POW commemorations in 1954   190

FIGURE 13. An enthusiastic welcome of returned POWs in the
Hessian town of Eschwege in October 1955   205

FIGURE 14. Poster advertisement for the film *The Bells of Friedland*
a documentary on the experience of returned POWs produced
by the Association of Returnees (VdH) in 1957   208

FIGURE 15. East German officials assisting returnees in crossing
the border from East to West Germany in September 1953   220

Acknowledgments

It is with great pleasure that I am finally able to acknowledge the considerable debts that I have accumulated while writing this book.

At various stages of this project, the German Historical Institute in Washington, D.C., has provided crucial support: first with the summer archive tour in 1995–96, then with a dissertation fellowship in 1998, and finally, with the first Thyssen-Heidenking Fellowship in 2002–3. As a graduate student, I benefited greatly from the support of the Institute of European History in Mainz and from the Watson Institute of International Studies at Brown. An Academic Senate research grant and a faculty career development grant from the University of California–San Diego as well as a UC-President's Fellowship provided the resources and the time to convert a dissertation into a book.

I cannot possibly name all the archivists and librarians in Germany and the United States who went out of their way to help me find materials and sources for this project. But I would like to mention the generosity of Linda Orth, who gave me access to the files of the Bonn psychiatry. I would also like to thank the men and women who were willing to share with me their experiences of war, captivity, and return home. We did not always arrive at the same conclusions about the meaning of their experiences, but I respect their genuine efforts to come to terms with their complex and contradictory past.

My first and deepest academic debt is to my advisor at Brown University, Volker Berghahn. His personal and professional support went far beyond the duties of a *Doktorvater*, and he remains a model of integrity in the academe. Carolyn Dean and David Kertzer, each in her or his own way, provided crucial advice and support. For almost a decade, Robert Moeller has followed the gestation of this project from the first dissertation proposal to the final version of this book. First as an outside reader, then, more recently, as a colleague, friend, and neighbor, he has read and reread numerous drafts. His astute and generous comments have been tremendously helpful at every stage.

I am also deeply grateful to Omer Bartov and Matt Matsuda for inviting me to spend a year as a postdoctoral fellow at the Rutgers Center for Historical Analysis. The extremely stimulating atmosphere at the Center allowed me to rethink my project and, equally important, to find a job.

Since my arrival in the fall of 2000, the University of California at San Diego has been an extraordinary—and very beautiful—place to be a historian. In particular, I would like to thank my colleagues Robert Edelman, Judith Hughes, Rebecca Plant, and Pamela Radcliff for their insightful comments on individual chapters. David Luft generously read the entire manuscript, provided many helpful suggestions, and worked much too hard in order to turn my sometimes Germanic prose into readable English. Special thanks go to Rachel Klein and Robert Westman for their warm friendship, stimulating conversations, and hospitality in San Diego.

I greatly benefited from the discussions in Hans Peter Ullmann's and Bernd Weisbrod's colloquia in Cologne and Göttingen, as well as from the inspiring conversations with Dagmar Herzog. Two colleagues from graduate school, Jonathan Wiesen and Pamela Swett, continue to serve as honest critics and close friends, a combination that is not easy to find. The same applies to Pertti Ahonen. Paul Lerner, another friend, gave me the benefit of his expertise in the history of psychiatry and trauma. Joe Busby and Evelyn Range, two excellent graduate students, offered invaluable help during the final preparation of the manuscript.

Brigitta van Rheinberg's commitment to this project was crucial, as was her patience with the author. As readers for Princeton University Press, Elizabeth Heineman and Eric Weitz provided very important feedback and much constructive criticism. I would also like to thank Richard Isomaki for his excellent editing skills.

All of these individuals made this a much better book than it otherwise would haven been. Any remaining errors and shortcomings remain, of course, my responsibility alone.

Debts of a different kind I have accumulated from friends on both sides of the Atlantic. Peter Schwartz and Silvia Beier have remained loyal friends over the years. Many thanks also to Tracy Musser, my oldest friend in this country. In Southern California, Elizabeth Allen, Charlie Chubb, Alice Fahs, Erik Kongshaug, and Heidi Tinsman did much to turn an initially foreign place into a *Heimat* of sorts. In Germany, I continue to rely on the indispensable friendship and hospitality of Bernd Pieper and Melanie von der Wiesche.

My deepest gratitude is to my family. My brother Armin has been a constant source of moral support and intellectual inspiration. Our many conversations convinced me that, at least within our family, the dialogue between the humanities and the sciences is alive and well. Visiting him and his partner Ya'ara in Israel also reminded me of the moral responsibilities that come with my job. Noah was present throughout the writing of this book, if not always physically, then certainly in my heart and mind. Without the unfailing emotional and financial support of my parents, Peter and Gudrun Bieß, I would never have been able to write these lines. Early on, my father's stories about his youth in postwar Germany inspired my interest in the period. To this day, my mother's intellectual curiosity and newspaper clipping skills keep me abreast of current events in Germany. Neither of them ever ceased to believe in my academic endeavors at faraway places, and they even provided crucial last-minute research assistance. Nobody has contributed more to this project than Ulrike Strasser. Her eloquence and intelligence have improved virtually every page of this book, and her humor and affection have sustained its author. Over the last few years, I have too often relied on her patience and generosity. This is why, as a small token of appreciation, this book is dedicated to her.

This book offers a much revised and expanded interpretation of materials included in the following publications: " 'Pioneers of a New Germany': Returning POWs from the Soviet Union and the Making of East German Citizens, 1945–1950"; *Central European History* 32 (1999): 143–80; "Men of Reconstruction, the Reconstruction of Men: Returning POWs in East and West Germany," in *Home/Front: The Military, War, and Gender in Twentieth-Century Germany*, ed. Karen Hagemann and Stephanie Schüler-Springorum, 335–58 (Oxford: Berg, 2002); "Between Amnesty and Anti-Communism: The West German *Kameradenschinder* Trials, 1948–1961," in *Crimes of War: Guilt and Denial in the Twentieth Century*, ed. Omer Bartov, Atina Grossmann, and Mary Nolan, 138–60 (New York: New Press, 2002). I would like to thank the publishers for their permission to reuse some of these materials.

Homecomings

On May 8, 2005, the world commemorated the sixtieth anniversary of the ending of World War II in Europe. The global celebrations of the defeat of Nazism marked a moment in the larger process of consigning to history the most destructive of all global conflicts in the modern era.[1] For more than half a century, the war's abiding legacies cast a long shadow over postwar societies in Europe and beyond. These multifaceted consequences of the war assumed different temporalities that have made it difficult to proclaim an end to the "postwar" period.[2] Yet the late twentieth century nevertheless marked a series of "endings" in the history and memory of the war and its consequences. The end of the Cold War brought to an end the division of Germany and Europe as the most important territorial consequence of the Second World War. The collapse of Communism led to the demise of an antifascist politics that had gained its central legitimacy from the struggle against European fascism.[3] And the bitter fights over the memory of the Second World War point to ongoing efforts at shaping a lasting, more ritualized cultural memory of the war at the moment when the voices of the remaining survivors are in the process of being silenced forever.[4] This rendering into history and cultural memory enables a new historical vantage point on the war and its aftermath. Precisely because some of its most important consequences are coming to an end, it has become possible to assess the ways in which the war and its legacies structured the postwar period. Thus, this book probes the precise meaning and historical specificity of the elusive and indeterminate category of the "postwar."

This study employs the return of the POWs to East and West Germany as a vehicle to write a comparative history of post-1945 Germany as *postwar* history. The book focuses primarily on the reception, treatment, and experience of more than two million German POWs returning from Soviet captivity to East and West Germany, but occasionally also considers returnees from Western captivity. Returning POWs from the Soviet Union constituted one of the most important, long lasting, and highly visible consequences of war and defeat. Their service first as soldiers in the war of annihilation on the Eastern front, then as German POWs in Soviet captivity, combined, in a dramatic fashion, active and passive experiences of violence.[5] Their delayed homecoming—the last POWs did not return until January 1956—literally transported these experiences of violence back into postwar society and ensured the presence of the war's consequences throughout both postwar societies' formative period of postwar reconstruction.

When I first conceived of this project almost exactly a decade ago, I was struck by the discrepancy between the rich historiography on the political, social, economic, cultural, and psychological consequences of the First World War and the virtual absence of a similar literature for the post-1945 period.[6] The suspicion that this omission did not result from mere oversight but was rooted in systemic features of postwar historiography—together with my desire to make use of the recently opened East German archives and write a comparative postwar history—led first to my dissertation and then to this book. To be sure, over the last few years, several works have investigated the second German "postwar," and others are in the process of being completed.[7] But the analytic and topical possibilities for exploring the myriad aftereffects of the Second World War are far from exhausted, and few studies have employed the "postwar" paradigm comparatively for both East and West.

While this is neither a history of the war on the Eastern front nor of German POWs in Allied or Soviet captivity, this study draws on the considerable literature that has emerged on both of these themes over the past decade.[8] The book asks what happened when the Eastern front "came home" to postwar Germany. By focusing on returning POWs, it investigates the social and moral burdens that total war and total defeat imposed on both German societies in the postwar period. To fully appreciate these challenges, a brief synopsis of returnees' experience in war and captivity will be required.

To Stalingrad and Back: History and Memory

When German troops invaded Poland in the early morning hours of September 1, 1939, and unleashed what was to become the Second World War, they embarked not only on a conventional war but also on a much broader campaign of terror and ethnic cleansing. Moving into the occupied territory in the rear of the army, SS units liquidated thousands of members of the Polish elites as well as many Jews. While some Wehrmacht leaders articulated their opposition to these criminal transgressions, army units also lent logistical support and participated in these mass killings.[9] After the German army had swept through France, Scandinavia, and the Balkans, the attack on the Soviet Union in June 1941 became the centerpiece of Nazi Germany's effort to impose a "new order" on the European continent. From its onset, "Operation Barbarossa" was designed as a racial war of annihilation. Its aim was the complete subjection of Eastern European societies in order to create "living space" for an ostensibly superior German "master race."[10] There can be no doubt that the Wehrmacht as an institution was involved in this project at all levels. The Wehrmacht was not only Hitler's "instrument"—a metaphor that suggests too passive a relationship—but actively fostered and promoted this genocidal project. The overwhelming majority of military commanders, for example, endorsed and willingly executed Hitler's "commissar orders," which mandated the shooting of captured "political commissars" of the Red Army.[11] The Wehrmacht leadership also expressed its utter disregard for "subhuman" Soviet soldiers by providing no provision whatsoever for millions of Soviet POWs captured during the early stages of the war. Instead, Soviet POWs were either killed immediately—as happened with Jewish POWs under Wehrmacht supervision—or deliberately starved to death. By 1942, out of 3.9 million Soviet POWs, a staggering 2.8 million had died. By the end of the war, out of 5.7 million Soviet POWs, approximately 3.3 million (or almost 58 percent of) Soviet POWs died in German captivity.[12]

As part of the effort to secure and exploit the occupied territories in the East, Wehrmacht units committed countless massacres against Soviet civilians, including women and children. These murderous practices occurred under the guise of "antipartisan" warfare and were part of the systematic economic exploitation of occupied territories. They were first implemented on the Eastern front but later also spilled over to the West.[13] The result of these brutal policies was an extremely violent and lethal intervention in occupied societies in the East whose consequences still defy adequate historical understanding. In his massive study of German occupation policy in Belarus, historian Christian Gerlach estimates that among the 1.6–1.7 million murdered POWs and civilians (out of a population of nine million), a "little bit more than half . . . had been killed by Wehrmacht units."[14] The slow German retreat from the Eastern front with its corresponding scorched-earth policies as well as the Wehrmacht's tenacious fighting up until the very end further drove up Soviet civilian and military casualties, which, according to recent estimates, amounted to a staggering 27 million dead.[15]

The war of racial annihilation on the Eastern front also provided the essential context for the Nazi project to murder all European Jews.[16] The Wehrmacht was directly involved in the implementation and execution of the Holocaust. The army's conquest of vast territories in the East not only provided the context and the opportunity for the murder of European Jews by mobile killing units; the army leadership also identified itself with "mass slaughter for ideological reason."[17] In addition, army units provided crucial logistical and organizational support for the killing squads from the SS or the police. Army units identified, ghettoized and rounded up Jews, and they supervised and secured killing actions. Finally, Wehrmacht soldiers directly participated in the killing of Jews, often under the guise of antipartisan activity.[18] The Wehrmacht's structural implication in genocidal warfare does not imply that every German soldier became a perpetrator, and the precise extent of ordinary soldiers' participation (as well as their motivations) remains an open and highly contested area of research.[19] Still, the quest for nuance in studying a huge collective comprising up to nineteen million men should not distract us from the basic historical fact: the soldiers of the Wehrmacht were deeply implicated in a genocidal project that brought unspeakable suffering and irretrievable losses to millions of Europeans.

For most Wehrmacht soldiers, the war did not end with unconditional surrender but led into a period of captivity of varying length and hardship. The global spread of some eleven million German POWs from Egypt to Scandinavia and from the Rocky Mountains to Siberia reflected the extent of the failed imperialist aspirations of the Third Reich. A veritable boom of "POW studies" over the last decade or so has brought into focus the experience of captivity during and after World War II, including such aspects as the POW policies of captor nations, political reeducation efforts, living conditions, the inner functioning of the "camp society," and the impact of captivity on the attitudes of POWs.[20] The experience of German POWs depended largely on time and place of captivity. POWs in British and American captivity generally encountered—with only a few exceptions[21]—circumstances that compared favorably with the situation of German civilians in the early postwar period.[22] By contrast, POWs in Eastern European, Soviet, and, to a lesser extent, French captivity, experienced a period of deprivation and forced labor that resulted in death rates ranging from 2.6 percent in French captivity to more than a third in Soviet captivity.[23] Official Soviet sources confirm the death of 356,687 German POWs in Soviet captivity, yet recent estimates place the additional death toll of unregistered German POWs—in transport to POW camps or in front camps—as high as 750,000.[24] Among the approximately three million German POWs, one-third did not survive Soviet captivity.

It is important to emphasize, however, that, in contrast to the German treatment of Soviet POWs, the mass death of German POWs in Soviet captivity was not the result of a deliberate Soviet policy of mass killing or even of passive negligence.[25] Many German soldiers were already utterly exhausted and sick when they fell into Soviet captivity. This was especially true for the approximately 110,000 POWs captured at Stalingrad, of whom only 5,000 survived.[26] In general, Soviet authorities were primarily interested in enlisting German POWs for the enormous task of postwar reconstruction, not in letting them die. The release of hundreds of thousands of sick and exhausted POWs in 1945–46 testifies to this priority. During the early postwar period, official food rations for German POWs were only slightly below the ratios accorded to Soviet civilians. Deaths of German POWs in Soviet captivity appear to have been largely the result of bureaucratic inefficiencies and corruption, an extremely bad harvest in 1946, and inadequate medical resources.[27] Mortality rates in Soviet captivity, moreover, declined significantly after 1947.[28] During their period of internment, German POWs were integrated into the vast universe of forced labor in Soviet industry. They worked primarily in industry, coal mining, or in the rebuilding of the Soviet infrastructure.[29] However, compared to the massive destruction of the German occupiers, German POWs' actual contribution to the Soviet economy amounted to only to 4.8 percent of the national income.[30]

Former soldiers and POWs were not the only group to experience the consequences of defeat. Total defeat brought back to ordinary Germans the violence that Germans had previously meted out all over the European continent. German civilian losses during the last two years of the war were considerable. They included approximately five hundred thousand civilian victims of the Allied air war as well as another five hundred thousand deaths among the approximately twelve million ethnic Germans who fled or were expelled from territories in Eastern Europe during the last months of the war and in the immediate postwar period.[31] Tens of thousands of German civilians fell victim to violent transgressions of the advancing Red Army in the East, and German women were subjected to mass rape by Soviet soldiers.[32] These were the collective experiences of suffering and defeat that shaped the German transition from war to the postwar period. They also constituted the social and emotional context for the postwar confrontation with fascism, war, and genocide.

The "many faces of defeat" notwithstanding, this book argues that returning POWs, especially from the Soviet Union, represented a particularly potent symbol for the consequences of war and defeat in postwar Germany.[33] Apart from historians' tendency to identify their own particular object of study as central to the period under investigation, certain aspects of returnees' collective experience substantiate this claim. First, returnees' active and passive experiences of violence exemplified, in a dramatic fashion, the experience of most ordinary Germans, which often included implication in and collaboration with the Nazi dictatorship as well as suffering from the consequences of total defeat. From today's perspective, the experience of returning POWs transcended the binary categories of perpetrator and victim. More so than other war-damaged groups, returnees exemplified the moral, social, and political challenges of confronting the legacies of defeat in postwar Germany. Moreover, returnees from the Soviet Union assumed a larger functional and symbolic significance for postwar reconstruction. These were "men in their best years" who represented a cross-section of the entire male segment of postwar German society.[34] In addition, returnees' experiences of Soviet captivity became symbolically significant in the context of the Cold War, when both Germanys defined their postwar identities largely with respect to the Soviet Union: either as an "ever present Other" in the West or as a Socialist "big brother" in the East.[35]

By focusing on returning POWs from the East, this book addresses the morally and methodologically difficult problem of German suffering in the aftermath of World War II. It cannot be emphasized strongly enough that the violence that Germans had to endure during the final stages of the war was a direct consequence of the unprecedented violence that Germans had previously inflicted all over the European continent. Any moral equation between German losses and German violence is misleading and necessarily obscures the relationship between cause and effect.[36] German violence was the cause and the precondition for violence against Germans, even if the German targets of violence were not always identical with those responsible for German violence.

This book does not condone recent interventions claiming that postwar Germans never sufficiently confronted German suffering. At least with respect to returning POWs and expellees, such criticism is based on a profound misreading of the postwar history of memory. As Robert Moeller's work has shown, the experience of returning POWs (and of expellees) formed the key reference points for a German discourse of victimization that revolved around German suffering.[37] Rather than contributing to this discourse of victimization (in either its 1950s or its contemporary version), this book seeks to historicize it. It highlights the commemorative function of narratives of victimization but also underlines, based on the example of returning POWs, the real experiences of suffering and hardship that informed these memories and made them plausible for ordinary Germans. In so doing, the book seeks to delineate—and historicize—the possibilities as well as the limitations of memory in a postwar society reemerging from total defeat.

If removed from the safe abstractions of statistics and figures, human suffering is always unique and cannot easily be classified into hierarchical categories. Collective experiences of suffering and loss leave indelible marks on individual lives and collective memories, and they reshape the moral and social fabric of societies that undergo them.[38] As a result, German suffering needs to be taken seriously as a formative force in shaping the postwar period and as an important social and emotional context for German confrontations with guilt and responsibility. From a moral and political point of view, a focus on German suffering and its consequences does not necessarily serve the purpose of relativization and apology, although it often has. Instead, such an analysis can reveal the extent to which both East and West German postwar societies remained infused with the violence and destructiveness that had preceded them.[39]

By focusing on the persistent legacies of war and defeat, this book calls into question widespread assumptions of a quick overcoming of the war's consequences as they still inform standard narratives of postwar Germany. Both postwar societies not only needed to muster considerable ideological work to manage German guilt and responsibility. They also needed to come to terms—and this aspect has not yet received the attention it deserves—with the consequences of defeat, that is, with a past that included fascism and genocide *as well as* a history of massive suffering, irretrievable loss, and mass death.[40] In both postwar societies, the return of the POWs prompted social and discursive strategies that sought to erase the consequences of German violence *and* of violence against Germans. This book is centrally concerned with tracing these social and discursive strategies of redemptive transformation. It discusses the costs and benefits of these efforts for returnees and for German society at large, and it highlights the difficulties and limitations of moving beyond defeat. In so doing, the book places the lingering aftereffects of war and defeat—as well as individual and collective efforts to overcome them—at the center of the analysis.[41]

A Comparative History of Postwar Germany

This book's path of inquiry follows two conceptual axes: first, it focuses on the German "postwar"; and second, it investigates the aftereffects of the war comparatively for both East and West Germany. Even though the field of post-1945 German history initially constituted itself as postwar history, this label tended to assume a more temporal than conceptual meaning. Apart from some very important exceptions that have defined the contours of this study, the focus on the abiding legacies of war and defeat has not occupied a prominent place in the historiography of post-1945 Germany.[42] In recent syntheses, the "postwar" is either virtually absent or appears as a temporary moment of a "German chaos" that then quickly became the "starting point for a better future."[43] Such conceptualizations bespeak a tangible pride in the achievements of the "old Federal Republic," its "remarkable stability" over fifty years.[44] They are also informed by the contrast to the experience of the Weimar Republic, which, as Richard Bessel has shown, never managed to make the transition from a postwar to a peacetime society and was characterized by an "inner denial of peace."[45] To be sure, there were important differences between the two German postwar periods that resulted, not the least, from different international contexts.[46] "Bonn," and for that matter, "East Berlin" did not become "Weimar," as the publicist Rene Alemann had declared, with a considerable sigh of relief, in 1957.[47] By contrast, Hans Peter Schwarz's suggestion to write the history of the Federal Republic as the history of a "catastrophe that did not happen" restores more contingency to postwar history. Yet at the same time, this perspective tends to downplay the considerable material and ideological costs of postwar stability, and it also underestimates the significant fissures between public affirmation and acquiescence and a persistent private unease that was constitutive for both German postwar societies.[48]

More recent approaches in post-1945 historiography have also tended to sideline the lingering consequences of war and defeat. Employing paradigms such as modernization, Westernization, or Americanization for the West, Sovietization or Stalinization for the East, historians have persuasively identified the 1950s as a period of decisive political, social, and cultural change.[49] While these approaches have significantly enhanced our understanding of the post-1945 period, they are less well suited to capture the lingering consequences of war and defeat. To be sure, the focus on the dynamic transformations in both postwar societies is not incompatible with a renewed attention to the war's aftermath. Indeed, the peculiar juxtaposition of unprecedented violence and unprecedented prosperity may well constitute the decisive hallmark of twentieth-century Germany. In this perspective, the longing for normality, security, and prosperity that marked much of the 1950s resulted from collective experiences of violence, insecurity, and loss.[50] Still, this book shifts the emphasis from what both German postwar societies have become to what they emerged from. It seeks to portray the 1940s and 1950s not only as the fulcrum of a liberal-democratic and increasingly Americanized consumer society in the West and a Stalinist dictatorship in the East but as the posthistory of unprecedented experience of violence, suffering, and mass death.

Defining the nature and the contours of the German "postwar" is no easy undertaking.[51] Given the collapse of most boundaries between front and home front, between soldiers and civilians during the Second World War, postwar societies needed to face more than just the classical tasks of reintegrating returning soldiers or even of converting a wartime to a peacetime economy. In light of the "extensity" (Roger Chickering) of warfare during the First and, even more so, the Second World War, postwar societies also needed to come to terms with the legacies of mass displacement, ethnic cleansing, and, most importantly, genocide.[52] If the signature of the epoch of European civil war during the first half of the twentieth century was the "socialization of violence," then postwar societies necessarily lived in the shadow of this large-scale mobilization of entire societies for the purpose of destruction.[53] The indeterminacy of the category "postwar" thus points to the all-pervasiveness of the war's legacies in postwar society.[54] The goal of a "postwar" history, then, is to identify the aftereffects of those experiences of violence—both active and passive—and to analyze coping strategies of both individuals and societies at large.

This book builds on the boom in memory studies over the last decade that has convincingly demonstrated the presence of the past in postwar Germany. As many studies have shown, Germans did not repress the past after 1945 but rather engaged in selective remembering and often very conscious effort to manage and mold the past.[55] In this perspective, the history of post-1945 Germany does not just appear as a history of a radical transformation but also as a "history burdened by the past" (Belastungsgeschichte).[56] Yet, as Klaus Naumann has argued, both German societies were not just *postfascist* societies that needed to confront the shared legacy of National Socialism and the Holocaust but also *postwar* societies that were centrally preoccupied with the legacies of total war and total defeat.[57] To be sure, given the Wehrmacht's extensive implication in the National Socialist genocidal project, "postfascism" and "postwar" cannot be neatly separated and always remained closely intertwined. This book does not intend to complement a history of postfascism that focused on Germans as perpetrators with a postwar history that emphasizes German suffering. Instead, it seeks to delineate the tensions and constant renegotiation between these two defining characteristics of East and West German societies after 1945.

This analytic focus on the postwar nature of both German societies offers new conceptual possibilities for a comparative history of East and West Germany. Since the collapse of the GDR in 1989, historians have not only invested tremendous energies in writing the history of the East German dictatorship, they have also debated the ways in which that history can be incorporated into the larger narrative of twentieth-century German and European history.[58] While persuasive arguments have been marshaled for comparing East Germany to other Communist societies or for a diachronic comparison between the Nazi and the East German dictatorship, this book argues for the continuing validity of the East/West German comparison.[59] In so doing, however, this study does not merely seek to add an East German story to a more familiar West German one, nor does it intend to contrast a West German success story with an East German narrative of failure. Instead, the book focuses on common problems that both German societies needed to address as a result of a shared past, and it elucidates the dialectical interrelationship between East and West.[60] This "separation and interconnection" between both postwar societies, as Christoph Klessmann has called it, was always asymmetrical—the West was more important for the East than vice versa—even though this contrast was less pronounced in the late 1940s and 1950s than it became later on.[61]

By emphasizing the shared postwar nature of both German societies, my analysis reveals surprising functional and structural similarities between East and West German responses to returning POWs that were located below the rhetorical antagonisms of the Cold War. I argue that the Cold War by no means completely overshadowed the consequences of war and defeat but rather shaped the ways in which East and West Germans confronted them.[62] This approach does not deny the considerable differences between liberal democracy in the West and dictatorship in the East. But it seeks to contribute to an ongoing critical investigation of the "old" Federal Republic that remains important for both political and historiographical reasons.[63] At the same time, the comparison between East and West also helps to bring into sharper focus the very real achievements of postwar West Germany.

Finally, this book places the German postwar within the larger context of a European postwar period. Arguably, Germany stands at the center of both postwar European history and historiography. German violence plunged the European continent into disaster, yet Germany was also central to Europe's postwar recovery. Clearly, postwar East and West Germany faced unique challenges in the postwar period, with total defeat and responsibility for genocide being the most important ones. Yet East and West German confrontations with the legacies of the Second World War also followed more general European rhythms.[64] While this book does not attempt to write a comparative history of the European postwar period, it draws on an emerging cross-national European historiography that has begun to bring into focus the war's aftermath as a central feature of European postwar societies.[65] It seeks to delineate the specificities of the German "postwar," yet also points to commonalities with larger European developments. As such, this comparative history of postwar Germany hopes to contribute to a yet-to-be-written integrated European "history of the aftermath" that would encompass both halves of the divided continent.

Memory, Masculinity, and Citizenship

This book is the product of a historiographical moment that seeks to transcend the divide between social and cultural history. No theoretically informed history, it seems to me, can afford to ignore some of the central insights of the "new cultural history," especially regarding the definition of culture as a "symbolic, linguistic and representational system" that itself constitutes reality rather than simply reflecting it.[66] At the same time, the book seeks to follow methodological and theoretical suggestions that, for some time now, have advocated new efforts to reconcile the focus on narrative, representations, and discourses with a renewed attention to subjectivity, agency, and experience.[67] I do not seek to propose a general theoretical resolution as to how these categories are related to each other at all times and at all places. The point is that they are, indeed, interrelated—"experiences" take shape within available discursive frameworks even though they are not completely determined by those frameworks.[68] The precise nature of this interrelationship, however, needs to be analyzed in specific historical settings and depends, not the least, on specific political contexts.

The argument proceeds on three distinct yet interrelated analytical levels. First, it investigates cultural representations of returning POWs as part of larger discourses— that is, culturally established and meaningful narratives—about war and defeat in postwar Germany. Second, it analyzes social and political strategies toward returnees and shows how they constituted a central aspect of sociopolitical reconstruction in East and West. Third, I demonstrate how returnees formed their own male subjectivities within the social and discursive contexts they encountered. The book is not designed primarily as a social history of integration. By definition, the concept of "integration" is too closely associated with the notion of overcoming the war's consequences that this book seeks to problematize.[69] Instead, the book combines the political history of postwar reconstruction with the social history of returnees and the cultural history of war memories and gender identities.

I deploy three conceptual terms to connect these different levels of analysis for both the East and West German case: memory, masculinity, and citizenship.[70] First, the project is inspired by the concern with memory as a central aspect of the "new cultural history."[71] Unlike many studies of memory that remain primarily on the level of representations, this book seeks to reconnect public representations of the past to social and political strategies as well as to the (re)constitution of subjectivities. My analysis follows a recent suggestion by Alon Confino and Peter Fritzsche "to destabilize the boundaries between memory as representation and memory as social action."[72] I demonstrate that public memories of returnees' experience were, at every turn, interrelated to social and political strategies of incorporating them into new communities of belonging. As such, public memories did indeed constitute, to quote Fritzsche and Confino again, "efforts to manage the social order." [73]

While the link between memory as representation and memory as social action constitutes one methodological premise of this study, another one concerns the relationship between public and private memories. Like many other historians, I have been centrally influenced by Maurice Halbwachs's concept of "collective memory," which defined memory as a social act that was shaped by available social frameworks.[74] Yet I also agree with the criticism that Halbwachs's model leaves too little room for the variances of individual memory.[75] Public and private memory are not necessarily identical, nor can their relationship simply be characterized as one of "production" and "reception," even though this is often necessary for narrative purposes. Instead, the transformation of individual memory into collective remembrance needs to be understood as a process of contestation, appropriation, and mutual influences that often also results in incongruities between public and private memory. This was certainly the case in East Germany, where the institutions of civil society did not mediate between the individual and the state, and public memories were largely imposed "from above" by Communist elites. Still, the assumption of a complete divergence between public and private memories in the East underestimates processes of appropriation and accommodation in the East German dictatorship, just as the thesis of a complete convergence between public and private memories in the West overestimates, in my view, the extent of consensus in postwar West Germany. By investigating the degree to which official East and West German memories succeeded in allowing former soldiers and POWs to connect their past and their present, the book explores the interrelationship of public and private memory in the different political contexts of democracy and dictatorship.

Second, this book draws on the central insight that the use of "gender as a category of analysis"—in Joan Scott's now famous phrase—also needs to incorporate the study of men and masculinities. The significance of the emerging history of men and masculinities for this study is twofold.[76] First, this book studies men *as men*, that is, as gendered subjects whose experience and behavior were crucially shaped by culturally and historically specific conceptions of masculinity. Total defeat called into question not only the racialized masculinities of the Nazi period but also the more general link between masculinity and militarism that had formed the basis of male citizenship since the early nineteenth century.[77] To be sure, historians of masculinity have warned against overusing and diluting the topos of a "crisis of masculinity"— the persistence of patriarchal relations of power, after all, hardly squares with a masculinity supposedly in permanent crisis.[78] But in both postwar societies, the return of exhausted, weak, and often traumatized POWs triggered widespread (and divergent) diagnoses of a masculinity in crisis as well as parallel processes of social and symbolic "remasculinization."[79] My analysis demonstrates that responses to returning POWs were primary sites for the formation of new "hegemonic masculinities" in East and West.[80] I also show that returnees were often not able (or willing) to live up to normative conceptions of masculinity. Persistent discrepancies between norm and reality thus posed distinctive challenges to male subjectivities in the postwar period. At the same time, parallel processes of social and symbolic "remasculinization" also yielded "patriarchal dividends" for returnees as well as for men in general.[81]

Besides investigating men as gendered subjects, the book also utilizes masculinity for analyzing East and West German confrontations with war and defeat as inherently gendered processes. Along with other recent studies, this study emphasizes gender and sexuality as primary sites for the experience and memory of war, genocide, and defeat.[82] Concerns over masculinity and male authority drove East and West German efforts to move out of the shadow of defeat. The renegotiation of masculinities structured the formation of postwar memories and shaped sociopolitical reconstruction. In particular, the rehabilitation of a male narrative of war and defeat legitimized the reassertion of male authority over women in both postwar societies. By demonstrating how reformulated and rehabilitated masculinities promoted the recreation of men's (social and symbolic) authority over women, this study seeks to alleviate concerns that histories of masculinity might replicate the marginalization of women.[83] Even though my primary concern here is with men and masculinity, this study hopes to contribute to an integrated and truly relational gender history of the postwar period.

Citizenship constitutes the third conceptual term that I employ to connect the multiple layers of my analysis. Postwar confrontations with the legacies of war and defeat were inextricably intertwined with parallel strategies of making East and West German citizens on opposite sides of the Cold War. My usage of the term *citizen* differs from T. H. Marshall's classic definition, which understands citizenship as a progression from civil to political to social rights.[84] Given the absence of important citizenship rights in East Germany, a merely rights-based, legal concept of citizenship is not conducive to the comparative framework of this book. However, the massive theoretical literature on citizenship has moved the concept away from the liberal-democratic context in which it originally emerged. Citizenship is now also construed as a concept of belonging and as a marker of subjectivity that is located at the intersection between state and society.[85]

This book draws on these expanded meanings of citizenship by demonstrating how the transformation of returnees into citizens entailed their incorporation into new postwar communities of belonging.[86] In the aftermath of war, genocide, and total defeat, when the relationship between the state and the individual had been severely strained if not completely ruptured, public memories of war and defeat were central for reforging those symbolic bonds between postwar polities and male subjectivities. Memory assumed a crucial significance in this process. In particular, membership in both postwar communities of belonging crucially depended on the "decontamination" of returnees from active and passive experiences of violence; and my analysis focuses on the narrative strategies that both societies deployed in order to achieve this goal.[87]

While East and West German responses to the return of the POWs were central to defining ideal male "posttotalitarian" or "antifascist" citizen, former soldiers and POWs actively participated in this process of renegotiating postwar citizenship. They did so more in the West, where returnees shaped public narratives of war and defeat through their self-organization in interest groups, than in the East, where returnees' agency manifested itself in a defensive posture towards the increasingly expansive claims of the totalitarian state. Still, in both societies, national belonging provided returnees with rhetorical and political tools that they employed in making claims to the state for material and ideological compensation. Finally, my analysis demonstrates the limitations of returnees' full integration into postwar communities of belonging. In both societies, the persistent consequences of defeat engendered more "passive" forms of citizenship that reflected these persistent gaps between normative discursive constructs and lived experience. These incongruencies between public discourse and private sensibilities constituted one of the hallmarks of the condition of the "postwar" in both societies.[88]

THE SCOPE OF THE BOOK

The book analyzes East and West German efforts to make "citizens" out of "returnees" as a comparative and transsocietal process. The temporal frame reaches from the defeat at Stalingrad in 1942–43 into the late 1950s. The study traces the origins of the postwar period back into the last years of the war, when ordinary Germans first began to face the massive consequences of defeat, and it ends with the return of the last POWs in 1955–56. Historians of the *longue durée* might object that this temporal focus privileges short and midrange upheavals at the expense of more salient, long-term structural change. But, as Konrad Jarausch and Michael Geyer have written, "focusing on the long run average does not account for the intense fluctuations that mattered at a given time—the extraordinary upheavals that ripped apart a nation, and all the exertions required to allow a people to pull itself back together." This book thus addresses precisely the "intense labors of undoing and belonging," which, as Jarausch and Geyer write, "ultimately made history."[89]

This book adopts a mixture of chronological and thematic organization. Part 1 discusses the German transition from war to postwar. Focusing on the increasing number of MIAs and POWs after 1943, chapter 1 analyzes official and popular responses to increasing losses, and it reveals the emergence of a privatized perspective on the future that anticipated postwar confrontations with war and defeat. Chapter 2 demonstrates how the return of the POWs gave rise to different versions of German victimization that gradually displaced an indigenous German discourse on guilt and responsibility. Based on an analysis of returnees' own encounter with a devastated homeland, the chapter also argues that narratives of victimization constituted a problematic basis for the reconstitution of male subjectivities and for postwar reconstruction at large. Chapter 3 elaborates on these tensions between victimization and postwar reconstruction by focusing on medical and psychiatric responses to the trauma of the returned POW. Returnees' pathologies represented a central site of the war's aftereffects in both postwar societies, and the ways in which East and West Germans diagnosed and treated these symptoms reveal much about their specific confrontations with the often traumatic legacies of total war and total defeat.

Part 2 analyzes how East and West Germans sought to overcome total defeat by transforming returning POWs into functioning male citizens on opposite sides of the Cold War. Chapters 4 and 5 analyze the emergence of redemptive memories in East and West respectively, which then translated into social and political strategies of "making citizens." I argue that redemptive memories in both societies did not fully succeed in incorporating returnees into new communities of belonging, thus pushing their adjustment to postwar society into the less public spheres of the workplace and the family. Chapter 6 highlights the exclusionary aspects of East and West German efforts at making citizens by focusing on returnees who were denied access to redemptive memories. The chapter compares the West German trials of former POWs who had assumed official functions in camp administration or had participated in antifascist activity in Soviet captivity, with the East German purges of returnees from Western captivity.

Part 3 shows how East and West German confrontations with the consequences of defeat increasingly diverged in the first half of the 1950s. Chapter 7 contrasts East German efforts to declare an end to *all* confrontations with the war's consequences after the end of POWs mass repatriations in May 1950 with the intense public and private concern with missing POWs that moved the war's consequence to the center of West German public life. In both societies, however, the issue of missing POWs prompted significant social and political tensions between political authorities and family members of missing POWs and MIAs. As chapter 8 shows, these tensions were only resolved with the return of the last POWs in 1953–54 and 1955–56. The return of these last POWs represented a preliminary end-point of East and West German confrontations with war and defeat. It brought into focus distinct strategies of coming to terms with defeat in East and West, and it offered a window into the self-perception of both societies a full decade after the end of the Second World War and at the height of the Cold War.

Finally, a word on terminology is in order. Throughout this study, I use the term *returnee* (*Heimkehrer*) to refer to former Wehrmacht soldiers returning from captivity to East and West Germany. This is not an innocent term. In German, its etymology is linked to the concept of *Heimat* (homeland) and thus tends to emphasize former soldiers' status as civilians, thereby distracting from their military service in the war of annihilation. "Returnee," moreover, also constituted a rather opaque category. Besides former Wehrmacht soldiers, its contemporary usage also included civilian internees who had never served in the military as well as, in its feminine form (*Heimkehrerinnen*), Red Cross nurses and female auxiliary forces of the Wehrmacht.[90] At various points in this study, I therefore make clear which groups were subsumed under the category of "returnee," and I discuss the implications of such categorizations. With these caveats, it seems justified to employ the term *returnee* here. It is the term used by contemporaries in East and West to refer to my object of study, and it was this identification as a distinct group with a shared collective experience that then defined "returnees" as a significant social and political problem in both postwar societies.

PART ONE

From War to Postwar

CHAPTER ONE

Impending Defeat: Military Losses, the Wehrmacht, and Ordinary Germans

The onset of the postwar period coincided only in a very literal sense with the unconditional surrender of the German military on May 8, 1945. Long before the end of the war, ordinary Germans had begun to experience the consequences of defeat. The decisive defeats of the Wehrmacht on the Eastern front and in North Africa in 1942–43 not only set in motion a social transformation from "Stalingrad to the currency reform," but also ushered in a period of "brutal peacemaking" that extended far into the postwar period.[1] Impending defeat brought back to ordinary Germans the massive and unprecedented violence that they had previously meted out to the nation's victims all over the European continent. Civilian and military casualties figures on all sides exploded during the last two years of the war. German casualties took a sudden jump with the defeat of the Sixth Army at Stalingrad in January 1943, when 180,310 soldiers were killed in one month. Among the 5.3 million Wehrmacht casualties during the Second World War, more than 80 percent died during the last two years of the war. Approximately three-quarters of these losses occurred on the Eastern front (2.7 million) and during the final stages of the war between January and May 1945 (1.2 million).[2]

Apart from the dramatic surge of casualty figures, Stalingrad also brought to the fore a problem that was to preoccupy Germans long after Soviet troops had raised the Red Flag on the Reichstag in May 1945: soldiers missing in action and POWs in Soviet captivity. The problem of German MIAs and POWs became one of the key links between the last years of the war and the postwar period.[3] After 1943, MIAs and POWs represented an increasingly large segment of German military losses. In part, this was a result of the military leadership's deliberate practice of downplaying German casualties and ascribing them to the category of MIAs.[4] At least since 1943, moreover, casualties could often not be confirmed with final certainty. As a result, MIAs accounted for more than 40 percent of all German losses on the Eastern front in 1943 and close to 60 percent in 1944. At the end of the war, the total number of soldiers missing in action amounted to 1.5 million. According to recent estimates, half of them had died on the Eastern front, the other half in Soviet captivity.[5] As with the MIAs, the growing number of German POWs in Allied or

Figure 1. German POWs in Berlin being marched off into Soviet capitivity (April/May 1945). German casualty figures escalated during the final stages of the war, and most German POWs were captured during this period. (Courtesy of Landesbildstelle Berlin.)

Soviet captivity represented another widely visible reminder that the war's fortunes had turned against the Third Reich. Whereas the Wehrmacht had captured millions of Soviet POWs during the early stages of the war, approximately 110,000 German soldiers fell into the hands of the Red Army at Stalingrad. But most of the more than three million German POWs in Soviet captivity were captured during the last months of the war in eastern Prussia and Kurland (200,000–250,000), in eastern Germany and Poland (800,000), in the Berlin area (330,000), and in Bohemia (630,000). The largest segment of approximately eight million German soldiers, however, managed to avoid Soviet captivity and ended up in the custody of the Western allies, often after a panic-stricken effort to reach British and American lines.[6]

This chapter analyzes official, popular, and private responses to rising military losses after Stalingrad. It inserts the hitherto largely neglected issue of German MIAs and POWs into the larger story of the German transition from war to the postwar period. Official and popular reactions to the increasing number of MIAs and POWs reveal much about ordinary Germans' confrontation with impending defeat. The liminal status of MIAs and POWs threatened to undermine the Nazi cult of heroic death, and it inspired family members to search for alternative vision for the future that no longer centered on an increasingly unlikely "final victory" but on a reunion with a missing or captured soldier. These "privatized" responses to impending defeat were based on predominantly female experiences on the home front, and they generally did not extend to (male) soldiers on the front. Even though Nazi authorities took this "private" dissent very seriously, it ultimately did not challenge the Nazi regime's remarkable ability to hold on to power in the face of certain defeat. The Wehrmacht's tenacious resistance up to the last minute not only produced the escalating casualties on all sides but also allowed for the continuation of the Holocaust up until May 8, 1945. My argument does not seek to divert from this important historical reality, nor does it attempt to belittle the considerable popular support that large segments of ordinary Germans extended to the Nazi regime, even though this consensus began to erode after Stalingrad.

What requires explanation, however, is not just the failure of popular resistance before defeat but also its complete absence *after* the war's end in 1945. Despite Allied and Soviet expectations to the contrary, ordinary Germans did not offer any sustained resistance to military occupation in the aftermath of total defeat.[7] The absence of any popular allegiance to National Socialism after 1945 points to processes of popular disengagement from it that originated in the last years of the war. The chapter demonstrates how popular responses to growing losses during the last two years of the war anticipated confrontations with total defeat after 1945. It also stresses the significance of the Christian churches in shaping this transition from war to postwar. Despite their strong ideological support for the war in the East, Germany's religious institutions provided an alternative set of meanings for coping with uncertainty and loss after 1943; in so doing, they forged interpretive patterns that then assumed even greater significance in the postwar period. The chapter thus offers an essential prehistory to the protracted aftereffects of war and defeat that form the central subject of this book.

OFFICIAL AND POPULAR RESPONSES TO RISING LOSSES

The rising casualty figures on the Eastern front posed new challenges to the political and military authorities of the Third Reich and transformed popular attitudes toward the war. Different kinds of casualties, however, prompted a variety of official and popular responses. In a straightforward manner, the Nazi regime incorporated the increasing number of fallen soldiers into its political mythology. In the aftermath of Stalingrad, the dead Wehrmacht soldier replaced the "old fighter" as the central object of the Nazi cult of the fallen hero.[8] Death on the battlefield became the ultimate sacrifice for the promised "final victory." This myth of the "fallen hero" served to extract new sacrifices from civilians and soldiers alike. In line with the more general "partification" of the Third Reich during the last years of the war, Nazi Party officials took over the business of communicating German losses to bereaved family members beginning in July 1942.[9] For the Nazi Party, increasing German losses did not signal the necessity to end the war but rather represented a means for further mobilizing the population. Ultimately, Hitler and the Nazi regime categorically refused to even conceive of a compromise peace as had been concluded in the aftermath of the First World War. Instead, the Nazi leadership set in motion an escalation of violence against internal and external "enemies" and ultimately orchestrated the nation's own self-destruction.[10]

It is difficult to assess how ordinary Germans responded to this official call for even greater sacrifices and, eventually, collective suicide in the face of rising casualties. Even if they subscribed to other key ingredients of Nazi ideology, many front soldiers resisted specific National Socialist interpretations of death and dying. Family members found little solace in the official portrayal of their relatives as fallen heroes. Even before Stalingrad, death announcements tended to omit the "*Führer*" from the standard line that a soldier had died for "Führer," "Volk," and "Fatherland"; and family members of fallen soldiers often refused to give the "Hitler salute." In the face of deep personal loss, the Hitler myth began to crumble.[11]

At the same time, German soldiers and civilians exhibited a remarkable tenacity during this period. Until the very end, large sections of the German population simply denied the possibility of defeat. As Robert Gellately has argued, despite numerous signs of disintegration and dissolution, "many people, and not just the died-in-the-wool Nazis, showed themselves anxious to interpret events in the most optimistic way possible."[12] Nazi Party membership actually rose from 6.5 million to 8 million between 1943 and 1945. For many ordinary Germans, the realization that past sacrifices and losses might have been in vain was simply too painful too accept.[13] In April 1942, Martha S., a sixty-six-year-old widow, denounced to the Gestapo the soldier Herbert N., who had told her that the war was lost. As the motive for her denunciation, she explained that "it would simply be inconceivable to experience that all the sacrifices of this war would have been in vain."[14] Like Martha S., large sections of the German population were incapable of conceiving of a future beyond Hitler and National Socialism despite increasing casualties.[15] Rising death tolls on the Eastern front thus did not prompt opposition and resistance to the Nazism. Instead, collective experiences of loss bound ordinary Germans to the regime or fostered, at best, widespread apathy and depression.[16]

In contrast to fallen soldiers, the liminal position of MIAs and POWs between active soldiers and mythical fallen heroes rendered these casualties more difficult to incorporate into the political mythology of Nazism. The widespread uncertainty about an increasing number of soldiers missing in action ran counter to the finality of official tales of heroic sacrifice. Likewise, captivity signaled the individual's desire for—as well as the actual possibility of—survival and thus threatened to undermine the National Socialist myth of heroic death. Consequently, the Wehrmacht command never prepared German soldiers for captivity, nor did the Nazi leadership ever try to integrate this possibility into its worldview.[17] Initially, the regime even tried to deny that any German soldiers had fallen into Soviet captivity at Stalingrad. The official Wehrmacht proclamation on Stalingrad from February 3, 1943, asserted that the members of the Sixth Army had "fought to the last bullet" and had died a heroic death "so that Germany will live."[18] The decision of the commander of the Sixth Army, General Paulus, to go into Soviet captivity rather than to commit suicide infuriated the Nazi leadership. Shortly after the surrender at Stalingrad, Goebbels noted in his diary the "depressing news that Paulus and fourteen of his generals had fallen into Bolshevist captivity."[19] Some days later, he worried that "it would be the most severe shock to the army's prestige that we have experienced during the entire National Socialist regime" if "several German generals had indeed voluntarily entered Bolshevist captivity."[20] As Goebbels's reaction makes clear, the liminal nature of German MIAs and POWs threatened to "pollute" the purity of the National Socialist "all or nothing" logic.[21]

Such concerns over detrimental influences emanating from Soviet captivity were further aggravated by the founding of antifascist organizations among German POWs in Soviet captivity: the National Committee for a Free Germany (NKFD) in July 1943 and the League of German Officers (BdO) in September of the same year.[22] The existence of these organizations turned Soviet captivity into an even more delicate political issue for the Nazi regime. By trying to win over German soldiers for the struggle against Hitler and National Socialism, these organizations gave Soviet captivity a more explicitly political dimension. The Army High Command (OKW) and the Nazi leadership took these organizations very seriously and were concerned about their negative propagandistic impact on both front and home front.[23] In National Socialist memory, the NKFD and the BdO evoked the specter of 1918 and of defeat not on the battlefield but through a "stab in the back"—this time not by a revolutionary home front but by "treacherous" generals such as Walter von Seydlitz, one of the founding members of the BdO.[24] As a result, the Nazi regime simply denied, until early, 1944, the existence of the BdO and of Seydlitz's participation.[25] When news about the NKFD and the BdO was confirmed through Soviet flyers and radio broadcasts, the Nazi regime engaged in extensive counterpropaganda and denounced both organizations as the creation of "Communist emigrants, mostly of the Jewish race."[26]

Popular concerns about the increasing number of missing and captured soldiers also entailed the potential of drawing ordinary Germans away from the regime's insistence on a "final struggle." Among family members of MIAs, the existential uncertainty about the fate of a missing relative produced, above all, a massive desire for information. Official statements that a "segment of the missing comrades in the Soviet Union has died a heroic death for the fatherland" appeared premature to many family members and failed to alleviate their nagging concerns about the fate of relatives missing on the Eastern front.[27] In contrast to the depressing certainty of an official death notification or the uncertainty of having a relative classified as MIA, captivity—even Soviet captivity—clearly represented "good news." "I wish Kurt were in Russian captivity; it would be better for him than to have died a heroic death for nothing," wrote the brother of a soldier missing in the East to his mother in June 1943, and, in so doing, willingly or unwillingly undermined the Nazi myth of heroic sacrifice.[28] Throughout the last years of the war, family members of MIAs and POWs confronted the political and military authorities with pressing demands to account for the fate of their sons, brothers, or husbands. In addition, they also began to develop their own activities that served one primary goal: to discover reliable information about the fate and the living situation of a son, brother, or husband. Sooner or later, these efforts brought them into contact with the main official agency for registering and communicating war losses, the Wehrmacht Agency for War Losses and POWs (Wehrmachtsauskunftsstelle für Kriegsverluste und Kriegsgefangene, WAST).

THE SEARCH FOR MISSING SOLDIERS:
POPULAR RUMORS ON THE HOME FRONT

The task of the WAST was to record all German losses—casualties, missing soldiers, and prisoners of war—and to provide Wehrmacht agencies as well as individual family members with information about German losses.[29] The massive losses at Stalingrad prompted the establishment of a separate "working agency" (*Abwicklungsstab*) that was supposed to determine the identities of the fallen soldiers at Stalingrad. While the "working agency" did not engage in active search operations for missing soldiers, it extensively communicated with family members in order to establish the location and date of the last news of each missing soldier.[30] After additional losses in northern Africa and on the Eastern front in

June 1944, its responsibilities were extended to all German casualties that could no longer be reported by military units themselves.[31] The skyrocketing casualty rates during the last stages of the war, however, meant that an increasing number of Wehrmacht soldiers were reported as "missing in action" without any more definitive information. Other losses were left unclassified after contact between family members and soldiers on the front had simply ceased to exist. Hitler's failure to conclude any agreement with the Soviet Union regarding the exchange of information about POWs further aggravated this situation.[32] As a result, family members were left in a state of fundamental uncertainty that often lasted into the postwar years.[33] The false postwar rumors about "missing divisions" in the East or hundreds of thousands of German POWs languishing in "secret camps" in the Soviet Union originated in this basic uncertainty about MIAs and POWs during the last years of the war.[34]

The Nazi regime not only failed to alleviate these popular anxieties but also deliberately concealed available information about MIAs and POWs. While the Nazi leadership was very much aware of the popular discontent that might originate from family members of MIAs and POWs, Goebbels and the propaganda ministry were even more concerned about hostile propaganda emanating from enemy sources.[35] The WAST shared information about MIAs and POWs gleaned from enemy sources only if family members directly contacted the agency.[36] In addition, the Nazi regime undermined the few existing avenues for establishing contact with German POWs. From August 1942 on, some German POWs managed to write letters and postcards to their relatives in Germany. But most of this mail from Soviet captivity never reached the intended recipients. The Reich Security Main Office (RSHA)—the administrative center of the Nazi security and terror apparatus—ordered that all mail from Soviet POW camps be held back by the censorship office (*Auslandsbriefprüfstellen*) for "state political reasons" (*staatspolitische*) and forwarded to the RSHA for further evaluation. By October 1943, an RSHA report listed seven thousand such letters from Soviet captivity; the total number for the entire duration of the war is estimated to be twenty thousand.[37] The authorities never notified family members of these letters and postcards. The potentially detrimental propagandistic impact of news about the survival in Soviet captivity took precedence over the existential worries and grief of family members of MIAs and POWs.

The regime's (dis)information policy prompted widespread popular discontent among relatives of missing soldiers. From the defeat at Stalingrad virtually to the end of the war, they suspected military and political authorities—correctly as it turned out—of withholding information about the number and identity of missing soldiers and POWs.[38] In December 1943, military authorities in Dresden reported that families of missing

Stalingrad soldiers felt "not sufficiently supported, and even abandoned or almost betrayed" by the political and military authorities. The report estimated that the number of affected persons in that army district alone amounted to more than one hundred thousand. In light of the "serious general situation," this "loss of confidence in the Wehrmacht among wide sections of the population" entailed "serious dangers."[39]

As a result of their frustration with official efforts to provide information, family members began to undertake their own efforts at investigating the fate of missing soldiers and POWs. One potential source of information consisted of Soviet flyers listing the names of alleged German POWs. Although the Army High Command asserted that the names on these flyers were probably forged or belonged to soldiers who had actually been killed on the Eastern front, family members of missing POWs nevertheless regarded them as a valuable source of information.[40] In March 1943, for example, Karl R. brought home with him a Soviet flyer encouraging soldiers to inform the families of missing soldiers that their loved ones were in Soviet captivity and that they were "doing well" (*sind wohlauf*). His parents subsequently contacted the families of several soldiers listed on the flyer, who then spread the information even further. When this communication was eventually intercepted by the Gestapo, Karl R.'s mother explained that her actions had been motivated by her own loss of two brothers in the First World War and of her youngest son Kurt's death on the Eastern front in 1942. "I wanted to help the affected persons, and I felt sorry for them that they did not have any news of their relatives." The "good reputation" that Frau R. had earned in the eyes of the Gestapo through her service in Nazi welfare organizations as well as her role as bloc leader of the local branch of the Nazi Women's League saved her from prosecution. But her case illustrates how private experiences of loss fueled empathy with other (German) losses and led even otherwise loyal Germans to transcend the codes of acceptable behavior in Nazi Germany.[41]

Soviet radio broadcasts represented an even more readily available, though also illegal, source of information about MIAs and POW. With the beginning of the war in September 1939, listening to foreign radio became a criminal offense punishable with several years in prison.[42] The threat of persecution, however, did not prevent family members from resorting to this news source, even if they were otherwise loyal to the Nazi regime. A report from June 1943 stated that "undoubtedly, a large number of faithful National Socialist Germans are listening to the Russian radio station night after night hoping to receive any news about missing soldiers."[43] Ever concerned about hostile influences on the "people's comrades," Goebbels worried that this illegal practice might leave "political traces" among family members of missing soldiers.[44] The case of Fritz M. illustrates just how widespread this practice had become by the spring of 1943.[45] A World War I veteran and former SPD member who also suffered from multiple sclerosis, Fritz M. began to listen to Soviet radio broadcasts in January 1943 and then sent forty-six letters to relatives of German POWs. Because he signed the letters with his real name and address, the Gestapo eventually arrested him in May 1943.[46] In addition, the Gestapo also traced the recipients of his letters, who were hard pressed to explain why they had not reported these communications earlier. One woman declared that she had already received thirteen such letters regarding the fate of her husband from different sources.[47] In October 1943, Fritz M. was charged with having engaged in "Communist propaganda" by countering the "common assumption . . . that German soldiers in Russian captivity were treated badly" and by telling family members "that the allegedly missing German soldiers were in captivity and doing well." This, the Gestapo asserted, was tantamount to undermining the "morale of the troops on the front." As a result, Fritz M. was sentenced to two years in prison.[48]

Family members not only sought information about MIAs and POWs, they also began to contact each other and shared the scarce bits of information that were available. The months after Stalingrad saw the emergence of an entire subculture of informal networks among family members of missing soldiers. In a liberal-democratic or even authoritarian system, these networks would have represented the preliminary stages of legitimate interest-group formation.[49] Yet within the context of the Nazi dictatorship, these informal contacts assumed a subversive quality. They promoted a plethora of rumors about the fate of MIAs and POWs in order to compensate for the deficiencies of officially available information.[50] Such rumors represented a less than public countersphere in which it was possible to articulate alternative responses to impending defeat. When the war assumed a more personal meaning for an increasing number of ordinary Germans, official and private visions for the future began to diverge. Rumors and informal networks among family members of missing soldiers pointed to a gradual erosion of the popular consensus on which the war had rested since the early military triumphs in 1939–40.

The most prominent of these rumors centered on the former commander of the Eighth Army Corps of the Sixth Army, Generaloberst Walter Heitz. At Stalingrad, Heitz had lived up to his reputation as one of the most loyal Nazi generals by threatening to execute everybody who surrendered to the Red Army.[51] Yet on January 31, Heitz himself capitulated to Soviet forces and even managed to write a letter from a Soviet POW camp, which reached his wife Gisela in April 1943 due to a mistake of the censorship office in Vienna. After Frau Heitz had inquired with several agencies as to how to respond to her husband's letter, the OKW finally referred her to the WAST while also cautioning that "due to the completely negative attitude of the Soviet Union, there have been no agreements whatsoever regarding contact with German POWs in the Soviet Union." Yet, as it did with all such requests, the WAST never attempted to contact Heitz or any other German POW in Soviet captivity but rather forwarded Frau Heitz's letter to the Reich Security Main Office (RSHA) in Berlin.[52] Rather than seeking to explore the possibilities for communication with German POWs, the military leadership intentionally deceived family members of missing soldiers and relied on the security organs of the Third Reich to suppress such communications.[53]

Official repression notwithstanding, the Heitz letter quickly became the stuff of popular rumors and informal communications. Frau Heitz began to pass on the news about her husband to other wives of missing soldiers. Some months later, she reported that she had received "hundreds of inquiries" regarding this matter.[54] Hedwig Strecker, another general's wife, managed to establish similar contacts with her captured husband and passed on the information to other family members of missing soldiers.[55] The Heitz rumor gained new currency as a result of an ever increasing number of missing soldiers in 1944. In February, the father of a missing Stalingrad soldier portrayed Heitz as a liaison person for MIAs and POWs in the East. He developed a questionnaire that family members were supposed to send to Heitz through the WAST.[56] The collapse of Army Group Center in June 1944 promoted further rumors surrounding General Heitz, who, at that time, was no longer alive.[57] In June 1944, for example, Claire R. inquired with military authorities whether it was possible to receive information through General Heitz about her husband, who had been reported missing since January 1943.[58] In response to persistently high numbers of inquiries, the Army High Command finally issued a statement in which it firmly denied the possibility of learning about missing soldiers in the East through Generaloberst Heitz. From that point on, inquiring family members received a form letter indicating that "not in a single case was it possible to confirm the receipt of a letter sent from Germany by a German POW in the Soviet Union," thus discouraging any further requests.[59] Still, military and political authorities never succeeded in suppressing these inquiries, and the Heitz rumor accompanied the fighting almost until the end of the war.[60]

These informal communications about MIAs and POWs threatened to undermine the ideological cohesion of German society. By stating that "no officer has committed suicide up to the very end," the letters circulating among family members of Stalingrad soldiers flew in the face of the myth of heroic sacrifice.[61] These rumors carried the danger that a growing number of ordinary Germans might follow the example of highly decorated Wehrmacht generals and simply refuse to die a heroic death for the sake of an increasingly elusive "final victory." This was all the more true since these letters also established the possibility of survival in Soviet captivity and asserted that German POWs "must be treated by the Russians over there fairly humanely."[62]

Besides the figure of General Heitz, family members of missing soldiers also placed high hopes on neutral countries as potential intermediaries between Nazi Germany and the Soviet Union. In March 1943, one affected "family father" of a missing Stalingrad fighter even contacted the Führer's headquarters and suggested the use of a neutral power in order to encourage Russian officials to release the names of fallen and captured Wehrmacht soldiers.[63] Other rumors speculated that the Vatican had offered to establish contact with ninety thousand German POWs in the Soviet Union, yet the German government had rejected this offer.[64] The German embassy in Turkey and the Turkish branch of the Red Cross, the Red Crescent, also featured prominently in rumors about German POWs in Soviet captivity. Letters circulating among family members stated that it was possible to contact German POWs in the Soviet Union through the German embassy in Ankara. This rumor was based on at least one case in which the German ambassador to Turkey and former chancellor Franz von Papen had personally confirmed the internment of a German soldier in Soviet captivity.[65] Within a short period of time, however, this information spread like wildfire and led to hundreds of inquiries with the German embassy and the Red Crescent in Turkey, sometimes even with the encouragement of local Nazi Party leaders.[66] At the same time, family members exhibited considerable frustration that officials did not support them in their endeavors to find information about missing loved ones. When her inquiry to the Red Crescent was returned without any response about her missing fiancé in April 1943, Irmgard D. bitterly complained to the OKW in Berlin: "Why should we not make an inquiry [through the Red Crescent]? At least one should be allowed to try!" Frustrated about the lack of an official reply to her query, she charged that such ineffective and useless communications were detrimental to "total war," in which "every working hour is needed." As in earlier cases, this woman quite easily reconciled her frustration with the regime's (dis)information policy regarding MIAs and POWs with a public commitment to the war effort.[67] Still, like the Heitz rumor, the persistence of the "Turkey rumor" through the last two years of the war underlined the massive popular desire for information about MIAs and POWs.[68]

Informal networks among family members of MIAs and POWs also gave voice to private visions for the future that increasingly diverged from those of the Nazi regime. One letter reporting rumors about contacts with POWs in the Soviet Union took them as an inspiration to "look into the future with much more hope and to expect a good ending."[69] This hope

for a positive outcome, however, was no longer predicated on the expectation of a "final victory" in the distant and indeterminate future.[70] Instead,
family members began to define their expectations for the near future in
primarily private terms. They were hoping for a quick conclusion to the
war that would presumably result in a reunion with their captured or
missing husbands, sons, and brothers.[71] "If only this war were finally over,
and those poor people were freed," wrote one family member of a German POW.[72] The same popular sentiment was reported in March 1943
from Bensheim an der Bergstrasse in March 1943, a military district with
a particularly high concentration of relatives of Stalingrad fighters. This
report noted an increasingly "defeatist tendency" among the population
that manifested itself in frequent expressions of the wish "that the war
will be over soon."[73] Here, private concerns over family cohesion gave
rise to the imagination of alternative futures that superseded the Nazi
regime's scenario of national sacrifice. Within the admittedly limited milieu of family members of former Stalingrad fighters, the congruence between private interests and Nazi expansionary policies began to split
apart in the spring of 1943.[74] The potentially highly subversive quality of
these hopes for a compromise peace is manifest in the fact that they were
also adopted in flyers of the White Rose, the Munich-based resistance
organization whose student members were caught in February 1943 and
executed a few months later.[75]

In most cases, however, widespread dissatisfaction over the Nazi regime's failure to account for missing soldiers and POWs did not translate
into opposition to the regime. These concerns, after all, often remained
highly individualized and limited to one specific issue, and they were generally not linked to nonconformist viewpoints. In some cases, criticism of
official information policy even went along with an affirmative stance
toward Nazism. Moreover, as Detlev Peukert has argued, widespread rumors did not necessarily indicate the existence of broad-based popular
opposition to the regime, but rather represented an extreme "fragmenta-
tion of public opinion," which disintegrated into several subspheres. The
increasing discrepancy between public statements and private communications had a disorienting effect that ran counter to goal-oriented opposition and resistance.[76] While family members engaged in myriad activities
to investigate the fate of missing relatives, these activities remained scat-
tered and devoid of a more unified political direction.

Moreover, the security organs of the Third Reich were highly successful
in preventing such private communications from coalescing into political
opposition. To be sure, family members of missing soldiers enjoyed, unlike those groups excluded from the Nazi racial community, significant
protective barriers. Yet the threat of repression remained always present,
and often a mere admonition by a Gestapo officer or SS man sufficed to

convince a family member of a missing soldier to cease all independent activities. In addition, the Gestapo and the SD (Sicherheitsdienst), the intelligence division of the SS, also benefited from close cooperation with Wehrmacht agencies, and vice versa, in prosecuting these activities. The "working agency" for Stalingrad and the counterintelligence division of the Wehrmacht, the Abwehr, regularly exchanged information about the activities of family members of missing soldiers with the Gestapo and the SD.[77] Finally, the security organs of the Nazi regime drew on the willing collaboration of individual Germans. This was, for example, the choice of the Field Marshal Paulus's wife and brother, who denounced a letter from Soviet captivity as "propaganda for Russian captivity" and reported it to the authorities.[78] In so doing, they replicated the general's own disastrous commitment to the National Socialist ideals at Stalingrad.

The personal nature that gave popular concerns about MIAs and POWs their urgency also limited their potential political significance. For the most part, these concerns remained confined to the immediate range of one's own kin. Increasing losses and uncertainty did not open up ordinary Germans to larger questions of politics and morality but instead fostered a narrowing of one's perspective to the exclusive focus on the survival of the family. This "inward turn" was far from innocent. Given widespread knowledge about the Nazi regime's genocidal policies, the focus on one's own personal grievances facilitated a virtually complete moral and emotional disengagement from the victims of Nazism precisely at the moment when the regime unleashed its most destructive energies. Ordinary Germans' increasing self-referentiality and desire for peace did not just reflect a basic indifference toward the victims of Nazism but could also go along with a persistent belief in central aspects of anti-Semitic propaganda.[79] These popular responses to impending defeat also anticipated postwar Germans' denial of empathy with the victims of Nazism that so shocked outside observers like Hannah Arendt.[80]

This blocking out of the fate of Germany's victims did not constitute the only possible popular response to the mounting losses during the last years of the war. The remarkable, albeit highly unusual, case of Dr. Christian Schöne illustrates the range of popular responses to the increasing number of MIAs and POWs, which reached from fantasies of revenge to outspoken empathy with Germany's victims.[81] It also illuminates that these responses left, at least in part, room for an individual's choice and volition. Schöne was a medical doctor who headed a small military hospital near Frankfurt an der Oder. When his brother Konrad Schöne was reported missing at Stalingrad in January 1943, Christian Schöne began to participate in the informal network of family members of missing soldiers and, in March 1943, started to send out chain letters to other family members of MIAs in which he recounted his activities to research the fate of his missing brother. In the first letter, he told of his efforts to contact former members of the German embassy in Moscow as well as the Swiss and Swedish representative in Berlin, hoping that these neutral countries would be able to "help people who got into a difficult situation through no fault of their own."[82]

Up to this point, Schöne's efforts did not differ significantly from similar activities by family members of missing soldiers. Yet in a third chain letter sent out on 3 May, 1943 (the birthday of his missing brother), Schöne made a most unusual rhetorical move: he linked the fate of German MIAs to the killing of Jews on the Eastern front. Schöne recounted suggestions from other family members of missing soldiers to take revenge on the "6–7 million Jews in our hands" if Moscow's "Jewish rulers were to harm our captured soldiers."[83] This proposal reflected the popular acceptance of the Nazi regime's genocidal logic that blamed and punished Jews for German military losses. Unlike other family members of missing soldiers, Schöne, however, was adamantly opposed to such fantasies of revenge. Instead, he reported in his chain letter that Soviet Jews "have already been shot by us in numbers for which the pits of Katyn would be insufficient." He related that his missing brother had told him of the killing of sixty-four thousand Jews, including women and children, from Kiev and that he knew from an SS man, who had participated in 150 executions per day, that these killings were still going on. Rather than advocating reprisals against Jewish victims, Schöne feared that "our prisoners will have to pay the price for this." In addition—and this was the truly significant part of his letter—he declared that mass murder was dishonorable and unmoral, and thus demanded that these "morally reprehensible" actions cease. As a result, he encouraged the recipients of his letter to confront official party, state, and military authorities with two demands: first, petitioners should insist that "responsible military experts" lead the military operations in order to prevent another Stalingrad, and second, insist upon an end to the killing of the Jews.

This was a remarkable intervention. Schöne's letter clearly bespeaks the extensive knowledge about mass killings of Jews in the East that was available inside Nazi Germany by early 1943, as well as the different conclusions that contemporaries drew from this knowledge.[84] In contrast to many ordinary Germans' moral disengagement or sense of revenge, Schöne's personal concern for his brother did not lead him to ignore or deny what was happening at the same time to the victims of Nazi Germany. Instead, his personal loss enabled him to empathize with Jewish victims and to move toward a morally grounded opposition to National Socialism. Second, the outcome of the case was just as surprising as the letter itself. In November 1943, a military court tried Schöne for his activities but meted out a relatively mild sentence of one year in prison. Significantly, the verdict never questioned the truth of Schöne's assertions about mass killings on the Eastern front, but simply argued that these utterances threatened to subvert German morale. This ruling might have constituted an exception in the otherwise increasingly lethal military justice system. But the court might also have feared the negative propagandistic impact of punishing more harshly a member of the "national community" for his concern for his missing brother. Schöne survived war and dictatorship but died in March 1947, shortly before his brother was able to send a postcard from a POW camp in Siberia.[85]

Knowledge about Soviet Captivity and Wehrmacht Morale

The proliferation of informal networks among family members of missing soldiers fueled official concerns that these rumors might spill over to the front itself and undermine the morale of the troops. Partly to counter these proliferating rumors about Soviet captivity, Wehrmacht and party agencies undertook extensive efforts to compile information about the situation and treatment of German POWs. Such knowledge about Soviet captivity was important to military and political officials also in light of intensified NKFD propaganda that openly encouraged German soldiers to desert.[86] The credibility of NKFD efforts centrally depended on the perception of Soviet captivity among Wehrmacht soldiers. For only if German POWs had a decent chance of survival did captivity appear as a legitimate alternative to service in Hitler's army. A positive portrayal of Soviet captivity as "the shortest way home" thus formed a key element in NKFD propaganda.[87] As a "countermyth" to the National Socialist myth of heroic sacrifice, NKFD propaganda promised German soldiers an alternative time horizon. Whereas National Socialist authorities like Hermann Göring in his crucial speech on 30 January, 1943 gestured toward redemption in the long and indeterminate future ("in a thousand years, every German will still speak of this battle"), the NKFD portrayed the defeat at Stalingrad as the prehistory to liberation through the Red Army in the foreseeable future.[88]

Official efforts to investigate the treatment and conditions of German POWs in the Soviet Union drew on three types of sources: interrogations of captured Soviet soldiers, reports of escaped or liberated German POWs, and evaluations of Soviet propaganda.[89] Their interest in accurate information notwithstanding, military and political authorities processed this information through the lenses of racist and anti-Semitic stereotypes.[90] Military officials, for example, discredited the account of a captured Russian pilot by concluding that "he was Jewish" and made a "dishonest (*verschlagene*) impression."[91] In another case, a captured female

Soviet soldier was interrogated several times until her revised account approximated preconceived notions of atrocities by "Jewish officers" in the Red Army against German POWs.[92] Such stories of alleged Soviet atrocities also featured prominently in two confidential reports on POWs in Soviet captivity that were compiled by the Reich Security Main Office (RSHA) and the Wehrmacht counterespionage division Fremde Heere Ost in 1944. These reports told of political selections by "NKVD commissars, German emigrants, and Jews" who separated "fascists" from "anti-fascists" and "Communists" among German POWs. They reported frequent executions and mass deportations to Siberia in "cattle trains that resembled animal cages," which then led to "mass death."[93] While recent research indicates that shootings of German POWs did occur occasionally, German POWs were not subjected to a policy of deliberate annihilation.[94] Instead, the military and political authorities of the Third Reich projected their own practices of genocidal warfare onto their Soviet enemy. Reports of political selections, executions, and mass deportation of German POWs in Soviet captivity legitimized the similar criminal transgressions by German SS and regular army units in the war of annihilation on the Eastern front.[95] They also anticipated postwar tendencies to use the Jewish experience as a narrative frame for German suffering.[96]

Both reports also conceded that Soviet treatment of German POWs had improved considerably, largely as a result of Soviet efforts to exploit the labor force of German POWs. According to the Wehrmacht report, German POWs were "treated relatively well when they reached the camps," while the RSHA report granted that "the Bolshevists" have recently tried "to integrate the POWs as quickly as possible into the work process" and "to exploit this workforce as long as possible." Finally, both reports revealed officials' concerns regarding the susceptibility of German POWs to the activities of the NKFD. While the Wehrmacht report came to the conclusion that "only a very small number of German POWs decide to participate in the treacherous activity of these elements," the RSHA evaluated the political loyalty of German soldiers in captivity much more skeptically. "Most prisoners," the RSHA report stated, "sooner or later succumb to these influences."[97]

These confidential findings were highly explosive. Just as popular uncertainty about soldiers missing on the Eastern front threatened to subvert morale on the home front, this information about improved conditions in Soviet captivity raised official anxieties about the cohesion among soldiers on the front. Impressionistic evidence suggests that these concerns were not completely unfounded. In May 1943, a soldier writing from the front reported that "for some time, Russian captivity has sounded a bit better than earlier." In January 1944, another soldier reckoned that "the Russians no longer shoot all the injured POWs. They probably need them too."[98] The possibility of Soviet captivity as an alternative conclusion of the war also emerged in communications between soldiers on the front and family members on the home front. In September 1943, Margareta K. wrote to her thirteen-year-old son that his father was in Russian captivity, adding—and this was the phrase that caught the attention of the Gestapo—that her husband had always maintained that "he would rather be in captivity than have his bones shot to pieces." When interrogated by the Gestapo, Margareta K. vehemently denied that her husband had ever expressed any intention to desert, even though she conceded that his last letter from August 1943 indicated an increasing unwillingness to continue fighting because "he had been through so much already."[99]

An order by the head of the OKW, Wilhelm Keitel, from January 1944 prohibiting any statements regarding the allegedly good treatment of German POWs indirectly confirmed the increasing prevalence of such sentiments among Wehrmacht soldiers.[100] Nazi propaganda about Soviet atrocities also became less credible the longer the war lasted. When the propaganda ministry evoked the violent transgressions of the advancing Red Army in eastern Germany in 1944–45, ordinary Germans reportedly refused to believe these stories of Soviet atrocities precisely because they were played up so strongly in Goebbels's propaganda.[101] At least to a segment of ordinary soldiers, Soviet captivity no longer appeared as an utterly horrifying conclusion to the war, equal to or even worse than death. This assumption is borne out by the extremely high number of soldiers who were either reported missing in action or captured by enemy forces on the Eastern front during the last stages of the war. It is well known that rumors about the good treatment in British or American captivity contributed to the mass surrender of German forces on the Western front.[102] But beginning in the second half of 1944, voluntary surrender or at least a more passive refusal to fight also began to constitute a mass phenomenon on the Eastern front.[103]

Despite these indications of soldiers' searches for an exit from the war, the salient fact about the Wehrmacht during the last years of the war was not dissent and disintegration but remarkable cohesion. Historians have struggled to explain this behavior of ordinary soldiers, which, from today's perspective, seems difficult to fathom. The acceleration of terror and repression during the final stages of the war certainly contributed to the Wehrmacht's tenacity. A dramatic expansion of military justice led to the execution of more than twenty thousand German soldiers.[104] The Nazi regime, moreover, also sought to sever subversive communication between front and home front by extending punishment, including execution, to family members of successful deserters.[105] In November 1944, an order by the Wehrmacht High Command formally held family members liable "with property, freedom, or life" for the desertion of a son, brother, or husband.[106] Similarly radical measures were adopted against the families of German POWs who were suspected of collaborating with Soviet authorities. As early as January 1942, the Gestapo began to investigate the backgrounds of soldiers whose names appeared on Soviet flyers.[107] If it became known that individual German POWs had joined the NKFD, the Reich Security Main Office began to check their political backgrounds and family situation.[108] Wehrmacht agencies closely cooperated with the SS and SD in prosecuting cases of disloyalty among German soldiers in Soviet captivity.[109] In 1944, especially after the failed conspiracy against Hitler on July 20, the regime also began to prosecute and arrest family members of Wehrmacht officers who had joined NKFD and BdO. The wife of General Seydlitz was forced to divorce her husband.[110] Confirming the close link between desertion and Soviet captivity, these provisions were finally extended to all alleged "traitors" in captivity, thus making family members responsible for the conduct of German POWs.[111] By turning its destructive forces against Germans themselves, the Nazi regime revealed its final inability to provide perspective and meaning to the German population in the last stages of the war.

Terror and coercion alone, however, do not suffice to explain the ferocity with which ordinary soldiers fought to the end of the war. By 1943, the Wehrmacht had indeed become Hitler's army, and the bulk of its leadership as well as large segments of ordinary soldiers had come to share the ideological assumptions that drove the war of annihilation on the Eastern front.[112] Besides ideological indoctrination "from above," more recent interpretations assign more agency to ordinary soldiers' own motivations during the final stages of the war. To explain ordinary soldiers' purpose and commitment, historians have invoked a perverted sense of "comradeship,"[113] an unbroken emotional investment in the "myth of the Führer,"[114] or a desperate effort to hang on to communal bonds in the face of defeat, a "catastrophic nationalism."[115] This historiography, then, makes clear that Soviet captivity did not represent a viable alternative to most Wehrmacht soldiers. Rumors about improving conditions in Soviet captivity ultimately did not supersede soldiers' own cultural and often racist sense of superiority over "the Russians," which prevented them from voluntarily surrendering to the Red Army.[116] In addition, many soldiers must have witnessed the mass death of Soviet POWs in German captivity during the early stages of the war.[117] Here too, German soldiers' own guilty conscience lay behind their own fears of "revenge" if they ended up in captivity.[118] For these reasons, "Siberia" did not seem like an acceptable outcome for many ordinary soldiers, and hence, they continued to fight. In the end, official anxieties about collapsing Wehrmacht morale proved unfounded, and most German soldiers followed the Nazi regime into total defeat.

Popular responses to the increasingly personal quality of the war thus diverged on front and home front. For civilians, the "privatization" of the war implied an inward turn and an almost exclusive focus on kinship relations. For the vast majority of soldiers, by contrast, the same process often inspired an ethics of ferocious fighting that militated against voluntary surrender as an alternative conclusion to the war. The Nazi regime's most important achievement during the last years of the war resided in its ability to mobilize ordinary soldiers' personal motivations for its own self-destructive logic. It was precisely this increasingly "personal" quality of the war—combined with an utter dehumanization of the enemy—that accounted for its increasing lethality on all sides.

These diverging responses to increasing losses shaped postwar confrontations with total war and total defeat. The gradual and partial disengagement from National Socialism among family members of MIAs and POWs, as well as their focus on a private future centered on the family, provided emotional and experiential bridges across 1945. Informal communications among family members over the fate of MIAs and POWs also anticipated the postwar discourse on German victimization that completely severed German losses from previous German aggression.[119] Women's prominence in these informal networks on the home front also points to the gender-specific dimension of this particular transition from war to postwar. Ironically, the National Socialist emphasis on women's significance in the private sphere ultimately turned against Nazism itself: during the last years of the war, the family (and kinship relations more broadly) constituted a repository of alternative futures that fostered a disengagement from National Socialism.[120] This was true despite women's prominence in the war industry and air-defense battalions.[121] Postwar memories of women's experiences blocked out their significant participation in the war effort as well as their willful ignorance of Nazi genocide. Instead, these memories drew on predominantly female experiences of personal loss and private resilience, which then were easily transformed into national narratives of German innocence and victimization.[122] By contrast, the parallel male experience of fighting to the end was much more difficult to incorporate into postwar memories of defeat, not the least because it was a narrative of abysmal failure on both the individual and the collective level. The collapse of the Nazi regime paralleled the failure of German men to protect the homeland and their families against the Red Army. This absence of an adequate male narrative of the war's ending also deprived any potential postwar resistance to the victors of its ideological basis. It also meant, as the ensuing chapters of this book will demonstrate, that the rehabilitation of the male narrative of war and defeat became one of the central ideological projects of postwar reconstruction in both Germanys.

THE ROLE OF THE CHRISTIAN CHURCHES

The Christian churches crucially shaped this process of a gradual distancing from the Nazi regime among civilians at home and—to a much lesser extent—among soldiers on the front. As the last semiautonomous institution of the Third Reich, the churches alleviated the crisis of meaning that had opened up as a result of increasing losses since Stalingrad. Church organizations responded to ideological and emotional needs of the population that the Nazi regime increasingly left unsatisfied. Given the churches' historic role of providing a space, albeit highly confined and regulated, for action specifically for women, church organizations were well suited for articulating specifically female concerns regarding missing or captured soldiers. The churches addressed fundamental experiences of uncertainty and loss and, in so doing, prefigured confrontations with the consequences of total defeat in the postwar period. In this way, the churches represented a crucial institutional and discursive link between the last years of the war and the postwar period.

Two Christian welfare organizations illustrate the churches' role in the transition from the war to the postwar particularly well: the Catholic Church War Aid (Kirchliche Kriegshilfe) and the Protestant Aid Society for POWs and Internees (Evangelisches Hilfswerk für Kriegsgefangene und Internierte, EHIK). Initially closely linked to the Nazi war effort and highly supportive of the ideological crusade against Bolshevism, both organizations undertook extensive efforts to help ordinary Germans in coping with rising military losses beginning in 1943. They also continued to exist nearly unchanged after 1945 and assumed crucial roles in caring for MIAs, POWs, and returnees as well as their family members in postwar Germany.

The Catholic Kirchliche Kriegshilfe was formed within the Catholic Caritas and was initially responsible for providing religious literature to fifteen thousand Catholic soldiers, military chaplains, and theology students.[123] Until 1943, it was headed by Heinrich Höfler, who was subsequently drafted into the army and interned by the Gestapo in Berlin between June 1944 and May 1945. The explicit purpose of the EHIK, by contrast, was religious care for Protestant POWs and internees. Bishop Theodor Heckel, who, since 1934, also had headed the Foreign Office of the German Protestant Church, presided over the EHIK throughout the Nazi period.[124] From the beginning of the war, both organizations had lent crucial ideological and logistical support to the Nazi war effort. This was especially true after the onset of the National Socialist "crusade" against Bolshevism in June 1941. In his "letters to comrades," Heinrich Höfler wrote in October 1941:

In the land of the Red Star, you German soldiers have witnessed the invasion of a demonic power into the realm of history. The devilish evil and the terrifying bestiality that has been experienced in the East remains in your memory as a historical lesson on the . . . culturally destructive effect of a fanatical hatred and destructive will against Christian thinking, Christian symbols, and popular traditions.[125]

Bishop Heckel also preached a fervent anti-Bolshevism in public speeches as well as in individual communications with soldiers on the front, in which he often referred to his own front experience during the First World War.[126] Christian affinities to National Socialist ideology were not limited to a shared anti-Bolshevism but also derived from the Catholic hope for the coming of a new *Reich* or from the national Protestant emphasis on obedience to state authorities. Finally, the boundaries between a religiously motivated, traditional anti-Judaism and Nazi racial anti-Semitism always remained fluid.[127] Sermons for Catholic priests serving on the Eastern front sent out by the Kirchliche Kriegshilfe, for example, evoked biblical anti-Semitic motifs that provided legitimacy to the racial war of annihilation in the East.[128] Heckel articulated his anti-Semitism even more explicitly by denouncing the "Jewish clique in the United States" in a letter to a Protestant minister serving on the Eastern front.[129]

Despite this congruence between Nazi ideology and the Christian churches, both the Kirchliche Kriegshilfe and the EHIK came into conflict with the regime during the final years of the war. Höfler was interned by the Gestapo because he was accused of giving secret military details to the Vatican.[130] And even Heckel, whose affinity to Nazism was much stronger than Höfler's, ultimately clashed with the Nazi leadership over the efforts of the SS to push back the influence of the church in the occupied territories in the East.[131] These conflicts with the regime allowed both organizations to portray themselves as having remained immune to National Socialism, thus conveniently bracketing their earlier affinity to it.[132] While this postwar narrative of resistance was grossly exaggerated and, indeed, a myth, the last few years of the war did see an increasing divergence between Christian and National Socialist responses to mounting losses and impending defeat. In particular, the ever-increasing losses on the Eastern front (including MIAs and POWs) since the defeat at Stalingrad produced massive popular desire for consolation and meaning that the Christian churches were able to exploit. After years of decline, church membership soared, especially among family members of fallen soldiers.[133] During the last two years of the war, more and more ordinary Germans turned to Christian rituals of mourning again.

This new popularity of the churches did not remain hidden from the watchful eye of Nazi authorities. In the aftermath of Stalingrad, SD observers noted the popular appeal of Christian commemorations of fallen soldiers, which "sought to surpass National Socialist commemorations of the fallen hero in every respect." According to the SD, the Catholic Church, in particular, developed "extraordinary creativity in honoring the dead." Priests offered special sermons for fallen and missing soldiers, to which family members were personally escorted. The church established symbolic graves for dead soldiers—even for those soldiers who had left the church. In Göttingen, the local church community set up a specific altar that displayed a red candle for each fallen soldier and a green candle for every three soldiers missing in action.[134] Gestapo officials reported similar church activities in the wake of Stalingrad. At a special sermon for Stalingrad fighters, a Catholic priest read aloud a letter from one of them; the content was reportedly "so terrible" that "most of the audience began to cry." "This," the local propaganda chief commented, "is not the right way to prepare our countrymen (*Volksgenossen*) for a total war."[135]

The popularity of church commemorations filled the ideological void that resulted from the disintegration of the National Socialist myth of heroic sacrifice. Unlike the cult of the fallen hero, the Christian concept of suffering as a precondition for redemption was not tied to a National Socialist victory. Instead, the Christian notion of sacrifice—based on the model of the crucifixion of Christ—assumed a redemptive quality independent of the outcome of the war.[136] A Catholic sermon for Easter 1944 sent out by the Kirchliche Kriegshilfe, for example, explicitly rejected the notion that a final victory would ultimately justify sacrifices in the present. By contrast, the sermon argued that loss of a relative could never by compensated for by earthly gains but that true consolation could only be found in "God's eternal love."[137] Given the approaching Allied armies on all fronts, belief in religious salvation may have been easier than increasingly desperate hopes for a final victory. In fact, the (self-) destructive energies unleashed by the regime during the final stages of the war suggested that the collapse, not the ultimate triumph, of the Nazi regime was the precondition for the "return to God." These divergences in Christian and National Socialist interpretation of loss and suffering, then, also paved the way for the Christian interpretation of war and defeat in the postwar period. The Nazi regime now appeared as the epitome of a secular turn away from God and religion in the modern world, whose collapse was to usher in a new era of re-Christianization.[138]

The renewed appeal of the Christian churches during the last years of the Third Reich not only resulted from a rather desperate turn toward religion in the face of impending defeat. It also derived from the fact that church organizations like the Kirchliche Kriegshilfe and the EHIK addressed fundamental experiences of uncertainty and loss to which the Nazi regime no longer gave satisfying answers. This was true especially regarding the fates of German MIAs and POWs. The Catholic Easter sermon for 1944, for example, included a "prayer for missing soldiers," which sought to console family members who were anxious about missing loved-ones.[139] While the prayer appealed to God's power to comfort the missing soldier wherever he might be, it also addressed the possibility that he might no longer be alive and thus pleaded for the salvation of his soul. Through sermons and prayers, church representatives sought to alleviate popular concerns that the military and political leadership of the Third Reich tended to ignore or to address in a cursory and formal fashion.

This was also the function of a series of letters that Bishop Heckel sent to family members of MIAs and POWs. The EHIK established contact with ministers and theology students in Western captivity and then sought to provide these individual POWs with religious literature. As a result, an extensive correspondence emerged among the EHIK in Berlin, family members of POWs, and individual POWs from places as far away as Canada or New Zealand.[140] The EHIK, to be sure, was unable to establish similar contacts with German POWs in Soviet captivity. Still, family members of missing soldiers in the East frequently contacted the EHIK and Bishop Heckel personally, seeking to explore every possible option to gain information regarding their missing relatives. While Heckel and EHIK were unable to provide any more information than official state or Wehrmacht agencies, they responded with very personal, individual letters that sought to take seriously the desperate uncertainty of the predominantly female letter writers.[141] In one case from May 1943, the EHIK representative, for example, encouraged the letter writer not to abandon hope that "over the course of the war, there will be a possibility to conduct detailed investigations regarding the fate of German POWs in Soviet captivity."[142] These letters assumed a very different tone from official statements by Wehrmacht and party authorities, which tended to perceive the activities of family members of missing soldiers and POWs as a nuisance at best, as propagandistic subversion of morale at worst. Church organizations like Heckel's EHIK thus provided solace and support where the regime offered increasingly unconvincing propaganda. In so doing, these organizations sought to bridge the chasm that had opened up between the Nazi regime and ordinary Germans as a result of the rising German losses since 1943.

These semiofficial communications between church organizations and ordinary Germans anticipated the discursive communities that were to shape postwar confrontations with war and defeat. They gave expression to German losses, yet, unlike the Nazi propaganda, they did not seek to use these painful experiences for further mobilization. At the same time, these communications reflected ordinary Germans' increasingly narrow and selective perception of external reality. They separated private pain from previous German aggressions and thus dehistoricized and decontextualized German losses. Long before the collapse of the Nazi regime, these conversations prefigured the postwar proclivity of ordinary Germans to see themselves as the true victims of war and dictatorship.

The ascendancy of the Christian churches during the last years of the war thus gave the popular disengagement from National Socialism a distinct meaning. In particular, it promoted a crucial shift in the meaning of "sacrifice": from an active sacrifice for "final victory" that had been dominant in the National Socialist imagination to a more passive endurance of suffering that was compatible with Christian discourse. The postwar concept of "the victim" as an all-encompassing personal and collective identity represented the most important product in this discursive shift, and both East and West German postwar societies drew on this shift in their confrontations with total defeat after 1945.[143] At the same time, this period also gave rise to more redemptive narratives, which then informed postwar reconstruction in East and West. In the East, the NKFD narrative of liberation and conversion to antifascism through Soviet forces provided one of the central legitimating narratives of the postwar period. In the West, by contrast, the Christian concept of redemption through suffering assumed key significance for postwar efforts to move beyond defeat.

CHAPTER TWO

Confronting Defeat: Returning POWs
and the Politics of Victimization

ON 8 MAY 1945, Germany's defeat was total. The Nazi regime had collapsed, the Wehrmacht had surrendered unconditionally, and Allied occupation authorities ruled over four occupation zones while permanently severing about one-quarter of the prewar German territory. The human balance sheet of defeat included 5.3 million fallen soldiers, 1.5 million MIAs, and more than one million civilian deaths as a result of bombing, flight, and expulsion. Allied bombing directly affected some twenty million Germans and had reduced German cities to rubble.[1] Beyond the human losses and physical destruction, the German moral collapse was, arguably, even worse. The Allied liberation of Nazi concentration and extermination camps began to expose the inhumanity and destructiveness of National Socialism; its full extent would take years if not decades to become apparent.[2]

To be sure, 1945 was no "zero hour; it did not constitute a complete break with the past."[3] The enormity of the German defeat, however, needs to be emphasized. Unlike in 1918, there was no room for a "stab in the back" legend of an undefeated army.[4] Indeed, rarely has a modern society faced such utter military, physical, and moral collapse. Amidst the more general devastation and destruction, returning POWs represented one of the most telling symbols of the Third Reich's failed ambitions: while only a few years ago, the former soldiers of Hitler's army had subjected Europeans to a Nazi racial empire, they were now streaming back into the four occupation zones as exhausted, undernourished, and sick POWs. The reception and treatment of these returning POWs, then, constituted one of the most important sites for processing and coming to terms with the legacies of war and defeat.

This confrontation with defeat took place within the larger international context of the emerging Cold War. By 1946–47, Allied and Soviet occupation policies quickly shifted from punishing to rebuilding postwar Germany. Together with their respective German allies, occupation authorities in East and West promoted their antagonistic visions of postwar reconstruction and thus deepened the division of Germany. The overarching context of the Cold War, however, should not lead us to separate neatly the wartime from the postwar period. In East and West, "1945" did not signal a completely new beginning. As we have seen in the preceding chapter, popular responses to increasing losses since 1942–43 anticipated postwar confrontations with total defeat after 1945. Moreover, both postwar societies sought to harness shared experiences of defeat to efforts at postwar reconstruction on opposite sides of Cold War. This chapter, then, demonstrates how both postwar societies employed the return of the POWs to develop memories of war and defeat that severely limited, in different ways, notions of German guilt and responsibility, revealing the interrelationship of such defensive memories with sociopolitical reconstruction in both postwar societies. Shifting the perspective to returnees themselves, the chapter also investigates former soldiers' and POWs' own responses to the encounter with a devastated and destroyed homeland. It identifies significant tensions between postwar narratives of victimization and returnees' self-perceptions.

The Infrastructure of Repatriation

The return of some 11 million POWs was part of massive population movements in the postwar period. Nazi Germany's plan for a violent remaking of the ethnic composition of the European continent had subjected millions of people to forced migration, deportation, and, ultimately, mass death. After the defeat of Nazi Germany, the reversal of these huge population transfers became necessary. On the territory of the former Third Reich, between 10.5 and 11.7 million former slave laborers and concentration camp survivors, now labeled "displaced persons," waited to be repatriated to their home countries or decided to emigrate to North America, Australia, or Palestine.[5] Their movement out of the four Allied occupation zones that now comprised "Germany" was met by an equally massive population movement in the other direction: some 12.5 million ethnic Germans who fled the advancing Red Army in the East or were systematically expelled by postwar governments in Poland, Czechoslovakia, Romania, Hungary, and Yugoslavia.[6] Inside the occupation zones, more than 3 million wartime evacuees who had been transferred to rural areas to escape the Allied bombing of German cities sought to return home.[7] Another 3.8 millions inhabitants of the Soviet occupation zone and later the German Democratic Republic decided to cross the border to the West before the construction of the Berlin Wall in 1961 ended this inter-German migration.[8] Finally, the small yet significant group of German emigrants who had fled political or racial persecution by the Nazi regime began to trickle back to postwar Germany.[9]

The repatriation policies of the Allied victors set the pace of the POWs' return. In theory, the Geneva Convention of 1929 demanded the immediate release of POWs after the cessation of hostilities. In light of the massive death and destruction caused by German forces all over the European continent, however, the victors decided to employ former German soldiers for the purpose of reconstruction.[10] At the Moscow foreign minister conference in 1947, the Allies agreed to repatriate all German POWs by 31 December 1948, and the Western allies largely lived up to this agreement.[11] By contrast, the repatriation of German POWs from Eastern European countries and from the Soviet Union lasted until the spring of 1950. Like its Western counterpart, Soviet authorities released more than one million Wehrmacht soldiers from provisional POW camps in the rear of the front line shortly after the end of the of the war. The first mass repatriation of German POWs from camps inside Soviet Union started in mid-1946. From this point onward, a total of 1,125,352 POWs returned from the Soviet Union, 737,513 of whom went to West Germany and Berlin, while 387,839 stayed in East Germany.[12] According to recent estimates, the total number of returnees from the Soviet Union amounted to approximately two million.[13] These "returnees" were not just former Wehrmacht soldiers but also included at least 60,000 of civilian internees who had been deported—with or without conviction by Soviet military tribunals—to POW camps in the Soviet Union. In addition, some 25,000 of the more than 500,000 women employed in the Wehrmacht were captured by the Red Army and returned together with ordinary POWs.[14] The mass repatriation of POWs and internees from Soviet camps ended in May 1950. Some 26,000 POWs and civilian internees, who had been convicted by Soviet courts as "war criminals," returned between 1950 and 1956, the bulk of them in two waves in 1953–54 and 1955–56.[15]

In the immediate postwar period, the return of the POWs proceeded in a disorderly fashion since many were released without proper discharge certificates and procedures. It was only after the first mass release of POWs from camps in the Soviet Union that German authorities in East and West began to establish a comprehensive network of release and transition camps that imposed a greater degree of order and control on the repatriation process. In the summer of 1946, a transition camp was established in Gronenfelde near Frankfurt an der Oder for POWs returning from the Soviet Union.[16] Similar transition camps emerged all over the Western zones, with the Friedland camp in Lower Saxony serving as the main processing point for East returnees to the British zone and for West returnees to the Soviet zone of occupation.[17] The comprehensive network of release and transition camps ensured a relatively smooth demobilization of millions of returning soldiers. Unlike after World War I, German soldiers did not just simply "return home" but were, after mid-1946, systematically discharged from the Wehrmacht.[18]

During their brief stay of one or two days at the transition camps, returnees received food, clothing, and medical first aid. They also were issued crucial discharge certificates, which entitled them to residency permits and food-rationing cards in their home communities.[19] Former POWs had to return to their previous places of residence or to the communities where their families now resided. "Homeless" returnees with no information about their families were distributed among the four occupation authorities according to a predetermined ratio.[20] The camps in Gronenfelde and Friedland also assumed an important symbolic significance in shaping the first encounter between returning POWs and postwar German society. For authorities in East and West, the transition camps represented the first opportunity for influencing the minds and attitudes of returning POWs, and the reception in the camps also shaped returnees' own perception of a radically changed homeland.[21]

DISCOURSES OF GUILT AND RESPONSIBILITY (1945–46)

The return of millions of former Wehrmacht soldiers and POWs to the four occupation zones coincided with Allied efforts to assign guilt and responsibility for the horrific crimes of National Socialism. It was this coexistence between the confrontation with guilt and responsibility, on the one hand, and the ever-present consequences of defeat, on the other, that constituted, as Habbo Knoch has argued, the peculiar "double structure" of the postwar German commemorative culture.[22] The key problem for postwar Germans was to render intelligible and assign meaning to their own experience of defeat after the previous National Socialist legitimations had not only collapsed but had also been exposed as utterly criminal by the Allies.[23] East and West German responses to return of the POWs assumed a key significance in these postwar negotiations of the meanings of war and defeat.

The fresh memories of the disastrous ending of the war and its high casualties among soldiers and civilians alike shaped the first public responses to returning POWs. They prompted a surprising, though rather brief, willingness to address guilt and responsibility for Nazi crimes and military defeat of which Karl Jaspers's philosophical reflections on the "question of guilt" represented only the most prominent example.[24] Public and private responses to the first returnees often arrived at a surprisingly differentiated assessment of the POWs' individual culpability. Precisely because these efforts quickly gave way to a ubiquitous discourse of German victimization, they deserve close attention. They illuminate the degree of memory and justice that could be possible in the midst of the postwar devastation, and they reduce the seeming inevitability and linearity that is often assigned to postwar memories.

One response to the arrival of sick and utterly exhausted POWs was to renounce military force once and for all. Following a prohibition of wearing uniform, issued by the American Military Government in August 1945, the *Landrat* of the Hessian district St. Goarshausen called on returning soldiers to donate their uniforms to charity since "they will not be able to use them for the next hundred years."[25] Such antimilitarist, even pacifist sentiments reflected an indigenous German resentment against a "Prussian militarism," a common early explanation for the disastrous course of German history. The antimilitarism of the immediate postwar period also accounted for critical perceptions of the Wehrmacht and especially of its former leadership.[26] This popular "anger at the *Wehrmacht*" represented one aftereffect of the last months of the war, when Wehrmacht officers had frequently demanded pointless military defenses of towns and villages at the cost of considerable military and civilian casualties.[27] Newspaper reports about Allied trials of the Wehrmacht leadership also brought surprising details of war crimes on the Eastern front to the public's attention.[28]

Critical awareness of the nature of the war on the Eastern front also affected early perceptions of returning POWs. Commenting on the arrival of nine hundred German POWs from the Soviet Union, the antifascist Protestant Propst Grüber, himself a survivor of the Sachsenhausen concentration camp, left no doubt that "Hitler's criminal conduct" in the East was ultimately responsible for the miserable health of returnees.[29] Even more explicitly, an article in the (West) Berlin *Tagesspiegel* from November 1946 outlined the disastrous consequences of German occupation in discussing the treatment of German POWs in Soviet captivity. "Russia is the country where the war has left the most serious devastation. Huge areas were completely burned down, numerous villages and cities were destroyed. . . . These facts should be taken into consideration when comparing the conditions of German POWs in different countries."[30] In marked contrast to later perceptions, such observations placed the predicament of German POWs squarely within the larger historical context of the war of annihilation on the Eastern front.

A variety of public and private voices also employed the issue of German POWs as one way to differentiate between degrees of German guilt and responsibility. Writing on behalf of the parents and wives of German POWs, a petitioner to the Catholic archbishop of Cologne, Joseph Frings, strongly criticized the Allied policy of repatriating German POWs in November 1945. "So far," he argued, "precisely those soldiers have been released from captivity who have worshiped and glorified National Socialism and thus have become—willingly or unwillingly—responsible for the larger course of the war," whereas others "who had maintained their distance from National Socialism" were still held in captivity. To remedy this injustice, he demanded that the release of POWs privilege those least implicated in National Socialism.[31] While such proposals usually served the purpose of exonerating one's own kin, they also demonstrate a basic willingness to probe former soldiers' and POWs' individual pasts.

The emerging state governments in the Western zones also promoted proposals to exchange German POWs in Allied or Soviet captivity for former Nazi activists. In November 1945, the Hessian state government suggested to the American Military Government the release of antifascist POWs from Allied or Soviet captivity in exchange for active National Socialists, "militarists," and individuals "who joined the Nazi Party for personal benefit or who supported it financially." This proposal explicitly recognized the right of the Allies "to employ Germans for the purpose of reconstruction or to hold them in captivity"; and it demanded "that primarily those Germans should perform these tasks who had become particularly responsible for the destruction brought about by Germans in the liberated European countries."[32] The Bavarian state government, city councils, and individual petitioners put forth similar proposals, thus documenting their popularity in the immediate postwar period.[33] Logistic and legal problems ultimately blocked the realization of these plans.[34] By juxtaposing "Nazis" with innocent POWs, moreover, these initiatives drew on the erroneous assumption that the "real Nazis" had been active above all on the home front, where they had committed their offenses against presumably innocent German civilians, while Wehrmacht soldiers had remained largely immune to National Socialism and thus deserved to be repatriated as soon as possible.[35] Despite these apologetic aspects, these plans still accepted Soviet captivity as appropriate retribution for political failings, thus signaling an at least limited acceptance of German guilt that would soon be lost.

Finally, public statements of the two Christian churches crucially contributed to this indigenous discourse on guilt and responsibility: the first pastoral letter (*Hirtenbrief*) of Catholic bishops of August 1945 and the Stuttgart "confession of guilt" of the Protestant church of October 1945. Both statements served important strategic purposes: they distanced the churches from National Socialism and helped claim a singular moral authority for the churches. Both statements also exhibited different patterns of selectivity. Although the Catholic declaration named more specific degrees of guilt and responsibility than the Protestant one, neither proclamation mentioned Jewish victims, while each emphasized church resistance to National Socialism.[36] Significantly, however, the Christian notions of sin allowed, in principle, for a discussion of former soldiers' guilt and responsibility. Thus, in 1946, the magazine of the Bistum Osnabrück, in an article on the Easter confession of the returnee, encouraged former Wehrmacht soldiers to engage in a thorough soul-searching and ask themselves whether they had committed "moral transgressions" including "looting, drunkenness, and the murder of an innocent civilian, a defenseless prisoner, or an injured person."[37] This space for a differentiated discussion of German guilt and responsibility never completely disappeared from Christian discourse, even though it was gradually relegated to a marginal position.[38]

It is very difficult to ascertain the popularity of self-critical impulses among postwar Germans in the Western zones. The quest for a differentiated assessment of guilt and responsibility, as it also manifested itself in Allied denazification policies, always coexisted with other, more apologetic attitudes. Still, occupation authorities did not merely impose this limited quest for memory and justice on reluctant Germans.[39] Initial responses to returning POWs sought to determine individual *political* responsibilities of German soldiers and civilians alike, and locate the experience of POWs in the larger contexts of a German war of aggression. By 1946–47, however, this limited public and private willingness to assess individual guilt and responsibility gradually gave way to an ubiquitous discourse of victimization that elided most distinctions between victims and perpetrators as well as between different kinds of suffering. This shift to German (self-)victimization was neither inevitable nor natural nor merely a functional by-product of postwar democratization.[40] Instead, it resulted from the confluence of popular responses to the consequences of defeat "from below" and quite conscious strategies of (West) German commemorative elites.

The significance of political authorities in shaping the postwar politics of memory was even more pronounced in the Soviet zone of occupation, where political developments diverged from those in the West. Endowed with the support of Soviet occupation authorities, the German Communist Party (KPD) or—after its merger with East German Social Democrats in April 1946, the Socialist Unity Party (SED)— soon emerged as the dominant political authority. Having survived the Nazi years in concentration camps or in emigration, East German Communists did not need to be persuaded of German guilt and hence participated in the zonal-wide discourse on guilt and responsibility.[41] Former soldiers of the "fascist Wehrmacht" ranked high on the Communist list of those groups primarily responsible for war and fascism. Communist officials had already identified that guilt before the end of the war. In April 1945, the postwar leader of the Communist Party, Wilhelm Pieck, stressed in a speech before German POWs in Soviet captivity the "sickness" of the German people and their "deep implication" in Nazi crimes.[42] The KPD leadership was especially disappointed by the failure of German workers and soldiers to contribute to the defeat of Nazism, a contribution they had considered "likely" as late as November–December 1944.[43] For the KPD, the failure of the NKFD to instigate a popular revolt against National Socialism suggested that the former Wehrmacht soldiers strongly identified with fascist ideology; it was one reason for the dissolution of the NKFD in November 1945.[44]

The KPD's most pronounced statement on German guilt—the "appeal to the German people" of June 1945—charged "broad layers of the [German] population" with "following Hitler when he promised them a bountiful lunch and dinner table put together by war and thievery at the cost of other peoples." The millions of German soldiers who saw in "wild militarism, marching, and drill the sole blessing of the nations" bore a particular responsibility. The KPD's appeal thus replicated the antimilitarist attitudes from the Western zones but extended them to a wholesale condemnation of the German past and of ordinary Germans. Contrary to the classical emphasis in Marxist-Leninist ideology on the power of socioeconomic elites, the "appeal" came close to what Western commentators falsely accused the Western allies of propagating: a thesis of German collective guilt.[45]

This Communist memory helped legitimize the KPD/SED's official program for postwar reconstruction. The KPD/SED aspired to create an "antifascist-democratic" order in the Soviet zone of occupation that represented a historical antithesis to the preceding twelve years of German fascism. Initially, this project focused on the establishment of liberal-democratic structures—a completion of the bourgeois revolution of 1848–49, as the "appeal" called it. Yet from the outset, "antifascist" reconstruction entailed plans for a Socialist transformation of East German society and hence for a complete break with the German past.[46] At the same time, the citizens of this putative new order had served until 1945 as mostly loyal members of the National Socialist *Volksgemeinschaft*. The continuity of the East German population countered the Communist quest for a radical transformation of East Germany.

Returnees from the Soviet Union exemplified this very problem. Their experience as soldiers in the racial war of annihilation on the Eastern front and as POWs in Soviet captivity hardly prepared them to become loyal citizens of an "antifascist-democratic," Soviet-oriented postwar Germany. Accordingly, the KPD reacted to the return of the first POWs from the Soviet Union with a sense of panic. When the first returnees appeared in the Eastern zone in December 1945, the Communist Party functionary Karl Lewke sent an alarming report to the KPD leadership in Berlin. It was entitled "One Million Anti-Bolshevists Are Approaching. The Democratic Reconstruction of Germany Is Threatened by the Greatest Dangers!"[47] Lewke's description of the mentality and the attitudes of these returning POWs cannot have been comforting for his party superiors:

Every one of them [is] an agitator against "Communist" conditions, and because of his appearance, every one of them is a living demonstration against those very "Communist" conditions. . . . There is no recognition of the co-responsibility of the German people, no rational, political discussion. There is no talk of reconstruction and cooperation among them. They see the consequences of a total war and of an even more total defeat only as the result of the evil intentions of Bolshevism. They have forgotten Hitler, forgotten Nazism, and even the terrible horrors of the battlefields . . . are far remote to them. . . . All their anger, all their hate is directed only against the present situation. . . . All Nazi whisperings find an open ear. [They] act as a brake on the difficult work of reconstruction.

To Communist officials, the ardent anti-Bolshevism of returning POWs reflected their previous indoctrination by National Socialism. Upon their arrival, former soldiers were just beginning to awaken "from a kind of frenzy and dream in which National Socialist propaganda had put them," as another observer described it.[48] East German officials feared that this situation would render returnees easily susceptible to "the influence of former Nazis and other hostile elements."[49] The return of the POWs thus raised the frightening specter of a revival of Nazism in postwar Germany.[50]

While Communist officials emphasized returnees' guilt, their perceptions of former soldiers' "anti-Bolshevism" and, indeed, "fascist" attitudes did not lead them to resignation, nor did they simply turn to outright repression. To East German officials, the mentalities of returning POWs underlined, above all, the dire need for political reeducation. If former soldiers and POWs had indeed been deluded by fascist (and Western) propaganda, then extensive political agitation might succeed in reversing this process and in winning over returning POWs for the project of "antifascist-democratic" reconstruction. Most diagnoses of returnees' hostility thus included a plea for propagandistic party efforts toward this group. The above-cited Karl Lewke, for example, ended his bleak portrayal of returning POWs' hostile mentality by calling for the construction of a "party apparatus" that would be solely devoted to the task of bringing returning POWs into the ideological fold. He considered this task even more important than party work among the KPD/SED's prime constituency—industrial workers and labor unions.[51] Moreover, party officials extended these calls for political agitation to returnees from the West who were encouraged "to align themselves with the antifascist-democratic forces" in the Eastern zone.[52]

This project of ideological persuasion also entailed the transformation of the Communist politics of memory. The KPD/SED sought to make the presence of former soldiers of Hitler's army compatible with its vision for postwar reconstruction. The result of these adjustments was a specific Communist narrative of victimization.

NARRATIVES OF VICTIMIZATION, EAST AND WEST

In September 1947, Frau R. from the West German town of Hildesheim wrote a letter to a Catholic priest in which she bemoaned her "great suffering" and especially the uncertain fate of her eighteen-year-old son. He had been missing in action on the Eastern front since March 1945, and she believed him to be in Soviet captivity.[53] Conversations with POWs who had returned from the Soviet Union led Frau R. to believe that the situation of German POWs there was "not comparable with the German concentration camps." It was, in fact, "much worse." "One and a half to two million," she reported, "are believed to have starved to death and perished." "Is this a better treatment than in the German concentration camps?" she asked rhetorically and quickly added her own assessment: "In the concentration camps, people were immediately anaesthetized in the gas chambers, even though it was not nice to treat human beings like this." For Frau R., Allied treatment of German POWs clearly equaled and even exceeded the crimes of the Nazi regime. For what the victors had done to "innocent Germans" also constituted a "crime against humanity" and "belongs to the Nuremberg trials as well." Allied war crime trials only smacked of hypocrisy and had failed to console her sorrows: "My son-in-law was killed through terror. . . , I lost five nephews in this war. . . . And where is my son?"

Frau R.'s reflections, and many similar statements by ordinary Germans, encapsulate the peculiar failings of German memory in the postwar period.[54] Extensive knowledge of Nazi crimes did not translate into an awareness of German moral responsibility but rather led to blaming the Allied victors for German suffering. Why, therefore, did the awareness of German guilt and responsibility in the immediate postwar period turn into ubiquitous narratives of victimization? The emotional context of loss palpable in Frau R.'s example surely must have contributed to this transformation of popular memory.[55] In keeping with comparable popular sentiments from the last years of the war, ordinary Germans' own experiences of suffering and, often, irretrievable loss completely overshadowed any residual empathy with Germany's victims. These experiences assumed a very direct and personal quality, whereas any personal responsibility for National Socialism remained, in many cases, abstract and mediated by the anonymous institutions of the modern bureaucratic state.[56] As such, the link between ordinary Germans' own political failings and their own experience of suffering often remained elusive.

Stories of German victimization, as Frau R.'s example demonstrates, were grounded in social and emotional contexts of hardship, suffering, and loss. But the emergence of the victim trope in public discourse also resulted from a defensive response to Allied efforts at assigning individual guilt at a time when the consequences of defeat were more visible than ever. The mass repatriations of German POWs from the Soviet Union in mid-1946, for example, coincided with the Allied war crime trials at Nuremberg and the policy of denazification. As in Frau R.'s letter, the emphasis on German suffering now became the most compelling rhetorical tool to repudiate Allied accusations of guilt. In other words, the focus on the consequences of defeat began to displace any residual discussion of guilt and responsibility for Nazi crimes.[57]

In the Western zones, the press and popular culture played a crucial role in transforming individual narratives of suffering into public discourses of victimization. Newspapers and magazines began to publish autobiographical accounts of returned POWs from the Soviet Union and often highlighted the alleged similarity with the experience in Nazi concentration camps. One of the first autobiographies published by a returned POWs, Helmut Bohn's account of Soviet captivity, portrayed former soldiers as disillusioned "victims of totalitarianism" who had suffered from both Nazism and Stalinism.[58] In what became the most popular theatrical piece of the postwar period, Wolfgang Borchert's *Draussen vor der Tür*, the protagonist, a returning POW from the East, was transformed into an emblematic figure of suffering and alienation from postwar society.[59] Finally, the "movies of the rubble" of the early postwar period—most prominently Wolfgang Liebeneiner's cinematic adaptation of Borchert's piece in *Liebe 47*—popularized notions of German victimization by depicting devastated and shattered returnees finding their way home to destroyed cities.[60]

What gave these private and popular sentiments of German suffering their larger political significance, however, was the extent to which powerful social-political forces tried to harness notions of German victimization for their own specific purposes of postwar reconstruction. Discourses of victimization were compatible with the three most important concepts for postwar reconstruction: Christian conservative, Social Democratic, and Communist. Although they defined returnees' victim status very differently and employed it for very different purposes, multiple political traditions drew on the trope of Germans as victims to promote their divergent concepts of postwar reconstruction.[61] It was this convergence of stories of victimization "from below" and "from above" that turned the victim trope into such a compelling rhetorical device for postwar Germans' confrontations with defeat.

Figure 2. A mother welcoming her son home from Soviet captivity. The emotional context of suffering and loss crucially shaped ordinary Germans' memories of the Nazi past in the postwar period. (Courtesy Bundesarchiv Koblenz.)

Figure 3. This photo, entitled *Without Home, Without Possessions* was taken by the Berlin photographer Friedrich Seidenstücker. Sick, exhausted, and disoriented POWs returning from Soviet captivity constituted one of the most important markers of total defeat in postwar Germany. Such representations also served as important reference points for discourses of German victimization. (Courtesy Bildarchiv Preussischer Kulturbesitz.)

The most influential promoters of narratives of victimization were the Christian churches. The predominant historiographical focus on secular actors and institutions has obscured the significance of explicitly Christian concepts in shaping (West) German memories of the Second World War. As the only institutions that had weathered the collapse of Nazi Germany nearly unchanged, the Christian churches assumed a crucial moral and political authority in postwar Germany and, for that matter, in (Western) Europe more generally.[62] In addition, the Christian churches enjoyed the support of the occupation authorities while also taking on the role of quasi-state authorities, especially vis-à-vis the occupation authorities.[63] Despite internal regional and political division, both Christian churches developed parallel and often shared responses to the consequences of war and defeat.

Within both Christian denominations, the resurgence of national Catholic and Protestant traditions gradually superseded the churches' initial emphasis on guilt and responsibility.[64] As early as June 1945, the Munich cardinal Faulhaber called on church representatives to extend a warm welcome to returning soldiers that should include a sermon thanking them for their "unspeakable achievement and suffering." He also requested a requiem for soldiers who had not returned and a prayer for victims of war both on the front and at home.[65] Church authorities also increasingly shifted their focus from German guilt to "The Guilt of Others," as the title of a widely circulating memo by Hans Asmussen, the head the newly formed chancellery of the Evangelical church in Germany (EKD) put it as early as February 1946.[66] Church authorities leveled particularly harsh indictments against the Allied policy of denazification.[67] In this context, the withholding of German POWs represented yet another important vehicle for the churches to affirm their claims as legitimate representative of the German people. The POWs issue enabled the churches to criticize alleged Allied "injustices" while also allowing them to identify with German popular suffering.[68]

By emphasizing German victimhood, the Christian churches maintained their status as sites of popular mourning into the postwar period. After the collapse of Nazism, many ordinary Germans continued to place their hopes on the churches in confronting uncertainty about the whereabouts of missing family members. They flooded Protestant and Catholic authorities with petitions to obtain information about missing soldiers or to enlist the churches in effecting their release. The wife of one POW declared that the "church has become strong again," and "this is why it will be listened to if it speaks out for justice in matters relating to POWs."[69] Just as the churches' efforts on behalf of missing or captured soldiers during the last years of the war had led to a surge in popular religiosity, the concern for German MIAs and POWs after 1945 represented one of the primary means by which the churches identified with the sentiments of ordinary Germans. When Catholic bishops alerted the Allied Control council to the fact that the repatriation of POWs met the "needs" and "desires" of the German people, church leaders felt authorized by their "particular knowledge of the people."[70] Similarly, the EKD petitioned the same institution in February 1946 to ease the "tremendous pain" that burdened "millions" in the face of the uncertainty about the number and identity of German POWs, adding a selection of the "cries for help that we receive on a daily basis."[71]

Church efforts on behalf of German POWs did not end with appeals to the occupation authorities. In September 1946, the Protestant church organized its first "week of prayer" for German POWs.[72] This event turned into another occasion for indicting alleged Allied injustices and for showcasing German suffering. Bishop Wurm, in his sermon for this occasion, stressed the "great misery" that has "come over our communities and our entire people" because "one and a half years after the ending of hostilities, millions of German men are still held in captivity."[73] The considerable popularity of such appeals became apparent only a few weeks later in December 1946, when both Protestant ministers and the Catholic priests asked Sunday worshippers to sign lists demanding the immediate release of German POWs: nine million Germans in the American and British zone signed what constituted the most popular petition in occupied Germany.[74]

By portraying returning POWs unambiguously as victims, church publications departed from the more differentiating perceptions of the early postwar period. Residual references to German aggression now served primarily as a yardstick for the extent of German suffering. A Protestant welcoming speech delivered to POWs bemoaned how the "injustice that has originated from our people" now "falls back upon us and we are suffering much injustice ourselves."[75] In strong continuity with religious rhetoric during the war, the trope of German victimization also allowed for a reaffirmation of Christian anti-Bolshevism in the context of the emerging Cold War. In a sermon for POWs in 1949, Bishop Heckel attributed the "dehumanization" of POWs in captivity to the fact that "Russia was a country without church bells."[76] Christian constructions of returnees as victims also drew on biblical motifs of captivity. In particular, church representatives often invoked Psalm 126 on the Babylonian captivity of the people of Israel as biblical analogy for the plight of German POWs.[77] In the aftermath of the Holocaust, such references had anything but innocent connotations. They reflected the peculiar mixture of anti- and philo-Semitic elements in Christian and especially in Protestant discourse. Denunciations of the Soviet treatment of German POWs enabled Christian conservatives to hold on to central beliefs of anti-Bolshevism and, more or less explicitly, of anti-Semitism while, at the same time, distancing themselves from National Socialism.[78]

Elaborating on the Christian narrative of the German past, church representatives perceived returning POWs not just as the victims of Allied injustice but also as victims of the larger forces of modernity that had given rise to National Socialism in the first place. A Catholic report on the "religious and spiritual situation of our POWs" thus described the "inner life of these men" as a "field of rubble." They had become *Massenmenschen*—a "classical example for the completely secularized modern man who no longer has any sense for Christianity whatsoever." Far from attributing these attitudes to the aftereffects of war and National Socialism, the report highlighted the devastating "materialism," "subjectivism," "collectivism," and "secularization" that had "penetrated deeply into the [German] people."[79] In the churches' view, returnees were not just victims of Soviet injustice but also victims of the pathologies of modernity in general.

Significantly, these Christian confrontations with war and defeat transcended the confessional divide. To be sure, Protestant and Catholic responses to the return of the POWs were not completely identical—Protestants, for example, quickly tended to assume a more aggressive political tone especially vis-à-vis the occupation authorities. But their diagnosis of the German postwar condition—like their interpretation of the roots of Nazism—drew on a series of shared concepts, especially anti-Bolshevism and the victim trope. As such, shared Christian responses to war and defeat prepared the discursive ground for the central political innovation of the postwar years: the formation of the CDU/CSU (Christian Democratic Union/Christian Social Union) as a biconfessional, bourgeois, and antisocialist party.[80]

Concepts of German victimization extended beyond the boundaries of Christian conservatism and also reached the opposite end of the political spectrum, where the Social Democratic Party promoted a left wing-version of the victim trope. Social Democrats, to be sure, were among the most ardent proponents of memory and justice in postwar Germany, joining the few public voices that advocated the interests of the victims of Nazism.[81] At the same time, leading SPD politicians embraced concepts of German victimization for their own reason. In 1947, the leader of the SPD in the Western zones, Kurt Schumacher, proclaimed: "The SPD holds the opinion that German POWs are not the bearers but the victims of Hitler fascism." As they sought to identify with the predicament of German POWs, Social Democrats compared their own experience of persecution and internment during the Third Reich with the situation of German POWs in Allied or Soviet captivity. In a 1947 Christmas letter to German POWs, a member of the SPD executive committee, Hans Stephan, assured its recipients of the party's solidarity by referring to "numerous friends from our ranks who had been subjected to the same fate in concentration camps and prisons during the twelve years before the capitulation."[82] Linking their own experience to other collective experiences of suffering among ordinary Germans, Social Democratic survivors of the Nazi dictatorship tried to prepare the moral ground for a future coexistence with those Germans who had tolerated or even enforced their exclusion from the Nazi *Volksgemeinschaft*. Yet the equation of Nazi concentration camps with Soviet POW camps also powerfully promoted narratives of victimization.[83]

The SPD's appropriation of the victim trope served multiple political purposes. Much like the Christian churches, the SPD viewed the issue of German POWs as a national (if not nationalistic) issue. "The POWs are a part of us" and "we cannot live without them," Schumacher declared in 1948.[84] He saw immediate release of German POWs as an essential national demand that nobody was better positioned to articulate than the SPD.[85] The party's engagement on behalf of POWs was not just rhetoric. Since 1947, the SPD ran its own POW aid program, which provided local party branches with information on POW issues. In the same year, this organization also conducted a registration of German POWs and MIAs to establish their precise numbers.[86] The majority of German POWs, party officials were hoping, would honor these efforts by voting for the SPD in postwar elections. Test elections among German POWs in British captivity yielded large majorities for the SPD and were subsequently published in the party press.[87] Very early on, the party leadership also appealed especially to former Wehrmacht soldiers as a potential constituency. In January 1948, Schumacher distanced himself from "defamations of those who had borne arms during the Third Reich."[88] Such appeals to former Wehrmacht soldiers factored in the changing social composition of the Wehrmacht and especially of the officer corps, which had come to include many members from working-class or petit bourgeois backgrounds.[89] Sympathizing with the predicament of former soldiers and POWs, Social Democrats sought to create a political coalition that encompassed Nazi victims as well as war veterans.[90] Finally, the issue of German POWs in Soviet captivity also allowed the SPD to assert its own ardent anti-Communism. The focus on German POWs in the Soviet Union made it possible for the party to distance itself both from the SED in the Soviet zone of occupation and from the Communist Party in the West. This also included a vehement condemnation of antifascist activists in Soviet captivity and of the "Prussian officers" within the National Committee for a Free Germany (NKFD) who, according to the SPD, had misused German soldiers in the interest of the Soviet Union just as they had previously done in Hitler's interest.[91]

West German stories of victimization also drew on the experience of female returnees from the Soviet Union. Different aspects of the victim trope converged in West German perceptions of this group. On the one hand, West German observers characterized the internment of German women as the most outrageous offense against humanity and as an indication of "Bolshevist equalization of the sexes."[92] They also immediately suspected that these women were victims of rape in Soviet captivity, even though evidence for such offenses remained sparse.[93] This suspicion was often articulated indirectly with allusions to the "very severe experiences" that returning women were "too shy" to report.[94] Such veiled references to rape not only illustrate how deeply stories of mass rape permeated the (West) German imagination; they also display a profound inability to name these offenses as a gendered experience.[95] As a result, female returnees represented a problematic reference point for narratives of victimization. The common association of their experience with sexual violence accentuated men's failure to protect these women in the predominantly male sphere of the military and the POW camp. This helps to explain why female returnees were never fully incorporated into German memories of the Second World War or, for that matter, into the historiography of the postwar period.[96]

By the time of the founding of the Federal Republic in September 1949, the perception of (male) returning POWs as victims had been firmly established in West German public discourse and formed, as Robert Moeller has shown, a crucial building block for the reconstitution of West German identity.[97] The convergence of conservative and left-wing versions of German victimization left little discursive space for an alternative politics of memory in the West. It foreshadowed the "black-red" voting coalition that drove the postwar politics of memory.[98]

Parallel to the formation of West German narratives of victimization, Communist officials in the East busily forged their own version of German victimization. In the West, Communist officials did not identify the Allies or Soviet victors but rather the "fascist dictatorship" as primary victimizers. Communist narratives of victimization took shape against the backdrop of the first mass repatriation of German POWs from the Soviet Union. Between July and December 1946, some 150,000 German POWs returned to East and West Germany.[99] Confronted with hundreds of thousands of returning POWs in the Eastern zone, East German officials gradually moved away from their earlier assertions of collective guilt and held an increasingly narrow segment of the German population responsible for Nazi crimes. Conversely, they attempted to build ideological bridges to the former Wehrmacht soldiers by incorporating them into the expanding community of Hitler's victims.

Figure 4. Female auxiliary forces after their capture by Red Army, 1945. Approximately 25,000 women, mostly former members of auxiliary forces and Red Cross nurses, returned with former Wehrmacht soldiers from Soviet captivity. (Courtesy of Bundesarchiv Koblenz.)

A welcoming speech by Wilhelm Pieck, the chairman of the SED and later president of the GDR, to six thousand returnees in Gronenfelde on 10 August 1946 exemplified this shift.[100] Pieck made clear who was to blame for the "pile of rubble" to which the POWs were now returning: it was the "Hitler clique" that had "brought its war to the German people" and was therefore responsible for this "tremendous misery." In notable contrast to the earlier KPD appeal, Pieck confined German guilt to a small circle and exculpated "the German people" from any active participation in war and fascism. In a stunning rhetorical move, his speech in fact asserted a parallelism of suffering between "millions of German people" who "had been driven into death on the battlefields and in the Heimat by the Hitler government" and other "millions" (whose nationality or ethnicity he did not mention) who "had been murdered and tortured to death by an inhuman terror in the concentration camps." Not unlike Western Social Democrats, East German Communists evoked their own experience of suffering and persecution during the Third Reich to appeal to former soldiers and POWs. He also extended his offer of integration to former "nominal members" of the Nazi Party, indicating that the SED was willing to forgive political failure in the past in exchange for political loyalty in the present.

Pieck's speech was indicative of the SED's efforts to attract large sections of the population on the eve of the first local and regional elections in the Soviet zone of occupation on 20 October 1946. Pieck explained to returning POWs that they were immediately eligible to vote, and SED leaders particularly addressed "youth, women, and returning POWs."[101] Although the party did not have any significant impact on Soviet repatriation policies, the SED celebrated the return of the first 120,000 POWs as the result of its intervention with Soviet occupation authorities.[102] Party officials saw the POW issue as a good "campaign instrument" and deployed the issue especially in their efforts to appeal to the largest population group in the Eastern zone: women.[103] At meetings with women, party officials invited returned POWs to report about their experience in Soviet captivity—an idea that was reportedly "well received."[104] But SED representatives also needed to face women's daunting questions about the whereabouts of missing POWs—queries to which they often could only respond by urging women to "think of 1933" when they voted again.[105]

The election results turned out to be very disappointing to the SED. Despite severe administrative and organizational impediments for competing parties, the SED did not win a majority of the vote in the five provinces of the Soviet zone. The party suffered a particularly crushing defeat in the Greater Berlin election, where it faced the competition of the West German Social Democratic Party.[106] In particular, the POW issue seems to have hurt rather than helped the SED, especially among women.[107] To East German officials, the disappointing election results indicated the political immaturity of returning POWs, and indeed, most East Germans, who could not be entrusted with democratic powers. Thus, the ongoing difficulty of persuading the population of the party's view of the POW issue fostered belief of SED officials in the need for a small enlightened elite that would impose an "educational dictatorship" on East German society.[108] On the other hand, the official perception of returnees' alleged political immaturity spurred renewed efforts of reeducation. The SED's distrust of democratic politics thus did not put a stop to official efforts to win over returning POWs and, by extension, East German society at large, for the project of building an antifascist and Socialist order.

Despite their ideological antagonisms, official perceptions of returning POWs on both sides of the gradually descending "iron curtain" exhibited similar structural patterns. In both East and West, defensive memories that tended to portray returnees as passive victims of forces beyond their control gradually superseded discussions of returnees' individual or collective guilt and responsibility. These defensive memories distanced returnees from their previous roles as bystanders, collaborators, or perpetrators during the Nazi period.[109] This emphasis on victimization, to be sure, was not an exclusively German phenomenon. All over the continent, postwar societies reemerging from Nazi occupation developed their own similar memories as a way of balancing their own implication in Nazi violence. These societies constructed narratives of victimization that downplayed indigenous histories of collaboration and complicity and externalized guilt and responsibility by blaming the German occupiers.[110] As Tony Judt has noted, "they [the Germans] did it" was the dominating refrain in postwar European commemorative culture.[111] Yet nowhere was the push toward (self)-victimization as pronounced and as comprehensive as in postwar Germany. The unique burden of guilt and responsibility that both East and West German postwar societies needed to carry thus also manifested itself in a particularly forceful assertion of German suffering and victimization.

Different versions of narratives of victimization—Christian, Social Democratic, and Communist—made returnees central to East and West German confrontations with defeat. In both societies, this symbolic recognition translated into palpable benefits for former soldiers and POWs. Narratives of victimization informed, for example, the virtual exclusion of all returnees from denazification procedures in all four occupation zones.[112] In East and West, extensive amnesties and preferential treatment of former POWs turned an initial and reasonable impulse towards integration into a virtually indiscriminate exoneration of all returning POWs, including, as one Bavarian official feared, "highly compromised, well-known, fanatic, and feared" returnees.[113] These practices stood in marked contrast to early postwar efforts at differentiating returning POWs' individual guilt and responsibility.

Still, while returnees drew considerable symbolic and political benefits from narratives of victimization, they did not necessarily embrace a self-perception as "victim." How, then, did returnees themselves respond to these social and symbolic strategies they encountered in both societies? Did narratives of victimizations help them to reconstitute their male subjectivities in the aftermath of total war and total defeat?

Encountering Heimat or Victimization and Its Discontents

For former soldiers and POWs, "homecoming" often brought into the open a massive gap between their past and their present. What historian Reinhart Koselleck has identified as a hallmark of modernity in general—the increasing gap between what he called the "space of experience" and the "horizon of expectation"—applied to former soldiers of Hitler's army as well: their experience in war and captivity provided little guidance for

the encounter with a devastated and divided homeland.[114] Especially for
returnees from the East, information about conditions in postwar Germany had been scarce or distorted by rumors and biased camp newspapers.[115] Mail contact between POWs in Soviet captivity and family members at home did not start until 1946 and remained sparse and irregular
thereafter.[116] Upon their return, former soldiers and POWs faced a radical
historical rupture while also struggling to maintain a continuous sense of
self. More eloquently than most other returnees, the theologian Helmut
Gollwitzer articulated this difficulty of connecting past and present in his
autobiographical account of Soviet captivity.

> What kind of wall of glass is this, that divides the past from the present, which
> can yet touch each other within me, since I still am both the "then" and the
> "now," the former no less than the latter? What is time? What is the meaning
> of past and present? What does our existence in time mean?[117]

My focus here is not on reconstructing a wide range of individual homecoming experiences, which were too diverse and shaped by too many
variables to allow for meaningful historical generalizations. Instead, this
section probes how and by what means returnees addressed the existential
issues raised by Gollwitzer, that is, how they sought to connect their past
and their present. Clearly, the conditions that former soldiers and POWs
encountered in postwar Germany lend immediate plausibility to narratives of victimization. Returnees were often shocked by the confrontation
with a completely devastated and destroyed homeland.[118] Although some
returnees had either experienced bombing raids while on furlough or had
been informed about the conditions in Germany in captivity, others were
completely stunned when they faced the extent of the destruction.[119] A
former pilot who had been shot down over the Soviet Union in 1943 and
returned to the Western zones in 1948 found that the "misery and poverty
was much greater than we had ever envisioned in captivity."[120] Several
decades later, a Berlin returnee still professed to being utterly speechless
when realizing that the war's destructions had hit his hometown too: "Everything was completely gone. . . . There in Russia, in the big city, where
they also bombed so much, that was somehow war, that was different.
But now that one was back home again and found one's hometown in
such strange condition, that was somehow devastating; it is difficult to
put all this in words."[121]

The destruction that former soldiers and POWs encountered upon their
return was not only physical and public but also private and even inti-
mate. This was true especially for those returnees who experienced double
displacement of both captivity and expulsion from the former German
territories in the East. When Johann S. returned from Soviet captivity in
1948, his "biggest pain" was not "being able to return to his beautiful
Heimat in the Sudetenland." Returnees also encountered primitive living

conditions with a "seven person family" living in "two small and humid rooms."[122] Concepts of German victimization further allowed returnees to relate their own experience of deprivation and displacement to experiences of women on the home front. Consider the case of Eduard G., who was released from Soviet captivity in 1948 and could not return to his native Silesia. After a long odyssey, he found his family in a West German refugee camp. His wife was "sick and starving," his children "psychologically disturbed." He attributed this predicament to the expulsion, which he assumed "must have been the worst thing that any human being had to endure" and, even worse, to the "multiple horrible rapes" that his wife had to suffer "in front of the children."[123] Here, the language of shared victimization provided the basis of confronting and—perhaps—overcoming shared yet specifically gendered experiences of defeat.

Divergent sexual cultures—shaped by mass rape in the Soviet zone and by so-called fraternization in the Western zones—assumed crucial significance for the reconstitution of returnees' male subjectivities.[124] To be sure, due to their own previous experiences as occupiers, former soldiers must have been well aware of the sexual aspects of military defeat and foreign occupation.[125] Yet rumors about rape and fraternizations nevertheless triggered severe anxieties among POWs even before their return to the homeland. On the last stretch of their transport from Brest Litovsk to Frankfurt an der Oder, returnees were reportedly "shaken" when they were confronted with rumors that "the Russians are stealing everything from Germany" and that they "rape German women and drive them into concentration camps."[126] Such forewarnings, however, did not necessarily lead the men to adopt an understanding attitude toward female rape victims. On the contrary, oral history evidence suggested that German men often blamed women for having become a victim of rape.[127] Such accusations served a purpose similar to that of the widespread charge of "fraternization" against women entering sexual relationships with mostly American occupation soldiers: they deflected the blame for military defeat away from former Wehrmacht soldiers and onto women on the home front. As such, stories of male victimization in captivity also detracted from what constituted perhaps the decisive male trauma of the postwar period: the failure of former soldiers to protect their wives and the families against the Allied occupiers.[128]

Concepts of victimization thus clearly helped returning POWs to make sense of their return to a devastated homeland. At the same time, the victim trope was not the only rhetorical device that former soldiers and POWs employed to connect their past and their present. They also resorted to another concept that complemented but also went beyond self-perceptions as victims: the concept of Heimat. As a distinct language and set of images, Heimat had served as a way of expressing communal belonging since at least the early nineteenth century and was also invoked by authorities in East and West after 1945.[129] Former POWs often drew on Heimat in describing their subjective experiences of returning home. They framed their homecoming as a return not to the nation but rather to a distinct locality that promised meaning, coherence, and continuity. After passing through the transition camp Kienlesberg in Ulm, Wilhelm D. declared it was "only in Ulm that we finally began to realize that we were again in our cramped yet all the more beloved fatherland, our Swabian lands (*Schwabenländle*)."[130] In similar ways, the returnee Dr. Heinz S. from Weimar described his homecoming in 1946 as a return to a peaceful local community:

> There were German women and children who accompanied our march into freedom with happily brightened faces. These were the houses of peaceful German people, surrounded by gardens in which colorful sunflowers blossomed and ripe fruit was still hanging on the trees. There were fields and meadows on which a farmer was working. The soft waves of the Oder mountains and the dark green forests greeted us. It was the Heimat that welcomed us.[131]

In these accounts, Heimat appears as an imaginary and—given the less severe destructions of rural areas—real space that had ostensibly remained unaffected by the consequences of war and defeat. Precisely because it stood in marked contrast to the devastation that was most apparent in Germany's urban centers, Heimat represented an attractive fantasy for overcoming the massive ruptures that characterized returnees' experience and sense of self. Heimat stood for the persistence of seemingly transhistorical values and customs that had remained untainted by the catastrophes of the twentieth century. For the returnee Gustav M., the return to a "beloved Heimat" was also the return "to the old customs, the German language, the German song that we had been deprived of even on Christmas Eve."[132] For another returnee, this form of essential and untainted "Germanness" was represented by the "scent of *heimatliche* forests" and the "products of our skilled and precision workers, which due to the decade-long training of our workers, are second to none in the world."[133] While the concept of the "nation" had not only been utterly discredited by National Socialism but had also become highly elusive as a result of defeat, division, and occupation, Heimat offered an alternative way of imagining "Germanness." It constituted, in Celia Applegate's apt phrase, "one of the least suspicious expressions of togetherness" and offered, as Alon Confino has written, "a wide variety of rhetorical means to speak about the nation without breaking taboos."[134]

Heimat was also a distinctly male fantasy. It entailed the comforting promise of clearly defined gender boundaries that had been preserved by German women, who had served as caretakers of the Heimat and thus ensured men's return to a familiar social context. In his poem "the German woman," the East German returnee Karl T. thanked her for facilitating men's return to the Heimat:

> You German woman, so pure, so good
> you will remain loyal to the Heimat with unfailing courage
> You never rest you never spare pains nor time
> to alleviate the lot, the pains of returning men
> who found the way back to the Heimat from faraway places
> with sick bodies but strong hearts.[135]

For returnees like Karl T., the Heimat appeared as a distinctly feminine sphere that provided an explicit counterweight to the exclusively male world of the military and the POW camp. The association of Heimat with a feminine sphere untainted by the upheavals of war and defeat, however, clashed with the actual erasure of most boundaries between the "female" home front and the "male" front during the last years of the war.[136] As an ideal and as a project, Heimat thus held out the promise of psychological compensation for men's weakened position upon their return; and it served as a restorative model for the reconstruction of gender relations in postwar society. At the same time, the imagination of a female sphere divorced from war and defeat also promised relief from a traumatic past. To the previously mentioned Dr. Heinz S., Grotewohl's slogan "Work and Heimat" entailed the possibility of "forgetting the war with all its dangers, all its horrors, of forgetting captivity with all its bodily sufferings and all its misery of the soul."[137] As such, the imagined return to a peaceful and idealized *Heimat* helped to evade daunting memories of complicity in National Socialism, genocidal warfare on the Eastern front, and ensuing suffering in Soviet captivity.

Heimat, in short, represented an escapist fantasy that diametrically opposed the reality of death and destruction—as well as the significantly altered changed gender relations—that former soldiers and POWs encountered upon their return. It was precisely this contrast to returnees' active and passive experiences of violence that made Heimat such an attractive and adaptive concept to embrace. Heimat distanced returnees—and, by extension, all Germans—from the violence associated with total war and total defeat. As such, the recourse to Heimat reflected but also transcended narratives of victimization. It indicated returnees' desire for overcoming and leaving behind the war and its consequences.

Self-perceptions as victims thus did not reflect the whole range of returnees' own subjectivities. Instead, many former soldiers and POWs also displayed attitudes and mind-sets that were at odds with the hopelessness and desperation of a victim status. They were simply relieved to have survived the carnage of the final stages of the war and the ensuing deprivations of captivity. To the returnee Gustav M., the "long awaited" release from Polish captivity in April 1949 represented the "most dignified day of our lives" when "the barbed wire gates opened to a golden freedom."[138] In similar ways, many returnees employed, in retrospect, metaphors of rebirth to describe this moment. They felt like a "newborn," and homecoming appeared to them as a "second birthday" or as the "year of my rebirth."[139] If returnees were fortunate enough to find their homes intact and their families alive, such sentiments were even more pronounced. One returnee was "overjoyed to find [his family] in such good condition and could not believe his good fortune."[140] In other cases, returnees articulated their relief of having arrived in the Western zones. According to American occupation officials, many returnees from the East exhibited an "absolutely positive attitude toward the U.S." and felt like "being in heaven after all they had gone through in Russian captivity."[141] Even those returnees who considered the U.S. occupation as a "lesser evil than Russian rule" still felt "a little more friendly [toward the United States] than the general population because of their actual experience with the Russians."[142] In October 1947, more systematic interrogations of over two hundred POWs returning from the Soviet Union by American occupation officials also confirmed the largely optimistic and forward-looking attitude of returnees.[143] The report came to the conclusion that "repatriated PWs . . . are relatively hopeful about conditions at home. Nine out of ten expect to get started in their new life without encountering major obstructions."[144]

While such sentiments might have been influenced by the anti-Communism of both observers and observed, they also reflected the popularity of the trope of "fortunate survival" in postwar Germany.[145] Even the recollections of female returnees did not necessarily replicate the public emphasis on suffering and also cast the experience of captivity as hard yet also adventurous.[146] Conversely, the self-perception of male returnees mirrored the masculine ideals of endurance and stoicism in the face of hardship into which the former soldiers of Hitler's army had been socialized. When asked specifically about the long-term consequences of four years in Soviet captivity in an oral-history interview, one returnee still asserted, as late as 1995, that he "did not want to indulge in the past" (*in das Vergangene hineinsteigern*) and did not want to start again "all the suffering and all the lamentation."[147] Although returnees drew considerable symbolic and material benefits from narratives of victimization, they did not necessarily revel in their own real or imagined suffering in the past. Instead, the wide range of returnees' subjectivities points to the need to historicize the victim trope itself: for the men of the 1940s and 1950s, it was not necessarily the only or even the most attractive basis of personal or collective identity. The concept of "the victim" stood in uneasy tensions to both past ideals of masculinity as well as to former soldiers' and POWs' own hopes for the future. In general, the emergence of "victimization" as primary basis for collective and personal identity appears to have been a later development that was intrinsically linked to the rise of a politics of identity and should not be projected back onto the postwar period.[148]

On a more general symbolic level, stories of victimization distanced postwar Germans only insufficiently from the violence associated with total war and total defeat. In many case, these stories incidentally brought into view, as in a mirror image, the violence that Germans had inflicted onto others. As we saw in the case of Frau R., narratives of victimhood were constructed from knowledge of German violence. The "language of millions" that (West) Germans referred to in their portrayals of German suffering betrayed their own awareness of the quantitative dimensions of German violence.[149] The hyperbole with which West Germans condemned the treatment of German POWs derived from a deep-seated fear that the Allied victors would subject ordinary Germans to the same logic of annihilation that Germans had inflicted upon their victims.[150] Similarly, in the East, the focus on returnees' fascist indoctrination indirectly confirmed the enormity of the German Left's defeat in fighting fascism. Even in their self-construction as a nation of victims, postwar Germans did not completely succeed in obliterating all traces of their own past as victimizers and ended up reinscribing it into the increasingly popular tales of their own suffering. As a "negative memory" (Michael Bodemann) of German violence, memories of victimization still reflected ordinary Germans' own implication in fascism, war, and genocide.[151]

Narratives of victimization hence constituted an unstable and ambivalent ideological foundation for postwar reconstruction on both the personal and the collective level. The trope of Germans as victims, to be sure, continued to serve important functions throughout the 1950s; it did not simply fade away and was often deployed strategically. But the appeal of concepts like Heimat also pointed towards the need for more redemptive memories beyond an exclusive focus on suffering and victimization. What Pieter Lagrou has observed for postwar memory in Western Europe more generally—that "mourning without triumphalism would undermine postwar national recovery"— applied to postwar Germany as well.[152] By the late 1940s, powerful symbolic and functional needs pushed both German societies under reconstruction to move beyond defeat rather than embrace it. This desire, however, stood in uneasy contrast with the ever-present consequences of total war and total defeat that also remained inscribed in returnees' minds and bodies. This struggle over the articulation and recognition of returning POWs' physical and psychological weaknesses in East and West forms the subject of the next chapter.

CHAPTER THREE

Embodied Defeat: Medicine, Psychiatry, and the Trauma of the Returned POW

When Wilhelm L. returned from war and Soviet captivity in October 1948, he was no longer the man he used to be. After serving in France and Denmark, he had been deployed on the Eastern front, where he had contracted cholera and typhus and, in 1944, was actually buried alive. In Soviet captivity, he had suffered from severe malnutrition, water edema, and a heart condition. After his release in October 1948, his mother reported severe changes in her son's personality. Although he had always been a lively, alert, and sociable person, he had become reclusive and conspicuously silent, and he often stared vacantly into space. He was no longer interested in frequenting bars, did not talk to his parents, and refused to take up any kind of work. As Wilhelm L. described it, he did "not feel completely healthy," "often felt dizzy" and "weak," and was "incapable of performing any kind of heavy labor." Asked about the origins of his symptoms, he replied that he "had been in the war, in captivity," and that he "could not understand what was happening to him," the "whole course of life" that he had behind himself, "then the seizures, the dizziness, the fatigue."[1]

War and captivity also left a lasting impact on Rudolf G.'s mind and body. Born in 1912 into a working-class family, he had been a very ambitious student, passed his exam as a master tailor at the unusually young age of twenty-four, and then opened a successful business. In 1940, he was drafted into the army and spent most of the war as a medical orderly. In 1945, he fell into Soviet captivity from which he did not return until October 1949. When Rudolf G. tried to reopen his business after his return, he began to notice significant changes in his moods, behaviors, and health. He began to suffer from headaches, sweating, and back pain and also experienced psychological difficulties. He became extremely shy and often wanted to go outside only at night. He preferred to be alone or with his wife, and he did not even want to see his siblings. He was often irritable and angry, yet also frequently broke into tears for no apparent reason, only to feel deeply embarrassed by his emotional outbursts.[2]

These examples open a window on the dramatic impact of total war and total defeat on returnees' physical and mental health.[3] Such stories of prolonged physical and psychic suffering indicate the extent to which war and defeat remained inscribed on former soldiers' and POWs' minds and bodies far into the postwar period. They challenge assumptions of a quick "overcoming" of the war's consequences, and they represent a crucial indicator of the "postwar" condition of both German societies after 1945. A close analysis of East and West German responses to returnees' pathologies, in turn, reveals much about the specific ways in which both societies tried to come to terms with the consequences of total war and total defeat. In the West, medical doctors and psychiatrists served as privileged interlocutors for demarcating the war's impact on both individuals and society at large. Their diagnoses defined the range of symptoms that legitimately counted as a "consequence" of the war, and they delineated the boundaries of acceptable public speech in discussing the war and its aftereffects.[4] The significance of this medical-psychiatric literature in the West stands in contrast to the virtual absence of such a discourse in the East. East German authorities defined returnees' deficiencies not in terms of psychopathological disorders but rather as forms of political and ideological deviance. In both societies, however, interpretations of returnees' ailments both shaped and reflected larger public narratives of war and defeat. They also reflected East and West German perceptions of returnees' challenged or even shattered masculinities, thus generating divergent yet parallel strategies of "remasculinization."

Dystrophy and the Ambiguity of Victim Status

A large segment of POWs returned from Soviet captivity in abysmal health. Many of them were already sick and exhausted when the Red Army captured them, and the deprivation and malnutrition endemic to the Soviet Union in the early postwar years exacerbated their condition. When the first mass transports of German POWs from the Soviet Union arrived in Frankfurt an der Oder in August 1946, hundreds died within weeks of their return from exhaustion and disease.[5] Of ten thousand returnees from the East in November 1947, only 7 percent were capable of work; 60 percent were malnourished, and 30 percent exhibited water edema.[6] Returnees suffered from a wide variety of diseases such as a malaria, tuberculosis, dysentery, and typhus.[7] The most common diagnosis for their condition, however, was dystrophy.

Dystrophy entered the diagnostic arsenal of the German medical and psychiatric professions only after the Second World War. The term was reportedly adopted from the Russian, and it drew on previous research on "barbed wire disease" during the First World War by the Swiss physi-

Figure 5. A returnee in the Friedland transition camp. POWs from the East often returned in abysmal health. They exhibited severe psychological and physical deficiencies that West German doctors and psychiatrists diagnosed as "dystrophy." The extensive medical and psychiatric literature on returnees' lasting pathologies denoted the persistent significance of the consequences of defeat in postwar West Germany. (Courtesy Bundesarchiv Koblenz.)

cian Ernst T. Vischer.[8] Supposedly, the primary cause of dystrophy had been malnutrition in Soviet captivity. The lack of protein in the diet of POWs, in particular, was believed to cause a wide range of physical deficits, including water edema, heart disease, high blood pressure, liver and kidney damage, as well as metabolic and hormonal disorders.[9] But most commentators also cited a wide range of psychological symptoms, such as depression, apathy, irritability, a general lack of motivation, and a reduced ability to perform.[10] In postwar Germany, dystrophy was defined as an insufficient functioning, narrowing, and "dedifferentiation" of returnees' personalities resulting from deprivation and starvation in Soviet captivity.[11] As a result of gradually improving nutritional levels in Soviet captivity, POWs who returned after 1948 no longer exhibited the profound physical symptoms displayed by earlier returnees. But they still continued to suffer from a wide array of physical and psychological ailments that sometimes only manifested themselves after their return from war and captivity.[12] While there are no statistics as to how many returnees were affected by these symptoms, the extensive medical and psychological literature on dystrophy suggests that the condition was quite pervasive.

Did dystrophy equal what today would be called "post-traumatic stress disorder"? At least some psychiatrists retroactively identify returnees' condition as PTSD, which, of course, was not available as a diagnostic category in the 1950s.[13] Historians have also attempted to employ PTSD for analyzing the consequences of extreme violence during World War II on European societies more broadly.[14] And indeed, many of the symptoms West German doctors and psychiatrists described as "dystrophy" resemble contemporary conceptions of PTSD. Definitions of PTSD vary, but they usually include the following symptoms: "recurrent re-experiencing of a trauma," "avoidance of reminders of trauma and emotional numbing," and "increased arousal."[15] In particular, dystrophy symptoms came close to the "kind of atrophy in the psychological capacities" that Judith Hermann has identified as the central psychological response to different kinds of "captivity" situations among Holocaust survivors, former POWs, and battered women.[16] Along similar lines, Michael Geyer has identified "apathy" and the "extinction of emotive capacities of body and soul" as "paradigmatic reaction to mass death in the Second World War."[17] Seen in this way, dystrophy symptoms might also denote the emotional precondition for participation in genocidal warfare as well as for living in its aftermath.

Yet despite the similarity of symptoms, identifying dystrophy with PTSD obscures the historical specificity of definitions and experiences of trauma.[18] Trauma does not represent a timeless fact with a clearly discernable "psycho-biological" essence. It is rather, as Alan Young explains, a "historical product" that is "glued together by the practices, technologies, and narratives with which it is diagnosed, studied, treated, and represented and by the various interests, institutions, and moral arguments that mobilized these efforts and resources."[19] Following Young, the ensuing analysis does not seek to retroactively diagnose returning POWs with PTSD, nor does it seek to invalidate such diagnoses. My analysis instead engages contemporary discussions of returnees' trauma and places them in the historical context of postwar Germany. It explores the meanings that patients and psychiatrists attached to returnees' symptoms, and, in so doing, it elucidates the ways in which postwar societies in East and West Germany processed the aftereffects of war and defeat.

The dystrophy diagnosis was closely intertwined with West German narratives of victimization. By attributing returnees' symptoms solely to the deprivations in captivity, the diagnosis precluded, by definition, any extended discussion of the potentially traumatic impact of the military experience itself. Instead, dystrophy offered a seemingly objective, scientific justification for ascribing a victim status to returning POWs. Medical authors frequently equated the physical and psychological consequences of internment in Nazi concentration and Soviet POW camps. One of the earliest discussions of returnees' symptoms, for example, posited the notion of a larger "pathology of captivity" that included "captives of all categories, the inmates of concentration, labor and POW camps."[20] Such equations informed dystrophy literature throughout the postwar period.[21] Until the late 1950s, the reference to Holocaust survivors served as a mere yardstick for German suffering and did not inspire actual research into the physical and psychological condition of Nazi victims, although such research had begun to appear outside of Germany in the late 1940s.[22]

In fact, there is evidence that postwar publications on dystrophy drew, at least in part, on Nazi medical experiments with concentration camp survivors. The medical doctor Heinrich Berning, for example, was able to publish a comprehensive study of "dystrophy" as early as 1949 by drawing on starvation experiments that he had conducted with Soviet POWs in German concentration camps.[23] Similarly, the author of a multivolume publication on "life under extreme conditions" and advisor to the West German returnee association, Ernst Günter Schenck, had served as SS food inspector of concentration camps during the Nazi period. After having spent ten years in Soviet captivity, he was tried for directing starvation experiments with inmates in the Mauthausen concentration camps but acquitted due to a lack of evidence.[24] Schenck's postwar publications fueled narratives of German victimization by severely distorting the lethal nature of the Nazi Holocaust and foregrounding the suffering of German POWs in Soviet captivity.[25] Both Schenck and Berning managed to reinvent themselves in the postwar period by applying their previous research on starvation and malnutrition among inmates of Nazi concentration camps to the considerably more "popular" cause of returning POWs from the Soviet Union.

While dystrophy literature contributed to narratives of German victimization, the discussion of returnees' pathologies inadvertently pointed to some of the more problematic implications of casting former soldiers and POWs as "victims." Drawing on a continuity with eugenic categories, doctors and psychiatrists identified returnees' individual pathologies as a threat to the health of the national body and as detrimental to postwar reconstruction. According to one doctor, it was of "supreme importance for the health of our general population that hundreds of thousands of returnees regain their physical and psychological productivity."[26] The ongoing salience of eugenic and racial categories also manifested itself in diagnoses of returnees from the East as completely "Russified." Analyzing the "somatic" and "psychological consequences" of malnutrition, the Lübeck psychiatrist Erich Funk underlined the "often noted Slavization" (*Slawisierung*) of prisoners of war. Swellings of the salivary gland had allegedly "widened" and "flattened" returnees' facial features while also "narrowing" their eyelids and pupils, thus giving them an "Eastern face" (*ostisches Gesicht*).[27] Social workers and cultural commentators echoed these observations. A representative of a church-run "returnee home" observed that the "terrible existence in captivity in Russia" and the "completely different way of life" had transformed returnees so profoundly that their "nature and their facial features have become Russian" and that they have lost "much of their actual humanity."[28] Writing in the periodical *Die Wandlung*, Paul Herzog argued that returnees had not "rid themselves of the features of the country from which they return" and therefore made an "Eastern impression."

> Most of them still have shaved heads and have been deprived of all the features of Western civilization and personality. Their uniformity indicates the collective existence from which they return. . . . Some of them could be brothers or relatives of Tartars or Siberians, certainly of Great Russians. . . . The physiognomy of the East arrives with our returnees for the time being.[29]

Such anxieties about the "Russification" of German POWs continued a long- standing trope of captivity narratives according to which the captive gradually assumed the characteristics of the captors.[30] This trope bespeaks the abiding power of assumptions about essential racial differences between Slavs and Germans. In the aftermath of the racial war of annihilation on the Eastern front, however, such perceptions also represented a particularly powerful marker of defeat: in a peculiar inversion of racialist discourse, these diagnoses inscribed on the former soldiers of Hitler's army the allegedly "subhuman" features of their former enemies on the Eastern front.[31] Moreover, the perception of former POWs as

"Russianized" and "dehumanized" also raised the troubling question: how could returnees ever become functioning West German citizens? Even anti-Nazi psychiatrists like Alexander Mitscherlich shared these concerns. Summarizing the result of a study among six hundred returnees from the East in 1948, he reported that they had been "rendered uncomplaining and dumb by a collectivized existence" and let themselves "be ordered around without the slightest inner resistance." "How these human beings now can take charge of their lives again," he argued, was a "serious problem."[32]

Diagnostic and Therapeutic Continuities in the West

While most observers agreed that returnees suffered massively from physical and psychological deficits, they diverged in their assessment of the nature and etiology of these symptoms. Did returnees' deficiencies derive from "exogenous" factors such as the consequences of war and captivity, or were these symptoms the result of "endogenous" conditions, that is, constitutional weaknesses or preexisting illnesses? Did these symptoms represent "normal" responses to extreme circumstances or were they indicative of "abnormal reactions" to stressful events? Were returnees' symptoms rooted in organic deficiencies or should they be classified as a form of mental illness? These were by no means merely academic questions but shaped the daily practices of doctors and psychiatrists, who needed to pass judgment on individual returnees' eligibility for state pensions. Doctors and psychiatrists needed to decide whether returnees' symptoms fell under the provisions of the Federal War Victim's Law (BVG) of 1950, which granted pensions only for physical deficiencies that were causally related to the war and its consequences, including postwar captivity. For most of the 1950s, however, the law excluded claims that were solely based on psychological symptoms.[33]

Significant diagnostic and conceptual continuities shaped medical and psychiatric responses to returnees' pathologies after 1945. These continuities included National Socialist conceptions of health and illness, but also reached back to the pre-1933 period by drawing on previous experiences with "shell shock" during and after the First World War.[34] Concurrent with standard responses to soldiers' psychological difficulties after the First World War, the dystrophy diagnosis consistently disavowed the potentially traumatic impact of military service. By its very definition, dystrophy located the etiology of returnees' trauma solely in the deprivations of captivity, never in the experience of genocidal warfare on the Eastern front. Yet at the same time, the emphasis on the traumatic nature of an external influence such as postwar captivity also ran counter to diagnostic traditions in the medical and psychiatric profession. As Paul Lerner has shown, from the First World War onward, German doctors and psychiatrists had come to locate individual suffering not in an "external traumatic event" but rather in the "patient's pathological mind."[35] In fact, German psychiatrists took credit for the relative absence of "war neurosis" among the soldiers of the Second World War. They claimed that it was precisely the stern rejection of external traumatic origins of these symptoms during the First World War that had prevented the recurrence of psychological breakdowns among soldiers of the Second World War.[36]

After 1945, many German doctors and psychiatrists echoed Karl Bonhoeffer's belief that the First World War had demonstrated the "extraordinary capacity of the healthy brain for resistance and adjustment."[37] According to this view, any prolonged psychic suffering in response to external events was "abnormal" and resulted primarily from individual constitutional or possibly hereditary illness. This theory also shaped early responses to returnees' pathologies. Writing in 1946, the Hamburg physician Hans W. Bansi identified a disproportionate number of "dysplastics," "slightly feeble-minded" and "not fully adequate human beings" among dystrophic returnees. These individuals, he argued, "quickly grow weary in the hard struggle with the difficulties of our time" and were thus more likely to succumb to dystrophy in Soviet captivity.[38] Similarly, the medical doctor Hans Malten identified a specific "neurosis of the returned POW" that, as he argued, derived primarily from "endogenous factors" and "manifested itself in an insufficient capacity toward all the demands of the new life."[39] In this view, returnees' symptoms derived from their individual inadequacy and not from the external conditions of captivity and homecoming.

Significantly, such traditional diagnostic categories also allowed psychiatrists to relegate intense feelings of guilt and fear among German POWs to the realm of psychopathological disorders. The psychiatrist Nikolaus Jensch, for example, reported "states of intense agitation" among German POWs in France who feared "collective sentencing," "imaginary execution commandos," and "plans for mass annihilation," yet he interpreted these symptoms as analogous to the "hysterical reactions" of German front soldiers during the First World War.[40] Along similar lines, the psychiatrist Johannes Gottschick reported fantasies of German POWs in American captivity. They believed that they were being held responsible for the German military defeat, or they thought they were being accused of being war criminals by the lights of passing American cars. A former submarine commander and bearer of the Knight's Cross (Ritterkreuz) reportedly believed that "several Americans and three Jews" transmitted orders to him how to "mitigate the consequences of German military collapse and save the German people."[41] Psychiatrists squarely placed *these* feelings of guilt for both Nazi crimes and German defeat outside the range of normal "reactive" responses to the captivity situation and relegated them to the status of "endogenous psychosis" or a "schizophrenic-paranoid condition."[42] For most German doctors and psychiatrists, such sentiments of guilt and fear amounted to nothing more than signs of mental illness.

Even as doctors and psychiatrists classified returnees' responses to captivity and homecoming as pathological and abnormal, they still expected these symptoms to evaporate upon the POWs' return.[43] If malnutrition indeed constituted the primary causal factor for dystrophy, then returnees were bound to recover due simply to higher nutrition levels and improved living conditions. The expectation of quick recovery also corresponded to international psychiatric conventional wisdom. The 1952 manual of the American Psychiatric Association, for example, described psychological responses of soldiers to combat situations as "gross-stress reaction," yet also denied any delayed aftereffects of such stressful experiences.[44] To the dismay of West German doctors and psychiatrists, however, returnees' symptoms persisted beyond their return from captivity or manifested themselves at that very moment. "Many returnees," one doctor observed, "only become ill when they are at home" and notice the "reduction of their ability to perform." Even years after their return, former POWs continued to suffer from intestinal disorders, circulatory problems, and other physical symptoms.[45] Moreover, doctors and psychiatrists also reported tenacious psychological symptoms among returnees, such as "lack of motivation," "apathy," "irritability," "absent-mindedness," "insomnia," "nightmares," and a general "inability to perform."[46] In some cases, these symptoms lasted throughout the 1960s.[47]

Returnees' "post-traumatic" conditions raised even thornier problems than the POWs' initial response to captivity and homecoming, especially with respect to material compensation. The German welfare state was historically ill disposed toward granting compensation for the delayed aftereffects of traumatic events. In 1926, the Reich Insurance Office passed a landmark ruling against so-called pension neurosis that outlawed all material compensation for symptoms deemed to arise only from the patient's desires to secure financial aid from the state. In fact, the ruling identified the pension application process itself as detrimental to the patient's health, since it was believed to contribute to the neurotic fixation of his or her alleged ailments. The 1926 ruling remained binding throughout the Nazi period and was eventually incorporated into the BVG.[48]

Conceptual and legal frameworks dating back to the Nazi and the pre-Nazi periods determined the evaluation of returnees' condition in the postwar period. These continuities became apparent in the practices of the Bonn psychiatrist Friedrich Panse. Panse was a prominent representative of the professional tradition that categorically rejected any traumatic aftereffects of external stressors. One of his earliest publications had significantly contributed to the 1926 landmark decision by linking neurotic illnesses after accidents to the availability of pensions.[49] During the Nazi period, Panse was heavily invested in locating the source of psychological difficulties in hereditary deficits rather than in external events.[50] He also functioned as a psychiatric evaluator for the Nazi euthanasia program, in which approximately eighty thousand handicapped and mentally ill people were killed by August 1941.[51] Panse then also served as the head of a reserve military hospital near Cologne, where he revived—and intensified—electroshock treatment of "war neurotics" as practiced during the First World War. His method of applying higher and more intense electroshocks to soldiers eventually evolved into a standard treatment of "war neurotics" in the German army known as "pansen."[52] In a 1952 study, Panse reaffirmed his rejection of war-related trauma by examining ninety-five individuals who had been subjected to Allied bombing during the war. He concluded that all psychological difficulties had disappeared with the termination of the external stressor and classified any remaining symptoms as "abnormal reactions" that did not qualify for material compensation.[53]

Despite his compromised past, Panse was able to reassume his positions as professor at Bonn University and director of the Bonn psychiatric institute for brain-injured patients.[54] In this capacity, he continued to apply his belief in the hereditary basis of mental illness as well as his categorical rejection of traumatic or post-traumatic conditions to psychiatric evaluations of returned POWs. In October 1954, the social welfare court in Cologne commissioned Panse to evaluate the case of Wilhelm L., whose story opened this chapter. Asked to determine the extent to which Wilhelm L.'s massive symptoms resulted from war and captivity and hence entitled him to a state pension, Panse flatly rejected L.'s pension claim. He diagnosed L. with an inherent mental illness, most likely schizophrenia, which had begun to manifest itself during and after Wilhelm L.'s return from Soviet captivity. Even though he evaluated Wihelm L. as 100 percent disabled, Panse denied that his disability was caused or even aggravated in any way by the war and its consequences.[55]

Hereditary mental illness was not the only argument that psychiatrists like Panse invoked to reject returnees' pension claims.[56] Confronted with the persistence of massive physical and psychological symptoms among former soldiers and POWs, doctors and psychiatrists also revived the traditional charge of "pension neurosis," especially in cases in which a temporal gap existed between the alleged traumatic event and the first occurrence of symptoms.[57] In the absence of clearly discernable organic deficiencies, psychiatrists argued that the granting of pensions would "fixate" returnees' symptoms rather than helping them.[58] Studies that documented an alleged increase of "unjustified" pension applications in the aftermath of the currency reform seemed to suggest a causal link between worsening economic conditions and "pension neurosis."[59] Finally, the emphasis on stamina, endurance, and eventual overcoming of hardship as indicators of a healthy reaction to external stressors reflected the enduing significance of soldierly ideals of masculinity. Conversely, psychiatric evaluations portrayed any lasting form of psychic suffering as an index of an effeminate "exhaustibility" and "sensitivity."[60]

Long-standing diagnostic categories also shaped doctors' and psychiatrists' therapeutic strategies toward returnees. In particular, they resorted to "suggestive" therapies that had been employed during both world wars. These therapies were based on the assumption that the patient's suffering did not derive from any external influences but was based solely on his imagination. Therapy, accordingly, aimed at freeing the patient from his symptoms through rapid and forceful intervention. The mechanism for shaking up the patients' emotional state ran the gamut from persuasion to hypnosis to more forceful—and more painful—measures such as electroshock therapy or insulin treatment.[61] Psychiatrists continued to apply these therapeutic strategies in the aftermath of the Second World War.[62] If unsuccessful, doctors and psychiatrists did not call into question their strategies for healing. Instead, they emphasized the irreversibility of returnees' condition and explained therapeutic failure as the result of severe organic deficits or of hereditary mental illness.[63] In severe cases, psychiatrists recommended the returnee's admission to a psychiatric institution.[64]

Patients' responses to psychiatric diagnoses ranged from embarrassment and resignation to outright resistance. Tellingly, not all former soldiers and POWs embraced their symptoms and actively pursued their pension claims. Especially if they suffered from predominantly psychological symptoms, the widespread stigmatization of mental illness led them to downplay their difficulties. The returnee Hans E., for example, at first remained silent about the seizures he experienced upon his return from captivity, stating that he would soon become healthy again and that "nobody needed to know."[65] In these cases, it was often wives and other family members who urged returnees to seek help. They also appealed to medical officials on returnees' behalf to grant more favorable pension rulings, sometimes without the knowledge of their husbands.[66] These examples demonstrate that patients too subscribed to conceptions of masculinity that militated against an acceptance of physical and especially psychological injuries.[67]

Many returnees, however, publicly articulated their frustration with pension verdicts. Such complaints were a returning theme in interviews that the Frankfurt Institute for Social Research conducted with more than five hundred returnees in the mid-1950s.[68] "We all came back with some disease," one returnee exclaimed, "and when one files these claims with the welfare offices, one gets the wonderful response: 'constitutionally predisposed.' "[69] Even if claims were initially evaluated positively, former soldiers and POWs feared a reduction of their benefits as a result of periodic reexamination. "Just the thought of again standing in front of a doctor," another returnee lamented, "makes people nervous and anxious."[70] In some cases, returnees even offered violent resistance. When Josef K.'s pension was gradually reduced from 100 to 30 percent disability, he physically attacked a doctor who had asked him "to run up stairs" as part of his medical exam.[71] Other returnees appealed negative pension verdicts in the courts. Over a period of thirteen years, Karl G. tried unsuccessfully to convince medical and psychiatric examiners that his general weakness, frequent headaches, high blood pressure, and depression stemmed from the deprivation and malnutrition in Soviet captivity. Yet time and again, medical and psychiatric evaluators contested the attribution of his symptoms to exogenous factors and interpreted them in terms of constitutional weakness and "pension neurosis."[72] Responding to a similarly negative verdict, another returnee even complained to Chancellor Konrad Adenauer: "The examining doctor did not even look at or touch my body," Franz B. complained and appealed to Adenauer's commitment to "give returnees any conceivable support."[73] As returnees' individual experiences with the West German pension bureaucracy indicate, narratives of victimization did not necessarily translate into a recognition of their physical and psychological deficiencies as war-related. Instead, diagnostic and conceptual continuities within the medical and psychiatric relegated returnees' symptoms to merely individual pathologies unrelated to the war and its consequences.[74]

THE EMERGENCE OF PSYCHIC TRAUMA IN THE WEST

Significant continuities notwithstanding, medical and psychiatric responses to returnees' post-traumatic condition also exhibited subtle yet important transformations. Facing the pervasiveness of returnees' psychic suffering, some doctors and psychiatrists found it difficult to ascribe these symptoms entirely to constitutional weaknesses or hereditary illness. In particular, the strong public emphasis on German POWs' victimization in Soviet captivity pushed them towards a greater recognition of exogenous factors in diagnosing and evaluating returnees' symptoms. While the psychiatric casualties of the First World War had fueled an increasing emphasis on soldiers' constitutional weakness, the ideological parameters of the Cold War redirected psychiatrists' attention to the external causes of psychic suffering, notably the deprivations associated with Soviet captivity.

Against the background of pervasive public narratives of German POWs' suffering in Soviet captivity, some medical and psychiatric experts began to understand the weakening of the POWs' physical and psychological capacities not as an indication of "failure" but rather as a quite appropriate "compensatory emergency measure" to external hardship and deprivation. In fact, shutting off all nonessential functions appeared as essential for returnees' survival in captivity, much like animals in hibernation.[75] Moreover, the intense physical deprivation of Soviet captivity naturally required an extended period of readjustment after the POWs' return from captivity. The Marburg psychiatrist Wilhelm Schmitz, who had himself spent one and a half years in captivity, thus argued that it was "completely understandable" that "even previously not neurotic natures" might experience some difficulties upon their return from captivity. He also argued that returnees' psychological symptoms might result from organic deficiencies caused by severe malnutrition, such as edema of the brain.[76] This somatic basis of returnees' psychological difficulties, then, also explained the slow recession of these symptoms after the return from captivity.

The etiological link between returnees' psychic symptoms and organic changes in the brain was most pronounced in the work of the psychiatrist Walter Schulte.[77] Schulte focused on a "small group" of former POWs whom he had treated as patients in the psychiatric institution in Bethel. Contrary to all expectations, these patients did not recover from the physical and psychological deficits associated with dystrophy.[78] Instead, they continued to show reduced "physical and psychological capacities," including reduced sexual functions. Their personalities had "grown weary" and become "dedifferentiated," but most of them were also keenly aware of their "reduced ability to perform" and sometimes even became suicidal.[79] In the larger debate within West German psychiatry over the somatic or psychic origins of mental illness, Schulte took a middle position and conceded that it was not always easy to delineate "neurotic-psychoasthenic failure" from "organic characterological changes" caused by dystrophy.[80] But he shifted the emphasis from "abnormal reactions" to pathological changes inside the brain as the primary etiological factor of returnees' conditions. Schulte also claimed that it was possible to document these organic pathologies with medical tests, such as an encephalogram of the brain.[81] By attributing returnees' psychic symptoms to an "objectively" discernable physical cause, Schulte's interpretation gave legitimacy to returnees' symptoms and divorced them from the stigma of mental illness. In so doing, Schulte revived a focus on somatic origins of psychological suffering that the German psychiatric profession had largely abandoned during the First World War.[82]

His diagnosis of an organic etiology of dystrophy led Schulte to a more skeptical assessment of therapeutic possibilities. Psychotherapy and electroshock treatment might alleviate returnees' condition but could not cure the irreversible damage to the brain. The flip side of this assessment, however, was a more generous evaluation of returnees' pension claims. If their symptoms were indeed caused by an organic problem, then returnees qualified for material compensation as defined in the BVG. Schulte was very much aware of the potential financial implications of this diagnosis. He attempted to restrict the number of potential beneficiaries by insisting that such "permanent cerebral damage" was very rare. But he also criticized the frequent misdiagnosis of such conditions as "pseudodementia" and proposed a disability rate of 40–50 percent for those afflicted.[83]

Schulte's research had an immediate impact on compensation practices, even among psychiatrists like Panse who had previously rejected any notion of prolonged traumatic suffering. In July 1954, Panse served as psychiatric evaluator of Rudolf G., the second case cited at the beginning of this chapter. Upon his return from captivity in 1949, Rudolf G. was initially granted a 50 percent disability because of the organic consequences of dystrophy. But three years later, his pension was eliminated and his ongoing psychological problems were diagnosed as symptomatic of a constitutional weakness. Despite his earlier hostility to the recognition of any delayed psychological symptoms, Panse reversed this verdict. After an encephalogram of Rudolf G.'s brain, Panse pronounced—with explicit reference to Schulte—that G. suffered from "organically induced psychological changes" and reinstated his 50 percent disability rate.[84] In subsequent cases, Panse consistently granted pensions to returnees when he believed he had detected organic changes in the brain and when there was no family history of mental illness.[85] This practice reflected a subtle yet significant adjustment of psychiatric diagnosis to a new historical context: Panse did not abandon his belief in the organic basis of psychopathological disorders, but he now recognized not only hereditary factors but also external influences such as dystrophy in Soviet captivity as possible etiological factors of such pathologies.[86] Conversely, if no such changes could be detected, or if patients refused to submit to an encephalogram, Panse and his colleagues in the Bonn psychiatry consistently denied returnees' pension claims.[87]

The emphasis on organic damages, however, did not completely resolve the puzzle of returnees' post-traumatic condition. Contrary to Schulte's expectation, increased medical testing of returnees did not yield more evidence for pathological changes in the brain, which remained very rare and difficult to prove. Surveys among fifty-six thousand returnees in Schleswig-Holstein documented only eight such cases.[88] In another 1954 study, the Hamburg psychiatrist Hans-Harro Rauschelbach, who later served as medical evaluator for the Federal Labor Ministry, identified pathological changes in the brain in only one out of twenty-four returnees who suffered dystrophy after Soviet captivity.[89] This gap between return-ees' frequent psychological symptoms and the few cases in which these symptoms could actually be traced to organic deficiencies provided an opening for alternative diagnostic and therapeutic approaches, such as psychotherapy and psychoanalysis.

Just like mainstream psychiatry, psychotherapy and psychoanalysis ex-hibited numerous continuities to the Nazi period. Both disciplines under-went a rapid process of professionalization during the Third Reich and managed to adjust rather well to National Socialism.[90] It is therefore not too surprising that the most comprehensive psychotherapeutic approach to returnees' condition came from an outspoken supporter of the Nazi regime, the psychotherapist Kurt Gauger. In 1934, Gauger had delivered an enthusiastic commitment to National Socialism in a speech on "psycho-therapy and political worldview."[91] While his actual career in the Third Reich fell short of his ideological ambitions, he was deeply involved in the propagation of National Socialist concepts of health and illness. As the head of the Institute for Films in Science and Education, Gauger presided over the production of nine hundred medical research and teaching films that advocated the policy of compulsory sterilization as well as the prac-tice of children's euthanasia.[92] After 1945, Gauger was briefly interned by American occupation authorities but ultimately exonerated in his denazi-fication proceedings in 1947.[93] And while Gauger was "shunned" in the psychotherapeutic profession after 1945, he—like some of his compro-mised colleagues—managed to reinvent himself professionally through his work on dystrophy.[94]

Gauger's analysis of dystrophy incorporated many elements of his pre-vious analysis of psychological pathologies during the Nazi period, even though he now sought to distinguish returnees' curable "psychic illness" from more severe forms of mental illness. Gauger attributed returnees' symptoms less to malnutrition in Soviet captivity than to a severe defor-mation of their personality. For Gauger, dystrophy resulted, above all, from a "qualitative and quantitative narrowing of the POWs' libidinal instincts," a "depersonalization" and "loss of ego" in response to the captivity situation and the "shock" of homecoming.[95] Due to this "libidi-nal autism," returnees were incapable of establishing healthy object rela-tionships.[96] These deficiencies, Gauger argued, not only rendered return-ees incapable of making judgments or of pursuing their own interests; they also turned them into a potential threat to the social and moral order of postwar society.[97] In light of these dramatic effects of dystrophy, Gauger even warned of "mass dystrophication" as a weapon in the Cold War, which would turn individuals into "willing and passive objects of history" and hence render them susceptible to communism.[98]

Psychotherapy and psychoanalysis were no more likely to attribute returnees' symptoms to external events than mainstream psychiatry.[99] Consequently, Gauger advocated therapy instead of pensions as the appropriate response to returnees' conditions. In contrast to mainstream psychiatry, however, Gauger rejected the use of "shock therapies" for treating returnees' condition.[100] Instead, he advocated a specific kind of psychotherapy that he applied to approximately 750 returnees in a "returnee hospital" near Uelzen in northern Germany.[101] The main goal of his therapy was to assist returnees in overcoming their "autistic self-centeredness" and in enabling them to rebuild their "personality" and their "capacity for community." This therapeutic concept drew heavily on contemporary fears of "massification," as Gauger strove to help returnees in moving beyond their experience of "collectivism" in Soviet captivity while maintaining a healthy distance from (Western) "individualism."[102] Gauger's therapeutic strategies included sports, working groups, discussion evenings, communal singing, and, especially, dancing lessons. Dancing appeared to be particularly well suited for restoring returnees' masculinity by fostering their ability to form "libidinal object relations" while, at the same time, requiring a "restraining of desire."[103] Gauger claimed stunning therapeutic success. In one case, he allegedly not only transformed a twenty-year-old returnee from an infantile "kid" (*Bubi*) to a "self-conscious young man" but also allegedly effected seven inches of belated physical growth.[104] Gauger documented such processes with a series of "before" and "after" photos, which eerily resembled his earlier techniques of visualizing alleged mental and physical deficiencies in Nazi propaganda films.[105]

The psychiatric profession reacted rather coolly to Gauger's muddled application of psychoanalytic theory.[106] According to one critic, his concept of "psychic dystrophy" went "too far and completely diluted the term *dystrophy*."[107] While Gauger's influence within the psychiatric profession remained limited, his analysis exerted an important influence on the public discourse on the "returnee disease." Important news media such as *Die Zeit* und *Spiegel* popularized Gauger's theories and pondered whether dystrophy lay at the heart of many supposed social and cultural ills of postwar society.[108] By the early 1950s, West German officials recognized Gauger as *the* authority on returnee diseases. In a meeting with religious welfare organizations in October 1953, a representative of the ministry of expellees cited Kurt Gauger's book as the authoritative treatment of this issue and underscored the severe physical and psychological damages that returning POWs suffered as a result of dystrophy.[109] Gauger's compromised Nazi past and his marginal standing within the West German psychiatric profession notwithstanding, he became one of the most widely recognized experts on dystrophy in the early Federal Republic.

While medical and psychiatric authorities did not incorporate Gauger's concept of "psychic dystrophy" in their evaluation of returnees' pension claims, general practitioners at West German welfare offices (*Versorgungsämter*) adopted less restrictive compensation practices than university psychiatrists like Panse. In 1953, a doctor from the compensation office in Wiesbaden professed his sympathy for returned POWs by declaring that "because we were in the war as well, everything is done on our part to help the comrades to get their rights."[110] Medical evaluators generally granted partial disability for a period of two to three years as a result of the late consequences of dystrophy even if no pathological changes in the brain could be discerned.[111]

In addition, doctors and psychiatrists also developed new diagnostic categories to capture returnees' persistent pathologies. By the mid-1950s, the diagnosis of "vegetative dystony" referred to prolonged psychosomatic symptoms such as dizziness, nausea, weather sensitivity, sweating, fatigue, high blood pressure, and intestinal disorder.[112] Vegetative dystony illustrated the difficulty of isolating the physical and psychological consequences of war and captivity from other external factors. The diagnosis was situated at the boundary between health and illness, and it appeared as a "fashionable diagnosis," as a "stigma of our century," and as consequence of our "high-speed civilization" that affected large sections of the civilian population as well.[113] Still, a disproportionate percentage of former soldiers and POWs continued to suffer from psychosomatic symptoms that were subsumed under this category.[114] Thus, "vegetative dystony" became a distinct diagnosis for returnees' post-traumatic condition. It also signaled an increasing recognition of external factors in the discussion about the etiology of returnees' symptoms. This broadening of the medical-psychiatric perspective also began to include the socioeconomic circumstances that awaited the returnee at home. One study found that of the two hundred POWs who still suffered from vegetative dystony five years after their return, two-thirds were expellees who had difficulty finding appropriate employment and housing.[115] Returnees' lasting symptoms, this study suggested, were not merely a function of their individual inadequacy but also crucially depended on the larger socioeconomic environment they encountered.

The emergence of "vegetative dystony" and the increasing recognition of external factors by the early 1950s were not completely accidental. Given the standard practice of granting two to three years of partial disability for the late consequences of dystrophy, many pensions threatened to expire at that time. As a result, former soldiers and POWs directed medical and psychiatric attention to their ongoing symptoms by filing lawsuits and asking for renewed medical evaluations to prevent the elimination of their benefits. Moreover, during the early 1950s, the Association of Returnees (VdH) embarked on a public campaign to achieve a more generous recognition of the medical and psychological deficits among its constituency.[116] In 1953, the VdH organized the first congress on prisoner of war diseases that brought together leading experts on dystrophy, including Kurt Gauger, H. W. Bansi, and Walter Schulte.[117] Participants highlighted the rudimentary state of medical and psychiatric research, which was only beginning to discover the myriad physical and psychological consequences of dystrophy. They stressed the long-term impact of dystrophy on the functioning of the entire organ system, but also underlined psychosomatic and psychological consequences.

The VdH subsequently pushed further towards recognition of the medical and psychological consequences of dystrophy in Soviet captivity. Arguing that these aftereffects of dystrophy affected not only individuals with a "deficient brain" (Hirnschwache) or "weaklings" but also highly educated people, VdH representatives sought to shield their constituency against the stigma of mental illness.[118] The activities of the VdH eventually also attracted the attention of West German officials to the variety of "returnee diseases." In 1956, the Federal Labor Ministry commissioned a collection of essays on dystrophy as a "particularly widespread, significant, and for each patient very threatening syndrome," which had "thus far been relatively unknown" and "puzzled medical science."[119] Most of the contributions, however, focused on the wide variety of organic deficiencies as a result of dystrophy. While West German officials were thus quite receptive to further study—and eventually also material compensation—of returnees' organic deficiencies, purely psychological or psychosomatic conditions were still denied material compensation. This practice only changed in response to the last returning POWs in 1953–54 and 1955–56. Their public celebration as masculine heroes allowed for recognition of independent psychic trauma, which, in turn, increased West German receptivity for the trauma of Holocaust survivors as well.[120]

Male Sexuality as a Site of Trauma

In West German discussions of returnees' pathologies, gender and sexuality were privileged sites of trauma. Returnees from the East did not just appear as less masculine but, indeed, as wholly desexualized. Virtually all dystrophy authors emphasized the loss of the sexual instinct in captivity as a central element of returnees' pathologies. Upon their return from captivity, former soldiers and POWs purportedly exhibited a "eunuch-like lack of sexual desire" and frequently suffered from impotence.[121] Kurt Gauger even argued that captivity had altered the sexual nature of returnees' bodies, which began to exhibit feminine shapes and features with "pubic hair of the female type" as well as the "first signs and fully developed forms of the female breast."[122] As late as 1956, the German Society for Sexual Research devoted its annual congress entirely to the theme of "returnee sexuality" and addressed sexual "deficiencies," "maladjustments," and "perversions" that continued to plague former soldiers and POWs more than ten years after the end of the war.[123] Significantly, most observers argued that female returnees had been less affected by dystrophy and its impact on sexuality due to the "passive role of women in the sexual partnership."[124] Dystrophy appeared as a distinctly male disease, and male sexuality furnished a unique site through which postwar Germans discussed—and experienced—the consequences of total war and total defeat.

The sexual difficulties of returnees threatened their full participation in the central project of West German reconstruction: the reconstruction of the family.[125] Returnees' desexualization fundamentally undermined their ability to reassume their positions as fathers and husbands within reconstructed (or newly formed) families. Thus, the transformation of returnees into functioning male citizens crucially hinged on their successful "resexualization." Indeed, doctors and psychiatrists defined the restoration of returnees' heterosexuality as a crucial indicator for postwar societies' ability to move beyond defeat. This was one reason why, as Dagmar Herzog has aptly observed, "male bodies were called to a kind of public visibility and accountability that most scholars of the history of sexuality generally assume to be reserved for women."[126]

The diagnosis of returnees' sexual deficits was based on a conception of sexuality that emphasized the fluidity and fundamental openness of the sexual instinct. Doctors and psychiatrists assumed that normative "mature" heterosexuality did not constitute an inborn, "natural" disposition but needed to be consolidated during adolescence. In this view, culture and society played central roles in shaping sexuality.[127] Consequently, external social and cultural factors assumed much greater explanatory weight in assessing the etiology of returnees' sexual deficiencies than they did with reference to their more general post-traumatic condition. Moreover, most observers tended to agree that returnees' sexual deficits were not based in organic deficits but rather derived "primarily from psychic factors."[128] One doctor, for example, failed to detect any pathologies in his examination of the sperm of five hundred returnees suffering from severe impotence.[129] As a result, more so than in their diagnosis of returnees' psychological deficiencies, doctors and psychiatrists looked to external factors in seeking to explain their sexual problems.

Commentators left no doubt that total defeat had fundamentally undermined returnees' masculinity and hence also their sexuality. According to one psychiatrist, it was precisely the former members of the ostensibly "manliest" military branches—pilots, tank commanders, and submarine officers—who suffered disproportionately from impotence.[130] Doctors also invoked the "rape and impregnation of the German women" by Soviet soldiers in explaining returnees' sexual deficiencies, thus discussing the violation of female bodies primarily in terms of its impact on male psyche.[131] Finally and most importantly, doctors and psychiatrists blamed returnees' sexual problems on the changed gender relations of the postwar period. The psychiatrist Erwin Stransky speculated that the "increasing legal and moral equality of the woman" prompted "growing anxiety and pressure among the male partner," which then produced male impotence.[132] Another observer argued that returnees' sexual problems did not derive from hormonal disorders but rather from "an unnatural equality of the sexes" that placed undue burdens on women while also depriving men of important aspects of their masculinity.[133] Confirming their persistent antimodern bias, some psychiatrists also identified the changed gender relations as indications of the pathogenic effects of modernity more generally. They deplored the fact that most former soldiers and POWs returned to the "big city" rather than to a rural environment, which was considered more conducive to returnees' postwar readjustment.[134]

Just as diagnostic practices identified larger social and cultural factors primarily responsible for returnees' sexual difficulties, therapeutic suggestions tended to focus on social transformation rather than on individual pathologies. Beyond a general call for the restoration of more traditional gender relations, commentators identified women as decisive agents for therapeutic intervention. The returnee's wife, as one medical doctor put it, represents the "sole and usually the only effective medicine for the wounded soul of the returnee."[135] Her responsibility began with monitoring and providing an appropriate diet. Wives (or mothers) were to ensure that returnees would not indulge in their "understandable desire for food" but rather increase their calorie intake through small and easy-to-digest portions.[136] More importantly, women were also the key to remedying returnees' psychological and sexual problems. It was only through women—and especially through "resumption of sexual unification"—that men were to overcome their emotional coldness and asocial autism.[137] Such advice to the returnee's wife often included the suggestion that she should overcome her "shame and shy passivity" and initiate sexual activities with "a gentle stroke by a female hand."[138] At the same time, women should refrain from making too explicit sexual demands.[139] Commentators also warned wives' against infantilizing returnees by adopting the attitude of an "overprotective mother."[140] Independently of their specific—and often contradictory—suggestions, these therapeutic strategies defined the restoration of female domesticity as precondition for restoring male sexuality.

Postwar observers, however, were keenly aware that the reconstruction of an imaginary private sphere alone would not guarantee returnees' successful resexualization. Precisely because human sexuality appeared as fluid and indeterminate, the process of resexualization appeared fraught with danger. In particular, West German authorities worried that returnees' reawakened sexuality might be diverted from normative heterosexuality into "perversion" and crime. These concerns informed a memorandum of the Arbeiterwohlfahrt from March 1950 that alerted state and federal ministries of justice to the disproportionate representation of returnees among sex and property offenders in Lower Saxony. The memo drew heavily on Kurt Gauger's analysis; and it cited approvingly the case of a returnee who had been acquitted of incest with his twelve-year-old daughter due to extenuating circumstances as a result of dystrophy in Soviet captivity.[141] As expert witness in a series of trials, Gauger himself exculpated returnees who had committed sex offenses. In a 1951 case, he argued that only six months in Soviet captivity were sufficient to produce an "infantile regression" of one returnee's sexual instinct, who then molested two ten-year-old girls five years later.[142] Dystrophic returnees were believed to suffer from a "retardation of the sexual constitution, which . . . may give the undirected sexual impulse a perverted goal" and thus rendered them legally not responsible for their actions.[143] This argument eventually became widely accepted and was also applied to divorce and criminal cases involving former soldiers and POWs.[144]

While the invocation of dystrophy shielded returnees against criminal prosecution, it did not protect them against the most serious—and criminalized—diversion of the sexual instinct in postwar West Germany: homosexuality. There was, to be sure, no uniform agreement as to whether homosexuality represented an inborn, hereditary condition or whether it was shaped by social and cultural contexts.[145] But the widespread anxieties over returnees' resexualization clearly underlined concerns about heterosexual stabilization in the postwar period.[146] Postwar observers identified powerful external forces that threatened to divert returnees' sexual instinct into a homosexual direction. They argued that the all-male environment in war and captivity had fostered returnees' "digression into masturbation and homosexuality."[147] Another doctor interpreted key symptoms of returnees' post-traumatic condition—anxieties, compulsive behavior, eating and sleeping disorders, heart problems, lack of willpower, and the inability to work—as indications of unconscious homosexual desires.[148] By the mid-1950s, medical doctors estimated that 15 to 20 percent of returnees had engaged in homosexual acts in captivity, while another author feared that the actual number may have been considerably higher and "remained in the dark."[149]

To postwar observers, the specter of returnees' homosexuality was threatening on several levels. It was not only that homosexuality appeared to be incompatible with the reconstruction of the family. The widespread recognition of sexual orientation as mutable also fueled anxieties that returnees might become either agents or "victims" of homosexual seduction. These fears drove the continued application of the radicalized version of paragraph 175 from the Nazi period, which criminalized not just homosexual acts but any kind of same-sex activity, including mutual masturbation, touches, and even suggestive glances.[150] Homosexuality, moreover, appeared as "compulsive," "rigid," and "addictive" and thus ran counter to the ideal of restraint in masculinity.[151] Commentators emphasized not just the proclivity of homosexual men to crime but also their susceptibility "to political, religious, and criminal fantasies" and to "isms of all kind."[152] The reconstruction of male heterosexuality as a basic element of liberal democratic citizenship helped to create distance from the homoeroticism and male bonding that postwar commentators associated with Nazism.[153] Finally, sociologists like Helmut Schelsky also cast male homosexuality as an indication of the "tremendous social dislocation . . . that German society had suffered in the postwar period."[154] In this view, returnees' "resexualization" and the reconstruction of normative heterosexuality more generally became an integral part of West German efforts to overcome defeat.

POLITICS AND PSYCHIATRY IN THE EAST

The bodies and psyche of returning POWs assumed an equally important, albeit very different significance for defining the meaning of war and defeat in the East. While images of depraved and emaciated returnees both fueled and reflected Western narratives of victimization, the same representations discredited the SED's project of antifascist reconstruction. Initially, party officials tried to repress public representations of sick returnees. In a discussion over a poster advertisement for a collection on behalf of returning POWs in Berlin, the SED representative Kurt Ziegenhagen rejected the portrayal of a returnee as a "completely pathetic and desperate figure" and advocated a more upbeat representation.[155] Similarly, East German popular magazines published photos of smiling, well-fed, and optimistic returnees who were supposedly already well on their way toward building "a future for themselves and for their families with the same toughness that helped them to survive the horrors of the war."[156]

East German officials, however, were painfully aware of the fact that this official portrayal of healthy, optimistic, and forward-looking returnees stood in stark contrast to their actual condition. Even before the arrival of the first POWs, officials in Brandenburg sought to make available hundreds of hospital beds anticipating that the POWs would return exhausted and sick.[157] In August 1946, the medical doctor of a returnee camp in the Soviet zone reported to the central administration in Berlin that returning POWs were suffering from a variety of physical and psychic ailments, including severe malnutrition, tuberculosis and a "depressive attitude" that often led them to collapse "without any discernable organic suffering."[158] Within the population at large, party officials noted that the "the wildest rumors" were "circulating about the moral attitudes and health of returning POWs from the Soviet Union."[159] Even SED functionaries criticized official press reports about the health of returning POWs as "utter nonsense" and described the condition of returning POWs as "catastrophic."[160]

In contrast to the West, the East German medical and psychiatric profession remained largely excluded from analyzing or diagnosing returnees' pathologies. While East German medical doctors and psychiatrists addressed some of the physical and psychological symptoms that their West German counterparts associated with dystrophy, they never did so with explicit reference to returnees from the East.[161] East German reviews of West German dystrophy literature also never mentioned that this condition primarily referred to returnees from the East.[162] Instead, the main East German psychiatric periodical published some West German analyses on the mental health of returnees from *Western* captivity; and psychiatric textbooks discussed symptoms of war-related trauma—a reduced ability to perform, fatigue, lack of concentration—exclusively with reference to victims of Nazism and POWs in the West.[163] East German authorities (possibly on order from their Soviet superior) suppressed a similarly extensive medical and psychiatric discourse on returnees from the Soviet Union as it emerged in the West.[164]

Silence and repression, however, were not the only ways in which East German doctors and psychiatrists sought to disavow returnees' symptoms. A combination of professional continuities and specific developments of East German psychiatry further eroded the discursive space for the recognition of returnees' trauma. As in the West, East German medicine and psychiatry experienced an incomplete denazification after 1945.[165] Consequently, the traditional hostility in the German psychiatric profession to recognizing war-related trauma survived in East Germany as well. In 1946, a former military psychiatrist advised—with explicit reference to the experience of the First World War—against the recognition of any psychological damage among former soldiers and argued that all of these symptoms derived either from constitutional weakness or the "hunt for a pension."[166] This emphasis on the "steeling of the will" in East German psychiatry was, then, also easily compatible with the SED's interest in restoring individual and collective productivity.[167]

Any residual openness to war-related trauma in East German psychiatry that still existed in the late 1940s fell victim to official efforts at imposing the theories of the Soviet psychiatrist Ivan Petrovic Pavlov as the new
orthodoxy.[168] The Pavlovan emphasis on external societal factors as shaping individual psyche was now contrasted to the "subjective irrational-
ism" of Western psychoanalysis.[169] Any persistent psychological symptoms no longer appeared as consequences of war and defeat but rather as
pathological maladjustment to the real existing "antifascist-democratic"
or "Socialist" order. The work of one leading psychiatrist in the Soviet
zone, Dietfried Müller-Hegemann, clearly reflects these developments. A
KPD member since 1931, Müller-Hegemann served in a military hospital
during the war and then spent three years in Soviet captivity as the leader
of an "antifascist committee."[170] Müller-Hegemann asserted a direct cor-
relation between psychic structure and the evolution of "societal consciousness." He identified, for example, a "psychology of German fascists" that resulted from the socioeconomic structures of "imperialism"
and "monopoly capitalism."[171] Conversely, Müller-Hegemann attributed
the alleged absence of schizophrenia among German POWs in the Soviet
Union to the stimulating conditions in Soviet captivity, such as "regular
and intensive work, sufficient supplies . . . , comprehensive medical treatment, and permanent cultural stimulation." It was only after the POWs'
return that psychiatric illnesses became more frequent, and they appeared
to have been almost epidemic among German POWs in U.S. captivity.[172]

As a result of these developments within East German psychiatry, former soldiers with psychic symptoms stood little or no chance of receiving
material compensation. Without access to patient files of East German
psychiatric institutions, the actual treatment of mentally disturbed former
soldiers and POWs in East Germany is difficult to trace. If they were
referred to a psychiatric institution, they were likely to have been diagnosed with traditional categories of schizophrenia or "feeble-mind-
edness" and treated with "work therapy" or electroshock.[173] In some
cases, sick and mentally ill returnees were treated in church-run institutions that partly compensated for the lack of official attention.[174] Most
returnees, however, were left alone with their conditions and forced to
cope privately within the family and at the workplace.

To remedy returnees' pathologies, East German officials resorted not
to psychotherapy but to political enlightenment. They incorporated returnees' individual predicament into the larger antifascist narrative of war
and defeat. In this view, deprivations and hardship in Soviet camps directly resulted from the massive destruction of Soviet resources. Returnees' poor health and miserable appearance derived from their already
weakened and exhausted state when they had fallen into Soviet captivity.[175] In addition, party officials asserted that many German POWs had

become ill "naturally" due to the extreme climate in the Soviet Union or had purposefully ruined their health to effect an earlier release from captivity.[176] By claiming that returnees' conditions resulted from *anything but* Soviet captivity, East German officials sought to counter Western claims that these conditions derived *solely* from internment in Soviet POW camps.

Although they substituted the political for psychiatric deviance, East German officials also associated returnees' pathologies with deficient masculinity, which, however, they defined differently than their West German counterparts. When the SED representative Edith Höding visited a group of returning POWs in the Gronenfelde transition camp, she was shocked by their sense of desperation and self-pity. "Almost all of them," she reported, "were '[dy]strophics,' and they have completely internalized the notion that they will be a wreck forever and never become fully capable human beings again." She sternly informed the men that "we women in Berlin went through a lot as well" and that "we expect them to be good comrades (*Kameraden*) who will diligently help us with the reconstruction of the country."[177] Such apathy and indifference stood in direct contrast to the militant activism that had formed the core of Communist conceptions of masculinity from the 1920s on.[178] In both postwar societies, perceptions of returnees' deficiencies exposed a severe crisis of masculinity. Yet, whereas in the West deficient masculinity was defined primarily in relation to returnees' sexuality, East German officials characterized it exclusively in terms political ignorance and apathy.[179]

The implications of this diagnosis were clear: "therapy" needed to focus not on individual deficiencies but on political and ideological reeducation. Returnees were supposed to overcome their "limited barbed-wire" perspective by placing their suffering in the larger historical context of German aggression.[180] Party officials were to foster this political transformation through a "psychologically sensitive combating of the romantic martyr-psychology of the *Landser* [ordinary soldier]."[181] Confronted with largely hostile and traumatized former soldiers and POWs, East German officials adopted a primarily defensive strategy. They sought to counteract subjective and "bodily" memories that appeared incompatible with antifascist reconstruction under Soviet auspices.[182] This was an *anti*-fascist strategy in the sense that it sought to neutralize the perceived remnants of returnees' "fascist" and "militarist" predispositions. It was only with the deepening of the German division and the gradual establishment of a Communist dictatorship that East German officials embarked on more offensive strategy: they now actively aimed to reshape the former soldiers of Hitler's army into male citizens of an "antifascist-democratic" republic.

PART TWO

Making Citizens

Survivors of Totalitarianism: Returning POWs and the Making of West German Citizens

With the gradual waning of Allied accusations of German guilt and the slow improvement of living conditions, postwar Germans sought to move out of the shadow of defeat and focus on postwar reconstruction. Rather than simply containing the consequences of defeat, both societies now sought to transform former soldiers and POWs into male citizens on opposite sides of the Cold War. An essential part of this process was the formation of redemptive memories that partially displaced earlier, defensive memories. By turning German experiences of defeat into universal tales of moral regeneration, redemptive narratives sought to distance postwar society from the violent remnants of the war. Redemptive memories provided what John Dower has called "bridges of language" between the past and the present.[1] These narratives sought to incorporate, in very different ways, returnees into communities of belonging on opposite sides of the Cold War.

This shift from victimizing to more redemptive memories was not unique to postwar Germany. In most European postwar societies, commemorative practices did not stop with references to victimization by Nazi occupiers.[2] Instead, Europeans in East and West searched for more heroic narratives that would meet the functional and symbolic requirements of postwar reconstruction. In much of postwar Europe, this was the basis of the myth of the "resistance," which provided a "usable past" across the political spectrum precisely because it exaggerated the popularity and military significance of the resistance.[3] At the same time, European memories of the Second World War increasingly drew on the experience of survival. As Pieter Lagrou has shown in his pathbreaking work on Western Europe, the memory of deportation soon superseded the memory of resistance. The central point of reference of this "metaphorical memory" was the survivor of the *universe concentrationnaire*, the (usually male) "hero-victim" whose experience in Nazi concentration camps was transformed into a tale of moral renewal and political inspiration.[4] While memories of resistance were available to postwar Germans only to a very limited extent, they could latch on to such broader European memories of survival.[5] Indeed, West German redemptive representations of returnees bear a striking resemblance to Western European images of returning concentration camp survivors. In both cases, survival in the camps served as the basis for regenerative and redemptive memories of the Second World War that would largely erase the humiliating experience of occupation and defeat. The structural similarity of these redemptive memories was not accidental: they projected the war' s deprivation onto the (Nazi or Soviet) "camp" as the central symbol of the totalitarian "other" in the Cold War. In so doing, redemptive memories assimilated West German memories of the Second World War to the larger antitotalitarian project of the "West."

This chapter demonstrates the ascendancy of redemptive memories of the Second World War in postwar West Germany. It shows how these memories crucially shaped social strategies of transforming former soldiers and POWs into posttotalitarian citizens, and it discusses the achievements and shortcomings of these efforts. The reconstruction of masculinity was central to this process. Redemptive memories crucially contributed to the formation of new prescriptive ideals of masculinity in both postwar societies that differed from the overtly militarized masculinities of the Nazi period *as well as* from the shattered masculinities of the early postwar period. Finally, the chapter highlights the persistent incongruities between public and private memories. The analysis follows returnees' postwar adjustment from public memory to the realms of the workplace and the family. The war's abiding legacies in these more private spheres severely constrained returnees' transformation into postwar citizens and hence limited West German efforts to move beyond defeat.

REDEMPTIVE MEMORIES

In the West, the Christian concept of conversion and rebirth stood at the center of redemptive narratives of war and defeat. Christian tropes gave redemptive meaning to collective experiences of suffering by linking them to a distinct program for postwar reconstruction: the concept of "re-Christianization." "Re-Christianization" had featured prominently in Catholic and Protestant critiques of modern society since the early nineteenth century. It advocated a return to explicitly religious ways of life to counter the ongoing process of secularization. Yet after 1945, re-Christianization became the most important interconfessional response to war, fascism, and defeat. The concept propagated a return to Christian principles as the most promising concept for overcoming National Socialism as well as for safeguarding postwar society against the Communist East.[6]

Former soldiers and POWs played an important role in Christian visions for a religious revival. "In the year 1914, we went to war with God and returned without God. In the year 1939, we went to war without God and returned with God," as a Catholic analysis from November 1946 declared.[7] Similarly, a Protestant welcoming speech depicted returnees as religiously inspired survivors, as a "secret order for our torn people" with "a mission in the center of Europe."[8] The Christian interpretation of captivity turned returnees into protagonists of postwar re-Christianization. Captivity even appeared as a form of "soul-searching" during which former Wehrmacht soldiers had realized their previous "distance from God."[9] Christ himself offered the model for this concept of redemptive suffering. As modern Christ figures, returning POWs wore a "crown of thorns made out of barbed wire."[10] Returnees were, as a Catholic priest told them in a West German transition camp, "to thank God for their suffering" because "Christ too had to suffer before he entered his glory."[11]

This Christian imagery turned returned POWs into a potent symbol for a society in the aftermath of total defeat. In a treatise *Christians in Captivity*, the founder of the Protestant Academy in Berlin Brandenburg, Erich Müller-Gangloff, portrayed the POWs as "symbols for our present situation," when the "entire German people was captured spiritually and religiously in a barbed-wire existence." Yet it was precisely this humiliating experience that provided the starting point for reflection and conversion. Postwar society should follow the example of former Wehrmacht soldiers who supposedly had managed to survive Soviet captivity by returning to their Christian faith.[12] Adopting one of the tropes of "cultures of defeat," these Christian commentators stressed the regenerative and redemptive potential inherent in military defeat.[13]

Despite their universal language, Christian narratives of redemptive suffering were closely linked to the visions of bourgeois reconstruction. Church authorities portrayed the POWs' conduct in captivity as emblematic for the assertion of the individual personality against the forces of "massification." According to Müller-Gangloff, this capacity was only available to "valuable" and "moral" (*wertvolle und wesenshafte*) human beings who managed to transcend their physical desires of hunger and thirst and succeeded in processing their barbed-wire existence as a peculiar form of *Bildung*.[14] In a similar vein, the Catholic psychologist Walter Hemsing detected a strong attachment to culture and education among German POWs. According to him, the "deep educational value of captivity" had manifested itself in the reading of Goethe's *Faust*, the key text of Germany's educated bourgeoisie, "wherever German men were held in captivity." This strong attachment to German culture, he contended, also distinguished German POWs from "more primitive peoples."[15] As a replacement for more traditional forms of nationalism, redemptive memories identified ostensibly timeless German cultural values as a source of postwar identity while maintaining a sense of cultural superiority towards Slavic peoples in the East.

The appeal of redemptive memories also derived from the fact that they masked significant mental and ideological continuities behind a facade of change. Although these narratives subscribed to the trope of returnees' "inner transformation," they obliquely facilitated mental and ideological continuities across the divide of 1945, above all anti-Bolshevism. Ostensibly distancing themselves from Nazi ideology, church officials argued that returnees' anti-Bolshevism was no longer rooted in an abstract ideology but stemmed from the personal experience of having "seen the devil in his ugly face."[16] According to this view, POWs were better capable of honoring the family and the "purity of German women" because they had witnessed the destruction of these values by a "satanic power" in the Soviet Union.[17] Returnees from the Soviet Union were therefore uniquely positioned to prevent the "Bolshevik hatred of God" from threatening again "your children, your family, your profession, your church, and your God."[18] They were ideal representatives of a Christian *Abendland* (Occident), who would immunize postwar society against the temptations of "godless materialism" of both Eastern and Western origin.[19]

In postwar West Germany, the Christian trope of redemptive suffering exerted a powerful effect on secular commemorative culture as well. In fact, the boundaries between secular and religious memories were always fluid.[20] Christian concepts of redemptive suffering shaped the commemorative activities of the Association of Returnees (VDH), the largest interest organization of former POWs in West Germany. Two exhibitions on the POW experience, entitled "Prisoners of War Speak" and "We Admonish," formed the centerpiece of the VdH's public activities during the 1950s. The exhibitions toured through sixty German cities and were seen by at least 750,000 visitors, including many local dignitaries and representatives of the Bundestag.[21]

These exhibitions oscillated between presenting memories of victimization and of redemption. On the one hand, the exhibitions clearly appealed to public empathy with the POWs' suffering. In 1952, "Prisoners of War Speak" featured a reconstructed Soviet POW camp, including a wooden watchtower and a four-meter-high barbed-wire fence. One year later, the VdH advertised for the successor exhibition "We Admonish" with a poster that depicted a shaved head behind barbed wire. This image unmistakably evoked the emaciated bodies of concentration camp survivors and reflected, as Robert Moeller has persuasively argued, "the ways in which, by the early 1950s, these symbols were associated in West German popular consciousness not with victims of Nazi concentration camps but with German prisoners of war in the Soviet Union."[22] At the same time, the exhibitions not only presented stories of deformed and victimized German POWs but also tales of moral resistance and inner strength. According to the official exhibition guide to "We Admonish," the shaved head behind barbed wire was selected because "no other image of the exhibition seemed to represent so clearly the will to self-assertion out of inner tranquility and self-assurance (*innerer Ruhe und Sicherheit*)."[23] Indeed, the exhibitions portrayed captivity, especially in the Soviet Union, as an existential crisis situation that the POWs had mastered morally and spiritually. They gave testimony of the POWs' capacity to maintain their "humanity amidst inhumanity."[24] The VdH's narrative of the POW experience drew on the same trope of regeneration through suffering as Christian narratives. The goal of the exhibit was to document the "suffering and the misery of the POWs" but also to reveal "to an even greater extent" the "human self-assertion in captivity" fueled by "hitherto unknown and unconscious resources of the soul."[25] In the POW exhibitions, this message of redemption eventually supplanted a mere emphasis on suffering.

Similar to the Christian narrative, the POW exhibitions identified a set of cultural values that had enabled the POWs to assert their individual and collective identity in captivity. One section of the exhibitions displayed a series of handicraft works that had been produced by the POWs in the camps. Nothing demonstrated better, as the exhibition guide suggested, the POWs' resistance against "the brutality of power," the "meaninglessness of being," the "idleness within us," and the "influence of the foreign" than these simple items.[26] The POWs' dexterity under primitive conditions was a testimony to German "quality work" and, as such, affirmed German cultural superiority over Soviet labor practices of norms and quota. In addition, the POWs' simple and basic life in captivity served as an important moral counterweight to the "materialism" and "superficiality" that were associated with the "economic miracle" and Western-style consumerism.[27] This profoundly antimodernist, culturally pessimistic message of the exhibition fit well into intellectual climate of the 1950s, a resonance not lost on Germany's preeminent philosopher, Martin Heidegger. When "Prisoners of War Speak" opened in Freiburg, he encouraged his students to "listen to the silent voice" of the POWs and keep it in their "inner ear."[28]

The iconography of "the returnee" further illustrates the congruence between Christian and secular memories. One entire section of "We Admonish" was in fact devoted to religious issues, documenting the "strength" that POWs had found in a "renewed encounter with God."[29] Along the same lines, the 1952 Berlin exhibition featured a bronze relief by the sculptor Fritz Theilmann, himself a returnee from Soviet captivity, which depicted a POW crucified in a fence of barbed wire. Another image showed a POW wearing a crown of thorns made out of barbed wire.[30] Visitors of the exhibition could not help but notice this allusion to Christian concepts of redemptive suffering. One visitor remarked in a letter to a Catholic priest that the exhibition "expresses the same language that we have repeatedly heard from our Reverend Cardinal."[31] Christian motifs and tropes provided essential components for West German commemorations of the Second World War, even in seemingly secular settings.

Representations of returnees as noble survivors of totalitarianism both shaped and reflected new West German ideals of masculinity. By the early 1950s, these images gradually replaced representations of emasculated and emaciated returnees associated with the "crisis of masculinity" of the early postwar period.[32] According to the president of the VdH, August Fischer, the typical representative of his constituency was no longer the "ragged returnee" in the streets but rather the "realistic, quiet, but tough man of the future."[33] Postwar ideals of masculinity did not draw on the front experience but rather on survival under conditions of extreme adversity; they were based not on military service but on the adherence to allegedly timeless and essential German values such as Heimat, family, and Freedom.[34] Transformed and re-Christianized returnees were to prove their masculinity not as soldiers on the battlefields but as fathers and husbands within reconstructed families.[35] Their strength resided primarily in the moral and religious qualities that had enabled them to survive both forms of totalitarianism, even though returnees' rejection of Bolshevism was always much more passionate than their criticism of National Socialism.[36] Still, as survivors of totalitarianism, returnees were destined to become ideal posttotalitarian citizens of the West German state.

Precisely because POWs in Soviet captivity represented such a central symbol for the war's legacies, redemptive memories of their experience took on a larger significance for West German efforts to overcome defeat. It was one key function of these narratives to establish greater distance between the unprecedented violence of genocidal warfare and postwar society. Narratives of victimization had still reflected, as in a mirror image, the tremendous violence of the war on the Eastern front, even if they projected its effects from Germany's victims onto German victims.[37] Redemptive narratives, by contrast, dissolved this experience of violence in universal categories of religious transformation and moral purification. These narratives "decontaminated" former soldiers and POWs from any implication in genocidal violence on the Eastern front.[38] In so doing, redemptive memories significantly contributed to the myth of the "clean Wehrmacht."[39] Men who had mastered the ordeal of captivity with such inner moral strength, these representations suggested, could not possibly have been implicated in genocidal warfare on the Eastern front. This shift from victimizing to redemptive memories was also noticeable in popular representations of the POW experience. The "movies of the rubble" from the late 1940s gave way to filmic representations that depicted heroic (and often highly sexualized) POWs, thus erasing most traces of active *and*

Figure 6. *The Crowned*, a drawing by K. Sieth also exhibited at the POW exhibitions during the 1950s. In a clear analogy to representations of Christ with a crown of thorns, it depicts a POW with a crown of barbed wire, illustrating the significance of Christian iconography in West German memories of the Second World War. (Courtesy Verband der Heimkehrer.)

Figure 7. *The Crucified*, bronze relief by Fritz Theilmann. His work was displayed in the POW exhibitions organized by the Associaton of Returnees (VdH) in the 1950s. Depicting a POW as crucified Christ figure, the work denoted the prominence of Christian motifs in redemptive representations of German POWs. It was also included on postcards produced by the VdH. (Courtesy Bärbel Rudin.)

passive experiences of violence.[40] By the early 1950s, it was left to writers like Heinrich Böll to remind his West German compatriots that the "destructions in our world are not just of an external nature and that they are not so insignificant that one could assume to heal them within only a few years."[41]

By employing religious, moral, and psychological categories, redemptive narratives dehistoricized and depoliticized the consequences of a highly ideological war. The indeterminacy of these categories made it possible to integrate returnees' complex and contradictory experiences into a transhistorical narrative that was not linked to any specific political order.[42] As such, redemptive narratives allowed for the continuity of national identifications without resorting to language of the nation.[43] These memories asserted the persistence of transhistorical and essentially German values—Christianity, Heimat, German culture—that had ostensibly remained unaffected by total war and total defeat. It was the allegiance to these values that had made possible the POWs' survival in captivity, and the same values were to serve as moral guideposts for the process of postwar reconstruction. Thus, redemptive narratives sought to alleviate the consequences of total defeat, on both the individual and the collective level. By asserting a persistent cultural superiority of the defeated over the victors, these narratives transformed total military defeat into a moral victory.[44] German soldiers may have lost the war on the battlefields, but redemptive narratives of their experience in captivity asserted that they had won the postwar battle over memory and morality.

Redemptive narratives, finally, shaped the inclusionary and exclusionary patterns of the West German commemorative culture. The belief in the redemptive consequences of internment made these narratives accessible to those individuals "who in their youth had never spoken of God," including Nazi perpetrators and convicted war criminals.[45] Redemptive narratives informed the strong political engagement of the Christian churches on behalf of these groups.[46] While these memories made possible the integration of perpetrators, they simultaneously facilitated the exclusion of non-Christian victims. Sacralized memories always serve a community-building function, independently of whether they apply to religious or national communities.[47] As such, they exclude groups and individuals who do not subscribe to the specific faith of the community. In postwar West Germany, commemorative practices that were so clearly based on Christian concepts of redemption through sacrifice were, by definition, difficult to apply to non-Christians and non-Germans, such as Jews and atheist "Bolshevists." Therefore, the exclusion of the victims of Nazism from West German memory did not even require active acts of repression and forgetting. Instead, this elision was already grounded in the very discursive structures of redemptive memories of war and defeat.

Making Citizens I: Re-Christianization as Project

Public memories of war and defeat were inextricably intertwined with social and discursive strategies of transforming former soldiers and POWs into ideal posttotalitarian citizens. Making citizens out of returnees consisted of two interrelated yet distinct steps: first, fragmented and decentralized efforts sought to contain the most severe consequences of defeat and provide essential assistance to returnees in need; second, more redemptive narratives shaped official strategies of incorporating returnees into new communities of belonging. In the West, a variety of actors and institutions were involved in these processes. Semipublic church organizations, reemergent state authorities, and, eventually, returnee interest organizations interacted in making citizens out of returnees. West German strategies toward returnees, in other words, were formulated at the intersection of state and civil society. The emergence and partial incorporation of civil society into the structures of the state in West Germany contrasted with its wholesale repression in the East.

Because of the Allied authorities' suspension of all special benefits to former Wehrmacht soldiers, many of the former soldiers of Hitler's army initially depended on donations of food and clothing.[48] Paralleling their significance in shaping public memories, the Christian churches also assumed crucial functions in meting out charity to displaced populations.[49] Church welfare organizations benefited from international donations and also could draw on institutional and organizational continuities with the war years. The Kirchliche Kriegshilfe of the Catholic Caritas, for example, became the Caritas Kriegsgefangenhilfe after 1945 and remained under the leadership of Heinrich Höfler, until he was elected to parliament for the CDU/CSU in 1949.[50] Similarly, Bishop Heckel's Hilfswerk für Kriegsgefangenen und Internierte was integrated as an independent division into the newly formed Evangelische Hilfswerk.[51] Both organizations participated extensively in the social care for returning POWs and their family members. Heckel's Hilfswerk in particular continued to cultivate postal communications with POWs in captivity and family members at home.[52] These organizations also provided food and clothing to returning POWs and distributed these goods in the major transition camps.[53] Such aid was crucial not only in a material but also in a larger symbolic sense. In the absence of state authorities, the initial assistance for returning POWs came from within civil society and thus may have prevented an alienation of veterans from postwar society similar to that which occurred after the First World War.[54]

Church organizations, however, not only provided essential support to returnees but also fostered their conversion into ideal West German citizens that would serve as agents of postwar re-Christianization. As early as March 1946, the Protestant Academy in Bad Boll organized a seminar that was to provide moral and religious orientation to former soldiers and POWs who had "survived the horrors of war through the grace of God."[55] Presentations during the weeklong colloquium addressed more general religious or political issues but also focused on themes specifically pertaining to the situation of returned POWs, such as "Jesus' Answer to Our Marriage Problems," "The Hopes of the Churches for the Returnees," or "Thoughts of a Returnee regarding the German Future."[56] Along similar lines, specific "men's circles" sought to mobilize "Christian men" as "active parts of the community." Their goal was to free former POWs from their tendency toward self-isolation and "nihilism" and inspire them toward religiously motivated activism. Former Wehrmacht soldiers often headed these circles and actively sought to recruit returning POWs.[57] In Bremen, a "men's circle" of former POWs tried to establish connections between still interned POWs and their home communities and also organized care for POWs after their return—an approach that the chancellery of the Protestant church praised as a model for other communities in West Germany.[58] Similarly, at a Catholic conference on pastoral care for men (*Männerseelsorge*) in 1950, one speaker advocated the "inner transformation from *Landser* and sick camp inmate into the true father of his family, the active member of his church, and the responsible citizen of the community and the state."[59] In contrast to the often-noted "feminization," especially of Catholicism, since the nineteenth century, the postwar churches were specifically concerned with restoring men's positions *as men*.[60]

Protestant and Catholic welfare organizations also tried to give a distinctly Christian meaning to the experience of war, captivity, and homecoming. Like West German psychiatrists, church officials assumed that returnees' "inner healing process" would last at least five years after their return.[61] Only after this period of time would returnees' "personality break through again" and enable former POWs to reenter new "religious and human communities."[62] Christian relief organizations worked hard to have this long-term adjustment take specifically Christian forms. Church-run "returnee homes" that offered temporary shelter for homeless returnees provided an opportunity for "spreading the word of Paul among returnees who had been deprived of religious instruction for years."[63] Specific "returnee camps," lasting from one to four weeks, were to serve a similar purpose. These camps were supposed to provide physical recreation to exhausted returnees, but they should also demonstrate to returnees "by deed" what "Christian charity is able to do," thus "leading them again to the community of Jesus Christ."[64] While the precise relationship between social assistance and missionary activity remained contested in both Christian churches, church responses to returning POWs always sought to combine the care for "body and spirit."[65]

This link between social and religious care also manifested itself in parallel concerns over specific confessional influences on returning POWs. Representatives of the Catholic Caritas asserted, for example, that the "returnees have a right to be taken care of by the forces of the Catholic Caritas" and worried about losing out to the larger and better-staffed Protestant Aid Society.[66] In 1951, the head of the Caritas Prisoner of War Aid bemoaned that the Protestant church "has attended to the POWs question to a particular extent, frequently for reasons that do not have anything to do with the POWs themselves."[67] Similar concerns also existed with respect to the Social Democratic Arbeiterwohlfahrt which, according to a Caritas representative at the POW transition camp in Hof, engaged "in increased publicity for its cause among returning POWs."[68] Both Christian churches shared similar responses to war and defeat, and they both sought to transform former soldiers and POWs into protagonists of a re-Christianized republic. Yet their persistent rivalries in practical welfare work also reflected the salience of a lingering confessional conflict in postwar Germany that was petering out only gradually.[69]

How successful were the churches' discursive and practical efforts at re-Christianizing returning POWs and, by extension, postwar Germany? In retrospect, the concept of re-Christianization appears as an anachronistic and illusionary response to what became a period of accelerated secularization and modernization. But in the aftermath of defeat, church representatives had many indications that these hopes for a re-Christianized republic were not delusionary. Many individual returnees thanked church representatives for their material and spiritual support. These letter writers confirmed the significance of Christian religion, which, in the words of one letter writer, "especially in suffering forms the only solid basis of our life."[70] Other such letters emphasized the extent to which the POWs had "again learnt to pray" in captivity, or described how only the sight of the Erfurt cathedral had signaled arrival in the homeland.[71] At least for some returnees, the return to Christian beliefs offered a possibility for a radical break with National Socialism.[72] While it is difficult to quantify such evidence, these responses must have fueled the confidence of church authorities in re-Christianization as a viable aim for postwar reconstruction.

By the late 1940s, however, church authorities received less optimistic signals regarding the religiosity of former Wehrmacht soldiers and POWs. Former camp priests returning from Soviet captivity had at best mixed reports about POW piety that mentioned a brief initial impetus toward religion that only a small minority of camp inmates had sustained.[73] Antireligious "Communist propaganda" as well as the aftereffects of Nazi ideology reportedly further undermined German POWs' religiosity.[74] Christian life in captivity thus had continued only in "depth rather than width," with a strong core of devout POWs that remained limited to only 5 or 6 percent of all POWs.[75] After their return, many former POWs were not receptive to a Christian interpretation of their experience. They quickly abandoned the "good lessons regarding church and captivity" and wanted to "disappear in anonymity."[76] Only a "small segment of returnees" asked for further pastoral care. "The largest segment of returnees," another report noted, "does not want to be addressed as 'returnee' but wants to return as quickly and as unnoticeably as possible to normal conditions."[77] Church membership statistics, which never reached pre-1933 levels, confirmed these more negative impressions. In light of such reports, church officials had to concede that their desired "return to God" had not taken place.[78]

Still, declining church membership or attendance did not necessarily equal declining religiosity either among returning POWs or in postwar society at large. Instead, the prominence of Christian motifs in postwar memory reflected the centrality of the Christian churches in giving meaning to existential experiences of loss, suffering, and survival in postwar society. Charitable activities of Christian welfare organizations helped to confront the persistent consequences of defeat and thus anchored the significance of religion in civil society. Even if these efforts did not fully translate into the desired re-Christianization, they secured the cultural hegemony of the Christian churches in postwar society. This was one of the major reasons for the electoral successes of Christian Democracy in West Germany (and Western Europe at large) throughout the 1950s and into the 1960s.[79]

MAKING CITIZENS II: THE STATE AND CIVIL SOCIETY

The Christian churches were not the only forces to promote returnees' transformation into postwar citizens. By 1946–47, state authorities reasserted themselves and began to complement these relief efforts by the churches, initially on the local level. In the Western zones, many city administrations established specific agencies for returning POWs, which were often headed by former POWs themselves. These agencies organized food and clothing collections on behalf of returnees and even arranged short welcoming ceremonies to recognize "the sacrifices that former POWs had made during a long period of captivity."[80] By October 1947, the state government in North Rhine-Westphalia granted modest financial support to returnees in need for thirteen weeks.[81] Notwithstanding frequent complaints by returnees, public officials exhibited considerable sympathies toward former soldiers and POWs and often equated them with the victims of Nazism.[82] In this sense, public discourses of victimization also shaped the day-to-day activities of local bureaucracies.

In April 1947, a Committee for POW Issues began to coordinate the reception and treatment of returning POWs at the South German federal council in Stuttgart. This committee included representatives of the state governments in the U.S. zone. It drew on the work of several state committees for POWs that encompassed all the major private welfare organizations and charities involved in POW and returnee issues.[83] By February 1949, this committee expanded into a bizonal agency, and it eventually evolved into the Division for POW and Returnee Issues within the newly formed Federal Ministry of Expellees.[84] Parallel to the establishment of state agencies for POW issues, former soldiers and POWs began to form their own organization. This was made possible by the decision of the Allied occupation authorities, in 1948, to lift some of the restrictions against the formation of veterans' organizations. In March 1950, all of these organizations merged to form the Association of Returnees and Family Members of POWs and MIAs (VdH).[85] In both German societies, state institutions increasingly shaped parallel efforts to transform returnees into postwar citizens. Yet whereas East German authorities gradually repressed the activities of private welfare organizations and prohibited the formation of interest groups, these actors were partially incorporated into the structures of the liberal democratic state in the West. For example, a separate POW advisory board that was comprised of church and VdH representatives continued to lobby state agencies on issues relating to POWs and returnees after the formation of the Federal Republic.[86]

In postwar West Germany, the struggles for the POWs' material compensation were always closely intertwined with memories of war and defeat. From the late 1940s on, returnee organizations pushed for a "returnee law" that would address the immediate material needs of former soldiers and POWs.[87] To substantiate these demands, these organizations deployed well-established narratives of victimization. They underlined the "POWs' long years of suffering as reparation workers in Soviet POW camps" as well as their difficult situation upon their return, arguing that "our former jobs are occupied or gone" and "many of us lack clothing, underwear, and shoes."[88] These efforts resulted in the passage of the Returnee Law (Heimkehrergesetz) in March 1950. The bill stipulated one-time cash payments of DM 100, the provision of material goods for up to DM 250, and a series of other benefits that were to facilitate the former POWs' return to the workplace.[89] It was only with the passage of this law that public assistance to returning POWs began to diverge significantly between East and West.

The newly founded central organization of returnees, the Association of Returnees (VdH), however, soon concentrated its efforts on a provision that had not been included in the 1950 Returnee Law nor in the 1952 Equalization of Burdens Law designed for refugees and expellees: the compensation of former POWs for time spent in captivity. This campaign stood at the center of the VdH's activities during the early 1950s, and it reflected the shift from victimizing to redemptive memories. VdH leaders, to be sure, continued to emphasize the suffering of German POWs, but they were also at pains not to portray returnees solely as needy victims of war and captivity. Instead, they honed in on the POWs' achievements in captivity, which qualified returnees as the "best citizens" of the West German state. German POWs, so the VdH argued, had performed reparations for the entire German people and, in so doing, "had conquered new moral ground" as well as "elevated the reputation of the German people." Compensation for time spent in captivity represented a just "legal and moral claim" and not simply an "act of social welfare."[90] Therefore, the association strongly rejected any social welfare component that would tailor compensation payments according to social need. Instead, the VdH demanded a flat rate of one German mark for every day spent in captivity after 1 January 1946 and two German marks for every day spent in captivity after 1 January 1949 regardless of the social situation to which the POWs had returned.[91]

The campaign for a POW compensation law enjoyed tremendously popularity among returnees and significantly increased the VdH's organizational basis. Precisely because it was not linked to social need, the demand for compensation appealed to all former POWs irrespective of their material situation. As a result, VdH membership soared during the first half of the 1950s. Shortly before the founding of the VdH, 31,000 returnees were organized in regional associations. By September 1951, VdH membership reached 160,000. Due to the agitation for POW compensation, this figure tripled during the ensuing years, and the VdH reached its greatest expansion in the fall of 1955 with 500,000 organized returnees. Since most of the VdH members had been former POWs in the Soviet Union or Eastern Europe, the VdH may well have succeeded in organizing almost half of the returnees from the East.[92]

Despite the VdH's increasing political clout, the association still needed to enter into a fierce competition with other "war-damaged" groups over the scarce resources of the federal budget.[93] In February 1953, the federal government decreed that "the issue [of POW compensation] cannot be solved during the present legislative period since the funds for the required high expenditures do not exist."[94] Just at that moment, however, the opposition Social Democrats (SPD) took up the cause of POW compensation. Undoubtedly with an eye to the impending federal elections, the SPD submitted a proposal for a Prisoner of War Compensation Law in May 1953 that was nearly identical to the VdH's draft.[95] In the decisive parliamentary debate of the VdH/SPD proposal, the CDU/CSU deputy Maria Probst rejected the notion that material compensation constituted a "right" of former POWs. She instead proposed more individual compensation according to social needs that should help to "overcome a difficult fate" rather than provide a "lump sum for the past."[96] In contrast to Probst, the SPD expert on POW issues, Hans Merten, supported the VdH's position and argued that POWs should receive compensation not "for their suffering" (*Erlittenes*) but rather for "what they have achieved" (*Geleistetes*). To him, the recognition of the POWs' labor in captivity represented a "matter of honor" for the entire German people and would determine whether "this generation of POWs will gain confidence in the institutions of our democratic state."[97]

Ultimately, the political pressure of the VdH proved to be successful, and a broad majority in the West German parliament, including a significant number of CDU/CSU deputies, passed the Prisoner of War Compensation Law.[98] Few members of parliament wanted to alienate an association that represented millions of voters. And even though Finance Minister Fritz Schäffer initially invoked his constitutional right to delay the implementation of the law, the strong parliamentary support for this measure eventually forced the federal government to put the law into effect in January 1954.[99] The driving force behind the POW compensation law, however, were the Social Democrats. The party's strategy to forge ties with the war generation did not lead to electoral victories in the 1950s, but it crucially contributed to the political stability of the Federal Republic.[100] The SPD channeled some of the dissatisfaction among former soldiers and POWs that might otherwise have formed a political basis for antidemocratic forces on the right.

The POW compensation law marked the greatest political success of the VdH. It was a success not only in terms of securing material benefits but also in ideological terms. The 1954 law granted official recognition of the status of returnees as survivors who were largely compensated for their service rather than for their suffering. The passage of the POW compensation law in 1954, however, did not end the association's efforts to promote the image of the returnee as the ideal West German citizen. The VdH's Mehlem Program of 1955 called for the "formation, conservation, and utilization of experiences and insights that had been gained in war, captivity, and returning home for the entire German people as well as for a free and peaceful Europe." After its most important social policy goal had been met, the VdH increasingly became a citizens' association that advertised the advantages of West German democracy to former soldiers and POWs. This was the explicit purpose of the "Mehlem Conversation," where local and regional functionaries of the association met with representatives of West German politics and society to discuss issues such as the Basic Law, "the free market economy," "German history from Weimar to Bonn," the "Bolshevist danger," and rearmament.[101]

Did the VdH's ideological efforts—combined with the material benefits meted out by the West German welfare state—reconcile former soldiers and POWs to postwar West German democracy? A study by the Frankfurt Institute of Social Research from 1957 on the "political consciousness of former POWs" casts some doubt on the official portrayal of returnees as ideal, posttotalitarian citizens.[102] Based on sixty-two group discussions with more than five hundred VdH members, the study identified strongly authoritarian dispositions among the returnees. While returnees were united in their opposition to Bolshevism, more than half of them argued that National Socialism had "as many" or "more" good sides than bad sides.[103] The study also found deep resentments toward parliamentary democracy among former soldiers and POWs. Many of them preferred a vision of communal solidarity and authoritarian "order" that clearly reflected the ideological aftereffects of the National Socialist "national community."[104]

While the Frankfurt study attributed these authoritarian attitudes specifically to middle-class returnees, the interview transcripts reveal a series of recurrent preoccupations and resentments that were not necessarily class-specific.[105] Returnees exhibited a strong desire for national identification as well as an equally strong frustration with the Federal Republic as a problematic community of national belonging. Despite the rather extensive symbolic and material benefits for returnees in West Germany, they felt that the postwar polity continued to deny them full validation of their past. "Today's state is the same as the state of 1945," one returnee exclaimed, "and this state of 1945 tore everything into the dirt that had to do with being a soldier."[106] Nothing contributed more to the alienation of returnees from West German democracy than the alleged defamation and prosecution of Wehrmacht soldiers as "war criminals" by the Western allies, even though this prosecution had largely ended by the mid-1950s.[107] One returnee, for example, professed to have been deeply disappointed by "so-called democracy, which denied we participants in the war were good Germans and which denounced us . . . as war criminals."[108] While returnees constantly sought to sever the links between military service and Nazi crimes, the Allied prosecution of German war criminals seemed to reaffirm precisely those links. Consequently, many interviewees denied Nazi crimes altogether,[109] attributed them to Allied "fairy tales"[110] or to the necessity of "following orders."[111] Charges of Nazi atrocities were not compatible with returnees' sense of personal identity and national belonging. They could "simply not imagine," as one returnee stated, "that the German human being was barbaric enough to commit such atrocities."[112] Hence, it was not just denial but their very sense of self-respect and moral integrity that dictated former soldiers' emotional distance from a state that many of them considered, at least initially, complicit with Allied accusations of German war crimes.

Located at the intersection of state and civil society, interest organizations such as the VdH served a crucial function in defusing and channeling returnees' resentment against the West German state. Yet the association itself needed to walk a thin line between maintaining its public position as an association of loyal citizens and representing its constituency. This became clear at the first meeting of former members of the Armed SS (Waffen SS) in October 1952. Although the event was supposed to demonstrate the loyalty of former Waffen-SS members, Herman Bernhard Ramcke, a radical parachute general and VdH member, subverted the purpose with a vehement attack against the Western allies, calling them "real war criminals."[113] Ramcke's speech was scandalous less for its content than for its performative nature at a high-profile, closely watched event. But opinions about the appropriate response to this incident diverged within the VdH. Whereas the head of the local VdH district called for Ramcke's immediate exclusion from the association, the chairman of the North Rhine-Westphalian branch, Josef Reichmann, considered criticism of Ramcke's speech an indication of a deficient "democracy": "[We all] need to know that in a true democracy, everything can be said, yet since we are not yet and also must not be a democracy, we must not say everything."[114] It is unclear how this controversy ended. But the rousing applause as well the extensive public support that Ramcke's speech received clearly illustrated that the loyalty of the VdH's constituency—and of the larger veterans' culture—towards the Federal Republic was tenuous at best. During the1950s, the acceptance of the Federal Republic by the VdH and the larger veterans' culture could not be taken for granted but needed to be secured by a complex process of material and symbolic exchange whose external boundaries were often drawn by the Western allies.[115]

The true litmus test for organized returnees' attitude toward the West German was the issue of West German rearmament. Since the early nineteenth century, the link between military service and male citizenship was a constitutive feature of the modern territorial state.[116] In the aftermath of total defeat, this link was not easily reestablished. It was only the emerging Cold War that once again put the issue of West German rearmament on the agenda of domestic and international politics. For the VdH, rearmament turned into a difficult and divisive issue, not in the least because the association wanted to maintain its political neutrality. Still, at the height of the national debate about rearmament, the VdH leadership came out in qualified support of a new German army.[117] The fear of

Communism and the conviction that a "free people cannot renounce in principle the protection of a Wehrmacht" were cited as the main justification for a new German army. This was to be a distinctly national army, even carrying the name Wehrmacht.[118] In addition, the VdH made its support of West German rearmament dependent on the release of all POWs and a general amnesty for German war criminals imprisoned by the Western allies.[119]

These conditions, however, failed to secure the support of the VdH's rank-and-file members for a new West German army.[120] According to the Frankfurt study, a strong minority of 39 percent opposed West German rearmament, which almost exactly reflected the extent of opposition on the national level.[121] This significant opposition did not simply stem from "tactical considerations," nor was it primarily fueled by pacifist sentiments.[122] Instead, the opposition to rearmament reflected a more far-reaching aversion to the state itself or, as Michael Geyer has aptly called it, a sense of "injured citizenship."[123] In his letter to the VdH leadership, Karl Heinz K., for example, invoked his fear that a "new Wehrmacht" threatened to "turn us back into tyrannized human beings and slaves ready to be used in combat."[124] Along similar lines, another returnee reported that he was opposed to rearmament because he had experienced during the war "how often human lives had been wasted" and how often "comrades had been sacrificed senselessly."[125] Such oppositional attitudes did not derive from a general rejection of military service but rather resulted from a distrust of Western authorities.[126] Many returnees simply did not want to be used as "cannon fodder" for the Western allies in a new war, which they feared would take place on German soil and which they doubted could be won.[127] They denied postwar authorities the right to make decisions about their own life and death: "We are no longer willing, not even under the best of circumstances, to direct a weapon against other human beings for you gentlemen of the higher categories. Our life is to too precious to be sacrificed again for an unreal and spiritless struggle," as another returnee explained to the VdH leadership.[128] Not all returnees, to be sure, shared these sentiments, and many of them also converted their anti-Bolshevism into a willing embrace of rearmament. For former professional soldiers, a deeply engrained ethics of service as well as a simple lack of political alternatives could facilitate the transfer of loyalty from the Third Reich to the Federal Republic.[129] Still, the substantial and deeply personal opposition to West German rearmament points the persistent fissures between returnees' subjectivities and the West German state. While returnees did not openly challenge the legitimacy of West German democracy, many of them simply refused to risk their health and possibly their lives for the state in which they were living.[130]

Redemptive memories of war and defeat served important functions for the social and symbolic reconstruction of postwar society, and they shaped new postwar ideals of masculine citizenship. Contrary to the assumption of an older historiography, postwar society *did* generate pervasive yet also highly selective "structures of meaning" for processing the war and its consequences.[131] The persistent incongruity between public and private memory did not result from a lack but from the perceived inadequacy of public narratives of war and defeat. Neither victimizing nor redemptive narratives offered returnees a framework to make sense of their complex and contradictory experiences. In part, returnees' reluctance to fully embrace public memories originated from their abiding nationalist—if not National Socialist—attitudes. These sentiments lay outside the confines of acceptable public discourse and thus needed to remain "private," even in the widely "integrationist" political culture of the early Federal Republic.

But many former soldiers and POWs also exhibited a desire to shed the identity as "returnee" altogether and did not want to assign a redemptive or even lasting meaning to war and defeat.[132] This was one reason why the membership in the VdH dropped by almost 40 percent after the passage of the POW compensation law in 1954.[133] More informal contacts between former POWs also petered out by the late 1950s.[134] Most former soldiers and POWs exhibited a deep skepticism about formal political organizations and all-encompassing explanations of their experience.[135] Highly complex and often traumatic experiences may never be adequately addressed in public narratives. While West German redemptive memories tried to turn defeat into a retrospective moral victory, they largely failed in promoting an individual "working through" of returnees' active and passive experiences of violence.[136] As a result, returnees' confrontation with the consequences of a lost war was transferred from public discourse to the private spheres of the workplace and the family.

RETURNEES AND THE WORKPLACE

A successful return to the workplace was a central element of transforming former soldiers and POWs into postwar citizens.[137] In both German postwar societies, the capacity for productive labor appeared as the core of masculine citizenship. Postwar officials agreed that for the defeated soldiers of Hitler's army, the only way to restore an independent selfhood was through productive labor. Gainful employment, then, constituted the precondition for reestablishing men's authorities as breadwinners and husbands within reconstituted families. It also corresponded to the task of rebuilding a devastated society in the aftermath of total defeat.

Disabilities, in turn, were measured by the percentage to which they reduced an individual's capacity to work.

Based on a law of 1 September 1939, all Wehrmacht soldiers had a legal right to be reinstated in their old jobs. Even though Allied Control Council Law abolished all special privileges for former members of Hitler's army, employment offices generally honored former returnees' right to return to their workplace.[138] Companies also kept track of employees who were still missing and reserved jobs for them.[139] In addition, employment offices established specific agencies to assist returned POWs. According to reports from North Rhine–Westphalia, employment officials wanted to provide "special assistance to returning POWs" and displayed a keen sensitivity to returnees' peculiar "psychological condition."[140] In March 1950, the federal Returnee Law formalized the preferential treatment that returning POWs had enjoyed on the West German labor market. Returnees were protected against layoffs for six months after their return; they were to receive priority in referrals to open jobs; and they were eligible for educational support (*Ausbildungsbeihilfen*) and retraining measures.[141]

The efforts of West German officials to facilitate former soldiers' and POWs' return to the workplace were matched by returnees' own eagerness to take up work again. Employment officials in all occupation zones reported returnees' generally high motivation to (re)enter the world of work.[142] These professional ambitions reflected the same hopes of upward mobility that Wehrmacht soldiers had articulated during the war.[143] Military defeat and captivity dealt a severe blow to these expectations, but they most likely did not destroy these plans for the future. Instead, years of additional exposure to coercion and military discipline in captivity enhanced many returnees' determination to finally realize their professional goals in the postwar period. Many former soldiers and POWs who had a job to return to did not encounter serious professional difficulties.[144]

This does not mean, however, that the absorption of *all* returnees into the labor market proceeded smoothly and without difficulties. In fact, wartime destructions and social displacements prevented at least a segment of former soldiers and POWs from reassuming their old positions. This was especially true for those returnees from the lost Eastern territories who had suffered double displacements of captivity and expulsion and thus had neither a home nor a job to return to. In other cases, Allied bombings or postwar dismantling of German industries had eliminated returnees' old jobs.[145] The widespread housing shortage also affected returnees' ability to take up work again. Former POWs often returned to where their families resided, but then could not find work at those places. If they wanted to take up a job elsewhere, they needed to apply for a change of a discharge certificate, which was usually only possible within a period of three months.[146] Returnees frequent complaints about "excessive bureaucracy" often stemmed from these additional obstacles to reentering the workplace.[147]

Returnees' prospects on the West German labor market also crucially depended on their time of return. Prior to 1948, a considerable shortage of labor, especially in mining and agriculture, provided alternative opportunities for employment even for those returnees who were not able to return to their old jobs. At the same time, food shortages and rationing rendered monetary wages less significant and meant that employment itself did not necessarily enable returnees to again provide for their families.[148] After the currency and economic reforms in mid-1948, however, the West German labor market tightened again. Unemployment rose significantly and remained high into the early 1950s.[149] POWs returning from Soviet captivity after 1948 were disproportionately affected by these worsening economic conditions. They not only had to endure a longer and more strenuous period of captivity, but they also encountered greater problems in finding employment. POWs who had returned between 1948 and 1950 thus often felt that they had arrived too late to find open jobs yet also too early to benefit from more extensive state aid as well as from the later activities of the VdH.[150] Conversely, POWs who had returned in 1945–46 resented later—and sometimes older and better qualified—returnees for again pushing them out of their newly gained positions.[151]

The postwar reconstruction economies placed a high premium on skilled blue-collar workers in sectors such as the building trades, coal mining, and heavy industry. The 1950s constituted the last decade in which hard manual labor remained the predominant form of occupation.[152] Yet because of their miserable health, returnees were often barred from taking up physically demanding labor.[153] And even after they had found jobs again, former soldiers and POWs needed to confront the limitations of their own ability to perform. While they quickly realized that "the same was expected from us as from everybody else," they also needed to concede that they were "not completely fit healthwise" or even incapable of performing certain kinds of job.[154] One returnee reported that he took up a job as boilerman in order to "show some backbone" only to collapse after two years due to a heart condition.[155] Persistent physical and psychological weaknesses rendered returnees unable to live up to normative conceptions of working-class masculinity, which were predicated on long hours of strenuous labor. By contrast, if former POWs managed to return without major disabilities, their survival in war and captivity also engendered a more assertive attitude toward employers and management.[156]

Likewise, former soldiers and POWs seeking to return to traditional middle-class professions as civil servants and white-collar employees also encountered serious obstacles.[157] The influx of bourgeois elites from the

Soviet zone of occupation increased the demand for white-collar jobs in the West, while fiscal constraints forced administrations on all levels in the Western zones to adopt a rather cautious hiring policy.[158] Professional displacement and the shortage of housing in postwar Germany also rendered it difficult to reconstruct a distinctly bourgeois lifestyle in the aftermath of total war and total defeat.[159] "When I got married in 1942," a pharmacist wrote to the social welfare ministry in North Rhine–Westphalia in 1951, "I was well established in a bourgeois setting and believed that my future was secured." Yet when he returned from Soviet captivity in 1949, he found his home destroyed and his family living in an old shack with no floors. Although he was ultimately able to return to his old profession after having worked for years in coal trading, this returnee inquired about the possibility of a loan that would help him to establish an independent household and "to lead a family life after thirteen years." "As a man and as a father," this returnee added, "I cannot tolerate that my wife and my children are morally and psychologically depressed and that their health is being ruined."[160] A similar desire to escape the existence of being a "mere number" in captivity and becoming a "bourgeois citizen" (*ein Bürger*) motivated the protest of another middle-class returnee.[161] Such petitions to authorities illustrated the existential challenges—economically and psychologically—of reconstructing bourgeois subjectivities in the aftermath of war and defeat. As with respect to more muscular working-class masculinities, returnees found it difficult to reinsert themselves into a bourgeois gender order in which male authority was based on the uncontested position as breadwinner and provider for the family.

Social statistical research indicates that the impact of war and captivity on professional life-courses was most pronounced among younger returnees. In the highly stratified West German occupation system, the disruption of younger returnees' educational or occupational careers at an early stage significantly influenced their long-term prospects for social advancement.[162] As a result, some of them never achieved a middle-class status. Hans W. had joined the army in 1940 right after his high-school exam (*Abitur*) and returned from Soviet captivity in 1946. Thereafter, he was forced to work as a construction worker. In December 1950, four years after his return, lack of money, appropriate clothing, and housing and a larger sense of disorientation still prevented him from obtaining a university education, as he had originally planned. "To have to work far below my skills and to have virtually no possibility to get a professional education which would correspond to my education and to my talents" was deeply troubling to Hans W.[163] Yet his experience of thwarted ambitions was not unusual. Former soldiers and POWs often inquired with West German officials about the possibility of acquiring an *Abitur* and pursuing an academic career.[164] Oral history studies also confirm that structural economic conditions pushed a significant segment of returnees into unfamiliar and unwanted industrial labor.[165]

Of course, economic expansion and public policies combined over the course of the 1950s to reverse some of these experiences of middle-class displacement. In keeping with the decade's dominant gender ideology, state employers deliberately laid off working women to free up public service positions for returning men.[166] The Federal Labor Ministry also encouraged the preferential hiring of returnees in the public sector, while postwar anti-Communism and the undoing of Allied denazification policies further improved the prospects of middle-class returnees to reassume their positions in the public sector.[167] In February 1951, an amendment to the West German constitution mandated that 20 percent of all positions in public administrations and civil service go to former civil servants who had lost their positions because of denazification, expulsion, or flight from East Germany.[168] This law enabled former civil servants to return to positions within the West German bureaucracy, often in spite of a compromised past. By the middle and late 1950s, a rapidly expanding economy generated further opportunities for upward mobility.[169] Among 389 returnees who were interviewed for the Frankfurt study in 1957, only one-third reported "some" or "great" difficulties in finding suitable employment upon their return; 74 percent of interviewed returnees were satisfied with their economic situation—a figure that was only slightly below the national average.[170]

Still, returnees' permanent or temporary social displacement mirrored the profound and ubiquitous social uncertainty in postwar West German society. Former soldiers and POWs often experienced not the war itself but the return and adjustment to postwar society as traumatizing. Postwar narratives of victimization thus not only derived from experiences and memories of defeat and captivity. They also reflected specific middle-class experiences of disappointed expectations and downward mobility in the early postwar period. At the same time, the eventual overcoming of this kind of socioeconomic uncertainty also explains the particularly forceful thrust of ordinary West Germans into a modern consumer society.[171] For many former soldiers and POWs, the hopes for the "good life" that had been fueled by Nazi economic recovery in the 1930s and the promises of German imperialism in the 1940s finally became true in the context of an expanding consumer society starting in the late 1950s.

Privatizing War and Defeat: Returnees and the Family

Like the workplace, the family was a key site for the transformation of returnees into postwar citizens.[172] In the West, the reconstruction of the family became virtually synonymous with the reconstruction of the nation at large. The postwar liberal-democratic polity wanted to distance itself from both Nazism and Communism by protecting an allegedly "private sphere" against the intrusion of totalitarian ideologies.[173] The reconstruction of the family also united the Christian churches, political elites, and influential medical and social experts. In addition, this focus on the family was not just imposed "from above" but also reflected the desires of ordinary Germans seeking to restore normalcy to their private lives. Thus, public discourse and private longings charged the institutions of the family with tremendous energies. It was to carry the main burden of postwar reconstruction, and it also became a crucial arena for confronting the legacies of war and defeat.

The ideal family, however, greatly diverged from the social reality of millions of families that had been shattered or broken apart by the war and its consequences. The return of millions of soldiers and POWs was supposed to narrow this gap between ideal and reality. Approximately 40 percent of returnees were married, and their arrival was to transform hitherto "incomplete" into "complete" families.[174] In many cases, the strains of readjustment between men and women proved to difficult to master. Rather than promoting a "return to normalcy," the release of the POWs exposed a profound and pervasive "crisis of the family" in the postwar period. This crisis manifested itself, above all, in the skyrocketing divorce rates, which reached a high point in 1948 with 18.7 divorces per 10,000 residents (compared to 8.9 in 1939).[175] The figures for "returnee marriages" were considerably higher. In Lower Saxony, for example, every third returnee marriage ended in divorce.[176]

Postwar commentators identified a wide variety of reasons for the specific difficulties of returnee marriages. The factors they cited ran the gamut from cramped living quarters to women's newly gained independence to modernity and secularization more generally.[177] But observers such as the well-known psychologist Walter von Hollander also identified a specific "crisis of the German man" as the source of marriage difficulties.[178] He stressed the decline of military ideals of manliness as a result of total defeat and also underlined men's genuine incompetence in the postwar period. Other commentators identified returnees' psychological predicament, their emotional impoverishment and apparent "coldness," as main reasons for the crisis of the returnee marriage.[179] These diagnoses showed that the reconstruction of the family not only demanded the restoration of specific conceptions of femininity but also hinged upon restoring the position of former soldiers and POWs as fathers and husbands. West German public discourse thus rendered the transformation of returnees into citizens virtually synonymous with the task of making them "capable of living in a family."[180]

This was especially true for the Christian churches. For the churches, the family was the key institution for the practice of a Christian life and for the transmission of Christian values to the children.[181] Accordingly, the Christian churches and their affiliated organizations concerned themselves with assisting returnees in (re)adjusting to postwar family life. An entire network of church-run returnee homes, for example, provided temporary shelter to those returnees who had lost their families due to bombings or expulsions. These homes were supposed to create a "family atmosphere" to aid returnees in "adjusting to and mastering their new environment in a healthy manner."[182] With similar intentions, the churches also supported and promoted the "sponsorship" (*Patenschaft*) campaign of the Munich journalist Erich Wollenberg. Wollenberg tried to locate individual families who would "adopt" a "homeless returnee" for several weeks or months to help the former POW to orient himself in a new environment. Protestant authorities instructed parish ministers to advertise these sponsorships in their sermons and to supervise individual sponsors.[183] The campaign mobilized more than six hundred individual sponsors during the first eight months. The goal was to change the returnee from his former self as "soldier and prisoner" to "the civilian of tomorrow, the German citizen with whom we want to build a new, happier, and better Germany."[184]

The effort to reestablish men's authority as fathers and husbands, however, did not equal a mere restoration of patriarchy. War and defeat rendered a simple return to an imaginary prewar "normalcy" all but impossible.[185] Even Christian conservatives began to advocate more equal relationships between men and women in postwar society. Catholic authorities, for example, encouraged returnees to adopt a gentle and, if necessary, forgiving attitude toward their wives and children. Former soldiers and POWs should regain a "deep respect for his wife in marriage life" and to refrain from a "military tone" toward their children. In particular, Christian publication strongly encouraged returnees to forgive their wives for any possible "missteps," especially since "50 to 80 percent of men had committed adultery" during the war.[186] These suggestions sought to reorient returnees' masculinities away from the overtly militarized masculinities of the Nazi period as well as from the homosocial world of the military and the POW camp. Instead, they propagated civilian, even soft, masculinities within the firmly heterosexual realm of reconstituted families.

Despite the extensive public debate over the "marriage miseries" of returnees, the predominant response to the upheavals of war and defeat was not a permanent separation but rather a shift in intra-familial relations. The high divorce rates of the late 1940s were the inevitable backlog of the war years and also often affected marriages formed during the war that lacked a solid emotional basis.[187] Oral history evidence suggests that both men and women remembered the renegotiation of marital terms as just that—a process of negotiation and compromise rather than the return to a "natural" order. One returnee remembered that "we wanted to continue where we had stopped" but then added that this "unfortunately had not been the case."[188] Another returnee recalled that, after having spent only 231 days in eleven years together with his wife, "they needed to work things out together if they wanted to stay together."[189] Even in retrospect, these recollections testify to the tremendous efforts that both men and women needed to make in establishing a new equilibrium.

These shifts in intrafamilial relations—both on the normative and on the experiential level—did not end patriarchy in West Germany but rather made it, in the words of Thomas Kühne, "more flexible."[190] Marriages might have moved closer toward a "more equal, cooperative relationship," but they still reflected what Hanna Schissler has called "harmonious inequalities."[191] Contemporary sociological studies confirm the continued existence of traditional and highly gendered divisions of labor even within the new "cooperative families."[192] Despite the erosion of masculine authority, the West German civil law guaranteed male paternal authority until 1959.[193] By the early 1950s, moreover, popular magazines as well as marriage advice literature took a conservative turn and advocated the voluntary subordination of wives to male authority.[194] Yet while historians have often emphasized this conservative reconstruction of gender relations in postwar West Germany, they have paid less attention to persistent concerns over male weaknesses that lingered well into the 1950s.[195] While postwar society was indeed undergoing a process of social and symbolic remasculinization, nagging doubts persisted about actual men's capability of living up to new ideals of masculinity as fathers and husbands.

Postwar commentators identified a whole range of long-term forces that weakened male authority, such as the growing bureaucratization of the world or the increase in leisure time. But the aftereffects of war and defeat often exacerbated these secular tendencies.[196] According to a study from 1954, 64 percent of families cited war and postwar as the most difficult period they had undergone, and 30 percent noted that these aftereffects were still present.[197] Especially in returnee families, the consequences of war and defeat maintained a tangible presence. Physical and mental impairments often eroded returnees' ability to serve as breadwinners and providers in the reconstruction economy. As Vera Neumann has persuasively argued, women's "family labor" needed to compensate for the burdens men's disabilities imposed on the postwar family.[198] Women were largely left alone in coping with these deficiencies of their partners. In 1954, for example, Frau B. petitioned the West German parliament to raise the pension for her husband, who had suffered from periodic fever attacks since his return from Soviet captivity in 1945. "He has now been lying here again since Christmas 1953," she wrote, adding that in "the first few weeks he could not work at all. Then we were without money for five weeks."[199] Another woman described the numerous afflictions her husband brought with him from Soviet captivity that forced her "to consider his health constantly. His stomach no longer tolerates all kinds of food as used to be the case; he comes home from work in the afternoon at a quarter to five, and then only wants rest; more is not possible."[200] Often, the multiple tasks of caring for a sick husband and possibly older parents, raising children, and perhaps even holding a job completely overtaxed women's physical and emotional capacities, leaving them with little energy for other family members. "My mother was preoccupied for years with getting my father on his feet again," one daughter of one returnee recalled.[201]

Men, in turn, experienced their persistent weaknesses as deeply humiliating. Occasionally, they even confessed to impotence, which they attributed to the fact that they were "internally shattered." "We have been lying in the dirt," the same returnee declared, "and could not be the elegant men we were supposed to be."[202] The failure to fully participate in the West German reconstruction effort bred feelings of inferiority and resentment against other family members. "I never heard a nice word from him; he was always grumpy and argumentative," one woman recalled.[203] Children remembered their fathers as emotionally disengaged, ill tempered, and irritable, and they often attributed these unpleasant character traits to their fathers' experience of defeat.[204] Historians of West German reconstruction have emphasized the relatively smooth integration of former Wehrmacht soldiers into postwar society. This positive assessment needs to be complemented with greater attention to the considerable private costs that the public acquiescence of former soldiers and POWs entailed. Their experiences of defeat may not have led to an open rejection of the postwar public order but permeated the inner fabric of interpersonal relations in postwar society. This "privatization" of the consequences of the war channeled a great deal of frustration and resentment resulting from a lost war into the family and towards women.

The displacement of postwar adjustments into the family also shaped relations between generations.[205] In about 10 to 15 percent of families, children grew up without their biological father because he had died in war or captivity.[206] But even in families where the father returned, oral history interviews testify to conflicts between older children who had often assumed the position of "surrogate partners" and returning POWs, who resented the emotional symbiosis between mothers and children.[207] Children also remembered the daily confrontation with their fathers' persistent physical and psychological impairment. They remembered the sad atmosphere at home or felt that their own problems paled in comparison to their father's disability.[208] This tangible presence of the war and defeat in postwar families, moreover, did not translate into an open conversation about the past, with the result that failure or lack of communication undermined intergenerational attachment and empathy.[209] Often, fathers attempted to compensate for their apparent weaknesses with excessive authoritarianism.[210] In many cases, it was again left to women to smooth out these differences between returnees and their children.[211] Given this state of affairs, it is not surprising that West German youth sought to escape the stifling family atmosphere by seeking refuge in a different set of values. American popular culture, in particular, offered German adolescents idols and role models that differed markedly from the ones represented by their own fathers.[212] Conversely, returnees were often critical of the Americanized youth culture of the 1950s and advocated a more authoritarian educational style.[213] The deepest fault line in postwar society existed not between genders but between generations.

The projection of the consequences of the war into the family significantly contributed to the moral and political stabilization of postwar West German society. The confrontation with the collective experience of total defeat took place not in the public sphere or even within a homogenous social-cultural milieu but rather in a highly individualized and "atomized" fashion within postwar families. As a result, the consequences of a highly ideological war were discussed—and experienced—primarily in the thoroughly deideologized realm of the family. Such privatized confrontations with the consequences of the war left little room for a discussion—or even an awareness—of questions of moral and political responsibility for genocide and mass murder. Instead, the (re)construction of returning POWs as civilian fathers, gentle husbands, and upstanding bourgeois citizens in effect eroded the public space that would have allowed a confrontation with their distinctly "uncivilian" past. At the same time, the channeling of all these tasks into the private sphere clearly overburdened the family. It prompted severe tensions between genders and generations, which, in the long run, also became socially and politically disruptive. The pacification of West German society through privatizing the consequences of the war thus already contained the seeds for the massive sociopolitical disruptions and generational conflicts of the 1960s and 1970s.

CHAPTER 5

Antifascist Conversions: Returning POWs and the Making of East German Citizens

In January 1948, Paul Merker, the SED's authority on all matters relating to POWs, published an article that signaled a crucial shift in official perceptions of returning POWs from the East. Moving away from earlier concerns over their alleged fascist indoctrination and political apathy, Merker now depicted former soldiers and POWs as "pioneers of a new Germany" who would work with "the united working-class movement and other progressive forces for the peaceful recovery of our entire people."[1] As Merker's article indicated, official East German literature began to portray returnees as future ideal citizens of a separate "antifascist-democratic" state.[2] While East German official memories differed in content and were largely imposed "from above," they assumed a redemptive quality that is comparable to West German memories. In spite of their antagonistic political systems, the shared postwar nature of both German societies led to important structural and functional similarities in their respective efforts to overcome defeat.

The emergence of East German redemptive memories was closely tied to domestic and international turning points in 1947–48. It was part of the larger Soviet effort to impose a Soviet-centered, Communist master narratives of World War II on Eastern Europe, and it reflected the gradual establishment of the SED dictatorship in East Germany.[3] The SED now gave up its earlier strategy of seeking a broad coalition of progressive forces and transformed itself into a Leninist "party of the new type." Abandoning its earlier quest for a "German road to Socialism," the party now promoted the Stalinization of East Germany according to the Soviet model. Reeducated and converted returnees from the East assumed a crucial role in this project. They illustrated the virtually unlimited ideological malleability of human beings on which the SED counted in its attempt to win over ordinary Germans. If it was possible to transform the former soldiers of Hitler's army, who had come close to annihilating the Soviet Union, into loyal citizens of a Sovietized East German state, then the SED's project of "antifascist-democratic" reconstruction along the Soviet model might indeed be feasible. Narratives of antifascist conversion in Soviet captivity crucially contributed to forging a Soviet-centered antifascism as the legitimatory ideology of the East German state.

This chapter demonstrates how the incorporation of returnees' experience shaped official East German memories of the Second World War. It also investigates the institutional and ideological strategies that East German officials deployed in order to transform former soldiers and POWs into loyal antifascist citizens, and it explores returnees' adjustment to postwar society in different realms of citizenship. Finally, the chapter analyzes returnees' responses to their reception in the East as examples of broader patterns of resistance, refusal, accommodation, and consensus in the East German dictatorship.

FORGING EAST GERMAN ANTIFASCISM: THE *Heimkehrer* CONFERENCES IN 1949

In the summer and fall of 1949, a series of "returnee conferences" took place in East Germany. Hundreds of such conferences on the local level and five regional conferences in the East German states led up to the central *Heimkehrer* conference in Berlin on 29 October 1949.[4] These meetings were organized by the Society for German-Soviet Friendship (GDSF). They were staged propaganda events that featured only carefully selected speakers who were supposed to elaborate on main themes such as "Why we have become and will forever remain friends of the Soviet Union."[5] These events represented constitutive acts in the formation of the East German state. Scheduled around the formal founding of the German Democratic Republic on 7 October 1949, the *Heimkehrer* conferences universalized the experience of antifascist POWs and applied it to the nation at large. In his opening speech to the central conference in Berlin, the president of the GDSF, historian Jürgen Kuczynski, conceded that it is a "complicated process if one wants and needs to convert an entire people." But he also portrayed the antifascist returnee as a central symbol for this project of national conversion. According to Kuczynski, the return of antifascist POWs signified a return to the positive traditions of German history, a "return to everything that was great and progressive in our history, to everything that had been destroyed by the enemies in our country, to everything that constitutes the great future of Germany." In this sense, he argued, "all Germans must become returnees."[6]

The content of the POW narratives presented at the *Heimkehrer* conferences differed fundamentally from parallel redemptive narratives in the West. But they nevertheless followed similar tropes. Much like Christian memories in the West, official East German memories portrayed returnees' experience in terms of a pseudoreligious progression leading from confession to conversion and redemption. At the heart of returnees' transformation lay a recognition and a confession of guilt for their past actions as members of the "fascist army." Speakers pleaded guilty to having participated in the Nazi war of destruction against the Soviet Union. "Seven million deaths, 1,700 destroyed cities, 70,000 destroyed villages, 6 million destroyed houses," as one returnee listed the disastrous consequences of the German occupation of the Soviet Union.[7] Although East German memories named the destruction on the Eastern front far more explicitly than the dehistoricized memories in the West, they ultimately also served the purpose of evading guilt and responsibility. Returnees' confessions referred only to guilt by association and never contained admissions of individual guilt implying individual responsibility. Instead, newly converted antifascist returnees portrayed themselves as passive objects of Hitler's policies. They had been "handed a gun by Hitler" and had, as one returnee claimed, "unconsciously" participated in the campaign against the Soviet Union, allegedly ignorant as to why and what they were fighting for.[8] Speakers also adopted the SED's focus on the responsibility of German elites for war and fascism by blaming a "small group of war profiteers" and exonerating German workers who had allegedly "not want[ed] the war."[9] In the East German antifascist narrative, confessions of an abstract historical guilt enabled an exoneration of former soldiers' individual pasts.

What exculpated returnees' from their participation in genocidal warfare was their alleged conversion in Soviet captivity. Speakers described their experience in Soviet captivity as a form of "secondary socialization" during which they had internalized a completely different political and social reality.[10] They affirmed their POW experience as a decisive "university of life" through which they had become "new human being[s]."[11] They had, as yet another returnee declared, "encountered a moral and political truth" in the Soviet Union, which had given a "new meaning" to their lives.[12] Against the background of this pseudoreligious conversion in Soviet captivity, returnees' past experience as soldiers of the Wehrmacht appeared as part of a previous life that almost seemed as if it had not been their own. This externalization of the "fascist past" in individual biographies of antifascist returnees corresponded to its similar externalization in the emerging national narrative of the GDR, which exempted the East German state from all continuities of German history and projected them onto the Federal Republic.[13]

The *Heimkehrer* conferences constructed East German antifascism as a Stalinist antifascism in which the Soviet Union thus took center stage both as fascism's primary victim and, even more importantly, as the source of postwar Germany's redemption.[14] Antifascist returnees exhibited a strong philo-Sovietism, which converted the negative features that Nazi propaganda had assigned to the Soviet Union into positive ones. The "Soviet human being" no longer appeared as "subhuman" but rather as a "model for selflessness, a model for the love of the fatherland and of a Socialist homeland."[15] German POWs and the entire German people, as another returnee asserted, resembled Lilliputians who looked up to the giant Soviet Gulliver and who initially only saw the "little dirt" that "necessarily stuck to the soles of the powerful Soviet Union on its march through history."[16] Such lionizing of the "great, one may even say gigantic task of reconstruction in the Soviet Union" then also served the purpose of minimizing the East German reconstruction effort.[17] In East German antifascist memory, an idealized image of the Soviet Union compensated for the lack of a distinctly German authority in the postwar period.[18] It was only through their experiences in the Soviet Union as the "land of the future" that returnees would be able to overcome shortcomings of their own fathers, who "in their delusions, their insufficient understanding and their uncritical, naive confidence had brought worries and misery to our lives."[19]

Official East German antifascism was a distinctly masculine concept. It entailed a militaristic emphasis on "struggle" and "fighting," and it propagated a Manichaean division of the world into hostile camps engaged in permanent struggle. Antifascist returnees claimed to be the most ardent "fighters for peace" and pledged to align themselves with the "fighting front (*Kampffront*) of the democratic forces," whereas "everybody who does not fight for peace" became "a soldier in the hostile camp."[20] Fitting this emphasis on militarized masculinities, the *Heimkehrer* conferences were almost exclusively male events and featured only a few short speeches by women. None of the presenters addressed the experience of thousands of women returning from Soviet captivity. The official focus on the ideological transformation of returnees in Soviet captivity validated predominantly male experiences and incorporated them into the emerging East German national narrative. Similar to the West, redemptive narratives of the POW experience fostered the symbolic "remasculinization" of East German society at large.

The reconstruction of East German masculinity was based on the alleged contrast between enlightened and politically transformed men on the one hand and politically ignorant women on the other.[21] At the regional returnee conference in Brandenburg, the Stalingrad general and NKFD member Dr. Otto Korfes cited "resentment and emotions" particularly among German women towards the Russians and emphasized that "it was easier to win over and convince men" since they appeared "calmer in their judgments."[22] Even female party activists contributed to this portrayal of women as politically indifferent. A female speaker in Dresden noted, for example, that "much of what had been said" at the conference was new to women and that "they may have understood many things for the first time."[23] None of the speakers, however, addressed the major reason *why* East German women may have found it difficult to convert to Soviet-centered official antifascism. In sharp contrast to antifascist return-ees' "life changing" experience of ideological transformation in Soviet cap-tivity, the key experience of East German women with the Soviet occupier was, in Norman Naimark's words, the "ubiquitous threat and reality of rape over a prolonged period of time."[24] Any serious effort to publicly discuss the mass rape of German women remained outside the confines of permitted public discourse in the Soviet zone of occupation.[25] While East German men and women shared the very physical experience of defeat by the Red Army, only the (male) POW experience in the Soviet Union was integrated into the emerging East German national narrative. By contrast, the issue of rape remained, in Atina Grossmann's words, a "question of silence" until the very end of the GDR.[26]

Finally, official antifascism, as it was forged at the *Heimkehrer* confer-ences, marginalized experiences of suffering that were difficult to incorpo-rate into the redemptive, Soviet-centered narrative. Like redemptive mem-ories in the West, it was based on hierarchies and exclusions.[27] In the East, former persecuted Communists received prime victim status at home, while the Soviet Union was privileged among the non-German victims of National Socialism. The German attack on the Soviet Union represented the "greatest national catastrophe," of which Auschwitz merely appeared a "consequence."[28] Official East German memories clearly subordinated the Holocaust to the war against the Soviet Union. Unlike the Holocaust, the war against the Soviet Union entailed the possibility of building a bridge into the postwar period through the transformative experience of Soviet captivity. The murder of European Jews, on the other hand, simply did not lend itself to the redemptive narratives that both East and West German officials were busily constructing in the postwar period.[29]

"A DRIVE AND ENTHUSIASM THAT OLDER FUNCTIONARIES
    OFTEN HAVE LOST"

Official representations of returnees as ideal antifascist citizens consti-tuted more of a political project than an actually existing social reality. With the gradual extension of the SED's dictatorial powers in 1947–48, state and party officials engaged in sustained efforts to make actual re-turnees conform to officially propagated ideals of antifascist citizenship. The focal point of these efforts were those former POWs who had partici-pated in antifascist reeducation courses in Soviet captivity. As early as 1941, Communist emigrants to the Soviet Union had identified German POWs in Soviet captivity as important cadres for the reconstruction of an antifascist Germany.[30] The first antifascist schools for German POWs were established in 1942–43. It is estimated that approximately seventy thousand German POWs participated in three- or six-month courses at 120 camp schools, 50 regional schools, and 2 central schools.[31] The courses offered a doctrinaire Marxism that highlighted the advantages of the Stalinist model of social and political organization. Courses usually consisted of three segments addressing "basic questions of scientific Socialism," the "history of the Soviet Union and the Communist Party," and "German history and the history of the labor movement."[32]

From the early postwar period onward, Communist Party officials attempted to recruit graduates of these antifascist schools for the SED. Initially, this project turned out to be much more difficult than both East German and Soviet authorities had expected. In March 1948, the SED's personnel policy department indicated that among 1,240 graduates of antifascist schools, it held specific information only for 304.[33] A few months later, the SED leadership conveyed similarly sobering results in a comprehensive report to the Soviet Administration for Prisoners of War and Internee Camps (GUPVI). "The impact of these schools," as the report concluded, "has not yielded the results that one might have expected in light of your comprehensive efforts." Among 2,300 antifascist returnees, 70 to 80 percent "at most" had joined the SED in the Eastern zones, and even this figure appears to have been a high estimate. Among antifascist returnees in the Western zones, only 25 percent had become a member of the Communist Party. Many antifascist returnees who had not returned in specific transports from Soviet captivity, moreover, had "gotten lost (*versandet*) in the Heimat without control and without help from the party."[34]

The SED blamed these disappointing results—with surprising openness—on the deficiencies of reeducation efforts in Soviet captivity, such as the selection of too many candidates from "bourgeois and petit bourgeois circles" or a too theoretical focus of the courses. Soviet authorities, in turn, were quite receptive to this criticism, and the SED subsequently also expanded its own efforts to recruit antifascist returnees.[35] Party officials welcomed antifascist returnees upon their arrival in Gronenfelde and asked them to fill out a questionnaire. The personnel policy department entered this information into a central card catalog and forwarded it to the regional and the district party leaderships. The local district executive committees (*Kreisvorstände*) then were to motivate and recruit antifascist returnees for party work.[36]

By late 1948, these heightened ideological and organizational efforts yielded somewhat better results.[37] In March 1951, the latest statistic listed 8,094 registered antifascist returnees, of whom 6,584 occupied political functions and 3,464 had become members of the SED.[38] Yet these improved results still fell short of both Soviet and East German expectations.

Figure 8. Paul Merker, the SED's expert on POW issues, addresses a group of returned POWs in October 1948. The SED aggressively tried to recruit returned POWs as functionaries for the party, partly in order to compensate for the loss of members as a result of the extensive party purges. Ironically, Merker himself eventually became a victim of the purges. (Courtesy Bundesarchiv Koblenz.)

In 1950, the Soviet occupation official Semjonow concluded that "only weak use is being made . . . of those POWs who had attended antifascist schools in the Soviet Union" and complained—not quite accurately—that only about 10 percent of the 18,000 antifascist returnees in East Germany were politically engaged.[39] Later historians have arrived at a similar negative assessment.[40] It is important, however, to measure the impact of antifascist returnees not only in quantitative but also in qualitative terms. Antifascist returnees were strongly committed functionaries who had deeply internalized the authoritarian principles of Stalinist ideology. They occupied primarily midlevel positions within the party and state bureaucracies, which put them into closer contact with the population than functionaries from higher echelons of the party.[41] According to one report, antifascist returnees could be found "everywhere in our party, in the mass organizations, in the economic and administrative sectors, in the police, etc."[42] Most antifascist returnees were employed within People-Owned Companies (VEBs) and as officers within the newly formed People's Police, while the district and provincial administrations, the GDSF (Society for German-Soviet Friendship), and the FDJ (Free German Youth) constituted other primary areas of occupation.[43] As highly motivated and visible activists, antifascist returnees shaped the public image of the SED to a greater extent than their limited number might suggest.

The recruitment of antifascist returnees as party activists reveals a great deal about the subterranean mentality and ideological makeup of the "party of the new type" as it was emerging in 1948–49. It also illuminates the difficult reality behind officially propagated narratives of antifascist conversion. For party officials recognized quickly that returning POWs' "antifascism" was based on a rather thin ideological foundation. In September 1949, an SED official from Saxony complained about the low "theoretical and ideological level" of recently arrived antifascist returnees, who had not been able to explain the concept of a "people-owned company."[44] Another antifascist returnee criticized the conditions in Soviet camps and reportedly stated that "in the winter 1946–47, half of the people in the camps had died"—a statement that SED authorities immediately identified as dangerous "anti-Soviet agitation."[45] Even more shockingly, a third antifascist returnee reportedly ended a conversation with SED functionaries from Saxony by giving the Hitler salute.[46]

Party meetings with antifascist returnees not only exposed their ideological deficiencies but also revealed their severe problems in encountering ordinary East Germans. Much to their dismay, antifascist returnees needed to realize that they did not enjoy a very favorable reputation within the East German population. "The opinion prevails," one returnee reported, "that 90 percent of students at antifascist schools were scoundrels who sought only personal advantages."[47] Such negative reactions targeted especially antifascist returnees' philo-Sovietism. One returnee reported that "talking about the Soviet Union easily produces distrust" and one needed to be "careful."[48] Antifascist returnees were particularly shocked to confront the hostility of ordinary workers towards the SED. One returnee was surprised that workers "ask such strange questions" and began to wonder whether "there still are any honest comrades around at all."[49] Another returnee complained about the "strange attitude" of older workers in particular who were "only concerned about food."[50] When he realized how difficult it was "to convince the workers," a third antifascist returnee admitted that he begun to waver in his ideological commitment.[51] Resentment toward antifascist returnees extended far into the ranks of the SED itself. Most antifascist returnees lacked deep roots in the labor movement and had been, for the most part, socialized in the Hitler Youth and Wehrmacht. When they presented themselves as converted and committed antifascists, they faced hostility and rejection from older party members with lifelong records of political activism. One antifascist returnee, for example, was asked whether he "already had such a big mouth in the Hitler Youth"; another one complained that "older comrades from the KPD and the SED" focused "one-sidedly on the past and not on the new ideology" and refused to "make room for new cadres."[52] While historians have often portrayed the power structure of the SED as a symbiosis between veteran Communists in leadership positions and members from the "Hitler Youth generation" as "antifascist foot soldiers," the recruitment of antifascist returnees also brought into the open massive intergenerational conflicts and tensions.[53]

Significantly, some leading party authorities stressed the merits of antifascist returnees and were highly critical of older functionaries. To the Moscow faction of the SED around Ulbricht, antifascist returnees represented the then ascendant Soviet-centered version of official antifascism. It was no coincidence that heightened efforts to recruit them coincided with the onset of extensive party purges in the fall of 1948. Antifascist returnees were to compensate, at least in part, for the heavy losses of the SED as a result of the purges.[54] As a result, the party leadership made it easier for antifascist returnees to join the ranks of the SED by shortening or even abandoning the newly introduced waiting period for "candidates" prior to full party membership.[55] From the perspective of the party leadership, antifascist returnees exhibited numerous advantages over "older comrades" who still suffered from the "consequences of twelve years of fascism" and thus tended to display "sectarian" and "opportunistic" (i.e., more independent) attitudes. By contrast, young people who were "new to the party" were often "more committed than those from before 1933."[56] They displayed, as one official concluded, a "drive and an enthusiasm that older functionaries often have lost."[57]

Antifascist returnees also promised to become highly malleable party functionaries who were likely to follow the party line at every turn. Their socialization in the Hitler Youth and Wehrmacht had taught them the virtue of subordination to authority. A report from Brandenburg praised antifascist returnees for "standing firm for the party," "making no demands in terms of salary," and being willing "to go wherever the party considers it necessary."[58] Even in the case of potential conflicts, antifascist returnees remained aware of their compromised past and were therefore easier to discipline than longtime Communists.[59] Any alleged political mistake or ideological deviation could simply be attributed to antifascist returnees' "bourgeois" social background or to their "fascist" past. The party leadership's proclivity for antifascist returnees illuminated the increasingly authoritarian nature of East German antifascism. It demonstrated that loyal obedience to the party authorities in the present represented a more important component of East German antifascist citizenship than an antifascist record in the past.

"Leading Them Back to the Proletarian Class to Which the Overwhelming Majority of Them Had Belonged"

East German efforts to forge ideal antifascist citizens out of returnees from the East did not remain limited to graduates of antifascist schools but concerned all returnees, especially those from the East. Party officials engaged in a sustained campaign of winning over returnees from the East that coincided with the establishment of the SED dictatorship. Just as millions of working-class Germans had been "misled" by fascist propaganda, political agitation in the Soviet zone was to reinforce antifascist reeducation in captivity and to reverse this historical process among returning POWs. The SED wanted, as another party official put it, to lead returnees "back to the proletarian class to which the overwhelming majority of them had belonged."[60]

Official strategies toward returnees built on earlier party efforts from the immediate postwar period to control and coordinate the reception of returning POWs. As early as September 1945, a Central Administration for German Resettlers (ZVU) was established to organize the care for so-called resettlers (i.e., expellees and refugees) as well as returnees. Since it was controlled by Communists and also enjoyed a close relationship with Soviet occupation authorities, the ZVU was supposed to extend the KPD/SED's influence over these displaced populations in the Eastern zone, especially vis-à-vis the provincial administrations.[61] Yet the party's organizational weakness during the early postwar period meant that it needed to rely on intermediate organizations to facilitate returnees' transition to civilian life. As in the West, Christian welfare organizations played a crucial role in providing charity and essential assistance to returnees and expellees. Food shortages forced SED officials to rely on church welfare organizations despite their ideological concerns.[62] Given these external pressures, church welfare organizations cooperated well with the SED's own welfare organization People's Solidarity (Volkssolidarität) in distributing food donations to returning POWs.[63] Besides church organizations, some six thousand antifascist democratic women's committees played a crucial role in providing assistance to returning POWs.[64] They cooked warm meals, dyed and repaired old uniforms, organized food and clothing collections, and also offered more general orientation.[65] While male party officials were primarily concerned with returnees' ideological deficiencies, it was women's responsibility to restore former soldiers' ability to function in everyday life.

By 1948, official strategies toward returning POWs began to reflect the strengthened position of the SED in East Germany. In a letter to all regional party organizations in April 1948, Paul Merker complained that party work among returnees had generally been limited to a "modest social care" and had generally not included any "political guidance" of returnees and their families.[66] Party officials should now embark on more extensive efforts to reshape the minds and mentalities of the former soldiers of Hitler's army. Party work among returnees assumed a variety of forms. Party officials were to accompany the return of the POWs from their arrival at the train stations, their stay in the transition camps, and their final travel to their home communities with systematic campaigns for "information" and political education. Party efforts toward returnees began in the Gronenfelde transition camp. Political slogans, information boards, and welcoming speeches were to communicate to returning POWs the SED's interpretation of the German past and the party's proposals for the future.[67]

Party officials emphasized that only the "best-trained functionaries" should be employed in Gronenfelde since "the first conversations of returnees after such a long absence were of tremendous significance for their future development."[68] As in Soviet captivity, a small vanguard of activists was to lead the mass of indifferent returnees to political enlightenment.[69] These strategies often reflected rather patronizing and even infantilizing attitudes, describing returnees, for example, as "sick people" who "needed to be helped" or even as "childlike."[70] At the same time, SED officials were supposed to avoid the "ideological sledgehammer" and remain politically sensitive.[71] When visiting returned POWs in their homes, one official suggested, SED functionaries should inquire about problems of daily life and bring a small gift, even if it was only two cigarettes. Only after the returnee had gained the impression "that the SED takes care of him and wants to help him" were they supposed to address political issues.[72] Ultimately, however, party work among returnees should entail, as Paul Merker insisted, a "systematic general campaign for the party."[73]

A realignment of the SED's organizational apparatus accompanied this program for systematic political agitation among returnees. As with policies toward resettlers (i.e., refugees and expellees from the lost German eastern territories), the party sought to coordinate and control all party efforts within the central party bureaucracy.[74] This strategy spelled the end of specific bureaucratic agencies outside of the party structure, such as the Central Administration for Resettlers (ZVU). While this agency had initially assisted the SED in extending its influence over policies toward war-damaged groups, it now threatened to become an institutional locus for the propagation of specific group identities. As a result, the ZVU was dissolved on 31 March 1948, and responsibilities for dealing with returnees were shifted to a new commission for POW and returnee issues within the Central Secretariat of the SED.[75] The inclusion of representatives from the crucial personnel policy department in this commission

Figure 9. Returnees leaving the transition camp in Gronenfelde in April 1949. The camp was the site of the first encounter between returning POWs from the East and postwar German society. East German state and party officials undertook considerable ideological and organizational efforts to give returnees a positive first impression of conditions in the Soviet zone of occupation. (Courtesy Bundesarchiv Koblenz.)

reflected the shift from social welfare work to political indoctrination in official policies toward returnees.[76] Within a period of several weeks, similar POW/returnee commissions were also formed within the regional and the district party organizations.[77] This shift of competences from specific administrative agencies to the central power structure of the SED represented, as Michael Schwartz has written, a "moment of Stalinization."[78] It denoted the SED's new ideological ambitions of thoroughly transforming returning POWs and, by extension, East German society.

By 1948, institutional arrangements for dealing with returning POWs began to diverge between East and West: whereas former soldiers and POWs began to form powerful interest organizations in the Western zones, East German authorities repressed the formation of such organizations. Yet even within the SED, this strategy was not uncontested. In November 1948, an SED official and representative of the German Interior Administration proposed the formation of an "Association of Former POWs for the Struggle Against War." This association was supposed to keep former soldiers and POWs from forming "war associations," and it should prevent their "lapse . . . into the reactionary camp."[79] The party

Figure 10. Returnees in the Gronenfelde transition camp reading a party advertisement for the SED, October 1948. The party deployed considerable organizational and ideological efforts toward returnees, and sincerely believed in the possibility of converting them into antifascist citizens. The official caption to this photo reads, "Returnees follow with great interest the daily news and have long discussions about it."

leadership, however, rejected this proposal, even though the proposed association was conceived as another SED-dominated mass organization. The SED was opposed to any "special organization" and wanted to strengthen the existing mass organizations.[80] Rather than cultivating returnee-specific interests, the SED's ultimate goal was the "dedifferentiation" of East German society, that is, the dissolution of separate group identities and their replacement by new identities as citizens of the East German state.[81]

To promote this transformation, the party relied on another political transmission belt: the National Democratic Party (NDPD). Concurrently with the larger ideological and institutional shifts in SED policies toward returnees, the NDPD was founded in June 1948. The party was supposed to align bourgeois and "national" segments of the population with the larger transformation of East German society under the auspices of the SED and Soviet occupation forces. In particular, the NDDP was to appeal to former Nazis and former Wehrmacht soldiers, and become the political "home of many returnees."[82] Unlike representatives of other bloc parties such as the Liberal Democratic Party (LDPD), NDPD officials were granted access to the transition camp in Gronenfelde to recruit returnees for their party.[83] East German officials, however, soon realized that the NDPD was a problematic instrument for the transformation of returnees into antifascist citizens. A report to Walter Ulbricht criticized the "inevitable remnants of the fascist ideology, nationalist divergence, and low ideological level" among NDPD party members.[84] To counteract these alleged tendencies, the SED infiltrated the NDPD with loyal antifascist returnees from the Soviet Union who were supposed to report about the inner development of the new bloc party.[85]

Such usage of covert operations points to another crucial aspect in SED responses to returnees: a significant degree of paranoia. The flip side of party officials' confidence in the ideological transformability of returning POWs was their constant worry about potential outside forces that might subvert this political healing process. To SED functionaries, persistent signs of indifference or even hostility among returning POWs did not signal a lack of legitimacy of their own vision but were rather the product of ideologically damaging forces. As a result, East German officials constantly sought to "shield" returning POWs against supposedly "hostile" influences. Thus, SED strategies toward returnees were indicative of the larger mixture of "paternalism and paranoia" that Mary Fulbrook has identified as a typical "mentality of power" in the GDR.[86]

Throughout the postwar period, SED officials were deeply concerned about the detrimental influence that German train personnel exerted on German POWs during their transport from the last Russian station in

Brest Litovsk to Frankfurt an der Oder. A report from July 1947 illustrates how seriously the SED took this issue:

> The railwaymen on the way from Brest to Frankfurt an der Oder engage freely in an open profascist propaganda. . . . [They] agitate against the antifascist-democratic Germany, openly display their fascist attitude, and recklessly criticize the problems in our country. We therefore urge strong provisions and making available antifascist train personnel . . . who can replace their fascist colleagues. We should not wait until we have to climb the gallows or populate the prisons and concentration camps again. That is why we need to confront these elements in time.[87]

The dramatic language employed in this report indicates the extent of official anxieties about "hostile" political influences. These apprehensions also extended to the Gronenfelde transition camp. Party officials complained about the camp's medical personnel, who allegedly consisted primarily of "military doctors and Nazi doctors," and they were similarly concerned about the nurses and even about the cook, allegedly an "active Nazi."[88] In mid-1949, a comprehensive review of ostensible "fascist influences" in the returnee camps revealed rather mundane political impediments, such as the sale of high-alcohol beer in Gronenfelde, which reportedly allowed "returnees to get drunk, get together in groups, and sing military songs."[89] The persistent and ultimately rather paranoid fears over ubiquitous "fascist" influences ultimately revealed the SED's own distrust of the ideological and political reliability of former soldiers and POWs, and by extension, of East German society more generally.

Even more than internal "fascist" dangers, the lure of the West appeared as a grave danger to returnees' ideological conversion. The SED's intensified political campaign toward returnees after 1948 coincided with the gradual improvement of the West German economy under the auspices of Marshall Plan and the currency reform. The presence of a West German parallel society with increasingly higher living standards and better social policy benefits posed a constant challenge to the SED's quest for legitimacy. In seeking to counter the West's attraction, some party officials began to portray conditions in the Western zones in the darkest possible colors.[90] Other party officials, however, sought to teach returnees the virtue of resisting these material temptations by associating consumption with the rise of fascism. According to one SED official, popular desire for a "warm meal" and a bowl of chickpea soup "had turned the SA and SS into huge organizations." It was therefore only by becoming "politically conscious beings" that returning POWs would be able to forsake higher living standards in the West for their long-term political and ideological redemption in the East.[91]

While the existence of the more prosperous West represented a permanent and insoluble problem for the SED, the party tried to eliminate countervailing forces within East German society that threatened to subvert returnees' transformation into antifascist citizens. In particular, the SED identified the Christian churches as a severe threat to this project. At a regional meeting in Brandenburg on POW and returnee issues, an SED representative vehemently criticized the attempt of church organizations to "transform the POWs into pious human beings, into hypocrites."[92] As a result, the SED sought to reduce the influence of the church-related welfare organizations Caritas, Innere Mission, and Evangelisches Hilfswerk, which, as we have seen, had provided crucial social assistance and material aid for returning POWs during the early postwar period. The party tried to do so by strengthening its own welfare organization, the Volkssolidarität (People's Solidarity) vis-à-vis church-affiliated welfare organizations. By early 1948, leading functionaries of the Volkssolidarität sought to "contain" (*abdämmen*) church organizations like Caritas and Innere Mission by forging "closer ties to the party."[93]

In light of the SED's persistent dependency on church donations in providing essential assistance to displaced populations, this strategy was never completely successful. In the summer and fall of 1947, the Volkssolidarität was no longer able to provide food and first aid to returnees at East German train stations, and needed to relinquish—to the great dismay of the SED—these services to Caritas and Evangelisches Hilfswerk.[94] Party officials subsequently tried to regain control of, or at least to participate in, the distribution of those food donations, but church organizations managed to retain a significant degree of autonomy.[95] As a result, the conflict over welfare work in the Eastern zones lingered, and the relationship between the churches and the SED dictatorship remained one of the unresolved tensions of the formative period of the GDR.[96]

Finally, the independent role of the East German women's organizations fell victim to the SED's efforts to centralize the reception of returning POWs within the central party administration.[97] In November 1947, the party dissolved the "antifascist-democratic" women's committees because of their independent agenda and the involvement of too many bourgeois women. Their functions were transferred to women's advisory committees within the central state and party bureaucracies.[98] In addition, the SED established a new mass organization for East German women, the Democratic Women's Union (DFD). Women continued to provide social and political assistance for returning POWs through the DFD. But they did so in a less autonomous manner and under the firm control of the party and state bureaucracies. The SED leadership, for example, suggested it as a "beautiful task" for women of the DFD to organize "friendly evenings or afternoons with coffee for returnees and their families."[99] Still, women carved out specific areas of activity within and through the DFD despite this curtailed autonomy. In addition, a trip by a DFD delegation to POW camps in the Soviet Union in the fall of 1948 was made to soothe widespread anxieties about the treatment of German men in Soviet captivity.[100] As primarily organizations of married women, local DFD branches assisted returning POWs in overcoming marriage problems after a long period of separation. In so doing, they addressed an issue that East German state and party officials continued to ignore almost completely.[101]

Women, moreover, not only lost influence on returning POWs' reception in the East, they were also increasingly criticized for their alleged political underdevelopment. Women increasingly stood for the persistence of a nonpolitical private sphere that that tended to subvert the returnee's political transformation. "Politically blind wives," as one party official argued, allegedly failed to grasp their husbands' political commitment and were thus deemed responsible for the breakup of many marriages in East Germany.[102] In contrast to the early postwar period, these accusations juxtaposed a renewed male revolutionary enthusiasm to an innate female political apathy. Official SED strategies toward returnees went along with the revival of traditional Communist gender stereotypes in which the men's functions as party activists were always at odds with their domestic roles as father and husband.[103] Similar to their counterparts in the West, East German officials blamed women for preventing men from living up to postwar ideals of masculine citizenship, which, however, they defined differently: in the East, these ideals focused on political activism and on men's working lives, whereas in the West, they centered on men's functions as fathers and husbands.

The party's ongoing concerns with "hostile influences" emanating from within East Germany as well as from the West reflected the persistence of countervailing forces, which severely limited the party's capacity to remake "returnees." While SED strategies toward returnees evolved in conjunction with the establishment of the SED dictatorship in East Germany, they also revealed the persistent "limitations of the East German dictatorship" that continued to subvert the party's totalitarian aspirations.[104]

Living Antifascist Memories: Resistance, Accommodation and Consensus in the East German Dictatorship

The responses of returnees to the SED's offer for antifascist integration reveal much about resistance, accommodation, and consensus in the East German dictatorship. A variety of anecdotal and "oral history" evidence points to returnees' rejection of East German official memories both at the time and in retrospect.[105] They took umbrage not only at the content of the SED's interpretation of their experience but also resented its political implications. As in the West, many returnees exhibited a strong skepticism regarding any form of political engagement. But while this attitude was quite compatible with the emerging conservative democracy in the West, it undermined the SED's efforts at political mobilization. In August 1946, an SED activist experienced this difficulty in a Berlin movie theater. When he began to praise the SED's accomplishments, all he encountered was laughter and loud protest, especially from former POWs, who, as he reported, "wanted to be left alone at least in a movie theater" and "did not want to be bothered with political issues after the deprivations of war and captivity."[106] Short of this kind of public protest, another strategy of avoiding the SED's call for political mobilization was the refusal to join the Society for German-Soviet Friendship, for which returnees were considered particularly desirable candidates. In so doing, returnees denied the party a visible and public display of loyalty that formed the basis for conformist behavior in East Germany.[107]

The SED's master narrative of Soviet captivity as antifascist conversion also encountered more explicit oppositional attitudes. Too wide was the chasm between this official memory and the POWs' individual experiences of suffering and deprivation, which often could only be articulated within the private realm of the family.[108] But some returnees also did not hesitate to articulate this chasm between public and private memory in public. At the VEB in Plauen, former returnees interrupted a speech by a SED functionary, yelling that "we were hungry all the time and many of us perished" and that "we do not want to have anything to do with the Russians."[109] In the Berlin district of Prenzlauer Berg in early 1950, a similar incident occurred at a returnee meeting that was modeled on the *Heimkehrer* conferences of the previous fall. After the usual speeches about "why we have become friends of the Soviet Union," the question by an audience member about many "innocent POWs" still held in the Soviet Union provided the signal for a "general disturbance of the meeting," which "demonstrated the weakness of our party."[110]

Throughout the 1950s, flight to the West represented another possible consequence of this gap between public and private memory. Having returned to East Germany in 1949, Werner J., for example, went to the West three years later because he saw no career possibilities in the GDR without compromising his personal and political conviction, that is, without joining the SED or one of its mass organizations.[111] Returnees in East Germany were also very much aware of specific material assistance for former POWs in the Federal Republic. Better social policy benefits thus constituted an important pull factor in leaving East Germany.[112] Nevertheless, the available statistics do not indicate that former soldiers and POWs were overrepresented among the refugees from East to West.[113] A large segment of returnees to East Germany thus actively chose or at least passively adjusted to life in East Germany. These choices point to sources of popular accommodation and even consensus in the East German dictatorship.

One such source consisted of the SED's official master narrative of antifascist conversion, which not only provoked returnees' resistance but also offered considerable opportunities for ideological integration. East German redemptive memories entailed, as we have seen, strongly apologetic dimensions that tended to exonerate "nominal" Nazi Party members and ordinary Wehrmacht soldiers rather easily. In addition, antifascist integration offered a convenient and highly compatible new political identity to former soldiers and POWs. This was all the more true since the notion of antifascist conversion in Soviet captivity was not only an ideological construct but also had an experiential basis. Participation in antifascist activity was not just motivated by opportunism or material needs, but also by a genuine search for new meaning after the collapse of National Socialism. A postwar antifascist identity thus could also be seen as a compensation for and consequence of previous political errors.[114]

The East German writer Franz Fühmann is a case in point. In December 1949, shortly after returning from Soviet captivity, where he had attended several antifascist schools, he assumed political functions within the NDPD and openly identified with the East German state.[115] In his autobiographical account from 1982, Fühmann recalled the attractiveness of his new antifascist identity, but he also pondered the ease with which he had converted to the new creed. He remembered how even he, as "the son of a local Nazi functionary and petit bourgeois," could become a member of "the class of the future" and how he felt "as on a morning, when the world was bright, and I was walking toward the light, at last aligned with the right forces."[116] It was this capacity for a retrospective, self-critical reflection on their own conversion to the "winning side of history" that set writers like Fühmann apart from the orthodox antifascist master narrative as it had been forged in the late 1940s and early 1950s.[117]

As Fühmann's critique illustrated, antifascist integration by no means required a complete break with earlier beliefs and attitudes despite its emphasis on ideological conversion. What Lutz Niethammer and others have pointed out for members of the Hitler Youth generation also applied especially to antifascist returnees: they could easily incorporate their earlier conditioning to "fight" for a "final victory" into normative conceptions of male antifascist citizenship in the GDR. Thus, "learning from the Soviet Union how to be victorious," as the famous Stalinist slogan went, also provided an opportunity to go over, by way of a political leap of faith, to the winning side of history.[118] Such mental continuities from the Third Reich to the "antifascist-democratic" order became apparent in the poem that the antifascist returnee Werner K. dedicated to the SED upon his return to East Germany in December 1948. It was entitled "Fight" (*Kampf*) and described a spring storm inevitably driving away the last remnants of winter. It ends by equating this fight between natural forces with the fight between the human forces of "reaction" and "progress":

> We see in this struggle between the elements
> a parable of our own struggle
> a glance at the future opens up
> and the certainty reaches all of us:
> Ours, the victory
> Ours, the victory
> because time is ripe
> and everybody takes an oath anew at this hour
> fight! fight and victory!
> loyally following the red flag
> through the roaring into the last battle
> until it breaks through the night of the peoples
> as a shining signal.[119]

Clearly, the antifascist returnee Werner K. had neither abandoned his earlier belief in a "final victory" nor his willingness to fight for it. He had simply transferred both of them to a new cause. Thus, antifascist returnees could see themselves as engaged in a new struggle against a new enemy whose inferiority was no longer defined in terms of race but determined by the laws of history. This persistent emphasis on fighting, then, allowed antifascist returnees to hold on to their militaristic ideal of manliness, which had determined their socialization in the Hitler Youth and in the Wehrmacht and continued to shape their lives as political activists. In East Germany, as in Eastern Europe more generally, Communist revolutions did not constitute a complete break with the past but rather drew on social and political transformation from the wartime period.[120] To meet normative conceptions of masculine citizenship in East Germany, antifascist returnees did not have to undergo a radical change but needed rather to integrate their already existing mental dispositions into new symbolic, social, and political contexts.

SPHERES OF EAST GERMAN CITIZENSHIP: THE MILITARY, THE WORKPLACE, AND THE FAMILY

As in the West, the transformation of returnees into postwar citizens took shape not only in the realm of public discourse and politics. This last section of the chapter discusses former soldiers' and POWs' functional significance within other sites of citizenship, such as the military, the workplace, and the family. It also analyzes returnees' adjustments to the specific challenges they confronted in these realms.

By the late 1940s, East German conceptions of masculine citizenship began to include a military dimension as well. Parallel to the West German debate over rearmament, the escalating Cold War in 1947–48 provided the context for the expansion of already existing police forces into paramilitary units. These forces became the nucleus for the "barracked people's police" (*kasernierte Volkspolizei*) in 1952 and the East German military, the National People's Army (Nationale Volksarmee) in 1956.[121] From the onset, returning POWs from the Soviet Union assumed a key role in the East German rearmament. These former Wehrmacht soldiers had been shielded from Western influences for years and, given the belief of SED officials' in the transformative impact of Soviet captivity, they could be expected to support the East German project of antifascist reconstruction. As early as April 1948, SED general secretary Walter Ulbricht declared that returning POWs "should be primarily won for the police."[122] After high-level talks between Wilhelm Pieck and Soviet occupation officials, Soviet authorities agreed to provide five thousand German POWs for service in the East German armed forces. POWs needed to sign up for three years of service in exchange for their release from Soviet captivity. The main criteria for selecting these POWs was working-class background and residence in (and willingness to return to) the Soviet zone of occupation. In addition, Soviet officials also recruited one hundred former Wehrmacht officers and five generals, primarily former members of the National Committee "Free Germany" or the League of German Officers, for service in the East German *Volkspolizei*.[123]

In September and October 1948, four transports with a total of 4,933 POWs destined for service in the *Volkspolizei* arrived in the Soviet zone of occupation. Party commissions were there to evaluate the political and ideological qualifications of the new recruits to serve in the East German armed forces. To the dismay of SED officials, however, many returnees of the first POW transport arriving on 18 September 1948 were reluctant to join a new military formation. Much like their counterparts in the West, many returnees had had, as one report concluded, "enough of wars and uniforms and wanted to return to their old jobs."[124] Returning POWs were particularly shocked to realize that they were to be enclosed in military barracks and not allowed to see their families for another six to eight weeks. Farmers in particular wanted to return to their homes. Some returnees felt deceived and even betrayed by Russian officials, who had put considerable pressure on them or had lured them into signing applications to the *Volkspolizei* under false pretenses.[125] As a result, out of 898 returnees of the first transport, 272 were initially barred from entering the *Volkspolizei* for political or health reasons or because "they strictly refused to join the police forces."[126] The Soviet military government, however, valued the POWs' military expertise more than their alleged ideological deficiencies.[127] Upon a renewed evaluation of the POWs, it ordered the acceptance of all but 32 POWs who had concealed their former Nazi Party membership and were subsequently sent back to labor camps in the Soviet Union. Soviet officials made sure to communicate this practice to returnees from ensuing transports, who, undoubtedly out of fear of experiencing the same fate, "tried very hard" to be accepted into the police. A total of 4,774 POWs were therefore ultimately integrated into units of the new *kasernierte Volkspolizei*. They accounted for about half of the ten thousand new recruits who formed the core of the emerging East German military.[128]

While antifascist citizenship had always included a militant dimension, the establishment of East German armed forces explicitly turned the military experience of former soldiers and POWs from an ideological burden into an asset.[129] For Walter Ulbricht, it was clear that "we need people with front experience."[130] The SED's careful evaluations of individual returnees underscored the traits that East German officials considered necessary if they wanted to entrust former soldiers with bearing arms again. Working-class background and membership in KPD or SPD before 1933 still constituted the most important feature of an individual's biography. But, by the late 1940s, returnees' socialization in the Wehrmacht by no means excluded them from service in the *Volkspolizei*. The transformative impact of Soviet captivity and the confidence of SED officials in future political reeducation made it possible to regard such returnees as "capable of development."[131] While former members of the Nazi Party and other National Socialist organizations constituted only a small segment of the East German police force, returnees from the Soviet Union comprised 12.3 percent of the *Volkspolizei* by the late 1950s. The figures for officers and functionaries for ideological indoctrination (*Politkultur* officers) were still higher, amounting to 23 percent and 31.7 percent respectively.[132]

The emphasis on military expertise as a central component of antifascist citizenship also enhanced the career prospects of former professional soldiers in the future East German military, the Kasernierte Volkspolizei (KVP) and later the National Volksarmee (NVA). Former Wehrmacht sergeants and noncommissioned officers in particular enjoyed good prospects for promotion through the ranks of the East German military. To be sure, the number of former Wehrmacht officers and generals serving the East German army was always much lower than in the West, and it also declined over the course of the 1950s. But former Wehrmacht officers nevertheless assumed crucial functions in the administrative and educational sections of the newly emerging armed forces in the East.[133] For them, the experience of Soviet captivity and possible participation in antifascist work remained an important source of political capital. It conferred onto them an antifascist nimbus that allowed the continuity of professional military careers from Hitler's army to the East German People's Army.

Apart from staffing the first units of the East German *Volkspolizei*, returning POWs also represented the most important resource of male skilled labor in postwar East Germany.[134] Their recruitment into the workforce was crucial for coping with the devastating consequences of the war. Participation in antifascist-democratic reconstruction through work also represented the ideal path to postwar citizenship in the East German "labor society" (*Arbeitsgesellschaft*). A photo series by the "returnee committee" in East Berlin sketched out the exemplary trajectory of a returnee that led from the Gronenfelde transition camp straight to "integration into the production process" in key sectors of the East German economy such as the Bergmann-Borsig locomotive works.[135] This strong emphasis on the workplace derived from Marxist doctrine, which identified work as the core of human identity. In the absence of any specific material compensation, gainful employment also became a sheer material necessity for POWs returning to East Germany.

Given their firm belief in economic planning, East German officials refused to leave the POWs' return to the workplace to the contingencies of the labor market. Instead, they adopted a comprehensive program of labor regulation (*Arbeitslenkung*), which they portrayed as superior to the "chaotic" functioning of the capitalist labor market.[136] This also included resorting to coercive mechanisms, such as recruiting workers against their will for specific tasks for a limited period of time, usually for about six months. In so doing, East German authorities tried to fill the labor demand for Soviet-owned companies (especially the uranium mines in Aue) and for other key sectors such as coal mining, transport, and heavy industry.[137] The zonal average for such coercive recruitment amounted to 12.7 percent of all job placements. The considerably higher figure for Brandenburg (32.8 percent), where the main returnee transition camp in Gronenefelde was located, points to returning POWs as an important target group for coercive recruitment.[138] "Homeless" returnees from the lost German eastern territories, in particular, were prime candidates to fill the ever increasing Soviet demands for workers in mines in Aue, even though their had health often prevented from performing heavy labor.[139]

By 1948, East German officials largely abandoned these coercive means. Returnees were often too weak to perform heavy labor, and officials shifted to voluntary recruitment. The establishment of the German Economic Commission in June 1947 and the promulgation of the first Two-Year Plan in July 1948 provided the administrative means for central economic planning. Labor direction now relied on mechanisms such as retraining, freeing up male workers by replacing them with women or disabled workers, and incentives through higher wages and better housing.[140] By 1949, the rate of coercive recruitments for the East German labor market had dropped to less than 1 percent.[141] Because most POWs from Western captivity had already returned by 1948, labor regulation especially targeted returnees from the Soviet Union during the decisive restructuring of the East German economy in 1948.[142] Official attempts to mobilize former soldiers and POWs for the SED thus coincided with a sustained effort at recruiting them for East German economic reconstruction.

Labor regulation entailed a deliberate recasting of the gender composition of the East German workforce. In contrast to the West, East German authorities did not simply advocate the replacement of working women by returning men. Instead, they sought to draw women into the workforce in order to free up men for more physically demanding and essential jobs in coal mining and heavy industry. Despite official statements to the contrary, these efforts often implied the assignment of women to subordinate positions. The Brandenburg provincial government, for example, advised regional employment offices that "men could be trained more easily for qualified tasks than women who are new to the production process."[143] Women, in turn, resented their transfer to less demanding jobs. Female workers performing heavy labor at the Lenzo factory in Spremberg "were absolutely opposed to leaving their firms," arguing that they "earned more than in any other factory" and that they "lived close to their workplace."[144] Despite an official commitment to gender equality at the workplace, labor regulation ultimately worked in returnees' favor. Precisely at the moment when the introduction of economic planning and the first Two-Year Plan in 1948 limited employment opportunities and prompted a sharp increase in female unemployment, returning POWs enjoyed privileged access to the East German labor market.[145] Their health conditions had improved considerably by 1948, and their labor in captivity was now officially recognized as an apprenticeship.[146] As a result, returnees were prime candidates for jobs as skilled workers in heavy industry and coal mining that received the highest material compensation and were invested with considerable social prestige. Coal mining, after all, was a job only for "tough guys."[147] In addition, these positions entailed the opportunity to rise in the union and party bureaucracies. They therefore also included the prospect, for former middle-class returnees, of resuming management or administrative positions after an intermediary period as blue-collar worker.

Such possibilities for upward mobility go a long way in explaining former soldiers' and POWs' accommodation to the SED dictatorship. Systematic social mobility studies as well as oral history interviews suggest extraordinary possibilities for social advancement in postwar East Germany. This was true especially for young men, who were able to pursue careers that, according to Heike Solga, "would have been inconceivable under different circumstances."[148] Moreover, the—voluntary or involuntary—exodus of East German middle-class professionals to the West also opened up spaces for middle-class returnees in the East. By mid-1948, East German officials appealed especially to "doctors, pharmacists, medical students, engineers, technicians, and intellectuals who are returning from captivity" to stay in the Soviet zone of occupation.[149] By focusing on their professional careers, it was possible for individual returning POWs to accommodate themselves quite successfully with the situation in East Germany while still maintaining a neutral or even a critical attitude toward the SED.[150] And once they had established a professional identity in East Germany, they became increasingly unwilling to again jeopardize these accomplishments by moving to the West.[151] Such acquiescence also built on important habitual continuities among former soldiers, who tended to favor personal advancement over political engagement and were willing to assume professional functions on the basis of orders "from above."[152]

This desire for upward mobility was not incompatible with an at least outward demonstration of loyalty to the SED regime. The activist movement that was inaugurated with Soviet Military Government Order No. 234 and based on a piecework system for wages appealed precisely to this sense of individual achievement.[153] Since former POWs had already familiarized themselves with the possibility of improving their material circumstances through better individual performance in captivity, they were well positioned for becoming activists. Official messages such as "Returnee: You used to be the best worker and activist—now show that you've remained the same" appealed precisely to these continuities.[154] A quest for social advancement also motivated antifascist activists, who joined the SED after their return from captivity. Some of them exhibited a rather unsocialist desire to move from manual labor to administrative positions. One antifascist returnee working as a forester's apprentice requested a more "responsible position"; a gardener "felt qualified" to become a manager (Betriebsleiter) in a horticulture business; while a former saddler wanted to participate in a training course for becoming a "people's judge" (Volksrichter). The SED leadership took these individual ambitions very seriously and instructed the district party organizations "to check whether their wishes can be realized."[155] Their individual aspirations exemplified the strong subjective desires as well as the actually existing possibilities for social advancement in the early GDR.

What made this quest for individual advancement politically acceptable and morally attractive in the eyes of East German Communists was the link to the larger communal project of "building Socialism."[156] This emphasis on (national) community tied in well with many returnees' allegiance to communal visions of society that, as we have seen, were also popular among returnees in the West. Bernd W., for example, remembered how he was attracted, upon his return from Soviet captivity, by the communal reconstruction effort during the early GDR while feeling "betrayed" by the formation of the Federal Republic. These normative demands of East German citizenship drew on socialization patterns from the Nazi period when individual performance had always been closely associated with the well-being of the Nazi *Volksgemeinschaft*.[157] As one of his first impressions upon returning to East Germany, one returnee stated, "Under the Nazis, there was much talk about *Volksgemeinschaft*, but one did not act accordingly. Now we talk less about it but prove all the more the existence of this *Volksgemeinschaft* through action."[158] In this sense, it was also possible for returning POWs to create a continuity between their "achievements" for the National Socialist *Volksgemeinschaft* and their "achievements" in reconstructing East Germany. No one symbolized these mental continuities better than a returnee, who, during an oral history interview, proudly presented his wartime decorations (including the Iron Cross, First Class) that he had received as tank commander on the Eastern front next to the several medals he had received as factory director for his contribution to the building of socialism in the GDR.[159] As this example illustrates, both German dictatorships welcomed and honored an abstract ethic of performance despite their mutually antagonistic ideologies.

How did returning men's adjustment to the demands of antifascist citizenship affect East German family life? For East German authorities, the family assumed a much less important place in postwar reconstruction than in the West. As Thomas Lindenberger has argued, a "family-centered citizenship" in the West stood in contrast to the predominance of the "state-citizen" relationship in the East.[160] In East German efforts to transform returnees into citizens, the family was either largely ignored or featured as a serious obstacle to political mobilization. For example, some returnees resisted official efforts to channel them into heavy industry and insisted that after "years of separation from their families as a result of war and captivity," they at last wanted to "lead a family life."[161] Unlike the Federal Republic, the East German state did not provide any specific material support for former POWs or war victims. As a result, the East German family became, even more so than in the West, a key site for coping with the consequences of war and captivity in addition to the numerous challenges posed by the East German dictatorship.[162]

The family in East Germany, however, did not serve only as a private counterworld, as the much-cited "niche" opposed to the public world dominated by the totalitarian demands of the SED. Instead, the public world of the state and the private world of the family always remained intertwined and interrelated.[163] Former returnees who successfully adjusted to the new environment in East Germany functioned as important mediators between, on the one hand, the world of the state and politics and, on the other, the family and private life. They were, in Dorothee Wierling's words, "state fathers" who transported the norms and expectations of the new state into the family, even if they themselves often fell short of these norms because of their problematic past in the Hitler Youth and Wehrmacht.[164]

For succeeding generations, "state fathers" represented a highly ambivalent object of identification or rebellion. On one level, they represented the opportunities and benefits of the GDR, which allowed them to transfer their ideological or at least pragmatic allegiance to their children.[165] At the same time, their alleged ideological conversions and numerous concessions to the official demands for political loyalty provoked resentment and resistance among children. Commenting on her father's switch from membership in the Nazi Party to membership in the SED after 1945, one East German woman questioned how it was possible for him to "become a 'fighter for peace' even though [he] had been a Nazi before." "I am extremely bothered by this dishonesty," she added.[166] The experience of "state fathers" prompted a search for more straightforward ways of life that manifested themselves either in a more dedicated loyalty to the SED regime or a move into the opposition camp.[167] Both reactions reflected the next generation's efforts to overcome the moral and political ambiguities that had shaped their parents' survival under two German dictatorships.

CHAPTER 6

Parallel Exclusions: The West German POW Trials and the East German Purges

Parallel exclusions of certain groups of returnees from postwar communities of belonging constituted an integral part of making citizens out of returnees. These exclusionary practices were part of a much wider European effort to mete out retributive justice in the wake of war and defeat. All over the European continent, first spontaneous purges and then more formal political and judicial procedures sought to exclude from postwar polities those individuals who were deemed responsible for crimes associated with the Nazi regime. The courtrooms became the site of protracted battles over the meaning of war, defeat, occupation, and liberation.[1] After the conclusion of major war crime trials and the gradual abandonment of denazification, however, former Nazis were no longer the primary targets of legal prosecution but became the prime candidates for integration. Instead, the increasingly rigid ideological parameters of the Cold War increasingly determined exclusionary practices in East and West. For POWs returning to East and West Germany, inclusion in and exclusion from postwar polities did not primarily depend on their activities during war and fascism but rather on their behavior in Allied or Soviet captivity. For those POWs who needed to cross the gradually descending "iron curtain" on their return to East or West Germany, contacts and cooperation with Allied or Soviet captors now became a major liability.

The first section of this chapter analyzes the little-known *Kameradenschinder* trials (trials of those who abused their comrades) in West Germany. These trials focused on German POWs who had collaborated with their Soviet or Eastern European captors by either assuming official functions in the camp administration or by actively engaging in political reeducation efforts as "antifascist activists." The second part of the chapter addresses the functional equivalent to these trials in East Germany: the extensive purges of the party and state apparatus between the late 1940s and early 1950s. These purges targeted, among other groups, returnees from Western or (since Tito's defection from the Soviet camp in March 1948) Yugoslav captivity, especially if they had participated in reeducation efforts. In both postwar societies, the emerging Cold War antagonism delegitimized specific POW experiences in Allied or Soviet captivity. In West Germany, compromised returnees from the East suffered political marginalization, moral condemnation, and, in some cases, criminal prosecution, whereas in East Germany, West returnees were subjected to outright political persecution.

BETWEEN AMNESTY AND ANTI-COMMUNISM:
THE WEST GERMAN POW TRIALS

Between 1948 and 1956, West German courts sentenced approximately one hundred former POWs as *Kameradenschinder* (torturers of their comrades) to prison terms ranging from several months to fifteen years.[2] Most cases were initiated by former POWs who charged their former comrades either with mistreating them in their function as camp officials or with denouncing them to their Soviet or Eastern European captors. Convictions were usually based on paragraphs 223 and 224 of the German criminal code (StGB) ("bodily injury" and "grave bodily injury") or on paragraph 239 StGB ("deprivation of liberty"). "Bodily injury" was invoked in cases of violent transgressions by German camp officials against other POWs. "Deprivation of liberty" was applied to cases of knowingly false denunciations to camp authorities, which had prolonged the plaintiffs' internment in the Soviet Union or Eastern Europe. In several cases, the courts also judged these offenses as having been based on a particularly "reprehensible character" and withdrew the offenders' citizenship rights for several years.[3]

These trials fell precisely into the period between the late 1940s and the late 1950s when the legal prosecution of Nazi crimes came to a virtual standstill. After a brief and quite vigorous prosecution of Nazi crimes under the auspices of the occupation authorities, the willingness of the West German judiciary to call to task Nazi perpetrators declined sharply during the early Federal Republic. In 1955, 239 preliminary proceedings led to the conviction of only twenty-one persons for crimes committed under Nazi dictatorship.[4] Thus, the number of convicted Nazi perpetrators may have roughly equaled the number of returned POWs who were convicted for their actions in Soviet captivity in the same year. The POW trials, to be sure, *did* prosecute German perpetrators. But these were perpetrators who had acted under auspices of the Soviet, not the Nazi, dictatorship, and who were accused of victimizing other Germans rather than non-Germans. Thus, the trials displaced the legal, political, and moral confrontation with the homegrown Nazi dictatorship onto a confrontation with the foreign, Communist, Soviet dictatorship.

The link between Nazi perpetrators and accused former POWs was forged in public discourse. When, in the summer of 1949, a West German Social Democratic paper bemoaned the fact that many war criminals had escaped justice, it referred not to perpetrators of the Nazi regime but instead to one of the first convicted former POWs in West Germany.[5] In July 1949, the Wuppertal district court had sentenced Otto S., a former commandant of a prison unit in a Soviet POW camp, to ten years in prison and loss of his citizenship rights for six years for "bodily injury" in ten cases, one of them leading to the death of a fellow POW.[6] The same article did not hesitate to place him in the same category as Ilse Koch, the infamous concentration camp guard from Buchenwald, as well as the "beasts of Auschwitz, Buchenwald, Ravensbrück, and Sachsenhausen." It celebrated the verdict against Otto S. as the "first atonement by a German court of a crime against humanity that had been committed under the auspices of Communism."[7]

Public and legal discourse did not remain separate but mutually influenced each other. Reporting on another POW trial in 1950, the popular weekly *Stern* denounced the "torture of comrades in the service of an inhuman power" as one of the "most miserable of postwar issues with which our people is confronted."[8] Inside the courtroom, prosecutors indicted returnees with "crimes against humanity," and judges compared the function of German camp officials in Soviet camps to the "system that was also practiced in German concentration camps."[9] The invocation of "crimes against humanity" in POW trials stood in marked contrast to German courts' reluctance to employ this accusation in prosecutions of Nazi perpetrators.[10] The charge was also legally inappropriate. As one judge correctly noted, it could be leveled against those "inhumanities that were linked to National Socialist rule" and hence could not be applied to offenses committed in Soviet POW camps.[11] Yet this insight did not prevent another judge from characterizing the offenses of one former POW in Soviet captivity as "bordering on crimes against humanity."[12] Inside and outside of the courtrooms, the trials offered one more opportunity to deflect charges of "crimes against humanity" away from postwar (West) Germans and toward Soviet Communism.[13]

Most of the preliminary proceedings and actual prosecutions were set in motion by accusations of returned POWs against other returnees. At times, potential culprits were already identified during their brief stay in the returnee transition camps. In Friedland, for example, the camp police repeatedly needed to protect returned POWs who had been identified as potential offenders against violent attacks from their comrades. In these cases, camp officials alerted the attackers to the possibility of formally pressing charges against suspected offenders or, in what appeared to be particularly grave cases, decided to press charges themselves.[14] Other offenders, such as the previously mentioned Otto S., were identified by returnees during his stay in a returnee hospital.[15] Most cases, however, were initiated by former POWs shortly after their return to their hometown.[16]

In some cases, family members or POW interest organizations pressed charges on behalf of POWs still in captivity.[17] These accusations were leveled as late as 1961, when a potential offender was identified in a carnival procession in Cologne that was broadcast on television.[18]

The identity of the accusers varied widely and ran the gamut from former SS volunteers to German Communists. In a 1950 case, the SS volunteer Hermann R. presented himself as a victim of "crimes against humanity" and charged a fellow POW with denouncing him to Soviet authorities, which had then precipitated his prolonged internment.[19] Often, tangible bitterness over real experiences of hardship, suffering, and even death of a fellow POW in Soviet captivity informed these accusations. One Karl S., for example, blamed his former German capo in a work brigade in a Stalingrad POW camp for his physical deterioration that reduced his body weight from 140 to 88 pounds within less than three months.[20] If the accused had been involved in antifascist reeducation efforts, accusations also assumed an explicitly political bent. In the case of Franz G., a witness for the prosecution claimed to be solely motivated by the "worldwide danger of Communism" and the need to "observe and eliminate such unscrupulous mercenaries of Communism."[21] In at least one case, moreover, the accusation came from a former member of the German Communist Party who had been interned in Dachau and, from 1944 onward, in Auschwitz. After the liberation of the camp, he was captured by Red Army troops and treated like an ordinary German POW. He eventually blamed the head of the antifascist group and camp doctor, Dr. T., for denouncing him to Soviet authorities and pressed charges against him in January 1950, thus seeking justice for what was undoubtedly a very unhappy life story.[22]

Most defendants flatly rejected these allegations and sought to explain their actions in Soviet or Eastern European captivity. Former camp officials either completely denied any beating or abusing of fellow POWs or admitted only minor incidents of physical violence, which they then justified with the need to maintain camp discipline as well as with their accountability toward Soviet officials.[23] The leader of a work brigade, for example, claimed that Soviet authorities forced him to extract additional labor from already malnourished POWs.[24] Even if the defendants confessed grave mistreatment of fellow POWs, they evoked the "general conditions in the camp" as a mitigating circumstance for their behavior.[25] Similarly, defendants in denunciation cases either refuted the charges or argued that NKVD agents had coerced them into informing on fellow POWs.[26] Defendants with a compromised past as SS members or military judges claimed a "putative emergency" situation, which had allegedly left them no choice but to cooperate with Soviet authorities.[27]

For West German courts, these trials posed thorny logistic and legal problems. They needed to reconstruct events that had taken place years ago and in faraway places on the basis of often scarce and fragmentary testimonies. Moreover, the accusations of returnees by their former fellow POWs raised a series of difficult questions. Should former POWs be held responsible for actions that they had committed under the oppressive conditions of Soviet or Eastern European captivity? Did POWs act as a result of coercion by Soviet authorities and were thus entitled to the "privilege of necessity"? Did denunciations of POWs to Soviet authorities for war crimes have a factual basis? And if so, were POWs morally and legally entitled to inform Soviet authorities of these offenses? These logistic, moral, and legal difficulties were remarkably similar to the issues raised in trials of Nazi perpetrators. In both cases, courts needed to reconstruct past events on the basis of often limited evidence; and in both cases, courts were faced with exculpatory strategies of the defendants that cited coercion and oppression as mitigating if not exonerating circumstances.[28] Similar to the trials of Nazi perpetrators, the moral and legal issues at stake in the POWs trials assumed a larger symbolic significance that exceeded individual cases. As Peter Steinbach has argued with respect to Nazi trials, the "question of a diminished guilt simply as a result of external circumstances concerned, in essence, all Germans."[29] During the 1950s, however, West Germans found it easier to negotiate these complicated issues with reference to offenses that had occurred in faraway POWs camp rather than on their own doorsteps during the Nazi dictatorship.

The sociopolitical composition of the West German judiciary crucially shaped the manner in which courts approached the trials.[30] The incomplete denazification of the West German judiciary had left many former Nazis in their official positions as judges or prosecutors. By 1948, 80–90 percent of the judges in the British zone of occupation—from where most of the cases analyzed here are drawn—were former Nazi Party members.[31] Despite these continuities within the judicial system, the Federal Republic was founded on the rule of law. Individual guilt could only be established on the basis of clear and sufficient evidence. In prosecuting accused POWs, courts thus assembled as much evidence as possible, interrogating, as in one case, up to seventy witnesses.[32] Still, the evidence often remained inconclusive and left much room for interpretation. More so than in other criminal persecutions, the biases of judges and prosecutors influenced the conduct and outcome of the POW trials. To be sure, these biases did not necessarily consist of National Socialist sentiments, especially since jurists whose training reached back to the Weimar or even the imperial era occupied the leading positions in the West German judiciary. These judges and prosecutors often adhered to a conservative worldview dating back to the pre-1933 period, which, however, was also very compatible with the virulent anti-Communism of the Cold War.[33]

A central problem of the POW trials concerned the extent to which individual POWs could be held legally responsible for their actions under the coercive conditions in captivity. Courts did not arrive at a consistent position regarding this issue. In some cases, judges and prosecutors exhibited a remarkable empathy for the difficult position of German camp officials who needed to reconcile the conflicting demands of fellow POWs and Soviet authorities.[34] This was especially true when witnesses confirmed the defendants' efforts on behalf of other POWs.[35] Strenuous living conditions in the camp were then attributed not to the "German officials" but to the "Russian administration" of the camp.[36] Courts also counted noninvolvement in political reeducation efforts as a mitigating factor. When Erwin F., a former camp official who was accused of mistreating fellow POWs, stressed that he had "never participated in political schooling" and had "never been a propagandist in any camp," the prosecutor ascribed to him an "honorable character and attitude" and exculpated him of all the charges.[37]

In most cases, however, courts adopted a less understanding attitude and placed greater emphasis on the individual responsibility of German camp officials. Hans-Josef K., the leader of a work camp in Siberia, was sentenced to one year in prison for "bodily injury" in five cases. While the court recognized the defendant's difficult position as intermediary between Soviet authorities and German POWs, the judge argued that he could have employed alternative means such as "friendly words" or "engagement on behalf of other POWs" in order to fulfill Soviet work norms.[38] Courts also denied incriminated POWs mitigating circumstances in order to deter German camp officials still in Soviet captivity from resorting to violence.[39] Finally, in a 1952 decision, the Bundesgerichtshof (BGH), the highest legal authority for criminal and civil offenses, officially confirmed this stricter interpretation regarding the individual responsibility of German camp officials in Soviet captivity. The BGH denied that a former camp official had sufficiently evaluated whether the "infringement on the rights of others" had been "necessary in order to escape danger himself."[40]

The denial of mitigating circumstances to indicted returnees also resulted from the influence of external pressure groups such as the Association of Returnees (VdH). The VdH newspaper, *Der Heimkehrer*, reported regularly on ongoing POW trials and generally voiced harsh criticism if sentences appeared too lenient.[41] Courts also cooperated closely with the VdH in gathering evidence for the prosecution of accused POWs and in identifying potential witnesses.[42] The association maintained a special committee that provided expert testimony on conditions in Soviet captivity. In that function, VdH functionaries tended to emphasize the possibility of free choice and argued that any POW who had assumed an official function in captivity had done so voluntarily and was therefore fully responsible for his actions.[43] This uncompromising attitude stood in stark contrast to the leniency that the VdH and other pressure groups advocated toward convicted war criminals.[44] In general, West German courts and the West German public denied accused former POWs the extenuating circumstances that were routinely invoked in trials of Nazi perpetrators. In virtually every one of these trials, defendants accused of Nazi crimes claimed an emergency situation (*Befehlsnotstand*) to justify their actions, and courts often accepted these defenses. Judges and prosecutors tended to afford a greater degree of individual agency and, hence, legal accountability to German POWs in Soviet captivity than to Nazi perpetrators during the Third Reich. Inside and outside the courtroom, offenses that were committed under the Soviet dictatorship were evaluated more harshly than often more serious offenses committed under the Nazi dictatorship.[45]

This imbalance was also reflected in the respective sentences. Especially in the earlier POW trials, courts meted out rather harsh sentences, such as in the 1948 cases, when Adolf G. and Otto S. were sentenced to four and ten years in prison respectively.[46] The latter sentence was considerably higher than the one that the same court meted out in the first trial of concentration camp personnel in West Germany, the Kemmna trial, which had taken place parallel to Otto S.'s trial in 1949.[47] This is why, in 1955, the head of the Wuppertal prison petitioned the chief prosecutor to grant parole to Otto S. after he had served two thirds of his sentence. He substantiated this request with the concern "that [S.] would get the feeling that he had been judged according to political criteria."[48] Even after his release, however, Otto S.'s conviction for offenses committed in Soviet captivity weighed more heavily than a conviction for Nazi or war crimes. Otto S., for example, was automatically disqualified from receiving benefits according to the 1954 POW compensation law whereas the same benefits were routinely extended to convicted war criminals who had been interned by the Western allies.[49]

Apart from the problem of individual responsibility in coercive situations, the criminal prosecution of denunciations constituted another similarity between trials of POWs and of Nazi perpetrators. After Allied authorities had handed over most of the jurisdiction for Nazi crimes to German courts, denunciations to Nazi authorities represented one of the most contested problems of German criminal law. While the late 1940s saw quite vigorous prosecution of such offenses, the willingness of courts to prosecute these cases declined significantly by the early 1950s. According to Martin Broszat, "convictions only occurred when the consequences of these denunciations had been very drastic," while acquittals amounted to about 60 percent of the cases.[50] At the same time, courts began to devote increasing attention to denunciations in Soviet captivity. According to the BGH, such acts constituted a criminal offense because they extradited German citizens to "Russian military justice" that was incompatible with the "dominating legal sensibility in our cultural sphere" *(in unserem Kulturkreis herrschenden Rechtsempfinden).*[51] Courts thus saw the consequences of denunciations—deprivation of liberty or even death—as criminal offenses for which the denunciators could be held legally responsible.[52]

The practice of denunciation, moreover, was widely established among Wehrmacht soldiers and had been a driving force for the murderous extension of military justice.[53] It is therefore not surprising that German soldiers continued to resort to denunciations in Soviet captivity. This was true especially for those former soldiers who had assumed a more prominent role in the racial war of annihilation on the Eastern front. These soldiers faced a higher risk of being prosecuted by Soviet authorities for war crimes and hence were more susceptible to informing on their fellow POWs in captivity in order to escape prosecution themselves. At the same time, these former soldiers were likely to have witnessed, if not participated themselves in, German genocidal warfare. As a result, they were in a privileged position "to think and to narrate" stories of criminal transgressions on the Eastern front, regardless of whether their testimonies to Soviet authorities always identified the right culprits or not.[54]

The example of Franz K. is a case in point. He had volunteered for the Armed SS in the spring of 1940, had served as a member of the SS divisions Viking and Deathhead on the Eastern front beginning in 1941, and then fell into Soviet captivity in 1945. As a former SS member, he was at a high risk of being subjected to retaliation by Soviet authorities. As a result, he ultimately cooperated with Soviet investigators and accused Bernhard S., a fellow POW, of having executed 106 Jews in gas and torture chambers in the Kowno ghetto. Partly based on K.'s statement, Bernhard S. was convicted and sentenced to twenty-five years in prison and did not return from Soviet captivity until 1955. Upon his return, he charged Franz K. with denouncing him to the Soviet authorities. In the ensuing trial, Franz K. admitted that he had knowingly provided false testimony about Bernhard S., but he also claimed that Soviet NKVD agents had coerced him into collaboration. The courts, however, denied any emergency situation to K. and sentenced him to two and a half years in prison and forfeiture of citizenship for two years.[55]

Not all West German courts, however, denied the "privilege of emergency" to former informers in Soviet captivity. In 1960, the BGH overturned a 1954 decision of the Frankfurt district court and granted a "putative emergency situation" to Heinrich S., a high civil servant in Bonn and former military judge on the Eastern front. Heinrich S. confessed to having falsely accused Egon W. and Friedrich R. of participating in the execution of two hundred Russian civilians on the Eastern front. He justified this false testimony with his fear of Soviet punishment for the death sentences he had meted out to thirty members of a Russian Cossack unit who had subsequently been executed.[56] The BGH accepted this defense and argued that the defendant could not be held responsible for his actions. Ironically, it was precisely Heinrich S.'s rather compromised past on the Eastern front that ultimately served as the basis for his acquittal by the highest West German court.[57] In addition, courts exhibited a tangible bias in favor of middle-class defendants and witnesses like Heinrich S., and judges were probably also reluctant to mete out harsh sentences to a member of their own guild.[58]

Trials of denunciations in Soviet captivity not only negotiated past behavior in Soviet captivity but also addressed, at least indirectly, the violent transgressions of German soldiers on the Eastern front. Since the BGH recognized the obligation of witnesses to testify truthfully even before Soviet military courts, West German courts needed to clarify the factual basis of alleged denunciations in Soviet captivity.[59] In investigating these cases, West German judges and prosecutors needed to determine whether accusations of war crimes leading to Soviet convictions had, in fact, been true or not. Testimonies of participants in the trials—accusers, defendants, and witnesses—drew on the shared experience of participating in the war of annihilation on the Eastern front. Their stories often coalesced to a rather thick description of criminal transgression of German soldiers on the Eastern front. Thus, at a time when few West Germans wanted to address it, the violence associated with genocidal warfare entered West German courtroom through the back door of the POW trials.

Significantly, West German courts did not always succeed in proving that defendants had simply invented their testimonies on heinous war crimes in front of Soviet military courts.[60] And in one case, the Cologne district court actually confirmed that a German soldier had committed a war crime by tying three alleged Russian partisans to his tank and dragging them to death.[61] This case thus indirectly validated the Soviet verdict against a former Wehrmacht soldier and hence casts doubt on West German assertions—both then and now—that the Soviet convictions of German POWs were always unjustified.[62] While the POW trials yielded at least some evidence for criminal offenses of Wehrmacht soldiers against Russian civilians, POWs, and Jews on the Eastern front, West German courts rarely followed these leads. In contrast to the considerable energies West German judges and prosecutor invested in prosecuting crimes against German POWs in Soviet captivity, they were extremely reluctant to investigate or even prosecute criminal acts of German soldiers on the Eastern front.[63] This was clearly a deliberate omission that did not result from a mere lack of evidence. In one case, the court, for example, did not pursue unmistakable evidence that Adam H., the alleged victim of a denunciation to Soviet courts, had actually murdered his Jewish servant. This offense had not been part of his conviction by Soviet courts and hence did not interest the West German prosecutor.[64]

For much of the 1950s, the West German judiciary largely failed to capitalize on the availability of this kind of evidence. This judicial passivity was very much to the liking of former POWs as well as the public at large. Witnesses in the POW trials professed—undoubtedly because of their own involvement in criminal offenses on the Eastern front—that they "did not want to be brought into contact with this entire complex."[65] In addition, no former POW ever brought charges in a West German court against a former comrade for crimes committed during wartime rather than in postwar captivity.[66] Despite the evidence they produced on German war crimes on the Eastern front, the POW trials did not initiate a more comprehensive legal confrontation with this past and instead contributed to its increasing obfuscation.

Besides the dictates of a highly selective politics of memory, an equally important factor in shaping the trials consisted of the contemporary pressures of the Cold War. The POW trials did not take place in a vacuum but were crucially shaped by external political and ideological influences. In fact, as Martin Conway has argued, "historians have long seen in the records of judicial proceedings a privileged window into mentalities, structures, and internal tensions of diverse societies" precisely because the "definition and execution of justice is inextricably intertwined with, and molded by wider social and political forces."[67] This political dimension of some of these trials also did not remain hidden from contemporary observers. Writing in one of the most important West German legal journals, one commentator worried that the *Kameradenschinder* trials were inspired by "political antagonisms" and based on the "agitation of returnees, especially lawyers among them."[68] Accused returnees also often saw themselves as victims of a political campaign. A former antifascist activist, for example, castigated the charges against him as an attack on his "honor," "profession," and "family life."[69]

The most important external influence on the trials was the ideology of anti-Communism.[70] Yet anti-Communism shaped the trials not in overt and direct but in more subtle ways. After 1945, West German judges and prosecutors were extremely reluctant to employ explicitly political categories in legal proceedings. Instead, the reconstruction of the legal system in the Federal Republic was based on the central notion of its "depoliticization." It aimed to counter what was perceived as undue politicization of the law both during the Nazi dictatorship and during the occupation period.[71] This effort obscured the extent to which an allegedly apolitical legal positivism had facilitated the destruction of democracy before 1933. Still, in line with their efforts to keep politics out of the courtroom, judges and prosecutors refused to interpret the collaboration of German POWs with Soviet authorities as a consequence of explicitly political choices. In so doing, West German jurists sought to distance the POW trials from the simultaneous purges in East Germany. The prosecutor of the one of the first POW trials in 1949 publicly declared that he wanted "to avoid a show trial at all costs."[72] Rather than as outgrowth of political choices, courts tended to portray the actions of accused returnees as the result of pathological personality structures.

Several verdicts were explicitly based on the "characterization" or the "personality" of the defendants.[73] Judges argued that German POWs had collaborated with Soviet authorities solely from a desire to improve their living situation in captivity at the expense of fellow POWs. Defendants in the *Kameradenschinder* trials were thus described as having exhibited a "weak character" as well as "mean" and "reprehensible" behavior. They had followed "base urges" and had pursued "reprehensible goals."[74] In one case, the prosecutor did charge the antifascist activist and camp doctor Rudolf T. with excessive political activism that "went far beyond anything that was permissible among civilized peoples."[75] Yet in this case too, the prosecution linked the charge of political fanaticism to homosexuality and to possible morphine addiction, thus underlining the alleged pathologies of the defendant's personality.[76] Courts also employed questionable moral constructs as normative yardsticks. In the case of Hans-Josef K., for example, the court relied "to a particular extent" on "life experience, knowledge of human nature, and inference" in substantiating the verdict, while in another case the judge invoked the "moral principles of the general public" as the basis of his judgment.[77] The latter term eerily resembled the notion of the "healthy public sentiment" that had often served as the basis of the National Socialist practice of law. By deploying moral or psychological categories in their indictments and verdicts, West German judges and prosecutors individualized and depoliticized the behavior of German POWs in captivity.

Courts, however, were not alone in explaining the choices of accused returnees in captivity as outgrowth of pathological personality structures. Public commentators also argued that the reason for "failure in Soviet captivity" could be found "in the character of the respective persons." The observer just quoted, moreover, identified a more general "psychology of the *Kameradenschinder*" that, according to him, was not limited to "criminal natures" but had also affected "fathers, sons, and brothers of our own people. . . . colleagues in our professions and people in our daily lives."[78] In this view, the "torturer of comrades" became the "totalitarian enemy within" whose "name remained unknown" and whose identity—in clear reference to the difficulty of identifying assimilated Jews—could not be inferred from "physiognomic inferences."[79] Public commentators as well as judges and prosecutors, moreover, asserted a particular susceptibility of former Nazis to collaboration with Soviet authorities in captivity. Due to their shared pathological personality structures, the "local NS leader" (NS-Zellenleiter) was therefore most likely to become the "political educator" (Politbetreuer) in Soviet captivity.[80] In what Omer Bartov calls the larger process of "defining enemies" and "making victims," West German commentators constructed the collaborator in Soviet captivity as the "totalitarian other," who assumed the devious character traits of both "the Jew" and "the Nazi" as past and present "others."[81] This pathologization of alleged Kameradenschinder mirrored similar processes in the public representation of Nazi-perpetrators in the early 1950s, which also emphasized their primitive brutality and pathological sadism.[82] For the legitimacy of bourgeois reconstruction in West Germany, it was essential to draw clear boundaries between bourgeois values and violent perpetrators, thus obscuring the extent to which the popularity of the Nazi regime had been based on the appeal of these very bourgeois values of "order" and "cleanliness."[83]

The depoliticization of German POWs' behavior in captivity, however, served profoundly political purposes.[84] In particular, it delegitimized the antifascist organizations of German POWs such as the National Committee for a Free Germany (NKFD) and the League of German Officers (BdO) in Soviet captivity. Even though not all accused returnees had participated in these organizations and not all antifascist activists were charged with criminal offenses, antifascist activity featured as compromising fact in these trials. In 1955, Günter J., a founding member of the BdO in the Jelabuga POW camp, was charged with denouncing fellow POWs to Soviet authorities. When confronted with these allegations, Günter J. not only vehemently denied any wrongdoing but also defended his participation in NKFD and BdO as a form of resistance against Hitler. He asserted that he had not received any better treatment in Soviet captivity than ordinary POWs, and he cited his refusal to be repatriated to the Soviet zone of occupation in 1948 as evidence for his resistance to Soviet indoctrination efforts.[85] The prosecutor of the Bonn district court, however, completely discounted this defense. He portrayed the defendant as a "willing instrument in the hands of the Russians" who had not "refrained from making more difficult the life of his fellow inmates for purely egoistic reasons." According to the prosecution, Günter J. had acted "extremely abominably." Yet despite this moral condemnation, the prosecution failed to collect enough evidence that the defendant was actually guilty of any criminal offense. As a result, the prosecution dismissed the case.[86] Still, it demonstrated that the West German judiciary was unwilling to recognize any kind of collaboration with Soviet authorities as a legitimate form of resistance against Hitler—whether there was enough evidence for actual criminal offenses or not. Instead, the courts tended to portray any kind of disloyalty towards Hitler's army as a moral if not legal offense equaling treason and betrayal.

By pathologizing dissenting behavior in Soviet captivity, the POW trials promoted the notion of "comradeship" as a central, if highly ideological, component in West German memories of the Second World War. Several verdicts explicitly charged the defendants with having violated the bonds of "comradeship," which, according to one judge, had constituted the only "psychological support" for German POWs in Soviet captivity.[87] In this context, the ideal of comradeship not only stood for a "defensive community of suffering" but also for steadfastness in Soviet captivity.[88] The trials made clear that German POWs who had collaborated—for whatever reasons—with Soviet authorities disqualified themselves as "comrades." Courts, moreover, cast the violation of comradeship as a sign of deficient masculinity. Whereas ordinary POWs had displayed an "upright, manly attitude" and had resisted collaboration, cooperation with Soviet authorities was seen as giving in to personal desires for comfort and well-being and thus coded as feminine.[89] Postwar conceptions of masculinity, the trials demonstrated, were based not just on the redefinition of men's relationship to women but also on their relationship to other men. Moreover, by juxtaposing treacherous and feminized collaborators with virtuous and manly "comrades," the POW trials implied that firm allegiance to wartime beliefs and attitudes was the only ethically correct stance for German POWs in Soviet captivity. In so doing, the proceedings fostered and reflected the widespread assumption that German soldiers had remained aloof from National Socialist ideology all along, that they had served their country bravely and honorably, and that there was therefore no need to rethink their previous allegiances in Soviet captivity.[90]

While the trials clearly promoted the myth of the "clean Wehrmacht," they also reflected a gradual and subtle change toward military service from the late 1940s to the late 1950s. Verdicts of earlier trials interpreted lack of front experience as indication of the defendants' flawed character and of their insufficient preparation for withstanding the pressures in captivity.[91] By the late 1950s, however, military service no longer appeared as an unequivocally positive fact in POW trials. One of the last POW trials in 1957 targeted Hans-Dieter T., a former Wehrmacht officer with a distinguished military record that also included service in Hitler's headquarters. In 1949, Hans-Dieter T. had begun to serve as an interrogator in Yugoslavian captivity and allegedly extracted false confessions from fellow POWs. In 1955, four years after his return from captivity, he was sentenced to eighteen months in prison for aiding and abetting the deprivation of liberty.[92] A psychological evaluation still praised his "qualification as a brave and eager officer," yet also identified his military career as the source of his transgressions. As a "young professional soldier," he had been "destined to receive orders" from Yugoslav authorities; his "inflexible character" led him to live in a "military dream world," which prevented him from developing the "kind of thoughts that more complex and more sensitive human beings would have."[93] This case involved interrogating military values such as blind obedience to authority, and it indicated the ease with which traditional military virtues could be instrumentalized for totalitarian purposes. For the new West German army that began to recruit its new members at the time of Hans-Dieter T.'s trial, this case entailed important lessons. Unlike this veteran, the soldiers of the new army would not blindly "follow orders." Instead, they were to be "citizens in uniform" who were imbued with a firm set of democratic values and therefore immune to the totalitarian temptation.[94]

In spite of the efforts of judges and prosecutors to keep "politics" out of the courtroom, changing political and ideological contexts exerted a decisive influence on the POW trials. They were an integral part of the West German politics of memory by subordinating German violence to violence committed under the auspices of Communist dictatorships. Moreover, fueled by an implicit and often quite explicit anti-Communism, the proceedings pathologized dissenting behavior in Soviet captivity, thus preventing a more general debate on loyalty and resistance to the Nazi regime among former Wehrmacht soldiers. In this way, the trials used, in Otto Kirchheimer's words, "legal means for political ends," even though they differed "quantitatively and qualitatively" from the more blatant forms of political justice in East Germany.[95]

At the same time, the formal establishment of the rule of law imposed important constraints on the political instrumentalization of the courts in postwar West Germany. The courts were not simply the handmaidens of political interest, nor were these interests always completely monolithic. In January 1955, for example, the West German Foreign Office attempted to intervene in a planned trial of returnees from a Yugoslav POW camp. Diplomats worried that the trial might undermine the Federal Republic's relations with the only non-Stalinist country in Eastern Europe. As a result, they sought to pressure—unsuccessfully in the end—the Munich district court to postpone the trial.[96] Many investigations of accused returnees, moreover, did not lead to a trial because prosecutors simply failed to marshal enough evidence for an indictment, even though the investigations themselves sent a clear political message and often threatened the standing of the accused returnee in the local community.[97] Still, even if the accused returnees were tried in court, the trials often ended with an acquittal.[98]

Such outcomes also derived from the more general thrust toward amnesty in postwar West Germany that ended or least severely limited *any* judicial confrontation with the past. In several cases, courts actually concluded that defendants had been guilty of criminal offenses, yet acquitted them on the basis of the 1949 amnesty law. This was one of the first laws that the new West German parliament passed with a large majority. It aimed at exonerating all offenses that were to be punished with less than six months in prison. As Norbert Frei has shown, this amnesty served to exonerate "tens of thousands" of smaller and not so small Nazi offenders who had committed bodily injuries and even manslaughter during the Nazi dictatorship.[99] The same law, however, was also applied to POWs whose sentence was expected to remain below six months in prison.[100] Thus, the contradictory yet equally formative tendencies of anti-Communism and amnesty shaped the POW trials during the early Federal Republic.

Cleansing East German Antifascism: The Purge of Returnees from the West

In East Germany, exclusionary practices were part of the widespread purges that swept all Eastern European Communist parties during the late 1940s and early 1950s. The purges crucially contributed to the Sovietization of Eastern Europe by firmly establishing the dominance of a Stalinist leadership within the parties.[101] In East Germany, the purges were also an essential element of the SED's transformation into a Leninist "party of the new type."[102] They targeted those party members who resisted the increasing Stalinization of the SED, primarily former Social Democrats but also long-standing Communists, who had survived the war in Nazi captivity or in Western emigration.[103] The purges undoubtedly eliminated existing oppositional tendencies within the SED, and they ensured the dominance of the group of former Moscow emigrants around Walter Ulbricht and Wilhelm Pieck. But they also served as a crucial element of disciplining and terrorizing the party membership by inventing largely fictitious tales of political deviance and foreign subversion. These accusations were also supposed to distract attention from material hardship and economic difficulties associated with the introduction of the first Two-Year-Plan in 1948.[104]

The party agency in charge of the purges was the Central Party Control Commission (ZPKK). Founded in 1948 under the leadership of the Moscow émigré Hermann Matern, the ZPKK investigated alleged cases of political deviance and meted out punishment to purge victims. Sanctions included removal from certain key positions within the state and party bureaucracy or exclusion from the party altogether. In many cases, allegations of political opposition were linked to criminal charges of espionage or corruption that then could lead to arrest, imprisonment, and, in some cases, deportation to Siberia. It is difficult to establish how many East Germans fell victim to the purges. Estimates for the number of persecuted Social Democrats amount to five thousand arrests and four hundred deaths. Between December 1950 and December 1951, official SED membership figures dropped from 1,537,000 to 1,256,000.[105] The purges also significantly changed the composition of the SED. By 1952, only 15.9 percent of SED members had been affiliated with left-wing parties (only 6.5 percent with the SPD) before 1933, whereas 19 percent of the party membership consisted of former members of the Nazi Party (NSDAP) or of one of its branches. Thus, the purges transformed the SED from an antifascist mass party to the new party for the former followers of the Nazi regime.

Former POWs returning from Western or Yugoslav captivity to East Germany were not the most significant group that came under the purview of the ZPKK, nor did they suffer the most serious consequences among the victims of the purges. Still, the purge of returnees from the West constituted the functional East German counterpart to the POW trials in the West.[106] Both forms of exclusions reshaped experiences of war and captivity according to the new ideological antagonisms of the Cold War. Thus, on both sides of the gradually descending "iron curtain," previous wartime cooperation and contacts now increasingly assumed the odium of espionage, subversion, and treason.[107] This exclusion of returnees from the West from the antifascist tradition was by no means a foregone exclusion. During the early postwar period, East German officials saw "antifascist" (i.e., Communist or Socialist) POWs in Western captivity as an important future cadre resource for the SED, and they underlined the antifascist activities of POWs in Western captivity.[108] In March 1946, the SED official Kurt Ziegenhagen recounted his struggle "not just against fascism but also against capitalism" in French and American captivity. He concluded that "we can proudly say that we upheld the flag of the party far away from home and despite terror" and that "through our tireless efforts, we succeeded in integrating thousands of comrades and especially our youth into the antifascist unity front."[109]

By 1948, however, the emerging Cold War gave rise to paranoid fear of espionage and foreign subversion in East and West. Fantastic tales of Western agents and omnipresent foreign subversion as they were presented at the Budapest show trial of the Hungarian party leader, László Rajk, in September 1949 provided the spark for the purge of returnees from the West in East Germany. In October 1949, only two weeks after the founding of the GDR, the ZPKK and its regional branches began to screen all state and party officials who had spent more than three months in Western or Yugoslavian captivity. In particular, the PKKs targeted those former POWs who had participated in reeducation courses at one of the POW schools on American and British soil. These schools, as the PKK charged, had exerted a "corrupting" influence on German POWs and served as "training grounds for spies."[110] In addition, Tito's defection from the Soviet bloc in 1948 subjected returnees from Yugoslavia to increased ideological scrutiny by the PKK. According to the PKK, there were "comrades from Yugoslavian captivity who have been influenced by developments in Yugoslavia and thus got into opposition to our principal policies."[111] PKK officials thus noted that among all captivities "American and English captivity" as well as "the later Yugoslavian captivity" were the most dangerous—a finding that, according to these party officials, precisely corresponded to the "position of the individual powers within the larger camp of world imperialism."[112]

The screenings involved initially a secret evaluation of the personnel file of the targeted persons followed by a personal interview with PKK officials.[113] These procedures aimed at gaining a "comprehensive picture of [Western] emigration and [Western] captivity." In particular, officials were looking for "forms of political corruption" among returnees from the West as well as "political indoctrination," "opportunism in all its variants," "moral and political disorientation by commissioned agents," and "personal and collective ties to the imperialist civil and military administration." The PKKs moreover, not only scrutinized returnees' behavior during war and captivity, but also looked for any indication of political deviance before, during, and after the Nazi period. Any "membership in opposition groups before and after 1933" thus made returnees from the West appear even more suspicious. In addition, PPK officials saw returnees' "political and moral behavior" in the East German reconstruction effort as an important clue to their present ideological and political beliefs.[114]

These considerable efforts, however, yielded rather modest results. In May 1950, the ZPKK reported that it had investigated 4,068 returnees from Western emigration or captivity who occupied positions within the state and party apparatus; 91.4 percent of them had spent more than three months in Western captivity. Among them, the PKK formulated "reservations" or "strong reservations" about 344 persons, which equaled 1 in 18 screened individuals within the state apparatus and 1 in 7 within the party apparatus.[115] The regional PKK in Brandenburg investigated 850 personnel files of government officials, interviewed 117, and developed "reservations" or "strong reservations" about 27 persons.[116] Most of these individuals were removed from their positions in the state and party bureaucracy, although in several cases, they were assigned positions in politically less sensitive areas. Still, emigration or captivity in the West remained a permanent stain on the victims' biography and undermined their future careers in East Germany.

Although returnees from the West accounted for only a small section of the victims of the East German purges, their purge from state and party bureaucracies denoted the remaking of the antifascist tradition in East Germany. The ascendancy of a Moscow-centered master narrative of antifascism went along with an increasing marginalization of alternative antifascist traditions. Concurrently with the official propagation of Soviet captivity as antifascist conversion at the *Heimkehrer* conferences, the purges cleansed the official antifascism from any contamination with antifascist experiences in the West (or in Yugoslavia).[117] As a result, antifascist returnees from the West and from Yugoslavia, many of them with a long-standing allegiance to the Social Democratic or Communist parties, found it increasingly difficult to have their experiences of war and captivity integrated into official East German memories.

The purges often invalidated a lifelong dedication to left-wing parties and years of antifascist struggle in war and captivity. For the Communist Wilhelm G., participation in a three-month reeducation course in the antifascist school in Fort Ghetty, Rhode Island, was sufficient to nullify more than twenty years of membership in the Communist Party. He had joined the KPD in 1927 and worked in the illegal resistance movement against the Nazis beginning in 1933. He had been imprisoned by the Nazis between 1939 and 1941 and was drafted into the army in 1943. In American captivity, he had reportedly maintained his Communist convictions and was denied early repatriation because of his "Marxist discussion style." Despite G.'s "good illegal past," however, the PKK advocated his removal from party positions and his transfer to a People-Owned Company for "reasons of principle."[118]

The PKK also claimed to have uncovered large-scale conspiracies of former returnees from Western and Yugoslavian captivity. Members of a "platform group" of former antifascist POWs at the American reeducation school in Fort Devens, who now occupied party positions within the SED district association in Leipzig, were charged with being "American agents" often "denouncing and slandering" the Soviet Union and the Red Army. Similarly, the PKK charged one Herbert F. in the Interior Ministry in Thuringia with systematically hiring fellow POWs from Yugoslavian captivity. According to the PKK, he had displayed his "opportunism" through his membership in the SPD since 1920 and continued to diverge from the party line through his membership in the organization New Beginning.[119] For the PKK, it was therefore "absolutely impossible" that "people who had been actively engaged on behalf of the political business of the Tito bandits" could be employed in "responsible positions of the state apparatus of our GDR."[120] As these examples indicated, the East German purges rewrote individual and collective biographies from a story of lifelong dedication to the Communist Party or years of antifascist resistance during the Third Reich into a history of political deviance and collaboration with "Western imperialists."

A particularly telling (and tragic) case of shifting attitudes toward antifascist returnees from the West concerned the former members of the Penal Battalion 999. This battalion was put together between October 1942 and August 1944 from inmates of concentration camps in order to augment Nazi Germany's manpower resources.[121] Units of Battalion 999 were deployed in Africa, in the Balkans and, to a lesser extent, on the Eastern front. Many members of these battalions seized the first opportunity to desert to enemy lines and then resumed antifascist activities in American or British captivity, often against the resistance of committed Nazis among German POWs.[122] In 1949, East German officials estimated that among twenty-four thousand members of Battalion 999, twelve thousand had been political prisoners, of whom three to four thousand had returned.[123] Initially, SED officials identified "999ers" as an antifascist cadre resource and actively worked for their release to the Eastern zone.[124] In August 1946, the SED leadership in Saxony reminded party officials that a "large section of the Battalion 999 is politically trained" and that "none of these valuable comrades must get lost [for the party]."[125] Party officials promoted an unequivocally positive evaluation of the antifascist record. They underlined that "antifascist '999ers' [in Western captivity] had remained faithful to their ideas and their tasks despite terror and resistance" and had tirelessly pursued their goal of "educating the people for democracy and preparing them for socialism."[126] To East German officials, returnees from the Battalion 999 offered one of the few bright spots in what otherwise appeared as a catastrophic recent history. Consequently, the SED tried to make propagandistic use of 999ers in order to bolster its claim for moral and political leadership in the Eastern zone.[127]

By early 1947, however, the official attitude toward Battalion 999 began to change, and party officials started to view 999ers much more critically. In March 1947, officials highlighted the criminal past of some returning members of the battalion, characterizing them as "bootlickers" and "notorious drinkers."[128] But party officials also increasingly doubted the political reliability of 999ers and distinguished between "recommendable" and "uncertain 999s." One Georg N., for example, was characterized as a "strong opportunist" because he did not immediately return to the Soviet zone; a second former member of the battalion, Oskar H., was deemed a "typical Trotskyist" due to his membership in a Communist opposition group before 1933, while a third returnee was described as a "controversial personality" because he had joined the SPD rather than the KPD after 1945.[129] Such more critical attitudes ultimately also applied to the battalion as a whole. In April 1948, party officials commissioned a historical study that was supposed to document "the reasons for the formation of the 999ers, their peculiar conspiratorial methods, their common struggle with partisans against fascists, and their work in POW camps."[130] While this project still appeared to celebrate the battalion's record of antifascist resistance, it could also easily be turned into an investigation of 999ers' political record in war and captivity.

An anonymous and undated "political-critical" analysis of the Battalion 999 illuminated the outcome of this officially sponsored revisionism. The author seems to have been a former member of Battalion 999 himself, who now set out to demonstrate his own political reliability by destroying the "legend" of the "heroic history" of the 999ers that had been "created primarily by our émigré comrades in the United States."[131] This author rewrote the battalion's history from one of antifascist resistance under extremely difficult circumstances to a story of persistent ideological failure and political errors. According to him, many 999ers harbored pervasive doubts regarding the "question of Russia" and had been sympathetic to opposition left-wing groups during the Weimar Republic. Their ideological unreliability also manifested itself in American and British captivity when many members of the battalion allegedly overestimated the possibilities of cooperation with "American bourgeois democracy" and misperceived the "two-sided nature of the war" as a "war against fascism as well as capitalism." While attitudes toward the United States had indeed been contested among Communist and non-Communist members of Battalion 999, the larger antifascist alliance against Nazi Germany had justified such cooperation during the war.[132] In the new climate of the Cold War, however, the memory of this cooperation became increasingly incompatible with Soviet-centered narratives of World War II. Finally, this author did not shy away from resorting to traditional anti-Semitic stereotypes in discrediting the antifascist activity of 999ers in captivity. According to him, "Jewish emigrants of German descent" who were serving in the U.S. Army had tried to lure 999ers into military service for the Western allies; members then displayed a "spineless" and a "slavish attitude" toward the United States. The recourse to traditionally anti-Semitic code words anticipated an element of the purges that was to come into the open more fully during the "anticosmopolitan" campaign in 1952–53 and the concurrent show trial of the former leader of the Czech Communist Party, Rudolf Slánsky.[133]

How did individual returnees respond to the party's attack on their antifascist pasts? It bespeaks the tremendous loyalty especially of veteran

Communists to the party cause that many of them generally accepted the charges of political deviation.[134] In some cases, returnees from the West accepted the official party line but denied any individual implication in foreign subversion while denouncing fellow POWs. One graduate of the British reeducation school at Wilton Park declared, for example, that he "had only recently gained knowledge that former Wilton Park students let themselves be misused as espionage instruments." He insisted that he had not signed anything at Wilton Park and did not maintain any contacts with fellow graduates, but also conceded that these "saboteurs of the peaceful reconstruction in the GDR" had discredited all POWs who had "unknowingly" become Wilton Park students.[135] Collaboration and denunciation was one strategy to cope with the PKK's allegations; downplaying the accusations was another one. As a PKK report from Brandenburg stated, almost all the interviewed returnees from the West sought to portray their captivity experience as "politically insignificant," because they were afraid to lose their positions.[136] Others finally chose to keep secret their participation in reeducation courses in American or British captivity—a strategy that automatically cost them their positions if PKK officials found out about it.[137]

Some accused returnees from the West, however, also courageously challenged the underlying assumptions of the purges. In May 1950, Fritz B. from Dresden sent an angry letter to the SED party executive committee portraying himself as one of the "pitiable antifascists" who had been sent to the Western front by Hitler's High Command. Since he did not want to shoot anybody for Hitler, he seized the first opportunity to desert to the British army and subsequently attended the first reeducation course at Wilton Park in January 1946. While he was "still proud of the work at Wilton Park," which he had performed under "difficult conditions," he bitterly complained about the PKK's reservations, which prevented him from assuming a position in the Ministry of Education. "Had I known what the party had in store for me," he argued, "I would not have made myself known as an antifascist" in British captivity. In another letter to the ZPKK in November 1950, he adopted a somewhat more cautious tone and indicated a limited acceptance of the purge's legitimacy. But he still defied the "irresponsible" and "superficial" view that everybody who was "forced to fight fascism from the West rather than from the East" bore the odium of being a "Western agent."[138] While it is not clear how this case ended, it demonstrated the tremendous disillusionment and frustration that came with the streamlining of official antifascism in East Germany.

The West German POW trials and the East German purges exhibited significant procedural differences, and they also yielded different results. In the West, an at least formally independent judiciary conducted the trials; they were initiated by individual accusations of former POWs and pursued by sympathetic prosecutors and judges. The trials, moreover, employed individualized notions of guilt that allowed prosecution and sentencing only if there was sufficient evidence. By contrast, the purges in the East were state-sponsored prosecutions that were instigated "from above" by the leadership of the Communist Party. Unlike the West German trials, the purges were based on collectivized notions of guilt that saw mere contact with real or imagined enemies as grounds for political suspicion and prosecution.

Notwithstanding these important differences, the trial and the purges were part of parallel exclusionary mechanisms in the two postwar societies. Both forms of exclusion narrowed the range of politically acceptable biographies in East and West Germany. They aligned East and West German memories of war and captivity with the new ideological parameters of the Cold War. In the West, the trials contributed to the myth of the "clean Wehrmacht" by pathologizing and criminalizing any effort to withdraw loyalty from the armies of Nazi Germany in Soviet or Eastern European captivity. The East German purges, on the other hand, eliminated alternative antifascist traditions and secured the dominance of a Moscow-centered narrative of antifascism. Increasingly homogeneous official narratives left no room for either the BdO member Günter J., who saw his activities in captivity as a form of resistance against Hitler, nor for the antifascist returnee Fritz B., who declared that he had fought Hitler "from the West rather than from the East." As a result, both the trials and the purges served, in the words of Charles Maier, "to inhibit dissent" and "narrow the limits of political discussion."[139]

Exclusionary practices in East and West employed different means to define dissent and marginalize nonconformity: in the West, legal and public discourse "depoliticized" German POWs' choices in captivity by describing them in terms of moral or psychological categories. In so doing, West German legal positivism foreclosed any space for the recognition of legitimate political resistance to Hitler among German POWs. The East German purges, by contrast, saw the behavior of returnees from the West as exclusively determined by the political contexts in Soviet captivity. This belief in the formative and corrupting influence of the larger political context reflected East German Communists' own traumatic experience with the susceptibility of the German working class to political indoctrination during the Nazi period. Yet the SED also counted precisely on this malleability in its efforts to reshape the former members of the Nazi *Volksgemeinschaft* into citizens of the antifascist-democratic order.

Far from obscuring the crucial differences between democracy in the West and dictatorship in the East, the comparison between the trials and the purges points to functional similarities of two postwar and postfascist societies in the context of the Cold War. While POW trials illustrated the limits of legitimate political discourse in West Germany, the comparison with the East also highlights the distinct accomplishments of the Bonn republic. Because the Federal Republic was based on the "rule of law," marginalization and pathologization of politically deviant behavior did not necessarily translate into criminalization or political persecution. In light of the Nazi past and against the background of the SED's totalitarian ambitions in the East, this was no small achievement.

PART THREE

Divergent Paths

CHAPTER 7

Absent Presence: Missing POWs and MIAs, 1950–1955

On 5 May 1950, almost exactly five years after the unconditional surrender of the German army, the Soviet news agency TASS announced the end of POW repatriation from the Soviet Union. According to TASS, the Soviet Union had repatriated 1,939,063 German POWs since 1945, while 13,536 German POWs remained in custody because they had been convicted of war crimes or were awaiting trial for the same offense.[1] More recent research, however, tallies 34,000 German POWs convicted in Soviet captivity between 1948 and August 1950. The motivation for these trials was primarily Soviet fears that repatriated POWs might provide crucial information to Western intelligence or contribute to the remilitarization of West Germany.[2] The trials generally did not live up to Western legal standards and often used mere membership in military formations as justification for high sentences of up to twenty-five years. This does not mean that the trials did not also target perpetrators who had committed crimes in the war of annihilation on the Eastern front.[3]

East and West German responses to the TASS announcement differed widely. In the West, vehement protest erupted across the political spectrum (with the exception of the KPD), whereas in the East, the SED made the TASS position its own. In the aftermath of the TASS announcement, East and West German authorities increasingly employed the POW issue in the propaganda battles of the early Cold War. Despite sharp divergences in East and West German responses to the end of POW repatriations, the common preoccupation with missing POWs and MIAs in East and West reflected the shared "postwar" nature of both societies. Throughout the first half of the 1950s, West Germans insisted on the incompleteness of a postwar society that was still awaiting the return of hundreds of thousands of POWs. East German authorities took the opposite position and asserted that the TASS announcement signaled the completion of the postwar body politic. These divergent stances shaped commemorative practices in both Germanys, and they gave rise to different kinds of tensions between the authorities and family members of missing soldiers. In the West, the strong public presence of absent POWs and MIAs increased domestic political pressures on the Adenauer government to pursue a more proactive policy on behalf of the release of the POWs.

In the East, by contrast, the official assertion of a completed postwar society ran counter to the privately held hopes of many East Germans that a missing family member might still be alive and perhaps return from Soviet captivity.

"Incomplete" or "Complete"? East and West German Responses to the End of POW Repatriations

West Germans responded to the TASS announcement with utter shock, disbelief, and vehement protest. The TASS announcement shattered the hopes of ordinary Germans that hundreds of thousands of soldiers missing on the Eastern front might still return. Upon learning of the TASS declaration, Chancellor Adenauer interrupted an ongoing parliamentary debate and charged that the TASS statement left unclear the "the fate of 1.5 million POWs."[4] This number conflicted with the results of a national registration of POWs and MIAs from two months earlier, which had yielded 61,244 POWs, 161,668 missing civilian internees, and 1,068,089 MIAs.[5] Thus, Adenauer could only arrive at his number by conflating the categories of POWs and MIAs—a fallacy that had originated in Nazi efforts to disguise actual casualty figures and continued to shape public discussions of missing soldiers throughout the early 1950s. By implying that all MIAs were still alive and held in the Soviet Union, the chancellor clearly misled the public.

Adenauer, to be sure, was by far not the only West German official to publicly inflate numbers of POWs in response to the TASS announcement. An SPD press release described the withholding of 700,000 POWs "who had committed no crime except for being German" as the "largest war crime that has ever been committed in peacetime."[6] The West German Foreign Office, too, confounded POWs and MIAs by estimating that 450,000 German POWs were still alive. This figure also appeared in the West German government's official protest note against the TASS declaration to the Allied High Commission.[7] Even outspoken experts on POW issues such as the SPD parliamentary deputy Hans Merten suggested in October 1950 that beyond those POWs whose names were already known, "200,000 to 300,000 POWs are still expected to return from Soviet captivity."[8] Newspaper commentators joined this official protest, expressing their outrage in terms resonant with the language of annihilation and mass death. The liberal weekly *Die Zeit* denounced the TASS statement as a virtual "death sentence for half a million German POWs."[9] Another paper labeled the TASS declaration "Moscow's atomic bomb" and bemoaned that it had "wiped out the existence of at least half a million German POWs."[10] Extending the public protest to the local level, the city council of Ulm passed a resolution against the inhumane confinement of German POWs by the Soviet Union.[11]

These protests against the alleged captivity of hundreds of thousands POWs served profoundly political purposes.[12] Not surprisingly, the TASS declaration fueled West German anti-Communism. According to the SPD chairman, Kurt Schumacher, the "TASS declaration, if true, would render impossible any kind of Communist politics in Germany."[13] In the aftermath of the TASS announcement, initiatives to outlaw the West German Communist Party gained new currency. In 1950–51, the Bundestag passed a series of laws that severely restricted Communist activity in West Germany.[14] As a result, it became virtually impossible to hold dissenting views on German POWs. In 1952, a KPD member was sentenced to four months in prison because he declared publicly, with explicit reference to the TASS declaration, that all remaining German POWs in the Soviet Union were "war criminals."[15]

Not surprisingly, the alleged withholding of hundreds of thousands of German POWs quickly became a weapon in the propaganda battles of the Cold War. Just as it did in the domestic politics of memory, the issue of missing POWS served a defensive function on the international scene: West Germans could fend off accusations of guilt by the victors of the war by portraying themselves as victims of (postwar) Soviet inhumanity. One press article deployed this very logic, arguing that the "mass murder of German POWs" deprived the Soviet Union of any right to pass judgment on the "deeds of Hitler."[16] Yet the ideological battles of the Cold War did not fully account for the emotional intensity of West Germans' protests against the TASS announcement. The tenacious belief that hundreds of thousands of POWs might still return from Soviet captivity also reflected a profound refusal to come to terms with the human losses of the Second World War. The notion of "secret camps" (*Schweigelager*) in the Soviet Union, in particular, encapsulated this popular inability to accept the true consequences of total defeat. The "secret camp" was one of the central myths of the Cold War. It stipulated that hundreds of thousands of German POWs were still held in complete isolation and without the opportunity to contact their family members in Soviet camps. West German officials as well as the news media constantly invoked this idea to explain the discrepancy between Soviet figures and their own estimates of the number of German POWs.[17] The existence of very few individual cases in which returnees had indeed been unable to write from Soviet captivity additionally fueled the popular belief that hundreds of thousands of German POWs were still experiencing the same fate in the Soviet Union.[18]

What made the idea of the "silent camp" so popular was the way it helped to absorb the losses of the Second World War into the rhetoric and

ideology of the Cold War. Given the prevailing anti-Communist sentiment, West Germans were ready to charge the Soviet Union with any
conceivable inhumanity.[19] At the same time, the myth of the secret camps
allowed West Germans to deny the finality of their own losses. The belief
in the existence of silent camps made it possible for West Germans to
maintain at least a flicker of hope that a missing family member was still
alive and might eventually return home. As such, the myth of the silent
camp in essence served a function comparable to the propagandistic ma-
nipulation of casualty figures during the last years of Nazi period: it protected ordinary Germans from the full realization of their wartime losses.

Widespread popular hopes for the return of hundreds of thousands of
POWs from the Soviet Union persisted even when West German officials
began to revise their numbers for POWs. In January 1952, Chancellor
Adenauer lowered his estimate to 106,000 German POWs in the Soviet
Union, and even this figure was immediately contested by the head of the
Foreign Office of the Protestant church, Martin Niemöller, who asserted
there were no more than 60,000 German POWs still held in captivity."[20]
Some months later, the SPD POW expert Hans Merten offered an even
lower estimate of 45,000 POWs.[21] Along the same lines, West German
officials also began to debunk the myth of the silent camps. In July 1951,
the Ministry of Expellees and the Protestant Aid Society issued a warning
against "uncontrollable rumors regarding so-called secret camps in the
Soviet Union."[22] And in January 1954, the respectable *Frankfurter Allgemeine Zeitung* declared unmistakably: "There are no silent camps."[23]
But popular attitudes did not change as swiftly as official proclamations,
and many West Germans resolutely held onto their belief in silent camps.
Even ten years after the unconditional surrender of the Wehrmacht, ordinary Germans clung to the conviction that hundreds of thousands of soldiers might still return from Soviet captivity. On the eve of Adenauer's
trip to Moscow in 1955, which was supposed to bring about the release
of the last POWs, 27 percent of all West Germans expressed their hopes
for the return of one or several family members, another 73 percent questioned the accuracy of Soviet figures of German POWs, and 27 percent
estimated that more than 100,000 remained in Soviet captivity.[24] At that
time, West German officials were certain of the existence of no more than
8,477 POWs in Soviet captivity.[25]

East German responses to the end of POW repatriations were diametrically opposed to Western ones. Whereas West Germans insisted on the
"incompleteness" of postwar society and vigorously questioned the Soviet
numbers, East German officials employed the TASS announcement to declare the end of the direct consequences of the Second World War. As
early as January 1950, Soviet authorities had informed the SED leadership
about the impending end of POW repatriations. In the spring of 1950,

the SED began to dismantle the entire organizational apparatus for the reception of returning POWs in East Germany.[26] In so doing, the party made clear that it expected no further returnees from the Soviet Union and concurred with the Soviet characterization of missing POWs as "war criminals." The TASS announcement, moreover, followed on the heels of the release of 14,400 inmates from the last Soviet-run internment camps in Buchenwald, Sachsenhausen, and Bautzen.[27] To East German officials, both events—the end of POW repatriation from the Soviet Union and the closing of internment camps—marked the completion of the East German body politic. In this view, the Waldheim trials, which resulted in the conviction of 3,324 internees for Nazi crimes, represented the East German equivalent of the Soviet trials of German POWs in 1949–50.[28] According to this official perception, POWs or internees who had not returned by May 1950 were no longer alive or, alternatively, became ineligible for membership in the community of "antifascist-democratic" citizens on account of their past or present political offenses.

East German authorities' attempt to terminate the consequences of the war by decree did not remain uncontested, though. The official claim to a "completed" postwar society not only stood in contrast to the West German insistence on the "incompleteness" of postwar society. It also ran counter to the intense longing of ordinary East Germans for the return of missing family members. Concurrent with its preparations for the arrival of the last POW transports in January 1950, the SED leadership instructed the "mass agitation" division of the party to organize a campaign against the "lies" of the Western press regarding POWs in the Soviet Union.[29] By December, the Politburo had established a specific committee to counter the "agitation" relating to the POW question.[30] Conversely, East German counterpropaganda made it more difficult for West German officials to arrive at a realistic assessment of the number of POWs still held in the Soviet Union. In the West, any public statement that drastically reduced estimates for the number of POWs in the Soviet Union ran the risk of being discredited as aiding and abetting Communist propaganda.[31] While the public discussion of the POW issue put East German officials on the defensive, its politicization during the Cold War also constrained the West German ability to arrive at a realistic assessment of wartime losses. Such were the dialectics of the German-German confrontation with the shared legacies of defeat at the height of the Cold War.

The activities of tracing services in East and West also reflected distinct approaches to dealing with this shared past. In the West, a multiplicity of public and private organizations emerged in all four occupation zones and helped search for missing soldiers and POWs in the East.[32] These organizations gained in effectiveness once they were centralized under the auspices of the German Red Cross in Munich in January 1950. The Munich Tracing Service was instrumental in processing, with the help of early forms of computerization, the results of the national POW registrations in March 1950. Among other things, it produced a list of all POWs who were still writing from Soviet captivity. In addition, the Munich bureau undertook extensive efforts to determine the fate of MIAs on the Eastern front. Throughout the 1950s, it cooperated closely with veterans' associations, presenting lists of MIAs at veterans' meetings and directly consulting approximately 290,000 returnees. By 1958, the tracing service had produced two hundred volumes with pictures of missing soldiers that were distributed to local Red Cross bureaus. Between 1958 and 1965, representatives of the search service also visited 178 West German local districts, interviewing a total of 2.6 million former soldiers. In the end, the results of these considerable organizational efforts remained limited. They did not clarify the fate of the vast majority of more than one million MIAs. It was not until 1966 that the Red Cross began to compile final reports on each case, which informed family members that their missing relative had most likely been killed on the Eastern front.[33]

The tracing services were crucial in facilitating millions of family reunions in the aftermath of war and defeat, and they were indicative of an emerging liberal society to which the fate of every individual mattered.[34] But the very visible activities of these organization also delayed the process of accepting wartime losses into the mid-1960s and beyond. Tracing services operated on the assumption that in the absence of any conclusive proof of death either on the battlefield or in POW camps, "everything remained unclear."[35] This reluctance to resolve individual cases once and for all surely fueled popular hopes that some or many of the missing soldiers might still be alive. Many ordinary Germans were loath to abandon these hopes. Throngs of crooks, fortune-tellers, and outright swindlers, who claimed to be able to provide information about a missing soldier or even to liberate him—for a considerable fee—from a silent camp in the Soviet Union, found ample opportunity for employment not just immediately after the war but throughout the 1950s.[36] As much as the activities of these organizations helped Germans to clarify individual fates, they were also indicative of a society that refused to accept the finality of its wartime losses.

If West Germans engaged in myriad efforts to trace missing POWs and MIAs, East German authorities sought to curtail precisely those activities. A centralized tracing service had been established in the Eastern zone as early as July 1945, but its activities were confined to helping returning POWs and expellees to find their family members in postwar Germany. Unlike the West German tracing service, its East German counterpart was prohibited from searching for missing soldiers and POWs in the Soviet Union. To East German officials, any offering of hope that MIAs would be found on the Eastern front threatened to become politically disruptive. Whereas in the West efforts to research the fate of missing soldiers only began in the early 1950s, the East German tracing service terminated its activities in March 1951.[37] As a result, many East Germans turned to the West German tracing service to investigate the fate of a missing family member on the Eastern front.[38] Thus, the abolition of the institutional structures for dealing with the consequences of the war did not terminate the significance of these consequences in the private lives of East Germans.

Similar differences shaped official practices in issuing death certificates for missing soldiers in East and West. In the West, the absence of a formal peace treaty invalidated a 1939 law, which stipulated that soldiers missing in action could be pronounced dead one year after the conclusion of a peace treaty. But most West German states wanted to make it possible to apply for a death certificate of a missing family member after 1 July 1949.[39] In January 1951, a new federal law went into effect that coordinated the different state practices and made it possible to issue death certificates for soldiers missing in action and POWs if they had not send any news after 1 July 1948. If there was evidence that a missing person was interned, this period was extended to five years.[40] In light of widely circulating rumors about silent camps, these plans triggered grave anxieties about "irreversible moral and material damage" that might result from false death certificates.[41] Newspaper reports about individual cases, in which former POWs who had been presumed death did indeed return, fostered these concerns.[42] In reality, however, there were only seventy-five such cases between 1950 and 1953.[43] Still, West German officials put up various bureaucratic obstacles in order to "delay the issuing of death certificates for POWs and soldiers missing in the Soviet Union." They demanded, for example, verification with tracing services in East and West, or a potentially indefinite prolongation of the period during which the death certificate had to be made public before it actually went into effect.[44] In addition, West German legal commentaries invoked the notion of silent camps or at least "news barriers," which allegedly made it impossible to place MIAs on the Eastern front in the category of "missing" and hence to issue death certificates.[45] The West German approach to this problem was therefore ambivalent at best: official laws in principle made possible the issuance of death certificates for MIAs and missing POWs, while expert opinions and bureaucratic practices sought to delay the final recognition of war losses as long as possible.

The East German approach was, by contrast, straightforward: after 1 August 1949, courts could issue death certificates for every soldier still missing in action. This was to allow many families to draw a "painful final stroke" under their war losses. It would also counteract "anti-Soviet" agitation of "imperialist circles" asserting that German MIAs were still withheld in Soviet POW camps.[46] After the end of POW repatriations from the Soviet Union in 1950, the Foreign Office recommended that official death certificates be issued for soldiers missing in action.[47] In 1951, two Politburo decrees determined that missing soldiers or POWs could be declared dead solely on the basis of statements of other returnees, or if no news had been received from them in five years.[48] In East Germany, official efforts to declare an "end" to the war sped up the issuance of death certificates for missing soldiers and POWs even in the absence of final certainty.[49]

Although East and West German responses to the end of POW repatriations from the Soviet Union differed considerably, both approaches represented forms of denial. In the West, popular opinion refused to accept the death tolls on the Eastern front and continued to cling to increasingly unlikely scenarios of hundreds of thousands of POWs interned in "silent camps." In the East, in turn, the official assertion of a completed postwar society pitted the SED against ordinary East Germans who shared their West German compatriots' hope—often also based on the myth of the secret camps—that family members might still return from captivity.[50] While West Germans refused to accept the true losses of the Second World War or projected them onto the Soviet Union, East German authorities simply denied the persistent significance of these losses and sought to repress corresponding feelings of grief, longing, and hope. In so doing, they replicated a more general tendency, inherent in Communist ideology, to focus on reshaping the collective existence of the living rather than on mourning the dead.[51]

MAKING ABSENT POWs VISIBLE: THE POW COMMEMORATIONS IN THE WEST

Throughout the first half of the 1950s, West Germans sought to make absent POWs visible through specific commemorative efforts. Annual "weeks of remembrance" and "days of loyalty" served to remind all West Germans of the fate of POWs still held in the Soviet Union.[52] These commemorations illuminated that West Germans could (re)imagine themselves as a nation only through commemorating the shared experience of loss and incompleteness.[53] While West Germans were already embarking on the rapid national recovery that came to be known as the "economic miracle," the POW commemorations reminded everyone that the persistent consequences of defeat still shaped the inner fabric of West German society. Indeed, in the absence of a formal peace treaty and in light of the continuing division of Germany, the POW commemorations expressed a sense that the war itself had not yet come to an end. A Protestant memo in 1949 argued, for example, that one should not create war memorials "as long as the war still continues."[54]

The POW commemorations built on earlier "weeks of prayer" that the Christian churches had held for absent POWs since the early postwar period.[55] The events of the early 1950s were organized jointly by the Christian churches, state authorities, and the Association of Returnees (VdH). They aimed to demonstrate the unity of the entire nation in the demand for the release of the POWs. Indeed, the range of activities during the annual POW remembrance week ensured that virtually everyone in West Germany would be confronted with the issue of missing POWs during that period.[56] The VdH distributed thousands of leaflets and posters, collected seventy thousand signatures on behalf of the POWs, and encouraged every West German community to place a banner above its busiest streets demanding "freedom for the POWs." In movie theaters, slides about the "army behind barbed wire" were screened before the main film. By 1954, the VdH also produced an entire series of memorabilia—from green candles to be displayed in shop windows and private homes, to an anthology of POW poems and a record featuring the "song of the faithful hearts" specifically composed for these events.[57] In addition to the myriad activities of the VdH, the federal parliament decreed a two-minute work and traffic stoppage on one day during the remembrance week.[58] A radio address by federal president Theodor Heuss and a speech in parliament by Chancellor Adenauer underlined the official character of the POW commemorations. The commemorations ended with a "day of faith" that was exclusively reserved for church sermons on the fate of the POWs.

The POW commemorations enjoyed great popularity and broad participation. In the small Hessian town of Limburg, thousands of citizens marched in a torchlight parade through the old city center.[59] In Wolfsburg, the entire workforce of the Volkswagen factory participated in a "silent march" alongside four thousand citizens in 1952.[60] The commemorations also drew on key elements of ritualized politics during the Nazi period. Torchlight parades or the two thousand "fires of admonition" that the VdH organized alongside the German-German border closely resembled collective self-representation of the "national community" during the Third Reich.[61] These rituals were also easily assimilated to the ideological demands of the Cold War. Many commemorative efforts centered on West Berlin with its exposed location at the border between East and West. Every year an eight-meter-high "candle of memory" was lit in the center of Berlin, where it burned until the end of the year. Like the fires along the East-West border, it was supposed to serve as a symbolic point of orientation not only for German POWs in Soviet captivity but for all Germans held captive on the other side of the "iron curtain."[62] Here too,

Figure 11. A two-minute traffic stoppage in Berlin on the occasion of the POW remembrance week in 1952. Commemorations of missing POWs and MIAs were powerful reminders of the persistent legacies of defeat in postwar West Germany. West Germans also harbored largely futile hopes that hundreds of thousands of German POWs were still held in "secret camps" in the Soviet Union and would eventually return. (Courtesy: Landesbildstelle Berlin.)

the commemoration of German losses of the Second World War primarily served the purpose of indicting the new enemy in the Cold War.

The POW commemorations both shaped and reflected the nature of West German public memories of the Second World War. These events fostered the association of victimhood with female experiences by assigning a central symbolic role to wives and mothers of missing returnees, who felt more strongly than anybody else that "the wounds in our people are still bleeding."[63] On occasion of the POW commemorations in 1954, the wife of a missing POW was flown to West Berlin from West Germany, carrying with her a flame to light the memorial candle and handing it over to a former POW who was dressed in his POW uniform.[64] Static representations of waiting wives' resilience in suffering stood in contrast with the more dynamic representations of the (male) POW experience as regeneration and redemption. Whereas the "women of the rubble" had signaled the will to reconstruction in the early postwar period, suffering waiting wives now stood for the past of a defeated and victimized nation, while noble and heroic returnees became emblematic for moral and political reconstruction.

Notwithstanding the public image of a society united in solidarity with its absent members, the planning and organization of these events also exposed fissures and conflicting interests among the parties involved. While generally supportive of the commemorations, state authorities were increasingly concerned that too noisy protests might undermine more subtle diplomatic efforts on behalf of the POWs. In May 1951, for example, the West German Foreign Office blocked the VdH from organizing a "day of loyalty" for German POWs on the first anniversary of the TASS declaration because it might interfere with a major diplomatic initiative at the UN.[65] As a result, the "day of loyalty" took place on a much smaller scale than the VdH had originally planned it.[66] One year later, the federal government again intervened in VdH plans to let a "freedom run" of German youth demonstratively pass by the prisons in Werl, Wittich, and Landsberg, where the Western Allies had interned convicted German war criminals. The foreign office feared that such a demonstrative link between POWs in the Soviet Union and interned war criminals in the West might interfere with its own efforts to overturn Allied convictions of German war criminals.[67]

The unique position of the Protestant church as the only institution still present in both halves of divided Germany also complicated its cooperation with state officials and especially with the VdH in organizing the POW commemorations. The Protestant church extended the POW commemorations to the East by instructing East German ministers to deliver special sermons for missing POWs during the West German week of remembrance in September 1950.[68] East German church officials also organized collections for absent POWs and transferred the funds to the Berlin Office, the official representation of the Protestant church in East Germany.[69] Such activities flew in the face of SED efforts to terminate all public discussion of the POW issue in the East. As a result, party officials tried to prevent several Protestant ministers from delivering sermons on behalf of missing POWs in 1953.[70] In addition, the increasingly vulnerable position of the Protestant church in East Germany rendered its close cooperation with the VdH more problematic.[71] In light of the VdH's ardent anti-Communism, collaboration with the association exposed East German church officials to charges that they simply served as an arm of Western propaganda, thus offering the SED a pretext to curb all commemorations of absent POWs in East Germany. In the aftermath of the failed East German uprising in June 1953, East German church officials began to distance themselves from the practices of the POW commemorations in the West. A minister from Brandenburg, for example, criticized the Western use of the POW issue as a "means of political propaganda" that occa-

Figure 12. The wife of a still missing POW arrives in Berlin to hand the light for the memorial candle to be lit on the occasion of the POW commemorations in 1954. A returned POW in his original POW clothing welcomes her at the Berlin airport. (Courtesy: Landesbildstelle Berlin.)

sionally resorted to "vocabulary . . . derived straight from the language of the Third Reich."[72]

Along similar lines, Western church officials grew increasingly weary over the "big propaganda efforts" of the "returnee associations" as well.[73] The churches tried to assert their independence by restricting the ringing of church bells to strictly religious events and by refusing to use this device during purely "secular" events such as the commemorative traffic stoppage, as the VdH had demanded.[74] In 1954, the conflicts between the VdH and the Christian churches in the West came into the open when the churches decided to hold a separate "week of prayer" for missing POWs in November instead of participating in the official POW commemorations in October. This decision reflected what Protestant church officials perceived to be their obligation in a divided Germany. They saw the church as "one of the few ties between the Eastern and Western parts of our fatherland" and wanted to cultivate the POW issue as one of the "main common bonds of both parts of Germany." By emphasizing the "purely pastoral" nature of their concerns for missing POWs, church officials distinguished their commemorative efforts from parallel West German ones, which purportedly "turn[ed] the POW question into a political issue."[75] Ironically, even though the POW commemorations sought to give the impression of a united nation, their organization actually exposed the rather divergent interests that different actors pursued with and through the POW issue.

Despite these conflicts, the POW commemorations nevertheless served important symbolic and political functions. They also helped to erase crucial boundaries among victims, bystanders, and perpetrators. These events were part of a public campaign to dramatically extend POW status to imprisoned German war criminals convicted by the Western allies. Participants routinely linked demands for the release of POWs from Soviet hands with calls for an amnesty for imprisoned war criminals in the West.[76] By January 1952, 1,258 of such convicted war criminals were still interned by the Western allies, approximately 700 of them inside Germany in Allied prisons in Werl, Wittich, and Landsberg, the rest of them in France, the Benelux countries, Denmark, Norway, and Yugoslavia.[77] These prisoners included some former Wehrmacht generals, such as Erich von Manstein, Albert Kesselring, and Hermann Hoth, but they consisted primarily of members of police and Gestapo units, concentration camp guards, and participants in the euthanasia actions.[78] The POW commemorations attempted to transfer the emotional identification of all sections of West German society from German POWs in the Soviet Union to these convicted war criminals, even though most of them were highly compromised perpetrators.

The highest West German dignitaries promoted this conflation between POWs and convicted war criminals. On occasion of the 1952 week of remembrance, federal president Theodor Heuss criticized not only the Soviet Union for withholding German POWs, but also the "Western and European states," which had allegedly stripped "German POWs of their human rights" by subjecting them to an "evil" and "formalistic" justice simply out of "resentment and political considerations."[79] Such statements were much to the liking of the VdH, which placed itself at the forefront of the campaign to find a solution to what was now labeled the "POW question in the West."[80] The association cooperated closely with behind-the-scene pressure groups, often comprised of former Nazis, who lobbied on behalf of imprisoned war criminals. These groups argued that any "delay in the settlement of the 'war criminal' problem in the West" might be "at the expense of the prisoners in Russia."[81] When this issue gained new importance in connection with the debate over West German rearmament, the VdH leadership was quick to threaten the mobilization of its constituency if convicted prisoners were not set free. Writing to Werner Best, a leading former SS official and key advocate of Nazi perpetrators after 1945, VdH executive director Werner Kiessling anticipated "thus far unprecedented" demonstrations by returnees and former soldiers if the establishment of German troop contingents did not also entail a general amnesty for imprisoned war criminals.[82]

The rhetorical and symbolic incorporation of convicted war criminals in the demand for the release of the last POWs from the Soviet Union had important political ramifications. By effectively conferring POW status on convicted war criminals in Allied prisons, the POW commemorations paved the way for their actual recognition as "returnees" in West German social policy. Throughout the 1950s, the federal bureaucracy and especially the Ministry of Expellees gradually extended returnee status to released war criminals from Allied prisons in the West.[83] The very term *returnee* bestowed an aura of civility upon interned war criminals that stood in stark contrast to their highly compromised past. This extension of returnee status, then, not only called into question the validity of Allied war crime trials by implicitly equating them with the summary justice in the Soviet Union, it also entitled Nazi perpetrators to social policy benefits according to the 1950 Returnee Law and the 1954 POW compensation law. The same provisions were eventually also extended to family members of convicted war criminals who were still detained in Allied prisons.[84]

In public commemorations and in social policy measures, West Germans thus gradually extended the assumptions of innocence from POWs in the Soviet Union to virtually all Germans who had been interned by the victors of the Second World War. By granting imprisoned war criminals official status as POWs and returnees, West Germans included them, symbolically and materially, in the postwar community of solidarity. This virtually indiscriminate inclusion of Nazi perpetrators and convicted war criminals in postwar society went beyond the functional requirements of democratization that necessitated the exoneration of the bulk of Nazi fellow travelers.[85] Instead, the POW commemorations illustrated what Norbert Frei calls the "secondary confirmation of the National Socialist *Volksgemeinschaft*" or perhaps even its reinvention in the postwar period.[86] Whereas the ties among the Nazi Party, the Wehrmacht, and German society had actually began to crumble during the last years of the war, postwar commemorations reaffirmed these bonds of solidarity and elided most distinctions between ordinary soldier and Nazi perpetrators. Moreover, the inclusion of convicted war criminals in domestic POW commemorations erased most traces of the Western allies' prosecution of Nazi crimes, thus fostering the moral integration of the Federal Republic into the Western alliance.[87]

Between Propaganda and Realpolitik: Missing POWs in International Politics

A series of international protests against the internment of German POWs in the Soviet Union served a similar purpose of integrating West Germany into the Western Cold War alliance. Innocent POWs held in abysmal conditions in Communist captivity furnished a particular potent image in the propaganda battles of the early Cold War. American officials could easily fuse the alleged mistreatment of Western POWs in the Korean War with protests against the withholding of German POWs in the Soviet Union: German POWs of the Second World War and American POWs of the first military conflict of the Cold War both appeared now primarily as victims of Communist inhumanity.[88] American occupation officials were quick to point out this potential propagandistic value of the POW issue. In the aftermath of the TASS declaration, the assistant to U.S. high commissioner John McCloy, Charles Thayer, informed members of the West German Foreign Office about the U.S. intention "to activate the question of German POWs for the active defense propaganda against Russian Communism."[89]

The centerpiece of the broader Western campaign on behalf of German POWs consisted of a U.S.-led effort to bring the issue to the attention of the newly founded United Nations.[90] Against the diplomatic resistance of the Soviet Union, the UN established an international committee that was supposed to investigate the number of POWs who were not yet repatriated as well as the reasons for their ongoing internment. While the West German government initially was supposed to provide only extensive documentation about the number and identity of German POWs still held in the Soviet Union, officials at the U.S. High Commission in Bonn left no doubt that the UN initiative would also help in "further mobilizing anti-Soviet feelings among Germans, while giving them [a] real sense of participation with [the] West in the process of the UN."[91] Indeed, West German participation in the UN initiative was of eminent political significance. It implied a de facto recognition of the Federal Republic as the representative of all Germans before the United Nation, and made it possible for the representative of the Federal Republic, Walter Hallstein, to address the UN General Assembly directly in September 1953.[92] Only a few years after Germans had been tried for heinous crimes at the International Military Tribunal in Nuremberg, the UN initiative turned the world organization into a forum for showcasing German suffering in Communist captivity.[93] And while nothing came out of the UN initiative, it undoubtedly transformed the "vital question of German POWs . . . into a common cause for the unifying free world."[94] Just as the POW commemorations had ensured the presence of the POW issue in domestic politics, the UN initiative achieved the same goal in the international arena.

This increasing domestic and international visibility of the POWs issue, however, also extracted a toll. The numerous diplomatic activities raised popular expectations that it would indeed be possible to achieve the release of the last POWs. For family members of absent POWs, the negotiations at the highest international level assumed a deeply personal significance. Helene B., for example, worried that her husband was not properly registered as a POW and thus might not be included in the work of the "POW commission of the United Nations."[95] Such voices illustrated the increasing popular pressure on the Adenauer government to pursue a more proactive policy on behalf of German POWs and enter into direct negotiations with the Soviet Union. Family members floated quite unconventional suggestions about how to achieve the release of the POWs. One Heinrich B., for example, suggested to Adenauer an exchange of two ordinary criminals from West Germany for every released prisoner from the Soviet Union.[96] In March 1955, a group of students from Munich even offered themselves in the place of POWs in the Soviet Union if they were guaranteed a release after one to three years.[97]

These popular demands assumed greater political salience when they merged with mounting criticism of Adenauer's foreign policy from opposition Social Democrats as well as from some segments of the Free Democrats (FDP). These critics grew increasingly concerned that the Adenauer government—its official rhetoric notwithstanding—accepted not only the continuing division of Germany but also refused to undertake any concrete steps on behalf of POWs in the Soviet Union. Critics of Adenauer's foreign policy thus demanded direct negotiations with the Soviet Union over German unification and over German POWs. In fact, between 1951 and 1954, several Adenauer critics such as Martin Niemöller; the president of the West German Red Cross, Heinrich Weitz; and the maverick FDP deputy Karl Georg Pfleiderer planned (or, in Niemöller's case, went on) independent trips to Moscow to effect the release of the POWs.[98] The Adenauer government reacted ambivalently at best to these plans and may even have actively subverted some of these initiatives.[99] Any proposal for direct negotiation with the Soviet Union clashed with the fundamental principle of Adenauer's foreign policy, namely to advance the Federal Republic's political, economic, and military integration into the Western alliance.[100] These priorities prevented Adenauer from exploring the Soviet note of March 1952 that offered German unification in exchange for neutrality in the Cold War, and they also stood in the way of reaching an agreement with the Soviet Union over German POWs. Yet West German officials as well as their American counterparts were clearly concerned that popular longings for a return of the POWs might undermine the official parameters of Adenauer's policy of Western integration.[101]

The West German parliament's ratification of the Paris treaties in May 1955, which granted West Germany limited sovereignty and integrated the Federal Republic into the NATO alliance, finally put these concerns to rest. Yet a series of petitions sent to Chancellor Adenauer around the same time also demonstrate a great deal of popular frustration over the POW policy of the Adenauer government up to that point. Unlike West German expellee organizations, which were vehemently opposed to any direct contacts with the Communist East, the VdH had supported calls for a more active policy on behalf of German POWs.[102] Members of the Essen branch of the VdH, for example, reminded Adenauer that, despite all his previous accomplishments, he had not yet fulfilled "his highest human obligation toward his people"—namely "bringing home of our comrades to their wives and children."[103] This position also enjoyed the strong support of family members of missing POWs and MIA. Another petitioner, "in the name of all wives and mothers whose husbands and sons are still in Soviet captivity," reminded the chancellor of the significance of the POWs' return for the popular acceptance of his foreign policy. "Do you believe that we will give our sons for the new Wehrmacht so that they may face the same fate as their fathers?" she asked, stressing that "our patience has come to an end" and that "we finally want our government to fight for the release of the POWs."[104] Yet another woman reckoned that the POW question would have long been solved if the government had only engaged in official talks with the Soviet Union as the Red Cross and the VdH had demanded time and again.[105]

In light of these popular attitudes, it was clear that Adenauer had no choice but to accept an official Soviet invitation in June 1955 for a visit to Moscow. After the successful integration of the Federal Republic into the Western alliance, the chancellor finally needed to demonstrate his willingness to pursue a more active policy toward the Soviet Union.[106] According to an opinion poll from June 1955, 82 percent of West Germans felt that Adenauer should accept the invitation.[107] Hundreds of letters written by family members of POWs and MIAs to Adenauer illustrated the high expectations that accompanied the chancellor when he embarked on his trip to the Soviet capital in September 1955.[108] This time, petitioners were less critical and pleaded with Adenauer to bring back a missing family member. One mother of a POW counted on the chancellor's paternal empathy for the troubles of a "desperate, unhappy mother" who was anxiously awaiting the return of her son from Soviet captivity.[109] Erika K. appealed to Adenauer not to let concerns of high politics overshadow the "fate of the individual," stressing that "for me and my three children, the most important thing is that the husband and breadwinner will finally return."[110] Many petitioners also articulated their persistent belief in the myth of the "silent camp." A mother of a soldier who had been reported missing in action at Stalingrad in January 1943, for example, held on to her conviction that "my son still is in Russia" and asked Adenauer to "put in a good word for him with the Soviets."[111] Against this backdrop, popular hopes for the return of the last POWs promised different kinds of closure: it would either make incomplete families complete again, or it would at last put to rest all hopes for the return of a family member from the Eastern front. In both cases, however, the return of the POWs would signify, ten years after the capitulation of the Wehrmacht, a definitive end to the immediate consequences of the Second World War in the private lives of West Germans.

CITIZENS OR CRIMINALS? ABSENT POWS AND MIAS IN EAST GERMANY, 1950–55

In contrast to the integrationist approach in West Germany that came to encompass even the most compromised war criminals, the SED dictatorship tried to radically redraw the boundaries of postwar society. With the aid of Soviet occupation forces, East German authorities sought to remake the postwar body politic by excluding real or alleged Nazis, war criminals, and, increasingly, opponents of the SED.[112] While West Germans saw missing POWs and imprisoned war criminals as integral members of the West German political body, East German authorities denied these groups the status of "antifascist-democratic" citizens.

The SED's project of remaking East German society, however, found its limits in the makeup of the East German people who, together with the West German population, had constituted the National Socialist *Volks-gemeinschaft*. Many East Germans flouted the official boundaries between "citizens" and "criminals" and often displayed a strong sense of solidarity with missing POWs and MIAs. The persistence of private familial bonds but also a larger sense of identification with the POWs' collective experiences prevented many ordinary East Germans from cutting emotional ties with absent POWs. While the high public visibility of absent POWs in the West undermined the parameters of Adenauer's foreign policy, the wide chasm between the official exclusions of absent POWs from postwar society and popular longings for their return threatened to subvert the already tenuous legitimacy of SED rule in East Germany.

In the aftermath of the TASS announcement in May 1950, family members sent hundreds of petitions to East German authorities.[113] Most petitions were addressed to the first (and only) president of the GDR, Wilhelm Pieck. The aftereffects of charismatic rule during the Nazi period led East Germans, like their West German counterparts, to believe that direct appeals to the grandfatherly head of state promised the most success in issues of utmost importance.[114] Some of these letters demanded accountability for soldiers who had been missing in action for years on the Eastern front, yet most of them referred to POWs who had written from Soviet POW camps and hence were likely to be still alive. These petitions came from a very specific group—family members of absent POWs—and served a clearly defined purpose. But they nevertheless reveal much about popular attitudes toward the consequences of war and defeat in East Germany. They illustrate a significant popular resistance to official efforts to terminate public discussion of the war's consequences. The petitioners' rhetorical strategies, moreover, also demonstrated how ordinary East Germans appropriated official ideology to advance deeply personal causes.

These petitions brought into the open the discrepancy between the SED's assertion of a completed postwar society and popular sentiments in East Germany. In contrast to the West, where private longings for the return of the POWs corresponded to public commemorations (if not always to actual policies), East Germans faced a deep chasm between official ideals and their private predicaments. In particular, they contrasted official campaigns for "peace" with the persistent presence of the war's consequences in their private lives. Willi B., for example, assured Pieck that he was willing to vote for "peace" in an East German propaganda campaign for German unity in October 1950, yet at the same time, he demanded an "internal peace" that could be achieved only through the release of his brother from Soviet captivity.[115] In a similar way, Gisela B. drew parallels between her fight for peace in East Germany and her desire "to have peace in our family" through a reunion with her husband.[116] The SED's emphasis on the completion of postwar society notwithstanding, these petitioners asserted the war's ongoing significance in their private lives.

Although fathers, brothers, and even sons of missing POWs were among the petitioners, wives of absent POWs submitted most of the petitions. In both postwar societies, divergent official perceptions of missing POWs as either innocent "victims" of Soviet inhumanity (in the West) or as justly sentenced "war criminals" (in the East) defined the position of wives of missing POWs. Yet whereas in the West wives of absent POWs were central to POWs commemorations and also qualified for state support, they suffered symbolic marginalization and material hardship in the East. They also received no specific financial subsidiaries, and the East German state attempted to draw them into the workforce, like single women in general.[117] As a result, the return of a husband would significantly improve waiting wives' material situation. Klara B. spoke for many of them when she appealed to Pieck to return to "a severely tested mother and wife . . . the breadwinner for her family."[118] And in her letter to Pieck, Gerda B. explained that her weekly wage of fifty marks was insufficient to support her two children and that she was living in a "cold, dark apartment without living room or kitchen."[119]

The story of Dorothea B. demonstrated that wives of absent POWs were not just facing material hardship but also encountering social ostracism and emotional distress. Between 1950 and 1954, Dorothea B. sent numerous letters to East German authorities inquiring about the fate of her husband, who had written from Soviet captivity in 1947 and then again in 1951. Because of the uncertainty about her husband's future, she suffered a nervous breakdown and became dependent on welfare. She also told East German authorities that it "hurts to hear that there are only war criminals left in the Soviet Union." In addition, her daughter was denied an apprenticeship position because she was determined to be the daughter of an alleged "war criminal." After years of struggle and several visits to the East German Interior Ministry, she still had not received any explanation why her husband was held in Soviet captivity. As a result, she could "no longer bear the uncertainty" and gave in to official pressures by filing for divorce from her missing husband.[120]

Some petitioners transformed their private predicaments into more open challenges to East German authorities. Family members of missing POWs contested the official portrayal of their relatives as war criminals and questioned the legitimacy of further detainment in Soviet captivity. Letter writers argued that their sons or husbands had been involuntarily drafted into service for the Wehrmacht or the SS, where they had simply "done [their] duty" without committing any criminals offenses.[121] "If my son is a war criminal," one petitioner asserted, "then all of us who wore a uniform were war criminals."[122] "My husband was certainly not responsible for this terrible war," another wife of a missing POW wrote, adding that her "entire village was happy" when she received, after four years of silence, a letter from her husband in November 1950.[123] While the popular memories of war and defeat articulated in these petitions differed widely from the SED's official narrative, they were actually rather similar to popular memories in the West. Like their counterparts in the West, many ordinary East Germans asserted that Wehrmacht soldiers had fought an honorable war devoid of any ideological motivation and could therefore not possibly have been implicated in Nazi crimes.

Petitioners also demonstrated their keen awareness of normative conceptions of East German citizenship by emphasizing absent POWs' potential contributions to the East German reconstruction effort. Martha D. told Pieck how her husband would "become politically active" and devote all his labor "to the reconstruction of our GDR."[124] Similarly, Lisabeth S., a member of the SED and of the Democratic Women's Union (DFD), assured the leadership of the Free German Youth (FDJ) that her son would "immediately engage politically in the FDJ" upon his return.[125] By portraying missing POWs as potential producers and party activists, these petitioners contested the exclusion of their family members, as alleged war criminals, from the community of East German citizens. More so than West German petitioners, East German letter writers stressed absent POWs' potential impact on politics and public life rather than on their private lives, thus reflecting the contrast between the depoliticized and "privatized" West German society of the 1950s and the politicized "working society" (*Arbeitsgesellschaft*) in East Germany.

Petitioners frequently turned the SED's own ideological pronouncements against the party and insisted on the state's assistance in bringing home the last POWs. In his query to Grotewohl, Heinz D. listed his numerous accomplishments as the leader of a workers' brigade, which made him feel "a little bit proud of my unrelenting engagement for the German Democratic Republic, the five-year plan, and the building of socialism." Yet he was deeply dissatisfied that, over a period of two years, East German authorities had failed to respond adequately to his queries about his missing brother in the East. Such delays, he complained, "stand in stark contrast to the laws and the constitution of our German Democratic Republic, which commands that all petitions, complaints, and inquiries of the population have to be answered as swiftly as possible."[126] Another popular rhetorical strategy was to draw on the loudly trumpeted Soviet-German friendship, which, according to many petitioners, was hardly compatible with the persistent detainment of German POWs in Soviet captivity. Party authorities ought to at least employ their close contacts to Soviet authorities on behalf of these POWs. "On a friendship basis," one petitioner argued, it should be possible, "to reach an agreement with the Soviet Union in these cases."[127] Finally, petitioners reminded party authorities of their claims to represent the interests of working people. This is not a concern of "higher bourgeois circles," as Marianne H. explained to Pieck, but "rather a matter of the heart for ordinary people who see an undue hardship in the persistent detention of a number of men who have not committed any more serious crimes than those POWs who have already returned."[128] While the SED's own ideological claims provided family members with a language to advance their causes, the authorities' failure to deliver on these promises clearly subverted the party's credibility among ordinary East Germans.

Missing POWs represented a particularly troubling issue for outspoken SED activists, who were still awaiting the return of a family member. To Erwin H., a KPD member since 1924, the fact that his son was still being held in Soviet captivity seriously undermined his efforts to win over "many, many *Volksgenossen* who so far have remained aloof" from the SED.[129] A teacher from Saxony reported that her brother-in-law's detainment in the Soviet Union produced a "great inner conflict," which made it impossible for her to defend the "policy of the German Democratic Republic" and the "friendship with the Soviet Union" as "freely and as unconditionally as I would like to."[130] More than anyone else, party activists among family members of missing POWs needed to bridge the gap between official demands to display an optimistic, forward-looking attitude and their private feelings of loss, uncertainty, and frustration. Their predicament thus exemplified what Lutz Niethammer has identified as a paradigmatic problem for the postwar existence of East Germans in general: the difficulty or even impossibility of reconciling their private with their public existence.[131]

Official responses to these petitions were ill suited to alleviate the grievances of family members of missing POWs. East German authorities had little or no influence on the situation of German POWs in the Soviet Union, and they were in no position to effect their release.[132] As a result, East German officials either did not reply to these queries or sent out rather empty form letters.[133] The Interior Ministry, for example, told petitioners that the "government of the GDR seeks a clarification on these issues," yet asked for "patience" since it was unable to "deal with each individual case separately."[134] In other cases, state authorities responded in a more hostile manner and stated bluntly that "those persons who today still write from the Soviet Union are not POWs but rather criminals."[135] This mixture of silencing, evasion, and repression exhibited many similarities to Nazi responses to the POW/MIA issue during the last year of the Third Reich.[136] The liminal position of POWs and MIAs

threatened to subvert the policies of both German dictatorships: it undermined the Nazis' efforts to continue the war as well as the SED's efforts
to end it.

In East Germany, the stark divergence between official and popular
responses to absent POWs posed a severe problem to the SED. One party
official reported to Pieck that many families confronted him with the issue
of missing POWs and that "political education" in East Germany would
be considerably easier if this problem were solved.[137] The POW issue was
particularly troubling for the SED in light of mounting evidence that popular identification with absent POWs extended beyond their immediate
families.[138] One party activist told Pieck that the "problem of POWs in
the Soviet Union is frequently discussed in my hometown."[139] Similar to
officials during the Nazi period, the SED regime employed coercive means
to break up informal contacts among family members of missing soldiers.
In September 1950, for example, the *Volkspolizei* in Saxony arrested a
man who reportedly contacted family members of missing soldiers in the
East and spread "rumors" that allegedly promoted anti-Soviet feelings.[140]

Just as during the last years of the Third Reich, individual grievances
regarding missing soldiers rarely translated into open opposition and resistance against the East German dictatorship. Petitions to East German
authorities did not represent collective forms of civic protest but rather
drew on, and hence partly legitimized, official discourses. Individual petitions channeled, as Jonathan Zaitlin has persuasively argued, collective
grievances into a one-on-one communication between individual East
Germans and representatives of the state, thereby allowing East German
authorities to diffuse popular discontent about this issue.[141] Thus, while
the issue of missing POWs certainly undermined SED efforts to "win
over" the East German population, it fell short of challenging the founda-
tions of Communist rule in East Germany.

Nonetheless, the preoccupation with missing POWs prompted different
kinds of tensions in both postwar societies. In the West, public commemorations, diplomatic activities, and social policy all underlined the nature
of West German society as an incomplete society that was still awaiting
a reunion with its lost parts. The public longing for its completion coincided with private longings for the reconstitution of still incomplete families. Yet the high public visibility of missing POWs in West Germany increased popular pressures on the Adenauer government to engage in
direct negotiations with the Soviet Union and threatened to undermine
the parameters of Adenauer's foreign policy. In addition, the integration
of imprisoned war criminals into the still incomplete West German national body erased crucial differences among innocents, bystanders, and
perpetrators, thus further reducing the moral sensitivity of West German
society toward the Nazi past.

In East Germany, the issue of missing POWs put the SED on the ideological defensive. The SED needed to defend the Soviet Union's policy in POW matters without ever exerting any significant influence on it. The public visibility of missing POWs in the West as well as the Protestant church's transmission of POW commemorations to East Germany constantly undermined the SED's efforts at terminating any public discussion of missing POWs. More importantly, the official assertion of a completed postwar society clashed with the persistent private preoccupation of ordinary East Germans with absent family members. By exposing the discrepancies between the SED's political agenda and popular concerns, the issue of missing POWs further undermined East German Communists' tenuous popular legitimacy.

In both societies, the return of the last POWs in 1953–54 and in 1955–56 thus promised to resolve a multiplicity of grievances that still lingered from war and defeat ten years earlier. In the West, it signaled the end of the direct consequences of the war as well as the symbolic completion of postwar society. In the East, by contrast, the return of the POWs removed a potentially destabilizing issue from relations between the SED and the East German population. However, as the persistent tensions resulting from missing POWs in both German postwar societies indicated, bringing the Second World War to an end was a complicated social and symbolic process that lasted throughout the entire first postwar decade.

CHAPTER 8

Divided Reunion: The Return of the Last POWs

The return of the last POWs in 1953–54 and 1955–56 constituted a defining moment in the history of postwar Germany. A full decade after the war's end, the last POWs brought back the legacies of war and defeat to two German states that now were firmly integrated into opposing Cold War blocs. Only a few months before the return of the last POWs, the Federal Republic joined the Western military alliance (NATO) and received virtually full sovereignty in return. The simultaneous formation of the Warsaw Pact and the integration of the German Democratic Republic into the Eastern alliance cemented the Cold War division of Germany and of the European continent. Against this background, the highly symbolic return of the last POWs illustrated both societies' confrontation with the shared consequences of a lost war at the height of the Cold War.

In the West, the enthusiastic reception of the last POWs signaled the end point of returnees' transformation from "victims" into noble and heroic "survivors" in West German public memory. In the East, by contrast, official responses to the last POWs demonstrated the SED's increasing reliance on force and coercion in the aftermath of the uprising in June 1953. The return of the last POWs also accentuated tensions between public and private confrontations with the war's legacies in both postwar societies. In the West, the public image of mythical and heroic returnees often did not correspond to more ambivalent internal perceptions by West German officials, and it ran counter to returnees' own difficulties in adjusting to a completely changed society. In the East, the popular reception of the last POWs diverged significantly from their official portrayal as "war criminals," thus indicating the limitations of the SED's project of antifascist transformation. The divergent responses to the return of the last POWs further widened the gap between East and West that had emerged in the early 1950s.

Even though both German governments claimed to have been instrumental in effecting the release of the last POWs, they actually exerted little influence over Soviet policies. The repatriation of the last POWs resulted primarily from shifts in Soviet foreign policy in response to changing international contexts. After Stalin's death in March 1953, his temporary successor, Beria, sought to reduce the huge system of forced labor in the Soviet Union by granting widespread amnesties that included

German POWs and civilian internees. The actual Soviet decision to release 10,197 POWs as well as approximately 2,000 civilian internees came in the aftermath of the June 1953 uprising in East Germany and was supposed to bolster the SED's questionable legitimacy.[1] In 1955, Soviet policy sought to perpetuate the status quo in Europe—including the division of Germany—by establishing diplomatic relations with the Federal Republic. As early as July 1955, the Soviet leadership informed SED leaders Walter Ulbricht and Otto Grotewohl of its intention to release the last POWs in exchange for the achievement of this diplomatic goal.[2] The negotiations on the occasion of Chancellor Adenauer's visit to Moscow in September 1955 yielded the desired quid pro quo. As a result of this agreement, the last 9,262 returnees, including some 3,000 civilian internees, arrived in East and West Germany between October 1955 and January 1956.[3]

"A Common Joy Which Seized All Germans as Never Before"

"Germany's heart beats in Friedland," exclaimed a West German newspaper in October 1955 and thus captured the popular enthusiasm that accompanied the return of the last POWs to West Germany. More so than any time before, West Germans celebrated the return as a moment of national reunification by extending a triumphant and highly publicized welcome.[4] Jubilant crowds greeted the returnees on their bus ride on the "eighty most important kilometers of the world" from the German/German border station in Herleshausen to the Friedland transition camp.[5] Along the way, thousands of Germans flocked to the streets, stopped the buses, and showered returnees with flowers, fruit, candies, and cigarettes in order to "demonstrate their affection for the returnees."[6] In Friedland the highest West German dignitaries welcomed the last POWs. The federal president, Theodor Heuss, assured the returnees that popular sympathies "transcended all differences between parties and groups." Along similar lines, Archbishop Frings of Cologne welcomed the POWs in their "Christian Heimat" to which they had finally returned from the "godless world" of Bolshevism. Faced with this enthusiastic welcome, the last returnees could easily lay to rest nagging fears that the "Heimat would receive us as criminals."[7]

Given the relatively small number of returnees, the symbolic significance of this event by far exceeded its actual impact on West German society. Ten years after the end of the war, the return of the last POWs put an end to the public insistence on the "incompleteness" of West German society and signified the symbolic completion of the West German body politic. According to one commentator, "only the return of the last

Figure 13. An enthusiastic welcome for returned POWs in the Hessian town of Eschwege in October 1955. The return of the last POWs triggered an outpouring of national sentiments in West Germany. The last returnees' adjustment to postwar society, however, often turned out to be more troubled than their enthusiastic celebration upon return suggested. (Courtesy Bildarchiv Preussischer Kulturbesitz.)

POWs gives us the consciousness to be a nation with equal rights among other nations" since "no state that is forced to accept foreign captivity of a part of its members is really sovereign."[8] Along with the West German triumph in the 1954 soccer World Cup, the return of the last POWs was an event that allowed West Germans to experience positive national emotions.[9] As one commentator observed, "The returnees from Russia were welcomed with emotions (*Ergriffenheit*) that came from the bottom of people's hearts. This was a common joy . . . that seized all Germans completely and strongly as never before."[10] The depth of these national emotions manifested itself as late as 1967: shortly after Adenauer's death, 75 percent of West Germans cited the "liberation" of the POWs from the Soviet Union as the chancellor's most important political success.[11]

The return of the last POWs also underlined the Federal Republic's claims to be the only legitimate representative of the German nation. Most POWs chose to return to the West. In 1953, 8,137 out of 10,383 POWs went to the West, while in 1955–56, 7,250 out of 9,626 POWs did so, and an additional 589 returnees from East Germany requested to be released to the West after originally planning to return to their families in the East.[12] Public commentators stressed that these preferences shed light on the distance between "the ideology of Communist doctrinaires" and the "substance of our people."[13] Preference for the West even among returnees whose families still resided in the East showed that the "Moscow-sponsored 'GDR' cannot convey any feeling of Heimat."[14] The return of the POWs was an occasion to affirm what soon became the official guideline of West German foreign policy in the "Hallstein doctrine": there was to be only one legitimate representative of the German nation, and this was the Federal Republic of Germany.

More than any time before, West Germans projected their imagination of the nation onto the last returnees. In public discourse, the POWs embodied conceptions of "Germanness" that were divorced from National Socialism yet still incorporated redemptive memories of war and defeat. The POW commemorations of the early 1950s had long ingrained the POW's innocence in West German public consciousness. With only a few exceptions to be discussed below, public representations of the last POWs largely ignored their often compromised pasts and focused on the POWs' heroic resistance and survival in Soviet captivity. Public commentators celebrated them as men "baptized by fire" who had resisted Communist indoctrination by holding on to "old fashioned values" such as "comradeship," "loyalty," and "fatherland."[15] Such representations of the last POWs as heroic survivors not only overwrote memories of total defeat while highlighting the centrality of sustained anti-Communist resistance for all Germans. They also presented examples of masculine assertion, which, as contemporary observers bemoaned, had increasingly fallen victim to the corrosive effects of bureaucratization and a more general "disenchantment of the world."[16]

This public celebration of the last POWs as national icons was not only directed against Soviet Communism but also against perceived "materialist excesses" of the West. Many press accounts recounted returnees' surprise at "how Americanized Germany had become."[17] Returnees' reliance on allegedly timeless German character traits offered an important counterpoint and the possibility of asserting a distinctly German identity in the face of increasing American influences. In 1957, this function of returnees as a moral counterweight to Americanization found graphic expression in a poster advertisement for a documentary movie that the VdH produced. The poster juxtaposed a sad-looking returnee with a young couple—the girl taller than the boy—dancing "jitterbug style" and a jazz band with black musicians.[18] The message of this poster was clear: these returnees had reasserted their Germanness in captivity and thus offered an important corrective to foreign influences and gender disturbance. They served, in Robert Moeller's word, as a "repository of values that would prevent Germany from becoming another America."[19]

The public reception of the last POWs reaffirmed the exclusionary patterns of West German redemptive memories. Because returnees blamed their conviction and internment in Soviet captivity on denunciations by fellow POWs, the return of the last POWs prompted a new wave of POW trials.[20] In 1955, the accusation of treason and betrayal in captivity targeted especially the former general and cofounder of the League of German Officers, Walter von Seydlitz. Unlike most of the defendants in the POW trials, however, Seydlitz had actually refused any collaboration with Soviet authorities after 1945 and hence was interned for ten more years. Yet such subtleties were lost upon Seydlitz's return in the fall of 1955, when he faced an "iron rejection" and few commentators were willing to point out his contribution to the resistance against Hitler.[21] At the same time, public commentators distanced themselves not just from Seydlitz but also from General Schörner, who had returned in January 1955. Representatives from across the political spectrum called for Schörner's criminal prosecution in front of a West German court because of his well-known advocacy of gruesome military justice during the final stages of the war.[22] Ten years after the end of the war, both Seydlitz's resistance *and* Schörner's excessive loyalty to National Socialism lay beyond the confines of acceptable behavior.

While the return of the last POWs marked an important milestone in the symbolic and emotional reconstitution of West Germany as a nation, it also defined the internal and external boundaries of the postwar nation. Several commentators emphasized that the "mourning of our people over those who will not return anymore" casts a "deep shadow" over the "na-

Figure 14. Poster advertisement for the film *The Bells of Friedland,* a documentary on the experience of returned POWs produced by the Association of Returnees (VdH) in 1957. The poster illustrates the functions of the last returnees as a moral counterweight to the increasing Americanization of postwar West Germany. (Courtesy Verband der Heimkehrer.)

tional joy" associated with this event.[23] The return of the last POWs laid to rest most residual hopes for a return of missing soldiers. It largely ended popular speculations about missing soldiers in the East, which had originated in the last years of the Third Reich and persisted throughout the first postwar decade. Moreover, in 1953 and 1955, West German observers expressed new hopes that the Soviet Union's decision to release the last German POWs might eventually also lead to the "return of seventeen million men, women, and children" in the GDR as well.[24] Critics of Adenauer's policy, however, charged that the Moscow agreement had reduced rather than enhanced the prospects for national unification. Gustav Heinemann, for example, castigated Adenauer for rewarding the Soviet "policy of ransom" and "normalizing" the German division, while Marion Gräfin Dönhoff pointed out in *Die Zeit* that the freedom of ten thousand POWs had "sealed the servitude of seventeen million" Germans in the GDR.[25] As these interventions demonstrated, the return of the last POWs signified the reconstitution of West Germany as a nation while cementing the German division.

In 1955, however, the enthusiastic reception of the last POWs indicated that most West Germans favored the completion of West German society over national reunification. When a West German magazine added the headline "Reunification" to an image of a returning husband and waiting wife, it clearly indicated that in 1955, family reunions took precedence over national reunion.[26] Just as the increasing separation of families after 1943 had brought the war into the private lives of ordinary Germans, the tales of family reunions in 1955 suggested that the war's direct consequences had finally come to an end. Not all of those reunions, to be sure, had happy endings, and newspaper reports clearly blamed wives for not having waited for their husband.[27] At the same time, the return of the last POWs prompted intense longings for making whole again shattered private lives. In the fall of 1955, thousands of single women sent letters to the camp administration in Friedland seeking to attract a returnee as a potential husband and, often, as a father for their children. Most of these inquiries did not yield the desired results and were met with official indifference and ridicule in the popular press.[28] But the letters illuminate some of the popular hopes and expectations that were associated with the return of the last POWs. The letter writers were mostly women whose husbands had either been killed in the war or had been missing in action for more than a decade.[29] Others were women like Frida G., who explained that her husband had returned "deeply discontented" from war and captivity in 1947 and had filed for divorce in 1950.[30] Finally, in response to the return of several hundred female POWs in 1955, some men also wrote to Friedland inquiring for possible female companions among the returnees.[31] All of these letter writers expressed their desire for a "nice home and a happy family life" that been lost as result of the war.[32]

To many of these women, the last returnees appeared as ideal companions because their suffering in captivity reflected their own experience of displacement and deprivation. Letter writers told of their expulsion from the German territories in the East; evacuation from the cities to escape Allied bombing raids; political persecution in, and flight from, East Germany; and emotional and material hardship in the postwar period.[33] For these women, it was the shared experience of suffering that formed the emotional and experiential basis of future imagined partnerships. To Ursula D., a single mother of a six-year-old daughter, the last returnees were men who had "gone through such difficult times themselves" and thus "could empathize with my suffering." She therefore hoped that "we can find each other through this suffering."[34] The last returnees, however, stood not only for shared suffering but also for a restored and rehabilitated masculinity. Whereas in the early postwar period, returning POWs had appeared as central symbols of the defeated nation, survival in Soviet captivity had given these men, in the eyes of female letter writers, a sincerity that distinguished them from the alleged shallowness of their male compatriots. "I only want to marry a returnee," Maria Z. argued, because "they at least have reason" and "they have languished for years behind barbed wire only for us and our Heimat."[35] Chastened in captivity and appropriately skeptical about the "Americanization" of postwar Germany, the last returnees represented ideal partners for women like Gerlinde J., who professed to be "rather old-fashioned" and to prefer a "comfortable home to the dancing floor."[36]

Popular representations of the last returnees as ideal and "remasculinized" posttotalitarian citizens satisfied a wide variety of symbolic and emotional needs in postwar West Germany. But these were also highly idealized images that often did not reflect the last returnees' encounter with a drastically changed environment that was fraught with problems. These former soldiers and POWs had missed decisive transformations of postwar society, and their long period of captivity often seems to have led to a hardening of preexisting habitual attitudes rather than to a democratic transformation. According to the study of the Frankfurt Institute, the last POWs subscribed to an even more fervent anti-Bolshevism and were more strongly supportive of West German rearmament than earlier returnees.[37] They also displayed an unbroken attachment to the nation that stood in marked contrast to gradual yet important processes of denationalization that West German society underwent throughout the postwar period, notwithstanding the occasional outpouring of national sentiments, as in the fall of 1955.[38] One returnee, for example, declared that "after everything we had experienced in Russia . . . we were very concerned with our 'Germanness' and denounced everything that was not energetically 'German'" and also asserted that the "work of political parties" had done much to destroy the "soldierly spirit."[39] Another returnee articulated the contrast between his sense of national identification and postwar consumerism by stating that, upon his return, he had "searched Germany" only to find "refrigerators and cars."[40] Long years in war and captivity thus indeed strengthened the last returnees' nationalism. Yet it was precisely this intensified identification with the nation that set the last returnees apart from an increasingly "postnational" West German society and made them move in a different "social time."[41]

Such incongruities also rendered difficult the integration of a small number of late returnees into the newly formed West German army. While public representations cast them as ideal models for the "citizens in uniform" of the new Bundeswehr, their actual incorporation into the armed forces proved, as Klaus Naumann has demonstrated, highly problematic.[42] Like all applicants to the new West German army above the rank of colonel (*Oberst*), the last returnees needed to undergo a screening by a special parliamentary commission. While the final report of this commission acknowledged that the last returnees "may have maintained with remarkable energy their capacity of body, spirit, and soul," it also came to the conclusion that they had missed "a chunk of contemporary history" and worried that their "one-sided hatred of Communism" made it difficult for them to arrive at a "comprehensive assessment of our political situation."[43] Seeking to defend himself against vehement protests of returnee associations, the head of the parliamentary screening commission made it clear that returnees had not been discriminated against; the percentage of rejected applicants from this group was actually lower than the average rejection rate. Still, he also explained that some interviews with returnees from the Soviet Union had confirmed and even exceeded the commission's concerns regarding this group. In one case, a former general and returnee from Soviet captivity was asked about his attitude toward the "campaign against the Jews." After a brief pause, the returnee responded that "it was probably right that the Jewish spirit had finally been eradicated from Germany." When pressed specifically about the "annihilation" and "gassing" of the Jews, he confirmed that it was better that a "small percentage of the population had disappeared" rather than that "the entire people had been eradicated."[44] While some members of the commission were prepared to excuse even such unabashed attachment to National Socialist ideals as temporary (and still redeemable) deviations on the part of basically "honorable guys," this particularly egregious statement indeed disqualified the returnee from joining the Bundeswehr. Conversely, the commission had less difficulty in identifying "any membership in the 'Antifa' or the Officers' League" as incompatible with service in the West German army or, for that matter in the state bureaucracy.[45] The newly established West German secret service agency (*Verfassungsschutz*) recommended special screenings of all late returnees who applied for civil service positions because of concerns "that a considerable number of late returnees" had been recruited as Soviet spies."[46]

The public emphasis on a seamless reconstitution of the national body politic contrasted with the ambivalences and mutual skepticism that shaped the encounter between West German society and the last returnees. Returnees' individual adjustment to the more private aspects of citizenship in the workplace and in their families often did not proceed more smoothly. Returnees frequently commented on the contrast between the "triumphant" reception in Friedland and a more prosaic "reality [that] looks different than in big speeches and newspaper articles."[47] To be sure, much of the VdH's public emphasis on the difficult position of returnees served the purpose of supporting the association's campaign for the POW compensation law.[48] But a statistic in December 1955 indicated that 4,379 out of 10,059 registered "late returnees" were still unemployed.[49]

The publicity surrounding the 1955–56 return prompted West German authorities to devote considerable time and effort to facilitating the returnees' readjustment. In September 1956, the Ministry of Expellees sent out 8,753 detailed questionnaires inquiring about the financial situation, housing, and employment of 1955–56 returnees. Approximately 20 percent of the 5,384 respondents, it turned out, were dissatisfied with their living situation.[50] While returnees perceived this official attention to their situation as very positive, they often also articulated deep insecurities about their new living situation: "The many years behind barbed wire left their traces," as one returnee reported. "One feels completely different now that one is back in freedom. One needs to slowly get used to the economy, especially since one has also become older."[51] Here too, it was often the wives of returnees who facilitated their transition to a civilian life. "I am a broken man," wrote one returnee to the Caritas POW Aid, and added that "it would be completely impossible for me to orient myself in this new world without my loving wife."[52] Such private confession to their stark dependency on their wives stood in contrast to the public emphasis on their secure and reconstituted masculinities.

Public representations of the last returnees also tended to pay little attention to the last returnees' physical and psychological difficulties. Recognition of physical and emotional scars did not blend well with the public's desire to see the last POWs as chastened and regenerated heroes. To be sure, because of extensive packages from the West as well as generally improving living conditions in captivity, the last returnees no longer exhibited the massive physical deprivations of returnees from the early postwar period. Still, they suffered disproportionately from more psychosomatic symptoms of "vegetative dystony" that had also been diagnosed for earlier returnees.[53] According to the psychiatrist Hans Bürger-Prinz, the last returnees had experienced an irreversible "vital crack" (*vitalen Knick*), a damage from their long period of captivity that could not simply be categorized as "neurosis."[54] Unlike in the cases of earlier returnees, when psychosomatic symptoms were often interpreted as indications of constitutional weakness, such conclusions were difficult to maintain in these cases of extremely long internment.[55] Public representations of these last returnees as heroic survivors thus militated against diagnosing returnees' symptom as neurosis, failure, or abnormal reaction.[56] Psychiatric responses to the psychological problems of the last returnees subsequently promoted diagnostic shifts as well as changes in compensation practices already under way since the early 1950s.

Consider, for example, the case of returnee Erich D., who complained in 1959, six years after his return from more than nine years in Soviet captivity in 1953, about ongoing psychological symptoms such as inhibition, insecurity, and irritability. Unlike in earlier cases, the psychiatric evaluation stressed that his symptoms did not just indicate "psychological failure" but expressed "a long and extraordinary psychic burden that would lead to psychological deficits even among persons of a less robust psychic constitution." His "psychological symptoms" were accordingly categorized as "real health deficits," and Erich D. was awarded a minor disability of 30 percent. These psychiatric evaluations of the last returnees represented an important milestone towards the gradual recognition of independent psychic trauma in postwar West Germany. While doctors and psychiatrists continued to insist that purely "reactive" psychological symptoms did not entitle returnees to compensation, they now stressed the discrepancy between the extremely strong psychic stress of long captivity and the psychological capacities of the individual.[57] As a result, all returnees in 1953–54 and 1955–56 were diagnosed with an "experience-induced personality disorder" that was not differentiated according to physical and psychological symptoms. This diagnosis was coined by the Göttingen psychiatrist Ulrich Vetzlaff, who applied it to victims of Nazi persecutions as early as 1952. However, this diagnosis only gained wider currency when it was applied to the last returnees from the East.[58] On the basis of this diagnosis, returnees were granted an approximately 50 percent disability rate for a period of at least four to five years.[59]

Together with diagnostic practices, medical and psychiatric responses to the last returnees also transformed West German compensation law over time. The revision of the BVG of 1956 made room for the recognition of psychological pain accompanying organic deficiencies, even if these psychological symptoms significantly exceeded organic deficiencies.[60] The revised law continued to exclude "psychogenic" and "neurotic symp-

toms" that were located solely in the patient's mind. The criteria for distinguishing "normal" from "pathological" psychological symptoms were
based on "normal psychological empathy" (*normal psychologisch ein-
fühlbar*) and general medical experience.[61] In subsequent years, however,
the Federal Welfare Court (Bundessozialgericht) revised these guidelines
and allowed for a wider variety of individual responses to traumatic
events rather than relying on an elusive psychological "average."[62] Similarly, the Labor Ministry's evaluation guidelines reflected an ever more
differentiated understanding of "dystrophy's" impact on an entire series
of organic deficiencies. By 1965, these guidelines explicitly recognized a
more general "state of exhaustion" comprised of psychological and psychosomatic symptoms as the result of captivity.[63] Thus, the confrontation
with the pathologies of late returnees paved the way for a diagnostic and
legal recognition of psychic trauma due to external events.

Ironically, the medical and psychiatric response to the last soldiers of
Hitler's army significantly increased West German receptivity for the
trauma of Holocaust survivors. In 1956, the first medical advocate of
Holocaust survivors invoked experiences of late returnees from Soviet
captivity and compared them to symptoms that French and Danish re-
searchers had identified among Holocaust survivors. The etiological shift
from endogenous to external factors, from the patients' mind to traumatic events, then prompted a closer examination of the nature of these
external stressors. Max Michel strongly asserted the difference between
POW camps and the "total persecution" in concentration camps.[64] To be
sure, West German commentators fought a rearguard battle against these
slowly emerging calls for distinguishing between POW and concentration camps, and they continued to focus on the similarity of the "captivity situation."[65] Unlike former POWs, Nazi victims did not command a
powerful interest group that would lobby for recognition and material
compensation of physical and psychological consequences of persecution. Still, the gradual recognition of psychic trauma as a response to
external events eventually also prepared the ground for an emerging recognition of these conditions among Holocaust survivors.[66] Sadly, this
transformation came much too late for many of the unfortunate victims
of the Nazi dictatorship.

As in the realm of psychiatric diagnoses and compensation practices,
the return of the last POWs also prompted subtle yet important transformations in the West German politics of memory. The last "returnees"
were not just ordinary Wehrmacht soldiers but often also members of the
of the Armed SS and of police units.[67] Among 1,011 former returnees of
higher rank among 1953 returnees, there were 537 known former SS and
police officers, most of them from elite units such as the Deadhead Division or the Leibstandarte Adolf Hitler.[68] Similar detailed statistics did not

exist for the transports in 1955–56. But more critical observers identified some prominent Nazi perpetrators among the last returnees, such as the medical doctor Carl Clauberg, who had performed sterilization experiments in Auschwitz, the former police chief of Frankfurt, Adolf Beckerle, the former regional Nazi leader (*Gauleiter*) of Saxony-Anhalt, Rudolf Jordan, or the Hamburg Gestapo chief and high official of the Reich Security Main Office, Bruno Streckenbach.[69] In addition, a separate transport with 746 "nonamnestied POWs" arrived on 14 January 1956, with 471 of them going to the West and 275 to the East. Soviet authorities had refused to grant amnesty to these returnees because they were alleged to have committed particularly heinous crimes. According to a recent study, approximately 20 percent of these nonamnestied returnees had belonged to SS and police units.[70] The transport also included nonmilitary personnel, such as the former concentration camp guards from Sachsenhausen Gustav Sorge and Wilhem Schubert—better known as "Iron Gustav" and "Pistol Schubert"—who had tortured and killed numerous prisoners.[71] Other returnees of this transport were the deputy commandant and camp doctor of the Sachsenhausen concentration camp, August Höhn and Heinz Baumkötter; the SS officer Friedrich Panzinger, who had served as a high official in the Reich Security Main Office; and the SS man Otto Günsche, a personal adjutant of Adolf Hitler. Finally, this transport also included victims of the Stalinist purges in East Germany, such as the Social Democrats Karl Kapp, who had served as "camp oldest" in the Dachau concentration camp and was later denounced by Communist fellow prisoners, and Hermann M., who had been a critic of Communist and Soviet policies in the Eastern zones.[72]

As the personal composition of these transports demonstrated, many different pasts returned with the last "POWs," and public responses to them carried great symbolic weight. In 1955, British officials stressed the potential repercussions of the West German reception of the last returnees for the legitimacy of the Allied war trials program: "If the German authorities decide to prosecute some of the returnees, this will strengthen our own case for keeping our own prisoners in Werl until their sentences have expired. Alternatively, if the German authorities do nothing about some of the more notorious characters, this may well start another hostile press campaign at home."[73] Clearly, the reception of the last POWs immediately became a test case for how the newly sovereign Federal Republic would confront its difficult past one full decade after the ending of the war.

Initial reactions did not inspire much confidence in official and popular willingness to scrutinize individual returnees' pasts. When the head of the judicial committee of the Bavarian regional parliament, the SPD politician Jean Stock, proposed in 1953 that returnees undergo formal denazification procedures, he provoked a public outcry. Commentators echoed earlier denunciations of Social Democrats as "fellows without a fatherland" when they charged that politicians like Stock had "placed themselves outside of the nation in the hour of a reawakening *Volksgemeinschaft*."[74] Such popular identification with the last returnees reached into the West German working class as well. In 1955, an incident among workers of the Lemmerz factory in the Rhenish town of Königswinter brought to the fore just how unpopular dissenting views about the last returning POWs were. When the worker Hans Minzbach stated that "the returnees from Russia are all criminals" and "deserve a kick rather than a reception with flowers," his coworkers were so infuriated that they refused to continue to work with Minzbach and went on strike. "I was in Siberia for three years . . . while you were sitting at home for the entire war. You should therefore shut up now," charged one of his fellow workers. When Minzbach subsequently qualified his statement by indicating that he had only referred to people like Clauberg, his coworkers still were not appeased. All 1,350 employees of the factory ultimately refused to work with Minzbach, who was laid off with the approval of the factory council.[75]

West German officials at the highest level replicated these popular attitudes. Even though the Moscow agreement demanded careful scrutiny of "nonamnestied" returnees by West German courts, authorities in the Foreign Office quickly decided that "most of them had not committed any crimes according to German law."[76] However, especially in response to "nonamnestied" returnees, an increasing number of domestic and international voices advocated a more nuanced approach. In particular, the opposition Social Democrats began to move away from the bipartisan consensus that had characterized the politics of memory in the early Federal Republic.[77] In 1955, the Social Democratic *Vorwärts* argued that "whoever was implicated in the National Socialist terror regime cannot be integrated into the community of our democratic state, even if he was among the last returnees."[78] On a more formal level, the chairman of the Social Democratic Party, Erich Ollenhauer, attacked Jakob Kaiser of the Ministry for All German Affairs for not doing anything about the "real war criminals who are being sent back from Russia at the moment," adding that "there were quite a number of persons who really have committed atrocious crimes."[79] Likewise, the main Jewish newspaper in West Germany wondered whether the "national pathos" at the receptions in Friedland would give the impression that Germans were trying to replace the thesis of collective guilt with an assumption of collective innocence.[80] Protests from abroad joined this domestic criticism. In a letter to Chancellor Adenauer in January 1956, the members of a Danish association of former inmates of the Dachau concentration camp professed to be "outraged" by the fact that the West Germans welcomed the "slaughtermen from Sachsenhausen" with "gifts of money" and the "promises of good jobs and pensions."[81] In addition, the East German public campaign against "war criminals" in the West put pressure on West German officials to adopt a more differentiated attitude toward the last returnees.

It was partly in response to these domestic and international pressures that several 1955 returnees were indeed prosecuted and tried before West German courts. Carl Clauberg, for example, was arrested six weeks after his return in November 1955.[82] Because of the protests of "circles of Nazi victims at home and abroad" as well as the "attacks of the foreign press," officials in the West German foreign office also recommended a legal investigation of the Sachsenhausen concentration camp personnel. Shortly after the return of the "nonamnestied" prisoners, Chancellor Adenauer supported the arrest of "heavily compromised" concentration camp guardsmen.[83] Sorge and Schubert were arrested in February 1956 and sentenced to life in prison in 1959.[84] Both closely fit the profile of the so-called genuine criminals who had actually carried out the killings and the torture of victims. By contrast, West German courts tended to pay much less attention to the "bourgeois" administrators of genocide during the 1950s unless there was significant public pressure for prosecution, such as in Clauberg's case.[85] Some 1955 returnees were also prosecuted during the 1960s, often also for offenses that were unrelated to their convictions by Soviet courts. Others, however, benefited from the expiration of the statute of limitations in the 1960s.[86] Many highly compromised returnees thus never faced charges in West Germany.[87]

Still, official responses to the last returnees reflected subtle changes in the West German politics of memory, which, during the second half of the 1950s, brought about a more comprehensive confrontation with the Nazi past. The arrests and trials of some Nazi perpetrators among the 1955 returnees mirrored the increasing willingness of West German courts to resume the prosecution of Nazi crimes that had virtually ended by the mid-1950s. As Ulrich Brochhagen has convincingly argued, the compromised pasts of the 1955 returnees presented new challenges to the West German judicial system, which contributed to the founding of the Central Agency for the Prosecution of Nazi Crimes at Ludwigsburg in 1958.[88] Moreover, the return of the last POWs removed a significant ideological and psychological barrier to a more comprehensive confrontation with the Nazi past. As long as German POWs were still interned in Soviet camps, any suggestion in favor of a more vigorous prosecution of Nazi perpetrators in the West ran the risk of conceding legitimacy to Soviet trials of German POWs. The return of the last POWs nullified one of the most important and long-lasting consequences of defeat, and thereby opened up new possibilities for confronting German guilt and responsibility.

PROPAGANDA, PARANOIA, AND POPULAR OPINION:
THE RETURN OF THE LAST POWs TO THE EAST

The return of several thousand POWs from the Soviet Union in 1953–54 and 1955–56 to the East marked an equally important moment in postwar East German history. As in the Soviet Union, the return of the POWs was part of a careful retreat from the period of "high Stalinism" in East Germany. It coincided with large-scale amnesties of alleged "war criminals" who had been convicted by Soviet courts and were interned in East German prisons. In January 1954, the Soviet authorities released 6,143 persons who had been sentenced by Soviet courts after 1945.[89] In November 1955 Walter Ulbricht asked for Soviet approval for the release of 2,616 more prisoners who had been convicted by Soviet military tribunals (SMT).[90] In addition, 937 prisoners who had been convicted in the 1950 Waldheim trials were set free in 1955–56.[91]

The simultaneous release of POWs and internees allowed East German authorities to subsume both under the shared category of amnestied "war criminals." In 1955, Erich Mielke, then a high official in the Ministry of State Security, defined the term *war sentenced* as referring to those "persons who had been sentenced because of the crimes against humanity that they had committed during the war, independently of when, by what courts, and according to what laws they had been sentenced."[92] Much as in the West, official East German discourse elided distinctions between different kinds of "returnees." But whereas in the West, everybody, including convicted war criminals and civilian internees, became a "POW," in the East, everybody, including innocent POWs, became a "war criminal."

The official reception of the last returnees in the East featured a similar combination of ideological persuasion and vehement denunciations that had characterized SED responses to returning POWs throughout the postwar period. But in the aftermath of the popular uprising on 17 June 1953, the paranoia was much greater than the paternalism. This event marked the "internal foundation" of the GDR, and East German officials were henceforth determined to prevent "another 1953."[93] In particular, the SED began to expand its security apparatus in order to control and repress more effectively future dissent and opposition. This period therefore witnessed the expansion of the East German security police, the Stasi, which became one of the defining features of the East German dictatorship.[94]

Official reactions to the return of the last POWs reflected the heightened significance of the East German security apparatus. The 1953 transports arrived at night, and they were heavily guarded by the East German People's Police in order to prevent mutual ideological contamination between returning POWs and ordinary East Germans.[95] Yet this did not prevent individuals living near the transition camp in Fürstenwalde from showering returnees with questions about POWs still held in the Soviet Union.[96] In addition, they also reportedly told returnees "untrue stories about the events of June 17."[97] Even after East German authorities more carefully shielded the POW transports from encounters with the East German population, ordinary East Germans continued to display "great empathy for the fate of the returnees" by waving at and greeting them from afar.[98] In 1955, East German officials faced similar problems of preventing contacts between returning POWs and East German civilians. One of the first POW transports reportedly displayed banners with slogans such as "We thank you, Dr. Adenauer" and even the outlawed first verse of the German national anthem, "Deutschland, Deutschland, über alles."[99] Partly in response to Western criticism, East German officials adopted a more subtle approach than two years earlier. They tried to avoid "massive police cordons in uniform" and resorted to police in civilian clothes instead. Returning POWs were to be treated "properly and politely," yet security forces were still ordered to prevent any demonstrations or gatherings at the train stations "by all means."[100]

To counteract the enthusiastic reception of the last POWs in the West, East German officials engaged in massive counterpropaganda. In 1955, the SED published records of Soviet war crimes trials, which Soviet authorities had made available to them but not to West German authorities. These excerpts aimed at exposing these returnees as "inhuman creatures" who had committed the "ugliest crimes."[101] To East German commentators, the public celebration of the last returnees exposed the militaristic and essentially fascist nature of the Bonn republic. According to *Neues Deutschland*, the West portrayed those who had become "particularly guilty in Hitler's war and in the catastrophe of Germany" as "idols for German youth and the future Wehrmacht."[102] That the West German reception turned Wehrmacht generals and Nazi criminals into "heroes and martyrs" demonstrated unbroken continuities between the Third Reich and the West German state. The propagandistic attacks were supposed to highlight the affinity between Nazi perpetrators and the Federal Republic while, at the same time, casting the GDR as the "better" Germany.[103]

While some of these charges were not completely unfounded, the SED propaganda also failed to detect the subtle yet important changes within the West German politics of memory as discussed above. Moreover, East German officials' own responses to returning POWs revealed the largely instrumental nature of their attacks on the Federal Republic. Except for 275 nonamnestied returnees to East Germany in 1955, all former soldiers and POWs were immediately sent to their home communities.[104] East German authorities clearly valued returnees' political attitudes in the present

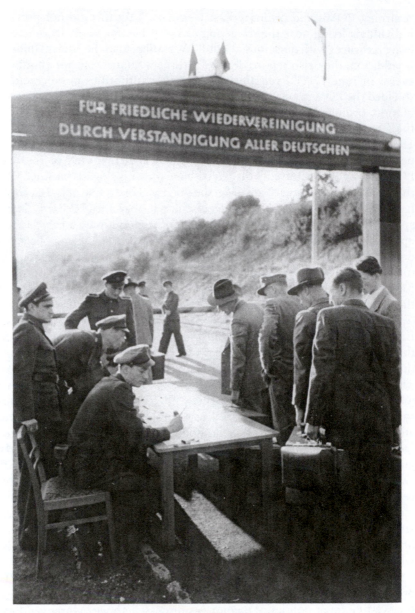

Figure 15. East German officials assist returnees in crossing the border from East to West Germany in September 1953. The caption on the border gate reads: "For peaceful reunification through an understanding between all Germans." Such officials were very suspicious of the "released war criminals" in 1953–54 and 1955–56. Paramilitary units of the People's Police tried to prevent any contact between the last returnees and the East German population. (Courtesy Bundesarchiv Koblenz.)

above their possible offenses in the past. Returnees simply needed to demonstrate that they had "learnt from the past" by returning to the East rather than to the West; then they would "no longer [be] considered criminals" but "citizens of our state with equal rights."[105] All that was expected from returnees was a general admission that their sentences had been "generally more or less justified" and that they "have changed." Beyond that, any preoccupation with the past would be finally laid to rest, and neither they nor their relatives would face any further discrimination.[106] According to official portrayals in the party organ *Neues Deutschland*, ideologically purified former war criminals smoothly assumed their new place within a society that had already made considerable headway on its path towards Socialism.[107]

Internal reports of the East German security forces, however, showed most returnees to be unlikely candidates for Socialist citizenship in the East. In 1953, many returnees reckoned that they did not owe their release to SED efforts but rather to Stalin's death and the removal of NKVD chief Beria.[108] Most returnees were also unwilling to deliver even the general admission of guilt that the SED required from them. Instead, they claimed that they were "completely innocent" and some said that they did not know why they had been sentenced to twenty-five years in prison. Comparisons between East and West German living standards rarely led to favorable results for the SED. "The population in East Germany has already been working hard for eight years and still does not have anything to eat," one returnee pointed out.[109] Finally, some returnees counteracted the official admiration of the Soviet Union by exhibiting a clear sense of superiority towards their Soviet captors. "We have turned Stalingrad from a dog kennel into a city," one of them exclaimed, adding that he would immediately join a new military campaign against "the Russians."[110] To their dismay, East German authorities noted that "a large segment of the returning prisoners still displays a strong allegiance to the fascist ideology" and that "the released prisoners do not have much confidence in the development of the GDR."[111]

Given these disconcerting reports, East German security forces followed returnees to their local communities. The Ministry of State Security (Stasi) received lists with all the names of returnees to the East and then instructed local Stasi officials to "keep these persons under permanent observation."[112] Returnees also needed to register with local People's Police officers who subsequently monitored their adjustment to conditions in East Germany.[113] Not surprisingly, most returnees tried to keep a low profile and were "frequently very reserved" in "discussions and conversations."[114] Rather than articulating any distinct political views, they emphasized that they wanted to "live in peace," "pursue their jobs," and "build themselves a new existence."[115] But secret informers also recorded some more negative statements. In private and public conversations, returnees refused any admission of wrongdoing and stated that they "did not know why [they] had been sentenced."[116] The returnee Josef F. declared that he did not agree with developments in the GDR and that he wanted to go to the West in order to write a book about his experience in captivity that, he hoped, would make him rich.[117] The Stasi also had an extremely long memory. It was only in 1961 that Stasi agents were willing to conclude that "no hostile activities have become apparent" among the last returnees.[118] Yet as late as 1973 and even 1980, Stasi officials proffered information about some of the last returnees.[119] Contrary to official assertions, the last returnees were not immediately accepted as citizens with equal rights in the East. Instead, their official labeling as war criminals tainted their biographies, and meant that the security police maintained extensive records that could be dug up at any given moment.

Notwithstanding its distrust of returnees' political attitudes, the Stasi also tried to recruit some returnees as informers and spies. In December 1955, Erich Mielke ordered the enlistment of returning POWs as Stasi agents. They were supposed to "spread panic, demoralization, and mistrust" in the West and write letters back to the GDR about the "bad conditions" in the West.[120] In some cases, these plans seemed to have been successful. As secret informant "GI Peter Holten," one returnee wrote several reports about POWs who had returned with him to East Germany in 1955.[121] In mid-1956, the same "GI Peter Holten" was instructed to observe two of his former fellow POWs and evaluate whether they could be recruited as "GIs" for the Stasi. In particular, he was to find out whether it would be possible to infiltrate the West German organization of former Armed SS members, the HIAG.[122] The Stasi thus subordinated all antifascist requirements to its struggle against the perceived "class enemy" at home and abroad, even if it mean recruiting former SS members and alleged war criminals as "fighters for peace."

East German officials, moreover, not only observed returnees' attitude but were even more concerned about their impact on East German society at large. Stasi and local police wrote extensive reports on the reception of the last returnees in East German communities.[123] These reports open an important window onto popular memories of the Second World War in East Germany ten years after the war's end, even as they reflected the biases of East German security officials.[124] They also illuminate the impact of ten years of party agitation on popular East German memories of war and defeat. Three major themes dominated East German popular responses to the last returning POWs. First, the return of several thousand POWs raised new questions about the numbers of POWs and MIAs still alive in the Soviet Union. Second, East Germans debated intensely the characterization of returnees as war criminals, and third, East Germans compared the different reception of these last returnees in East and West Germany.

For many East Germans, the return of thousands of POWs from the Soviet Union severely undermined the SED's official portrayal of the POW issue up to that point. In the fall of 1953, a woman from Mecklenburg-Vorpommern declared that she "could not understand how there could still be so many POWs in the Soviet Union." "Two years ago," she argued, "it was said that all have come home, but now I have to assume that more POWs are still being held there than is officially admitted."[125] The arrival of the POWs sparked new rumors about POWs still being held in Soviet "secret camps," often also inspired by letters from Western relatives.[126] The unexpected return of thousands of POWs thus also instilled new hope among family members that a missing soldier might still return, even though "they had never corresponded with them and even though they are most likely dead."[127] Still, the reports indicate that the return of the last POWs further undermined the SED's credibility among East German women. In Rostock, housewives who were still waiting for the return of a POW declared that "one needed to listen to West German radio stations in order to find out the truth."[128] Conversely, these reactions confirmed East German officials' own gender bias against women as politically indifferent and immature. They blamed it on women that the "agitation of the Western press and RIAS has found largely fertile ground."[129]

Most East Germans also rejected the official label of "war criminals" for the last returnees. In 1953, a Stasi official noted that the "population has not been enlightened enough, because it does not understand the difference between POWs and criminals."[130] These attitudes became even more pronounced in the fall of 1955. An official from Halle summarized that "discussions in the precinct are generally negative." He added that returnees are seen "not as war criminals but as prisoners of war who had been unjustly sentenced to long sentences" for theft in captivity rather than for war crimes.[131] Similar views even circulated within the ranks of the SED itself. In Halle, the SED member Otto W. explicitly disagreed with the party's position and declared that returnees "are human beings just like us" who "only had to follow orders."[132] Given the tendency of party officials to assign "progressive" attitudes to workers, incidents of working-class solidarity with returning POWs, which also occurred in the West, must have been particularly troubling to the authorities. When the local district SED chairman began his presentation on the "return of former war criminals from the Soviet Union" at a factory in Hallenberg, his deputy rose from his chair and declared that "they were not war criminals but soldiers just as everybody else had been." When the speaker attempted to counter this objection, all the workers immediately left the room.[133] As these examples demonstrated, popular memories of the Second World

War as a "people's war" cut across class lines and thwarted East German efforts to distance the working class from the "fascist Wehrmacht."

Because they generally disagreed with the official portrayal of returnees as war criminals, many East German advocated a similarly "dignified reception" of the last returnees as in the West.[134] In Cottbus, for example, there were "lively discussions as to why the former war criminals are received with ringing church bells and welcoming speeches [in the West], whereas they are only registered and processed in Frankfurt an der Oder." East Germans were also keenly aware of the compensation payments that returning POWs received in West Germany.[135] They indeed attributed most returnees' choice of the West over the East to the favorable reception and material benefits that awaited them there, not to returnees' alleged ideological affinity with the "fascist" Bonn republic, as the SED would have it.[136] Their dissatisfaction with the rather sober official reception of the POWs in the East led some East Germans to organize independent welcoming ceremonies for returning POWs in their local communities. When the news of the imminent arrival of the returnee Johannes F. reached the community of Wildenfels in the Zwickau district, relatives and friends gathered in the street and welcomed him with flowers.[137] Even some SED members advocated a more friendly reception of returning POWs in East Germany. An employee of the city administration in Magdeburg argued, for example, that if one of her relatives were among the returnees, she would scatter flowers in the street for his welcome as well.[138] Representatives of the Christian churches were frequently involved in the organization of such local welcoming ceremonies.[139] Protestant ministers welcomed returnees in their parishes and, if necessary, referred them to specific church-run rest homes in the Eastern zone.[140] They also lobbied quietly for the release of those "nonamnestied" POWs, who were detained in East German prisons after their return from the Soviet Union.[141] Church officials continued to compensate for the deficits of state policies in the East, and they tried to claim at least limited political independence. But they also operated within the constraints of the East German dictatorship and tried to achieve a modus vivendi with the SED.[142]

The popular sentiments recorded in these reports demonstrated that the SED largely failed in imposing official memory of war and defeat on the majority of the East German citizens. Ten years after the war, most ordinary East Germans were more willing to empathize with the last returning POWs than condemn them as war criminals. A decade of intense party agitation regarding returning POWs had largely failed in winning over the East German population to the SED position. Instead, the last returnees served as a rallying point for dissent and opposition to the SED. As the popular identification with the last POWs demonstrated, "counter"-memories of war and defeat severely limited the SED's transformative project. This was especially true for East German women, who lost much confidence in the SED as a result of the party's handling of the POW issue. Despite their popular breadth and intensity, such expressions of dissent, however, often remained limited to mere grumbling and did not involve an open challenge to party authority. As during the last years of the Third Reich, popular dissent over POWs and MIAs did not translate into political resistance. Fear of repression, especially in the aftermath of the June 17 uprising, may have prevented many East Germans from uttering any dissenting opinions at all.[143] In addition, for those East Germans who were not personally affected by it, the POW issue was not a problem of existential importance. Finally, the expanding East German security forces effectively controlled and curbed more open acts of defiance.

It would be misleading, though, to see East German responses to returning POWs only in terms of dissent and coercion. Official informers also recorded a minority of more critical responses to the returnees that came closer to the position of the SED. Observers noted a particularly strong popular resentment against the former regional Nazi Party chief (*Gauleiter*) in Magdeburg, Rudolf Jordan, who was among the last returnees. Citizens from that town demanded that Jordan "should not be let go to West Germany," or even that he should have received a "lethal injection" in order "to free humanity from such a scourge."[144] Undoubtedly because of Jordan's presence, popular opinion in Magdeburg was particularly divided: a "part of the population rejects the release of the POWs, another part wants to receive them with flowers."[145] Other East Germans criticized the release of General Paulus in 1953, who, on Hitler's order, had sacrificed the Sixth Army at Stalingrad in 1942–43.[146] In Cottbus, the farmer Emil M. voiced his belief that some of the war criminals were indeed guilty and had received their just sentence, yet that "most of them were innocent."[147] And a man from Halle who had spent five years in a concentration camp found that the returning POWs received "too much attention."[148] Ordinary East Germans were not quite ready to exonerate high Wehrmacht generals and Nazi officials, especially if they had victimized other Germans. While it is difficult to quantify these more critical voices, they nevertheless demonstrated that official and popular discourse did not remain completely separate in East Germany.

In both German postwar societies, the homecomings in 1953–54 and 1955–56 prompted a massive outpouring of national solidarity with the last returning POWs. These events served as crystallization points for shared popular memories of the Second World War. In East and West, ordinary Germans exhibited a remarkably similar emotional identification with the last soldiers of Hitler's army. In the East, these popular memories were diametrically opposed to the SED's official representation of the last POWs as "war criminals." The reactions of a majority of ordinary Germans to the return of the last POWs thus illustrated the deep fault lines between official and popular memories. They demonstrated the SED's failure to inculcate the narrative of antifascist conversion in large sections of the East German population. In the West, by contrast, popular memories largely coincided with official memories and thus demonstrated the greater extent of consensus between the government and the governed in the Federal Republic. It is important to emphasize, however, that one source of this popular consensus consisted precisely of the selective and highly apologetic memories of the Second World War as they manifested themselves in popular responses to the last POWs. As this case demonstrates, the demands of memory were not always identical to, but often also ran counter to, the process of West German democratization.

Still, the return of the last POWs also engendered more differentiated and more critical memories of the Second World War in both postwar societies. In the West, the completion of postwar (West German) society opened up a new discursive space, which made possible public demands for a more critical confrontation with the past, including the legal prosecution of highly compromised returnees. This opening set the stage for the dramatic transformation of the West German politics of memory in the late 1950s and early 1960s. As we have seen, a minority of East Germans also articulated similar criticism with respect to the last POWs. These more critical responses illustrated an at least partial identification with the SED's official narrative by a minority of the East German population. But because of the inherent limitations of that official narrative itself, these critical voices ultimately did not become an engine for the transformation of the East German politics of memory as a whole. Instead, East German official memory remained, for the most part, static and "cold" from the late 1940s to the eventual collapse of the GDR in 1989.[149]

Histories of the Aftermath

The return of the last POWs in 1955–56 did not signal the "end" of the postwar period, as contemporaries and later historians have often claimed. Too diffuse and too ubiquitous were the aftereffects of the Second World War to be contained in the first postwar decade.[1] Still, the return of the last POWs represented a turning point in the *public* confrontation with the *direct personal* consequences of the war, and hence also marks a logical end point of this book. Moreover, historians now agree that the second half of the 1950s was a period of crucial political, social, and cultural transformations, at least in the West.[2] By the end of the decade, these incremental yet important changes prepared the ground for a renewed confrontation with the Nazi past, such as the trial of members of killing squads in Ulm in 1958 and then the Auschwitz trial in 1963. Historians have offered various explanations for these transformations of the late 1950s, including the attainment of sovereignty in 1955, generational dynamics, or the development of "Cold War liberalism."[3] This study suggests that the return of the last POWs constituted an important precondition for these changes. It completed the (re)constitution of a (West) German national body that could then serve as the agent for a more critical confrontation with the past.[4]

Scholars are only beginning to unearth the internal dynamics of liberalization in postwar West Germany that started to unfold in the late 1950s.[5] Yet there is much evidence that these transformations often derived from internal changes within the key institutions that, as this study has shown, also crucially shaped West German responses to war and defeat: the Christian churches,[6] the professions of law, medicine, and psychiatry,[7] and the sphere of public discourse.[8] The combined effects emanating from several pluralist sites within West German society eventually also transformed state policy and official discourse at the national level. These changes did not simply lead to more "memory" and "justice" with respect to the legacies of war and genocide. They also entailed particular reinterpretations of Nazism and its memory, which often involved new patterns of selectivity and new distortions.[9] Still, there can be no doubt that West German memory became more inclusive and more pluralist by the 1960s. A similar transformation did not occur in East Germany's confrontations with the past. In East German state socialism, pluralist institutions could not serve as the engines of change, as in the West, nor were they able to channel and mediate popular demands emanating from within East German society. Instead, popular pressures "from below" managed to extract often grudging concessions from a regime that remained concerned about its popular legitimacy even though it was always willing to resort to coercion as well. And while the East German politics of memory did incorporate new elements, such as a distinct recourse to national traditions, over the course of the 1960s and 1970s, the basic elements of the foundational narrative of antifascist conversion, as it was forged in the late 1940s, changed little throughout the history of the GDR.[10]

The increasingly divergent paths of East and West, however, should not obscure the important structural and functional similarities between the two postwar societies during their formative decade of reconstruction. Throughout this period, East and West German confrontations with the Second World War exhibited a striking degree of internal homogeneity.[11] Before 1955, the pluralist interaction of a variety of actors and institutions in the West did not translate into more heterogeneous memories in the West. In both societies, the shared legacies of the war as well as the external pressures of the Cold War generated homogeneous memories. A battle over memory comparable to that of the Weimar Republic did not take place in post-1945 Germany, where the conflict over the interpretation of war and defeat was externalized to the antagonism between East and West.[12]

Arguably, the most significant parallel between East and West consisted of parallel strategies of overcoming the legacies of defeat as well as the limitations of this project in East and West. Redemptive memories in both postwar societies served the purpose of leaving behind the consequences of German violence *and* of violence against Germans. Postwar Germans' highly emotional investment in reconstruction, in security, and, increasingly, in consumption reflected this attempt to create distance from unprecedented experiences of violence, suffering, and deprivation.[13] In many ways, these East and West German strategies of overcoming were remarkably successful, and contemporaries as well as later historians have often credited both postwar societies for their achievements in these areas.

By contrast, this study has emphasized the costs and the limitations of this postwar stabilization for both individuals and society at large. On the level of society, the deformation and deficiencies of postwar memories in East and West resulted to a large extent from efforts to pacify war-damaged groups, such as professional soldiers, expellees, or, for that matter, returning POWs.[14] Meanwhile, the transformation of former soldiers into East and West German citizens was based on the erasure of violence and hence remained incomplete.[15] These problematic aspect of both postwar societies' commemorative cultures not only consisted of shared efforts to limit guilt and responsibility through narratives of victimization but also of efforts to overcome the war and its consequences through redemptive modes of remembrance.[16] These abstract and "forward-looking" narratives dissolved the war's violence into universal tales of regeneration and renewal that rendered all but impossible a confrontation with the war's losses. On the level of the individual, public memories stood in the way of an individual "working through" of the massive ruptures and contradictions that defined returnees' and other Germans' life histories.[17]

To be sure, it is not entirely clear how the violence of the war and its aftermath could have been adequately incorporated into public narratives. The war's destructive impact on both individuals and society at large simply may have exceeded the capacity for narrative integration, and any effort to further appease war-damaged groups may have accrued even steeper social and ideological "costs." Conversely, the prevalence of widely apologetic popular memories among returnees and their families illustrated the extraordinary difficulties that both German postwar societies faced in moving towards a more comprehensive and more critical memory of fascism, war, and genocide. The persistent gap between public and private memories had profound long-term consequences for both societies. It fostered merely "private" or "passive" forms of citizenship that shaped West German political culture and also persistently frustrated East German Communists in their efforts to mobilize the population for the construction of Socialism.[18] It was also a phenomenon that was symptomatic of a shared "postwar" condition.

As this book has further demonstrated, East and West German confrontations with the Second World War followed broader European patterns. To be sure, total defeat accentuated the "postwar" condition in Germany more strongly than in other European societies. The burden of guilt and responsibility for war and genocide prompted a particularly forceful assertion of defensive narratives of German victimization, and it may have weakened the transition to redemptive modes of remembrance. But these were differences in degree, not in kind, and hence should not distract from the underlying patterns of shared European confrontations with the legacies of the Second World War. All European societies embarked on a transnational quest for patriotic memories, which often also entailed the postwar rehabilitation of shattered masculinities. Moreover, actual experiences of loss and suffering were relegated to the margins of national memory. This was true, above all, for the Jewish victims of genocide, whose experience altogether refused redemptive resolution. They remained either excluded from postwar memory or were integrated into a larger antifascist memory; the latter still remained oblivious to the specificity of racial persecution in Nazi-dominated Europe.[19] This omission also applied to Eastern Europe and the Soviet Union, where, as Amir

Weiner has shown, the myth of the Great Patriotic War eradicated the memory of Jewish specificity.[20] Whether public memories were generated primarily from within civil society (as in Western Europe) or were primarily state-sponsored (as in Eastern Europe), they screened out experiences of genocide. The appeal of redemptive memories even extended to Jewish communities of Holocaust survivors in Israel and the United States, where the symbolic and functional demands of state building militated against a full recognition of past suffering and victimization.[21] By contrast, German suffering, as this study has stressed, was *not* excluded from postwar memory but often operated at its center. However, the key to the inclusion of collective experiences of suffering in national narratives was the possibility of redemptive resolution. Certain forms of feminized suffering, such as experiences of rape or exposure to strategic bombing, defied such resolution and hence featured much less prominently in postwar memories than the masculinist narratives of survival, conversion, and regeneration that focused on the POW experience.[22]

This all-pervasive discrepancy between public and private memory raises the question of the *lieux de mémoire* of individual experiences of loss and suffering. Where, in other words, did these experiences and memories go, and how did they manifest themselves in the postwar period? One possible answer to this question lies in localized forms of remembrance that might have compensated for the deficiencies and blank spots of national memory.[23] Another direction is trauma, the result of such failure of narrative integration. Notwithstanding the recent fascination with trauma as a site of privileged memory, the application of individual social-psychological concepts to entire collectives or societies remains deeply problematic. Yet, as the chapter on psychiatric responses to the trauma of the returned POWs in East and West Germany demonstrated, historically and culturally specific interpretations of physical and psychological injuries have much to reveal about broader patterns of coming to terms with the past. They illuminate the available categories for defining and articulating the war's consequences in a given society, and they point to mental and physical impairments that lack language and representation. The loquacious silence around returnees' psychological deficiencies in the East, finally, underlines the fact that concepts of "trauma" are inextricably intertwined with larger commemorative cultures. This historical and cultural specificity of trauma even extends to the level of individual experience. In her recent study on death and memory in twentieth-century Russia, Catherine Merridale warn us against the assumption of "universal patterns of psychological damage."[24] Despite a history of unimaginable suffering and mass death, she notes the virtual absence of concepts of trauma in Soviet culture on the level of official discourse or in the stories of individual lives.[25]

At the beginning of the twenty-first century, memories of the Second World War have lost much of their previous homogeneity and hence also some of their exclusionary tendencies. Most importantly, the period from the 1960s onward has seen the emergence of a distinct Holocaust memory, which now stands at the center of memories and histories of the Second World War. Parallel to this process, a proliferation of memories and narratives about the Second World War eroded the national narratives of the Cold War before it ended in 1989.[26] Although these developments entailed the troubling resurgence of openly apologetic and even fascist memories and histories, notably in West Germany and in Italy, these developments have also begun to bring into focus the multifaceted nature of the Second World War.[27] They have decentered the history of war and its aftermath by highlighting the local diversities and the multiplicity of experiences that made up this global conflict. Now the challenge for a comparative European history of aftermath is to represent such plural transitions from war to postwar on the level of individuals as well as on the level of nation-states. This history will have to do justice to individual and collective learning processes that informed postwar reconstruction in East and West, while also naming the silences, omissions, and exclusions on which these processes of overcoming were often based. At a time when the European continent faces new uncertainties and, possibly, new wars, such histories of the aftermath might help to recover the often devastating aftershocks of Europe's last conflict. They can reveal the ongoing significance of a "Europe in ruins," from which, as the German poet Hans Magnus Enzensberger has reminded us, we are "separated by only a few decades."[28] Such histories might also caution us against succumbing to the dangerous misconception that modern wars can be waged without long-term costs for both individuals and societies at large.

Notes

INTRODUCTION

1. Current estimates for the death toll of the Second World War, including the victims of the Holocaust, amount to sixty million; Weinberg, *A World at Arms*, 894.

2. Naumann, "Die Frage nach dem Ende"; Gluck, "The Long Postwar."

3. Hobsbawm, *Interesting Times*; Eley, *Forging Democracy*, 491–98.

4. For the distinction between "communicative" and "cultural memory," see Assmann, *Das kulturelle Gedächtnis*, 48–66.

5. This distinction between "active" and "passive" experiences of violence represents a rather crude way of distinguishing between different aspects of returnees' experience. Soldiers often experienced military service as a "passive" experience of violence, while captivity, as I show in chapter 6, also entailed active experiences of violence. Still, this distinction seems important in order to avoid a too general reference to "violence" without indicating the respective agents or recipients.

6. The pioneering study in English-language historiography was Diehl, *Thanks of the Fatherland*; for a similar point, see Lagrou, "The Nationalization of Victimhood," 243–44.

7. For comparative perspectives, see Thoß and Volkmann, *Erster Weltkrieg–Zweiter Weltkrieg*. On the period after World War II, see Geyer, "Das Stigma der Gewalt"; Heineman, *What Difference*; Moeller, *War Stories* and "Germans as Victims"; Naumann, *Nachkrieg in Deutschland*; Echternkamp, *Nach dem Krieg*; Greven and von Wrochem, *Der Krieg in der Nachkriegszeit*; Neumann, *Nicht der Rede Wert*; Bessel and Schumann, *Life after Death*; Kühne, "Kameradschaft"; Schwartz, "Vertreibung und Vergangenheitspolitik." On returning POWs specifically, see the older studies by Smith, *Heimkehr aus dem Zweiten Weltkrieg*; and Lehmann, *Gefangenschaft und Heimkehr*. Peter Steinbach has long advocated the study of captivity and returning home as central aspects of the postwar period; see Steinbach, "Jenseits von Zeit und Raum." More recent studies include Kaminsky, *Heimkehr 1948*; Moeller, "Last Soldiers" Badstübner, "Die Heimat grüsst Euch"; Hilger, *Deutsche Kriegsgefangene in der Sowjetunion*, which focuses primarily on captivity; Borchard, *Die deutschen Kriegsgefangenen in der Sowjetunion*, which analyzes the POW issue in diplomatic history. On returnees and psychiatry, see also the work of Goltermann.

8. See the useful reviews of the literature in Kühne, "Der nationalsozialistische Vernichtungskrieg und die ganz 'normalen' Deutschen" and "Der nationalsozialistische Vernichtungskrieg im kulturellen Kontinuum"; Overmans, "Ein Silberstreif am Forschungshorizont"; and "Kriegsgefangenschaft--ein vergessenes Thema?"

9. Mazower, *Dark Continent*, 160–66; Rossino, *Hitler Strikes Poland*.

10. On Hitler's planning for the war in the East, see Kershaw, *Hitler, 1936–1945,* 399–89; on the Eastern front, see Bartov, *The Eastern Front 1941–45* and *Hitler's Army*; Heer and Naumann, *Vernichtungskrieg*; Schulte, *The German Army*; Förster, "Das Unternehmen 'Barbarossa,' " 413–47; Müller and Überschär, *Hitler's War in the East, 1941–1945*; Müller and Volkmann, *Die Wehrmacht*; Gerlach, *Kalkulierte Morde*; Herbert, *Nationalsozialistische Vernichtungspolitik*; Rass, *"Menschenmaterial"*; Jarausch and Geyer, *Shattered Past,* 111–48.

11. Förster, "Das Unternehmen 'Barbarossa' als Eroberungs—und Vernichtungskrieg."

12. Streit, *Keine Kameraden*; Müller, "Die Behandlung sowjetischer Kriegsgefangener."

13. Farmer, *Martyred Village,* 31–60; Richter, "Wehrmacht und Partisanenkrieg"; and the literature cited in note 9.

14. Gerlach, *Kalkulierte Morde,* 1151.

15. The Soviet figure is based on Bergen, *War and Genocide,* 145. The history of the German retreat from the Eastern front deserves further study.

16. Ibid.

17. Quotation from Weinberg, *A World at Arms,* 303.

18. Bartov, *Germany's War,* 3–32; Förster, "Wehrmacht, Krieg und Holocaust"; Richter, "Wehrmacht und Partisanenkrieg"; Rass, *"Menschenmaterial."*

19. For different evaluations, see Graml, "Die Wehrmacht im Dritten Reich"; Latzel, *Deutsche Soldaten—Nationalsozialistischer Krieg*; Bartov, *Hitler's Army*; for examples of soldiers who resisted genocidal warfare, see Wette, *Retter in Uniform.*

20. These new publications have superseded the massive state-sponsored study of German POWs under the auspices of Maschke, *Die deutschen Kriegsgefangenen*; for an analysis of this project, see Moeller, *War Stories,* 177–80. The most important recent works on Soviet captivity are Hilger, *Deutsche Kriegsgefangene in der Sowjetunion*; and Karner, *Im Archipel GUPVI.* See also the essays in Bischof and Overmans, *Kriegsgefangenschaft im Zweiten Weltkrieg.*

21. On unsubstantiated speculations about mass death of German POWs in U.S. captivity, see Bischof and Ambrose, *Facts against Falsehood.*

22. For a more critical view that places German POWs in the context of race relations in the United States, see Reiss, *"Die Schwarzen waren unsere Freunde."*

23. Figures cited according to Overmans, "German Historiography," 155.

24. Hilger, *Deutsche Kriegsgefangene in der Sowjetunion,* 137; Karner, "Deutsche Kriegsgefangene," 1035; Overmans, *Deutsche militärische Verluste,* 288–89.

25. Hilger, *Deutsche Kriegsgefangene in der Sowjetunion,* 56.

26. Overmans, "Das andere Gesicht des Krieges".

27. Karner, *Im Archipel GUPVI,* 86–94; Hilger, *Deutsche Kriegsgefangene in der Sowjetunion,* 127–37.

28. Soviet sources recorded 17,484 deaths in 1947, 3,547 in 1948, and 907 in 1950; see Hilger, *Deutsche Kriegsgefangene in der Sowjetunion,* 404–5.

29. Karner, *Im Archipel GUPVI,* 135–70; Hilger, *Deutsche Kriegsgefangene in der Sowjetunion,* 173–219.

30. Hilger, *Deutsche Kriegsgefangene in der Sowjetunion,* 192.

31. Friedrich, *Der Brand*; Overmans, *Deutsche militärische Verluste*, 298–300, revises previous estimates that ran as high as two million victims of flight and expulsion.

32. See Zeidler, *Kriegsende im Osten*, 143–54; and on rape, Naimark, *The Russians in Germany*, 69–140; Grossman, "A Question of Silence." Estimates for the number of rapes range between tens of thousands and two million.

33. Peterson, *Many Faces of Defeat*.

34. Lange, "Alter und Beruf"; Altersaufbau der Kriegsgefangenen und Vermissten in der US Zone, 23 January 1948, EZA, 2/640. According to this statistic, close to 80 percent of POWs and MIAs were between twenty and forty years old.

35. Weitz, "The Ever Present Other."

36. This was the fallacy committed by Hillgruber, *Zweierlei Untergang*; see the incisive critique by Bartov, *Murder in Our Midst*, 71–88.

37. Moeller, *War Stories*, 186–98, and "Germans as Victims?"

38. Scarry, *The Body in Pain*; Domansky and Jong, *Der lange Schatten des Krieges*, 9–30.

39. Naumann, "Einleitung," 23.

40. Wolfgang Schivelbusch's notion of a "culture of defeat" has not yet been applied to the study of post-1945 Germany; see Schivelbusch, *The Culture of Defeat*. The masterly study by Dower, *Embracing Defeat*, does not yet have a German equivalent.

41. Bessel and Schumann, *Life after Death*.

42. See especially Naumann, *Nachkrieg in Deutschland*; Geyer, "Das Stigma der Gewalt"; Moeller, *War Stories*, as well as the literature cited above in note 7. Oral-history projects have also tended to emphasize the aftereffects of war and defeat; see the now classic studies by Niethammer, *Lebensgeschichte und Sozialkultur*; Niethammer, von Plato, and Wierling, *Die volkseigene Erfahrung*; see also Domansky and Jong, *Der lange Schatten des Krieges*. I have tried to develop this perspective in the introduction to my dissertation, "The Protracted War," 13–17.

43. First quotation, Birke, *Nation ohne Haus*, 23; second quotation, Görtemaker, *Geschichte der Bundesrepublik*, 31.

44. Görtemaker, *Geschichte der Bundesrepublik*, 13.

45. Bessel, *Germany after the First World War*, 283.

46. Maier, "The Two Postwar Eras"; and for Germany, Niedhardt, *Lernen aus dem Krieg?*

47. Allemann, *Bonn ist nicht Weimar*.

48. See Schwarz, "Die ausgebliebene Katastrophe." A consideration of subjective factors in writing contemporary history might increase sensitivity to these private dimensions of the past; see Schissler, "*Zeitgenossenschaft.*"

49. Jarausch and Siegrist, *Amerikanisierung und Sowjetisierung*; Schildt, *Ankunft im Westen*; on East Germany, see Ross, *The East German Dictatorship*, 19–43.

50. Bessel and Schumann, *Life after Death*, 1–13; Jarausch and Geyer, *Shattered Past*, 269–314; Betts and Eghigian, *Pain and Prosperity*; Braun, "Das Streben nach Sicherheit."

51. Naumann, "Einleitung"; Bessel and Schumann, *Life after Death*, 1–13; Deák, Gross, and Judt, *The Politics of Retribution*.

52. Quoted in Thoß, "Die Zeit der Weltkriege," 15.

53. Geyer, "Eine Kriegsgeschichte" and *Deutsche Rüstungspolitik, 1860–1980,* 12.

54. Naumann, "Die Frage nach dem Ende."

55. For excellent surveys of the recent literature, see Moeller, "Coming to Terms"; and Confino, "Telling about Germany." My thinking on postwar memory has been particularly influenced by Moeller, *War Stories*; Herf, *Divided Memory*; Gregor, "Is He Still Alive"; Wiesen, *West German Industry*; Frei, *Vergangenheitspolitik*; Marcuse, *Legacies of Dachau*; Herzog, *Sex after Fascism*; Wolfrum, *Geschichtspolitik in der Bundesrepublik*; Brochhagen, *Nach Nürnberg*; Danyel, *Die geteilte Vergangenheit.* This literature has revised the classic study by Mitscherlich and Mitscherlich, *Die Unfähigkeit zu trauern.*

56. This term comes from Schildt, "Fünf Möglichkeiten," 1240–42.

57. Naumann, "Einleitung."

58. Ross, *The East German Dictatorship,* 175–202.

59. For a more skeptical view of the East-West comparison, see Epstein, "East Germany and Its History," 656–57.

60. Bauernkämper, Sabrow, and Stöver, *Doppelte Zeitgeschichte*; Klessmann, *The Divided Past*; see also the insightful comments in Jarausch, "Die Teile als Ganzes erkennen."

61. Klessman, *The Divided Past,* 1–9.

62. Domansky, "A Lost War," argues the former.

63. See the respective introductions in Moeller, *West Germany under Construction,* 1–30; and Schissler, *The Miracle Years,* 3–16.

64. For a comparative perspective on postwar commoration, see Rousso, "Das Dilemma eines europäischen Gedächtnisses"; Lagrou, *Legacy of Nazi Occupation*; and Moeller, "Coming to Terms."

65. See especially Deák, Gross, and Judt, *The Politics of Retribution*; Bessel and Schumann, *Life after Death*; Wood, *Vectors of Memory*; Mazower, "Changing Trends."

66. Bonnel and Hunt, *Beyond the Cultural Turn.*

67. See, for example, Fass, "Cultural History/Social History"; and the discussion about the concept of "class" in *International Labor and Working Class History* 57 (2000).

68. On "experience," see Canning, "Feminist History after the Linguistic Turn"; Jarausch, "Towards a Social History of Experience"; see also the contributions in Buschman and Carl, *Erfahrungsgeschichtliche Perspektiven.* For a radical critique of the concept of experience, see Scott, "The Evidence of Experience"; for an insightful response, see Daniel, "Erfahrung"; for an excellent discussion of the history of the concept, see Jay, *Songs of Experience,* especially 241–55.

69. See, for expellees, Lüttinger, "Der Mythos der schnellen Integration."

70. These concepts are designed to allow meaningful comparisons between East and West; see Poiger, *Jazz, Rock, and Rebels,* 225.

71. Confino, "Collective Memory and Cultural History."

72. Confino and Fritzsche, *The Work of Memory,* 1–21, quotation on 7.

73. *Ibid.,* 6.

74. Halbwachs, *On Collective Memory*; Assmann, *Das kulturelle Gedächtnis*, 34–48.

75. Crane, "Writing the Individual"; Confino, "Telling about Germany"; Winter and Sivan, "Setting the Framework." For a philosophical discussion of the relationship between "personal" and "collective" memory, see Ricoeur, *History, Memory, Forgetting*, especially 93–132.

76. Scott, "Gender as Category"; for an excellent review of this field, see Ditz, "The New Men's History"; for the German context, see Kühne, "Männergeschichte als Geschlechtergeschichte."

77. Frevert, *Die kasernierte Nation*; Hagemann, *Männlicher Muth*; Mosse, *Fallen Soldiers*; Schilling, *Kriegshelden*.

78. Ditz, "The New Men's History"; Allen, "Men Interminably in Crisis?"

79. Jeffords, *The Remasculinization of America*, 51, defines this term as "regenerations of the concepts, constructions, and definitions of masculinity . . . and of the gender order for which [they are] formulated"; for the application of this concept to postwar Germany, see Moeller, "The 'Remasculinization' of Germany."

80. The term comes from Connell, *Masculinities*, 79; on this concept, see also Tosh, "Hegemonic Masculinity."

81. Connell, *Masculinities*, 79.

82. Grossmann, "Trauma, Memory and Motherhood"; Herzog, "Desperately Seeking Normality"; and *Sex after Fascism;* Heineman, "Hour of the Woman"; Moeller, *War Stories*.

83. Ditz, "The New Men's History"; Ramazanoglu, "What Can You Do?"

84. Marshall, *Citizenship and Social Class;* on the German context, see Gosewinkel, *Einbürgern und Ausbürgern*.

85. Canning and Rose, "Gender, Citizenship, and Subjectivity"; for a good introduction to the literature on citizenship, see Radcliff, "La ciudadania."

86. My thoughts here are influenced by Borneman, *Belonging in the Two Berlins*.

87. The term comes from Weisbrod, "Moratorium of the Mandarins," 66.

88. On the contrast between "active" and "passive" citizenship, see Turner, "Outline of a Theory of Citizenship."

89. Jarausch and Geyer, *Shattered Past*, 12.

90. Hilger, Schmeitzner, and Schmidt, *Sowjetische Militärtribunale*.

CHAPTER 1
IMPENDING DEFEAT

1. . For these conceptualizations, see Broszat, Henke, and Woller, *Von Stalingrad zur Währungsreform*; and Mazower, *Dark Continent*, 212–49.

2. Weinberg, *A World at Arms*, 454; Overmans, *Deutsche militärische Verluste*, 228, 265–66, 278–79.

3. Steinbach, "Die sozialgeschichtliche Dimension der Kriegsheimkehr," 325–40.

4. By late 1944, official casualty figures for the Eastern front were one million soldiers below actual casualty figures. The difference between official and actual casualty figures during the final stages of the war amounted to an additional one million soldiers; see Overmans, *Deutsche militärische Verluste*, 300.

5. Ibid., 285–89.

6. Zeidler, *Kriegsende im Osten*, 178–79; Henke, *Die amerikanische Besetzung Deutschlands*, 683.

7. On U.S. expectations of postwar resistance, see Henke, *Die amerikanische Besetzung Deutschlands*, 160–69.

8. Behrenbeck, *Kult um die toten Helden*, 458.

9. "Benachrichtigung von Angehörigen gefallener, verstorbener und vermisster Wehrmachtsangehöriger," 18 May 1943, BA-M, RW 48/10; see also Behrenbeck, *Kult um die toten Helden*, 498.

10. On Hitler's inability to make peace, see Wegner, "Hitler"; and, in general, Kershaw, *Hitler,1936–1945*.

11. Latzel, *Deutsche Soldaten—nationalsozialistischer Krieg*, 227–83; Kershaw, *Hitler Myth*, 188; Behrenbeck, *Kult um die toten Helden*, 533–91. See also the "oral history" evidence in Dörr, *Wer die Zeit nicht miterlebt hat*, 2:207–35.

12. Gellately, *Backing Hitler*, 253; Kershaw, *Hitler Myth*, 172, cites American surveys from 1945 according to which one-third of the population continued to believe in final victory up until the very end.

13. Heinemann, "Krieg und Frieden," 42; Steinert, "Stalingrad und die deutsche Gesellschaft," 182.

14. Interrogation of Martha S., 7 April 1942; 20 May 1942, NRWHStA, RW 58/30367, 7, 17; for similar examples of women's loyalty despite heavy losses, see Heineman, *What Difference*, 52.

15. See also the evidence presented in zur Nieden, "Chronistinnen des Krieges."

16. Herbert and Schildt, *Kriegsende in Europa*, 22; Schäfer, *Das gespaltene Bewusstsein*, 114–62.

17. Soldiers were told to volunteer only name, military rank, date of birth, and home address. Otherwise they were supposed to maintain an "upright attitude" and admonished that every further statement equaled "high treason" and the "murder of comrades"; see "Merkblatt für kriegsgefangene Soldaten für das Soldbuch," cited in Hilger, *Deutsche Kriegsgefangene in der Sonjetunion*, 74.

18. Cited in Behrenbeck, *Kult um die toten Helden*, 556.

19. *Goebbels, Tagebücher, part 2, Diktate 1941–1945, vol. 7: Januar-März 1943*, 239, 255; see also Welch, *The Third Reich*, 106–13.

20. Goebbels, Tagebücher, 253.

21. Douglas, *Purity and Danger*.

22. On these organizations, see Scheurig, *Free Germany*; and, with further references, Überschär, *Das Nationalkomitee "Freies Deutschland."*

23. Haider, "Reaktionen der Wehrmacht."

24. OKW counterpropaganda against the NKFD made frequent references to 1918; see Mitteilungen für das Offizierskorpes, Sondernummer 1943, in Überschär, *Das Nationalkomitee "Freies Deutschland,"* 269–79; and "Stellungnahme des OKW zu einigen Flugblättern des NKFD in 'Mitteilungen für die Truppe,' Nr. 351 vom August 1944," in Überschär, 281–83.

25. "Sondernummer der vom Oberkommando der Wehrmacht (OKW) herausgegebenen 'Mitteilungen für das Offizierskorpes' zum Moskauer Komitee 'Freies

Deutschland' vom Oktober 1943," in Überschär, *Nationalkomitee "Freies Deutschland,"* 269–78.

26. Quotation from Abt. Fremde Heere Ost (IIb), Behandlung der deutschen Kriegsgefangenen in der SU, 18 June 1944, BA-M, RH 2/2780, 7; Sonderdienst der Reichspropagandaleitung, HA Propaganda, Amt Propagandalenkung, Ausgabe B, Folge 11, 20 January 1944, BA-Berlin, R 55/517, 139.

27. Merkblatt für die Angehörigen der in Sowjetrussland vermissten deutschen Soldaten, BA-M, RH 15/291, 21. In a similar way, Martin Bormann asserted that missing soldiers had most likely been shot in captivity; cited in Absolon, *Die Wehrmacht im Dritten Reich*, 543.

28. Letter by "Pepi" to his "liebe schwer geprüfte Mutter," Basel, 10 June 1943, BA-M, RH 15/340, 30.

29. Overmans, *Deutsche militärische Verluste*, 23–43.

30. Between 11 and 20 November 1944, the agency recorded 689 inquiries, 1,288 responses by mail, OKH/Abwicklungsstab Gruppe A/B, Meldg. üb. d. Stand d. Ab-Arbeiten f.d.Zeit v. 11.–20.11.1944, 21 November 1944, BA-M, RH 15/290.

31. Overmans, *Deutsche militärische Verluste*, 36–37.

32. In July 1941, the Soviet Union had directed a note to the German government through the Swedish government in which it offered to honor the The Hague convention of 1907 under the condition of reciprocity. Hitler, however, had left this note unanswered. Unlike in the West, where the International Red Cross or the Allies themselves published the names of German POWs, such official channels for information did not exist for the Eastern front; Hilger, *Deutsche Kriegsgefangene in der Sowjetunion*, 65–66; Absolon, *Die Wehrmacht im Dritten Reich*, 541.

33. See the case cited in Dörr, *Wer die Zeit nicht miterlebt hat*, 2:237–38.

34. Overmans, *Deutsche militärische Verluste*, 300–301; Böhme, *Gesucht wird . . .*, 234–37.

35. *Propagandaparole Nr. 57 an alle Gauleiter, Gaupropagandaleiter und Leiter der Reichspropagandaämter, 26 May 1943, BA-Berlin, R 55/977 1–5; Leiter der Partei Kanzlei, Rundschreiben Nr. 83/43, 28 May 1943, BA-Berlin, N S6/341, cited in Absolon, Wehrmacht im Dritten Reich,* 543.

36. Oberkommando des Heeres, Betr. Namhaftmachung von deutschen Kriegsgefangenen in sowj. Flublättern (Abschrift), 29 October 1942; Aktenvermerk über Besprechung AWA am 15.10.1942 betreffend Benachrichtigung der Angehörigen von angeblichen deutschen Kriegsgefangenen in der UdSSR, BA-M, RW 48/10.

37. Boddenberg, *Die Kriegsgefangenenpost deutscher Soldaten*, 44. Rundschreiben des RSHA betr. Deutsche Kriegsgefangene in der Sowjetunion, 18 May 1943, BA-M, R58/268, 45–47, also cited in Boddenberg, 44.

38. Stellv. Generalkommando IV Ak (Wehrkreiskommando IV) IC/WVW Nr. 63/43 geh.-Aktion Stalingrad, Bericht über die Stimmung bei den Angehörigen der Stalingrad Kämpfer, 8 December 1943, BA-M, RH 15/340, 5; Notiz 27 March 1943, BA-M, RH 15/310, 134; Stellv Gen. Kdo, III, AK an Kommandeur Abwicklungsstab 6. Armee, Berlin, 28 June 1943, BA-M, RH 15/308; RPA Lüneburg, Vermisstenmeldungen, 11 December 1944, BA-Berlin, R55/604, 215.

39. Stellv. Generalkommando IV Ak (Wehrkreiskommando IV) IC/WVW Nr. 63/43 geh.-Aktion Stalingrad, Bericht über die Stimmung bei den Angehörigen der Stalingrad Kämpfer, 8 December 1943, BA-M, RH 15/340, 5; for another report, see OKH, Abwicklungsstab 6. Armee u. Hegru Afrika, Sachbearbeiter d. 24. Panzer-Div., Bericht über die Dienstreise vom 18.–25.10.1943, 26 October 1943, BA-M, RH 15/310, 67.

40. Oberkommando des Heeres, Betr. "Namhaftmachung von deutschen Kriegsgefangenen in sowjetischen Flugblättern," 29 October 1942 (Abschrift), BA-M, RW 48/10. For examples of flyers with names of German POWs, see Boddenberg, *Die Kriegsgefangenenpost deutscher Soldaten*, 54–62.

41. Flyer "Kameradschaftsdienst"; interrogation of August R., Gerard K, and Christine R.; Gestapo Stettin to Gestapo Düsseldorf, 21 May 1943; Schlussbericht, 6 August, 1943, all in NRWHStA, RW 58/26362.

42. Reuband, " 'Schwarzhören' im Dritten Reich." Death sentences were only meted out in combination with other offenses; see Hensle, *Rundfunkverbrechen*.

43. Stellv Gen. Kdo III Ak, Arbeitsstab Stalingrad u. Tunis to Kommandeur Abwicklungsstab 6. Armee, 28 June 1943, BA-M, RH 15/308.

44. Propagandaparole Nr. 57 an alle Gauleiter, Gaupropagandaleiter und Leiter der Reichspropagandaämter, 26 May 1943, BA-Berlin, R 55/977.

45. NRWHStA, RW 58/41982. See also the discussion of this case in Gellately, *Backing Hitler*, 237–38.

46. Unlike Gellately, *Backing Hitler*, 237–38, I have found no evidence that Fritz M. was actually denounced to the Gestapo. Instead, one recipient forwarded one of the letters to the "working agency Stalingrad," from which it found its way to the Abwehr and finally to the Gestapo; Wehrkreiskommando VI A.K., 19 April 1943; Abwehrstelle im Wehrkreis VI to Gestapo Düsseldorf, 4 June 1943, NRWHStA, RW 58/41982, 55.

47. Interrogation of Hildegard Z., 1 June 1943, NRWHStA, RW 58/41982, 39. Another declared that she had not denounced Fritz M. because he did not seem to be trying to convey a political message; interrogation of Anni H., 30 May 1943, NRWHStA, RW 58/41982, 31–32.

48. Wuppertal, 22 June 1943, 44–45, NRWHStA, RW 58/41982; Verdict, 16 October 1943, NRWHStA, RW 58/41982, 72–73. It is not clear whether Fritz M. survived the war.

49. For Vichy-France, see Fishman, *We Will Wait*.

50. On the function of rumors in the Third Reich, see Dröge, *Der zerredete Widerstand*.

51. On Heitz, see Wegner, "Der Krieg gegen die Sowjetunion 1942/43," 1060.

52. Rundschreiben des RHSHA, betr. Deutsche Kriegsgefangene in der Sowjetunion, 18 May 1943, BA-Berlin, R58/268, 45–47; Boddenberg, *Die Kriegsgefangenenpost deutscher Soldaten*, 38.

53. Oberkommando der Wehrmacht to Frau Gisela Heitz, 16 July 1943, BA-M, RH 15/310, 240; see also the recollections of Mady Feijn Schilling, a former secretary at the Abwicklungsstab Stalingrad, cited in Steinhoff, Pechel, and Showalter, *Deutsche im Zweiten Weltkrieg*, 259–61.

54. Gisela Heitz to Fräulein G., (no date), probably early 1944, BA-M, RH 15/310, 6.

55. Hedwig Strecker to Frau von P., 25 June 1943, BA-M, RH 15/310, 18. General Strecker did not return from Soviet captivity until 1955. The wife of Oberst Hollunder, Erika Hollunder, was also involved in spreading news about these letters; Erika Hollunder, no date (probably October 1943), BA-M, RH 15/310, 53.

56. For a copy of the questionnaire, see Fragebogen, 15 July 1944, BA-M, RH 15/316, 13; see also Boddenberg, "Der Kriegsgefangenenbrief des Generaloberst Heitz."

57. Heitz was transported to a Moscow hospital in January 1944 and probably died on 9 February 194; see Reschnin, *Feldmarschall im Kreuzverhör*, 104.

58. Claire R. to Generalkommando Berlin, 8 June 1944, BA-M, RH 15/316.

59. Oberkommando der Wehrmacht to Abwicklungsstab der 6. Armee und Hegru. Afrika, 8 July 1944, BA-M, RH 15/310, 150; form letter Wehrmachts-auskunftsstelle für Kriegsverluste und Kriegsgefangene beim Oberkommando der Wehrmacht, no date, BA-M, RH 15/311; see also Gaupropagandaleitung der NSDAP to Kreispropagandaleiter der NSDAP, 30 August 1944, NRWHStA, RW 23, 116–18.

60. The polycratic power structure of the Third Reich contributed to these failures. In October 1943, the working agency "Stalingrad" still awaited Hitler's decision as to how to respond to Heitz's letter; Stell. Gen. Kdo. III A.K. to Abtg Ic, 23 October 1943, BA-M, RH 15/316, 139. As late as October 1944, local officials conveyed the impression that it was indeed possible to contact German POWs in the Soviet Union; RPA Westfalen Süd to RPM, Berlin, 27 October 1944, BA-Berlin, R 55/613, 206.

61. Hedwig Strecker to Frau von P., 25 June 1943, BA-M, RH 15/310.

62. Quotation from Frau Gisela Heitz to Fräulein G., BA-M, RH 15/310, 6; see also Asta B. to Frau von J., 22 June 1943, BA-M, RH 15/310, 18; Erika Hol-lunder, no date, BA-M, RH 15/310, 53.

63. Max K. to Führer-Hauptquartier, 3 March 1943, BA-M, RH 15/310, 123.

64. RPA Koblenz to RPM Dr. Schäffer, 11 February 1943, BA-Berlin, R 55/613, 15. This rumor was explicitly denied in Bormann's confidential memo of May 1943; see Absolon, *Wehrmacht im Dritten Reich*, 544.

65. Erna B. to Deutsche Rote Kreuz, 2 August 1943, BA-M, RH 15/310, 50; Lübbert, Delegierter für die Türkei der Firma Lasson & Co, Istanbul, 21 August 1943, BA-M, RH 15/310, 104; Botschaft, Militärattache, Betr. Nachrichtenüber-mittlung von Kriegsgefangenen in der UdSSR, 21 December 1943, BA-M, RH 15/316, 155; Deutsche Botschaft to Frau Maria P. (Abschrift), 31 March 1954, BA-M, RH 15/310, 13.

66. Geheime Staatspolizei Chemnitz to Reichssicherheitshauptamt Amt IV, Berlin, 19 April 1943, BA-M, RH 15/310. In November 1943, a local party offi-cial told Frau Cläre S. that "all soldiers who had been captured in Stalingrad were alive and well" and were under the supervision of Turkish and Swiss authorities;

Frau Cläre S. to liebe Kameradeneltern und Kameradenfrauen, 24 November 1943, BA-M, RH 15/310, 207.

67. Irmgard D. to Oberkommando der Wehrmacht (Abschrift), 9 April 1943, BA-M, RW 48/10.

68. Boddenberg, *Die Kriegsgefangenenpost deutscher Soldaten*, 90.

69. Letter Erika Hollunder, 29 June 1943, BA-M, RH 15/310, 65.

70. Kumpfmüller, *Die Schlacht von Stalingrad*, 71–73.

71. This evidence runs counter to Susanne zur Nieden's findings in diaries of women, which, according to her, demonstrated the "incapability to imagine a future beyond National Socialist idea"; zur Nieden, "Chronistinnen des Krieges," 848.

72. Käte B. to Frau R., 1 May 1943, NRWHStA, RW 58/26362.

73. Notiz, 27 March 1943, BA-M, RH 15/310, 134.

74. Wette, "Zwischen Untergangspathos und Überlebenswillen," 13–15. It is important here to distinguish between relatives of POWs/MIAs and soldiers' wives; for the latter, see Kundrus, *Kriegerfrauen*.

75. Moll, "Die Weisse Rose," especially, 464–65; see also Bald, *Die Weisse Rose*.

76. Peukert, *Volksgenossen und Gemeinschaftsfremde*, 55–77.

77. Wehrkreiskommando VIII Arbeitstab Stalingrad to Abw. Stab 6. Armee und Hegru. Afrika, 2 March 1944, BA-M, RH 15/311; for cooperation between the Abwicklungsstab and the Sipo, see Chef der Sicherheitspolizei und des SD to OKW, Abwicklungsstab VI. Armee und Hegru. Afrika, 16 March 1944, BA-M, RH 15/392, 199; Abwicklungsstab 6. Armee und Hegru Afrika to Chef der Sicherheitspolizei und des SD, 19 April 1944, BA-M, RH 15/316, 121; Chef der Sicherheitspolizei und des SD to Oberkommando der Wehrmacht, Abwicklungsstab der VI. Armee und Hegru. Afrika, 19 February 1944, BA-M, RH 15/311.

78. Hptm. Ernst Paulus to stellvertr. Generalkommando XVIII A.K., 10 July 1944, BA-M, RH 15/316.

79. My thoughts here are influenced by the discussion of "indifference" in Dean, *The Fragility of Empathy*, 76–105.

80. Arendt, "The Aftermath of Nazi Rule."

81. Apart from the evidence cited below, see "Kettenbriefe gegen die deutschen Verbrechen im Zweiten Weltkrieg," *Frankfurter Allgemeine Zeitung*, 91, 18 April 1996, 13–14, cited in Wette, *Die Wehrmacht*, 321–22 n. 75.

82. Dr. Chr. Schöne, An Angehörige von Stalingradkämpfern, Fürstenwalde/Spree, 28 March 1942 [*sic*], BA-M, RH 15/310, 169.

83. All quotations, unless otherwise indicated, are from the verdict of the military court in Berlin against Schöne, 22 November 1943, reproduced in "Kettenbriefe gegen die deutschen Verbrechen im Zweiten Weltkrieg," *Frankfurter Allgemeine Zeitung*, 91, 18 April 1996, 13–14. Such suggestions echoed a similar proposal to subject Jews to reprisal measures for Allied bombing attacks; see Stargadt, "Opfer der Bomben."

84. See Bankier, *Germans and Final Solution*, 101–15.

85. Verdict cited in "Kettenbriefe gegen die deutschen Verbrechen im Zweiten Weltkrieg," *Frankfurter Allgemeine Zeitung*, 91, 18 April 1996, 13–14; Albrecht Schöne, "Lesehilfe für Nachgeborene," *Frankfurter Allgemeine Zeitung*, 15 April 1996, 13–14.

86. Überschär, "Das NKFD und der BDO."

87. "Wie lebt der deutsche Kriegsgefangene in Russland," BA-M, RH 15/346, 179; Front-Illustrierte für den deutschen Soldaten, Nr. 15–16, June 1943, BA-M, RH 15/340, 237.

88. Cited in Behrenbeck, *Kult um die toten Helden*, 553; Kumpfmüller, *Die Schlacht von Stalingrad*, 156–57.

89. Martin Bormann, Bekanntgabe 30/44g, Betr.· Deutsche Kriegsgefangene in der Sowjetunion, 8 February 1944, BA-Berlin, NS 6/350, 38–41. For a report of escaped German soldiers, see Heerwesenabteilung beim General zbV beim OKH to Fremde Heere Ost., 31 October 1944, BA-M, RH 2/2783.

90. See Volkmann, *Das Russlandbild im Dritten Reich*; Messerschmitt, *Die Wehrmacht im NS-Staat*, 326–47, 353–61.

91. Oberkommando der Heeresgruppe Süd, 23 February 1943, BA-M, RH 15/392.

92. Vernehmungsniederschrift, Gruppe Geheime Feldpolizei 626, Sekretariat in Tschassow-Jar., 21 July 1943, BA-M, RH 15/392, 142. The files do not provide any evidence of torture in this case, even though it may have been applied.

93. M. Bormann, Leiter der Parteikanzlei to Gauleiter, Betr. Deutsche Kriegsgefangene in der Sowjetunion, 8 February 1944, BA-Berlin, NS 6/350, 38–41; Abt. Fremde Heere Ost, "Behandlung der deutschen Kriegsgefangenen in der SU," 18 June 1944, BA-M, RH 2/2780, 2. See also the material in BA-M, RH 2/2780–85.

94. Hilger, *Deutsche Kriegsgefangene in der Sowjetunion*, 103–5.

95. On this argument more generally, see Bartov, *Hitler's Army*.

96. See Moeller, *War Stories* and "Germans as Victims"; see also Welzer, Monteau, and Plass, *Was wir für böse Menschen sind*.

97. M. Bormann, Leiter der Parteikanzlei to Gauleiter, Betr. Deutsche Kriegsgefangene in der Sowjetunion, 8 February 1944, BA-Berlin, NS 6/350, 38–41; Abt. Fremde Heere Ost, "Behandlung der deutschen Kriegsgefangenen in der SU," 18 June 1944, BA-M, RH 2/2780, 2.

98. Cited in Latzel, *Deutsche Soldaten—nationalsozialistischer Krieg*, 199.

99. NRWHStA, RW 58/37037; for another case in which Nazi authorities suspected family members of inciting a soldier to desertion, NRWHStA, RW 58/1016.

100. Keitel, Oberkommando des Heeres (Abschrift), 5 January 1944, BA-M, NS 6/350, 43.

101. See Bajohr, "Hamburg," 323. On the Soviet conquest of eastern Germany, see Zeidler, *Kriegsende im Osten*, 135–54; and Naimark, *The Russians in Germany*, 69–140.

102. See Wette, Brenner, and Vogel, *Das letzte halbe Jahr*, 149, 168, 308; on mass surrender along the Elbe, see Henke, *Die amerikanische Besetzung Deutschlands*, 674–94.

103. Ziemann, "Fluchten aus dem Konsens zum Durchhalten," 608. On voluntary surrender on the Eastern front, see also the evidence cited in Hilger, *Deutsche Kriegsgefangene in der Sowjetunion*, 78; and Messerschmitt, "Wehrmacht in der Endphase," 43. On desertion in general, see Haase and Paul, *Die anderen Soldaten*; for a report of large-scale desertion, see Grünewald, Generalrichter und Abt. Chef, Vortragsvermerk für Herrn Feldmarschall, BA-M, RW 4/725, 7.

104. Messerschmidt and Wüllner, *Die Wehrmachtsjustiz im Dienste des Nationalsozialismus*; Haase, "Wehrmachtsangehörige vor dem Kriegsgericht."

105. This happened as early as February 1943, when the mother, wife, and two brothers of the grenadier Wenzelaus M., who had deserted to Soviet lines in 1942, were executed; see Haase and Paul, *Die anderen Soldaten*, 144; NRWHStA, RW 58/74304.

106. Chef OKW Keitel to Reichsführer SS und Leiter der Parteikanzlei, 7 November 1944, BA-M, RW 4/725; WFsT/Qu. Betr. Massnahmen gegen Überläufer, 17 November 1944, BA-M, RW 4/725, 16; Fernspruch an Oberstl. Hass, Wolfschanze, 17 November 1944, BA-M, RW 4/725.

107. See case of Friedrich S., NRWHStA, RW 58/55465.

108. OKW to Reichsministerium für Volksaufklärung und Propaganda, 21 September 1943, BA-Berlin, R 55/799.

109. Abwicklungsstab 6. Armee und Hegru. Afrika to Chef der Sicherheitspolizei und des SD, 26 January 1944, BA-M, RH 15/34.

110. Überschär, "Das NKFD und der BDO," 39–40. Seydlitz's divorce was reversed after his return from Soviet captivity in 1955.

111. WFSt/Qu.2 (I), Betr. Massnahmen gegen Wehrmachtsangehörige, die in der Kriegsgefangenschaft Landesverrat begehen, 2 February 1945, BA-M, RW 4/725, 49; Chef des Oberkommande der Wehrmacht, Betr. Massnahmen gegen Wehrmachtsangehörige, die in der Kriegsgefangenschaft Landesverrat begehen (Entwurf), January 1945, BA-M, RW 4/725, 38. These measures were implemented even in a desperate military situation; see Heeresgruppe Kurland, OKH Generalleutnant Foertsch to OKW, WFSt, 4 April 1945, BA-M, RW 4/725.

112. On ideological indoctrination, see Messerschmitt, *Die Wehrmacht im NS-Staat*; Berghahn, "NSDAP und 'Geistige Führung' der Wehrmacht"; on ideological motivation of ordinary soldiers, see Bartov, *The Eastern Front, 1941–1945* and *Hitler's Army*.

113. Kühne, "Kameradschaft."

114. Wehler, *Deutsche Gesellschaftsgeschichte*, 869; Kershaw, *Hitler, 1936–1945*, 699.

115. Geyer, "There Is a Land."

116. Latzel, *Deutsche Soldaten—nationalsozialistischer Krieg*, 138–96. This attitude often persisted throughout captivity into the postwar period; see Hilger, *Deutsche Kriegsgefangene in der Sowjetunion*.

117. Streit, *Keine Kameraden*.

118. Geyer, "There Is a Land"; for a discussion of the variety of soldiers' responses to impending defeat, see also Kunz, *Wehrmacht und Niederlage*. This study appeared too late to be integrated into the analysis here.

119. Moeller, *War Stories*.

120. For a discussion of this significance, see Koonz, *Mothers in the Fatherland*; for an excellent discussion of women on the home front, see Kundrus, *Kriegerfrauen*.

121. See Hagemann, "Jede Kraft wird gebraucht."

122. Heineman, "Hour of the Woman."

123. Missalla, *Für Volk und Vaterland*; see also Heinrich Höfler, "Kirchliche Hilfe im Krieg, 1939–1949," BA-M, B 205/1473.

124. Kunze, *Theodor Heckel*. Theoretically, this mission should also include foreign Protestant POWs in German captivity. However, I have found no indication that the EHIK indeed was involved in caring for non-German POWs.

125. "Lieber Kamerad," 26 October 1941, ADCV, 370.17, Fasz. 1; also cited in Missala, *Für Volk und Vaterland*, 150.

126. On Heckel's anti-Bolshevism, see Kunze, *Theodor Heckel*, 170, whose own evidence runs counter to his rather apologetic interpretation; for a more critical view, see Boyens, "Lernen aus der Geschichte"; on Heckel's communications with front soldiers, see BA-M, Msg 194/52.

127. Missalla, *Für Gott und Vaterland*, 119; Brakelmann, "Nationalprotestantismus und Nationalsozialismus"; Greschat, "Begleitung und Deutung"; and in general, Friedländer, *Nazi Germany and the Jews*.

128. See, for example, Predigtskizze Nr. 2 zum 3. Adventssonntag, ACDV 370.17, Fasz. 3.

129. Theodor Heckel to Dolmetscher E. Burghard (1942?), BA-M, Msg 194/52; on religious anti-Semitism in general, see the contributions in Bartov and Mack, *In God's Name*.

130. This was his own explanation in "Kirchliche Hilfe im Krieg, 1939–1945," BA-M, B 205/1473.

131. Bergen, *Twisted Cross*, 54; and Kunze, *Theodor Heckel*, 174–81.

132. Höfler portrayed the work of the Kirchliche Kriegshilfe as a permanent subversive struggle against the Gestapo; see "Kirchliche Hilfe im Krieg, 1939–1945," BA-M, B 205/1473.

133. Steinert, *Hitlers Krieg und die Deutschen*, 390, 409; Blessing, "Deutschland in Not."

134. Boberach, *Meldungen aus dem Reich*, Nr. 363, 1 March 1943, 4869–79.

135. Gestapo Düsseldorf to Aussendienststelle in Mönchengladbach, 1 April 1943, NRWHStA, RW 58/5727.

136. Behrenbeck, *Kult um die toten Helden*, 561.

137. "Selig sind die Trauernden, denn sie werden getröstet werden," Predigtskizzen XXIX. Reihe, Osterwoche 1944, ADCV 370.17, Fasz. 3; see also the sermon of the Munich cardinal Faulhaber, "Heimgeholt. Ansprache des Herrn Kardinal nach dem Pontifikal Requium im Dom am 1. August 1944 für die Opfer der Luftangriffe," HEK, CR II, 25, 18, 1.

138. See chapter 4.

139. Kirchliche Kriegshilfe, "Gebet für einen Vermissten," ADCV 370.17, Fasz. 3.

140. See the material in BA-M, Msg 194/35.

141. See the letters and the EHIK's responses in BA-M, Msg 194/21.

142. Theodor Heckel to Margarete D., 11 May 1943, BA-M, Msg 194/21.

143. On changing conceptions of "victimhood" and "sacrifice," see Behrenbeck, "The Transformation of Sacrifice," and, with further references, Münkler and Fischer, "Nothing to Kill or Die For."

CHAPTER 2
CONFRONTING DEFEAT

1. Figures based on Wehler, *Deutsche Gesellschaftsgeschichte*, 932, 941–50; Overmans, *Deutsche militärische Verluste*.

2. On Allied failures to recognize the true extent of the Holocaust, see Bloxham, *Genocide on Trial*.

3. This has been amply demonstrated by an older literature; see Kocka, "1945: Neubeginn oder Restauration?" and Broszat, Henke, and Woller, *Von Stalingrad zur Währungsreform*.

4. Diehl, *Thanks of the Fatherland*, 227–37; Levy and Roseman, *Three Postwar Eras*.

5. Figure cited in Jarausch and Geyer, *Shattered Past*, 209; see also Grossmann, "Victims, Villains, and Survivors."

6. On this context, see Jarausch and Geyer, *Shattered Past*, 197–220.

7. On evacuees, Krause, *Flucht vor dem Bombenkrieg*.

8. Figure according to Jarausch and Geyer, *Shattered Past*, 210.

9. Krauss, *Heimkehr in ein fremdes Land*.

10. Borchard, *Die deutschen Kriegsgefangenen in der Sowjetunion*, 30–33.

11. Ibid., 63–64. All German POWs from British and U.S. captivity had returned by the end of 1947, all POWs from French captivity by the end of 1948; see Overmans, "German Historiography"; Statistisches Bundesamt Wiesbaden, Volkszählung vom 6. Juni 1961, 8–9.

12. Rückblick auf das Heimkehrerlager Gronenfelde, 15 May 1950, BA-Berlin, DO 1/10/47, 1–29. The registration in Gronenfelde constitutes the only reliable figure of returning POWs from the Soviet Union after August 1946; Die angekommenen Heimkehrer bis zum 30. Juni 1951, BA-Berlin, DQ 1/HA 0.34/33291. For slightly different figures based on Soviet sources, see Hilger, *Deutsche Kriegsgefange in der Sowjetunion*, 328–39.

13. Karner, *Im Archipel GUPVI*, 79, cites a total figure of 2,031,743 repatriated POWs. This figure roughly corresponds to an earlier estimate of 1,959,000 returnees cited by Böhme, *Die deutschen Kriegsgefangenen*, 150. I have found no information on how many POWs went to the West after initially returning to the East.

14. Hilger, Schmeitzner, and Schmidt, *Sowjetische Militärtribunale*, 671, cite the figure of seven thousand individuals convicted by Soviet courts. East German sources cite 60,754 civilian returnees (32,120 men, 28,120 women, 514 children) between July 1947 and May 1950; see Rückblick auf das Heimkehrerlager Gronenfelde, BA-Berlin, DO 1/10/47, 28; on women in the Wehrmacht, see Kundrus, "Nur die halbe Geschichte." Estimates for the number of female POWs are extremely vague; see Böhme, "Zum Schicksal der weiblichen Kriegsgefangenen," 344.

15. See below, chapter 8.

16. Bericht von der Besprechung der Provinzialvertreter, 27 August 1946, BA-Berlin, DO 1/10/47, 53–54; Rückblick auf das Heimkehrerlager Gronenfelde bei Frankfurt/Oder, 1 May 1950, BA-Berlin, DO 1/10/47; and Kaminsky, "Frankfurt, das glückliche Frankfurt," 82–95.

17. Flüchtlingslager Friedland/Leine to Hermann L., 20 January 1948, NHStA, Nds. 386/Acc. 16/83/Nr. 97; Kleineke, "Entstehung und Entwicklung."

18. On demobilization after World War I, see Bessel, *Germany after the First World War*, 69–90.

19. Innenministerium Baden-Württemberg to Landratsämter des Landbezirkes Württemberg, 30 March 1948, Stadtarchiv Ulm B 422/30, Nr. 2; Lager Friedland,

"Achtung! An alle entlassenen Kriegsgefangenen aus der russischen Zone!" 13 August 1946, NHStA, Nds. 386, Acc. 16/83, Nr. 97.

20. Informationsdienst für Kriegsgefangene, herausgegeben von den Landesarbeitsgemeinschaft für Kriegsgefangene der US-Zone, Nr. 2, BWHStA, EA 2/801, Bü. 250.

21. Josef Krahé, Lagerpfarrer, Bericht der Caritasstelle im Heimkehrer- und Flüchtlingslager in Friedland vom 1. April bis 30. Juni 1948, 1 August 1948; ADCV, 372.20, Fasz. 1.; Abt. Arbeit und Sozialfürsorge to Kreisleitung der SED, 11 October 1948, "Heimkehrerarbeit in Frankfurt/Oder," BLHA, Rep. 332/576, 289; see also Kaminsky,"Frankfurt, das glückliche Frankfurt."

22. Knoch, *Die Tat als Bild*, 27.

23. The Allied definition of "criminality," however, always focused more strongly on waging a war of aggression than on the Holocaust per se; see Bloxham, *Genocide on Trial*.

24. On Jaspers and discourses of guilt, see Rabinbach, *Shadow of Catastrophe*.

25. Der Landrat von St. Goarshausen to die Herren Bürgermeister des Kreises, 16 November 1945, HHStA, 360/258.

26. Echternkamp, "Wut auf die Wehrmacht," 1058–90.

27. For echoes of such memories fifty years later, see Naumann, *Der Krieg als Text*, 129–42.

28. Echternkamp, "Wut auf die Wehrmacht," 1070.

29. Heimkehrer aus dem Osten! Wie helfen wir ihnen? (1946), ADW, HGSt, Allg. Slg./C23.2. Propst Grüber was one of the few Protestant officals advocating aid for Holocaust survivors and later became the representative of the Protestant church in East Germany; see Hockenos, *A Church Divided*, 144–48; Besier, *Der SED-Staat und die Kirche*, 61–65.

30. Hebert Gessner, "Die Kriegsgefangenen," *Der Tagesspiegel*, 14 November 1946, newspaper clipping in ADCV, 511/W Fasz. 03, III.

31. J. Windhagen to Cardinal Frings, 23 November 1945, HEK, CR II, 25, 19, 2.

32. Grosshessisches Staatsministerium. Der Minister für Wiederaufbau und politische Bereinigung, Betrifft: Austausch von Kriegsgefangenen gegen Aktivisten, 29 November 1945, HHStA, 502/1001.

33. L. Mayer to Minister Heinrich Schmitt in München, 12 June 1946, BHStA, Sonderministerium MSO/1450; for a similar proposal, SPD Hersching to MP Högner, 8 Dezember 1945, BHStA, Stk, 114832; Stadt Ulm to Staatsministerium, Betr. Kriegsgefangenenaustausch, 29 November 1945, Stadtarchiv Ulm, 422/31, Nr. 3. In the summer of 1946, the later chancellor Adenauer added an interesting twist to these proposals by suggesting an exchange of, not former Nazis, but rather German Communists against POWs in the Soviet Union, see Borchard, *Die Deutschen Kriegsgefangenen in der Sowjetunion*, 73.

34. Dr. Werner Hilpert to Herrn Ministerpräsident Prof. Dr. Geiler, 22 November 1945, HHStA, 502/1001.

35. See Bartov, *Mirrors of Destruction*, 116, "Defining Enemies, Making Victims."

36. Schildt, "Solidarisch mit der Schuld des Volkes"; Bücker, *Die Schulddiskussion im deutschen Katholizismus*; Wolgast, *Die Wahrnehmung des Dritten Reiches*, 179–284; Hockenos, *A Church Divided*, 75–100.

37. Cited in Schildt, "Solidarisch mit der Schuld des Volkes," 279–80.

38. See especially the Darmstadt statement of the Council of Brethren of August 1947, Hockenos, *A Church Divided*, 118–30; Greschat, "The Potency of Christendom."

39. This is the argument in Domansky, "A Lost War," 245.

40. Lübbe, "Der Nationalsozialismus im deutschen Nachkriegsbewußtsein"; for another argument linking deficient memory and democratization, see Herf, *Divided Memory*.

41. Epstein, *Last Revolutionaries*, 44–99.

42. Ansprache Piecks vor Absolventen des 6. Kurses der antifaschistischen Schule für deutsche Kriegsgefangene beim Lager 27 in Krasnogorsk (Abschrift von handschriftlichen Notizen), 17 April 1945, BA-SAPMO, NY 4036/421.

43. "Über das Verhältnis von Kommunisten und Kriegsgefangenen im NKFD (November/Dezember 1944)," in Erler, Laude, and Wilke, *Nach Hitler kommen wir*, 304–10.

44. Benser, "Zur Auflösung des Nationalkomitees 'Freies Deutschland' 1945"; see also Morré, *Hinter den Kulissen des Nationalkomitees*.

45. "Aufruf des ZK der KPD vom 11. Juni 1945," in Erler, Laude, and Wilke, *Nach Hitler kommen wir*, 390–97; for an analysis of the "appeal," see Herf, *Divided Memory*, 27–33.

46. On the definition of antifascism, see Meuschel, *Legitimation und Parteiherrschaft in der DDR*, 29–40.

47. Karl Lewke to KPD-ZK, 2 December 1945, BA-SAPMO, DY 30/IV2/11/211, 3–7.

48. Unsere Aufgaben rbeit unter den entlassenen Kriegsgefangenen, Vo./R., 3 December 1945, BA-SAPMO, DY 30/IV2/11/196, 19.

49. Report from Gronenfelde, 15 November 1945, BA-SAPMO, DY 30/IV2/11/211,1.

50. Fulbrook, *Anatomy of a Dictatorship*, 27.

51. Karl Lewke to KPD-ZK, 2 December 1945, BA-SAPMO, DY 30/IV2/11/211, 3–7.

52. Dahlem to Sekretariat, Betrifft Annahme eines Aufrufs an die zurückkehrenden Kriegsgefangenen vom Ausschuss der vier Parteien, 29 March 1946, BA-SAPMO, NY 4036/718, 206–8; FDGB Provinzialvorstand to SED Provinzialvorstand Brandenburg, 11 July 1946, BLHA, Rep. 332/576, 60–61; ZVU to Provinzialverwaltung Mark Brandenburg, 9 March 1946, BA-Berlin, DO 2/78, 1–2.

53. Frau R., Hildesheim to Herr Dkp. Müller, 2 September 1947, HEK, CR II 29, 19, 8. One year earlier, she had also written to the Protestant bishop Wurm; see Frau R. to Bishop Wurm, 2 October 1946, EZA, 2/527.

54. See, for example, the petitions in Anträge auf vorzeitige Entlassung aus der Kriegsgefangenschaft and den Magistrat in Berlin, Abteilung Umsiedler und Heimkehrer, 29 April 1947, LAB, Rep.118/874.

55. Gregor, "Is He Still Alive."

56. Bauman, *Modernity and the Holocaust.*

57. Moeller, *War Stories.*

58. Peitsch, *Deutschlands Gedächtnis an seine dunkelste Zeit,* 221–26.

59. On Borchert, see Reemstma, *Mord am Strand,* 369–80; Weckel, "Spielarten der Vergangenheistbewältigung"; Reichel, *Erfundene Erinnerung,* 45–51.

60. On movies, see Moeller, *War Stories,* 125, with further references.

61. See Herf, "Multiple Restorations."

62. See, with further references, Conzemius, Greschat, and Kocher, *Die Zeit nach 1945;* Blessing, "Deutschland in Not"; Vollnhals, "Die Evangelische Kirche"; Greschat, *Die evangelische Christenheit;* and, most recently, Hockenos, *A Church Divided;* Köhler and van Melis, *Siegerin in Trümmern;* for the European context, see van Melis, " 'Strengthened and Purified.' "

63. Thierfelder, "Die Kirchenpolitik der vier Besatzungsmächte."

64. Bücker, *Die Schulddiskussion im deutschen Katholizismus.*

65. M. Cad. Faulhaber, Ezbischof München, "Pastorale Richtlinien an den Klerus der Erzdiözese München, Mitte Juni 1945," HEK, CR II, 25, 18,3. For similar statements, see Wolgast, *Die Wahrnemung des Dritten Reiches,* 204–8, 224.

66. Greschat, *Die evangelische Christenheit,* 185; Hockenos, *A Church Divided,* 101–17.

67. Vollnhals, *Evangelische Kirche und Entnazifizierung;* Bücker, *Die Schulddiskussion in deutschen katholizismus,* 67–77; on the emergence of the "collective guilt" thesis, see Frei, "Von deutscher Erfindungskraft."

68. In general, see Foschepoth, "German Reactions to Defeat and Occupation."

69. Anna P. to Oberkirchenrat, 8 May 1946, EZA, 2/469.

70. Katholische Bischöffe to Alliierten Kontrollrat für Deutschland zu Händen des derzeitigen Vorsitzenden General Eisenhower, Fulda, 23 August 1945, HEK, CR II, 25, 18, 3.

71. Eingabe der EKD to the Allied Control Council, 26 February 1946, EZA, 2/471.

72. Kanzlei der EKD, Asmussen, to alle Mitglieder der EKD, 12 July 1946, EZA 4/750; "Die Kirche und die Kriegsgefangenen," *Evangelisches Kirchenblatt für Rheinhessen,* 20 October 1946; "Vergesst unsere Gefangenen nicht," *Sonntagsblatt der evangelisch-reformierten Gemeinden,* 29 September 1946.

73. Wurm, "An die Gemeinden zur Gebetswoche für die Kriegsgefangenen," 28 August 1948, EZA, 7/4234.

74. Greschat, *Die evangelische Christenheit,* 185–88.

75. Liebe Heimkehrer, 24 April 1948, EZA, 2/600.

76. Kriegsgefangenen-Gottesdienst, 1949, BA-M, Msg 194/394.

77. Predigt bei dem Heimkehrer- und Vermissten Gottesdienst in der Südkirche zu Heilbronn am 8.Mai 1950 von Pfarrer Werner Reininghaus, BA-M, Msg 194/102.

78. Stern, "Evangelische Kirche zwischen Antisemitismus und Philosemitismus"; on the blatant anti-Semitism of Bishop Wurm, see Hockenos, *A Church Divided,* 149–52.

79. Zur religiös-geistigen Lage unserer Kriegsgefangenen (n.d., probably 1946), ADCV, 372.059, Fasz. 2; for a similar Protestant perception, see "Kirche und Heimkehrer," ADW, HBB 22.

80. On the formation of the CDU, see Bösch, *Adenauer-CDU*, 21–72; and Mitchell, "Materialism and Secularism"; on the reconciliation of conservatism and democracy, see Solchany, "Konservative Interpretationen des Nationalsozialismus."

81. Herf, *Divided Memory*, 239–66, 301–12.

82. Hans Stephan, SPD Parteivorstand, Referat: Kriegsgefangenenhilfe, Weihnachten 1947, HHStA, 1213/53; for a similar comparison, see Rede des Herrn Staatssekretärs Dr. Brill zur Kriegsgefangenensendung am Neujahrssonntag 1948 über Radio Frankfurt (Abschrift), HHStA, 1213/106.

83. Moeller, *War Stories*.

84. "Kriegsgefangenschaft-menschliches Unrecht. Worte von Dr. Kurt Schumacher zum Jahresende 1947," SPD Kriegsgefangenenhilfe. Informationsblätter für die Ortsvereine, Nr. 6, Januar 1948, ASD, O44 "Kriegsgefangene," 1947.

85. On Schumacher's "patriotism," see Erdinger, *Kurt Schumacher*.

86. SPD Kriegsgefgangenenhilfe, Informationsblätter für die Ortsvereine, Nr. 1, 27 April 1947, ASD, O44 "Kriegsgefangene," 1947.

87. "Kriegsgefangene wählen," Sopade Informationsdienst, 29 Juli 1947, ASD, O44 "Kriegsgefangene," 1947.

88. "Kriegsgefangenschaft-menschliches Unrecht. Worte von Dr. Kurt Schumacher zum Jahresende 1947," SPD Kriegsgefangenenhilfe. Informationsblätter für die Ortsvereine, Nr. 6, Januar 1948, ASD, O44.

89. Kroener, "Auf dem Weg zu einer nationalsozialistischen Volksarmee."

90. On affinities of war veterans with the SPD, see Holtman, "Die neuen Lassalleaner."

91. "Die kommunistische Antifa in jugoslawischen Kriegsgefangenenlagern," SPD Kriegsgefangenhilfe, Nr. 4, 2 October 1947; "Brigardiere, Aktivälteste und Verwandte," Kriegsgefangenendienst der SPD, ASD, O44, 1948/49, "Kriegsgefangene"; "Ein Nachwort zur Heimkehrerversammlung der SPD," 18 March 1949, ASD, O43, 1949–52.

92. "Das Schicksal einer deutschen Frau in russischer Kriegsgefangenschaft," EZA, 2/599; see also the newspaper clippings in BA-M, B 205/1404.

93. Most newspaper articles explicitly stated that returning women had *not* been raped; see clippings in BA-M, B 205/1404.

94. EHiW Brit. Zone to OKR Ranke, 25 March 1949, EZA, 2/585; for a more explicit reference to rape, see report by Tamara Strauss, 2 December 1946, BA-M, B 205/1640.

95. Heineman, "Hour of the Woman"; Grossmann, "A 'Question of Silence.'"

96. Kundrus, "Nur die halbe Geschichte"; and see Klier, *Verschleppt ans Ende der Welt*, which is based on interviews.

97. Moeller, *War Stories*; see also Behrenbeck, "Between Pain and Silence."

98. Frei, *Vergangenheitspolitik*, 398.

99. Rückblick auf das Heimkehrerlager Gronenfelde bei Frankfurt/Oder, 1 May 1950, BA-Berlin, DO 1/10/47, 1; Bericht an Ulbricht über Heimkehrerarbeiten, 20 January 1947, BA-SAPMO, NY 4182/1160, 62–70.

100. Wilhelm Pieck, "An die Heimkehrer," 10 August 1946, BA-SAPMO, NY 4036/428, 20–24.

101. SED Brandenburg, Protokoll der Sekretariatssitzung, 28 May 1946, BLHA, Rep. 332/90.

102. Campaign poster, "Durch Fürsprache der SED: 120,000 Kriegsgefangene kehren aus der UdSSR heim," BA-SAPMO, DY 30/IV2/2.027/35.

103. Resolution des Kommunalen Frauenausschusses Hartmannsdorf, 18 November 1946 (Abschrift), BA-SAPMO, DY 30/IV2/17/54, 118; SED Landesverband Thüringen, 23 July 1946, BA-SAPMO, DY 30/IV2/2.027/35.

104. SED-LV Sachsen, Abt. Frauen, "Überblick über die Arbeit des Jahres 1946," BA-SAPMO, DY 30/IV2/17/54, 157–61.

105. Bericht über die Frauenversammlung in Niederbarnim, 2 June 1946, BLHA, Rep. 332/953, 161; Bericht über die Frauenveranstaltung der Wohngruppe 2 im Café Bismarck, 26 August 1946, BLHA Rep. 332/954, 97.

106. In the Berlin elections, the SED received 19.8 percent of the vote (SPD 48.7 percent); in the regional elections, the SED remained below 50 percent in all five provinces; Broszat and Weber, *SBZ-Handbuch*, 383–90.

107. Harsch, "Approach/Avoidance," 163.

108. This is the main argument in Herf, *Divided Memory*, 13–39.

109. Bartov, *Mirrors of Destruction*; Moeller, *War Stories*.

110. Judt, "Past Is Another Country," 296; Lagrou, "The Nationalization of Victimhood"; Farmer, *Martyred Village*.

111. Judt, "Past Is Another Country," 296.

112. On returnees and denazification, see Smith, *Heimkehr aus dem Zweiten Weltkrieg*, 129–31; Krüger, *Entnazifiziert*, 131; Vollnhals, *Entnazifizierung*, 34–42; Vogt, *Denazification in Soviet-Occupied Germany*, 199–200, 224–25; see also Gesetz über die Anwendung des Befreiungsgesetzes auf Heimkehrer ("Heimkehrer-Amnestie"), Amtsblatt des Hessischen Ministeriums für politische Bildung 40/2, 21 April 1948, BA-K, B 150/336a.

113. Dr. Hans Müller, Staatssekretär, Staatsministerium der Finanzen to Staatsministerium für Sonderaufgaben, 16 August 1949, BHStA, Stk/113897. Due to Soviet practices of interning Nazi perpetrators in Soviet POW camps and repatriating them with ordinary POWs, these concerns were not unfounded; see Niethammer, "Alliierte Internierungslager in Deutschland"; Possekel, "Einleitung: Sowjetische Lagerpolitik in Deutschland," 45–46.

114. Koselleck, " 'Erfahrungsraum' und 'Erwartungshorizont.' "

115. On rumors, see Lehmann, *Gefangenschaft und Heimkehr*, 101–6; Reiss, "*Die Schwarzen waren unsere Freunde*," 163–65; on rumors among West POWs returning to the East, see Lewke, "Entlassungen aus der britischen Besatzungszone," 12 March 1946, BA-Berlin DO 2/78; on the content of camp newspapers in Soviet captivity, see the material in BA-SAPMO, DY 34/21402.

116. Hilger, *Deutsche Kriegsgefangene in der Sowjetunion*, 308–9.

117. Gollwitzer, *Unwilling Journey*, 310.

118. Interview with "Thomas G.," 4 November 1996, OH 2.

119. Schröder, *Die gestohlenen Jahre*, 726–69; interview with Willy F., IfGB.

120. G. Fr., Erlebnisbericht, 22 March 1949, ADW, HGSt, Allg. Slg./B456; for a similar statement from the East, see Günter L. to "Heinz," 25 November 1946, BA-SAPMO, DY 30/IV2/4/156, 3.

121. Sibylle Meyer and Eva Schulze Interview Collection, Interview 26, Hr. Lu., Institut für Sozialforschung, Technische Universität Berlin.

122. Johann S. to EHiW, ADW, HGSt, Allg. Slg./B454; for a similar report, see Klaus-Dieter L., 14 May 1949, ADW, HGSt, Allg. Slg./B454; on living conditions in general, see Thurnwald, *Gegenwartsprobleme Berliner Familien.*

123. Eduard G. to Evangelisches Hilfswerk (no date, probably 1949), ADW, HGSt, Allg. Slg/B454.

124. Heineman, *What Difference,* 75–82, 95–106.

125. Beck, "Rape."

126. Alwin Wild, "Bericht über die Eisenbahnerbrigaden von Brest nach Frankfurt/Oder," 26 June 1947, BA-Berlin, DO 2/76; on similar anxieties in Western captivity, see Reiss, *"Die Schwarzen waren unsere Freunde,"* 323.

127. Heineman, *What Difference,* 119.

128. Heineman, "Hour of the Woman"; zur Nieden, "Erotic Fraternization."

129. Applegate, *A Nation of Provincials;* Confino, *Nation as Local Metaphor,* and specifically for the post-1945 period, Knoch, *Das Erbe der Provinz;* Koshar, *Germany's Transient Pasts,* 271–73; Palmowski, "Building an East German Nation."

130. Wihelm D. to Landesbischof in Stuttgart, 26 December 1948, EZA, 4/474.

131. Dr. Heinz S. aus Weimar, "Heimkehr aus der Kriegsgefangenschaft," 1 September 1946, BA-SAPMO, NY 4182/1160, 46–49.

132. Gustav M., Heimkehrer aus Polen, to Ausschuß für Kriegsgefangenenfragen, 4 June 1949, BA K, B 150/331a.

133. Morach, "Heimkehr 1948," 5 September 1948, BA-SAPMO, DY 30/IV2/11/211, 287–88.

134. Applegate, *A Nation of Provincials,* 240; and Confino, "This Lovely Country," 251.

135. Gedicht des Heimkehrers Karl T., "Die deutsche Frau," BA-SAPMO, DY 34/40/61/4508.

136. On women on the home front, see Kundrus, *Kriegerfrauen.*

137. Dr. Heinz S., "Heimkehr aus der Kriegsgefangenschaft," 1 September 1946, BA-SAPMO, DY 32/10057.

138. Gustav M., Heimkehrer aus Polen, to Ausschuß für Kriegsgefangenenfragen, 4 June 1949, BA-K, B 150/331a.

139. Karsten, *Glückliche Heimkehr,* 57; interview with "Thomas G.," 4 November 1996, OH 2; Jonitz, "In amerikanischer und französischer Kriegsgefangenschaft," 130.

140. Intelligence Control Staff, Berlin, Intelligence Summary No. 53, 17 July 1946, PRO, FO 371/55880; also quoted in Diehl, *Thanks of the Fatherland,* 71. One of my interviewees began to cry when he recalled this moment.

141. OMGB, Field Operations Division, Essential Information No. 48-2 on the Subject of German Prisoners of War, Ebersberg, 30 June 1948, BHStA, OMGB 10/51-3/6.

142. OMGB, Field Operations Division, Essential Information No. 48-2 on the Subject of German Prisoners of War, Koetzing, 30 June 1948, BHStA, OMGB 10/51-3/6; Office of Military Government for Hesse, Information Control Division, Research Branch, Opinion Surveys, "Survey of PW Returnees from Russia," 21 October 1947, HHStA, RG 260 OMGH 8/64-1/3.

143. Echternkamp, "Kameradenpost bricht auch nie ab," 458–59.

144. Office of Military Government for Hesse, Information Control Division, Research Branch, Opinion Surveys, "Survey of PW Returnees from Russia," 21 October 1947, HHStA, RG 260 OMGH 8/64-1/3.

145. On the significance of such "survival stories," see also Jarausch and Geyer, *Shattered Past*, 320–25.

146. Interview with "Annemarie R.," 28 November 1996, OH 5. Another interview with a female returnee however, very much focused on suffering, including possible rape; see interview with "Waltraud Heimann," February 27, 1997, OH 7.

147. Interview Hans G., 24 March 1995, 90–91, IfGB.

148. Bruckner, *Ich leide also bin ich;* on the emergence of the victim status as a basis for collective identity, see Chaumont, *La concurrence des victimes*; for a critical perspective on this debate, see Bartov, *Mirrors of Destruction*, 71–75.

149. Moeller, *War Stories*, 21.

150. On popular knowledge of the Holocaust in Nazi Germany and beyond, see Laqueur, *The Terrible Secret*; on these fears, see Gellately, *Backing Hitler*, 253–54 and Geyer, "There Is a Land."

151. Bodemann, "Negativ-Gedächtnis"; see also Weigel, "Pathologisierung und Normalisierung," 262.

152. Lagrou, *Legacy of Nazi Occupation*, 2.

CHAPTER 3
EMBODIED DEFEAT

1. Patient Record Wilhelm Lu., ARLK.

2. Patient Record Rudolf G., ARLK.

3. This chapter is based on the published medical and psychiatric literature and on patient records from the Archiv der Rheinischen Landeskliniken (ARLK) in Bonn.

4. On this significance of psychiatry for defining cultural norms, see Lunbeck, *The Psychiatric Persuasion*. Svenja Goltermann is currently completing a major study on psychiatric responses to war trauma in postwar West Germany; see Goltermann, "Verletzte Körper," "Die Berherrrschung der Männlichkeit," "Im Wahn der Gewalt," and "Psychisches Leid und herrschende Lehre." For an earlier analysis of the published medical and psychiatric discourse on "returnee diseases," see my dissertation, "The Protracted War," 63–90, 155–66; see also Biess, "Survivors of Totalitarianism" and "Men of Reconstruction."

5. Between August and November 1946, more than two hundred returnees died in Frankfurt an der Oder; see Totentagebuch aus Frankfurt/Oder, 23 August 1946 to 20 November 1946, ADW, CA/O/351.

6. Protokoll Länderrat, Ausschuss für Kriegsgefangenfragen, Besprechung der Lagerärzte über Mangelerscheinungen bei Heimkehrern und ihre Behandlung, 18 November 1947, EZA, 2/627.

7. Fischer, "Der praktische Arzt"; Wetzel, "Die Tuburkulose bei Heimkehrern."

8. Weiss, "Ernährungsstörungen"; Brasche, "Ärztliche Beobachtungen in der Kriegsgefangenschaft," 1–9; Berning, *Die Dystrophie* 4–11; Gauger, *Die Dystrophie*, 3.

9. Weiss, "Ernährungsstörungen"; Bansi, "Die Ödemkrankheit"; Malten, "Heimkehrer"; Sedlmayer, "Erfahrungen in der Behandlung kranker Heimkehrer."

10. Balderman, "Psychischen Grundlagen" and "Wesen und Beurteilung der Heimkehrerdystrophien"; Bansi, "Die Ödemkrankheit"; Malten, "Heimkehrer."

11. Schulte, *Hirnorganische Dauerschäden nach schwerer Dystrophie*, 20; Gries, *Abbau der Persönlichkeit*.

12. Sedlmayer, "Wandlungen im Krankheitsbild der Ostheimkehrer."

13. Oral history interview with Heinz-Harro Rauschelbach, OH 9. On the emergence of PTSD during the 1970s and its eventual inclusion in DSM-IIII, see Shepard, *A War of Nerves*, 355–68; Young, *The Harmony of Illusions*, 89–175.

14. Förster and Beck, "Post-Traumatic Stress Disorder and World War."

15. McNally, "Posttraumatic Stress Disorder."

16. Hermann, *Trauma and Recovery*, 74–95, quotation on 187.

17. Geyer, "Das Stigma der Gewalt," 681.

18. Bullinger, "The Culture of Survivors."

19. Young, *The Harmony of Illusions*, 5; see also Lerner and Micale, "Trauma, Psychiatry, and History."

20. Malten, "Heimkehrer," 593.

21. As late as 1957, a medical doctor compared the increase in blood pressure among German POWs in the Soviet Union to similar processes among the civilian population of Leningrad during the German siege; Dietze, "Der Verlauf der Blutdruckschwankungen."

22. See, for example, Hottinger, *Hungerkrankheit, Hungerödem, Hungertuberklulose*.

23. Berning, *Die Dystrophie*; on this context, see Aly, *Macht-Geist-Wahn*, 57–69.

24. See Klee, *Auschwitz*, 179–89. Schenck's actual biography contrasts markedly with his very positive portrayal in the recent German film Downfall.

25. Schenck and v. Nathusius, *Extreme Lebensverhältnisse und ihre Folgen*; Schenck, *Das menschliche Elend im 20. Jahrhundert*. This publication never mentions gassing as a means of mass extermination but instead suggests that death rates in Auschwitz largely resulted from disease and lack of hygiene.

26. Sedlmayer, "Wandlungen im Krankheitsbild der Ostheimkehrer"; see also Bonhoeffer, "Vergleichende psychopathologische Erfahrungen"; on these continuities, see also Goltermann, "Verletzte Körper" and, for West German family policy, Moeller, *Protecting Motherhood*, chapter 4.

27. Funk, "Somato-psychologische Beobachtungen," 234.

28. Die psychische und physische Situation der Ostheimkehrer (Beobachtungen und Erfahrungen im Heimkehrerhotel Willingen), EZA, 2/529.

29. Herzog, "Heimkehr aus russischer Gefangenschaft," 71–79.

30. For the eighteenth-century United States, see Demos, *The Unredeemed Captive*.

31. West German newspapers in the early 1950s also claimed that inhabitants of the Soviet zone began to exhibit "broad noses" and "slanted eyes"; see Wolfrum, *Geschichtspolitik in der Bundesrepublik*, 72.

32. Mitscherlich report, "Untersuchung durchgeführt im Kriegsgefangenenentlassungslager Münster," 24 May to 9 July, 1948, BA-M, B 205/1409. For similar perceptions of Jewish "displaced persons" in the immediate postwar period, see Grossmann, "Victims, Villains, and Survivors," 297–99.

33. On the passage and provision of the BVG, see Diehl, *Thanks of the Fatherland*, 109–40.

34. On shell shock, the key study now is Lerner, *Hysterical Men*; on National Socialist health policies, see Weindling, *Health, Race, and German Politics* and Schmuhl, *Rassenhygiene, Nationalsozialismus, Euthanasie*.

35. Lerner, *Hysterical Men*, 2.

36. Interview with Dr. Heinz-Harro Rauschelbach, 16 and 22 April 1998, OH 9; Bonheoffer, "Vergleichende psychopathologische Erfahrungen."

37. Ibid., 2; Janz, "Psychopathologische Reaktionen der Kriegs- und Nachkriegszeit."

38. Bansi, "Die Ödemkrankheit," 278. Bansi served as expert witness in the trial of Ernst Günter Schenk. He was also implicated in typhus fever experiments in the Buchenwald concentration camp; see Klee, *Auschwitz*, 189, 295.

39. Malten, "Heimkehrer," 598; Baldermann, "Psychischen Grundlagen."

40. Jensch, "Über psychogene Störungen der Kriegsgefangenschaft," 369.

41. Gottschick, "Kriegsgefangenschaft und Psychosen," 130–31. For a more extensive discussions of feelings of guilt and shame among former soldiers and POWs, see Goltermann, "Im Wahn der Gewalt."

42. Schmitz, "Bemerkungen zum Aufsatz von J. Gottschick 'Kriegsgefangenschaft und Psychosen.' " Significantly, the same psychiatrists categorized other psychological responses of German POWs to captivity within the realm of "normalcy"; see below.

43. Schmitz, "Kriegsgefangenschaft und Heimkehr"; Malten, "Heimkehrer."

44. See Shepard, *A War of Nerves*, 364.

45. Sedlmayer, "Erfahrungen in der Behandlung kranker Heimkehrer," 258.

46. Baldermann, "Psychischen Grundlagen," 2186; R. Weiss, Der Mangelschaden des Spätheimkehrers," ACDP, VII-005/47/1.

47. Leonhardt, "Erscheinungsbilder des postdystrophischen psychoorganischen Dauerschadens."

48. Lerner, *Hysterical Men*, 243–44; Eghigian, "German Welfare State," 109–10; Goltermann, "Psychisches Leid und herrschende Lehre."

49. Lerner, *Hysterical Men*, 243.

50. Panse, *Das Erb- und Erscheinungsbild des Psychopathen*; Heyll, "Friedrich Panse."

51. Figure is based on Friedlander, "The Exclusion of the Disabled," 156. The killing continued secretly, and estimates for the total number of victims are as high as two hundred thousand.

52. Riedesser and Verderber, *Maschinengewehre hinter der Front*, 126–49.

53. Panse, *Angst und Schreck*.

54. In 1947, Panse was tried for crimes against humanity for his involvement in the euthanasia program, but he was later exonerated. The court largely followed his argument that he had participated in the program only to save patients; see Heyll, "Friedrich Panse," 333–35.

55. Patient Record Wihlelm Lu., ARLK.

56. For a diagnosis of schizophrenia, see Patient Record Theodor B., ALRK.

57. Patient Record Kurt L., ARLK.

58. Baldermann, "Wesen und Beurteilung der Heimkehrerdystrophien," 124; Balderman, "Psychische Grundlagen," 2188–89.

59. Kayser, "Über das Verhältnis berechtigter und unberechtigter Kriegsrentenansprüche."

60. Patient Record Wilhelm E., ALRK. On the significance of masculinity in defining returnees' conditions, see Goltermann, "Die Beherrschung der Männlichkeit."

61. Lerner, *Hysterical Men*, 86–123; and Riedesser and Verderber, *Maschinengewehre hinter der Front*, 43–67; on World War II, Roth, "Die Modernisierung der Folter."

62. For a report on the "considerable success" of hypnosis in treating dystrophic returnees, see Baldermann, "Psychische Grundlagen," 2188; see also "Ich weiss wieder was war. Russland Heimkehrer erhält durch Hypnose Behandlung sein Gedächtnis zurück," *Quick* 4/34 (1951): 1109–11; for a electroshock and insulin treatments, see Rauschelbach, "Spätfolgezustände nach Hungerdystrophie," 225.

63. Rauschelbach, "Spätfolgezustände nach Hungerdystrophe," 225. Responsiveness to electroshock therapy was also seen as proof of the endogenous etiology of returnees' condition; see Schmitz, "Bermerkungen zum Aufsatz von J. Gottschick 'Kriegsgefangenschaft und Psychosen.' "

64. Patient Record Gerhart G., ARLK.

65. Patient Record Hans E., ARLK.

66. Anneliese B. to Regierungspräsident Arnold, 7 November 1952, NRWHStA, NW 47/63, 102–4, also cited in Neumann, *Nicht der Rede Wert*, 118; Frau Kornelia B. to Petitionsausschuss des Deutschen Bundestages, 25 August 1954, NRWHStA, NW 47/61, 20.

67. See also Neumann, *Nicht der Rede Wert*.

68. The findings of these interviews were summarized in Institut zur Sozialforschung, *Zum Politischen Bewusstsein ehemaliger Kriegsgefangener*. Here I am drawing on the original interview transcripts housed in the Archive of the Institute of Social Research, Frankfurt. On the context of this study, see also below, chapter 4.

69. Interview H3, 37–38, ISF; see also interviews H1, 6; H13, 3; H51, 6.

70. Interview H1, 21, ISF.

71. Patient Record Josef K., ARLK.

72. Patient Record Karl G., ARLK.

73. Franz B. to Konrad Adenauer, NRWHStA, NW 47/61, 65–66.

74. For a similar point, see Goltermann, "Im Wahn der Gewalt," 356; and Ackermann, "Das Schweigen der Flüchtlingskinder."

75. Meyering and Dietze, "Wandlungen im Bild der Dystrophie." On the comparison to hibernation, see Funk, "Somato-psychologische Beobachtungen," 245.

76. Schmitz, "Kriegsgefangenschaft und Heimkehr."

77. Schulte, "Cerebrale Defektsyndrome"; *Hirnorganische Dauerschäden*. On Schulte, see also Goltermann, "Psychisches Leid und Herrschende Lehre," 267–69.

78. Schulte, *Hirnorganische Dauerschäden*, 50.

79. Ibid., 20–24.

80. Schulte, "Cerebrale Defektsymptome," 417; on the larger psychiatric debate, see Hanrath, *Zwischen Euthanasie und Psychiatriereform*, 305–7.

81. Schulte, *Hirnorganische Dauerschäden*, 27. He conceded that not all psychological symptoms could be documented in this way.

82. See Lerner, *Hysterical Men*, 61–85.

83. Schulte, *Hirnorganische Dauerschäden*, 56–58.

84. Patient Record Rudolf G., ARLK.

85. See the similar case of Wi. B., who had returned from Soviet captivity in 1949, was initially denied a pension, but eventually was granted an 80 percent disability by Panse in March 1955 due to organic changes in the brain; Patient Record Wi. B., ARLK.

86. Heyll, "Friedrich Panse," 322.

87. Patient Records Wilhelm E., Josef K., and Eugen E., ALRK.

88. Meyeringh, "Über Spätfolgen der Dystrophie"; Rauschelbach, "Zur versorgungsrechtlichen Beurteilung der Spätheimkehrer."

89. Rauschelbach, "Spätfolgezustände nach Hungerdystrophie."

90. Cocks, *Psychotherapy in the Third Reich*; Geuter, *Die Professionalisierung der deutschen Psychologie*; Nitzschke, "Psychoanalyse als 'un'-politische Wissenschaft"; Lockot, *Erinnern und Durcharbeiten*; Rickels, *Nazi Psychoanalysis*.

91. On Gauger, see Cocks, *Psychotherapy in the Third Reich*, 120–27; Gauger, "Psychotherapy and Political Worldview"; 215–17; Gauger, *Politische Medizin*.

92. Schmidt, *Medical Films* and "Der medizinische Forschungsfilm im Dritten Reich." This evidence revises Cocks's assessment that Gauger was simply a "noisy ideologue, who tried to jump on the National Socialist bandwagon but whose own personal deficiencies allowed him only the most transitory roles"; Cocks, *Psychotherapy in the Third Reich*, 127.

93. Schmidt, *Medical Films*, 282–83.

94. Cocks, *Psychotherapy in the Third Reich*, 235.

95. Gauger, *Die Dystrophie*, 30, 43.

96. Ibid., 36. This diagnosis corresponded to Gauger's definition of mental illness from the 1930s.

97. Ibid., 37.

98. Ibid., 128.

99. On the role of psychoanalysis during the First World War, see Lerner, *Hysterical Men*, 163–89.

100. Gauger, *Die Dystrophie*, 119.

101. The Fischerhof clinic was run by the Arbeiterwohlfahrt. Gauger served as the director of the clinic between 1948 and 1952; see brochure "Der Fischerhof," HHStA Abt. 503/456; "Acht Wochen Fischerhof bereiten auf das Leben vor,"

Hannoversche Presse, 11 August 1949, NSHStA, Nds. 386, Acc. 16/83; Donat, "Männer kommen 'zu sich' "; Strobel, "Der Fischerhof."

102. Schildt, *Moderne Zeiten*, 324–50; Gauger, *Die Dystrophie*, 87.

103. Gauger, *Die Dystrophie*, 90.

104. Ibid., 115.

105. Ibid., 207. Gauger left the Fischerhof in 1952 under somewhat unclear circumstances. He continued to publish on dystrophy, published a medical-anthropological study on criminal youth in 1957, and died two years later; see Schmidt, *Medical Films*, 283.

106. On Gauger's attitude toward Freud, see *Psychotherapie und Zeitgeschen*.

107. Rauschelbach, "Spätfolgezustände nach Hungerdystrophie," 224.

108. See the reviews of his book by Dietrich Zekorn, "Heimkehrer, die keine sind. Das Buch eines Arztes über die Kriegsgefangenendystrophie," *Die Zeit*, 14 May 1953, clipping in NRWHStA, NW 48/56, 218, and "Dystrophie. Die Krankheit der Heimkehrer," *Der Spiegel* 40 (1953): 26.

109. EKD to Leitungen der deutschen evangelischen Landeskirchen in Westdeutschland, 4 November 1953, EZA, 4/447.

110. Dr. med Keller, Kriegsgefangenenkrankheiten, 97, VdH Archive. Rauschelbach also reports that medical evaluators generally felt a "sense of solidarity" with sick returnees; interview with Dr. Heinz-Harro Rauschelbach, 16 and 22 April 1998, OH 9.

111. This practice was confirmed by the central guidelines of the Labor Ministry, Bundesministerium für Arbeit, *Anhaltspunkte für die ärztliche Gutachtertätigkeit*, Neuausgabe 1954, 78.

112. Dietze, "Zur Frage der langdauernden vegetativen Regulationsstörungen"; Bansi, "Spätschäden nach Dystrophie, 3. Teil"; Hochrein and Schleicher, "Die vegetative Dystonie," Bericht über sämtliche im Krankenhaus für Heimkehrer behandelten Heimkehrer, BA-M, B 205/1560.

113. Hochrein and Schleicher, "Die vegetative Dystonie," 2018; see also "Modekrankheit: Das Leiden der Gesunden," *Der Spiegel*, 22 April 1953, 28–29.

114. Hochrein und Schleicher, "Die vegetative Dystonie."

115. Dietze, "Zur Frage der langdauernden vegetativen Regulationsstörungen."

116. The VdH was founded in March 1950; for a more detailed discussion of the emergence of the VdH, see below, chapter 4.

117. Verband der Heimkehrer, Kriegsgefangenenkrankheiten.

118. Wolf v. Nathusius, "Erforschung der Heimkehrerkrankheiten," newspaper clipping in LAK 930/4780; Nathusius, "Sind die Gesundheitsschäden bei den Heimkehrern aus Kriegsgefangenschaft und Internierung überwunden?"

119. Bundesministerium für Arbeit- und Sozialordnung, *Die Dystrophie*, preface.

120. See below, chapter 8.

121. Quotation from Malten, "Heimkehrer," 597; Baldermann, "Wesen und Beurteilung der Heimkehrerdystrophien"; Funk, "Somato-psychologische Betrachtungen."

122. Gauger, *Die Dystrophie*, 64.

123. Bürger-Prinz and Giese, *Die Sexualität des Heimkehrers*, preface; see also Lehmann, *Gefangenschaft und Heimkehr*, 149–51.

124. Sedlmayer, "Erfahrungen in der Behandlung kranker Heimkehrer," 259; Stransky, "Mehrfachdeterminationen der Sexualstörungen," 26. Kurt Gauger, by

contrast, also analyzed dystrophy among female returnees, see Gauger, *Die Dystrophie*, 116.

125. Moeller, *Protecting Motherhood.*

126. Herzog, "Pleasure, Sex, and Politics," 398.

127. Schelsky, "Die soziale Formen der sexuellen Beziehungen," 16, and *Soziologie der Sexualität.*

128. Stransky, "Mehrfachdetermination der Sexualstörungen," 23.

129. Steen, "Ergebnisse aus 500 Sperma Untersuchungen"; Bansi, "Die 'interne Klinik' der Heimkehrer," 9–18.

130. Hoff and Schindler, "Die psychohygienische Aufgabe im Heimkehrerproblem," 896.

131. Mayer, "Zur Heimkehrerfrage."

132. Stransky, "Mehrfachdeterminationen der Sexualstörungen," 21.

133. Schaetzing, "Die Frau des Heimkehrers," 47.

134. Kilian, "Das Wiedereinleben des Heimkehrers," 37.

135. Schaetzing, "Die Frau des Heimkehrers," 42; on similar prescriptive guidelines in the United States, see Hartmann, "Prescriptions for Penelope."

136. Aufruf an entlassene Kriegsgefangene und ihre Angehörigen, EZA, 2/600.

137. Hemsing, "Der Heimkehrer und seine Ehe," 207–8.

138. Schaetzing, "Die Frau des Heimkehrers," 48.

139. Frankl and Roth, "Zur Therapie reaktiver Sexualneurosen." On advice literature for women more generally, see Herzog, *Sex after Fascism*, 119–20.

140. Hoff and Schindler, "Die psychohygienische Aufgabe im Heimkehrerproblem," 896. These were echoes of the discourse of "momism" in the United States; see Plant, "Repeal of Mother Love."

141. Hauptausschuss der Arbeiterwohlfahrt, Strafverfahren gegen Heimkehrer, BA-M, B 205/1560; see also Strafverfahren gegen Heimkehrer, *Neues Beginnen. Zeitschrift der Arbeiterwohlfahrt* 5 (1950): 7. The memo was sent to all attorneys general in the West German states and to the Federal Ministry of Justice.

142. Gauger, *Die Dystrophie*, 194–205.

143. Gerchow, "Über die Ursachen sexueller Fehlhaltungen und Straftaten," 454; for similar comments on returnees' proclivity toward sexual crime as a result of dystrophy, see Schulte, *Hirnorganische Dauerschäden*, 45–46.

144. Kohlhaas, "Die Problematik des Spätheimkehrers im Strafrecht"; Frenzel, "Der Heimkehrer im Straf und Ehescheidungsprozess."

145. For opposing views, see Lang, "Die Homosexualität als genetisches Problem" and Schultz, "Bemerkungen zu der Studie von Lang."

146. Herzog, *Sex after Fascism*, 64–100.

147. Stransky, "Mehrfachdetermination der Sexualstörungen," 24; see also Suhren, "Sexuelle Probleme in der Kriegsgefangenschaft."

148. Cernea, *Sexualbiologische Studien*, 122–23.

149. Kilian, "Das Wiedereinleben des Heimkehers"; quotation from von Henting, *Die Kriminalität des homophilen Mannes*, 33.

150. Herzog, *Sex after Fascism*, 88–95. If caught with male prostitutes, former soldiers and POWs were often granted extenuating circumstances; see Evans, "Bahnhof Boys," 632–33. On postwar applications of paragraph 175, see Moeller, "Homosexual Man."

151. Bürger-Prinz, "Psychopathologie der Sexualität," 543.

152. Wiethold, "Kriminalbiologische Behandlung von Sittlichkeitsverbrechern," 37–45; Henting, *Kriminalität des homophilen Mannes*; quotation from Laszlo, "Zur Soziologie der Homosexualität," 84.

153. See Heineman, "Sexuality and Nazism," 33–42; on the association of homosexuality with totalitarian political convictions in Western liberal discourse, see Dean, *Sexuality in Modern Western Culture*, 60.

154. Schelsky, *Soziologie der Sexualität*, 75–82, quotation on 82; on Schelsky's views and postwar discussions of homosexuality see Moeller, "Homosexual Man."

155. Protokoll über Sitzung des Heimkehrerausschusses Groß Berlin, 19 September 1946, BA-SAPMO, DY 3/6, 242–43.

156. Illustrierte Rundschau, 13 July 1947, newspaper clippings, "Heimkehrerlager Gronenfelde," Stadtarchiv Frankfurt/Oder; "Sie kehren zurück," *Neue Berliner Illustrierte* 2/27 (1946): 5; "Wir sind daheim," *Neue Berliner Illustrierte* 2/14 (1946): 6–7.

157. Provinzialverwaltung Mark Brandenburg, Abt. Gesundheitswesen, to Präsidenten der Provinzialverwaltung Mark Brandenburg, 20 July 1946, BLHA, Rep. 211/1164.

158. Lagerarzt Dr. Elisat to Zentralverwaltung für Arbeit und soziale Fürsorge, 12 August 1946, BA-Berlin, DQ2/2018.

159. Vogt, 13 September 1946, BA-Berlin, DO 1/10/87, 177.

160. Eggerath von SED Thüringen to Ulbricht: "Bericht des Kreisvorsitzenden der SED Walter Peters zu den Verhältnissen in dem Quarantänelager No.22 Unterwellenborn," 1 November 1946, BA-SAPMO, NY 4182/1160, 56–58.

161. Straunzenberg, "Über das Hungerödem"; Ratschow, "Zur Oedemkrankheit und ihrer Beeinflussung durch Cystin"; Lemke, "Über die vegetative Depression"; Henssge, "Reaktive psychische Erkrankungen."

162. Review of H. W. Bansi, "Die Ödemkrankheit" in *Das Deutsche Gesundheitswesen* 1 (1946): 750–51 and of Heinrich Berning, "Die Dystrophie" in *Das Deutsche Gesundheitswesen*, 4 (1949): 1278–79.

163. Lewin, "Neurologisch-psychiatrische Untersuchungen"; Gottschick, "Die 'experimentellen' Neurosen"; Müller-Hegemann, *Neurologie und Psychiatrie*, 652–56.

164. This was similar to the status of psychiatry in the Soviet Union; see Krylova, "Healers of Wounded Souls," 317–19; see also Merridale, *Night of Stone*. While I have found no evidence for political intervention regarding this issue, there can be no doubt that such intervention did occur; see Hanrath, *Zwischen Euthanasie und Psychiatriereform*, 212.

165. On medicine, see Ernst, *Die beste Prophylaxe*; on psychiatry see Eghigian, "Communist Psychiatry"; Hanrath, *Zwischen Euthanasie und Psychiatriereform*.

166. Kröbe, "Der praktische Arzt."

167. Quotation from Lindenberg, "Lebensmut oder Renten-Neurose?" 91; see also Eghigian, "Psychologization of Socialist Self."

168. A brief moment of openness toward psychoanalysis and psychotherapy in the late 1940s allowed for a limited recognition of war-related trauma as long as it did not refer to returnees from the East; see Henssge, "Reaktive psychische

Erkrankungen"; Lemke, "Über die vegetative Depression"; on the general context, see Hanrath, *Zwischen Euthanasie und Psychiatriereform*, 228–32.

169. Hanrath, *Zwischen Euthanasie und Psychiatriereform*, 400–410.

170. On Müller-Hegemann, see the biographic profile at *http://www.uni-leipzig.de/~psy/geschichte.htm*.

171. See Müller-Hegemann, *Zur Psychologie deutscher Faschisten*; on the reception of this work, see Barck, *Antifa-Geschichte(n)*, 115–21.

172. Müller-Hegemann, *Die Psychotherapie bei schizophrenen Prozessen*, 109.

173. Hanrath, *Zwischen Euthanasie und Psychiatrie*, 369–81.

174. On caring for returnees with brain damage, see Erholungsfürsorge, ADW, CA/O/288; Bevollmächtigte des Hilfswerk der EKD im Bundesland Sachsen, Dr. Brachman, to EHiW, Zentralbüro Ost, 14 September 1946, ADW, ZB/151.

175. Rededisposition für Heimkehrerversammlungen, BLHA, Rep. 332/542, 221–25; Vogt, 13 September 1946, BA-Berlin, DO1/10/87, 177.

176. Rededisposition für Heimkehrerversammlungen, BLHA, Rep. 332/542, 221–25.

177. Edith Hönig, "Stimmungsbild aus dem Rückkehrerlager der aus russischer Kriegsgefangenschaft heimkehrenden Deutschen in Frankfurt/Oder Gronenfelde," 2 August 1946, BA-SAPMO, DY 30/IV2/17/56, 12.

178. On gender notions within the Communist Party, see the intriguing analysis in Weitz, *Creating German Communism*, 188–223.

179. This does not mean that East German authorities were not concerned with regulating sexual behavior more generally; for an instructive comparison of East and West German efforts to regulate male prostitution, see Evans, "Bahnhof Boys."

180. W. Käferstein, Rededisposition für die Einleitung in Versammlungen mit Berichten von Heimkehrern aus der SU, 7 November 1947, BLHA, Rep. 332/578, 119.

181. SED-ZK to all Landes- und Provinzialvorstände der SED, Merkblatt für die Betreuung der heimkehrenden Kriegsgefangenen, 27 June 1946, BA-SAPMO, DY 30/IV2/2.027/46, 2–4.

182. Such defensive mechanisms also shaped official responses to female returnees. East German officials and East German publications explicitly rejected Western accusations of their bad treatment in Soviet captivity and especially emphasized the absence of rape; SED-Kreisvorstand Frankfurt-Oder, Abt. Frauen to SED-ZK, 22 August 1947, BA-SAPMO, DY 30/IV2/17/11; see also "Das ist die Wahrheit," *Für Dich*, 13 August 1947, BA-M, B 205/1404.

CHAPTER 4
SURVIVORS OF TOTALITARIANISM

1. Dower, *Embracing Defeat*, 168–200.

2. Rousso, "Das Dilemma eines europäischen Gedächtnisses."

3. Judt, "Past Is Another Country"; Sasson, "Italy after Fascism"; Rousso, *The Vichy Syndrome*.

4. Lagrou, *Legacy of Nazi Occupation*, 251, "The Nationalization of Victimhood," 254–56.

5. On the resistance as basis of postwar memory, see Danyel, "Die Opfer und Verfolgtenperspektive als Gründungskonsens?"

6. On Christian memory, see Mitchell, "Materialism and Secularism"; Schildt, "Solidarisch mit der Schuld des Volkes"; on Protestants, see Greschat, *Die evangelische Christenheit*, 310–14, and " 'Rechristianisierung' und 'Säkularisierung' "; on Catholics, see Repgen, "Die Erfahrung des Dritten Reiches"; Löhr, "Rechristianisierungsvorstellungen im deutschen Katholizismus 1945–1948."

7. Über die geistig-religiöse Lage in Deutschland (5 November 1946), HEK, CR II, 25, 18, 8.

8. Grusswort an die Heimkehrer, hrsg. vom Evangelischen Hilfswerk, EZA, 2/600.

9. Der Heimkehrer fragt—Was antwortet die Kirche? EZA, 2/532.

10. Quotation in Predigt des im Oktober 1948 aus russischer Gefangenschaft heimgekehrten Priesters Robert Dörflinger, Augsburg, DA-EB, I/9–22–4; see also Niederschrift über die Tagung "Kirche und Heimkehrer" in der britischen Zone, 1 September 1948, EZA, 2/601.

11. Schwester Richarda, Bericht über die Betreuung der Heimkehrer in der Waldschänke, 14 October 1946 to 1 September 1947, ADCV, 372.2.056, 1946–51.

12. Müller-Gangloff, *Christen in Kriegsgefangenschaft* , 8, 48–49.

13. Schivelbusch, *The Culture of Defeat*, 1–35.

14. Müller-Gangloff, *Christen in Kriegsgefangenschaft*, 11, 16, 51–62.

15. Hemsing, "Der deutsche Geistesmensch," 294, 297; along similar lines, see Hemsing, "Über die seelische Gesundung des Heimkehrers."

16. Grusswort an die Heimkehrer, hsrg. vom Evangelischen Hilfswerk, EZA, 2/600; Krahé, "Männerseelsorge und Heimkehrer," 37.

17. Krahé, "Männerseelsorge und Heimkehrer," 47.

18. Predigt des im Oktober 1948 aus russischer Gefangenschaft heimgekehrten Priesters Robert Dörflinger, Augsburg, DA-EB, I/9–22–4.

19. On the notion of a Christian *Abendland*, see Mitchell, "Materialism and Secularism," 297–99.

20. See, for examples, the speeches in Zusammenfassung der Ergebnisse der Tagung über die Notstände entlassener Kriegsgefangener auf der Comburg, 10–12 June 1948, BA-K, B 150/339; see also Kurt Krüger, "Die vergessenen Heimkehrer," *Der Tagesspiegel*, 21 June 1951.

21. Aufstellung der Besucherzahlen der Ausstellung "Wir Mahnen" seit März 1951, VdH Archive, File Kulturarbeit, No. 4. On these exhibitions, see also Moeller, *War Stories*, 40–41; and Beil, "Erfahrungsorte des Krieges," citing two million visitors by the mid-1960s.

22. Moeller, *War Stories*, 40–41.

23. Wegweiser durch die Ausstellung des VdH "Wir Mahnen," VdH Archive, Kulturarbeit, Nr. 5.

24. Ibid.; "Wir Mahnen. Zur VdH Ausstellung in Gießen," *Gießener Anzeiger,* 17 November 1959, VdH Archive, File Kulturarbeit Nr. 4.

25. Rede zur Eröffnug in Iserlohn der Ausstellung "Wir Mahnen," 1957, VdH Archive, File Kulturarbeit, Nr. 4.

26. Wegweiser durch die Ausstellung "Wir Mahnen," VdH Archive.

27. "Wir mahnen. Zur VdH-Ausstellung in Giessen," *Gießener Anzeiger*, 17 November 1959; "Innere Haltung überwand äussere Not," *Rheinische Post*, 22 April 1958, newspaper clipping, VdH Archive, Kulturarbeit, Nr. 4.

28. "Kriegsgefangene reden," hrsg. vom VdH, 2, ACDP, I-369–012/1. On the cultural pessimism of the 1950s, see Schildt, *Moderne Zeiten*, 324–50.

29. "Dokumente unzerstörten Menschentums," *Krefelder Stadtpost*, no date, VdH Archive, Kulturarbeit, Nr. 5; Wegweiser durch die Ausstellung "Wir Mahnen," VdH Archive.

30. See figures 6, 7; see also Fritz Theilmann, "Kunst hinter Stacheldraht," in Fritz Theilmann, "Bildhauer des Gegenständlichen (1902–1991)," 18–19 (http://www.fritz-theilmann.de/; last accessed 26 February 2005).

31. Günter Battke to Hochwürdigen Msr Dr. Bernsdorff, 3 March 1952, HEK, CRII, 25, 19, 13. See also the organization of specific "returnee pilgrimages" by VdH branches in Bavaria, Josef Hofbauer, "Die Wallfahrt zu unserer Lieben Frau auf den Bogenberg in der Zeit von 1945 bis heute," Zulassungsarbeit, University of Regensburg, 1977, VdH-Archive, BV Oberpfalz-Niederbayern.

32. See also Knoch, *Die Tat als Bild*, 314–23.

33. August Fischer to Harald Boldt, no date, VdH Archive, Kriegsgefangene Nr. 6.

34. Rede zur Eröffnug in Iserlohn der Ausstellung "Wir Mahnen," 1957, VdH Archive, File Kulturarbeit, Nr. 4.

35. Moeller, "Last Soldiers."

36. Institut zur Sozialforschung, *Zum Politischen Bewusstsein ehemaliger Kriegsgefangener*, 39–43, 83–84.

37. For these projections see Bartov, *Mirrors of Destruction*; and Moeller, *War Stories*.

38. Weisbrod, "Moratorium of the Mandarins."

39. Wette, *Die Wehrmacht*.

40. On POW movies, see Moeller, *War Stories*, 148–70.

41. Böll, "Bekenntnis zur Trümmerliteratur," 35.

42. Kühne, "Zwischen Vernichtungskrieg und Freizeitgesellschaft."

43. Frevert, "Die Sprache des Volkes"; for a stronger emphasis on the continuity of nationalism, see Echternkamp, "Verwirrung im Vaterländischen."

44. On parallels to postwar Japan, see Dower, *Embracing Defeat*, 499–502; see also Schivelbusch, *The Culture of Defeat*, 25–32.

45. Krahé, "Männerseelsorge und Heimkehrer," 39.

46. Frei, *Vergangenheitspolitik*, 137–63; Der Heimkehrer fragt—was antwortet die Kirche, EZA, 2/532.

47. Eschenbach, "Heilige Stätten—imaginierte Gemeinschaft," 119–20.

48. Diehl, *Thanks of the Fatherland*, 60–61.

49. Ther, "Vertriebenenpolitik," 146.

50. "Das Werk der Caritas Kriegsgefangenenhilfe," *Caritas* 48/1–2 (1947): 23; "Die Caritas Kriegsgefangenenhilfe," ADCV 372.059, Fasz. 2. Höfler then served as first chairman of the subcommittee on POW and returnee issues in the Bundestag.

51. Kunze, *Theodor Heckel*, 182–84, and "Das Evangelische Hilfswerk." Heckel was forced to resign from the position as head of the Foreign Office of the Protestant church because of his involvement with the pro-Nazi "German Christians" and was replaced by Martin Niemöller. See Heckel's letter to Niemöller, 21 January 1946, BA-M, Msg 194/436; on the EHiW in general Wischnath, *Kirche in Aktion*.

52. See the material in BA-M, Msg 194/224 and Msg 194/239.

53. Deutscher Caritasverband, Caritas Kriegsgefangenenhilfe, Anfang Februar 1948, HEK, CR II, 25, 19, 7; Die Caritas Kriegsgefangenenhilfe, ADCV 372.059, Fasz. 2; and for Protestants, Lagebericht, Vorschläge und Durchführung hinsichtlich der Betreuung der heimkehrenden Kriegsgefangenen, Juni 1947, EZA, 2/530; Hilfswerk der Evangelischen Kirche to Church World Service, Dankberichterstattung, 20 January 1949, ADW, HGSt, Allg. Slg., B45.6; see also Hilfswerk der Evangelischen Landeskirche in Württemberg, Handreichung für die Betreuung der Flüchtlinge und Heimkehrer, March 1946, June 1948.

54. Cohen, *The War Come Home*, 71–97.

55. Landesbischof Wurm an die Heimkehrer aus Gross-Stuttgart, February 1946, Heimkehrer-Tagung 9.–17.3.1946, EA/IBB.

56. Programm, Heimkehrer Tagung 9.–17.3.1946, EA/IBB. These meetings continued into the 1950s; see also Lockenour, *Soldiers as Citizens*, 85–92.

57. Männerarbeit der evangelischen Kirche in Deutschland, 3 May 1946, ADW, CA/W 394; Kirche und Heimkehrer, ADW, HBB/22; Dekan Pfeifle to Oberkirchenrat, 4 January 1949, BA-K, B 150/357; see also Vollnhals, "Die Evangelische Kirche."

58. Pfarrer Günter Besch aus Bremen to Pastor Damrath, Kanzlei der Evangelischen Kirche Deutschlands, 10 April 1947; Kanzlei der EKD to Herrn Pfarrer Besch, 20 June 1947, EZA, 2/530.

59. Dr. Egidius Schneider, "Was können wir praktisch tun?" 70.

60. Von Olenhusen, "Die Feminisierung von Religion."

61. Arbeitsbericht des Kirchlichen Dienstes für Kriegsgefangene und Heimkehrer, Bremen, 1 February 1950–1 January 1951, EZA, 2/617.

62. Evangelisches Jugendwerk Tübingen to Evangelisches Dekanat Tübingen, 25 January 1949, BA-K, B 150/337.

63. "Bericht über Errichtung eines Erholungsheimes für Russlandheimkehrer in Rentheim," in *Westfälische Nachrichten*, 17 June 1948, clipping in EZA, 2/602.

64. Zentralbüro des Hilfswerks der EKD to Hauptbüro des Hilfswerks in den Westzonen, 8 November 1947; Rundschreiben Nr. 130, Evangelisches Hilfswerk Westfalen, 15 August 1947, EZA, 2/530.

65. On the Protestant discussion, see Wischnath, *Kirche in Aktion*, 121–67; Kirche und Heimkehrer, ADW, HBB/22.

66. Deutscher Caritasverband, Caritas Kriegsgefangenenhilfe, Anfang Februar 1948, HEK, CR II, 25, 19, 7.

67. Hünerfeld, Caritas Kriegsgefangenenhilfe to Hauptvertretung der Caritasverbände, 22 June 1951, ADCV, 372.2 (497.1), 1954–56. At the camp in Friedland, the Evangelische Hilfswerk employed as many as sixty people; see the brochure *Das Evangelische Hilfswerk im Heimkehrerlager Friedland,* 4, ADCV, Library.

68. Bericht Caritasstelle Hof Moschendorf, 3 February 1949, ADCV, 372.2.056, 1946–1951.

69. Greschat, "Konfessionelle Spannungen in der Ära Adenauer"; and Blaschke, *Konfessionen im Konflikt.*

70. Jakob M. to Evangelisches Hilfswerk, 16 May 1949, ADW, HGSt, Allg. Slg., B 454.

71. Quotation from Arthur S. to Evangelisches Hilfswerk für Kriegsgefangene und Internierte, 28 May 1950, BA-M, Msg 194/241; for a similar reference to the dome in Cologne, Anton G. to Frings, 6 January 1949, HEK, CR II, 25, 19, 10. For other responses testifying to the POWs' religiosity, see Rudolf M. to Frings, 23 March 1948, HEK, CR II, 25, 19, 7; Johannes Heber, "Bericht über Gottesdienst und Seelsorge in der Kriegsgefangenschaft," EZA, 4/472 and, for POWs in Western captivity, Tätigkeitsbericht über die Seelsorgearbeit bei den deutschen Kriegsgefangenen in Italien (February–May 1946), HEK, CR II, 25, 19, 2.

72. See also the "oral history" evidence in Rosenthal, *Wenn alles in Scherben fällt,* 338–79.

73. Caritasverband Kriegsgefangenenhilfe to Caritasverbände der deutschen Erzdiözesen und Diözesen, June 1947, HEK, CRII, 25, 19, 8; Bericht über meine Erlebnisse in russischer Kriegsgefangenschaft, insbesondere über die Zustände im Kriegsgefangenenlager Minsk 168, EZA, 2/527.

74. Karl A., "Bericht über die seelsorgerischen Verhältnisse in deutschen Kriegsgefangenenlagern in Rußland," 3 December 1949, HEK, CR II, 25, 19, 11.

75. Pfarrer Schiele to Krummacher, Oberster Kirchenrat, 29 March 1948, Arnold Zywicki, Priester des Bistums Berlin to OKR Krummacher, 9 April 1948, ADCV, 511/W, Fasz. 03, Akte III; Lehmann,*Gefangenschaft und Heimkehr,* 112, also emphasizes the POWs' low religiosity.

76. First quotation Hilfswerk der Evangelischen Kirche to Hessische AG für Kriegsgefangenenfragen, Erfahrungsberichte über die Heimkehrerbetreuung,12 August 1949, BA-K, B 150/357; second quotation, Evangelisches Stadtdekanatsamt to Oberkirchenrat, 31 December 1948, BA-K, B 150/357a.

77. Dekan Pfeifle to Oberkirchenrat, 4 January 1949, BA-K, B 150/357a.

78. Greschat, *Die evangelische Christenheit,* 71; see also Repgen, "Die Erfahrung des Dritten Reiches," 141.

79. Pollack, "Secularisation in Germany after 1945"; on the European dimension, see Conway, "Western Europe's Democratic Age," 81–84.

80. On these local efforts, see Oberstadtdirektor Wuppertal, Flugblatt "Heimkehrerhilfe für entlassene Kriegsgefangene," September 1947, NRWHStA, NW 47/53, 58; and Jellinghaus, *Vorsorge und Fürsorge für unsere Kriegsgefangenen,* 41. For Berlin, see Aufruf an die Einwohner des Bezirks Kreuzberg, Public Welfare Branch, "Problems of Returned POWs," OMGBS 4/18–3/12, LAB and, in general, Matschenz, "Der Onkel da ist Dein Vater"; for Cologne, see Dülffer, "Aussichtslose Kämpfe, Kriegsgefangenschaft und Rückkehr"; quotation from report

by Dr. Muthesius, Deutscher Städtetag to Mitgliederstädte in NRW, Landesverbände, Berlin und Verbindungsstellen, 1 March 1949, Stadtarchiv Köln, Acc. 5.,
Nr. 860, 1–2.

81. Regierungspräsident Arnsberg to Sozialminister des Landes Nordrhein-
Westfalen, 15 November 1948, NRWHStA, NW 42/681.

82. Oberregierungsrat v. Kalm, Münster, West, "Was geschieht für die heimkehrenden Kriegsgefangenen?" (n.d), NRWHStA, NW 117/17, 220–23. For a
similar statement equating returnees with "victims of fascism," see Der Ober-
kreisdirektor des Kreises Wiedenbrück to Verwaltung des Provinzialverbandes der
Provinz Westfalen, Münster, Fürsorge für heimkehrende Kriegsgefangene, 19
March 1947, NRWHStA, NW 42/1157, 303.

83. Aufbau der Landesarbeitsgemeinschaften, des Ausschhusses für Kriegsgefangenenfragen und des Referats für Kriegsgefangenenfragen, BA-K, B 150/320a.

84. Hessisches Staatsministerium des Innern to Staatskanzlei, 19 December
1949, HHStA 502/1002; on this institutional history, see Smith, *Heimkehr aus
dem Zweiten Weltkrieg.*

85. On the emergence of these interest organizations, see Diehl, *Thanks of the
Fatherland,* 71; and my dissertation "The Protracted War," 137–39.

86. Bericht über die erste Siztung des Kriegsgefangenenbeirates am 6.12.1951
in Bonn, VdH Archive, Kriegsgefangene, Nr. 8. On institutional developments in
the East, see below, chapter 5.

87. Moeller, *War Stories,* 21–50; Hughes, *Shouldering the Burdens,* 73–82;
Diehl, *Thanks of the Fatherland,* 101. The VdH strongly resented the exclusion of
former POWs from these benefits; see Denkschrift des Verbandes der Heimkehrer,
Kriegsgefangenen- und Vermisstenangehörigen Deutschlands e.V. zum Lastenaus-
gleichgesetz, *Der Heimkehrer* 2/2 (February 1951): 1–2.

88. Bund der Russlandheimkehrer to Länderratsausschuss für Kriegsgefangenenfragen, 26 February 1949, Erste Entschliessung des Bundes der Russlandheimkehrer am 6. Februar 1949, BA-K, B 150/336b; Diehl, *Thanks of the Fatherland,*
101–2.

89. *Bundesgesetzblatt* 27 (1950): 221–24; on the discussion and passage of the
law, see Diehl, *Thanks of the Fatherland,* 101–7.

90. All quotations from August Fischer to Harald Boldt, no date, VdH Archive,
Kriegsgefangene Nr. 6. See also *Der Heimkehrer* 3/8 (August 1952):1. Expellee
organizations adopted a similar strategy and tended to play a "double game of
simultaneously asserting victimhood and self-reliance"; see Hughes, *Shouldering
the Burdens,* 102.

91. Verband der Heimkehrer, Entwurf zum Gesetz über die Entschädigung der
deutschen Kriegsgefangenen, NRWHStA, LANW 36II, 493–94.

92. These figures are based on Teschner, "Entwicklung eines Interessenverbandes," 36–42; see also Diehl, *Thanks of the Fatherland,* 172.

93. See the materials in VdH Archive, File Kriegsgefangenenentschädigunsgesetz.

94. 274. Kabinettssitzung, 10 February 1953, in *Die Kabinettsprotokolle der
Bundesregierung,* vol. 6, 1953, 159.

95. See Drucksache No. 4318, "Entwurf eines Gesetzes über die Entschädigung ehemaliger deutscher Kriegsgefangener, 15 May 1953," VDBT, 1. Wahlperiode, Drucksachen. The only difference from the VdH's draft was that all POWs

who had returned after 1 January 1947 rather than 1 January 1946 were to receive compensation; on the legislative history of POW compensation, see Diehl, *Thanks of the Fatherland*, 172–73.

96. VDBT, Stenographische Berichte, 1. Wahlperiode, 271. Sitzung, 12 June 1953, 13431–33.

97. VDBT, Stenographische Berichte, 1. Wahlperiode, 271. Sitzung, 12 June 1953, 13427–28, 13436–38.

98. See, for example, August Fischer to Heinrich von Brentano, 29 April 1953, VdH Archive, File Kriegsgefangenen-Entschädigungsgesetz, CSU.

99. Diehl, *Thanks of the Fatherland*, 126; 10. Kabinettssitzung, 1 December 1953, *Die Kabinettesprotokolle der Bundesregierung*, vol. 6, 535–37; "Bundeskabinett stoppt Entschädigungsgesetz," *Der Heimkehrer* 4/9 (1953): 1. In December 1953, the VdH threatened a "march on Bonn" to effect the implementation of the POW compensation law; see "Regierung kontra Bundestag," *Der Heimkehrer* 4/12 (1953): 1.

100. See also the contacts between Fritz Erler and the organization of former members of the Armed SS (HIAG) during the 1950s, ASD, NL Erler, Box 149. On the role of the SPD in attracting former soldiers, see also Holtman, *Politik und Nichtpolitik*, 246.

101. Teschner, "Entwicklung eines Interessenverbandes," 68–78; Diehl, *Thanks of the Fatherland*, 175–77. Both authors interpret these activities as part of the VdH's "organizational ideology" after its most important material demand had been met.

102. This study followed the methodological premises of the institute's "group study" that had been published two years earlier; Wiggershaus, *Die Frankfurter Schule*, 519–53.

103. Institut für Sozialforschung, *Zum politischen Bewusstsein ehemaliger Kriegsgefangener*, 39–50, 83.

104. Ibid., 119–37. Such authoritarian views were typical for large sections of the conservative milieu; see Kühne, "Zwischen Vernichtungskrieg und Freizeitgesellschaft," 106–7; and Bösch, *Das Konservative Milieu*, 185–213.

105. Institut für Sozialforschung, *Zum Politischen Bewusstsein ehemaliger Kriegsgefangener*, 128–65. This view also reflected the dominant interpretation of National Socialism as "radicalization of the middle class" (124). On the methodological difficulties of evaluating group interviews, see Wiggershaus, *Die Frankfurter Schule*, 528–34; The transcripts are housed in the Archive of the Institut für Sozialforschung, Frankfurt (ISF), H1-H51.

106. Interview H31, 21, H17, 14, ISF.

107. On the issue of "war criminals," see Frei, *Vergangenheitspolitik*, 133–306; see also below chapter 7.

108. Interview H4, 1, ISF.

109. Interviews H5, 6; H6, 7, 28; H18, 24, ISF.

110. Interview H18, 24, ISF.

111. Interview H2, 36–37, ISF.

112. Interview H12, 49, ISF.

113. Cited in Tauber, *Beyond Eagle and Swastika*, 352–53.

114. VdH Kreisverband Verden to Landesverband Niedersachsen, 28 October 1952; Josef Reichman, VdH Archive, File Kriegsgefangenfragen, Nr. 9.

115. This is the argument in Manig, *Die Politik der Ehre*; on the intervention of the Western allies, see Frei, *Vergangenheitspolitik*, 307–96.

116. Frevert, *Die kasernierte Nation*; Hagemann; *Männlicher Muth*.

117. Institut für Sozialforschung, *Zum Politischen Bewusstein ehemaliger Kriegsgefangener*, 45; on former officers' attitude toward rearmament, see also Lockenour, *Soldiers as Citizens*, 125–51.

118. "Wenn schon, dann Wehrmacht," *Der Heimkehrer* 6/8 (15 August 1955): 1.

119. "Aufruf zur Generalmnestie," *Der Heimkehrer* 3/3 (March 1952): 1; see also Frei, *Vergangenheitspolitik*, 234–65.

120. VdH Bezirksverband Mittelfranken to VdH Landeserband Bayern, August Fischer, 5 February 1952, Vdh Archive, Wehrbeitrag 1952. These internal debates extended into the second half of the 1950s; see VdH Informationsdienst, 24 September 1956, VdH Archive, Wehrbeitrag 1952.

121. Institut für Sozialforschung, *Zum Politischen Bewusstsein ehemaliger Kriegsgefangener*, 45.

122. For the first position, see Kühne, "Zwischen Vernichtungskrieg und Freizeitgesellschaft," 94.

123. Geyer, "Cold War Angst."

124. Karl-Heinz K., February 1952, to VdH, Bonn, VdH Archive, Wehrbeitrag 1952.

125. Interview H2, 39, ISF. See also letter to the editor in *Stern* 3/49 (1950): 42.

126. Interviews H2, 33; H51, 22; H5, 27, ISF.

127. Interviews H33, 31; H51, 39; H32, 35–36, ISF; Institut für Sozialforschung, *Zum politischen Bewusstsein ehemaliger Kriegsgefangener*, 45.

128. Paul Gerhard G. to Kamerad Boldt, VdH-Bundesverband, 8 February 1952, VdH Archive, Wehrbeitrag, 1952; similarly H32, 45, ISF.

129. Lockenour, *Soldiers as Citizens*.

130. Geyer, "Cold War Angst," 377.

131. This was one thesis in the otherwise seminal essay by Niethammer, "Heimat und Front," 228; see also Bude, *Bilanz der Nachfolge*, 69–71.

132. See the reports from local communities in BA-K, B 150/357a; for similar findings for Anglo-American soldiers, see Bourke, "Going Home."

133. Teschner, "Entwicklung eines Interessenverbandes," 63.

134. Echternkamp, "Kameradenpost bricht nie ab."

135. Besides the evidence offered above, see also Niethammer, "Heimat und Front," 227. For contrary evidence of political activities of former soldiers and POW below the level of formal political participation, see Holtman, *Politik und Nichtpolitik*; Boll, *Auf der Suche nach der Demokratie.*

136. On the concept of "working through," see LaCapra, *History and Memory*, 180–210.

137. This emphasis goes back to the interwar period; see Cohen, *The War Come Home,* 152–62; Diehl, *Thanks of the Fatherland*, 12–13.

138. Referat für Kriegsgefangenenfragen, Aufzeichnung Mugdan, Weiterbeschäftigung von entlassenen Kriegsgefangenen, August 1948, BA-K, B 150/

331a; Bayrische Staatsministerium für soziale Fürsorge to Herrn Präsidenten der Landesarbeitsämter, 20 July 1948, BA-K, B 150/320a; see also Ruhl, *Verordnete Unterordnung,* 117.

139. See the example from the Bayer works in Leverkusen, Sozialabteilung to Abteilungsvorstände, Betriebsleiter, Bürovorsteher und Hauptvertrauensleute, 10 August 1949, Bayer-Archive Leverkusen, Sozialabteilung, Wohlfahrtsangelegenheiten 1945–1951, 214/10.5; Personalstand der Angestellten am 1. Mai 1946, Bayer-Archive, Leverkusen, Sekretariat Haberland, 214/10.5.

140. Vermerk über Berichte der Arbeitsämter, 21 July 1949, NRWHStA, LANW 36/I, 156; Die Betreuung der Heimkehrer durch die Arbeitsämter. Erfahrungen und Vorschläge, Sonderbeilage zum Arbeitsblatt, NHStA, Nds. 386, Acc. 16/83, Nr. 36.

141. *Bundesgesetzblatt* 27 (1950): 221–24. Significantly, the law asserted the priority of the war-disabled and of victims of Nazism on the labor market.

142. Die Betreuung der Heimkehrer durch die Arbeitsämter, NHStA, Nds. 386, Acc. 16/83, Nr. 36, 29.

143. Latzel, "Freie Bahn den Tüchtigen"; and *Deutsche Soldaten-Nationalsozialistischer Krieg,* 330.

144. Vermerk über Berichte der Arbeitsämter, NRWHStA, LANW 36/I, 158.

145. Die Betreung der Heimkehrer durch die Arbeitsämter, NHStA, Nds. 386, Acc. 16/83, Nr. 36, 30.

146. Ibid., 30; Georg W., Bonn, to Bundesministerium, Referat für Kriegsgefangenen und Heimkehrerfragen, 7 May 1950, NRWHStA, NW 42/1183, 269; Willy Sporahn, "Die Zuzugsnehmigung," in *Der Heimkehrer* 1 (1947).

147. Institut für Sozialforschung, *Zum politischen Bewusstsein ehemaliger Kriegsgefangener,* 5–6.

148. Erker, *Ernährungskrise und Nachkriegsgesellschaft.*

149. Abelshauser, *Die langen 50er Jahre,* 29, 80.

150. See interviews H2, 7; H7, 35–37; H14, 18; H15, 7, ISF.

151. Interview H3, 6, ISF; interview "Paul Werner," 8, 23 June–4 July 1981, IfGB.

152. Mooser, "Arbeiter, Angestellte und Frauen," 363.

153. Die Betreung der Heimkehrer durch die Arbeitsämter, NHStA, Nds. 386, Nr. 36, 29.

154. First quotation interview H32, 6; second quotation interview H36, 10; see also interview H36, 7–8; interview H51, 6, ISF.

155. Interview H36, 7–8, ISF.

156. Interview "Fritz Enger," 8 June 1982, 10–11, IfGB; interview with "Werner J.," 20 January 1997, OH 6.

157. For West Germany: Arbeitsamt Bielefeld, 13 June 1949; Arbeitsamt Krefeld, 13 June 1949; Arbeitsamt Arnsberg, 14 June 1949; Präsident des Landesarbeitsamtes Niedersachsens an die Verwaltung des Vereinigten Wirtschaftsgebietes, 25 February 1949; all in NRWHStA-Kalkum, LANW 36/1; Die Betreuung der Heimkehrer durch die Arbeitsämter. Erfahrungen und Vorschläge, NHStA, Nds. 386, Acc. 16/83, Nr. 36, 31; Bundesministerium für Arbeit, Statistik über die arbeitslosen Heimkehrer in der Bundesrepublik Deutschland in der Gliederung nach Berufsgruppen, 31.1.1951–30.6.1951, BA-K, B 149/905.

158. Garner, "Public Service Personnel," 194.

159. Wehler, "Deutsches Bürgertum nach 1945"; Berghahn, "Reacasting Bourgeois Germany."

160. Friedrich Wilhelm W. to Sozialminister des Landes Nordrhein-Westfalen, 31 January 1951, NRWHStA, NW 42/1183, 111.

161. Friedrich W. to Innenminister des Landes Nordrhein-Westfalen, NRWHStA, NW 110/777, 169.

162. Mayer, "German Survivors," 229–46. He refers primarily to men born between 1926 and 1930.

163. Hans W. to Sozialministerium Nordrhein-Westfalen, 25 December 1950, NRWHStA, NW 42/1183, 151.

164. Hans S. to Zonenrat in US-Zone, 3 September 1949; Ewald G. to Arbeitsgemeinschaft für kulturelle Betreuung der Kriegsgefangenen und Heimkehrer, 11 September 1949, BA-K, B 150/332.

165. See also the reference to the large segment of returnees and expellees among the Volkswagen workforce in Uliczka, *Berufsbiographie und Flüchtlingsschicksal*, 167–68.

166. On the conservative gender ideology of the 1950s, see Moeller, *Protecting Motherhood*; on the replacement of working women by returning men, see Garner, "Public Service Personnel," 175–91; Ruhl, *Verordnete Unterordnung*; Heineman, *What Difference*, 155–62.

167. Der Bundesminister für Verkehr to Herrn Bundesminister für Arbeit, 14 February 1951, BA-K, B 149/905; Der Niedersächsische Ministerpräsident-Staatskanzlei, Bevorzugte Behandlung von Heimkehrern bei Einstellungen im Bereich des öffentlichen Dienstes, 6 February 1950, BA-K, B 149/905.

168. Garner, "Public Service Personnel," 157–75; on the significance of the 131 Law for the West German politics of memory, see Frei, *Vergangenheitspolitik*, 69–100.

169. The percentage of civil servants and white-collar employees increased steadily after the mid-1950s; see Abelshauser, *Die langen 50 Jahre*, 68–69, 88.

170. Institut für Sozialforschung, *Zum Politischen Bewußtsein ehemaliger Kriegsgefangener*, 18–19; Noelle and Neumann, *Jahrbuch der öffentlichen Meinung, 1957*, 230.

171. On the link between war and consumption, see Jarausch and Geyer, *Shattered Past*, 269–314.

172. See the excellent review of the historiography in Moeller, "Elephant in Living Room."

173. Moeller, *Protecting Motherhood*.

174. Heineman, *What Difference*, 118, who bases this estimate on registrations of MIAs.

175. Statistisches Jahrbuch 1952, 45.

176. Bericht der Arbeitsgemeinschaft für Jugend- und Eheberatung in Hannover für das Geschäftsjahr 1951/52, ADW, CA/W 408 A.

177. Bader, "Ehekrisen unserer Heimkehrer"; Wilm, "Die herrschende Ehekrise als Problem und Aufgabe"; Dirks, "Was die Ehe bedroht"; Thurnwald, *Gegenwartsproblem Berliner Familien*, 196–99.

178. von Hollander, "Der Mann in der Krise" in *Constanze* 1/3 (1948): 3, "Der Held und der Mann von Heute," *Constanze* 1/4 (1948): 3, and "Der Mann als Ballast," *Constanze* 1/5 (1948): 7. On Hollander, see also Herzog, *Sex after Fascism*, 87–88; on men's incompetence, Heineman, *What Difference*, 120–25. I would like to thank Dagmar Herzog for making the unpublished version of her manuscript available to me.

179. Hemsing, "Der Heimkehrer und seine Ehe," 206.

180. Spahn, "Heimkehrer ohne Heimat."

181. Rölli-Alkemper, *Familie im Wiederaufbau*, 51–84.

182. Thesen zu den Lehrgängen für Spätheimkehrer, EZA, 2/604.

183. Evangelischer Oberkirchenrat to sämtliche Dekanatsämter, Betreuung von Heimkehrern ("Patenschaften"), 11 December 1947, EZA, 2/603.

184. Erich Wollenberg, "Patenschaften für heimatlose Kriegsgefangene," September 1947, BAK, B150/335; Smith, *Heimkehr aus dem Zweiten Weltkrieg*, 116.

185. On gender relations during the war, see Kundrus, *Kriegerfrauen*.

186. Quotations from Richtlinien für die Pastoration der Heimkehrer, ADCV, 372.025, Fasz. 3 and "Ein Wort zum Ehebruch: Soll der Mann seiner Frau vergeben," *Der Heimkehrer* 1 (1947); see also Rölli-Alkemper, *Familie im Wiederaufbau*, 91–106.

187. Heineman, *What Difference*, 123; Niehuss, *Familie, Frau und Gesellschaft*, 102.

188. Interview H2, 15, ISF.

189. Sibylle Meyer and Eva Schulze Interview Collection, Interview 26, Frau und Herr Lu., Institut für Sozialforschung, TU-Berlin; Meyer/Schulze, *Von Liebe sprach damals keiner*, 181; Interview Collection, Frau. Pi, Institut für Sozialforschung, TU-Berlin.

190. Kühne, "Zwischen Vernichtungskrieg und Freizeitgesellschaft," 108; see also Dörr, *Wer die Zeit nicht miterlebt hat*, 3:36.

191. First quotation from Wierling, "Mission to Happiness," 115; second quotation Schissler, "Normalization as Project," 361.

192. Mayntz, *Die moderne Familie*, 50–51; Wurzbacher, *Leitbilder gegenwärtigen Familienlebens*, 114–49.

193. Moeller, *Protecting Motherhood*.

194. Heineman, *What Difference*, 131–34; Schneider, "Ehen in Beratung."

195. Herzog, *Sex after Fascism*, 119.

196. Mayntz, *Die moderne Familie*, 47–48; this is also the emphasis in Bodamer, *Der Mann von Heute*.

197. von Stackelberg, *Familie und Ehe*, 325, 411. Despite these numbers, however, the study came to the conclusion that, for most families, the burdens of the present were more significant than the aftereffects of the war.

198. Neumann, *Nicht der Rede Wert*, 117–30, and "Kampf um Anerkennung."

199. Frau Kornelius B. to Petitionsausschuss des Deutschen Bundestages (Abschrift), 25 August 1954, NRWHStA, NW 47/61, 20.

200. Frau Anneliese B. to Herr Regierunsgpräsidenten des Landes Nordrhein-Westfalen, 7 November 1952, NRWHStA, NW 47/63, 102–4; also quoted in Neumann, *Nicht der Rede Wert*, 118.

201. Bruns, *Als Vater aus dem Krieg heimkehrte*, 189; see also Dörr, *Wer die Zeit nicht miterlebt hat*, 3:37–41.

202. Interview H3, 18–19, ISF.

203. Meyer, *Von Liebe sprach damals keiner*, 163; see also Baumert, *Jugend in der Nachkriegszeit*, 38–39.

204. Bruns, *Als Vater aus dem Krieg heimkehrte*, 23–31, 57–66, 82–88, 89–99, 177–85.

205. Moser, *Dämonische Figuren*; Eckstaedt, *Nationalsozialismus in der "zweiten Generation."*

206. Kurz, *Lebensverhältnisse der Nachkriegsjugend*, 15–20.

207. Heineman, *What Difference*, 119–20; Benz, "Maikäfer Flieg!"

208. Bruns, *Als Vater aus dem Krieg heimkehrte*, 57–66, 185–95.

209. Anhalt. "Farewell to My Father"; and for the recollections of a historians, Niethammer, *Ego-Histoire?* 172–82. On the negative consequences of silence, see Schwan, *Politik und Schuld*; more recent studies have revised the notion of pervasive silence and emphasize instead the presence of highly selective "family memories"; see Welzer, Moeller and Tschugall, *Opa war kein Nazi*; Wierling, "Mission to Happiness."

210. Bruns, *Als Vater aus dem Krieg heimkehrte*.

211. Hemsing, "Der Heimkehrer und seine Kinder."

212. Poiger, *Jazz, Rock, and Rebels*.

213. Interviews H5, 1; H6, 53; H8, 45, 52–53; for a more moderate view, H8, 46, ISF.

CHAPTER 5
ANTIFASCIST CONVERSIONS

1. Paul Merker, "Die Kriegsgefangenen," Abschrift eines Artikels aus der Märkischen Volksstimme aus Potsdam, 7 January 1948, BLHA, Rep. 203/1075, 74–75.

2. The official designation of 1948 as the "year of the returnee" added to this emphasis; "Unsere Heimkehrer," *Die neue Heimat* 2 (1938): 10–11.

3. On Communist memory, see Judt, "Past Is Another Country"; Herf, *Divided Memory*; on 1947 as turning point, see Mazower, *Dark Continent*, 263–73; Naimark, *The Russians in Germany*, 308–16.

4. Wilhelm Pieck, Ansprache auf der Zentralen Heimkehrerkonferenz, 29 October 1949, BA-SAPMO, NY 4036/441, 140; Arbeitsplan der Gesellschaft für Deutsch-Sowjetische Freundschaft für August 1949, BLHA, Rep. 332/725.

5. Speakers were carefully selected by regional and local branches of the GDSF. Among the 736 participating in the central *Heimkehrer* conference in Berlin, 471 had attended antifascist schools, and 585 were members of the SED; GDSF Landesleitung Sachsen to Kreissekretariate, Rundschreiben 30/49, 31 August 1949, BA-SAPMO, DY 32/10058; Auswertung der am 29. Oktober 1949 stattge-

fundenen zonalen Heimkehrerkonferenz, BA-SAPMO, DY 30/IV2/11/204, 84–85; Diskussionspunkte für die Zentrale Heimkehrerkonferenz, BA-SAPMO, DY 32/10057. On the GDSF, see Naimark, *The Russians in Germany*, 408–19; and Dralle, *Von der Sowjetunion lernen*.

6. Jürgen Kuczinsky, Protokoll der Zentralen Heimkehrerkonferenz, 29 October 1949, BA-SAPMO, DY 32/10057.

7. Franze, Protokoll der Zentralen Heimkehrerkonferenz, 29 October 1949, BA-SAPMO, DY 32/10057.

8. Heimkehrer Ludwig Sulek, Protokoll über das Heimkehrertreffen im Saal des Landratsamtes Guben, 26 July 1949, BLHA, Landratsamt Guben, Rep. 250/284.

9. Heimkehrer Klaus Willerding, Protokoll der Zentralen Heimkehrerkonferenz, 29 October 1949, BA-SAPMO, DY 32/10057.

10. Berger and Luckmann, *Die gesellschaftliche Konstruktion der Wirklichkeit*, 168–69. These authors identify the "religious conversion" as the prototype of such a transformation and refer to the adoption of this model by "political ideologies."

11. Walter Knoff, Perleberg; Schult, Ludwigslust, Protokoll der zentralen Heimkehrerkonferenz, 29 October 1949, BA-SAPMO, DY 32/10057.

12. First quotation Herr Grimmer, Landesheimkehrerkonferenz in der Nordhalle zu Dresden, 23 September 1949, SHStA, SED, LV A 306, 80; second quotation Heimkehrer Beckenstein, Schmalkaden, Protokoll der Landeskonferenz der GDSF mit antifaschistischen Heimkehrern, Erfurt, 25 September 1949, BA-SAPMO, DY 32/10058.

13. On the "externalization" of the Nazi past in East Germany, see Frei, "NS-Vergangenheit unter Ulbricht und Adenauer," 125–32.

14. Herf, *Divided Memory*, 13–39; Barck, *Antifa-Geschichte(n)*, 14.

15. This East German "philo-Sovietism" finds an interesting parallel in West German "philo-Semitism" after 1945; see Stern, *Whitewashing of Yellow Badge*.

16. Hemzal, Protokoll der zentralen Heimkehrerkonferenz, 29 October 1949, BA-SAPMO, DY 32/10057.

17. Wilhelm Pieck, Ansprache auf der zentralen Heimkehrerkonferenz, 29 October 1949, BA-SAPMO, NY 4036/441, 142; Naimark, *The Russians in Germany*, 410.

18. On this theme of absent authority in East Germany, see Hell, *Post-Fascist Fantasies*.

19. Begrüßungsansprache Prof. Kellermann, Stenografischer Bericht der Heimkehrer Konferenz, 24 June 1949, BA-SAPMO, DY 32/10058.

20. First quotation from Heimkehrer Klaus Willerding, Protokoll der Zentralen Heimkehrerkonferenz, 29 October 1949, BA-SAPMO, DY 32/10057; second quotation from Gerhard Wallich, Landesheimkehrerkonferenz in der Nordhalle zu Dresden, 23 September 1949, SHStA, SED, LV A 306, 108; third and forth quotation, Karl Leitz, Protokoll über das Heimkehretreffen im Saal des Landratsamtes Guben, 26 July 1949, BLHA, Landratsamt Guben, Rep. 250/284.

21. Heukenkamp, "Das Frauenbild in der antifaschistischen Erneuerung der SBZ."

22. Stenografischer Bericht der Heimkehrer Konferenz in Potsdam, 24 June 1949, BA-SAPMO, DY 32/10058. For a similar example, see Heimkehrer Kruse, MAS, Gross-Bressen, Protokoll über das Heimkehrertreffen im Saal des Landratsamtes Guben, 26 July 1949, BLHA, Landratsamt Guben, Rep. 250/284.

23. Landesheimkehrerkonferenz in der Nordhalle zu Dresden, 23 September 1949, SHStA, SED, LV A 306, 41–42.

24. Naimark, *The Russians in Germany*, 107.

25. For brief moments of openness that were immediately repressed, see ibid., 132–40.

26. Grossmann, "A Question of Silence"; Dahlke, "'Frau Komm."

27. Danyel, "Die geteilte Vergangenheit."

28. Heimkehrer Willerding, Protokoll der zentralen Heimkehrerkonferenz, 29 October 1949, BA-SAPMO, DY 32/10057.

29. On the exclusion of Jewish victims from Communist memories, see also Herf, *Divided Memory*, 69–161.

30. See Erler, Laude, and Wilke, *Nach Hitler kommen wir*, 112–15.

31. Morré, *Hinter den Kulissen des Nationalkomitees*, 194; Hilger, *Deutsche Kriegsgefangene in der Sowjetunion*, 225, provides this figure based on Soviet sources.

32. Erler, Laude, and Wilke, *Nach Hitler kommen wir*, 114; Morré, "Kader für Deutschland," 219; Hilger, *Deutsche Kriegsgefangene in der Sowjetunion*, 226.

33. Statistik über Antifa-Schüler, 23 March 1948 *BA-SAPMO*, DY30/IV2/11/202, 33; also cited in Morré, "Kader für Deutschland," 224.

34. Bericht über Antifa Heimkehrer, 29 October 1948, BA-SAPMO, NY 4036/745, 115–26; also cited in Morré, "Kader für Deutschland?" 224–25.

35. Antifa-Schüler und antifaschistische Aktivisten aus sowjetischer Gefangenschaft (Anregungen für eine Aussprache mit zuständigen Genossen), early 1948, BA-SAPMO, DY 30/IV2/11/202 23–32; Morré, "Kader für Deutschland," 228.

36. Hentschke, "Was wurde unsererseits in der Frage der Erfassung, Einsatzes und Betreuung der ehemaligen Antifa-Schüler getan?" BA-SAPMO, DY 30/IV2/11/202, 28–32; Vorschläge zur Verbesserung der Kriegsgefangenenarbeit in der personalpolitischen Abteilung, BA-SAPMO, DY 30/IV2/11/196, 88–90. The party leadership continued to complain about the insufficient attention of the district leaderships to antifascist returnees; SED Landesvorstand Sachsen, Kaderabteilung, to Kreisvorstand der SED in Bautzen, 3 January 1950, SHStA, SED Kreisleitung Bautzen, IV/4/01/179; H. Sinderman to Kreisvorstände der SED, 14 December 1949, SHStA, SED Kreisleitung Bautzen, IV/4/01/179.

37. Out of 2,350 antifascist returnees arriving between December 1948 and January 1949, 1,108 stayed in East Germany and 90 percent joined the SED; Zusammenfassender Bericht über die Erfahrungen und Einsatz der ehemaligen Antifa-Schüler, BA-SAPMO, DY 30/IV2/11/202, 173–74. Among returnees to Berlin, 532 out of 791 had become party members. SED Landesverband Gross-Berlin, Betr. Heimkehrer und Antifaschüler, 9 July 1949, LAB, SED-LV, IV L-2/11/413; see also Morré, "Kader für Deutschland?" 225.

38. Bericht über die Tätigkeit der ehemaligen Lehrer, Assistenten und Antifa-Schüler, die in der DDR wohnen, 14 March 1951, BA-SAPMO, DY 30/IV2/11/202, 269–74, also cited in Morré, "Kader für Deutschland?" 229.

39. Bericht Semjonows vom 24 January 1950, in Badstübner and Loth, *Wilhem Pieck—Aufzeichnungen zur Deutschlandpolitik*, 331.

40. Morré, "Kader für Deutschland?" 229.

41. Among 523 antifascist returnees who engaged in party work, 285 worked for district associations and 114 in party cells in the East German companies; Bericht über die Tätigkeit der ehemaligen Lehrer, Assistenten und Antifa-Schüler, die in der DDR wohnen, 14 March 1951, BA-SAPMO, DY 30/IV2/11/202, 269–74.

42. Zusammenfassender Bericht über die Erfahrungen und Einsatz der ehemaligen Antifa-Schüler aus den Schulen 2041, 2040 und 9999, die im Dezember 1948 und im Januar 1949 entlassen wurden, BA-SAPMO, DY 30/IV2/11/202, 173–74.

43. Out of 6,584 antifascist returnees, 1,096 were employed in VEBs and 1,145 were integrated into the People's Police; Bericht über die Tätigkeit der ehemaligen Lehrer, Assistenten und Antifa-Schüler, die in der DDR wohnen, 14 March 1951, BA-SAPMO, DY 30/IV2/11/202, 269–74; on the use of returning POWs during the formative period of the People's Police, see below; on FDJ use of antifascist returnees, Abteilung Personalpolitik to Erich Honecker, 16 October 1949 and Edith Baumann to Genosse Daub, Kader-Abteilung, 14 December 1949, BA-SAPMO, DY 30/IV2/11/196, 288, 297.

44. SED-Kreisleitung Bautzen, Personalpolitische Abteilung to Landesvorstand Sachsen, PPA-Parteifunktionäre, 19 August 1949, SHStA, Kreisleitung Bautzen, IV/4/01/179.

45. Heimkehrerkonferenz im Gorkihaus zu Bautzen, 13 February 1951, SHStA, Kreisleitung SED Bautzen, IV/4.01.179; Untersuchung im Kreis Bautzen über den Einsatz und die Weiterentwicklung von Antifaschülern, 27 November 1951, SHStA, SED Kreisleitung Bautzen, IV/4/01/179.

46. Bericht über die Instrukteursfahrt zur Überprüfung des Einsatzes der Antifa-Schüler in Leipzig und Dresden, 12–14 January 1950, BA-SAPMO, DY 30/IV2/11/202, 224.

47. Protokoll über Erfahrungsaustauch der Heimkehrer aus der Sowjetunion, 17 February 1950, BA-SAPMO, DY 30/IV2/11/204, 64.

48. Protokoll der Heimkehrerkonferenz in Wanzleben, 17 January 1950, BA-SAPMO, DY 30/IV2/11/204, 28–30.

49. SED Kreisvorstand, Kaderabteilung Dresden, Versammlung mit Heimkehrern (Zentralschülern), 24 February 1950, BA-SAPMO, DY 30/IV2/11/204, 44.

50. Ibid., 43.

51. Ibid., 46.

52. Ibid., 50–51.

53. Quotation from Niethammer, "Erfahrungen und Strukturen," cited in Epstein, *The Last Revolutionaries*, 215; on generational conflicts, see Stadtland, *Herrschaft nach Plan*, 253–67; von Plato, "The Hitler Youth Generation"; Wierling, "The Hitler Youth Generation in the DDR."

54. Auszüge aus dem Referat des Gen. F.Sch., "Über die Kaderarbeit der Partei," n.d. (probably 1948), BA-SAPMO, DY 30/IV2/11/202, 350–51; Bericht über die Zonentagung der Lagerleiter und Politbetreuer am 22. und 23. Januar 1948 in Pirna, BLHA, Rep. 332/578, 189; on the purges, see below, chapter 6.

55. SED-ZK Organisationsabteilung to LV der SED in den Ländern, 5 July 1949, BA-SAPMO, DY 30/IV2/11/196, 277–78; Bericht über die Verwendung von Kriegsgefangenen, die in der Sowjetunion waren, Dresden, 17 November 1949, BA-SAPMO, NY 4182/1134, 230–32. This waiting period had been introduced in January 1949 to ensure more effective political control of party members; see Kaiser, "Die Zentrale der Diktatur," 69.

56. Kaderabteilung Dresden, Versammlung mit Heimkehrern (Zentralschülern), 24 February 1950, BA-SAPMO, DY 30/IV2/11/204, 54–55.

57. Auszüge aus dem Referat des Gen. F. Sch., "Über die Kaderarbeit der Partei," BA-SAPMO, DY 30/IV2/11/202, 350–51.

58. Bericht über den Einsatz der Antifa-Schüler der Antifa-Schule 2040 und 2041 vom Juli des Jahres, 15 September 1949, BLHA, Rep. 332/759.

59. At a party meeting in 1950, one antifascist returnee conceded a "black spot" in his biography as a musician in the SA in 1934; another one admitted that he had been a Nazi Party member since 1937. See SED Kreisvorstand, Kaderabteilung Dresden, Versammlung mit Heimkehrern (Zentralschülern), 24 February 1950, BA-SAPMO, DY 30/IV2/11/204, 39, 51.

60. Kurt Nettball, Berichte von Kreiskonferenzen im Bereich das LV-Sachsen-Anhalt mit dem Thema "Partei und Heimkehrer," 24 August 1948, BA-SAPMO, DY 30/IV2/11/204, 22–24.

61. ZVU to Vizepräsident Tschesno im Hause, Material für die Besprechung in Karlshorst (120,000 Heimkehrer), 10 July 1946, BA-Berlin, DO2/76; on the ZVU in general, see Schwartz, "Apparate und Kurswechsel"; Ther, "Vertriebenenpolitik in der SBZ/DDR und in Polen."

62. Bericht Zentralbüro Ost an der Jahreswende 1949/50, ADW, ZBB, 47B. Heimkehrerbetreuung im Hauptbahnhof Leipzig, Bericht des HiW der EVKD, Bezirk Leipzig, 15 March 1949, ADW, ZBB/77, Wölky, betr.: Heimkehrerlager Gronenfelde, Besichtigung am 3./4.7.1947, ADCV, 372.2.056, 1946–51; and Kösters, *Caritas in der SBZ/GDR.*

63. EHiW Pommern, Greifswald to EHiW, Zentralbüro Ost, 27 June 1947, ADW, ZBB/105; see also Bericht des Bevollmächtigten des EHiW Sachen to Zentralbüro Ost, EKD, 14 September 1946, ADW, ZBB/77.

64. On the women's committees, see Naimark, *The Russians in Germany,* 131–32. The committees were dominated by SED members but also included a significant number of politically unaffiliated women. See "Tätigkeitsbericht im Monat Dezember [1946]" and "Im Kreis Niederbarnim bestehende Frauenausschüsse," BLHA, Rep. 332/953, 30, 142.

65. On the activities of the women's committees in general, see BLHA, Rep. 332/953 and Rep. 332/954.

66. Paul Merker to Vorsitzende der Landesverbände der SED, 6 April 1948, BA-SAPMO, DY 30/IV2/17/23, 162.

67. Arbeitsplan der Landesleiter und der Verteter der Organisationen im Heimkehrerlager Gronenfelde, BA-Berlin, DQ2/130, 3–6.

68. Bericht über meine Tätigkeit als politischer Betreuer der Heimkehrer in Gronenfelde, 26 June 1946, BA-Berlin, DO2/77, 60.

69. Rudolf Müller to ZS der SED, "Kleinarbeit," 24 August 1948, BA-SAPMO, DY 30/IV2/2/211, 620–32.

70. Rudolf Müller, "Ihnen muss geholfen werden," BA-SAPMO, DY 30/IV2/11/211, 315–17; Willi Käferstein to Landesleitung der SED Potsdam, 30 March 1948, BLHA, Rep. 332/578, 126.

71. Carl Friedrich, betr. Heimkehrerlager Gronenfelde, BA-Berlin, DO 2/77, 66–67.

72. Willy Käferstein to Landesleitung der SED Potsdam, 30 March 1948, BLHA, Rep. 332/578, 126.

73. Paul Merker to Vorsitzende der Landesverbände der SED, 6 April 1948, BA-SAPMO, DY 30/IV2/17/23, 162–68.

74. On the institutional and ideological dynamics of SED policies toward expellees, see Schwartz, "Zwischen Zusammenbruch und Stabilisierung" and "Apparate und Kurswechsel"; Wille, "Die Vertriebenen und das politische System der SBZ/DDR" and "SED und 'Umsiedler'"; Ther, "Vertriebenenpolitik in der SBZ/DDR und in Polen" and *Deutsche und polnische Vertriebene*.

75. On the shifting functions of the ZVU, see Schwartz, "Zwischen Zusammenbruch und Stabilisierung."

76. Bericht über Beratung in der Kriegsgefangenenfrage am 26. März 1948, BA-SAPMO, DY 30/IV2/11/196, 173–75; Schwartz, "Apparate und Kurswechsel," 115.

77. Protokoll über gemeinsame Besprechung zwecks Schaffung einer ständigen Arbeitskomission für Heimkehrerfragen des SED-LV Berlin, 12 April 1948, LAB, SED-LV, IV L-2/11/413; Bericht über die konstitutierende Sitzung des Heimkehrer-Komitees im Kreis Friedrichshain, 30 April 1948, LAB, SED-LV, IV L-2/11/413.

78. Schwartz, "Apparate und Kurswechsel," 118.

79. Peter Peterson, "Vorschlag zur Schaffung einer überparteilichen Massenorganisation ehemaliger Kriegsgefangener in Deutschland zur Vorbereitung des Kampfes gegen den Krieg," 25 November 1948, BA-SAPMO, DY 30/IV2/2.027/35, 242–43.

80. Paul Merker to Genosse Peterson, 9 December 1948, BA-SAPMO, DY 30/IV/2.027/35, 245.

81. Meuschel, *Legitimation und Parteiherrschaft in der DDR*, 10–15. It is important to distinguish between the SED's aspirations and actual societal processes; see Jessen, "Die Gesellschaft im Staatssozialismus."

82. On the NDPD in general, see Haas, "Die National Demokratische Partei Deutschlands"; Staritz, "National-Demokratische Partei Deutschlands"; Bauer, "Krise und Wandel der Blockpolitik"; Grundsätze und Forderungen der Nationaldemokratischen Partei, BA-SAPMO, NY 4090/511, 1–2; Grundsätze und Forderungen der Nationaldemokratischen Partei, Zonenausschuss der NDDP, 19 June 1948, BA-SAPMO, NY 4090/511, 1–6. Quotation in SED Landesvorstand Sachsen-Abteilung Information, Bericht über die NDPD Versammlung im Hotel Demnitz zu dem Thema "Was wollen die Nationaldemokraten"? 26 July 1948, BA-SAPMO, NY 4090/511, 7–9.

83. Herr Lonscher, Schule für nationale Politik, 19 June 1949, BA-SAPMO, DY 16/2568; Notiz für Herrn Vogt, Beteiligung der Blockparteien des antifaschistischen Blocks an der kulturellen und politischen Betreuung in den Lagern der Ostzone, BA-Berlin, DO 1/10/48, 19.

84. Bericht über Aufbau und Entwicklung in der NDPD, 2 February 1950, BA-SAPMO, NY 4182/1134, 132–45.

85. Protokoll über Erfahrungstausch mit Heimkehrern aus der Sowjetunion, 17 February 1950, BA-SAPMO, DY 30/IV2/11/204, 69–73.

86. Fulbrook, *Anatomy of a Dictatorship*, 22.

87. Quotations from Heimkehrerlager Gronenfelde to FDGB, Berlin, 22 July 1947, BLHA, Rep. 332/578, 99, Bericht über meine Tätigkeit als politischer Betreuer der Heimkehrer in Gronenfelde, 7–21 June 1948 BA-Berlin, DQ2/130, 2.; Ciesla, "Auf Schienenwegen nach Hause," 64.

88. Janke, Lagerleiter Gronenfelde and Dr. Görn, Chefarzt Gronenfelde, Bericht über die Konferenz der Lagerleiter und der kulturellen Betreuer der Heimkehrerlager in der Zone bei der Zentralverwaltung Umsiedler (ZVU), 24/25 February 1948, BA-Berlin, DQ 2/3788, 95–105; Bericht über die Zonentagung der Lagerleiter und Politbetreuer in Pirna, 22–23 January 1948, BLHA, Rep. 332/ 578, 186–92. Soviet occupation forces had indeed often recruited former Nazis for service as railwaymen, while medical personnel had generally received very lenient treatment in denazification procedures; see Ciesla, "Auf Schienenwegen nach Hause," 62–63; Vogt, *Denazification in Soviet Occupied Germany*, 158–60.

89. Bericht über die Kontrolle des Heimkehrerlagers Gronenfelde bei Frankfurt/Oder, 9 June 1949, BStU, MfS, AS., 440/67, 7–21, quotation on 10.

90. H. Nuding to Genossen Grotewohl und Pieck, n.d., BA-SAPMO, DY 30/ IV2/2.027/35, 99–101, Information über die Betreuung der Heimkehrer im Westen, BA-SAPMO, DY 30/IV2/11/211, 448–50.

91. Rudolf Müller, "Ihnen muß geholfen werden," BA-SAPMO, DY30/IV2/ 11/211, 315–17.

92. Referat des Genossen Belke, Bericht Landeskonferenz über "Fragen der Heimkehrerbetreuung," 7 June 1948, BLHA, Rep. 332/542, 90–111, quotation on 103.

93. Protokoll der persönlichen Besprechungen einiger Genossen der Volkssolidarität bei Genossen Landessekretär Kleinert, Dresden, 11 November 1948 and 17 November 1948; AdVS, Berlin, VS/I/A1; on the People's Solidarity in general, see Springer, *Da konnt' ich mich dann so'n bisschen entfalten*.

94. Jahresbericht über Heimkehrerbetreuung, 10 March 1949, ADW, ZBB 206; Heimkehrerbetreuung im Hauptbahnhof Leipzig, 15 March 1949, ADW, ZBB 77; SED Landesvorstand, Abteilung Arbeit- und Sozialfürsorge to Kreisleitung Cottbus der SED, 8 October 1948, BLHA, Rep. 332/576, 288.

95. Aktenvermerk Tillich, 31 July 1947, EZA, 4/359. Foreign donations, however, were outlawed in 1950; the church train missions existed until 1953. See Springer, *Da konnt' ich mich dann so'n bisschen entfalten*, 164–65, 171.

96. On church-state relations during the early GDR, see Fulbrook, *Anatomy of a Dictatorship*, 87–106; and Besier, *Der SED-Staat und die Kirche*; on the role of church welfare organizations, see Kösters, *Caritas in der SBZ/DDR*.

97. On the larger context of Communist policies toward women, see Harsch, "Approach/Avoidance."

98. Naimark, *The Russians in Germany*, 132.

99. SED-ZK to alle Frauensekretariate, betr.: Rückkehr der Kriegsgefangenen, BA-SAPMO, DY 30/IV2/17/23.

100. Maria Rentmeister, "Bei unseren Kriegsgefangenen in der SU," *Frau von Heute* 3/20 (1948): 10–11.

101. Was hat der DFD in der Frage der Kriegsgefangenenbetreuung getan? 16 June 1949, BLHA, Rep. 332/576, 346–47.

102. Die Stellung der Frau zum Heimkehrer, BA-SAPMO, DY 30/IV2/11/211, 596; see also "Deutschland grüsste Euch," *Frau von Heute* 4/10 (1949): 12–13.

103. See Weitz, *Creating German Communism*, 227.

104. Bessel and Jessen, "Einleitung. Die Grenzen der Diktatur."

105. In oral history interviews with East German returnees after 1989, the collapse of the East German state clearly fostered more negative responses by returnees. One theme in the interview with "Bernd W.," for example, is the notion of having been "betrayed twice"—in 1949 and in 1990; Interview with "Bernd W.," 18 November 1996, OH 4; on oral history with East German interviewees before the collapse of the GDR, see Niethammer, von Plato, and Wierling, *Die volkseigene Erfahrung*, 9–73.

106. Bericht über den Verlauf der Ansprache im "Bali" am 14.8.1946; Bericht über das Auftreten der Genossen in Kinos zur Verkündigung der neuen Verfassung Berlins, LAB, SED-LV IV/L-2/9.01/323.

107. Interview with "Bernd W.," 18 November 1996, OH 4; see also the interview with "Herr Apel" in Niethammer, von Plato, and Wierling, *Die volkseigene Erfahrung*, 315.

108. See the example in Wierling, *Geboren im Jahr Eins*, 51. This was also true for any extensive preoccupation with the war itself. When I entered the apartment of one of my interviewees in Berlin, a former member of the SED, his entire living room was packed with books about the military history of the Second World War.

109. SED Landesvorstand Sachsen, Abt. Massenagitation (Information) to Parteivorstand, 7 February 1950, SHStA, SED, LV A 306, 192–94.

110. Kurt V., Bericht über die Veranstaltung des Heimkehrerausschusses Prenzlauer Berg, 25 April 1950, LAB, SED-LV L-2/11/502.

111. Interview with "Werner J.," 20 January 1997, OH 6.

112. Interview with "Hans M.," 8 November 1996, OH 3.

113. Heidemeyer, "Vertriebene als Sowjetzonenflüchtlinge."

114. Smith, *War for the German Mind*, 66. "Hermann B.," who attended an antifascist course in his camp in the Soviet Union, recounts that he simply wanted to remain intellectually active and did not want to withdraw into indifference; interview with "Hermann B.," 28 January 1997, OH 7. West German commentators, too, were willing to grant individuals the "right to political error"; see Kogon, "Das Recht auf den politischen Irrtum."

115. Braese, "Unmittelbar zum Krieg."

116. Fühmann, *Der Sturz des Engels*, 55–57, 63–67.

117. See, for example, Kehler, *Einblicke und Einsichten*.

118. Niethammer, "Erfahrungen und Strukturen," 105; von Plato, "The Hitler Youth Generation," Wierling, "The Hitler Youth Generation"; Stadtland, "Vergangenheitspolitik im Widerstreit."

119. Werner K., " 'Kampf', der SED Kreis Erfurt gewidmet," 26 December 1948, BA-Berlin, DO 2/77, 183–85.

120. On the general European context, see Gross, "Themes for a Social History"; Mazower, *Dark Continent*, 250–85.

121. On East German rearmament in general, see Thoß, *Volksarmee schaffen*; Bald, Brühl, and Prüfert, *Nationale Volksarmee*. On the origins of the Volkspolizei, see Bessel, "Grenzen des Polizeisstaates" and "Polizei zwischen Krieg und Sozialismus"; and Lindenberger, *Volkspolizei*, 38–49.

122. Quoted in Wenzke, "Auf dem Weg zur Kaderarmee," 205–72.

123. Morré, "Kader für Deutschland?" 229–30; Diedrich, "Das Jahr der Rückkehr."

124. Zusammenfassender Bericht über die Heimkehrer aus der SU, die für den Einsatz in die DVdI bestimmt sind, BA-SAPMO, DY 30/IV2/11/211, 327–28.

125. See the reports on returning POWs' attitudes in BA-Berlin, DO 1/7/227, 207–11.

126. Zusammenfassender Bericht über die Heimkehrer aus der SU, die für den Einsatz in die DVdI bestimmt sind, BA-SAPMO, DY 30/IV2/11/211, 327–28.

127. SED officials considered only 50 percent of returnees as qualified, but the SMAD insisted on recruiting all returning POWs; Landesregierung Sachsen, Ministerium des Inneren to Deutsche Verwaltung des Inneren, 22 September 1948, BA-Berlin, DO1/7/243, 76–78.

128. Zusammenfassender Bericht über die Heimkehrer aus der SU, die für den Einsatz in die DVdI bestimmt sind, BA-SAPMO, DY 30/IV2/11/211, 327–28; Wenzke, "Auf dem Weg zur Kaderarmee," 214, 219.

129. In 1949, recruitment of returnees was extended to the Gronenfelde camp; Werbung für die Volkspolizei in Gronenfelde, October and November 1949, BA-Berlin DO 2/77, 294–97.

130. Quoted in Wenzke, "Auf dem Weg zur Kaderarmee," 215.

131. See the characteristics of Paul T., Alfred B., Horst B., Gerhard B., Heinz G., BA-Berlin, DO 1/7/228, 192, 196, 197, 208, 290.

132. Figures according to Lindenberger, *Volkspolizei*, 226.

133. Wenzke, "Wehrmachtsoffiziere in DDR Streitkräften"; Diedrich and Wenzke, *Die getarnte Armee*, 190–211.

134. Zank, *Wirtschaft und Arbeit in Ostdeutschland*, 43–44; Erich Lange, "Alter und Beruf der Heimkehrer," *Arbeit und Sozialfürsorge* 9 (1949): 194–95.

135. Photo report "Frankfurt bis Bergmann Borsig," LAB Rep. 061, Nr. 3.

136. See Albert Voss, "Erfassung und Arbeitslenkung der arbeitsfähigen Bevölkerung," in *Arbeit und Sozialfürsorge,* Jahrbuch 1945–47, 29–45.

137. These priorities were determined by Soviet authorities; see Hoffmann, *Aufbau und Krise der Planwirtschaft*, 117.

138. Statistiken über Zwangseinweisungen, BA-Berlin, DQ 2/1936; Hoffmann, *Aufbau und Krise der Planwirtschaft*, 118–21; Willi Donau, "Probleme der Arbeitslenkung" *Die Arbeit* 3 (1949): 112–15.

139. Bericht über die am 5.8.1947 durchgeführte Dienstreise nach Frankfurt/Oder, BA-DY 30/IV2/2.027/25, 26–27; Hoffmann, *Aufbau und Krise der Planwirtschaft*, 126–53. Among the 5,555 "homeless returnees" sent to the uranium mines in Aue in the last quarter of 1947, only 1,108 could actually be employed; Landesregierung Sachsen, Ministerium für Arbeit und Sozialfürsorge, Abt. Arbeit to Deutsche Wirtschaftskommission, Hauptabteilung Arbeit und Sozialfürsorge, 21 April 1948, BA-Berlin, DQ 2/3393, 98.

140. Hoffmann, *Aufbau und Krise der Planwirtschaft*, 201.

141. Bericht des Herrn Willi Donau in der Sitzung des Unterausschusses Arbeitseinsatz und Arbeitskräftelenkung, 8 April 1949, BA-SAPMO, DY 34/21185.

142. In 1948, East German officials estimated that 600,000 skilled workers would still be returning from captivity, 280,000 of them to the Soviet zone of occupation; Hauptabteilung Umsiedler to Deutsche Wirtschaftskommission, 5 August 1948, BA-Berlin, DO 2/77, 74–75.

143. On the need to train women for skilled jobs, von Koschnegg to Herr Donau, 25 November 1949, BA-Berlin, DQ 2/2072; quotation from Ministerium für Arbeit- und Sozialfürsorge to Frauensachbearbeiterinnen der Arbeitsämter des Landes Brandenburg, 21 February 1949, BLHA Rep. 332/563, 180.

144. SED-LV Brandenburg to Redaktion "Freie Gewerkschaft," 16 January 1947, BLHA, Rep. 332/576, 8.

145. This period witnessed a sharp increase in female unemployment from 47,000 (1948) to 230,000 (March 1949); Hoffmann, *Aufbau und Krise der Planwirtschaft*, 112. This was partly a result of more restrictive granting of social welfare benefits; see Boldorf, *Sozialfürsorge in der SBZ/DDR*, 53–54.

146. Hauptabteilung Umsiedler to Deutsche Wirtschaftskommission, 5 August 1948, BA-Berlin, DO 2/77, 74–75.

147. See the advertising poster for coal mining reproduced in *Arbeit und Sozialfürsorge*; Jahrbuch 1945–47, 59.

148. Solga, *Auf dem Weg in eine klassenlose Gesellschaft?* 95.

149. Esser, Chefarzt/Willy Kalinke, Minsterialrat an alle Ärzte, Apotheker, Medizinstudenten, Ingenieure, Techniker und Geisteschaffende, die aus der Kriegsgefangenschaft zurückkehren, May 1948, BA-SAPMO, DY 30/IV2/11/211, 123.

150. Interview with "Thomas G.," 4 November 1996, OH 2.

151. See interview with "Ehepaar Apel," IfGB; Niethammer, von Plato, and Wierling, *Die volkseigene Erfahrung*, 302–28.

152. Weitz, *Creating German Communism*, 364, emphasizes this aspect of SED rule; Stadtland, "Vergangenheitspolitik im Widerstreit," 111.

153. Naimark, *The Russians in Germany*, 198–204; Stadtland, *Herrschaft nach Plan*, 469–79.

154. Losungen für evtl. Verwendung für Veranstaltungen, SED-LV, Abt. Arbeit und Sozialfürsorge, Rundschreiben, 1 May 1950, LAB, SED-LV, IV L-2/11/502.

155. All examples are drawn from An alle Landesvorstände, Kaderabteilung, Anlage: Mecklenburg: Gründe der 18 Heimkehrer für ihre Beschwerden, BA-SAPMO, DY 30/IV2/11/204, 81–83.

156. Interview with "Bernd W.," 18 November 1996, OH 4.

157. See Peukert, *Volksgenossen und Gemeinschaftsfremde*, 247.

158. Heimkehrer Heinz Pohl, "Der erste Eindruck in der Heimat!" BLHA, Rep. 332/578, 233.

159. Interview with "Hans M.," 7 December 1996, OH 3/2.

160. Lindenberger, "Everyday History," quoted in Moeller, "Elephant in Living Room."

161. Rat des Kreises Cottbus to Landesregierung Brandenburg, betr. Argumente der Kollegen gegen die Arbeitsaufnahme in der Grundstoffindustrie, BLHA, Landkreis Cottbus, Rep. 250/1275.

162. On the presence of the war in East German families, see Wierling, *Geboren im Jahr Eins*, 24–59.

163. The notion of a "niche society" derives from Gaus, *Wo Deutschland liegt*; see also Moeller, "Elephant in Living Room."

164. Wierling, *Geboren im Jahr Eins*, 76–90.

165. See the examples cited in ibid., 85.

166. Bruns, *Als Vater aus dem Krieg heimkehrte*, 76; and the examples in Wierling, *Geboren im Jahr Eins*, 85–86.

167. For such examples of generational conflict in East Germany, see von Plato and Meinicke, *Alte Heimat-Neue Zeit*, 153–60, 204–8; see also Wierling, *Geboren im Jahr Eins*, 171–334. East German literature represents a promising source for reconstructing these generational tensions, which I was not able to incorporate in this study.

CHAPTER 6
PARALLEL EXCLUSIONS

1. See Deák, Gross, and Judt, *The Politics of Retribution*; Henke et al, *Politische Säuberung in Europa*.

2. Zusammenstellung der im Bundesjustizministerium bekannten Fälle rechtskräftiger Verurteilungen von Heimkehrern wegen Kameradenmißhandlungen, BA-K, B 150/7123b. The actual number of such legal investigations, however, must have been considerably higher since the majority of these cases were dismissed due to lack of conclusive evidence or the defendants were acquitted of the charges. This section is based on forty cases primarily from the North Rhine-Westphalian Archive in Düsseldorf-Kalkum.

3. Case of Otto S., Staatsanwaltschaft Wuppertal, NRWHStA, Rep. 92/60; Verfahren gegen Rudolf T., Staatsanwaltschaft Köln, NRWHStA Rep. 231/401. This withdrawal of citizenship rights was a common sanction for collaborators in European countries; see Rousso, "L'Epuration."

4. Rückerl, *Investigation of Nazi Crimes*, 121; Steinbach, *Nationalsozialistische Gewaltverbrechen*, 21–30. For the occupation period, see Broszat, " 'Siegerjustiz' oder strafrechtliche 'Selbstreinigung.' "

5. "Schmitz fand seine Richter," *Der Sozialdemokrat*, 16 July 1949, ASD, O44, 1949. For a more equivocal analysis of this case, see "In der Heimat, in der Heimat," *Spiegel* 3/29 (1949), 5–6.

6. Case of Otto S., Staatsanwaltschaft Wuppertal, NRWHStA, Rep. 92/60.

7. "Schmitz fand seine Richter."

8. "Der 'Politruk von Jelabuga' vor Gericht," *Der Stern* 3/48 (1950): 5–7; see also "Kameradenschinder vor Gericht," *Abendpost*, 18 December 1951; cited in Zentner, *Aufstieg aus dem Nichts*, 83.

9. Quotation from trial of Willy K., Verdict, 19 April 1951, Staatsanwaltschaft Köln, 24 Kls 8/51, NRWHStA, Rep. 231/393, 519; for charges of "crimes against humanity," see Strafanzeige gegen den Heimkehrer Gustav T. wegen Verbrechen gegen die Menschlichkeit, 12 October 1949, Staatsanwaltschaft Krefeld, NRWHStA Rep. 8/211, 1–2; Amtsgericht Gelsenkirchen to Oberstaatsanwalt in Köln, 8 November 1949, Strafsache gegen K. wegen Verbrechens gegen die Menschlichkeit, Staatsanwaltschaft Köln, NRWHStA, Rep. 231/333, 4; for verdicts, see the case of Franz G., Verdict, 21 September 1953, Staatsanwaltschaft Kleve, NRWHStA, Rep. 224/39, 41 and case of Hermann O., Verdict, 1 June 1950, Staatsanwaltschaft Kleve, NRWHStA, Rep. 107/52, 111. In the North Rhine-Westphalien archives, the POW cases are stored together with Nazi trials under the common category of "crimes against humanity."

10. Boberach, "Die Verfolgung von Verbrechen gegen die Menschlichkeit."

11. Case of Otto E., Staatsanwaltschaft Köln, NRWHStA, Rep. 231/813, 113; see also "In der Heimat, in der Heimat," *Der Spiegel* 3/29 (1949): 5–6.

12. Trial of Hans K., Verdict, Staatsanwaltschaft Mönchengladbach, NRWHStA, Rep. 72/23, 93.

13. On the larger commemorative context, see Moeller, *War Stories*, 38.

14. Lagerleiter Friedland to Herrn Regierungspräsidenten, Flüchtlingsdezernent, 12 October 1949, NHStA, Nds. 386, Acc. 16/83, Nr. 105. Interestingly, East German officials also tried to collect material against returnees who had committed criminal offenses in Soviet captivity in order to be able to distinguish real offenders from antifascist activists. These efforts, however, were prohibited by Soviet authorities; Nettball to Merker, 29 April 1949, BA-SAPMO, DY 30/IV2/2.027/35/260–61.

15. Vermerk, 26 October 1948, Staatsanwaltschaft Eberfelde, NRWHStA, Rep. 92/60, 1–2.

16. Many returnees did initially not intend to press charges, but then changed their mind upon arrival in their home community; see Lagerleiter Friedland to Herrn Regierungspräsidenten, Flüchtlingsdezernent, 12 October 1949, NHStA, Nds. 386, Acc. 16/83, Nr. 105.

17. Max Viett to Staatsanwaltschaft Aachen, 18 January 1950, NRWHStA, Rep. 89/71; Beauftragte der Arbeitsgemeinschaft der Heimkehrer-Verbände to Herrn Oberstaatsanwalt in Bonn, 13 November 1949, Staatsanwaltschaft Köln, NRWHStA, Rep. 231/361, 1; Centralverband der Russland Heimkehrer to Oberstaatsanwalt Köln, 14 October 1949, NRWHStA, Rep. 231/333,1.

18. "Fernsehbild der Jungfrau brachte Stein ins Rollen," *NRZ*, Nr. 35, 9 February 1961, NRWHStA, Rep. 231/1409, 31.

19. Strafanzeige Heinrich R., 11 January 1950, Staatsanwaltschaft Köln, NRWHStA, Rep. 231/366.

20. Strafanzeige Karl S., 18 February 1950, Staatsanwaltschaft Köln, NRWHStA, Rep. 231/363, 2–3; Strafanzeige Bernhard E., 11 November 1949,

Staatsanwaltschaft Wuppertal, NRWHStA, Rep. 240/166, 1; Strafanzeige Gustav K., 12 October 1949, Staatsanwaltschaft Krefeld, NRWHStA, Rep. 8/211, 1–2.

21. Wilhelm B. to Staatsanwaltschaft Kleve, 5 September 1950, NRWHStA, Rep. 224/39, 129; see also Statement by Herbert S., 14 November 1953, Staatsanwaltschaft Bonn, NRHWHStA, Rep. 104/82, 5–6.

22. Statement Josef M., 18 January 1950 and Interrogation Josef M., 20 February 1950, Staatsanwaltschaft Köln, NRWHStA, Rep. 231/399, 1.

23. Statement of Helmut P., 27 April 1950, Staatsanwaltschaft Kleve, NRWHStA, Rep. 238/67, 13–16; Statement of Franz K., 29 January 1957, Staatsanwaltschaft Köln, NRWHStA, Rep. 231/1006, 55–58.

24. Statement Karl S., 6 May 1950, Staatsanwaltschaft Köln, NRWHStA, Rep. 231/363, 23.

25. Verdict Adolf G., 4 August 1950, Staatsanwaltschaft Wuppertal, NRWHStA, Rep. 240/167, 259.

26. Anklageschrift Franz K., 30 April 1957, Staatsanwaltschaft Köln, NRWHStA, Rep. 231/10006, 69.

27. Statement Heinrich S., 10 August 1954, Staatsanwaltschaft Frankfurt, HHStA, Abt. 461, Nr. 33147, 67.

28. See Hinrichsen, "Befehlsnotstand."

29. Steinbach, *Nationalsozialistische Gewaltverbrechen*, 71–72.

30. Steinbach, "NS-Prozesse nach 1945," 20.

31. Müller, *Hitler's Justice*, 201–98; Wrobel, *Verurteilt zur Demokratie*, 139–51; Heilbronn, "Der Aufbau der nordrhein-westfälischen Justiz"; Niermann, "Zwischen Amnestie und Anpassung."

32. Case of Willi K., Verdict, NRWHStA, Staatsanwaltschaft Köln, Rep. 231/393, 516–17.

33. Diestelkamp and Jung, "Die Justiz in den Westzonen."

34. Case of Franz G., Staatsanwaltschaft Kleve, Verdict, 21 September 1953, NRWHStA, Rep. 224/41, 55–57.

35. See "Brief an den Lieben Kameraden Franz," ibid, 139.

36. Verfügung 24 June 1950, Staatsanwaltschaft Köln, NRWHStA, Rep. 231/364, 89.

37. Statement Erwin F., 17 February 1950, Staatsanwaltschaft Köln, NRWHStA, Rep. 231/364, 56–57; Verfügung, 24 June 1950, NRWHStA, Rep. 231/364, 89.

38. Case of Hans-Josef K., Verdict, Staatsanwaltschaft Mönchengladbach, NRWHStA, Rep. 73/23, 84–94. Interestingly, the court did not take into consideration the defendant's prior history, which included conviction by a military court, internment in a concentration camp, and service in an SS penal battalion.

39. See case of Willi K., Verdict, Staatsanwaltschaft Köln, NRWHStA Rep. 231/395.

40. BGH Verdict, 12 July 1951, in Lindenmaier-Möhring, 1950–1985, §54, No. 1.

41. See *Der Heimkehrer* 1/6–7 (June-July 1950): 8 and *Der Heimkehrer* 2/3 (March 1951): 5.

42. Oberstaatsanwalt Kaiserslautern to VdH, 27 July 1957; Staatsanwaltschaft Stuttgart to VdH, 7 October 1954; Untersuchungsrichter beim Land-

gericht Regensburg to VdH München, 4 November 1954; Nr. 37 15/51–33, Kameradenmißhandlungen, VdH Archive.

43. See, for example, Werner Kiessling to Oberstaatsanwalt Verden/Aller, 7 March 1955, Nr. 37, 15/51–33, Kameradenmißhandlungen, VdH Archive.

44. On this campaign, see Frei, *Vergangenheitspolitik*, 133–306.

45. On NS trials, see Hinrichsen, "Befehlsnotstand" and Steinbach, *Nationalsozialistische Gewaltverbrechen*, 41.

46. Case of Adolf G., Verdict, Staatsanwaltschaft Wuppertal, NRWHStA, Rep. 240/167, 252; case of Otto S., Staatsanwaltschaft Wuppertal, NRWHStA, Rep. 92/60.

47. Steinbach, "NS-Prozesse nach 1945," 15.

48. Case of Otto S., Vorstand der Strafanstalt to Herrn Oberstaatsanwalt in Wuppertal, 10 June 1955, Staatsanwaltschaft Wuppertal, NRWHStA, Rep. 92/60.

49. Der Hessische Minister des Inneren, Schneider, to Hessische Ministerpräsidenten Dr. August Georg Zinn, 22 June 1956, HHStA, Abt. 502/1003; on POWs and "war criminals," see below, chapter 7.

50. Broszat, " 'Siegerjustiz' oder strafrechtliche 'Selbstreinigung.' "

51. Lindenmeier-Möhring, Nachschlagwerk des Bundesgerichtshofs, 1950–1985, Band 57, Nr. 2, § 3 StGB.

52. Broszat, " 'Siegerjustiz' oder strafrechtliche 'Selbstreinigung,' " and Luther, "Denunization als soziales und strafrechtliches Problem."

53. On denunciations and comradeship, see Kühne, "Zwischen Männerbund und Volksgemeinschaft" and "Kameradschaft." On denunciations during the Third Reich in general, see Gellately, *The Gestapo and German Society*, 130–58; on military justice, see Haase, "Wehrmachtsangehörige vor dem Kriegsgericht."

54. In my view, this is also how the evidence needs to be read in Heer, *Stets zu erschießen sind die Frauen*; quotation from Hilger, *Deutsche Kriegsgefangene in der Sowjetunion*, 300.

55. Case of Franz K., Verdict, Staatsanwaltschaft Köln, NRWHStA, Rep. 231/1006, 94–98.

56. Case of Heinrich S., Vernehmungsprotokoll, 10 August 1954, Staatsanwaltschaft Frankfurt, HHStA, Abt. 461/Nr. 33147.

57. Case of Heinrich S., Verdict Bundesgerichtshof, 29 January 1960, Staatsanwaltschaft Frankfurt, HHStA, Abt. 461/Nr. 33147.

58. In other cases, the verdict described witnesses for the defendant as "rather simple-minded people," whereas it praised witnesses for the prosecution as men who "due to their education and their responsible professions" were "of particular maturity, experience and of an independent way of thinking." Case of Rudolf T., Verdict, NRWHStA, Staatsanwaltschaft Frankfurt, Rep. 231/401, 407; on the West German judiciary's reluctance to prosecute Nazi jurists, see Müller, *Hitler's Justice*, 274–83.

59. See the BGH decision cited in *Neue Juristische Wochenschrift* 11/23 (1958): 874.

60. Case of Theodor B.,Verfügung, Staatsanwaltschaft Köln, NRWHStA, Rep.231/814, 48, 52.

61. Case of Rudolf S., Staatsanwaltschaft Köln, NRWHStA, Rep. 231/361.

62. This is the tendency in Wagenlehner, *Stalins Willkürjustiz gegen die deutsche Kriegsgefangenen*; on the Soviet trials of German POWs, see also below, chapters 7 and 8.

63. West German courts did have, in principle, jurisdiction for such offenses. However, not one single Wehrmacht officer seems to have been convicted for war crimes in the Federal Republic during the 1950s and 1960s, despite a considerable number of legal investigations in the 1960s; see Wette, *Die Wehrmacht*, 238.

64. Case of Theodor B.,Verfügung, Staatsanwaltschaft Köln, NRWHStA, Rep.231/814, 48.

65. Ibid., 49.

66. Hilger, *Deutsche Kriegsgefangene in der Sowjetunion*, 300.

67. Conway, "Justice in Postwar Belgium," 133.

68. Griebel, "Zu den Strafprozessen gegen Heimkehrer."

69. Günter J. to Polizeipräsidium Bonn, 7 May 1955, Staatsanwaltschaft Bonn, NRWHStA, Rep. 104/83, 316.

70. On West German anti-Communism, Major, *The Death of the KPD*; and Weitz, "The Ever-Present Other."

71. Stolleis, *Law under the Swastika*, 178; see also Wrobel, *Verurteilt zur Demokratie*, 225–31.

72. Cited in "In der Heimat, in der Heimat," *Spiegel* 3/29 (1949), 5–6.

73. Case of Otto S., Verdict, 8 July 1949, Staatsanwaltschaft Eberfelde, NRWHStA, Rep. 92/60, 252; case of Rudolf T., Verdict, Staatsanwaltschaft Bonn, NRWHStA, Rep. 231/399, 409.

74. Quotations from case of Hans-Josef K., Beschluss 27 June 1951, Staatsanwaltschaft Bonn, NRWHStA, Rep. 72/23, 118; case of Franz K., Verdict, Staatsanwaltschaft Köln, NRWHStA, Rep.231/1006, 98.

75. See case of Rudolf T., Verdict, Staatsanwaltschaft Köln, NRWHStA, Rep.231/401, 404, 408.

76. Case of Rudolf T., Anklageschrift, Staatsanwaltschaft Köln, NRWHStA, Rep.231/400, 233. He was ultimately cleared of these charges.

77. First two quotations, case of Rudolf T., Verdict, Staatsanwaltschaft Köln, NRWHStA, Rep. 231/401, 409; third quotation, case of Hans-Josef K., Verdict, Staatsanwaltschaft Mönchengladbach, NRWHStA, Rep. 72/23, 93.

78. Gorges, "Man muss leben," quotation on 602.

79. Ibid.

80. See Wurm, "Schuld und Niederlage der Antifa." There is some evidence that former Nazis were indeed more likely to collaborate with Soviet authorities, most likely because they faced greater risks of prosecution in captivity; see for example the case of the former National Socialist leadership officer (NSFO) Otto E., who later became an antifascist activist in Soviet captivity; case of Otto E., Staatsanwaltschaft Köln, NRWHStA, Rep. 231/813.

81. Bartov, "Defining Enemies, Making Victims" and *Mirrors of Destruction*.

82. See Weckel and Wolfrum, *Bestien und Befehlsempfänger*.

83. Knoch, *Die Bild als Tat*, 298–301.

84. For a similar argument, see Poiger, *Jazz, Rock, and Rebels*, 106–36.

85. Günter J. to Polizeipräsidium Bonn, 7 May 1955, Staatsanwaltschaft Bonn, NRWHStA, Rep. 104/83, 315–25.

86. Case of Günter J., Vermerk, 11 November 1955, Staatsanwaltschaft Bonn, NRWHStA, Rep. 104/83, 372–81.

87. Case of Rudolf T., Verdict, Staatsanwaltschaft Köln, NRWHStA, Rep. 231/40, 448.

88. On the meanings of comradeship, see Kühne, "Kameradschaft."

89. Case of Rudolf T., Verdict, Staatsanwaltschaft Köln, NRWHStA, Rep. 231/40, 404, 448.

90. On the myth of the clean Wehrmacht, see Wette, *Die Wehrmacht,*197–244.

91. On military service as extenuating circumstance, see Müller, *Hitler's Justice,* 233.

92. Case of Hans Dietrich T., Staatsanwaltschaft Wuppertal, NRWHStA Rep. 240/155–62.

93. Dr.med. Fritz Wawersik an Untersuchungsrichter beim Landgericht W-Elberfeld, 28 May 1955, Staatsanwaltschaft Wuppertal, NRWHStA, Rep. 240/158, 36; "Tallarek konnte nicht aus seiner Haut," *Westdeutsche Rundschau,* 4 December 1957, NRWHStA, Rep. 240/162.

94. On military reform, see Large, *Germans to the Front,* 176–204.

95. Kirchheimer, *Political Justice*; Werkentin, "Der politische und juristische Umgang mit Systemgegnern," 268; on political justice in the early Federal Republic, see Major, *The Death of the KPD,* 277–83; and Gössner, *Die vergessenen Justizopfer des Kalten Krieges*; on East Germany, see Werkentin, *Politische Strafjustiz in der Ära Ulbrich* and Wentker, *Justiz in der SBZ/DDR, 1945–1953;* for the larger European context, see Déak, Gross, and Judt, eds., *The Politics of Retribution.*

96. Von Trützscheler to Bundesministerium der Justiz, 5 March 1954, BA-K, B 150/7123; Bayrisches Staatsministerium to Bundesministerium der Justiz, 20 July 1954, BA-K, B 150/7123; Bundesministerium der Justiz to Bayrisches Staatsministerium der Justiz, Meldung über Schreiben des Auswärtigen Amtes vom 16.12.1954, 5 January 1955, BA-K, B 150/7123.

97. One returnee complained that "the police spreads rumors in his hometown that he had beaten comrades to death in Russian captivity"; Vermerk, 14 May 1955, Staatsanwaltschaft Köln, NRWHStA, Rep. 231/593.

98. See case of Gustav T., Staatsanwaltschaft Krefeld, NRWHStA, Rep. 8/211; case of Erwin F., 24 Js 87/50, Staatsanwaltschaft Köln, NRWHStA, Rep. 231/364; case of Otto E., Staatsanwaltschaft Köln, NRWHStA, Rep. 231/813.

99. Frei, *Vergangenheitspolitik,* 29–53.

100. Case of Franz G., Staatsanwaltschaft Kleve, NRWHStA, Rep. 224/41; case of Franz M., Staatsanwaltschaft Wuppertal, NRWHStA, Rep. 191/166. Courts applied this amnesty to accused returnees despite a Bundesgerichtshof decision from 1951 according to which the amnesty law should not be applied to criminal offenses among German POWs in Soviet captivity since these offenses could not be directly linked to the "political collapse" of Nazi Germany; see case of Willi K., BGH Verdict, 16 May 1952, Staatsanwaltschaft Köln, NRWHStA, Rep. 231/393, 746–47.

101. On the purges in Eastern Europe, see Foitzik, "Die stalinistischen Säuberungen"; Weber and Mählert, *Terror*; Mählert, "Schauprozesse und Parteisäuberungen," 38.

102. On the purges in East Germany, see Malycha, *Die SED*, 356–447; Klein, "Die Parteikontrolle in der SED"; Mählert, "Die Partei hat immer Recht"; and Epstein, *The Last Revolutionaries*, 130–57.

103. Malycha, *Die SED*, 372–35; Epstein, *The Last Revolutionaries*.

104. On the motivations, see Mählert, "Die Partei hat immer recht," 371; and Epstein, *The Last Revolutionaries*, 152–55.

105. Malycha, *Die SED*, 404, 446.

106. At first sight, the former capos of the Buchenwald concentration camp who, as a result of their function as camps officials, were sentenced by Soviet authorities in 1950 and deported to the Soviet Union might offer a more appropriate comparison for the West German POW trials. The prosecution of these "red capos" raised some of the same issues as the POW trials, such as the extent to which collaboration with captors was legally, morally, and politically appropriate. I have decided against pursuing this comparison because it runs the risk of endorsing the incorrect and apologetic equation of Soviet POW camps with Nazi concentration camps. In addition, my particular analytic focus here is on former soldiers and POWs and on the ways in which the experiences of war and captivity were incorporated into (or excluded from) the polities of both postwar Germanys. On Buchenwald and the "red capos," see Niethammer, *Der "gesäuberte" Antifaschismus* and Overesch, *Buchenwald und die DDR*.

107. See Herf, *Divided Memory*.

108. Personalpolitik Wöhl to Genosse Franz Dahlem, 13 July 1946, BA-SAPMO, DY 30/IV2/4/154, 47–48.

109. Kurt Ziegenhagen, "Der antifaschistische Kampf in der Kriegsgefangenschaft," 15 March 1946, BA-SAPMO, DY 30/IV2/4/154, 135–52. On antifascist activity in Western captivity, see also Steinbach, "Neuorientierung im Umbruch."

110. Erfahrungen und Ergebnisse der E[migranten] und K[riegsgefangenen] Überprüfungsarbeit, 8 March 1950, BA-SAPMO, DY 30/IV2/4/93, 7–23.

111. SED-ZPKK to LPKK beim LV Sachsen-Anhalt, 15 October 1949, BA-SAPMO, DY 30/IV2/4/156.

112. LPKK Brandenburg, Komission für die Regierung und Körperschaften, Gesamtbericht über die durchgeführten Arbeiten und Auswertungen, BA-SAPMO, DY 30/IV2/4/100, 2–11.

113. Ibid.

114. Erfahrungen und Ergebnisse der E[migranten] und K[riegsgefangenen] Überprüfungsarbeit, 8 March 1950, BA-SAPMO, DY 30/IV2/4/93, 7–23; Mählert, "Die Partei hat immer recht," 392–400. On the purges of left-wing dissidents, see Malycha, *Die SED*, 407–10; Klein, "Die Parteikontrolle in der SED," 140–53.

115. Gesamtergebnis der E-Kommission in der Regierung, den nachgeordneneren Dienstsellen und den Verwaltungen, BA-SAPMO, DY 30/IV2/4/94, 6–8.

116. LPKK Brandenburg, Komission für die Regierung und Körperschaften, Gesamtbericht über die durchgeführten Arbeiten und Auswertungen, BA-SAPMO, DY 30/IV2/4/100, 2–11.

117. On the *Heimkehrer* conferences in East Germany, see chapter 4; on the emergence of a Moscow-centered narrative of antifascism in East Germany, see Herf, *Divided Memory*.

118. Berichte der ZPKK über Heimkehrer aus England, BA-SAPMO, DY 30/IV2/4/94, 174.

119. *New Beginning* was the title of a newspaper published in East Berlin by a Communist opposition group. See Klein, "Die Parteikontrolle," 146–50; and Malycha, *Die SED*, 422–23.

120. Erfahrungen und Ergebnisse der E[migranten] und K[riegsgefangenen] Überprüfungsarbeit, 8 March 1950, BA-SAPMO, DY 30/IV2/4/93, 7–23.

121. On the history of Battalion 999, see Klausch, *Die Geschichte der Bewährungsbattallione 999*. The battalion did not include Jews, homosexuals, or alleged "asocials."

122. On the activities of political 999ers in American captivity, see Tulatz, "Exil hinter Stacheldraht."

123. This was the estimate of an East German official in 1946; see Karl Wloch, Memorandum über die 999er, 6 August 1946, LAB, Rep. 118/640.

124. Wöhl, Personalpolitische Abteilung to Dahlem, 2 August 1946, BA-SAPMO, DY 30/IV2/11/208; Wöhl, Personalpolitik to Dahlem, 22 May 1947, BA-SAPMO, DY 30/IV2/11/210, 47.

125. SED Landesvorstand Sachsen, Abteilung Werbung und Schulung, Problem der 999er, SHStA, LV Sachsen A 306, 4.

126. Rededisposition, "Die 999er und die politische Umerziehung der deutschen Kriegsgefangenen im Mittleren Osten-Ägypten," BA-SAPMO, DY 30/IV2/4/94, Karl Wloch, Memorandum über die 999er (vorläufiger Bericht), 6 August 1946, LAB, Rep. 118/640.

127. Party officials promoted a more comprehensive reporting on the 999ers. They organized public welcoming ceremonies in East Berlin for returning 999ers and commissioned a specific film on their experiences. I have not been able to locate this film; Bericht von einer Besprechung über die 999er; Karl Wloch, Memorandum über die 999er, 6 August 1946, LAB, Rep. 118/640; Bericht von einer Besprechung über die 999er am 28.12.1946, BA-SAPMO, DY 30/IV2/11/208, 105.

128. SED LV Sachsen to SED-ZK, 10 March 1947, BA-SAPMO, DY 30/IV2/11/209; SED Landesvorstand Sachsen to alle Kreisvorstände, Rundschreiben Nr. 5/62, 3 March 1947, SHStAD, SED-Kreisleitung Bautzen, IV/4.01.179.

129. Wöhl, Personalpolitik to Franz Dahlem, SED Hausmitteilung, 22 May 1947, BA-SAPMO, DY 30/IV2/11/210, 47; Unsichere 999er, BA-SAPMO, DY 30/IV2/4/154, 78; see also Tulatz, "Exil hinter Stacheldraht."

130. Kurt Nettball, Bericht über die 999er Tagung in Weimar, 10/11 April 1948, BA-SAPMO, DY 30/IV2/11/208.

131. Politisch-Kritisches zur Division 999, BA-SAPMO, DY 30/IV2/4/154, 257–71. All following quotations are from this document.

132. On these conflicts, see Tulatz, "Exil hinter Stacheldraht," 187.

133. For East German anti-Semitism, see Herf, *Divided Memory*, 159–60; Epstein, *The Last Revolutionaries*, 139–43.

134. This point is emphasized in Epstein, *The Last Revolutionaries*.

135. Fritz U., "Wie ich in das Schulungslager Wilton-Park kam und was dort gelehrt wurde," May 1951, BA-SAPMO, DY 30/IV2/4/95, 2–3.

136. LPKK Brandenburg, Komission für die Regierung und Körperschaften, Gesamtbericht über die durchgeführten Arbeiten und Auswertungen, BA-SAPMO, DY 30/IV2/4/100, 2–11.

137. See the cases reported in Statistik über Überprüfung in Ministerien, Einzelbewertungen, BA-SAPMO, DY 30/IV2/4/97, 9–15.

138. Fritz B., Dresden, to Kaderabteilung des Parteivorstandes der SED, 1 May 1950; Fritz B., Dresden, to ZPKK der SED, 19 November 1950, BA-SAPMO, DY 30/IV2/4/94, 49–54.

139. Maier, *Dissolution*, 20.

CHAPTER 7
ABSENT PRESENCE

1. Erklärung der Nachrichtenagentur TASS, *Neues Deutschland*, 6 May 1950, reprinted in Ihme-Tuchel, "Die Entlassung der deutschen Kriegsgefangenen."

2. On the Soviet trials of German POWs, see the contributions in Hilger, Schmidt, and Wagenlehner, *Sowjetische Militärtribunale*, vol. 1. For an argument that convicted German POWs were to serve as "bargaining chip" in negotiations over the "German question," see Borchard, *Die deutschen Kriegsgefangenen in der Sowjetunion.*

3. On the compromised past of some sentenced POWs, see below chapter 8.

4. Borchard, *Die deutschen Kriegsgefangenen in der Sowjetunion*, 107–8; VDBT, 1. WP, 62. Sitzung, 5 May 1950, 2282.

5. Die Kriegsgefangenen und Vermißten aus dem Bundesgebiet, *Statistische Berichte* Arb. No. VIII/11/1, 10 May 1950, Übersicht 1. On this registration, see also Overmans, *Deutsche millitärische Verluste*, 88–89; Mittermaier, *Vermisst wird*, 42–44; Böhme, *Gesucht wird . . .*, 108–10.

6. Sozialdemokratischer Pressedienst, "Es geht um 700,000 Menschen," 5 May 1950, ACDP, VII-005–047/1.

7. Aktenvermerk, 15 May 1950, PAA, B10/2/1977.

8. Vermerk nach Ausführungen von Pfarrer Merten, Bonn, 26.10. in Wiesbaden und 28.10. in Wetzlar, 30 October 1950, HHStA, Abt. 503/450a; similar estimate in Hans Heinrich, "Die nicht wiederkehren," *Frankfurter Rundschau*, 6 May 1950, PIB, MF 1566.

9. "Gefangene, die nicht heimkehren," *Die Zeit* 5/19 (1950): 1.

10. "Was Wir meinen: Moskaus Atombombe," *Volksblatt*, 6 May 1950, ASD, O44, 1950.

11. Auszug aus der Niederschrift über die Verhandlungen des Gemeinderates vom 6. Mai 1950, Stadtarchiv Ulm, Bestand 422/31, Nr. 7.

12. The preoccupation with missing POWs and MIAs never derived solely from "humanitarian concerns," as Borchard, *Die deutschen Kriegsgefangenen in der Sowjetunion*, argues. For the profoundly political functions of the POW/MIA myth in the United States after the Vietnam war, see Franklin, *M.I.A. or Mythmaking in America.*

13. Cited in "Aufklärung über 1,5 Millionen Kriegsgefangene gefordert," *Stuttgarter Nachrichten*, 6 May 1950, ASD, O44, 1950.

14. Major, *Death of the KPD*, 278–80; see also "3 Parties in Bonn Plan Red Ouster," *New York Times*, 6 May 1950, PIB, MF 1566. The Communist Party was banned in 1956.

15. "Nur 'Lumpen' und 'Verbrecher,' " *Rheinische Post*, 18 April 1952, PIB, MF 1567.

16. "Was Wir meinen: Moskaus Atombombe," *Volksblatt*, 6 May 1950, ASD, O44, 1950.

17. Schornstheimer, *Die leuchtenden Augen der Frontsoldaten*, 189–96; "Verschollen—nicht vergessen. Das Los der deutschen Gefangenen in der Sowjetunion," *Deutsche Zeitung*, 23 December 1950; "Schweigelager in Sibirien," *Der Tagesspiegel*, 16 May 1950; "Ein Keulenschlag," *Schwäbische Donauzeitung*, 6 May 1950.

18. See Böhme, *Gesucht wird die dramatische Geschichte*, 241–45.

19. Weitz, "The Ever-Present Other."

20. "106,000 Namen," *Hamburger Abendlatt*, 17 January 1952; "Niemöller: Nur 60,000 Kriegsgefangene in Russland," *Bremer Nachrichten*, 20 Feburary 1952, PIB, MF 1567.

21. "Merten schätzt Rußland-Gefangene auf 45,000," *Wiesbadener Kurier*, 18 April 1952, PIB, MF 1567.

22. "Die Kriegsgefangenen," *Frankfurter AllgemeineZeitung*, 31 July 1951, PIB, MF 1566.

23. Bernd Naumann, "Es gibt keine Schweigelager," *Frankfurter Allgemeine Zeitung*, 20 January 1954.

24. Noelle and Neumann, *The Germans*, 391–92.

25. Aufzeichnungen, "Deutsche Gefangene in der Sowjetunion," 2 September 1955, PAA, B 2/3, 258–60.

26. The Gronenfelde transition camp was closed in May 1950; see Rückblick auf das Heimkehrerlager Gronenfelde bei Frankfurt/Oder, Gronenfelde 1 May 1950, BA-Berlin, DO 1/10/41, 1–29.

27. Bericht an die Sowjetische Kontrollkommision, 27 July 1950, BA-Berlin, DO 1/11/960, 22–24; von Plato, "Zur Geschichte des sowjetischen Speziallager-systems in Deutschland. Eine Einführung."

28. Otto, "Die Waldheimer Prozesse" and Possekel, "Einleitung: Sowjetische Lagerpolitik in Deutschland, " 99–100.

29. SED Politbüro, Protokoll No.65, 4 January 1950, BA-SAPMO, DY 30/IV2/2, 4; also cited in Ihme-Tuchel, "Die SED und die deutschen Kriegsge-fangenen," 494.

30. SED Politbüro, Protokoll No. 50, 12 December 1950, BA-SAPMO, DY 30/IV2/2, 2; see also Borchard, *Die deutschen Kriegsgefangenen in der Sowjet-union*, 159–68.

31. See, for example, the sharp reaction of the VdH to a public statement by Bishop Heckel in 1953 that only sixteen thousand POWs were still held in the Soviet Union. VdH Landesverband Berlin to VdH Hauptgeschäftsstelle Bonn, 28 August 1953, VdH Archive, Kriegsgefangenenfragen Nr. 12.

32. Mittermaier, *Vermisst wird*, 42–44; Böhme, *Gesucht wird die dramatische Geschichte*, 108–10; see also Smith, *Die vermisste Million*, 51–66.

33. By 1991, 1.2 million of such reports had been issued; see Mittermaier, *Vermisst wird*, 48–52; and Böhme, *Gesucht wird . . .*, 301–4; see also Ampferl, "Verschollen im Zweiten Weltkrieg."

34. The tracing service eventually determined the fate of 1.8 million cases; see Overmans, *Deutsche militärische Verluste*, 92.

35. Böhme, *Gesucht wird . . .*, 160.

36. Ibid. 238–41; see also Lehmann, *Gefangenschaft und Heimkehr*, 120; "Seelenschinder," *Der Heimkehrer* 4/10 (1953): 1.

37. Overmans, *Deutsche militärische Verluste*, 75–76.

38. At the national registration of POWs and MIAs in March 1950, 190,000 of the 1.4 million entries came from East Germans; Böhme, *Gesucht wird . . .*, 110.

39. Overmans, *Deutsche militärische Verluste*, 115–16.

40. *Bundesgesetzblatt* (1951); 59–62, "Gesetz zur Änderung von Vorschriften des Verschollenheitsrechts," 15 January 1951; Nitsche, "Das Internationale Privatrecht der Todeserklärung," 12–45; Strebel, *Die Verschollenheit als Rechtsproblem*.

41. Dr. Karl Scharnagel, Präsident des Bayrischen Roten Kreuzes to Bayrisches Staatsministerium der Justiz, 16 February 1949, BA K, B 150/338.

42. "500 amtliche Toterklärte fanden den Weg zurück ins Leben," *Süddeutsche Zeitung*, 5 January 1951, cited in Zentner, *Aufstieg aus dem Nichts*, 81–82.

43. "Die standesamtlich beurkundeten Kriegssterbefälle und gerichtlichen Todeserklärungen in den Jahren 1939 bis 1954," *Wirtschaft und Statistik* 8 (1956): 303.

44. West German tracing services checked 841,500 applications for death certificates and sent 564,000 queries to the East German tracing service. In 12,200 cases, the concerned persons were alive; in 77,000 cases, the issuance of death certificates needed to be postponed. See Böhme, *Gesucht wird . . .*, 91; Baden-Württembergisches Justizministerium to Länderrat der amerikanischen Besatzungszone, 11 March 1949, BA-K, B 150/338; see also Mitteilungsblatt des Arbeitsministeriums von Württemberg-Baden, July–August 1949, which stipulated that it was possible to apply for a pension if there had been no information from an MIA for two years, a POW for three years; cited in Smith, *Die vermisste Million*, 128–29.

45. Strebel, *Die Verschollenheit als Rechtsproblem*, 93–94.

46. Benjamin, *Zur Geschichte der Rechtspflege*, 304.

47. SED-ZK, Beschlüsse Kleines Sekretariat, BA-SAPMO, DY 30/JIV2/3/147, 12.

48. SED-ZK, Kleines Sekretariat, Anlage zum Protokoll, 8 February 1951, BA-SAPMO, DY 30/JIV2/3/173, 22; SED-ZK, Kleines Sekretariat, Verordnung über die Abkürzung der Verschollenheitsfristen, 8 November 1951, BA-SAPMO, DY 30/JIV2/3/246, 32; Ihme-Tuchel, "Die SED und die deutschen Kriegsgefangenen," 495.

49. See the story of Frau N., who was issued a death certificate for her husband in 1950, remarried in 1951, and received confirmation of the death of her first husband in 1953; interview with Frau N., IFGB.

50. SED Kreisvorstand, Freiberg, Sachsen, to SED Landesvorstand, 26 September 1949, SHStA, SED, LV A 306, 185.

51. On similar tendencies in the Soviet Union, see Tumarkin, *The Living and the Dead*, 95–106.

52. On the POW commemorations, see the discussion in Moeller, *War Stories*, 41–42.

53. On the significance of the nation in the West German commemorative culture, see Wolfrum, *Geschichtspolitik in der Bundesrepublik*, 7.

54. Evangelische-Lutherische Landeskirche Hannover to Landeskirchenamt, 25 July 1949, EZA, 4/717.

55. Bischof Wurm to die Gemeinden zur Gebetswoche für die Kriegsgefangenen, 28 August 1946, EZA, 4/472; see also chapter 2.

56. Allgemeine Informationen, Anweisungen und Empfehlungen zur Kriegsgefangenengedenkwoche 1952, EZA, 2/84/6453/10.

57. VdH Rundschreiben 35/54, 15 September 1954; VdH-Rundschreiben 37/1954, 24 September 1954, Vdh-Archive, Kriegsgefangenen-Gedenktage 1954.

58. See a corresponding motion by the FDP faction in parliament, Antrag der Abgeordneten Frau Hütter, Dr. Schäfer und Fraktion der FDP, 16 September 1952, VDBT, 1. Wahlperiode, No. 3694.

59. See excerpts of Limburg local newspapers compiled in Verband der Heimkehrer, Hessen, "Die Verpflichtung der Heimekhrer," HHStA, Abt. 502/1005.

60. Ulickzka, *Berufsbiographie und Flüchtlingsschicksal*, 297.

61. Reichel, *Der schöne Schein des Dritten Reiches*, 119, 221.

62. "Mahnfeuer an der Zonengrenze," *Frankfurter Allgemeine Zeitung*, 27 October 1952, ASD, O44, 1951–52; "Gedenkfeuer mahnten die Welt," *Kölnische Rundschau*, 26 October 1953, NRWHStA, 48/56, 59; Moeller, *War Stories*, 41.

63. Entwurf zu einer Ansprache der Frauen anlässlich des Kriegsgefangenen-Gedenktages 1954, VdH Archive, Kriegsgefangenengedenktag 1954.

64. See figure 12.

65. On VDH requests for official support, see VDH to Herbert Wehner, 5 April 1951, PAA, B 10/2/1980; Vermerk von Trützscheler, 26 April 1951, PAA, B 10/2/1980. On the UN initiative, see below.

66. The event still featured public demonstrations and speeches but lacked official endorsement by high West German dignitaries; see Protestkundgebung gegen die Zurückhaltung der deutschen Kriegsgefangenen, Vorschlag für die Programmgestaltung des "Tags der Kriegsgefangenen—Tag der Treue" am 4.5.1951, BHStA, Stk 114829; Sonderrundschreiben zur Ausgestaltung des Jahrestages der TASS-Meldung, Bund ehemaliger Kriegsgefangener Berlin, 12 April 1951, LAB, Rep. 8, Acc. 741, No. 56.

67. Durchführung einer Kriegsgefangenen-Gedenkwoche vom 20. bis 26. Oktober 1952, PAA, B 10/2/1934; Herbert Blankenhorn to alle Ministerien und Presse/Informationsamt, 18 September 1953; Schnellbrief Auswärtiges Amt to Staatssekretär des Bundeskanzleramtes, 21 October 1953, PAA, B 10/2/1935; on this issue, see also below.

68. EKD (Berliner Stelle) to Kirchenleitungen der Gliedkirchen, 6 October 1950, EZA, 4/476. Evangelische Kirchenkanzlei, Berliner Stelle, to Kirchenleitungen der östlichen Gliedkirchen, 11 August 1953, EZA, 104/610.

69. See the transfers from Görlitz, Dresden, and Schwerin, EZA, 104/610.

70. Analyse über die Lage in den Kirchen, eingegangen, 20 January 1952, BA-SAPMO, DY 30/IV2/14/1, 74–76; Konsistorium, Berlin-Brandenburg to EKD, Berliner Stelle, 6 April 1954, EZA, 4/477.

71. Bischof Heckel, Evangelisches Hilfswerk, to Kirchenkanzlei der EKD, 29 May 1953, EZA, 2/84/6453/10.

72. Superintendent des Kirchenkreises Storkow to Kirchenleitung der evangelischen Kirche Berlin-Brandenburg (Abschrift), 9 November 1953, EZA, 4/477.

73. Bischof Heckel to Kirchenkanzlei der EkD, 12 September 1952; Braunschweigische-Lutherische Landeskirche to Kirchenkanzlei, EKD, 20 October 1952 EZA, 2/84/6453/10.

74. This was also the position of the Catholic Church; see Erzbistum Köln to VdH, 22 September 1952, HEK, CR II, 25, 19, 13.

75. Evangelische Lutherische Landeskirche to Herren Ephoren, Rundverfügung 50/54, EZA, 2/84/6453/15.

76. On this campaign, see Frei, *Vergangenheitspolitik*, 133–306.

77. Ibid., 235.

78. Ibid., 270.

79. Theodor Heuss, "Das Menschliche des Kriegsgefangenen-Problems. Rundfunkansprache des Bundespräsidenten zur Woche der Kriegsgefangenen," *Die Neue Zeitung*, 20 October 1952, ASD, O44, 1951–52.

80. Werner Kießling to Werner Best, 17 May 1952, VdH Archive, File Nr. 4, Generalamnestie.

81. Dr. Achenbach, Vorbereitender Ausschuß zur Herbeiführung der Generalamnestie, to Caritas Kriegsgefangenenhilfe, 12 March 1952, ADCV, 372.025, Fasz. 7; see also the VdH letter to members of the U.S. Senate, Association of Returnees, P.O.W.'s and Family Members of Missing Germans to "Dear Senator," 10 November 1953, VdH Archive, Nr. 52, Generalamnestie, Heimkehrer, Kriegsgefangene, 1952–56.

82. Werner Kießling to Werner Best, 17 May 1952, VdH Archive, File Nr. 4, Generalamnestie; a "general amnesty" did ultimately not materialize. In 1954, "mixed review boards" with Allied and German representatives were formed to review all the sentences for all the prisoners still held by the Western allies. The last internee was released in 1958, see Frei, *Vergangenheitspolitik*, 251–54.

83. Hessische Minister des Inneren Schneider to Hessische Ministerpräsident Zinn, 22 June 1956, HHStA, Abt. 502/1003, citing a letter from expellee minister Theodor Oberländer indicating that the granting of these benefits to "unworthy persons" was preferable to a comprehensive review of Allied convictions for war crimes; see also Ausschuss für Kriegsopfer- und Kriegsgefangenenfragen, 20 February 1952, PA/DB, 1. Wahlperiode, 26. Ausschuss, Protokoll Nr. 74.

84. Dr. Lukaschek, Minister für Vertriebene to Dr. Erhard, Bayrischer Ministerpräsident, 27 June 1951, BHStA, Stk 114834; Ausschuss für Kriegsgefangenenfragen, gemeinsame Sitzung mit dem Ausschuss für Fragen der öffentlichen Fürsorge, 15 March 1950, PA/DB, 1. Wahlperiode, 26. Ausschuss, Protokoll Nr. 13. For a more detailed discussion of the gradual extension of the returnee status, see my dissertation "The Protracted War," 370–81.

85. On this argument, see Lübbe, "Der Nationalsozialismus im deutschen Nachkriegsbewußtsein"; see also Herf, *Divided Memory*.

86. Frei, *Vergangenheitspolitik*, 304.

87. In light of the massive West German resistance to the prosecution and internment of war criminals, the Western allies eventually also abandoned these efforts. Allied intervention into German politics focused primarily on preventing the rise of new neofascist movements, not so much on punishing past Nazi crimes; see Brochhagen, *Nach Nürnberg*, 83–97; Frei, *Vergangenheitspolitik*.

88. On POWs in Korea, see Foot, *A Substitute for Victory*, 108–10; and Moeller, *War Stories*, 222 n.82.

89. Aufzeichnungen von Trützscheler, March 1950, PAA, B 10/2/1977.

90. For a detailed discussion of this initiative that, however, tends to underplay its political significance; see Borchard, *Die deutschen Kriegsgefangenen in der Sowjetunion*, 123–57.

91. Cited in Moeller, *War Stories*, 39.

92. Borchard, *Die deutschen Kriegsgefangenen in der Sowjetunion*, 128.

93. On the Hallstein-speech, see ibid., 149–50; on the significance of the UN intiative for the West German politics of memory, see Moeller, *War Stories*, 39.

94. John L. Morton, "Sie sind nicht vergessen. Die Kriegsgefangenenfrage vor den Vereinten Nationen," *Hamburger Echo*, 2 September 1950, ASD, O44, 1950.

95. Frau Helene B. to Evangelisches Hilfswerk, 30 August 1951, BA-M, Msg 194/111.

96. Heinrich B., Rentner, to Adenauer, 3 October 1952, PAA, B 10/2/1935.

97. Studentische Notgemeinschaft München to Adenauer, 29 March 1955, PAA, B 10/2/1989.

98. On these initiatives, see especially Borchard, *Die deutschen Kriegsgefangenen in der Sowjetunion*, 186–219; Bentley, *Martin Niemöller*, 205–8; Riesenberger, *Das deutsche Rote Kreuz*.

99. On this controversy, see Borchard, *Die deutschen Kriegsgefangenen in der Sowjetunion*, 199–203, 289–93; for a critique of Adenauer's policy regarding POWs, see also the analysis by a 1955 returnee, Meyer, *Kriegsgefangene im Kalten Krieg*.

100. The literature on Adenauer's foreign policy is vast and controversial. I am following here the argument put forth by Foschepoth, "Westintegration statt Wiedervereinigung."

101. West German officials, for example, compared U.S. concerns over eleven American pilots missing in action in Korea to "50,000 German families" who were still awaiting the return of a POW from Soviet captivity; Kessel, Washington to Foreign Office, 22 January 1955, PAA, B 10/2/1988.

102. On the influence of expellee organizations on West German foreign policy, see Ahonen, *After the Expulsion*.

103. Bruno R. und 124 Heimkehrer to Adenauer, PAA, B 10/2/2000.

104. Helene L. to Adenauer, 16 May 1955, PAA, B 10/2/1989.

105. Hedwig M. to Adenauer, 6 May 1955, PAA, B 10/2/1989.

106. Schwarz, *Adenauer*, 213; Borchard, *Die deutschen Kriegsgefangenen in der Sowjetunion*, 229–37. For an original analysis of the domestic meaning of Adenauer's visit, see Moeller, *War Stories*, 88–91.

107. Noelle and Neumann, *The Germans*, 246.

108. For an analysis of these petitions, see also Moeller, *War Stories*, 92–96.

109. Anna von V. to Adenauer, 3 September 1955, PAA, B 10/2/1995.

110. Erika K. to Prof. Dr. Hallstein, 23 June 1955, PAA, B 10/2/1990.

111. Viktoria W. to Adenauer, 10 June 1955, PAA, B 10/2/1990.

112. According to current estimates, 154,000 Germans were interned in the Soviet-run "special camps" in East Germany; see von Plato, "Zur Geschichte des sowjetischen Speziallagersystems in Deutschland," 54.

113. These petitions can be found in BA-Berlin, DO 1/HA34.0/08520.

114. On West German petitions, see Moeller, *War Stories*, 159–60. On "charismatic rule," see Kershaw, *Hitler Myth*; and Wehler, *Deutsche Gesellschaftsgeschichte*, 933–37. Other addressees included the East German prime minister Otto Grotewohl, the Interior Ministry, the Foreign Ministry, the German Democratic Women's Union, the Free German Youth but never the actual leader of the GDR, the SED general secretary Walter Ulbricht.

115. Wili B. to Pieck, 11 October 1950, BA-Berlin, DO 1/HA34.0/08520.

116. Gisela B. to Pieck, 8 June 1951 and Ilse D. to Pieck, 10 January 1952, BA-Berlin, DO 1/HA34.0/08520.

117. Heineman, "Gender, Public Policy, and Memory," 228–31.

118. Klara B. to Pieck, 17 August 1951, BA-Berlin, DO 1/HA34.0/08520.

119. Gerda B. to Pieck, 6 May 1952, BA-Berlin, DO 1/HA34.0/08520.

120. All quotations are from the correspondence of Dorothea B., BA-Berlin, DO 1/HA34.0/08520.

121. Martha D. to Grotewohl, 21 April 1952; quotation from Arthur B. to Pieck, 22 May 1952, BA-Berlin, DO 1/HA34.0/08520.

122. Horst K. to Pieck, 25 January 1951, BA-Berlin, DO1/HA34.0/08520.

123. Margarete B. to Ministerium des Inneren, 4 June 1951, BA-Berlin, DO 1/HA34.0/08520.

124. Martha D. to Pieck, 27 October 1950, BA-Berlin, DO 1/HA34.0/08520.

125. Lisabeth S. to Zentralrat der FDJ, 21 July 1950, BA-Berlin, DO 1/HA 34.0/33259.

126. Heinz D. to Grotewohl, 28 November 1952, BA-Berlin, DO 1/HA34.0/08520.

127. Joachim G. to Pieck, 13 October 1951, BA-Berlin, DO 1/HA34.0/08520.

128. Marianne H. to Pieck, 20 June 1951 and Marie E. to Pieck, n.d., BA-Berlin, DO 1/HA34.0/08520.

129. Erwin H. to Pieck, 12 October 1951, BA-Berlin, DO 1/HA34.0/08520.

130. Ursula B., Lauenstein, Sachsen, to Kanzlei des Präsidenten der DDR, 30 January 1951, BA-Berlin, DO 1/HA34.0/8523.

131. Niethammer, "Erfahrungen und Strukturen," 107.

132. Ihme-Tuchel, "Die SED und die deutschen Kriegsgefangenen, 1949–1955."

133. See Borchard, *Die deutschen Kriegsgefangenen in der Sowjetunion*, 159–60.

134. Ministerium des Inneren to Margarete B., BA-Berlin, DO 1/HA34.0/08520.

135. Büttner, MdI, Abt. Bevölkerungspolitik an Industriegewerkschaft Bau/Holz, 24 October 1951, BA-Berlin, DO 1/HA34.0/08520.

136. See chapter 1.

137. Joachim G. to Pieck, 13 October 1951, BA-Berlin, DO 1/HA34.0/08520.

138. Marianne H. told Pieck that many East Germans knew a POW in the Soviet Union and "felt deep empathy with those who remained behind"; Mariane H. to Pieck, 20 June 1951, BA-Berlin, DO 1/HA34.0/08520.

139. Inge H. to Pieck, 15 November 1951, BA-Berlin, DO 1/HA34.0/08520.

140. Rapportmeldung Nr. 39, 25 September 1950, BA-Berlin, DO 1/11/1150, 140.

141. Zatlin, "Ausgaben und Eingaben"; see also the general discussion on opposition and dissent in Ross, *The East German Dictatorship*, 97–125.

CHAPTER 8
DIVIDED REUNION

1. On the 1953 release, see Hilger, "Faustpfand im Kalten Krieg," 255–62; Ihme-Tuchel, "Die Entlassung der deutsche Kriegsgefangenen" and "Die SED und die deutschen Kriegsgefangenen"; Borchard, *Die deutschen Kriegsgefangenen in der Sowjetunion*, 169–80. The exact number of returnees is difficult to determine and seems to have been left deliberately vague by Soviet officials; see Ihme-Tuchel, "Zwischen Tabu und Propaganda."

2. N. Krushchev to ZK der SED, Ulbricht und Grotewohl, 14 July 1955, BA-SAPMO, DY 30/JIV2/202/61, 15–16; and on this context in general the work of Borchard and Ihme-Tuchel cited above.

3. Figures for civilian internees in 1953 and 1955 according to Hilger, "Haft in entlegenen Gebieten," 669.

4. Moeller, *War Stories*, 88–122, and "Last Soldiers."

5. Ingeborg Glupp, "Das Erlebnis der Freiheit," *Berliner Morgenpost*, 22 October 1955, PIB, MF 2191; "Willkommenssturm warf alle Pläne um," *Frankfurter Rundschau*, 28 September 1955, PIB, MF 2190.

6. Barbara Groneweg, "Willkommenssturm warf alle Pläne um," *Frankfurter Rundschau,* 28 September 1953, PIB, MF, 2190; "Ergreifender Empfang in Friedland," *Hannoversche Allgemeine Zeitung*, 10 October 1955; "Sonntag 6:31: Eine große Stunde unseres Volkes," *Die Welt*, 10 October 1955; "Deutschlands Herz schlägt in Friedland," *Hessische Nachrichten*, 16 October 1955; all in PIB, MF 2191.

7. These speeches are cited in KNA No. 246, 19 October 1955, PIB, MF 2191.

8. "Die Heimkehrer," *General Anzeiger für Bonn und Umgebung*, 8 October 1955, PIB, MF 2191.

9. On the significance of the nation in West German memory, see Wolfrum, *Geschichtspolitik in der Bundesrepublik Deutschland*; on emotions, see François, Siegrist, and Vogel, "Die Nation"; on the 1954 World Cup, see Brüggemeier, *Zurück auf dem Platz*.

10. "Ein einzig Volk," *Aachener Volkszeitung*, 11 October 1955, PIB, MF 2191.

11. Foschepoth, "Adenauers Moskaureise 1955," 31, quoting *Jahrbuch der öffentlichen Meinung*, 1967, 187.

12. On these numbers, see Scheib, "Gefangenschaft und Eingliederung von Heimkehren," 16. Morina, "Instructed Silence," 337, cites a lower number of 5,374 released POWs with 4, 057 POWs to the West. The numbers for 1955–56 are based on my own calculations from the Listen der übernommenen Kriegsverurteilten No. 1 and No. 2, BA-Berlin, D0 1/34.0/27117. Hilger, "Faustpfand im Kalten Krieg," 270, cites the lower number of 6,557 POWs returning to the West, 3,104 returning to the East.

13. Hanz Zehrer, "Volk ohne Heimkehr," *Die Welt*, 15 October 1955, ASD, O43, 1955.

14. "Das echte Deutschland," *Hamburger Anzeiger*, 11 October 1955, PIB, MIF 2191.

15. Irmgard Kühne, "Männer aus dem Feuerofen," *Christ und Welt* 8/42 (1955), PIB, MF 2191.

16. See, for example, Bodamer, *Der Mann von Heute*.

17. "Deutschland ist anders geworden," *Rheinisch-Westfälische Nachrichten*, PIB MF 2191; "Der Weg zurück ins Leben," *Hamburger Anzeiger*, PIB MF 2191, and the evidence cited in Moeller, *War Stories*, 110–11.

18. Movie poster, *Die Glocke von Friedland*, VdH Archive; see figure 14.

19. Moeller, *War Stories*, 122.

20. On these trials, see above, chapter 6.

21. "Die ersten Stunden in der Heimat," *Hamburger Abendblatt*, 8 October 1955, PIB MF 2191; Erich Kuby, "Mit dem Blick auf Friedland," *Süddeutsche Zeitung*, 11 October 1955, ASD, O43 (1955), also quoted in Moeller, *War Stories*, 114.

22. "Legende der Tausend Galgen," *Der Spiegel* 9/7 (1955): 11–18.

23. "Politisches Tagebuch," *Flensburger Tageblatt*, 11 October 1955, PIB, MF 2191.

24. Hans J. Reinowski, "Heimkehr nach Deutschland," 31 December 1953, *Darmstädter Echo*, ASD, O43, 1953.

25. Koch, "Heinemans Kritik an Adenauers Deutschlandpolitik," 223; Marion Gräftin Döhnoff, "Das Moskauer Ja-Wort," *Die Zeit*, 22 September 1955, also cited in Moeller, *War Stories*, 176; on the Moscow agreement, see Foschepoth, "Adenauers Moskausreise 1955," 44–46.

26. *Bonner Hefte für Politik, Wirtschaft und Kultur*, 24 October 1955, PIB, MF 2191; see Moeller, "Last Soldiers."

27. On failed reunions, see, for example, "Ihre Kinder tragen fremde Namen," *Hamburger Abendblatt*, 4 February 1956, ASD, O43, 1955; "Die einen werden im Mercedes abgeholt, die anderen trifft ein neuer Schicksalsschlag," *Abendpost*, Frankfurt am Main, PIB, MF 2191; see also Moeller, *War Stories*, 182.

28. "Heiratsmarkt Friedland," *Welt am Sonntag* 17/1953, 3, clipping in DHM 1989.439.166.

29. Charlotte B. to Friedland, n.d., DHM 1989/439.15; Luise M. to Lager Friedland, 4 December 1955, DHM 1989/439.138.

30. Frida G. to Lager Friedland, 18 December 1955, DHM 1989/439.29.

31. Hans R. to Lager Friedland, 28 February 1957, DHM 1989/439.61; Matthias v. L. to Lagerleitung, n.d., DHM 1989/439.30.

32. Trude L. to Lager Friedland, 24 October 1955, DHM 1989/439.138.

33. Dorothea L. to einen lieben Heimkehrer, 7 June 1956, DHM 1989/439.41; Marie Luise W. to Heimleiter des Heimkehrerlagers Friedland, 9 October 1955, DHM 1989/439.51; Annemarie W. to Lagerleitung, 18 May 1956, DHM 1989/439.11; Charlotte B. to Lager Friedland, n.d., DHM 1989/439.15.

34. Ursula D., 19 November 1956, DHM 1989/439.97; similarly Klara M. to Lager Friedland, November 1956, DHM 1989/439.1; Edelgard S. to HKL Friedland, 6 June 1956; DHM 1989/439.56; similarly Annemarie W. to Lagerleitung, 18 May 1956, DHM 1989/439.11.

35. Maria Z. to Lager Friedland, 11 October 1955, DHM 1989/439.77.

36. Gerlinde J. to Lager Friedland, 23 November 1955, DHM 1989/439.69.

37. Institut für Sozialforschung, *Zum politischen Bewusstsein ehemaliger Kriegsgefangener*, 43–45.

38. See Jarausch, *Die Umkehr*, 76–85.

39. Interview H6, 7; H12, 81, ISF.

40. Interview H1, 36, ISF.

41. On this argument, see Echternkamp, "Verwirrung im Vaterländischen"; on "social time," see Confino, "Telling about Germany."

42. Naumann, "Brave Nazis."

43. Die Arbeit des Personalgutachterausschusses, Drucksache 109, Deutscher Bundestag, 3. Wahlperiode, BA-M, BW 27/27, cited in Naumann, "Brave Nazis," 215; see also "Hass gegen den Kommunismus. Heimkehrer im Urteil des Personalgutachterausschusses," BA-M, BW 27/17.

44. Arbeitskreis der Heimkehrer und Kriegsgefangenen Angehörigen des Lagers Borowitschi, "Personalgutachterausschuss und Spätheimkehrer," 19 February 1958, BA-M, BW 27/17, 53; Stenographisches Protokoll der 8 Sitzung des Ausschusses für Verteidigung, 13 February 1958, BW 27/17, 116, cited in Naumann, "Brave Nazis." For a similar statement advocating a solution to the "Jewish problem" in a "more tactful manner," see interview H18, 28, ISF.

45. Final Report "Die Arbeit des Personalgutachterausschusses," 15, cited in Naumann, "Brave Nazis," 217.

46. Innenminister Nordrhein-Westfalen, Betr.: Übernahme von Spätheimkehrern in den öffentlichen Dienst, 1 June 1955, NRWHStA, NW 110/776, 143.

47. Karl Ahrnessen to Vertriebenen-Ministerium, 27 November 1956, BA-K, B 150/4524; Interviews H24, 4–5; H34, 3–4, ISF.

48. This was true especially for the "Müller of Rhöndorf," a 1953 returnee and neighbor of Chancellor Adenauer who had been unable to find work for months after his return; "Der Kanzler und der Müller von Rhöndorf," *Der Heimkehrer* 5/10 (1954): 1. On the experience of 1953 returnees, see also Scheib, "Gefangenschaft und Eingliederung von Heimkehrern."

49. Übersicht über die Vermittlungsbemühungen für Spätheimkehrer, NRWHStA, LANW46I, 679.

50. Form letter, betr. Eingliederung der Heimkehrer aus den Jahren 1955/56, Fragebogen für Heimkehrer aus den Jahren 1955/56, BA-K, B 150/4524a; Heimkehrer Fragebogenaktion, 3 November 1956, BA-K, B 150/2889; Stellungnahme

zu dem Schreiben des Bundestagsausschusses für Kriegsopfer- und Heimkehrerfragen, 4 January 1957, BA-K, B 150/2829. On the positive reception of this questionnaire among returnees, see H1, 22–23, ISF.

51. Interview H51, 22–23, ISF; quotation from Alois F. to Caritas-Kriegsgefangenenhilfe, 24 January 1956, ADCV 372.2.095, Fasz. 1955.

52. Valentin D. to Caritas-Kriegsgefangenenhilfe, 18 November 1955, ADCV 372.2.095, Fasz. 1955.

53. See chapter 3; whereas 62.5 percent of returnees from 1948–49 suffered from these symptoms, 80–100 percent of 1953 returnees exhibited the same symptoms; Meyeringh Dietze and Haessler, "Über den Gesundheitszustand der Spätheimkehrer der Jahre 1953/54," 1611.

54. "Der Vitalknick bei den Spätheimkehrern," *Münchner Merkur*, 17 February 1956, ASD, O43, 1956.

55. For such evaluations among earlier returnees, see patient record Karl G. and AlfreD Dra., ALRK.

56. Hochreich und Schleicher, "Die Beurteilung der Spätheimkehrerschäden."

57. Rauschelbach, "Zur versorgungsrechtlichen Beurteilung der Spätheimkehrer," 14.

58. See Venzlaff, *Die psychoreaktiven Störungen*, on this history. See also Pross, *Paying for German Past*, 85–88; and Goltermann, "Psychisches Leid und herrschende Lehre."

59. Rauschelbach, "Zu einigen gutachterlichen Problemen"; interview with Dr. Heinz-Harro Rauschelbach, 16 and 22 April 1998, OH 9. Late returnees still felt disadvantaged by the West German pension bureaucracy but were also aware that they received more favorable evaluations than earlier returnees; interviews H3, 39; H31, 4; H51, 6, ISF.

60. Tagung des Ärztlichen Sachverständigenrates für Fragen der Kriegsopferversorgung am 5., 6. und 7.3.1956, BA-K, B 149/1955.

61. Bundeminister für Arbeit to Arbeitsminister und Senatoren für Arbeit der Länder, 25 August 1956, BA-K, B 149/7078.

62. Rauschelbach, "Allegemeine Begutachtungsgrundsätze."

63. Bundesministerium für Arbeit, *Anhaltspunkte für die Ärztliche Gutachtertätigkeit*, 120 (1958 ed.) or 153 (1965 ed.). The 1965 edition also reflected a more skeptical attitude toward the "dystrophy diagnosis" more generally, which was retained only because it had become "common usage."

64. Michel, "Die Tiefe des psychologischen Traumas bei der Totalverfolgung."

65. Dr.med Gerhard Schreiber, "Zur Frage der Dauerschäden nach Dystrophie," in Bundesministerium für Arbeit- und Sozialordnung, *Die Dystrophie*, 139; see also Bansi, "Spätschäden nach Dystrophie, 3. Teil," 321; and in general, Pross, *Paying for the German Past*, 82–89.

66. Pross, *Paying for the German Past*, 94–104. The key publication was Herberg and Paul, *Psychische Spätschäden nach politischer Verfolgung*; on the earlier history, see Goschler, *Wiedergutmachung*.

67. Heimkehrer Transporte 1–6, September/Oktober 1953, Sogennante Kriegsverbrecher laut Heimkehrer-Erfassungsbogen; Bahnke, Bericht 1.–6. Heimkehrertransport, September/Oktober 1953, 28 December 1953, PAA, B 10/2/2026.

68. Bericht über die Heimkehr amnestierter ehemaliger deutscher Kriegsgefangener aus der Sowjetunion, 14 October 1953, ADW, ZB/203; on Streckenbach, see Wildt, "Differierende Wahrheiten."

69. "Friedland," *Vorwärts,* 21 October 1955, PIB, MF 2191; see also Artur Satenus, "Gefangene kehren wieder heim," *Welt der Arbeit,* 14 October 1955, PIB, MF 2191.

70. Schmidt, "Spätheimkehrer oder Schwerstverbrecher," 273–350.

71. See the press reports "Heimkehrerzug mit verriegelten Türen," *Stuttgarter Nachrichten,* 18 January 1956; "'Pistolenschubert' als Spätheimkehrer," *Freie Presse Bielefeld (SPD),* 24 November 1955, PIB, MF 2191; Hergt to BdI, 23 January 1956, PAA, B 10/2/2001.

72. Schmidt, "Spätheimkehrer oder Schwestkriegsverbrecher," 337–39.

73. British Embassy, Bonn, 28 October 1955, PRO, FO 371/11804.

74. Erik Rinné, "Sie erkannten die Größe der Stunde nicht. SPD fordert Entnazifizierung für Spätheimkehrer," f.d.K., 13 October 1953, PIB, MF 2190; *Die Freiheit,* 12 October 1953, ASD, O43, 1953.

75. "Der Aufstand der Empörten von Königswinter," clipping in ASD, O43, 1955.

76. Hergt, Aufzeichnungen Kabinettssitzung, 25 January 1956, PAA, B 10/2/2001.

77. Frei, *Vergangenheitspolitik,* 398, interprets the second amnesty law of 1954 as the end point of the "grand coalition" between SPD and CDU/CSU regarding the politics of memory.

78. Kurt Hirsch, "Friedland," *Vorwärts,* 21 October 1955, PIB, MF 2191; for similar evidence, see Moeller, *War Stories,* 192.

79. This conversation was reported by the British ambassador in Bonn, D. A. Wilkinson, British Embassy Bonn, 28 October 1955, PRO, FO 371/11804; also cited in Brochhagen, *Nach Nürnberg,* 250.

80. " 'Heimkehrer' und Heimkehrer. Eine Stellungnahme zum Problem der Kriegsverbrecher," *Allgemeine Wochenzeitung der Juden,* 9 December 1955, PIB, MF 2191.

81. Sven Busk vom Dachau Klubben to Bundeskanzler Adenauer, 22 January 1956, PAA, B 10/2/2002.

82. " 'Heimkehrer' und Heimkehrer. Eine Stellungnahme zum Problem der Kriegsverbrecher," *Allgemeine Wochenzeitung der Juden in Deutschland,* 9 December 1955, PIB, MF 2191. See also Jörg Müller, "Heimkehr des Monstrums," *Die Woche,* 6 October 1995; and Brochhagen, *Nach Nürnberg,* 250.

83. Die Kabinettsprotokolle der Bundesregierung, 1956, 115. Kabinettssitzung, 25.1.1956, 122–25, cited in Schmidt, "Spätheimkehrer oder Schwerstkriegsverbrecher," 311.

84. The Foreign Office may also have reacted to attacks from East Germany; Hergt, Aufzeichnungen Kabinettssitzung, 25 January 1956; Bundesministerium des Inneren, Dr. Pioch to Auswärtiges Amt, 15 March 1956, PAA, B 10/2/2001; Brochhagen, *Nach Nürnberg,* 250.

85. See Frei, *Vergangenheitspolitik,* 247.

86. Schmidt, "Spätheimkehrer oder Schwerstkriegsverbrecher?" 346.

87. In a 1959 testimony, Schubert himself complained that "only Sorge and I have been arrested and not the others as well"; see Vernehmungsprotokoll, Wilhelm Schubert, 27 February 1959, Zentralstelle der Landesjustizverwaltung Ludwigsburg, 401 AR 826/64. My thanks to Oliver Schröm for making this document available to me.

88. Borchhagen, *Nach Nürnberg*, 254–55.

89. Erler, "Zur Tätigkeit der Sowjetischen Militärtribunale (SMT) in der SBZ/DDR," 186.

90. Walter Ulbricht to ZK der KPDSU, 19 November 1955, BA-SAPMO, DY 30/JIV2/202/244.

91. Otto, "Die Waldheimer Prozesse," 552.

92. Erich Mielke to Leiter der Hauptabteilung, Genossen Oberst Scholz, 16 December 1955, BStU, MfS AS 2/59, 487.

93. Kowalczuk, Mitter, and Wolle, *Der Tag X*.

94. For an analysis of the 1953 uprising and the reactions of the SED, see Fulbrook, *Anatomy of a Dictatorship*, 177–87; on the role of the Stasi in the reception of returnees in 1953, see Morina, "Instructed Silence," 335–37.

95. Bericht vom Leiter des OP Stabs, VP Kittler und Leiter der Abteilung PM, VP-Rat Passlack, BA-Berlin, DO 1/08/30800; Situationsbericht über den in der Nacht vom 27.12. zum 28.12. eingetroffenen Transport begnadigter Kriegsverbrecher aus der SU, 28 December 1953, BA-Berlin, DO 1/11/438, 167–68.

96. Bericht vom Leiters des OP Stabs, VP Rat Kittler und Leiter Abteilung PM, VP Rat Passlack, BA-Berlin, DO 1/08/30800.

97. Staatssekretariat Innere Angelengenheiten, Abt. Bevölkerungspolitik, Bericht über den 2. Sondertransport aus der UdSSR, 29 September 1953, BStU, MfS AS 6/54, Bd. 36, 203.

98. Bericht vom Leiters des OP Stabs, VP Rat Kittler und Leiter Abteilung PM, VP Rat Passlack, BA-Berlin, DO 1/08/30800.

99. Bericht über den zweiten Transport aus der UdSSR, 10 October 1955, BA-SAPMO, DY 30/IV2/12/403.

100. Plan für die Übernahmen und Weiterleitung von Transporten aus der UdSSR (Gen. Fritzsche), BA-Berlin, DO 1/34.0/08293; Fritzsche, Besprechung bei der HVDVP, 5 October 1955, BA-Berlin, DO 1/34.0/08293.

101. "Sie verdienen die allerschwerste Strafe," *Neues Deutschland,* 20 December 1955; "Sollen solche Verbrecher wieder morden," *Neues Deutschland,* 21 December 1955. In general on East German "counterpropaganda" to the West reception of 1955 returnees, see Ihme-Tuchel, "Die SED und die deutschen Kriegsgefangenen," 501–2.

102. *Neues Deutschland*, 11 October 1955, cited in *SBZ Archiv* 6 (1955): 317; "Zweierlei Empfang," *Neues Deutschland*, 9 October 1955, PIB, MF 2191.

103. These attacks continued throughout the 1960s; see Lemke, "Kampagnen gegen Bonn."

104. Nonamnestied returnees were interned in Bautzen, but most of them were released in April 1956. In 1959, only twenty-four nonamnestied returnees were still interned; see Schmidt, "Spätheimkehrer oder Schwerstkriegsverbrecher?" 300–305.

105. Bericht vom Leiter des OP Stabs, VP Rat K. und Leiter der Abteilung PM, VP Rat P., betr. Zusammenfassender Bericht über die im Bezirk Frankfurt/Oder geleistete Arbeit bei der Aufnahme und Abfertigung der Rücktransporte ehemaliger Kriegsverurteilter aus der UdSSR, BA-Berlin, D 01/08/30800; Begrüßungsansprache 1955, BA-Berlin, DO 1/34.0/08293.

106. "Die Menschen ändern sich," *Neues Deutschland*, 13 October 1955; see also Ihme-Tuchel, "Die SED und die deutschen Kriegsgefangenen."

107. "Wie sie aufgenommen werden," *Neues Deutschland*, 15 October 1955; "Heimkehrer und Heimgekehrte," *Neues Deutschland*, 17 October 1955, "Die Menschen ändern sich," *Neues Deutschland*, 13 October 1955.

108. Stimmungsbericht über die am 1. und 2.10.1953 im Auffanglager Eisenach entlassenen begnadigten ehemaligen Kriegsverbrecher, 2 October 1953, BA-Berlin, DO 1/11/438, 159–61; Stimmungsbericht über den am 5.10.1953 eingetroffenen Transport entlassener Strafgefangener aus der Sowjet-Union, 6 October 1953, BA-Berlin, DO 1/11/438, 162–64.

109. Stimmungsbericht über die am 1. und 2.10.1953 eingetroffenen ehemaligen Kriegsverbrecher, 2 October 1953, BA-Berlin, DO 1/11/438, 160.

110. Stimmungsbericht über den am 5.10.1953 eingetroffenen Transport, 6 October 1953, BA-Berlin, DO 1/11/438, 162–63.

111. Ibid.; Stimmungsbericht über die am 1. und 2.10.1953 eingtroffenen Begnadigten ehemaligen Kriegsverbrecher, BA-Berlin, DO 1/11/438, 159–60.

112. Staatssekretariat für Innere Angelegenheiten to Ministerium des Inneren, 12 October 1953, MfS, AS 6/54, Bd. 35, 172. The list of names of the third returnee transport in 1955 was sent to the Interior Ministry, which then forwarded it to the Stasi; Grötschel, Hauptabteilungsleiter, Staatssekretariat für Innere Angelegenheiten to Ministerium des Inneren, 1 October 1955, BStU, MfS AS 6/54, Bd. 35.

113. Fernschreiben HDVP to Stellvertreter aller BDVP and to Präsidenten der Volkspolizei Berlin, BA-Berlin, DO 1/08/30800.

114. Kreisdienststelle Magdeburg to Bezirksverwaltung Magdeburg, Information über ehemalige Kriegsverurteilte, BStU, Magdeburg AOP 334/59, Bd. 1, 37.

115. Abteilung II to Abt. Information im Hause, Informationsbericht über die Aussprache mit dem Kriegsverurteilten XY, 5 January 1956, BStU, Magdeburg AOP 334/59, Bd. 1, 41; for examples of positive statements, see Vermerk betr. zurückgekehrte Kriegsverbrecher, 1 November 1955, BStU, Dresden AP 1059/74, Bd. 1, 15.

116. bdvp mgb, 22 October 1955, BA-Berlin, D0 1/08/30801.

117. bdvp cbs, 18 December 1955, BA-Berlin, DO 1/08/30801.

118. Ermittlungsbericht, Volkspolizeikreisamt Freital (Abschrift), 27 July 1973, BStU, Dresden AP 1059/74, 30; Oberleutnant Siegert, Abschlußbericht, 4 April 1961, BStU, Potsdam AOP 52/61, Bd. 1, 56.

119. Anfrage, 3 October 1980, BStU, MfS HA/IX/11 Ak 4356/80, Bd. 1. This request for information on a 1955 returnee may have been linked to his application for permission to leave the GDR.

120. Erich Mielke to alle Leiter der Bezirksverwaltungen einschließlich "W" und Groß-Berlin, 16 December 1955, BStU, MfS-AS 2/59, Bd. 1, 490.

121. Bericht "Peter Holten," BStU, Potsdam AIM 129/60, 12–14; Bericht "Peter Holten," Potsdam AOP 52/61, Bd. 1, 15.

122. Abteilung V/5, Operativ Plan, Beobachtungs Vorgang No. 5/56, BStU, Potsdam AOP 52/61, Bd. 1, 13–14.

123. Ministerium für Staatssicherheit, Erich Mielke, to alle Leiter der Bezirks-verwaltungen einschließlich "W" und Groß-Berlin, 16 December 1955, BStU, Potsdam MfS-AS 2/59, Bd. 1, 491; Aktenvermerk, 3.7.1953, betr. Rückkehr von Personen aus der UdSSR, die wegen Kriegsverbrechen verurteilt wurden, BA-Ber-lin, DO 1/11/962, 84. These reports are to be found in BA-Berlin, DO 1/08/30801.

124. This bias often manifested itself in strict correlations between political attitudes and "class positions" as either "bourgeois" or "proletarian"; BStU, MfS AS 6/54, 189. There is evidence that East German security officials tried to arrive at a fairly accurate portrayal of popular opinion. They recorded a wide variety of different opinions, and they often provided very detailed descriptions of specific local situations; on the relative accuracy of opinion reports during the 1950s, see also Fulbrook, "Methodologische Überlegungen," 275–81.

125. Fernschreiben, October 1953, BStU, MfS AS 6/54, Bd. 35, 180. For simi-lar voices, see Stimmung der übrigen Bevölkerung, BStU, MfS, AS 6/54, Bd. 35, 194.

126. See Fernschreiben vmin to hvdvp, 22 October 1955, BA-Berlin, DO 1/08/ 30801; BStU, MfS AS 6/54, Bd. 34, 113.

127. Fernschreiben, 5 October 1953, BStU, MfS AS 6/54, Bd. 35, 204.

128. Fernschreiben, Bezirksverwaltung Rostock, 3 October 1953, BStU, MfS AS 6/54, Bd. 35, 207.

129. Fernschreiben, BtSU, MfS AS 6/54, Bd. 13, 113.

130. BStU, MfS AS 6/54, Bd. 35, 210.

131. Fernschreiben bdvp, Halle, 23 October 1955, BA-Berlin, DO 1/08/30801.

132. Quotation from bdvp, Halle, 5 November 1955; see also bdvp, Potsdam, 24 October 1955, BA-Berlin, DO 1/08/30801.

133. Fernschreiben an hdv, op stab, 28 October 1955; a similar incident of working-class solidarity is reported in Auszug aus dem Lagebericht der BDVP, FFO No. 885, 16 December 1955, all BA-Berlin, DO 1/08/30801.

134. bvdp Halle and hvdp op stab, 25 October 1955; Fernschreiben, bdvp cottbus, 22 October 1955; bdvp Potsdam, 22 October 1955, BA-Berlin, DO 1/ 08/30801.

135. bdvp Leipzig, 16 October 1955; bdvp Halle to hdvp op stab, bitterfeld, 25 October 1955, BA-Berlin, DO 1/08/30801.

136. vpk, riesa, 24 October 1955; ssd bvp hle to hdvp, opstab, "Bitterfeld," 25 October 1955, BA-Berlin, DO 1/08/30801.

137. Bvdp, kms, 24 October 1955, BA-Berlin, DO 1/08/30801.

138. Bdvp mgdb to hdvp, 26 October 1955, BA-Berlin, DO 1/08/30801.

139. Bdvp, rostock, 21 October 1955; bdvp Halle, no date, BA-Berlin, DO 1/ 08/30801.

140. Bericht über die Heimkehr amnestierter ehemaliger deutscher Kriegsge-fangener aus der Sowjetunion, ADW, ZBB 203.

141. EKD, Berliner Stelle, to Herrn Propst Grüber, 9 December 1956, EZA, 104/610.

142. Fulbrook, *Anatomy of a Dictatorship*, 100.

143. This dissent may have presented no more than the "tip of the iceberg"; see Kershaw, *Popular Opinion*, 6.

144. Fernschreiben bdvp mgd, 22 October 1955, 24 October 1955, BA-Berlin, DO 1/08/30801; for similarly critical quotations from Magdeburg, see bdvp, mgd, 11 October 1955; bdvp mgd to hdvp, 26 October 1955, all in BA-Berlin, DO 1/08/30801; Jordan died in West Germany in 1984.

145. bdvp, mgdb, 22 October 1955, BA-Berlin, DO 1/08/30801.

146. bdvp halle, 10 October 1955, BA, DO1/08/30801; BStU, MfS-AS 6/54, Bd. 35, 113.

147. vdp Cottbus to HDVP, 22 October 1955; BA-Berlin, DO 1/08/30801.

148. vdp Halle to HDVP, 5 November 1955; BA-Berlin, DO 1/08/30801.

149. On "hot" and "cold" memory, see Assmann, *Kultur der Erinnerung*, 68–70.

Conclusion

1. Naumann, "Die Frage nach dem Ende."

2. Schild and Sywottek, *Modernisierung im Wiederaufbau*: Poiger, *Jazz, Rock, and Rebels*; Herbert, *Wandlungsprozesse in Westdeutschland*.

3. Marcuse, *Legacies of Dachau*; Poiger, *Jazz, Rock, and Rebels*.

4. On the significance of national reconstruction for critical confrontations with the past, see Koshar, *Germany's Transient Past*, 242–43.

5. Jarausch, *Die Umkehr*.

6. Ruff, *They Wayward Flock*.

7. On law, see Requate, "Vergangenheitspolitik in der Debatte um eine Reform."

8. von Hodenberg, "Die Journalisten und der Aufbruch."

9. See Herzog, *Sex after Fascism* and Moeller, *War Stories*, 171–98.

10. Fulbrook, *German National Identity after the Holocaust*.

11. On this homogeneity, see Lagrou "The Nationalization of Victimhood" and *Legacy of Nazi Occupation*.

12. Ulrich and Ziemann, *Krieg im Frieden*.

13. Braun, "Das Streben nach Sicherheit"; Schild, *Ankunft im Westen*, 87–105; Jarausch and Geyer, *Shattered Past*, 269–314.

14. On these costs, see Manig, *Politik der Ehre*; Ahonen, *After the Expulsion*; Moeller, *War Stories*.

15. See also Behrenbeck, "Between Pain and Silence."

16. One might even argue that narratives of victimization actually entailed an epistemological potential that could have served as a starting point for a more comprehensive confrontation with the past. A true acceptance of German losses instead of a defensive self-victimization might have cured the peculiar lack of empathy that characterized postwar German society and thus led to a recognition of the suffering and losses of others. This argument goes back to Mitscherlich and Mitscherlich, *Die Unfähigkeit zu trauern*; see also Domansky and Jong, *Der lange Schatten des Kriegs*, 9–30.

17. On this concept of "working through," see LaCapra, *History and Memory*.

18. Turner, "Outline of a Theory of Citizenship."

19. Lagrou, *Legacy of Nazi Occupation*, 251–61.

20. Weiner, *Making Sense of War*, 191–235.

21. See Segev, *The Seventh Million*; Novick, *Holocaust in American Life*; Greenberg, "Orthodox Jewish Thought after the Genocide."

22. In this respect, see Seebald, *On the Natural History of Destruction* may have had a point; see also the contributions in Kettenacker, *Ein Volk von Opfern?*

23. On such local memories see Lüdtke, "Histories of Mourning"; Farmer, *Martyred Village*.

24. Förster and Beck, "Post-traumatic Stress Disorder and World War II"; Merridale, *Night of Stone*, 334.

25. It is important to note, however, that the author's reliance on oral-history interviews might have influenced these findings. Oral-history interviews are not a good source through which to identify trauma since they are by definition the product of narrative integration.

26. This is also true for memories of the war in the Pacific; see Fujitani, White, and Yoneyama, introduction to *Perilous Memories*.

27. On these developments, see Maier, *The Unmasterable Past*; and Bosworth, *Explaining Auschwitz and Hiroshima*.

28. Enzensberger, "Europe in Ruins," 99.

Bibliography

UNPUBLISHED SOURCES

Archiv der Bayer-AG, Leverkusen
Sozialabteilung, Wohlfahrtsangelegenheiten 1945–51
Sekretariat Haberland

Archiv für Christlich-Demokratische Politik, St. Augustin (ACDP)

1–369	NL Hermann Ehlers
VII–005	CDU Bundespartei

Archiv des Diakonischen Werkes, Berlin (ADW)

CA/O	Central-Ausschuß (Ost)
CA/W	Central Ausschuß (West)
HGSt	Hauptgeschäftsstelle
HBB	Hauptbüro Berlin
HBBr	Hauptbüro Brandenburg
ZB	Zentralbüro des Hilfswerks

Archiv des Deutschen Caritas Verbandes, Freiburg (ADCV)

111.055	Protokolle des Zentralrates der DCV
372.0	Kriegsgefangenenhilfe
370.17	Kirchliche Kriegshilfestelle, Abt. Schriftum
372.2	Heimkehrerbetreuung
372.20	Heimkehrerlager Friedland
511	Bischöfe

Archiv der Evangelischen Akademie Bad Boll
Bestand Tagungen (EA/BB)

Archiv der Rheinischen Landeskliniken, Bonn (ARLK)

Patientenakten, Hirnverletzteninstitut

Archiv des Verbandes der Heimkehrer, Bonn–Bad Godesberg (VdH-Archive)

Kriegsgefangenenfragen
Kulturarbeit
Kriegsgefangenen-Entschädigungsgesetz
Evangelisches Hilfswerk, Stille Hilfe, Plangemeinschaft Ostsibirien
Kameradenmißhandlungen
Kriegsgefangenengedenktage/wochen
Generalamnestie, Heimkehrer, Inlandgefangene
BV Oberplatz-Niederbayern

Archiv der Volkssolidarität, Berlin (AdVS)

VS/I/A1   Kriegsgefangenen-und Heimkehrerbetreuung
VS/1/B1   Zuammenarbeit mit Einrichtungen der Kirche

Archiv der Sozialen Demokratie, Friedrich Ebert Stiftung, Bonn (ASD)

O43   Zeitungsausschnitsssammlung, "Heimkehrer und
           Heimkehrerfürsorge"
O44   Zeitungsausschnitsssammlung, "Kriegsgefangene"
NL   Fritz Erler

Bayrisches Hauptstaatsarchiv, Munich (BHStA)

Stk   Bestand Staatskanzlei
MSO   Bestand Sonderministerium (Entnazifizierungsministerium)
OMGB   Bestand Office of Military Government for Bavaria

Brandenburgisches Landeshauptarchiv, Potsdam (BLHA)

Rep. 203   Ministerium des Inneren
Rep. 206   Wirtschaftsministerium
Rep. 211   Ministerium für Gesundheitswesen
Rep. 250   Bestand Landratsämter
Rep. 256   Lager Gronenfelde
Rep. 332   Landesvorstand SED Brandenburg
Rep. 731   SED Kreisleitungen

Bundesarchiv, Berlin (BA-Berlin)

R 55   Reichsministerium für Volksaufklärung und Propaganda
R 58   Reichssicherheithauptamt
NS 6   NSDAP Parteikanzlei
DO 1   Ministerium des Inneren
DO 2   Zentralverwaltung für deutsche Umsiedler
DP 1   Ministerium der Justiz
DQ 1   Ministerium für Gesundheitswesen
DQ 2   Ministerium für Arbeit und Berufsausbildung

Bundesarchiv, Koblenz (BA-K)

B 150   Bundesministeriuum für Vertriebene
B 149   Bundesministerium für Arbeit und Sozialordnung
B 106   Bundesministerium des Inneren

Bundesarchiv-Militärarchiv, Freiburg (BA-M)

RH 2   Chef des Truppenamtes/Generalstabes des Heeres
RH 15   Oberkommando des Heeres—Allgemeines Heeresamt
RW 4   Wehrmachtsführungsstab
RW 48   Wehrmachtsauskunftsstelle für Kriegsverluste und
            Kriegsgefangene

Msg 194   Evangelisches Hilfswerk für Kriegsgefangenen und Internierte
B 205   Akten der wissenschaftlichen Kommission zur
            Kriegsgefangenengeschichte
BW 27   Personalgutachterausschuss

Bundesarchiv-Stiftung Parteien und Massenorganisationen
  der ehemaligen DDR, Berlin (BA-SAPMO)

NY 4036   NL Pieck
NY 4065   NL Erich Weinert
NY 4090   NL Grotewohl
NY 4182   NL Ulbricht
DY 3   Demokratischer Block, Verbindungsbüro
DY 16   Nationaldemokratische Partei Deutschlands (NDPD)
DY 30/IV2/2   SED ZK: Beschlüsse des Politbüros
DY 30/JIV2/3   SED-ZK: Beschlüsse des Kleinen Sekretariats
DY 30/JIV2/202   SED-ZK: Büro Ulbricht
DY 30/IV2/2.022   SED-ZK: Sekretariat Merker
DY 30/IV2/2.027   SED-ZK: Sekretariat Lehmann
DY 30/IV2/4   SED ZK: Zentrale Parteikontrollkommission (ZPKK)
DY 30/IV2/11   SED-ZK: Kaderfragen
DY 30/IV2/13   SED-ZK: Abteilung Staat und Recht
DY 30/IV2/14   SED-ZK: Kirchenfragen
DY 30/IV2/17   SED-ZK: Abteilung Frauen
DY 32   Gesellschaft für Deutsch-Sowjetische Freundschaft
DY 34   Freier Demokratische Gewerkschaftsbund (FDGB)
                   Bundesvorstand
DY 55/V278   Vereinigung der Verfolgten des Naziregimes (VVN)

Bundesbeauftragte für die Unterlagen des Staatssicherheitsdienstes
  der ehemaligen Deutschen Demokratischen Republik, Berlin (BStU)

MfS AS 689/66
MfS AS 440/67
MfS AS 6/54
MfS HA/IX/11
Magdeburg AOP 334 A
Dresden AP 1059
Potsdam AIM
Potsdam AU 43
Potsdam AOP 52/61
Potsdam MfS-AS 2/59

Bundespresse und -informationsamt, Bonn (PIB)

Microfilms, Reels 1566, 1567, 2190, 2191

Deutscher Bundestag—Parlamentsarchiv (PA/DB)

Ausschuss für Kriegsopfer und Kriegsgefangenenfragen—Kurzprotokolle

Deutsches Historisches Museum, Berlin (DHM)

Rep. XVIII/K1/F11/M19a (1)–(25), Konvolut Heimkehrerverband,
Friedlandbriefe.

Diözesanarchiv des Erzbistum Berlin, Berlin (DA-EB)

I/9–22   Kriegsgefangenenseelsorge

Evangelisches Zentralarchiv, Berlin (EZA)

Bestand 2   Kirchenkanzlei der Evangelischen Kirche in Deutschland
Bestand 4   Kirchenkanzlei der Evangelischen Kirche in Deutschland—
                 Berliner Stelle
Bestand 7   Evangelischer Oberkirchenrat
Bestand 104   Kirchenkanzlei der EKD für die Gliedkirchen in der DDR

Hessisches Hauptstaatsarchiv, Wiesbaden (HHStA)

Abteilung 360   Orts- und Gemeindebestände
Abteilung 463   Staatsanwaltschaft Limburg
Abteilung 461   Staatsanwaltschaft Frankfurt
Abteilung 502   Hessische Staatskanzlei
Abteilung 503   Hessisches Innenministerium
Abteilung 504   Hessisches Kulturministerium
Abteilung 508   Hessisches Sozialministerium
Abteilung 649   Office of Military Government for Hesse
Abteilung 1213   Nachlaß Anna Beyer

Historisches Archiv des Erzbistums Köln, Köln (HEK)

CR II, 25, 18   Bestand Cabinetts-Registratur II, Kriegsakten, 2. Weltkrieg
CR II, 25, 19   Bestand Cabinetts-Registratur II, Kriegsgefangenenseelsorge

*Institut für Geschichte und Biographie an der Fern-Universität
Hagen, Lüdenscheid (IfGB)*

Interviewsammlung

Institut für Sozialforschung, Technische Universität Berlin

Sibylle Meyer/Eva Schulze Interviewsammlung

Institut für Sozialforschung, Frankfurt am Main (ISF)

Materialien zur Heimkehrerstudie, Grupeninterviews H1–H40

Landesarchiv, Berlin (LAB)

Rep. 4   Inneres
Rep. 8   Soziales
Rep. 061   Personenfonds, Erika Lorazg
Rep. 118   Gesundheits- und Sozialwesen (Ost)
SED-LV   SED-Landesvorstand Berlin
OMGBS   Office of U.S. Military Government, Berlin Sector

Landeshauptarchiv, Koblenz (LAK)

930 Ministerium für Soziales, Gesundheit und Umwelt Rheinland-Pfalz

Niedersächsisches Hauptstaatsarchiv, Hannover (NHStA)

Nds. 386 Grenzdurchgangslager Friedland

Nordrhein-Westfälisches Hauptstaatsarchiv, Düsseldorf (NRWHStA)

RW 23	NS-Stellen
RW 58	Gestapoakten
NW 42	Arbeits- und Sozialministerium/Volks- und Jugendwohlfahrt
NW 47	Arbeits- und Sozialministerium/Kriegsopferversorgung
NW 48	Arbeits- und Sozialministerium/ Haushalt und Versorgungsangelegenheiten, Ostflüchtlinge,
NW 49	Arbeits- und Sozialministerium, Flüchtlingdurchgangslager
NW 110	Innenministerium, Personalangelegenheiten
NW 117	Arbeits- und Sozialministerium, Kriegsgefangenen- und Heimkehrerbetreuung
LANW	Landesarbeitsamt Nordrhein-Westfalen

Staatsanwaltschaft Kleve
Staatsanwaltschaft Krefeld
Staatsanwaltschaft Mönchengladbach
Staatsanwaltschaft Aachen
Staatsanwaltschaft Eberfelde
Staatsanwaltschaft Bonn
Staatswanwaltschaft Essen
Staatsanwaltschaft Köln
Staatsanwaltschaft Wuppertal

Politisches Archiv des Auswärtigen Amtes, Bonn (PAA)

B 10	Politische Abteilung des Auswärtigen Amtes
B 2	Büro Staatssekretär

Public Record Office, Kew (PRO)

FO 371	Political Departments. General Correspondence since 1906
FO 939	Control Office: Prisoners of War

Sächsisches Hauptstaatsarchiv, Dresden (SHStA)

LRS, MdI	Landesregierung Sachsen, Ministerium des Inneren, 1945–52
LRS, MAuS	Landesregierung Sachsen, Ministerium für Arbeit und Sozialfürsorge, 1945–52
SED, LV	SED Landesleitung Sachsen, 1946–52
IV/4/01	SED Kreisleitung Bautzen

Stadtarchiv, Frankfurt an der Oder

BA II   Rat der Stadt FfO, 1945–52, Oberbürgermeister,
             Zeitungsausschnittsammlung, Heimkehrerlager
             Gronenfelde

Stadtarchiv Köln

Acc. 2   Oberbürgermeister
Acc. 4   Oberstadtdirektor

Stadtarchiv Uelzen

Fach 10/Nr. 11   Fischerhof

Stadtarchiv Ulm

422   Kriegsfolgenhilfe

Württembergisches Hauptstaatsarchiv, Stuttgart (BWHStA)

EA 1   Staatsministerium
EA 2   Innenministerium

Oral History Interviews (OH)

The names of the interviewed persons have been changed. Tapes and notes are in
  my possession.

OH 1	"Stefan Kleinhans"	Berlin, 27 October 1996
OH 2	"Thomas Gielemann"	Berlin, 4 November 1996
OH 3/1	"Hans Martin"	Berlin, 8 November 1996
OH3/2	"Hans Martin"	7 December 1996
OH 4	"Bernd Weissman"	Berlin, 18 November 1996
OH 5	"Annemarie Rosen"	Berlin, 28 November 1996
OH 6	"Werner Johannsen"	Berlin, 20 January 1997
OH 7	"Waltraud Heimann"	Berlin, 27 February 1997
OH 8	"Gerold Hehrmann"	Berlin, 28 March 1997
OH 9	Dr. Heinz-Harro Rauschelbach	Bonn, 16 and 22 April 1998
OH10	"Erwin Rudolf"	Mainz, 24 June 1998
OH 11	"Werner Uhde"	Mainz, 24 June 1998

Magazines and Newspapers

Aachener Volkszeitung
Abendpost
Allgemeine Wochenzeitung der Juden in Deutschland
Die Arbeit
Arbeit und Sozialfürsorge
Bonner Hefte für Wirtschaft, Kultur and Politik
Berliner Morgenpost

Bremer Nachrichten
Caritas
Constanze
Christ und Welt
Darmstädter Echo
Deutsche Zeitung
Evangelisches Kirchenblatt für Rheinhessen
Der Heimkehrer (hrsg. Im Auftr. d. Deutschen Nationalkomitees des Weltbundes des CVJM (YMCA)
Der Heimkehrer (hrsg. vom Verband der Heimkehrer)
Hessische Nachrichten
Flensburger Tagblatt
Frankfurter Allgemeine Zeitung
Frankfurter Rundschan
Die Frau von Heute
Freie Presse Bielefeld
Die Freiheit
Gießener Anzeiger
Hamburger Abendblatt
Hambuger Anzeiger
Hannoversche Allgemeine
Hannoversche Presse
Kirchliches Jahrbuch für die Evangelische Kirche in Deutschland
Kölnsche Rundschau
Krefelder Stadtpost
Der Mittag
Münchner Merkur
Neues Beginnen, Zeitschrift der Arbeiterwohlfahrt
Neue Berliner Illustrierte
Neues Deutschland
Neues Frauenleben
Neue Juristische Wochenschrift
Die Neue Zeitung
Die Neue Heimat
The New York Times
Quick
Rheinisch-Westfälische Nachrichten
Rheinische Post
Die Rundschau der Stuttgarter Heimkehrer, Kriegsgefangenen und Vermisstenangehörigen
SZB Archiv
Schwäbische Donauzeitung
Sonntagsblatt der evangelisch-reformierten Gemeinden
Der Sozialdemokrat
Der Spiegel
Der Stern
Stuttgarter Nachrichten

Süddeutsche Zeitung
Der Tagesspiegel
Volksblatt
Vorwärts
Die Welt
Welt der Arbeit
Westfälische Nachrichten
Wiesbadener Kurier
Wirtschaft und Statistik
Die Zeit

PUBLISHED SOURCES

Abelshauser, Werner. *Die langen 50er Jahre. Wirtschaft und Gesellschaft in der Bundesrepublik Deutschland, 1949–1966.* Düsseldorf: Schwan, 1987.

Absolon, Rudolf. *Die Wehrmacht im Dritten Reich.* Vol. 6, *19. Dezember 1941 bis 9. Mai 1945.* Boppard am Rhein: Boldt, 1995.

Ackermann, Volker. "Das Schweigen der Flüchtlingskinder—Psychische Folgen von Krieg, Flucht und Vertreibung bei den Deutschen." *Geschichte und Gesellschaft* 30 (2004): 434–64.

Ahonen, Pertti. *After the Expulsion: West Germany and Eastern Europe, 1945–1990.* Oxford: Oxford University Press, 2003.

Allemann, Fritz Rene. *Bonn ist nicht Weimar.* Cologne: Kiepenheuer and Witsch, 1957.

Allen, Judith. "Men Interminably in Crisis? Historians on Masculinity, Sexual Boundaries, and Mannhood." *Radical History Review* 82 (2002): 191–207.

Aly, Götz. *Macht-Geist-Wahn. Kontinuitäten deutschen Denkens.* Berlin: Aragon, 1997.

Ampferl, Monika. "Verschollen im Zweiten Weltkrieg. Die Entwicklung des Suchdienstes des Deutschen Roten Kreuzes." *Zeitschrift für Geschichstwissenschaft* 50 (2002): 527–42.

Anhalt, Irene. "Farewell to My Father." In *The Collective Silence: German Identity and the Legacy of Shame,* ed. Barbara and Christoph J. Schmidt Heimansberg, 31–48. San Francisco: Jossey-Bass, 1993.

Applegate, Celia. *A Nation of Provincials: The German Idea of Heimat.* Berkeley and Los Angeles: University of California Press, 1990.

Arendt, Hannah. "The Aftermath of Nazi Rule." *Commentary* 10 (1950): 347–53.

Assmann, Aleida, and Ute Frevert. *Geschichtsvergessenheit-Geschichtsversessenheit: Vom Umgang mit deutschen Vergangenheiten.* Stuttgart: Deutsche Verlags-Anstalt, 1999.

Assmann, Jan. *Das kulturelle Gedächtnis: Schrift, Erinnerung und politische Identität in frühen Hochkulturen.* Munich: C. H. Beck, 1999.

Bader, Helmut. "Ehekrisen unserer Heimkehrer." *Neubau* 5 (1950): 51–54.

Badstübner, Evemarie. " 'Die Heimat grüsst Euch.' Heimkehrer in der sowjetisch besetzten Zone Deutschlands—ein kulturgeschichtliches Thema?" *Mitteilungen aus der kulturwissenschaftlichen Forschung* 19 (1996): 296–313.

Badstübner, Rolf, and Wilhelm Loth, eds. *Wilhem Pieck-Aufzeichnungen zur Deutschlandpolitik 1945–1953.* Berlin: Akademie, 1994.

Bajohr, Frank. "Hamburg—der Zerfall der Volksgemeinschaft." In *Kriegsende in Europa. Vom Beginn des deutschen Machtzerfalls bis zur Stabilisierung der Nachkriegsordnung, 1944–1948,* ed. Ulrich Herbert and Axel Schildt, 318–36. Essen: Klartext, 1988.

Bald, Detlef. *Die Weisse Rose. Von der Front in den Widerstand.* Berlin: Aufbau, 2003.

Bald, Detlef, Reinhard Brühl, and Andreas Prüfert, eds. *Nationale Volksarmee— Armee für den Frieden. Beiträge zu Selbstverständnis und Geschichte des deutschen Militärs, 1945–1990.* Baden-Baden: Nomos, 1995.

Balderman, Manfred. "Die psychischen Grundlagen der Heimkehrerdystrophien und ihre Behandlung." *Münchner Medizinische Wochenschrift* 93 (1951): 2817–90.

———. "Wesen und Beurteilung der Heimkehrerdystrophien." *Münchner Medizinische Wochenschrift* 93 (1951): 61–67.

Bankier, David. *The Germans and the Final Solution: Public Opinion under Nazism.* Oxford: Blackwell, 1992.

Bansi, H. W. "Die 'interne Klinik' der Heimkehrer." In *Die Sexualität des Heimkehrers. Vorträge gehalten auf dem 4. Kongress der Deutschen Gesellschaft für Sexualforschung,* ed. Hans Bürger-Prinz and Hans Giese, 9–18. Stuttgart: Ferdinand Enke, 1957.

———. "Die Ödemkrankheit." *Medizinische Klinik* 41, no. 14 (1946): 273–82.

———. "Spätschäden nach Dystrophie, 3. Teil." *Materia Medica Nordmark* 8, no. 9 (1956): 319–24.

Barck, Simone. *Antifa-Geschichte(n). Eine literarische Spurensuche in der DDR der 1950er und 1960er Jahre.* Cologne: Böhlau, 2003.

Barnouw, Dagmar. *Ansichten von Deutschland 1945: Krieg und Gewalt in der zeitgenössischen Photographie.* Frankfurt am Main: Stromfeld, 1997.

Bartov, Omer. "Defining Enemies, Making Victims." *American Historical Review* 103 (1998): 771–816.

———. *The Eastern Front, 1941–1945: German Troops and the Barbarisation of Warfare.* London: Macmillan, 1985.

———. *Germany's War and the Holocaust: Disputed Histories.* Ithaca: Cornell University Press, 2003.

———. *Hitler's Army: Soldiers, Nazis, and War in the Third Reich.* New York: Oxford University Press, 1990.

———. *Mirrors of Destruction: War, Genocide, and Modern Identity.* Oxford: Oxford University Press, 2002.

———. *Murder in Our Midst: The Holocaust, Industrial Killing, and Representation.* New York: Oxford University Press, 1996.

Bartov, Omer, Atina Grossmann, and Mary Nolan, eds. *Crimes of War: Guilt and Denial in the Twentieth Century.* New York: New Press, 2002.

Bartov, Omer, and Phyllis Mack, eds. *In God's Name: Genocide and Religion in the Twentieth Century*. New York: Berghahn, 2001.

Bauer, Theresia. "Krise und Wandel der Blockpolitik und Parteineugründungen 1948." In *Das letzte Jahr der SBZ. Politische Weichenstellungen und Kontinuitäten im Prozess der Gründung der DDR*, ed. Dierk Hoffman and Hermann Wentker, 65–83. Munich: Oldenbourg, 2000.

Bauernkämper, Arnd, Martin Sabrow, and Bernd Stöver, eds. *Doppelte Zeitgeschichte. Deutsch-deutsche Beziehungen*. Bonn: Dietz, 1998.

Bauman, Zygmunt. *Modernity and the Holocaust*. Ithaca: Cornell University Press, 1989.

Baumert, Gerhart. *Jugend in der Nachkriegszeit. Lebensverhältnisse und Reaktionsweisen*. Darmstadt: Ernst Roether, 1952.

Beck, Birgit. "Rape: The Military Trials of Sexual Crimes Committed by Soldiers in the Wehrmacht, 1939–1944." In *Home/Front: The Military, War, and Gender in Twentieth-Century Germany*, ed. Karen Hagemann and Stefanie Schüler-Springorum, 255–73. Oxford: Berg, 2002.

Behrenbeck, Sabine. "Between Pain and Silence: Remembering the Victims of Violence in Germany after 1949." In *Life after Death: Approaches to a Social and Cultural History of Europe during the 1940s and 1950s*, ed. Richard Bessel and Dirk Schumann, 37–64. New York: Cambridge University Press, 2003.

———. *Der Kult um die toten Helden. Nationalsozialistische Mythen, Riten und Symbole*. Viewrow: SH Verlag, 1996.

———. "The Transformation of Sacrifice: German Identity between Heroic Narrative and Economic Success." In *Pain and Prosperity: Reconsidering Twentieth-Century German History*, ed. Paul Betts and Greg Eghigian, 110–36. Stanford: Stanford University Press, 2003.

Beil, Christine. "Erfahrungsorte des Krieges. Kriegsgefangenenausstellungen in der Adenauerzeit." In *Erfahrungsgeschichtliche Perspektiven von der Französischen Revolution bis zum Zweiten Weltkrieg*, ed. Nicolaus Buschmann and Horst Carl, 239–60. Paderborn: Schönigh, 2001.

Ben-Ghiat, Ruth. "Unmaking the Fascist Man: Masculinity, Film, and the Transition from Dictatorship." *Journal of Modern Italian Studies* 10 (fall 2005), in press.

Benjamin, Hilde. *Zur Geschichte der Rechtspflege in der Deutschen Demokratischen Republik*. Berlin: Staatsverlag der DDR, 1976.

Benser, Günter. "Zur Auflösung des Nationalkomitees 'Freies Deutschland' 1945." *Zeitschrift für Geschtswissenschaft* 38 (1990): 907–14.

Bentley, James. *Martin Niemöller, 1892–1984*. New York: Free Press, 1984.

Benz, Ute. " 'Maikäfer Flieg! Dein Vater ist im Krieg.' " In *Heimkehr 1948. Geschichte und Schicksal deutscher Kriegsgefangener*, ed. Annette Kaminsky, 176–91. Munich: C. H. Beck, 1998.

Benz, Wolfgang, ed. *Dimension des Völkermords. Die Zahl der jüdischen Opfer des Nationalsozialismus*. Munich: Oldenbourg, 1991.

Benz, Wolfgang, and Angelika Schardt, eds. *Deutsche Kriegsgefangene im Zweiten Weltkrieg. Erinnerungen*. Frankfurt am Main: Fischer, 1995.

Bergen, Doris. *Twisted Cross: The German Christian Movement in the Third Reich*. Chapel Hill: University of North Carolina Press, 1996.

———. *War and Genocide: A Concise History of the Holocaust.* Oxford: Rowman and Littlefield, 2003.

Berger, Peter, and Thomas Luckmann. *Die gesellschaftliche Konstruktion der Wirklichkeit.* Frankfurt am Main: Fischer, 1997.

Berghahn, Volker. "NSDAP und 'geistige Führung' der Wehrmacht 1939–45." *Vierteljahreshefte für Zeitgeschichte* 17 (1969): 7–71.

———. "Recasting Bourgeois Germany." In *The Miracle Years,* ed. Hanna Schissler, 326–40. Princeton: Princeton University Press, 2001.

Berning, Heinrich. *Die Dystrophie.* Stuttgart: G. Thieme, 1949.

Besier, Gerhard. *Der SED-Staat und die Kirche.* Munich: Bertelsmann, 1993.

Bessel, Richard. *Germany after the First World War.* Oxford: Clarendon Press, 1993.

———. "Grenzen des Polizeistaates. Polizei und Gesellschaft in der SBZ und frühen DDR, 1945–1953." In *Die Grenzen der Diktatur. Staat und Gesellschaft in der DDR,* ed. Richard Bessel and Ralph Jessen, 224–52. Göttingen: Vandenhoek, 1996.

———. "Leben nach dem Tode. Vom Zweiten Weltkrieg zur zweiten Nachkriegszeit." In *Wie Kriege enden. Wege zum Frieden von der Antike bis zur Gegenwart,* ed. Bernd Wegner, 239–58. Paderborn: Ferdinand Schönigh, 2002.

———. "Polizei zwischen Krieg und Sozialismus. Die Anfänge der Volkspolizei nach dem Zweiten Weltkrieg." In *Von der Aufgabe der Freiheit: Politische Verantwortung und bürgerliche Gesellschaft im 19. und 20. Jahrhundert: Festschrift für Hans Mommsen zum 5. November 1999,* ed. Lutz Niethammer, Christian Jansen, and Bernd Weisbrod, 224–52. Berlin: Akadamie, 1995.

Bessel, Richard, and Ralph Jessen. "Einleitung. Die Grenzen der Diktatur." In *Die Grenzen der Diktatur. Staat und Gesellschaft in der DDR,* ed. Richard Bessel and Ralph Jessen, 7–23. Göttingen: Vandenhoek, 1996.

Bessel, Richard, and Dirk Schumann, eds. *Life after Death: Approaches to the Social and Cultural History of Europe during the 1940s and 1950s.* Cambridge: Cambridge University Press, 2003.

Betts, Paul, and Greg Eghigian, eds. *Pain and Prosperity: Reconsidering Twentieth-Century German History.* Stanford: Stanford University Press, 2003.

Biess, Frank. "Between Amnesty and Anti-Communism: The West German Kameradenschinder Trials, 1948–1961." In *Crimes of War: Guilt and Denial in the Twentieth Century,* ed. Omer Bartov, Atina Grossmann, and Mary Nolan, 138–60. New York: New Press, 2002.

———. "Men of Reconstruction—Reconstruction of Men." In *Home/Front: The Military, War, and Gender in Twentieth-Century Germany,* ed. Karen Hagemann and Stefanie Schüler-Springorum, 335–58. Oxford: Berg, 2002.

———. " 'Pioneers of a New Germany.' Returning POWs from the Soviet Union and the Making of East German Citizens, 1945–1950." *Central European History* 32 (1999): 143–80.

———. "The Protracted War: Returning POWs and the Making of East and West German Citizens, 1945–1955." Ph.D. diss., Brown University, 2000.

———. " 'Russenknechte' und 'Westagenten': Kriegsheimkehrer und die (De)legitimierung von Kriegsgefangenschaftserfahrungen in Ost- und Westdeutschland nach 1945." In *Nachkrieg in Deutschland*, ed. Klaus Naumann, 59–89. Hamburg: Hamburger Edition, 2001.

―――. "Survivors of Totalitarianism: Returning POWs and the Reconstruction of Masculine Citizenship in West Germany, 1945–1955." In *The Miracle Years: A Cultural History of West Germany*, ed. Hanna Schissler, 57–82. Princeton: Princeton University Press, 2000.

Birke, Adolf. *Nation ohne Haus. Deutschland 1945–1961*. Berlin: Siedler, 1989.

Bischof, Günter, and Stephen Ambrose, eds. *Facts against Falsehood: Eisenhower and German POWs*. Baton Rouge: Louisiana University Press, 1992.

Bischof, Günter, and Rüdiger Overmans. *Kriegsgefangenschaft im Zweiten Weltkrieg. Eine vergleichende Perspektive*. Ternitz-Pottschach: G. Höller, 1999.

Blaschke, Olaf, ed. *Konfessionen im Konflikt: Deutschland zwischen 1800 und 1970: Ein zweites konfessionelles Zeitalter*. Göttingen: Vandenhoeck und Ruprecht, 2002.

Blessing, Werner K. " 'Deutschland in Not, und wir im Glauben . . .' Kirche und Kirchenvolk in einer katholischen Region 1933–1949." In *Von Stalingrad zur Währungsreform*, ed. Klaus-Dietmar Henke, Martin Broszat, and Hans Woller, 2–111. Munich: Oldenbourg, 1990.

Bloxham, Donald. *Genocide on Trial: War Crimes Trials and the Formation of Holocaust History and Memory*. Oxford: Oxford University Press, 2001.

Boberach, Heinz. "Die Verfolgung von Verbrechen gegen die Menschlichkeit durch deutsche Gerichte in Nordrhein-Westfalen 1946 bis 1949." *Geschichte im Westen* 12 (1997): 7–23.

―――. "Stimmungsumschwung in der deutschen Bevölkerung." In *Stalingrad: Mythos und Wirklichkeit einer Schlacht*, ed. Wolfram Wette and Gerd Überschär, 61–66. Frankfurt am Main: Fischer, 1992.

―――, ed. *Meldungen aus dem Reich 1938–1945: Die Geheimen Lageberichte des Sicherheitsdienstes der SS*. Herrsching: Pawlak, 1984.

Bodamer, Joachim. *Der Mann von Heute. Seine Gestalt und Psychologie*. Stuttgart: Schwab, 1956.

Boddenberg, Werner. "Der Kriegsgefangenenbrief des Generaloberst Heitz." *Philatelie und Postgeschichte* 21, no. 94 (1987): 1–9.

―――. *Die Kriegsgefangenenpost deutscher Soldaten in sowjetischem Gewahrsam und die Post von ihren Angehörigen während des II. Weltkriegs*. Berlin: Selbstverlag, 1985.

Bodemann, T. Michael. "Negativ-Gedächtnis. Deutsche Darstellungen der Schoah in der Nachkriegszeit." In *In den Wogen der Erinnerung. Jüdische Existenz in Deutschland*, 7–21. Frankfurt am Main: dtv, 2002.

Böhme, Kurt. *Die deutschen Kriegsgefangenen in sowjetischer Hand. Eine Bilanz*. Bielefeld: Gieseking, 1966.

―――. *Gesucht wird . . . : Die dramatische Geschichte des Suchdienstes*. Munich: Süddeutscher Verlag, 1965.

―――. "Zum Schicksal der weiblichen Kriegsgefangenen." In *Die deutschen Kriegsgefangenen des Zweiten Weltkrieges. Eine Zusammenfassung*, ed. Erich Maschke, 317–45. Bielefeld: Gieseking, 1974.

Boldorf, Marcel. *Sozialfürsorge in der SBZ/DDR 1945–1953: Ursachen, Ausmass und Bewältigung der Nachkriegsarmut*. Stuttgart: Franz Steiner, 1998.

Boll, Friedhelm. *Auf der Suche nach der Demokratie. Britische und Deutsche Jugendinitiativen nach 1945*. Bonn: J.H.W. Dietz Nachf., 1995.

Böll, Heinrich. "Bekenntnis zur Trümmerliteratur." In *Essayistische Schriften und Reden*, vol. 1, *1952–1963*, 31–35. Cologne: Kiepenhauer and Witsch, 1978.

Bonhoeffer, Karl. "Vergleichende psychopathologische Erfahrungen aus den beiden Weltkriegen." *Der Nervenarzt* 18 (1947): 1–4.

Bonnell, Victoria E., and Lynn Hunt, eds. *Beyond the Cultural Turn: New Directions in the Study of Society and Culture*. Berkeley and Los Angeles: University of California Press, 1999.

Booms, Hans, ed. *Die Kabinettsprotokolle der Bundesregierung*. Boppard: Boldt, 1982–.

Borchard, Michael. *Die Deutschen Kriegsgefangenen in der Sowjetunion. Zur politischen Bedeutung der Kriegsgefangenenfrage, 1949–1955*. Düsseldorf: Droste, 2000.

Borneman, John. *Belonging in the Two Berlins: Kin, State, Nation*. New York: Cambridge University Press, 1992.

Bösch, Frank. *Die Adenauer-CDU. Gründung, Aufstieg und Krise einer Erfolgspartei (1945–1969)*. Munich: DVA, 2001.

Bösch, Frank (unter Mitarbeit von Helge Matthiesen). *Das konservative Milieu. Vereinskultur und lokale Sammlunsgpolitik in ost- und westdeutschen Regionen*. Göttingen: Wallstein, 2002.

Bosworth, R.J.N. *Explaining Auschwitz and Hiroshima: History Writing and the Second World War*. London: Routledge, 1993.

Bourke, Joanna. " 'Going Home.' The Personal Adjustment of British and American Servicemen after the War." In *Life after Death: Approaches to a Cultural and Social History during the 1940s and 1950s*, ed. Richard Bessel and Dirk Schumann, 149–60. Cambridge: Cambridge University Press, 2003.

Boyens, Armin. "Lernen aus der Geschichte. Bischof Dr. Theodor Heckel (1894–1967). Ein deutscher Lebenslauf." *Kirchliche Zeitgeschichte* 8 (1995): 365–79.

Braese, Stephan. "Unmittelbar zum Krieg—Alfred Andersch und Franz Fühmann." In *Nachkrieg in Deutschland*, ed. Klaus Naumann, 472–97. Hamburg: Hamburger Edition, 2001.

Brakelmann, Günter. "Nationalprotestantismus und Nationalsozialismus." In *Von der Aufgabe der Freiheit. Festschrift für Hans Mommsen*, ed. Lutz Niethammer, Bernd Weisbrod, and Christian Jansen, 337–51. Berlin: Akademie, 1995.

Brasche, Hellmut. "Ärztliche Beobachtungen in der Kriegsgefangenschaft unter besonderer Berücksichtigung psychopathologischer Fragen." Ph.D. diss., University of Marburg, 1953.

Braun, Hans. "Das Streben nach Sicherheit in den 50er Jahren. Soziale und politische Erscheinungsweisen." *Archiv für Sozialgeschichte* 18 (1978): 279–306.

Brochhagen, Ulrich. *Nach Nürnberg. Vergangenheitsbewältigung und Westintegration in der Ära Adenauer*. Hamburg: Hamburger Edition, 1994.

Broszat, Martin. " 'Siegerjustiz' oder stafrechtliche 'Selbstreinigung.' Aspekte der Vergangenheitsbewältigung der deutschen Justiz während der Besatzungszeit 1945–1949." *Vierteljahreshefte für Zeitgeschichte* 29 (1981): 477–544.

Broszat, Martin, Klaus Dietmar Henke, and Hans Woller, eds. *Von Stalingrad zur Währungsreform. Zur Sozialgeschichte des Umbruchs in Deutschland*. Munich: Oldenbourg, 1988.

Broszat, Martin, and Hermann Weber, eds. *SBZ-Handbuch: Staatliche Verwaltungen, Parteien, gesellschaftliche Organisationen und ihre Führungskräfte in der Sowjetischen Besatzungszone Deutschlands 1945–1949*. Munich: Oldenbourg, 1990.

Browning, Christopher. *Ordinary Men: Reserve Police Battalion 101 and the Final Solution in Poland*. New York: Harper Perennial, 1993.

Bruckner, Pascal. *Ich leide also bin ich. Die Krankheit der Moderne*. Berlin: Aufbau Verlag, 1996.

Brüggemeier, Franz-Josef. *Zurück auf dem Platz. Deutschland und die Fußball Weltmeisterschaft*. Munich: DVA, 2004.

Bruns, Ingeborg. *Als Vater aus dem Krieg heimkehrte: Töchter erinnern sich*. Frankfurt am Main: Fischer, 1998.

Bücker, Vera. *Die Schulddiskussion im deutschen Katholizismus nach 1945*. Bochum: Studienverlag Dr. N. Brockmeyer, 1989.

Bude, Heinz. *Bilanz der Nachfolge. Die Bundesrepublik und der Nationalsozialismus*. Frankfurt am Main: Suhrkamp, 1992.

Bullinger, Pamela. "The Culture of Survivors: Post-traumatic Stress Disorder and Traumatic Memory." *History and Memory* 10 (1998): 99–132.

Bundesministerium für Arbeit- und Sozialordnung. *Anhaltspunkte für die ärztliche Gutachtertätigkeit im Versorgungswesen*. Bonn: Köllen, 1951, 1954, 1958, and 1965 eds.

———, ed. *Die Dystrophie. Spätfolgen und Dauerschäden*. Stuttgart: Georg Thieme Verlag, 1958.

Bürger-Prinz, Hans. "Psychopathologie der Sexualität." In *Die Sexualität des Menschen. Handbuch der medizinischen Sexualforschung*, ed. Hans Giese, 539–47. Stuttgart: Ferdinand Enke Verlag, 1955.

Bürger-Prinz, Hans, and Hans Giese, eds. *Die Sexualität des Heimkehrers. Vorträge gehalten auf dem 4. Kongress der Deutschen Gesellschaft für Sexualforschung*. Stuttgart: Ferdinand Enke, 1957.

Buschmann, Nicolaus, and Horst Carl, eds. *Erfahrungsgeschichtliche Perspektiven von der Französischen Revolution bis zum Zweiten Weltkrieg*. Paderborn: Schönigh, 2001.

Canning, Kathleen. "Feminist History after the Linguistic Turn: Historicizing Discourse and Experience." *Signs* 19 (1994): 368–404.

Canning, Kathleen, and Sonya Rose. "Gender, Citizenship, and Subjectivity: Some Historical and Theoretical Considerations." *Gender and History* 13 (2001): 427–43.

Cernea, Radu. *Sexualbiologische Studien. Betrachtungen eines Arztes über das Wesen und die Bedeutung der Sexualität*. Munich: Akademischer Verlag Ausländischer Wissenschaftler, 1948.

Chaumont, Jean Michael. *La concurrence des victimes. Génocide, Identité, Reconnaissance*. Paris: Edition La Decouverte & Syros, 1997.

Ciesla, Burghard. "Auf Schienenwegen nach Hause." In *Heimkehr 1948. Geschichte und Schicksal deutscher Kriegsgefangener*, ed. Annette Kaminsky, 55–69. Munich: C. H. Beck, 1998.

Cocks, Geoffrey. *Psychotherapy in the Third Reich: The Göring Institute*. New York: Oxford University Press, 1985.

Cohen, Deborah. *The War Come Home: Disabled Veterans in Britain and Germany, 1914–1939*. Berkeley and Los Angeles: University of California Press, 2001.

Confino, Alon. "Collective Memory and Cultural History." *American Historical Review* 102 (1997): 1386–1403.

———. *The Nation as a Local Metaphor: Württemberg, Imperial Germany, and National Memory*. Chapel Hill: University of North Carolina Press, 1997.

———. "Telling about Germany: Narratives of Memory and Culture." *Journal of Modern History* 76 (2004): 389–416.

———. " 'This Lovely Country You Will Never Forget.' Kriegserinnerungen und Heimatkonzepte in der westdeutschen Nachkriegszeit." In *Das Erbe der Provinz. Heimatkultur und Geschichtspolitik nach 1945*, ed. Habbo Knoch, 235–51. Göttingen: Wallstein, 2001.

Confino, Alon, and Peter Fritzsche, eds. *The Work of Memory: New Directions in the Study of German Culture and Society*. Urbana: University of Illinois Press, 2002.

Connell, R. W. *Masculinities*. Berkeley and Los Angeles: University of California Press, 1995.

Conway, Martin. "Justice in Postwar Belgium: Popular Passions and Political Realities." In *The Politics of Retribution in Europe: World War II and Its Aftermath*, ed. István Deák, Jan T. Gross, and Tony Judt, 133–56. Princeton: Princeton University Press, 2000.

———. "The Rise and Fall of Western Europe's Democratic Age, 1945–1973." *Contemporary European History* 13 (2004): 67–88.

Conzemius, Victor, Martin Greschat, and Hermann Kocher, eds. *Die Zeit nach 1945 als Thema kirchlicher Zeitgeschichte*. Göttingen: Vandenhoek, 1988.

Crane, Susan. "Writing the Individual Back into Collective Memory." *American Historical Review* 102 (1997): 1372–85.

Creuzberger, Stefan. *Die sowjetische Besatzungsmacht und das politische System der SBZ*. Weimar: Böhlau, 1996.

Dahlke, Birgit. " 'Frau Komm.' Vergewaltigung, Zur Geschichte eines Diskurses." In *LiteraturGesellschaft DDR. Kanonkämpfe und ihre Geschichten*, ed. Martina Langermann, Birgt Dahlke, and Thomas Taterka, 275–311. Stuttgart: Metzler, 2000.

Daniel, Ute. "Erfahrung—(k)ein Thema der Geschichtstheorie." *L'Homme* 11 (2000): 120–23.

Danyel, Jürgen. "Die geteilte Vergangenheit: Gesellschaftliche Ausgangslagen und politische Dispositionen für den Umgang mit Nationalsozialismus und Widerstand in beiden deutschen Staaten nach 1949." In *Historische DDR-Forschung: Aufsätze und Studien*, ed. Jürgen Kochka, 129–48. Berlin: Akademie, 1993.

———. "Die Opfer und Verfolgtenperspektive als Gründungskonsens? Zum Umgang mit der Widerstandstradition und der Schuldfrage in der DDR." In *Die geteilte Vergangenheit. Zum Umgang mit Nationalsozialismus und Widerstand in beiden deutschen Staaten*, ed. Jürgen Danyel, 31–46. Berlin: Akademie, 1995.

———, ed. *Die geteilte Vergangenheit. Zum Umgang mit Nationalsozialismus und Widerstand in beiden deutschen Staaten*. Berlin: Akademie, 1995.

Deák, István, Jan Gross, and Tony Judt, eds. *The Politics of Retribution: World War II and Its Aftermath*. Princeton: Princeton University Press, 2000.

Dean, Carolyn. *The Fragility of Empathy after the Holocaust*. Ithaca: Cornell University Press, 2004.

———. *Sexuality in Modern Western Culture*. New York: Twayne, 1996.

Demos, John. *The Unredeemed Captive: A Family Story from Early America*. New York: Alfred A. Knopf, 1994.

Diedrich, Torsten. "Das Jahr der Rückkehr—ein Jahr der Aufrüstung." In *Heimkehr 1948. Geschichte und Schicksal deutscher Kriegsgefangener*, ed. Annette Kaminsky, 232–54. Munich: C. H. Beck, 1998.

Diedrich, Torsten, and Rüdiger Wenzke. *Die getarnte Armee. Geschichte der kasernierten Volkspolizei der DDR 1952 bis 1956*. Berlin: Links, 2001.

Diehl, James. *The Thanks of the Fatherland: German Veterans after the Second World War*. Chapel Hill: University of North Carolina Pess, 1993.

Diestelkamp, Bernd, and Susanne Jung. "Die Justiz in den Westzonen und der frühen Bundesrepublik." *Aus Parlament und Zeitgeschichte* 39 (1989): 19–29.

Dietze, A. "Der Verlauf der Blutdruckschwankungen bei alimentärer und seelischer Dystrophie." *Die Medizinsche* 46 (1957): 1715–17.

———. "Zur Frage der langdauernden vegetativen Regulationsstörungen nach alimentärere Dystrophie." *Münchner Medizinische Wochenschrift* 97 (1955): 1733–55.

Dirks, Walter. "Was die Ehe bedroht: Eine Liste ihrer kritischen Punkte." *Frankfurter Hefte* 6 (1951): 18–28.

Ditz, Toby L. "The New Men's History and the Peculiar Absence of Gendered Power: Some Remedies from Early American Gender History." *Gender and History* 16 (2004): 1–35.

Domansky, Elisabeth. "A Lost War: World War II in German Memory." In *Thinking about the Holocaust after a Half Century*, ed. Alvin H. Rosefeld, 233–72. Bloomington: Indiana University Press, 1997.

Domansky, Elisabeth, and Jutta de Jong, eds. *Der lange Schatten des Krieges. Deutsche Lebensgeschichten nach 1945*. Münster: Aschendorfsche Verlagsbuchhandlung, 2000.

Donat, Erna. "Männer kommen 'zu sich.' Die Arbeiterwohlfahrt gründete das erste Heimkehrerhaus, in dem auf psychotherapeutischer Grundlage gearbeitet wird." *Neues Beginnen* 2, no. 18 (1948): 1–2.

Donau, Willi. "Probleme der Arbeitslenkung." *Die Arbeit* 3 (1949): 112–15.

Donth, Stefan. *Vertriebene und Flüchtlinge in Sachsen. Die Politik der Sowjetischen Militäradministration und der SED*. Cologne: Böhlau, 2000.

Dörr, Margarete. *"Wer die Zeit nicht miterlebt hat . . ." Frauenerfahrungen im Zweiten Weltkrieg und in den Jahren danach*. 3 vols. Frankfurt am Main: Campus, 1998.

Douglas, Mary. *Purity and Danger: An Analysis of Concepts of Pollution and Taboo.* London: Routledge, 1978.

Dower, John. *Embracing Defeat: Japan in the Wake of World War II.* New York: Norton, 1999.

Dralle, Lothar. *Von der Sowjetunion lernen. . . : Zur Geschichte der Gesellschaft für Deutsch-Sowjetische Freundschaft.* Berlin: Duncker and Humboldt, 1993.

Dröge, Franz. *Der zerredete Widerstand. Soziologie und Publizistik des Gerüchts im Zweiten Weltkrieg.* Stuttgart: Bertelsmann Universitätsverlag, 1970.

Dülffer, Jost. "Aussichtslose Kämpfe. Kriegsgefangenschaft und Rückkehr—Soldatenerfahrungen im Westen 1944–46." In *"Wir haben schwere Zeiten hinter uns." Die Kölner Region zwischen Krieg und Nachkriegszeit,* ed. Jost Dülffer, 21–43. Vierow: SH Verlag, 1996.

Echternkamp, Jörg. " 'Kameradenpost bricht auch nie ab . . .' Ein Kriegsende auf Raten im Spiegel der Briefe deutscher Ostheimkehrer 1946–1951." *Militärgeschichtliche Zeitschrift* 60 (2001): 437–500.

———. *Nach dem Krieg. Alltagsnot, Neuorientierung und die Last der Vergangenheit, 1945–1949.* Zürich: Pendo, 2003.

———. " 'Verwirrung im Vaterländischen'? Nationalismus in der deutschen Nachkriegsgesellschaft 1945–1960." In *Die Politik der Nation. Deutscher Nationalismus in Krieg und Krisen, 1760–1960,* ed. Jörg Echternkamp and Sven Oliver Müller, 219–46. Munich: Oldenbourg, 2002.

———. "Wut auf die Wehrmacht." In *Die Wehrmacht. Mythos und Realität,* ed. Rolf-Dieter Müller and Hans-Erich Volkmann, 1058–1090. Munich: Oldenbourg, 1999.

Eckstaedt, Anita. *Nationalsozialismus in der "zweiten Generation." Psychoanalyse von Hörigkeitsverhältnissen.* Frankfurt am Main: Suhrkamp, 1989.

Eghigian, Greg. "The German Welfare State as a Discourse of Trauma." In *Traumatic Pasts: History, Psychiatry, and Trauma in the Modern Age, 1870–1930,* ed. Paul and Mark Micale Lerner, 92–112. Cambridge: Cambridge University Press, 2001.

———. "The Psychologization of the Socialist Self: East German Forensic Psychology and Its Deviants, 1945–1975." *German History* 22 (2004): 181–205.

———. "Was There a Communist Psychiatry? Politics and East German Psychiatric Care, 1945–1989." *Harvard Review of Psychiatry* 10 (2002): 364–68.

Eley, Geoff. *Forging Democracy: The History of the Left in Europe, 1850–2000.* New York: Oxford University Press.

Enzensberger, Hans Magnus. "Europe in Ruins." In *Civil Wars,* 73–99. London: Grante Books, 1994.

Epstein, Catherine. "East Germany and Its History since 1989." *Journal of Modern History* 75 (2003): 634–61.

———. *The Last Revolutionaries: German Communists and Their Century.* Cambridge: Harvard University Press, 2003.

Erdinger, Lewis J. *Kurt Schumacher: A Study in Personality and Political Behavior.* Stanford: Stanford University Press, 1965.

Erker, Paul. *Ernährungskrise und Nachkriegsgesellschaft. Bauern und Arbeiterschaft in Bayern, 1943–1953.* Stuttgart: Klett-Cotta, 1990.

Erler, Peter, Horst Laude, and Manfred Wilke, eds. *Nach Hitler kommen wir. Dokumente zur Programmatik der Moskauer KPD-Führung 1944/45 für Nachkriegsdeutschland.* Berlin: Akademie, 1994.

Ernst, Anna Sabine. *"Die beste Prophylaxe ist der Sozialismus." Ärzte und medizinische Hochschullehrer in der SBZ/DDR 1945–1961.* Münster: Waxmann, 1997.

Eschenbach, Insa. "Heilige Stätten—imaginierte Gemeinschaft. Geschlechtsspezifische Dramaturgien im Gedenken." In *Gedächtnis und Geschlecht: Deutungsmuster in Darstellungen des nationalsozialistischen Genozids,* ed. Insa Eschenbach, Sigrid Jacobeit, and Silke Wenk, 117–35. New York: Campus, 2002.

Evans, Jennifer. "Bahnhof Boys: Policing Male Prostitution in Post-Nazi Berlin." *Journal of the History of Sexuality* 12 (2003): 605–36.

Farmer, Sarah. *Martyred Village: Commemorating the 1944 Massacre at Oradour-sur-Glane.* Berkeley and Los Angeles: University of California Press, 1999.

Fass, Paula. "Cultural History/Social History. Reflections on a Continuing Dialogue." *Journal of Social History* 37 (2003): 39–46.

Fehrenbach, Heide. *Cinema in Democratizing Germany: Reconstructing National Identity after Hitler.* Chapel Hill: University of North Carolina Press, 1995.

Fischer, O. "Wie soll sich der praktische Arzt bei der Malaria der Kriegsteilnehmer und Kriegsgefangenen verhalten?" *Deutsche Medizinische Wochenschrift* 75 (1950): 1581–85.

Fishman, Sarah. *We Will Wait: Wives of French Prisoners of War, 1940–1944.* New Haven: Yale University Press, 1991.

Foitzik, Jan. "Die stalinistischen 'Säuberungen' in den ostmitteleuropäischen kommunistischen Parteien. Ein vergleichender Überblick." In *Kommunisten verfolgen Kommunisten. Stalinistischer Terror und "Säuberungen" in den kommunistischen Parteien Europas seit den dreissiger Jahren,* ed. Herrmann Weber and Dietrich Staritz, 401–23. Berlin: Akademie, 1993.

Foot, Rosemary. *A Substitute for Victory: The Politics of Peacemaking at the Korean Armistice Talks.* Ithaca: Cornell University Press, 1900.

Förster, Alice, and Birgit Beck. "Post-traumatic Stress Disorder and World War II: Can a Psychiatric Concept Help Us Understand Postwar Society?" In *Life after Death: Approaches to a Cultural and Social History of Europe during the 1940s and 1950s,* ed. Richard Bessel and Dirk Schumann, 15–35. Cambridge: Cambridge University Press, 2003.

Förster, Jürgen. "Das Unternehmen 'Barbarossa' als Eroberungs- und Vernichtungskrieg." In *Das Deutsche Reich und der Zweite Weltkrieg,* vol. 4, *Der Angriff auf die Sowjetunion,* ed. Militärgeschichtliches Forschungsamt, 413–47. Stuttgart: DVA, 1983.

———. "Wehrmacht, Krieg und Holocaust." In *Die Wehrmacht. Mythos und Realität,* ed. Rolf Dieter Müller and Hans Erich Volkmann, 948–63. Munich: Oldenbourg, 1999.

———. "Zum Rußlandbild der Militärs, 1941–1945." In *Das Russlandbild im Dritten Reich,* ed. Hans-Erich Volkmann, 141–63. Cololgne: Böhlau, 1994.

Foschepoth, Josef. "Adenauers Moskaureise 1955." *Aus Politik und Zeitgeschichte* 22 (1986): 30–46.

———. "German Reactions to Defeat and Occupation." In *West Germany under Construction*, ed. Robert G. Moeller, 73–89. Ann Arbor: University of Michigan Press, 1997.

———. "Westintegration statt Wiedervereinigung: Adenauers Deutschlandpolitik, 1949–1955." In *Adenauer und die deutsche Frage*, ed. Josef Foschepoth, 29–60. Göttingen: Vandenhoeck und Ruprecht, 1988.

François, Etienne, Hannes Siegrist, and Jakob Vogel. "Die Nation. Vorstellung, Inszenierung, Emotionen." In *Nation und Emotion: Deutschland und Frankreich im Vergleich 19. und 20. Jahrhundert*, ed. Etienne François, Hannes Siegrist, and Jakob Vogel, 13–35. Göttingen: Vandenhoeck und Ruprecht, 1995.

Frankl, Viktor E., and Gottfried Roth. "Zur Therapie reaktiver Sexualneurosen." In *Die Sexualität des Heimkehrers. Vorträge gehalten auf dem 4. Kongress der Deutschen Gesellschaft für Sexualforschung*, ed. Hans Bürger-Prinz and Hans Giese, 65–71. Stuttgart: Ferdinand Enke, 1957.

Franklin, Bruce. *M.I.A. or Mythmaking in America*. New York: Lawrence Hill, 1992.

Frei, Norbert. "NS-Vergangenheit unter Ulbricht und Adenauer." In *Die geteilte Vergangenheit. Zum Umgang mit Nationalsozialismus und Widerstand in beiden deutschen Staaten*, ed. Jürgen Danyel, 125–32. Berlin: Akademie, 1995.

———. *Vergangenheitspolitik. Die Anfänge der Bundesrepublik und die NS-Vergangenheit*. Munich: C. H. Beck, 1996.

———. "Von deutscher Erfindungskraft. Die Kollektivschuldthese in der Nachkriegszeit." *Rechtshistorisches Journal* 17 (1997): 621–34.

Frenzel. "Der Heimkehrer im Straf- und Ehescheidungsprozess." *Deutsche Richterzeitung* 28 (1950): 232–33.

Frevert, Ute. *Die kasernierte Nation. Militärdienst und Zivilgesellschaft in Deutschland*. Munich: C.H. Beck, 2001.

———. "Die Sprache des Volkes und die Rhetorik der Nation. Identitätssplitter in der deutschen Nachkriegszeit." In *Doppelte Zeitgeschichte. Deutsch-Deutsche Beziehungen*, ed. Arnd Bauernkämper, Martin Sabrow, and Bernd Stöver, 18–31. Bonn: Dietz, 1998.

Friedlander, Henry. "The Exclusion of the Disabled." In *Social Outsiders in Nazi Germany*, ed. Robert Gellately and Nathan Stolzfuss, 145–64. Princeton: Princeton University Press, 2001.

Friedländer, Saul. *Nazi Germany and the Jews*. Vol. 1, *The Years of Persecution, 1933–39*. New York: HarperCollins, 1997.

Friedrich, Jörg. *Der Brand. Deutschland im Bombenkrieg 1940–1945*. Munich: Propyläen, 2002.

Fritzsche, Peter. "The Case of Modern Memory." *Journal of Modern History* 73 (2001): 87–117.

Fühmann, Franz. *Der Sturz des Engels: Erfahrungen mit Dichtung*. Munich: dtv, 1985.

Fujitani, Takashi, Geoffrey M. White, and Lisa Yoneyama, eds. *Perilous Memories: The Asia-Pacific War(s)*. Durham: Duke University Press, 2001.

Fulbrook, Mary. *Anatomy of a Dictatorship: Inside the GDR, 1949–1989*. Oxford: Oxford University Press, 1995.

Fulbrook, Mary. *German National Identity after the Holocaust*. Cambridge: Polity Press, 1999.

———. "Methodologische Überlegungen zu einer Gesellschaftsgeschichte der DDR." In *Die Grenzen der Diktatur. Staat und Gesellschaft in der DDR*, ed. Richard Bessel and Ralph Jessen, 274–97. Göttingen: Vandenhoeck und Ruprecht, 1996.

Funk, Erich. "Somato-psychologische Beobachtungen bei chronischer Fehl- und Unterernährung in der Gefangenschaft." *Fortschritte der Neurologie, Psychiatrie, und ihrer Grenzgebiete* 17 (1949): 229–46.

Garner, Curt. "Public Service Personnel in West Germany in the 1950s: Controversial Policy Decisions and Their Effects on Social Composition, Gender Structure, and the Role of Former Nazis." In *West Germany under Construction: Politics, Society, and Culture in the Adenauer Era*, ed. Robert Moeller, 135–95. Ann Arbor: University of Michigan Press, 1997.

Gauger, Kurt. *Die Dystrophie*. Munich: Urban und Schwarzenberg, 1952.

———. *Politische Medizin. Grundriss einer deutschen Psychotherapie*. Hamburg: Hanseatische Verlagsanstalt, 1934.

———. *Psychotherapie und Zeitgeschehen. Abhandlungen und Vorträge*. Munich: Urban und Schwarzenberg, 1954.

———. "Psychotherapy and Political Worldview." In *Nazi Culture: Intellectual, Cultural, and Social Life in the Third Reich*, ed. George Mosse, 215–17. New York: Grosset and Dunlap, 1966.

Gaus, Günter. *Wo Deutschland liegt. Eine Ortsbestimmung*. Munich: Hoffmann und Campe, 1983.

Gellately, Robert. *Backing Hitler: Consent and Coercion in Nazi Germany*. Oxford: Oxford University Press, 2001.

———. *The Gestapo and German Society: Enforcing Racial Policy, 1933–1945*. Oxford: Clarendon, 1990.

Gerchow, Jochen. "Über die Ursachen sexueller Fehlhaltungen und Straftaten bei ehemaligen Kriegsgefangenen." *Deutsche Zeitschrift für gerichtliche Medizin* 42 (1953): 452–57.

Gerfeldt, Ewald. "Lebensform und Ehekrise." *Soziale Welt* 3, no. 1 (1951): 7–17.

Gerlach, Christian. *Kalkulierte Morde. Die deutsche Wirtschafts- und Vernichtungspolitik in Weissrussland 1941 bis 1944*. Hamburg: Hamburger Edition, 1999.

Geuter, Ulfried. *Die Professionalisierung der deutschen Psychologie im Nationalsozialismus*. Frankfurt am Main: Suhrkamp, 1984.

Geyer, Michael. "Cold War Angst: The Case of West German Opposition to Rearmament and Nuclear Weapons." In *The Miracle Years: A Cultural History of West Germany, 1949–1968*, ed. Hanna Schissler, 376–408. Princeton: Princeton University Press, 2001.

———. *Deutsche Rüstungspolitik, 1860–1980*. Frankfurt am Main: Suhrkamp, 1986.

———. "Eine Kriegsgeschichte, die auch vom Tod spricht." In *Physische Gewalt. Studien zur Geschichte der Neuzeit*, ed. Thomas Lindenberger and Alf Lüdtke, 57–77. Frankfurt am Main: Suhrkamp, 1995.

———. "Das Stigma der Gewalt und das Problem der nationalen Identität." In *Von der Aufgabe der Freiheit: Politische Verantwortung und bürgerliche Gesellschaft im 19. und 20. Jahrhundert: Festschrift für Hans Mommsen zum 5. November 1999*, ed. Lutz Niethammer, Christian Jansen, and Bernd Weisbrod, 673–98. Berlin: Akademie, 1995.

———. "There Is a Land Where Everything Is Pure: Its Name Is the Land of Death." In *Sacrifice and National Belonging in Twentieth-Century Germany*, ed. Greg Eghigian and Matthew Paul Berg, 118–47. College Station: Texas A&M University Press, 2002.

Gluck, Carol. "The "Long Postwar": Japan and Germany in Common and in Contrast." In *Legacies and Ambiguities: Postwar Fiction and Culture in West Germany and Japan*, ed. Ernestine Schlant and J. Thomas Rimer, 63–78. Baltimore: Johns Hopkins University Press, 1991.

Goebbels, Joseph. *Die Tagebücher von Joseph Goebbels. Sämtliche Fragmente. Im Auftrag des Instituts für Zeitgeschichte und in Verbindung mit dem Bundesarchiv*, ed. Elke Fröhlich. Munich: K.G. Saur, 1987–.

Gollwitzer, Helmut. *Unwilling Journey: A Diary from Russia*. Philadelphia: Muhlenberg Press, 1953.

Goltermann, Svenja. "Die Beherrschung der Männlichkeit. Zur Deutung psychischer Leiden bei Heimkehrern des Zweiten Weltkrieges 1945–1956." *Feministische Studien* 8 (2000): 7–19.

———. "Im Wahn der Gewalt: Massentod, Opferdiskurs und Psychiatrie 1945–1956." In *Nachkrieg in Deutschland*, ed. Klaus Naumann, 343–63. Hamburg: Hamburger Edition, 2001.

———. "Psychisches Leid und herrschende Lehre: Der Wissenschaftswandel in der deutschen Psychiatrie der Nachkriegszeit." In *Akademische Vergangenheitspolitik. Beiträge zur Wissenschaftskultur der Nachkriegszeit*, ed. Bernd Weisbrod, 7–19. Göttingen: Wallstein, 2002.

———. "Verletzte Körper oder 'Building National Bodies.' Kriegsheimkehrer, 'Krankheit' und Psychiatrie in der westdeutschen Gesellschaft 1945–1955." *Werkstatt Geschichte* 24 (1999): 83–98.

Gorges, Valentin. "Man muss leben. Ein Beitrag zur Psychologie der *Kameradenschinder*." *Deutsche Rundschau* 78 (1952): 599–604.

Görtemaker, Manfred. *Geschichte der Bundesrepublik. Von der Gründung bis in die Gegenwart*. Munich: C. H. Beck, 1999.

Goschler, Constantin. *Wiedergutmachung. Westdeutschland und die Verfolgten des Nationalsozialismus (1950–1954)*. Munich: Oldenbourg, 1992.

Gosewinkel, Dieter. *Einbürgern und Ausbürgern. Die Nationalisierung der Staatsangehörigkeit vom Deutschen Bund bis zur Bundesrepublik*. Göttingen: Vandenhoeck und Ruprecht, 2001.

Gössner, Rolf. *Die vergessenen Justizopfer des Kalten Krieges. Verdrängung im Westen-Abrechnung im Osten?* Berlin: Aufbau, 1998.

Gottschick, Johann. "Die 'experimentellen' Neurosen als psychiatrisches Erklärungsprinzip." *Psychiatrie, Neurologie, und Medizinische Psychologie* 1 (1949): 367–74.

Gottschick, Johann. "Kriegsgefangenschaft als Schädigung, insbesondere bei angeborenem Schwachsinn." *Der medizinische Sachverständige* 51, no. 9 (1954–55): 191–93.

———. "Kriegsgefangenschaft und Psychosen." *Der Nervenarzt* 21 (1950): 129–32.

Graml, Hermann. "Die Wehrmacht im Dritten Reich." *Vierteljahreshefte für Zeitgeschichte* 45 (1997): 365–84.

Greenberg, Gershon. "Orthodox Jewish Thought after the Genocide." In *In God's Name: Genocide and Religion in the Twentieth Century*, ed. Omer Bartov and Phyllis Mack, 316–49. New York: Berghahn, 2001.

Gregor, Neil. " 'Is He Still Alive, or Long Since Dead?' Loss, Absence, and Remembrance in Nuremberg, 1945–1956." *German History* 21 (2003): 183–203.

Greschat, Martin. "Begleitung und Deutung der beiden Weltkriege durch evangelische Theologen." In *Erster Weltkrieg–Zweiter Weltkrieg. Krieg, Kriegserlebnis, Kriegserfahrung. Ein Vergleich*, ed. Bruno Thoß and Hans Erich Volkmann, 497–518. Paderborn: Ferdinand Schönigh, 2002.

———. *Die evangelische Christenheit und die deutsche Geschichte nach 1945. Weichenstellung in der Nachkriegszeit*. Stuttgart: Kohlhammer, 2002.

———. "Konfessionelle Spannungen in der Ära Adenauer." In *Katholiken und Protestanten in den Aufbaujahren der Bundesrepublik*, ed. Thomas Sauer, 19–34. Stuttgart: Kohlhammer, 2000.

———. "The Potency of 'Christendom.' The Example of the Darmstädter Wort (1947)." In *The Decline of Christendom in Western Europe, 1750–2000*, ed. Hugh McLead and Werner Ustorf, 130–42. Cambridge: Cambridge University Press, 2003.

———. " 'Rechristianisierung' und 'Säkularisierung.' Anmerkungen zu einem europäischen interkonfessionellen Interpretationsmodell." In *Christentum und politische Verantwortung. Kirchen in der Nachkriegszeit*, ed. Jochen-Christoph Kaiser and Anselm Döring-Manteuffel, 1–24. Stuttgart: Kohlhammer, 1990.

———. "Zwischen Aufbruch und Beharrung. Die evangelische Kirche nach dem Zweiten Weltkrieg." In *Die Zeit nach 1945 als Thema kirchlicher Zeitgeschichte*, ed. Victor Conzemius, Martin Greschat, and Hermann Kocher, 99–126. Göttingen: Vandenhoek, 1988.

Greven, Michael Th., and Oliver von Wrochem, eds. *Der Krieg in der Nachkriegszeit. Der Zweite Weltkrieg in Politik und Gesellschaft der Bundesrepublik*. Opladen: Leske und Budrich, 2000.

Griebel, Alexander. "Zu den Strafprozessen gegen Heimkehrer." *Juristenzeitung* 6 (1951): 362–63.

Gries, Ulrich. *Abbau der Persönlichkeit. Zum Problem der Persönlichkeitsveränderung bei Dystrophie in sowjetischer Gefangenschaft*. Munich: Ernst Reinhardt, 1957.

Gross, Jan T. "Themes for a Social History of War Experience and Collaboration." In *The Politics of Retribution: World War II and Its Aftermath*, ed. István Deák, Jan T. Gross, and Tony Judt, 15–35. Princeton: Princeton University Press, 2000.

Grossmann, Atina. "A Question of Silence: The Rape of German Women by Occupation Soldiers." In *West Germany under Construction: Politics, Society, and*

Culture in the Adenauer Era, ed. Robert G. Moeller, 33–52. Ann Arbor: University of Michigan Press, 1997.

———. "Trauma, Memory, and Motherhood. Germans and Jewish Displaced Persons in Post-Nazi Germany, 1945–1949." *Archiv für Sozialgeschichte* 38 (1998): 215–39.

———. "Victims, Villains, and Survivors: Gendered Perceptions and Self-Perceptions of Jewish Displaced Persons in Occupied Postwar Germany." *Journal of the History of Sexuality* 11 (2002): 291–318.

Haas, Josef. "Die National Demokratische Partei Deutschlands. Geschichte, Struktur und Funktion einer DDR Blockpartei." Dissertation, University of Bamberg, 1987.

Haase, Norbert. "Wehrmachtsangehörige vor dem Kriegsgericht." In *Die Wehrmacht. Mythos und Realität*, ed. Rolf Dieter Müller and Hans Erich Volkmann, 474–85. Munich: Oldenbourg, 1999.

Haase, Norbert, and Gerhard Paul, eds. *Die anderen Soldaten. Wehrkraftzersetzung, Gehorsamsverweigerung und Fahnenflucht im Zweiten Weltkrieg.* Frankfurt am Main: Fischer, 1995.

Hagemann, Karen. " 'Jede Kraft wird gebraucht.' Militäreinsatz von Frauen im Ersten und Zweiten Weltkrieg." In *Erster Weltkrieg-Zweiter Weltkrieg. Ein Vergleich. Krieg, Kriegserlebnis, Kriegserfahrung in Deutschland*, ed. Bruno Thoß and Hans Erich Volkmann, 79–106. Paderborn: Ferdinand Schöningh, 2002.

———. *"Männlicher Muth und Teutsche Ehre." Nation, Militär und Geschlecht zur Zeit der Antinapoleonischen Kriege Preussens.* Paderborn: F. Schöningh, 2002.

Hagemann, Karen, and Stefanie Schüler-Springorum, eds. *Home/Front: The Military, War, and Gender in Twentieth-Century Germany.* Oxford: Berg, 2002.

Haider, Paul. "Reaktionen der Wehrmacht auf Gründung und Tätigkeit des Nationalkomitees Freies Deutschland und des Bundes Deutscher Offiziere." In *Die Wehrmacht. Mythos und Realität*, ed. Rolf-Dieter Müller and Hans-Erich Volkmann, 614–34. Munich: Oldenbourg, 1999.

Halbwachs, Maurice. *On Collective Memory.* Ed. and trans. Lewis A. Coser. Chicago: University of Chicago Press, 1992.

Hanrath, Sabine. *Zwischen Euthanasie und Psychiatriereform. Anstaltspsychiatrie in Westfalen und Brandenburg: Ein deutsch-deutscher Vergleich (1945–1964).* Paderborn: Schönigh, 2002.

Harsch, Donna. "Approach/Avoidance: Communists and Women in East Germany." *Social History* 25 (2000): 156–82.

Hartmann, Susan M. "Prescriptions for Penelope: Literature on Women's Obligations to Returning World War II Veterans." *Women's Studies* 5 (1978): 223–39.

Heer, Hannes. *"Stets zu erschiessen sind die Frauen, die in der Roten Armee dienen." Geständnisse deutscher Kriegsgefangener über ihren Einsatz an der Ostfront.* Hamburg: Hamburger Edition, 1995.

Heer, Hannes, and Klaus Naumann, eds. *Vernichtungskrieg. Verbrechen der Wehrmacht.* Hamburg: Hamburger Edition, 1997.

Hefner, H., and D. Wunneberg. "Körperschäden ehemaliger Russlandheim-kehrer." *Deutsche Medizinische Wochenschrift* 77 (1952): 1539–41.

Heidemeyer, Helga. "Vertriebene als Sowjetzonenflüchtlinge." In *Vertriebene in Deutschland. Interdisziplinäre Ergebnisse und Forschungsperspektiven*, ed. Dierk Hoffmann and Michael Schwartz, 239–47. Munich: Oldenbourg, 2000.

Heilbronn, Wolfgang. "Der Aufbau der nordrhein-westfälischen Justiz in der Zeit von 1945 bis 1948/49." *Juristische Zeitgeschichte* 5 (1996): 1–59.

Heineman, Elizabeth. "Gender, Public Policy, and Memory: Waiting Wives and War Widows in the Postwar Germanys." In *The Work of Memory: New Directions in the Study of German Society and Culture*, ed. Alon Confino and Peter Fritzsche, 214–38. Urbana: University of Illinois Press, 2002.

———. "The Hour of the Woman: Memories of West Germany's 'Crisis Years' and West German National Identity." *American Historical Review* 101 (1996): 354–96.

———. "Sexuality and Nazism. The Double Unspeakable?" *Journal of the History of Sexuality* 11 (2002): 22–66.

———. *What Difference Does a Husband Make? Women and Marital Status in Nazi and Postwar Germany*. Berkeley and Los Angeles: University of California Press, 1999.

Heinemann, Ulrich. "Krieg und Frieden an der 'inneren Front.' Normalität und Zustimmung, Terror und Opposition im Dritten Reich." In *Nicht nur Hitlers Krieg. Der Zweite Weltkrieg und die Deutschen*, ed. Christoph Kleßmann, 25–50. Düsseldorf: Droste, 1989.

Hell, Julia. *Post-Fascist Fantasies: Psychoanalysis, History, and the Literature of East Germany*. Durham: Duke University Press, 1997.

Hemsing, Walter. "Der deutsche Geistesmensch in der Kriegsgefangenschaft." *Psychologische Rundschau* 3 (1952): 291–302.

———. "Der Heimkehrer und seine Ehe." *Caritas* 49 (1948): 198–208.

———. "Der Heimkehrer und seine Kinder." *Caritas* 49 (1948): 172–79.

———. "Über die seelische Gesundung des Heimkehrers." *Caritas* 49 (1948): 44–51.

Henke, Klaus-Dietmar. *Die amerikanische Besetzung Deutschlands*. Munich: Oldenbourg, 1995.

———. "Die Trennung vom Nationalsozialismus. Selbstzerstörung, politische Säuberung, Entnazifizierung, Strafverfolgung." In *Politische Säuberung in Europa. Die Abrechnung mit Faschismus und Kollaboration nach dem Zweiten Weltkrieg*, ed. Klaus-Dietmar Henke and Hans Woller, 21–83. Munich: dtv, 1991.

Henke, Klaus-Dietmar, and Hans Woller, eds. *Politische Säuberung in Europa. Die Abrechnung mit Faschismus und Kollaboration nach dem Zweiten Weltkrieg*. Munich: dtv, 1991.

Hensle, Michael P. *Rundfunkverbrechen. Das Hören von Feindsendern im Nationalsozialismus*. Berlin: Metroprol Friedrich Veitl, 2003.

Henssge, E. "Reaktive psychische Erkrankungen der Nachkriegszeit." *Psychiatrie, Neurologie und Medizinische Psychologie* 1 (1949): 133–37.

Herberg, H. J., and H. Paul, eds. *Psychische Spätschäden nach politischer Verfolgung*. Basel: S. Karger, 1963.

Herbert, Ulrich. *Best. Biographische Studien über Radikalismus, Weltanschauung und Vernunft, 1903–1989*. Bonn: J.H.W. Dietz Nachf., 1996.

———, ed. *Nationalsozialistische Vernichtungspolitik 1939–1945. Neue Forschungen und Kontroversen*. Frankfurt am Main: Fischer, 1998.

———, ed. *Wandlungsprozesse in Westdeutschland: Belastung, Integration, Liberalisierung 1945–1980*. Göttingen: Wallstein, 2002.

Herbert, Ulrich, and Axel Schildt, eds. *Kriegsende in Europa. Vom Beginn des deutschen Machtzerfalls bis zur Stabilisierung der Nachkriegsordnung, 1944–1948*. Essen: Klartext, 1988.

Herf, Jeffrey. *Divided Memory: The Nazi Past in the Two Germanys*. Cambridge: Harvard University Press, 1997.

———. "Multiple Restorations: German Political Traditions and the Interpretation of Nazism, 1945–1946." *Central European History* 26 (1993): 21–55.

Herman, Judith. *Trauma and Recovery: The Aftermath of Violence—from Domestic Abuse to Political Terror*. New York: Basic Books, 1997.

Herzog, Dagmar. "Desperately Seeking Normality: Sex and Marriage in the Wake of War." In *Life after Death: Approaches to the Cultural and Social History of the 1940s and 1950s*, ed. Richard Bessel and Dirk Schumann, 161–92. Cambridge: Cambridge University Press, 2003.

———. " 'Pleasure, Sex, and Politics Belong Together.' Post-Holocaust Memory and the Sexual Revolution in West Germany." *Critical Inquiry* 24 (1998): 393–444.

———. *Sex after Fascism: Memory and Morality in Twentieth-Century Germany*. Princeton: Princeton University Press, 2005.

Herzog, Paul. "Heimkehr aus russischer Gefangenschaft." *Die Wandlung* 3 (1948): 71–79.

Hettling, Manfred. "Täter und Opfer? Die deutschen Soldaten in Stalingrad." *Archiv für Sozialgeschichte* 35 (1995): 515–31.

Heukenkamp, Ursula. "Das Frauenbild in der antifaschistischen Erneuerung der SBZ." In *"Wen kümmert's, wer spricht." Zur Literatur und Kulturgeschichte von Frauen aus Ost und West*, ed. Irene Stephan, Sigrid Weigel, and Kerstin Wilhelms, 3–13. Cologne: Böhlau, 1991.

———, ed. *Unerwünschte Erfahrung. Kriegsliteratur und Zensur in der DDR*. Berlin: Aufbau, 1990.

Heyll, Uwe. "Friedrich Panse und die psychiatrische Erbforschung." In *Die Medizinische Akademie Düsseldorf im Nationalsozialismus*, ed. Michal G. Esch, 318–40. Düsseldorf: Klartext, 1997.

Hilfswerk der Evangelischen Landeskirche in Württemberg. *Handreichung für die Weiterführung des Evang. Hilfswerks im Frühjahr und Sommer . . . insbesondere für die Betreuung der Flüchtlinge und Heimkehrer: An alle Pfarrämter d. Württ. Landeskirche u. an alle Helfer u. Helferinnen d. Hilfswerks*. Stuttgart: Hilfswerk, 1946.

Hilger, Andreas. *Deutsche Kriegsgefangene in der Sowjetunion Kriegsgefangenenpolitik, Lageralltag und Erinnerung*. Essen: Klartext, 2000.

———. "Faustpfand im Kalten Krieg? Die Massenverurteilungen deutscher Kriegsgefangener 1949/50 und die Repatriierung Verurteilter 1950 bis 1956." In *Sowjetische Militärtribunale*, vol. 1, *Die Verurteilung deutscher Kriegsge-*

fangener, 1941–1955, ed. Andreas Hilger, Ute Schmidt, and Günther Wagenlehner, 211–71. Cologne: Böhlau, 2001.

———. "Haft in entlegenen Gebieten." In *Sowjetische Militärtribunale*, vol. 2, *Die Verurteilung deutscher Zivilisten, 1945–1955*, ed. Andreas Hilger, Mike Schmeitzner, and Ute Schmidt, 663–84. Cologne: Böhlau, 2003.

Hilger, Andreas, Mike Schmeitzner, and Ute Schmidt, eds. *Sowjetische Militärtribunale*. Vol. 2, *Die Verurteilung deutscher Zivilisten, 1945–1955*. Cologne: Böhlau, 2003.

Hilger, Andreas, Ute Schmidt, and Günther Wagenlehner, eds. *Sowjetische Militärtribunale*. Vol. 1, *Die Verurteilung deutscher Kriegsgefangener, 1941–1955*. Cologne: Böhlau, 2001.

Hillgruber, Andreas. *Zweierlei Untergang. Die Zerschlagung des Deutschen Reiches und das Ende des europäischen Judentums*. Munich: Siedler, 1986.

Hinrichsen, Kurt. "Befehlsnotstand." In *NS-Prozesse. Nach 25 Jahren Strafverfolgung: Möglichkeiten-Grenzen-Ergebnis*, ed. Adalbert Rückerl, 131–61. Karlsruhe: Verlag CF Müller, 1971.

Hobsbawm, Eric. *The Age of Extremes: A History of the World, 1914–1991*. New York: Pantheon, 1994.

———. *Interesting Times: A Twentieth-Century Life*. New York: Pantheon, 2002.

Hochrein, M., and I. Schleicher. "Die Beurteilung der Spätheimkehrerschäden." *Die Medizinsche* 8 (1958): 1–31.

———. "Die vegetative Dystonie beim Spätheimkehrer. Pathogenese, Beurteilung, Begutachtung, und Behandlung." *Medizinische Klinik* 50 (1955): 2017–25, 2057–63, 2097–2103, 2137–45, 2177–79.

Hockenos, Matthew. *A Church Divided: German Protestants Confront the Nazi Past*. Bloomington: Indiana University Press, 2004.

Hoff, H., and R. Schindler. "Die psychohygienische Aufgabe im Heimkehrerproblem." *Wiener Medizinische Wochenschrift* 106, no. 43 (1956): 896–98.

Hoffmann, Dierk. *Aufbau und Krise der Planwirtschaft. Die Arbeitskräftelenkung in der SBZ/DDR 1945 bis 1963*. Munich: Oldenbourg, 2002.

Hoffmann, Dierk, and Herman Wentker, eds. *Das letzte Jahr der SBZ. Politische Weichenstellungen und Kontinuitäten im Prozess der Gründung der DDR*. Munich: Oldenbourg, 2000.

Holtman, Everhard. "Die neuen Lassalleaner. SPD und HJ Generation nach 1945." In *Von Stalingrad zur Währungsreform. Zur Sozialgeschichte des Umbruchs in Deutschland*, ed. Martin Broszat, Klaus-Dietmar Henke, and Hans Woller, 169–210. Munich: Oldenbourg, 1988.

———. *Politik und Nichtpolitik. Lokale Erscheinungsformen politischer Kultur im Nachkriegsdeutschland*. Opladen: Westdeutscher, 1989.

Hottinger, Adolf. *Hungerkrankheit, Hungerödem, Hungertuberkulose: Historische, klinische, pathophysiologische und pathologisch-anatomische Studien und Beobachtungen an ehemaligen Insassen aus Konzentrationslagern*. Basel: B. Schwabe, 1948.

Hughes, Michael. *Shouldering the Burdens of Defeat: West Germany and the Reconstruction of Social Justice*. Chapel Hill: University of North Carolina Press, 1999.

Ihme-Tuchel, Beate. "Die Entlassung der deutschen Kriegsgefangenen im Herbst 1955 im Spiegel der Diskussion zwischen SED und KPdSU." *Militärgeschichtliche Mitteilungen* 54 (1994): 449–65.

———. "Die SED und die deutschen Kriegsgefangenen in der Sowjetunion zwischen 1949 und 1955." *Deutschland Archiv* 27 (1994): 490–503.

———. "Zwischen Tabu und Propaganda: Hintergründe und Probleme der ostdeutsch-sowjetischen Heimkehrerverhandlungen." In *Heimkehr 1948. Geschichte und Schicksal deutscher Kriegsgefangener*, ed. Annette Kaminsky, 38–54. Munich: C. H. Beck, 1998.

Institut zur Sozialforschung. *Zum Politischen Bewusstsein ehemaliger Kriegsgefangener. Eine soziologische Untersuchung im Verband der Heimkehrer.* Frankfurt am Main, 1957.

Janz, Hans Werner. "Psychopathologie Reaktionen der Kriegs-und Nachkriegszeit." *Fortschritte der Neurologie, Psychiatrie und Ihrer Grenzgebiete* 17 (1949): 264–93.

Jarausch, Konrad. "Care and Coercion: The GDR as Welfare Dictatorship." In *Dictatorship as Experience: Towards a Socio-Cultural History of the GDR*, ed. Konrad Jarausch, trans. Eve Duffy, 47–69. Oxford: Berghahn, 1999.

———. " 'Die Teile als Ganzes erkennen.' Zur Integration der beiden deutschen Nachkriegsgeschichten." *Zeithistorische Forschungen/Studies in Contemporary History, Online-Ausgabe* 1, no. 1 (2004).

———. *Die Umkehr. Deutsche Wandlungen 1945–1995.* Munich: Deutsche Verlags Anstalt, 2004.

———. "Towards a Social History of Experience: Postmodern Predicaments in Theory and Interdisciplinarity." *Central European History* 22 (1989): 427–43.

Jarausch, Konrad, and Michael Geyer. *Shattered Past: Reconstructing German Histories.* Princeton: Princeton University Press, 2003.

Jarausch, Konrad, and Hannes Siegrist, eds. *Amerikanisierung und Sowjetisierung in Deutschland 1945–1970.* Frankfurt am Main: Campus, 1997.

Jay, Martin. *Songs of Experience: Modern American and European Variations on a Universal Theme.* Berkeley and Los Angeles: University of California Press, 2005.

Jeffords, Susan. *The Remasculinization of America: Gender and the Vietnam War.* Berkeley and Los Angeles: University of California Press, 1989.

Jellinghaus, Karl. *Vorsorge und Fürsorge für unsere Kriegsgefangenen, Vermissten und Heimkehrer. Gemeinschaftsarbeit öffentlicher und privater Fürsorge in Hagen von 1945 bis 31.12.1947.* Stuttgart: W. Kohlhammer, 1948.

Jensch, Nikolaus. "Über psychogene Störungen der Kriegsgefangenschaft." *Deutsche Medizinische Wochenschrift* 74 (1949): 368–70.

Jessen, Ralph. "Die Gesellschaft im Staatssozialismus. Probleme einer Sozialgeschichte der DDR." *Geschichte und Gesellschaft* 21 (1995): 96–110.

Jonitz, Hans. "In amerikanischer und französischer Kriegsgefangenschaft." In *Deutsche Kriegsgefangene im Zweiten Weltkrieg. Erinnerungen*, ed. Wolfgang Benz and Angelika Schardt, 93–131. Frankfurt am Main: Fischer, 1995.

Jordan, Rudolf. *Erlebt und Erlitten. Weg eines Gauleiters von München nach Moskau.* Leoni: Druffel, 1971.

Judt, Tony. "The Past Is Another Country: Myth and Memory in Postwar Europe." In *The Politics of Retribution*, ed. István Deák, Jan T. Gross, and Tony Judt, 293–323. Princeton: Princeton University Press, 2000.

Kaiser, Monika. "Die Zentrale der Diktatur-organisatorische Weichenstellungen, Strukturen und Kompetenzen der SED Führung in der SBZ/DDR 1946 bis 1952." In *Historische DDR Forschung. Aufsätze und Studien*, ed. Jürgen Kocka, 57–86. Berlin: Akademie, 1993.

Kaminsky, Annette. ". . . Frankfurt, das glückliche Frankfurt . . ." In *Heimkehr 1948. Geschichte und Schicksal deutscher Kriegsgefangener*, ed. Annette Kaminsky, 82–95. Munich: C. H. Beck, 1998.

———, ed. *Heimkehr 1948. Geschichte und Schicksal deutscher Kriegsgefangener*. Munich: C. H. Beck, 1998.

Karner, Stefan. "Deutsche Kriegsgefangene und Internierte in der Sowjetunion, 1941–1956." In *Die Wehrmacht. Mythos und Realität*, ed. Rolf-Dieter and Hans-Erich Volkmann Mülller, 1012–36. Munich: Oldenbourg, 1999.

———. *Im Archipel GUPVI*. Munich: Oldenbourg, 1995.

Karsch, Rainer. *Allein bezahlt? Die Reparationsleistungen der SBZ/DDR 1945–1953*. Berlin: Links, 1993.

Karsten, Heiner. *Glückliche Heimkehr nach grauenvollen Kriegserlebnissen. Kurzgeschichten und Erinnerungen*. Hamburg: Betzel, 1993.

Kayser, Alexander. "Über das Verhältnis berechtigter und unberechtigter Kriegsrentenansprüche auf psychiatrischem und neurologischem Gebiet." *Der Nervenarzt* 23 (1952): 256–57.

Kehler, Ernst. *Einblicke und Einsichten: Erinnerungen*. Berlin: Dietz, 1989.

Kershaw, Ian. *Hitler 1936–45: Nemesis*. New York: Norton, 2000.

———. *The "Hitler Myth": Image and Reality in the Third Reich*. Oxford: Clarendon Press, 1987.

———. *Popular Opinion and Political Dissent in the Third Reich, Bavaria, 1933–1945*. Oxford: Clarendon Press, 1983.

Kettenacker, Lothar, ed. *Ein Volk von Opfern? Die neue Debatte um den Bombenkrieg 1940–1945*. Berlin: Rohwolt, 2003.

Kilian, H. "Das Wiedereinleben des Heimkehers." In *Die Sexualität des Heimkehrers. Vorträge gehalten auf dem 4. Kongress der Deutschen Gesellschaft für Sexualforschung*, ed. Hans Bürger-Prinz and Hans Giese, 27–38. Stuttgart: Ferdinand Enke, 1957.

Kirchheimer, Otto. *Political Justice: The Use of Legal Means for Political Ends*. Princeton: Princeton University Press, 1961.

Klausch, Hans-Peter. *Die Geschichte der Bewährungsbattallione 999 unter besonderer Berücksichtigung des antifaschistischen Widerstands*. Cologne: Pahl Rugenstein, 1987.

Klee, Ernst. *Auschwitz, die NS-Medizin und ihre Opfer*. Frankfurt am Main: Fischer, 1997.

Klein, Thomas. "Die Parteikontrolle in der SED als Instrument der Stalinisierung." In *Sowjetisierung und Eigenständigkeit in der SBZ/DDR (1945–1953)*, ed. Michael Lemke, 119–61. Cologne: Böhlau, 1999.

Kleineke, Dagmar. "Entstehung und Entwicklung des Lagers Friedland, 1945–1955." Ph.D. diss., University of Göttingen, 1992.

Klessmann, Christoph, ed. *The Divided Past: Rewriting German History.* Oxford: Berg, 2001.

Klier, Freya. *Verschleppt ans Ende der Welt. Schicksale deutscher Frauen in sowjetischen Arbeitslagern.* Munich: Ullstein, 2000.

Knoch, Habbo, ed. *Das Erbe der Provinz. Heimatkultur und Geschichtspolitik nach 1945.* Göttingen: Wallstein, 2001.

———. "Das mediale Gedächtnis der Heimat. Krieg und Verbrechen in den Erinnerungsräumen der Bundesrepublik." In *Das Erbe der Provinz. Heimatkultur und Geschichtspolitik nach 1945*, ed. Habbo Knoch, 275–300. Göttingen: Wallstein, 2001.

———. *Die Tat als Bild: Fotografien des Holocaust in der deutschen Erinnerungskultur.* Hamburg: Hamburger Edition, 2001.

Kocka, Jürgen. "1945: Neubeginn oder Restauration?" In *Wendepunkte deutscher Geschichte 1848–1990*, ed. Heinrich-August Winkler, 159–92. Frankfurt am Main: Fischer, 1994.

Kogon, Eugen. "Das Recht auf den politischen Irrtum." *Frankfurter Hefte* 2 (1947): 641–55.

Köhler, Joachim, and Damian van Melis, eds. *Siegerin in Trümmern. Die Rolle der katholischen Kirche in der deutschen Nachkriegsgesellschaft.* Stuttgart: Kohlhammer, 1998.

Kohlhaas, Max. "Die Problematik des Spätheimkehrers im Strafrecht." *Süddeutsche Juristenzeitung* 5 (1950): 450.

Koonz, Claudia. *Mothers in the Fatherland: Women, the Family, and Nazi Politics.* New York: St. Martin's Press, 1987.

Koselleck, Reinhart. "Der Einfluss der beiden Weltkriege auf das soziale Bewußtsein." In *Der Krieg des kleinen Mannes. Eine Militärgeschichte von unten*, ed. Wolfram Wette, 324–43. Munich: Piper, 1992.

———. " 'Erfahrungsraum' und 'Erwartungshorizont'—zwei historische Begriffe." In *Vergangene Zukunft. Zur Semantik geschichtlicher Zeiten*, ed. Reinhart Koselleck, 349–75. Frankfurt am Main: Suhrkamp, 1987.

Koshar, Rudy. *Germany's Transient Pasts. Preservation and National Memory in the Twentieth Century.* Chapel Hill: University of North Carolina Press, 1998.

Kösters, Christoph, ed. *Caritas in der SBZ-DDR. Berichte, Erinnerungen, Forschungen. 1945–1989.* Paderborn: Schönigh, 2001.

Kowalczuk, Ilko-Sascha, Armin Mitter, and Stefan Wolle, eds.. *Der Tag X: 17. Juni 1953. Die "Innere Staatsgründung" der DDR als Ergebnis der Krise 1952–54.* Berlin: Ch. Links, 1995

Krämer, Richard. "Schwachsinn als Heimkehrerproblem." *Der medizinische Sachverständige* 51 (1954–55): 164–65.

Krahé, Josef. "Männerseelsorge und Heimkehrer." In Heimatvertriebene und Heimkehrer. *Vorträge und Anregungen der VII. überdiözesanen Aussprache-Konferenz für Männerseelsorge in Fulda*, 33–51. Augsburg: Winfried Werk, 1950.

Krause, Gerhard. "Deus semper major: Bericht eines Spätheimkehrers." *Zeitwende* 27 (1956): 145–49.

Krause, Michael. *Flucht vor dem Bombenkrieg: "Umquartierungen" im Zweiten Weltkrieg und die Wiedereingliederung der Evakuierten in Deutschland, 1943–1963.* Düsseldorf: Droste, 1997.

Krauss, Marita. *Heimkehr in ein fremdes Land. Geschichte der Remigration nach 1945.* Munich: Beck, 2001.

Kröbe, E. "Der praktische Arzt und die Beurteilung der Kriegsschäden des Nervensystems." *Das Deutsche Gesundheitswesen* 1 (1946): 347–52.

Kroener, Bernhard R. "Auf dem Weg zu einer nationalsozialistischen Volksarmee: Die soziale Öffnung des Heeroffizierskorps im Zweiten Weltkrieg." In *Von Stalingrad zur Währungsreform. Zur Sozialgeschichte des Umbruchs in Deutschland*, ed. Martin Broszat, Klaus-Dietmar Henke, and Hans Woller, 51–82. Munich: Oldenbourg, 1988.

Krüger, Wolfgang. *Entnazifiziert. Die Praxis der politischen Säuberung in Nordrhein-Westfalen.* Wuppertal: Hammer, 1982.

Krylova, Anna. " 'Healers of Wounded Souls': The Crisis of Private Life in Soviet Literature, 1944–1946." *Journal of Modern History* 73 (2001): 307–31.

Kühne, Thomas. "Kameradschaft—'das Beste im Leben eines Mannes.' Die deutschen Soldaten des Zweiten Weltkrieges in erfahrungs-und geschlechtergeschichtlicher Perspektive." *Geschichte und Gesellschaft* 22 (1996): 504–29.

———. "Männergeschichte als Geschlechtergeschichte." In *Männergeschichte-Geschlechtergeschichte. Männlichkeit im Wandel der Moderne*, ed. Thomas Kühne, 7–30. Frankfurt am Main: Campus, 1996.

———. "Der nationalsozialistische Vernichtungskrieg im kulturellen Kontinuum des Zwanzigsten Jahrhunderts. Forschungsprobleme und Forschungstendenzen der Gesellschaftsgeschichte des Zweiten Weltkrieges. Zweiter Teil." *Archiv für Sozialgeschichte* 40 (2000): 440–86.

———. "Der nationalsozialistische Vernichtungskrieg und die ganz 'normalen' Deutschen. Forschungsprobleme und Forschungstendenzen der Gesellschaftsgeschichte des Zweiten Weltkrieges. Erster Teil." *Archiv für Sozialgeschichte* 39 (1999): 580–662.

———. "Zwischen Männerbund und Volksgemeinschaft. Hitlers Soldaten und der Mythos der Kameradschaft." *Archiv für Sozialgeschichte* 38 (1998): 165–89.

———. "Zwischen Vernichtungskrieg und Freizeitgesellschaft. Die Veteranenkultur der Bundesrepublik (1945–1955)." In *Nachkrieg in Deutschland*, ed. Klaus Naumann, 90–113. Hamburg: Hamburger Edition, 2001.

Kumpfmüller, Michael. *Die Schlacht von Stalingrad. Metamorphosen eines deutschen Mythos.* Munich: Wilhelm Fink, 1995.

Kundrus, Birthe. *Kriegerfrauen. Familienpolitik und Geschlechtverhältnisse im Ersten und Zweiten Weltkrieg.* Hamburg: Christians, 1995.

———. "Nur die halbe Geschichte. Frauen im Umfeld der Wehrmacht." In *Die Wehrmacht. Mythos und Realität*, ed. Rolf-Dieter Müller and Hans-Erich Volkmann, 719–35. Munich: Oldenbourg, 1999.

Kunz, Andreas. *Wehrmacht und Niederlage. Die bewaffnete Macht in der Endphase der nationalsozialistischen Herrschaft 1944 bis 1945.* Munich: Oldenbourg, 2005.

Kunze, Rolf Ulrich. "Das Evangelische Hilfswerk für Internierte und Kriegsgefangene 1945–1955/56. Ein Beitrag zur evangelischen Diakonie- und Seelsorge-geschichte und zur Geschichte der deutschen Kriegsgefangenen in der Sowjetunion." *Zeitschrift für Bayrische Kirchengeschichte* 65 (1996): 32–84.

———. *Theodor Heckel, 1894–1967. Eine Biographie.* Stuttgart: Kohlhammer, 1997.

Kurz, Karl. *Lebensverhältnisse der Nachkriegsjugend.* Bremen: Friedrich Trüjen, 1949.

LaCapra, Dominick. *History and Memory after Auschwitz.* Ithaca: Cornell University Press, 1998.

Lagrou, Pieter. *The Legacy of Nazi Occupation: Patriotic Memory and National Recovery in Western Europe, 1945–1965.* Cambridge: Cambridge University Press, 2000.

———. "The Nationalization of Victimhood: Selective Violence and National Grief in Western Europe, 1940–1960." In *Life after Death: Approaches to a Social and Cultural History of Europe during the 1940s and 1950s,* ed. Richard Bessel and Dirk Schumann, 243–57. Cambridge: Cambridge University Press, 2003.

Lang, Theo. "Die Homosexualität als genetisches Problem." In *Die Sexualität des Heimkehrers. Vorträge gehalten auf dem 4. Kongress der Deutschen Gesellschaft für Sexualforschung,* ed. Hans Bürger-Prinz and Hans Giese, 79–86. Stuttgart: Ferdinand Enke, 1957.

Lange, Erich. "Alter und Beruf der Heimkehrer." *Arbeit und Sozialfürsorge* 9 (1949): 194–95.

Laqueur, Walter. *The Terrible Secret: Supression of Truth about Hitler's "Final Solution."* Boston: Little, Brown, 1980.

Large, David Clay. *Germans to the Front: West German Rearmament in the Adenauer Era.* Chapel Hill: University of North Carolina Press, 1996.

Laszlo, Carl. "Zur Soziologie der Homosexualität." *Zeitschrift für Psychotherapie und Psychologie* 6 (1956): 84–87.

Latzel, Klaus. *Deutsche Soldaten—nationalsozialistischer Krieg. Kriegserlebnis-Kriegserfahrung 1939–1945.* Paderborn: Schönigh, 1998.

———. " 'Freie Bahn den Tüchtigen.' Kriegserfahrung und Perspektiven für die Nachkriegszeit in Feldpostbriefen aus dem Zweiten Weltkrieg." In *Lernen aus dem Krieg? Deutsche Nachkriegszeiten 1918–1945,* ed. Gottfried Niedhardt and Dieter Riesenberger, 331–43. Munich: C. H. Beck, 1992.

Lehmann, Albrecht. *Gefangenschaft und Heimkehr. Deutsche Kriegsgefangene in der Sowjetunion.* Munich: C.H. Beck, 1986.

Lemke, Michael. "Kampagnen gegen Bonn. Die Systemkrise der DDR und die West Propaganda der SED." *Vierteljahreshefte für Zeitgeschichte* 41 (1993): 153–74.

Lemke, R. "Über die vegetative Depression." *Psychiatrie, Neurologie und Medizinische Psychologie* 1 (1949): 161–65.

Leonhardt, Wolfgang. "Erscheinungsbilder des postdystrophischen psychoorganischen Dauerschadens." Med. Diss., University of Tübingen, 1969.

Lerner, Paul. *Hysterical Men: War, Psychiatry, and the Politics of Trauma in Germany, 1890–1930.* Ithaca: Cornell University Press, 2003.

Lerner, Paul, and Mark Micale. "Trauma, Psychiatry, and History." In *Traumatic Pasts: History, Psychiatry, and Trauma in the Modern Age, 1870–1930,* ed. Paul Lerner and Mark Micale, 1–27. Cambridge: Cambridge University Press, 2001.

Levy, Carl, and Mark Roseman, eds. *Three Postwar Eras in Comparison: Western Europe 1918–1945–1989.* New York: Palgrave, 2002.

Lewin, Bruno. "Neurologisch-psychiatrische Untersuchungen und Beobachtungen an deutschen Kriegsgefangenen in Ägypten 1941–47." *Psychiatrie, Neurologie, und Medizinische Psychologie* 1 (1949): 230–35.

Lindenberg, W. "Lebensmut oder Renten-Neurose?" *Das Deutsche Gesundheitswesen* 1 (1946): 91–93.

Lindenberger, Thomas. " 'Aus dem Volk, für das Volk?' Bermerkungen zur
Entstehung der bewaffneten Organe der SBZ/DDR aus sozialhistorischer
Sicht." In *Nationale Volksarmee—Armee für den Frieden. Beiträge zu Selbstver-
ständnis und Geschichte des deutschen Militärs*, ed. Detlef Bald, Reinhard
Brühl, and Andreas Prüfert, 165–80. Baden-Baden: Nomos, 1995.

———. *Volkspolizei. Herrschaftspraxis und öffentliche Ordnung im SED-Staat
1952 bis 1968.* Cologne: Böhlau, 2003.

———, ed. *Herrschaft und Eigensinn. Studien zur Gesellschaftsgeschichte der
DDR.* Cologne: Böhlau, 1999.

Lockenour, Jay. *Soldiers as Citizens: Former Wehrmacht Officers in the Federal
Republic of Germany.* Lincoln: University of Nebraska Press, 2001.

Lockot, Regine. *Erinnern und Durcharbeiten: Zur Geschichte der Psychoanalyse
und Psychotherapie im Nationalsozialismus.* Frankfurt am Main: Fischer,
1985.

Löhr, Wolfgang. "Rechristianisierungsvorstellungen im deutschen Katholizismus
1945–1948." In *Christentum und politische Verantwortung. Kirchen in der
Nachkriegszeit*, ed. Jochen-Christoph Kaiser and Anselm Döring-Manteuffel,
25–41. Stuttgart: Kohlhammer, 1990.

Lübbe, Hermann. "Der Nationalsozialismus im deutschen Nachkriegsbewußtsein." *Historische Zeitschrift* 236 (1983): 579–99.

Lüdtke, Alf. "Histories of Mourning: Flowers and Stones for the War Dead, Con-
fusion for the Living—Vignettes from East and West Germany." In *Between
History and Histories: The Making of Silences and Commemorations*, ed. Gerald Sider and Gavin Smith, 149–79. Toronto: University of Toronto Press, 1997.

Lunbeck, Elizabeth. *The Psychiatric Persuasion: Knowledge, Gender, and Power
in Modern America.* Princeton: Princeton University Press, 1994.

Luther, Host. "Denunziation als soziales und strafrechtliches Problem in Deutschland in den Jahren 1945–1990." In *Denunziation. Historische, juristische und
psychologische Aspekte*, ed. Inge Marssolek, Gunter Jerouschek, and Hedwig
Röckelein, 258–78. Tübingen: Edition Diskord, 1997.

Lüttinger, Paul. "Der Mythos der schnellen Integration. Eine empirische Analyse
zur Integration der Vertriebenen." *Zeitschrift für Soziologie* 15 (1987): 20–36.

Mählert, Ulrich. " 'Die Partei hat immer Recht.' Parteisäuberung als Kaderpolitik
in der SED (1948–1953)." In *Terror. Stalinistische Parteisäuberungen, 1936–
1953*, ed. Ulrich Mählert and Hermann Weber, 351–457. Paderborn: Schönigh,
1998.

———. "Schauprozesse und Parteisäuberungen in Osteuropa nach 1945." *Aus
Politik und Zeitgeschichte* 37–38 (1996): 38–46.

Maier, Charles. "Consigning the Twentieth Century to History. Alternative Narratives for the Modern Era." *American Historical Review* 105 (2000): 807–31.

———. *Dissolution: The Crisis of Communism and the End of East Germany.*
Princeton: Princeton University Press, 1997.

———. "The Two Postwar Eras and the Conditions for Stability in Western Europe." *American Historical Review* 86 (1981): 327–52.

———. *The Unmasterable Past: History, Holocaust, and German National Identity.* Cambridge: Harvard University Press, 1988.

Major, Patrick. *The Death of the KPD: Communism and Anti-Communism in West Germany, 1945–1956.* Oxford: Clarendon Press, 1997.

Malten, Hans. "Heimkehrer." *Medizinische Klinik* 41, no. 24 (1946): 593–600.

Malycha, Andreas. *Die SED. Geschichte ihrer Stalinisierung, 1945–1953.* Paderborn: Schönigh, 2000.

———. *Partei von Stalins Gnaden? Die Entwicklung der SED zur Partei Neuen Typs in den Jahren 1946 bis 1950.* Berlin: Dietz, 1996.

Manig, Bert-Oliver. *Die Politik der Ehre. Die Rehabilitierung der Berufsoldaten in der frühen Bundesrepublik.* Göttingen: Wallstein, 2004.

Marcuse, Harold. *Legacies of Dachau: The Uses and Abuses of a Concentration Camp, 1945–2000.* Cambridge: Cambridge University Press, 2001.

Marshall, T. H. *Citizenship and Social Class.* Cambridge: Cambridge University Press, 1950.

Maschke, Erich. *Die deutschen Kriegsgefangenen des Zweiten Weltkrieges. Eine Zusammenfassung.* Bielefeld: Gieseking, 1974.

Matschenz, Andreas. " 'Der Onkel da ist Dein Vater.' " In *Heimkehr 1948. Geschichte und Schicksal deutscher Kriegsgefangener,* ed. Annette Kaminsky, 117–40. Munich: C. H. Beck, 1998.

Mayer, A. "Zur Heimkehrerfrage." In *Die Sexualität des Heimkehrers. Vorträge gehalten auf dem 4. Kongress der Deutschen Gesellschaft für Sexualforschung,* ed. Hans Bürger-Prinz and Hans Giese, 38–41. Stuttgart: Ferdinand Enke, 1957.

Mayer, Karl Ulrich. "German Survivors of World War II. The Impact on the Life Course of the Collective Experience of Birth Cohorts." In *Social Structure and Human Lives,* ed. Mithalda White Riley, 229–46. New York: Sage, 1988.

Mayntz, Renate. *Die moderne Familie.* Stuttgart: Ferdinand Enke, 1955.

Mazower, Mark, ed. *After the War Was Over: Reconstructing the Family, Nation, and State in Greece, 1943–1960.* Princeton: Princeton University Press, 2000.

———. "Changing Trends in the Historiorgraphy of Postwar Europe, East and West." *International Labor and Working-Class History* 58 (2000): 275–82.

———. *Dark Continent: Europe's Twentieth Century.* New York: Knopf, 1999.

McNally, Richard. "Posttraumatic Stress Disorder." In *Oxford Textbook of Psychopathology,* 144–65. New York: Oxford University Press, 1999.

Meckel, Christoph. *Suchbild: Über meinen Vater.* Düsseldorf: Claassen, 1980.

Merridale, Catherine. *Night of Stone: Death and Memory in Twentieth-Century Russia.* New York: Penguin, 2000.

Messerschmidt, Manfred. *Die Wehrmacht im NS-Staat. Zeit der Indoktrination.* Hamburg: G. Schenk, 1969.

———. "Die Wehrmacht in der Endphase. Realität und Perzeption." *Aus Politik und Zeitgeschichte* 32–33 (1989): 33–46.

Messerschmidt, Manfred, and Fritz Wüllner. *Die Wehrmachtsjustiz im Dienste des Nationalsozialismus—Zerstörung einer Legende.* Baden-Baden: Nomos, 1987.

Meuschel, Sigrid. *Legitimation und Parteiherrschaft in der DDR*. Frankfurt am Main: Suhrkamp, 1992.

Meyer, Heinz Heinrich. *Kriegsgefangene im Kalten Krieg. Die Kriegsgefangenenpolitik der Bundesrepublik Deutschland im amerikanisch-sowjetischen Machtkampf von 1950 bis 1955*. Osnabrück: Biblio Verlag, 1998.

Meyer, Sibylle. *Von Liebe sprach damals keiner: Familienalltag in der Nachkriegszeit*. Munich: Beck, 1985.

Meyeringh, Hans. "Über Spätfolgen der Dystrophie." *Deutsche Medizinische Wochenschrift* 79, no. 7 (1954): 241–42.

Meyeringh, Hans, and Andreas Dietze. "Wandlungen im Bild der Dystrophie." *Medizinische Wochenschrift* 75, no. 42 (1950): 1–6.

Meyeringh, Hans, Andreas Dietze, and W. Haessler. "Über den Gesundheitszustand der Spätheimkehrer der Jahre 1953/54." *Deutsche Medizinische Wochenschrift* 80, no. 44 (1955): 1606–11.

Michel, Max. "Die Tiefe des psychologischen Traumas bei der Totalverfolgung." In *Die Sexualität des Heimkehrers. Vorträge gehalten auf dem 4. Kongress der Deutschen Gesellschaft für Sexualforschung*, ed. Hans Bürger-Prinz and Hans Giese, 50–59. Stuttgart: Ferdinand Enke, 1957.

Missalla, Heinrich. *Für Volk und Vaterland. Die Kirchliche Kriegshilfe im Zweiten Weltkrieg*. Königstein: Athanäum, 1978.

Mitchell, Maria. "Materialism and Secularism: CDU Politicians and National Socialism, 1945–1949." *Journal of Modern History* 67 (1995): 278–308.

Mitscherlich, Alexander, and Margarate Mitscherlich. *Die Unfähigkeit zu trauern. Grundlagen kollektiven Verhaltens*. Munich: Piper, 1967.

Mittermaier, Klaus. *Vermisst wird . . . Die Arbeit des deutschen Suchdienstes*. Berlin: Links, 2002.

Moeller, Robert G. "The Elephant in the Living Room or Why the History of Twentieth-Century Germany Should Be a Family Affair." In *Gendering Modern German History: Rewritings of the "Mainstream,"* ed. Karen Hagemann and Jean Quartart, New York: Berghahn Books, forthcoming.

———. " 'Germans as Victims?' Thoughts on a Post–Cold War History of the Second World War." *History and Memory* 17, nos. 1–2 (2005): 147–94.

———. "Geschichten aus der 'Stacheldrahtuniversität': Kriegsgefangene im Opferdiskurs der Bundesrepublik." *Werkstatt Geschichte* 26 (2000): 23–46.

———. "The Homosexual Man Is a 'Man,' the Homosexual Woman Is a 'Woman.' Sex, Society, and the Law in Postwar West Germany." *Journal of the History of Sexuality* 4 (1994): 395–438.

———. "The 'Last Solders of the Great War' and Tales of Family Reunions in the Federal Republic of Germany." *Signs* 24 (1998): 129–45.

———. *Protecting Motherhood: Women and the Family in the Politics of Postwar West Germany*. Berkeley and Los Angeles: University of California Press, 1993.

———. "The 'Remasculinization' of Germany in the 1950s: Introduction." *Signs* 24 (1998): 101–6.

———. *War Stories: The Search for a Usable Past in the Federal Republic of Germany*. Berkeley and Los Angeles: University of California Press, 2001.

———. "War Stories: The Search for a Usable Past in the Federal Republic of Germany." *American Historical Review* 101 (1996): 1008–48.

————. "What Has Coming to Terms with the Past Meant in the Federal Republic of Germany?" *Central European History* 35 (2002): 223–56.

————, ed. *West Germany under Construction: Politics, Society, and Culture in the Adenauer Era.* Ann Arbor: University of Michigan Press, 1997.

Moll, Christiane. "Die Weisse Rose." In *Widerstand gegen den Nationalsozialismus*, ed. Peter Steinbach and Johannes Tuchel, 443–67. Berlin: Akademie, 1994.

Mommsen, Hans. "The Dissolution of the Third Reich: Crisis Management and Collapse, 1943–45." *Bulletin of the German Historical Institute* 27 (fall 2000): 9–23.

Moore, Bob, and Kent Fedorwich, eds. *Prisoners of War and Their Captors in World War II.* Oxford: Berg, 1996.

Mooser, Josef. "Arbeiter, Angestellte und Frauen in der 'nivellierten Mittelstandsgesellschaft.' " In *Modernisierung im Wiederaufbau. Die westdeutsche Gesellschaft der 50er Jahre*, ed. Axel Schildt and Arnold Sywotteck, 362–76. Bonn: J.H.W. Dietz, 1995.

Morina, Christina. "Instructed Silence, Constructed Memory: The SED and the Return of German Prisoners of War as 'War Criminals' from the Soviet Union to East Germany, 1950–1956." *Contemporary European History* 13 (2004): 323–43.

Morré, Jörg. *Hinter den Kullisen des Nationalkomitees. Das Institut 99 in Moskau und die Deutschlandpolitik der UdSSR, 1943–1946.* Munich: Oldenbourg, 2001.

————. "Kader für Deutschland?" In *Heimkehr 1948. Geschichte und Schicksal deutscher Kriegsgefangener*, ed. Annette Kaminsky, 217–31. Munich: C. H. Beck, 1998.

Moser, Timan. *Dämonische Figuren. Die Wiederkehr des Dritten Reiches in der Psychotherapie.* Frankfurt am Main: Suhrkamp, 1996.

Mosse, George. *Fallen Soldiers: Reshaping the Memories of the World Wars.* New York: Oxford University Press, 1990.

————. *The Image of Man: The Creation of Modern Masculinity.* New York: Oxford University Press, 1996.

Müller, Ingo. *Hitler's Justice: The Courts of the Third Reich.* Trans. Deborah Lucas Schneider. Cambridge: Harvard University Press, 1991.

Müller, Rolf-Dieter. "Die Behandlung sowjetischer Kriegsgefangener durch das Deutsche Reich 1941–1945." In *Kriegsgefangenschaft im Zweiten Weltkrieg. Eine vergleichende Perspektive*, ed. Günter Bischof and Rüdiger Overmans, 283–302. Ternitz-Pottschach: Verlag Gerhard Höller, 1999.

Müller, Rolf-Dieter, and Gerd R. Ueberschär. *Hitler's War in the East: A Critical Assessment.* New York: Berghahn, 2002.

Müller, Rolf-Dieter, and Hans-Erich Volkmann, eds. *Die Wehrmacht. Mythos und Realität.* Munich: Oldenbourg, 1999.

Müller-Gangloff, Ernst. *Christen in Kriegsgefangenschaft.* Berlin: Verlag die Schöpfung, 1948.

Müller-Hegemann, Dietfried. *Neurologie und Psychiatrie. Lehrbuch für Studierende und Ärzte.* Berlin: VEB Verlag Volk und Gesundheit, 1966.

Müller-Hegemann, Dietfried. *Die Psychotherapie bei schizophrenen Prozessen. Erfahrungen und Probleme.* Leipzig: S. Hirzel, 1952.

———. *Zur Psychologie deutscher Faschisten.* Rudolstadt: Greiffenverlag, 1955.

Münkler, Herfried, and Karsten Fischer. " 'Nothing to kill or die for . . .'—Überlegungen zu einer politischen Theorie des Opfers." *Leviathan* 28 (2000): 343–62.

Naimark, Norman. *The Russians in Germany: A History of the Soviet Zone of Occupation.* Cambridge: Harvard University Press, 1995.

Nathusius, Wolf v. "Sind die Gesundheitsschäden bei den Heimkehrern aus Kriegsgefangenschaft und Internierung überwunden?" *Berliner Gesundheitsblatt* 6 (1955): 206–8.

Naumann, Klaus. " 'Brave Nazis' für die Bundeswehr? Russlandheimkehrer als Generäle und Offiziere der bundesdeutschen Streitkräfte." *Zeitgeschichte* 30, no. 4 (2003): 211–24.

———. "Die Frage nach dem Ende. Von der unbestimmten Dauer der Nachkriegszeit." *Mittelweg 36* 8 (1999): 21–32.

———. *Der Krieg als Text. Das Jahr 1945 im kulturellen Gedächtnis der Presse.* Hamburg: Hamburger Edition, 1998.

———. "Nachkrieg: Vernichtungskrieg, Wehrmacht und Militär in der deutschen Wahrnehmung nach 1945." *Mittelweg 36* 7 (1997): 11–26.

———, ed. *Nachkrieg in Deutschland.* Hamburg: Hamburger Edition, 2001.

Neumann, Gerhard J. "Zur Religionssoziologie der Flüchtlinge." *Soziale Welt* 8, no. 2 (1957): 114–28.

Neumann, Vera. "Kampf um Anerkennung. Die westdeutsche Kriegsfolgengesellschaft im Spiegel der Versorgungsämter." In *Nachkrieg in Deutschland,* ed. Klaus Naumann, 364–83. Hamburg: Hamburger Edition, 2001.

———. *Nicht der Rede Wert. Die Privatisierung der Kriegserfahrung in der frühen Bundesrepublik.* Münster: Westfälisches Dampfboot, 1999.

Niedhardt, Gottfried, and Dieter Riesenberger, eds. *Lernen aus dem Krieg? Deutsche Nachkriegszeiten 1914 und 1945. Beiträge zur historischen Friedensforschung.* Munich: C. H. Beck, 1992.

Niehuss, Merrit. *Familie, Frau und Gesellschaft. Studien zur Strukturgeschichte der Familie in Westdeutschland 1945–1960.* Göttingen: Vandenhoek, 2001.

Niermann, Hans Eckhard. "Zwischen Amnestie und Anpassung: Die Entnazifizierung der Richter und Staatsanwälte des Oberlandesbezirksgerichts Hamm 1945 bis 1950." *Juristische Zeitgeschichte* 5 (1996): 61–94.

Niethammer, Lutz. "Alliierte Internierungslager in Deutschland. Vergleich und offene Fragen." In *Von der Aufgabe der Freiheit. Politische Verantwortung und bürgerliche Gesellschaft im 19. und 20. Jahrhundert. Festschrift für Hans Mommsen,* ed. Christian Jansen, Lutz Niethammer, and Bernd Weisbrod, 471–92. Berlin: Akademie, 1995.

———. *Ego-Histoire?* Cologne: Böhlau, 2002.

———. "Erfahrungen und Strukturen. Prolegomena zu einer Geschichte der Gesellschaft der DDR." In *Sozialgeschichte der DDR,* ed. Jürgen Kocka, Hartmut Kaelble, and Hartmut Zwahr, 95–113. Stuttgart: Klett-Cotta, 1994.

———. "Heimat und Front. Versuch, zehn Kriegserinnerungen aus der Arbeiterklasse des Ruhrgebiets zu verstehen." In *"Die Jahre weiss man nicht, wo man die heute hinsetzen soll." Faschismuserfahrungen im Ruhrgebiet*, ed. Lutz Niethammer, 163–232. Berlin: J.H.W. Dietz, 1983.

———, ed. *Der "gesäuberte" Antifaschismus. Die SED und die roten Kapos von Buchenwald*. Berlin: Akademie, 1994.

———, ed. *Lebensgeschichte und Sozialkultur im Ruhrgebiet, 1930–1960*. 3 vols. Berlin: Dietz, 1983–86.

Niethammer, Lutz, Alexander von Plato, and Dorothee Wierling. *Die volkseigene Erfahrung: eine Archäologie des Lebens in der Industrieprovinz der DDR: 30 biografische Eröffnungen*. Berlin: Rohwolt, 1991.

Nitsche, Hans Jürgen. "Das Internationale Privatrecht der Todeserklärung." Ph.D. diss., University of Munich, 1971.

Nitzschke, Bernd. "Psycholanalyse als 'un'-politische Wissenschaft." *Zeitschrift für psychosomatische Medizin und Psychoanalyse* 37 (1991): 31–44.

Noelle, Elisabeth, and Erich Peter Neumann, eds. *The Germans: Public Opinion Polls 1947–1966*. Allensbach: Verlag für Demoskopie, 1967.

———, ed. *Jahrbuch der öffentlichen Meinung*. Allensbach: Verlag für Demoskopie, 1957.

Novick, Peter. *The Holocaust in American Life*. Boston: Houghton Mifflin, 1999.

Otto, Wilfriede. "Die Waldheimer Prozesse." In *Sowjetische Speziallager in Deutschland 1945 bis 1950*, ed. Sergej Mironenko, Lutz Niethammer, and Alexander von Plato, with Volkhard Knigge und Günter Morsch. Vol. 1, *Studien und Berichte*, ed. Alexander von Plato, 533–53. Berlin: Akademie, 1998.

Overesch, Manfred. *Buchenwald und die DDR: Oder die Suche nach Selbstlegitimation*. Göttingen: Vandenhoeck und Ruprecht, 1995.

Overmans, Rüdiger. "Das andere Gesicht des Krieges. Leben und Sterben der 6. Armee." In *Stalingrad: Ereignis-Wirkung-Symbol*, ed. Jürgen Förster, 419–55. Munich: Piper, 1993.

———. *Deutsche militärische Verluste im Zweiten Weltkrieg*. Munich: Oldenbourg, 1999.

———. "German Historiography, the War Losses, and the Prisoners of War." In *Facts against Falsehood: Eisenhower and German POWs*, ed. Günter Bischof and Stephen Ambrose, 127–69. Baton Rouge: Louisiana University Press, 1992.

———. "Kriegsgefangenschaft—ein vergessenes Thema. Bibliographischer Essay." In *Kriegsgefangenschaft im Zweiten Weltkrieg*, ed. Günter Bischof and Rüdiger Overmans, 429–68. Ternitz-Pottschach: Gerhard Höller, 1999.

———. "Ein Silberstreif am Forschungshorizont. Veröffentlichungen zur Geschichte der Kriegsgefangenschaft." In *In der Hand des Feindes: Kriegsgefangenschaft von der Antike bis zum Zweiten Weltkrieg*, ed. Rüdiger Overmans, 483–551. Cologne: Böhlau, 1999.

Overy, Richard. *Why the Allies Won*. New York: Norton, 1996.

Palmowski, Jan. "Building an East German Nation: The Construction of a Socialist Heimat, 1945–1961." *Central European History* 37, no. 3 (2004): 365–99.

Panse, Friedrich. *Angst und Schreck in klinisch-psychologischer und sozialmedizinischer Sicht*. Stuttgart: G. Thieme, 1952.

———. *Das Erb- und Erscheinungsbild des Psychopathen*. Bonn: Universitätsbuchdruckerei, 1941.

Peitsch, Helmut. *Deutschlands Gedächtnis an seine dunkelste Zeit. Zur Funktion der Autobiographik in den Westzonen und den Westsektoren von Berlin 1945 bis 1949.* Berlin: Ed Sigma, 1990.

Peterson, Edward N. *The Many Faces of Defeat: The German People's Experience in 1945.* New York: Peter Lang, 1990.

Peukert, Detlev. *Volksgenossen und Gemeinschaftsfremde. Apassung, Ausmerze und Aufbegehren unter dem Nationalsozialismus.* Cologne: Bund, 1982.

Plant, Rebecca J. "The Repeal of Mother Love: Momism and the Reconstruction of Motherhood in Phillip Wylie's America." Ph.D. diss., Johns Hopkins University, 2002.

Poiger, Uta. *Jazz, Rock, and Rebels: Cold War Politics and American Culture in a Divided Germany.* Berkeley and Los Angeles: University of California Press, 2000.

Pollack, Detlef. "Secularisation in Germany after 1945." In *The Divided Past: Rewriting Postwar German History,* ed. Christoph Kleßmann, 105–25. Oxford: Berg, 2001.

Possekel, Ralf. "Einleitung: Sowjetische Lagerpolitik in Deutschland." In *Sowjetische Speziallager in Deutschland 1945 bis 1950,* ed. Sergej Mironenko, Lutz Niethammer, and Alexander von Plato, with Volkhard Knigge und Günter Morsch. Vol. 2, *Sowjetische Dokumente zur Lagerpolitik,* ed. Ralf Possekel, 15–110. Berlin: Akademie, 1998.

Pross, Christian. *Paying for the German Past: The Struggle over Reparations for Surviving Victims of Nazi Terror.* Baltimore: Johns Hopkins University Press, 1998.

Rabinbach, Anson. *In the Shadow of Catastrophe: German Intellectuals between Apocalypse and Enlightenment.* Berkeley and Los Angeles: University of California Press, 1997.

Radcliff, Pamela. "La ciudadania ante la transición a la democracia." In *La construcción de la ciudadania en la España contemporanea,* ed. Manuel Pérez Ledesma. Madrid: Alianza Editorial, in press.

Ramazanoglu, Caroline. "What Can You Do with a Man? Feminism and the Critical Appraisal of Masculinity." *Women's Studies International Forum* 15 (1992): 339–50.

Rass, Christoph. *"Menschenmaterial." Deutsche Soldaten an der Ostfront. Innenansichten einer Infrantriedivision, 1939–1945.* Paderborn: Schöningh, 2003.

Ratschow, M. "Zur Ödemkrankheit und ihrer Beeinflussung durch Cystin." *Das Deutsche Gesundheitswesen* 1 (1946): 362–65.

Rauh-Kühne, Cornelia. "Die Entnazifizierung und die deutsche Gesellschaft." *Archiv für Sozialgeschichte* 35 (1995): 35–70.

Rauschelbach, Heinz-Harro. "Allegemeine Begutachtungsgrundsätze bei der Beeurteilung von gesundheitlichen Schäden nach Haft und Gefangenschaft." *Der medizinische Sachverständige* 92 (1996): 8–13.

———. "Zu einigen gutachterlichen Problemen bei der Nachuntersuchung von Spätheimkehrern." *Die Kriegsopferversorgung* 10, no. 2 (1961): 31–34.

———. "Zur Klinik der Spätfolgezustände nach Hungerdystrophie." *Fortschitte der Neurologie, Psychiatrie und ihrer Grenzgebiete* 22 (1954): 214–26.

————. "Zur versorgungsrechtlichen Beurteilung der Spätheimkehrer, unter besonderer Berücksichtigung der Dystrophiefolgenzustände." *Die Medizinische* 50 (1954): 1678–82.

Reemstma, Jan Phillip. *Mord am Strand. Allianzen von Zivilisation und Barbarei.* Berlin: Siedler, 2000.

Reichel, Peter. *Erfundene Erinnerung. Weltkrieg und Judenmord in Film und Theater.* Munich: Hanser, 2004.

————. *Der schöne Schein des Dritten Reiches. Faszination und Gewalt des Faschismus.* 2nd ed. Frankfurt am Main: Fischer, 1993.

Reiss, Matthias. *"Die Schwarzen waren unsere Freunde." Deutsche Kriegsgefangene in der amerikanischen Gesellschaft, 1942–1946.* Paderborn: Schöningh, 2002.

Repgen, Konrad. "Die Erfahrung des Dritten Reiches und das Selbstverständnis der Katholiken." In *Die Zeit nach 1945 als Thema kirchlicher Zeitsgeschichte,* ed. Victor Conzemius, Martin Greschat, and Hermann Kocher, 127–79. Göttingen: Vandenhoek, 1988.

Requate, Jörg. "Vergangenheitspolitik in der Debatte um eine Reform der Justiz in den Sechziger Jahren." In *Geschichte vor Gericht. Historiker, Richter, und die Suche nach Gerechtigkeit,* ed. Norbert Frei, Dirk von Laak, and Michael Stolleis, 72–92. Munich: Beck, 2000.

Reschnin, Leonid. *Feldmarschall im Kreuzverhör. Friedrich Paulus in sowjetischer Gefangenschaft, 1943–1953.* Trans. Barbara Lehnhardt and Lothar Lehnhardt. Berlin: edition q, 1996.

Reuband, Karl-Heinz. " 'Schwarzhören' im Dritten Reich. Verbreitung, Erscheinungsform und Kommunikationsmuster beim Umgang mit verbotenen Sendern." *Archiv für Sozialgeschichte* 41 (2001): 245–70.

Richter, Timm C. "Die Wehrmacht und der Partisanenkrieg in den besetzten Gebieten der Sowjetunion." In *Die Wehrmacht. Mythos und Realität,* ed. Rolf-Dieter Müller and Hans-Erich Volkmann, 837–57. Munich: Oldenbourg, 1999.

Rickels, Laurence A. *Nazi Psychoanalysis.* 3 vols. Minneapolis: University of Minnesota Press, 2002.

Ricoeur, Paul. *History, Memory, Forgetting.* Trans. Kathleen Blamey and David Pellauer. Chicago: University of Chicago Press, 2004.

Riedesser, Peter, and Axel Verderber. *"Maschinengewehre hinter der Front." Zur Geschichte der deutschen Militärpsychiatrie.* Frankfurt am Main: Fischer, 1996.

Riesenberger, Dieter, ed. *Das deutsche Rote Kreuz, Konrad Adenauer, und das Kriegsgefangenenproblem. Die Rückführung der deutschen Kriegsgefangenen aus der Sowjetunion (1952–1955).* Bremen: Donat, 1994.

Rölli-Alkemper, Lukas. *Familie im Wiederaufbau. Katholizismus und bürgerliches Familienideal in der Bundesrepublik Deutschland, 1945–1965.* Paderborn: Schönigh, 2000.

Rosenthal, Gabriele. *". . . wenn alles in Scherben fällt . . ." Vom Leben und Sinnwelt der Kriegsgeneration. Typen biographischer Wandlungen.* Opladen: Leske und Budrich, 1987.

Ross, Corey. *The East German Dictatorship: Problems and Perspectives of Interpretation.* London: Arnold, 2002.

Rossino, Alexander B. *Hitler Strikes Poland: Blitzkrieg, Ideology, and Atrocity.* Lawrence: University Press of Kansas, 2003.

Roth, Karl-Heinz. "Die Modernisierung der Folter in den beiden Weltkriegen: Der Konflikt der Psychotherapeuten und Schulpsychiater um die deutschen 'Kriegs-neurotiker' 1915–1945." *1999. Zeitschrift für Sozialgeschichte des 20. und 21. Jahrhunderts* 2, no. 3 (1987): 8–75.

Rousso, Henry. "Das Dilemma eines europäischen Gedächtnisses." *Zeithistorische Forschungen/Studies in Contemporary History, Online-Ausgabe* 1, no. 3 (2004).

——. "L'Epuration. Die politische Säuberung in Frankreich." In *Politische Säuberung in Europe. Die Abrechnung mit Faschismus und Kollaboration nach dem Zweiten Weltkrieg*, ed. Klaus-Dietmar Henke and Hans Woller, 192–240. Frankfurt am Main: Fischer, 1991.

——. *The Vichy Syndrome: History and Memory in France since 1944.* Cambridge: Harvard University Press, 1991.

Rückerl, Adalbert. *The Investigation of Nazi Crimes, 1945–1978.* Trans. Derek Rutter. Hamden, Conn.: Archon, 1980.

Ruff, Mark Edard. *The Wayward Flock: Catholic Youth in Postwar West Germany, 1945–1965.* Chapel Hill: University of North Carolina Press, 2005.

Ruhl, Klaus-Jörg. *Verordnete Unterordnung. Berufstätige Frauen zwischen Wirtschaftwachstum und konservativer Ideologie in der Nachkriegszeit (1945–1963).* Munich: Oldenbourg, 1993.

Rütter, C. F., and D. W. De Mildt. *Die westdeutschen Strafverfahren wegen nationalsozialistischer Tötungsverbrechen 1945–1997. Eine systematische Verfahrensbeschreibung mit Karten und Registern.* Munich: KG Sauer, 1998.

Sasson, Donald. "Italy after Fascism: The Predicament of Dominant Narratives." In *Life after Death: Approaches to the Social and Cultural History of Europe during the 1940s and 1950s*, ed. Richard Bessel and Dirk Schumann, 259–90. Cambridge: Cambridge University Press, 2003.

Scarry, Elaine. *The Body in Pain: The Making and Unmaking of the World.* New York: Oxford University Press, 1987.

Schaetzing, Eberhard. "Die Frau des Heimkehrers." In *Die Sexualität des Heimkehrers. Vorträge gehalten auf dem 4. Kongress der Deutschen Gesellschaft für Sexualforschung*, ed. Hans Bürger-Prinz and Hans Giese, 42–49. Stuttgart: Ferdinand Enke, 1957.

Schäfer, Hans Dieter. *Das gespaltene Bewusstsein: Über deutsche Kultur und Lebenswirklichkeit, 1933–1945.* Munich: Hanser, 1981.

Scheib, Manfred. "Gefangenschaft und Eingliederung von Heimkehrern als soziologisches Problem. Eine Untersuchung der seit September 1953 aus der Sowjetunion nach der Bundesrepublik und West-Berlin heimgekehrten Personengruppe." Ph.D. diss., University of Heidelberg, 1956.

Schelsky, Helmut. "Die soziale Formen der sexuellen Beziehungen." In *Die Sexualität des Menschen. Handbuch der medizinischen Sexualforschung*, ed. Hans Giese, 241–78. Stuttgart: Ferdinand Enke, 1955.

——. *Soziologie der Sexualität. Über die Beziehungen zwischen Geschlecht, Moral und Gesellschaft.* Hamburg: Rowohlt, 1955.

———. *Das menschliche Elend im 20. Jahrhundert. Eine Pathographie der Kriegs-, Hunger und politischen Katastrophen Europas.* Herford: Nicolaische Verlagsbuchhandlung, 1965.

Schenck, E. G., and Wolf v. Nathusius, eds. *Extreme Lebensverhältnisse und ihre Folgen: Handbuch der ärztlichen Erfahrungen aus der Gefangenschaft.* 6 vols. Schrifenreihe des ärztlich-wissenschaftlichen Beirates des Verbandes der Heimkehrer Deutschlands, e.V. N.p., 1958–64.

Scheurig, Bodo. *Free Germany: The National Committee and the League of German Officers.* Trans. Herbert Arnold. Middletown, Conn.: Wesleyan University Press, 1969.

Schildt, Axel. *Ankunft im Westen. Ein Essay zur Erfolgsgeschichte der Bundesrepublik.* Frankfurt am Main: Fischer, 1999.

———. "Fünf Möglichkeiten, die Geschichte der Bundesrepublik zu erzählen." *Blätter für deutsche und internationale Politik* 44 (1999): 1234–44.

———. *Moderne Zeiten. Freizeit, Massenmedien und Zeitgeist in der Bundesrepublik der 50er Jahre.* Hamburg: Christians, 1995.

———. "Nachkriegszeit. Möglichkeiten und Probleme einer Periodisierung der westdeutschen Geschichte nach dem Zweiten Weltkrieg und ihrer Einordnung in die deutsche Geschichte des 20. Jahrhunderts." *Geschichte in Wissenschaft und Unterricht* 44 (1993): 567–80.

———. " 'Solidarisch mit der Schuld des Volkes.' Die öffentliche Schulddebatte und das Integrationsangebot der Kirchen in Niedersachsen nach dem Zweiten Weltkrieg." In *Rechtsradikalismus in der politischen Kultur der Nachkriegszeit. Die verzögerte Normalisierung in Niedersachsen,* ed. Bernd Weisbrod, 269–96. Hannover: Hahn, 1995.

Schildt, Axel, and Arnold Sywotteck, eds. *Modernisierung im Wiederaufbau. Die westdeutsche Gesellschaft der 50er Jahre.* Bonn: J.H.W. Dietz, 1993.

Schilling, Rene. *"Kriegshelden." Deutungsmuster heroischer Männlichkeit in Deutschland 1813–1945.* Paderborn: Schönigh, 2002.

Schissler, Hanna, ed. *The Miracle Years: A Cultural History of West Germany.* Princeton: Princeton University Press, 2001.

———. " 'Normalization as Project.' Some Thoughts on Gender Relations in West Germany during the 1950s." In *The Miracle Years: A Cultural History of West Germany, 1949–1968,* ed. Hanna Schissler, 359–75. Princeton: Princeton University Press, 2001.

———. "Zeitgenossenschaft. Some Reflections on Doing Contemporary History." In *Conflict, Catastrophe, and Continuity in Modern German History,* ed. Frank Biess, Mark Roseman, and Hanna Schissler. New York: Berghahn, forthcoming.

Schivelbusch, Wolfgang. *The Culture of Defeat: On National Mourning, Trauma, and Recovery.* New York: Metropolitan Books, 2005.

Schmidt, Ulf. *Medical Films, Ethics, and Euthanasia in Nazi Germany: The History of Medical Research and Teaching Films of the Reich Office for Educational Films/Reich Institute for Films in Science and Education, 1933–1945.* Husum: Matthiesen, 2002.

Schmidt, Ulf. "Der medizinische Forschungsfilm im Dritten Reich: Seine Institutionalisierung, politische Funktion und ethische Dimension." *Zeitgeschichte* 4 (2001): 200–214.

Schmidt, Ute. "Spätheimkehrer oder Schwerstverbrecher? Die Gruppe der 749 'Nichtamnestierten.'" In *Sowjetische Militärtribunale*, vol. 1, *Die Verurteilung deutscher Kriegsgefangener, 1941–1955*, ed. Andreas Hilger, Ute Schmidt, and Günther Wagenlehner, 273–350. Cologne: Böhlau, 2001.

Schmitz, Willi. "Bemerkungen zum Aufsatz von J. Gottschick 'Kriegsgefangenschaft und Psychosen'." *Der Nervenarzt* 22 (1951): 149–50.

———. "Kriegsgefangenschaft und Heimkehr in ihren Beziehungen zu psychischen Krankheitsbildern." *Der Nervenarzt* 20 (1949): 303–10.

Schneider, Egidius. "Was können wir praktisch tun?" In *Heimatvertriebene und Heimkehrer. Vorträge und Anregungen der VII. überdiözesanen Aussprache-Konferenz für Männerseelsorge in Fulda*, May 9–12, 1950, 67–70. Augsburg: Winfried Werk, 1950.

Schneider, Franka. "Ehen in Beratung." In *Heimkehr 1948. Geschichte und Schicksal deutscher Kriegsgefangener*, ed. Annette Kaminsky, 192–216. Munich: C. H. Beck, 1998.

Schmuhl, Hans-Walter. *Rassenhygiene, Nationalsozialismus, Euthanasie*. Göttingen: Vandenhoek and Ruprecht, 1987.

Schornstheimer, Michael. *Die leuchtenden Augen der Frontsoldaten. Nationalsozialismus und Krieg in den Illustriertenromanen der fünfziger Jahre*. Berlin: Metropol, 1995.

Schröder, Hans Joachim. *Die gestohlenen Jahre. Erzählgeschichten und Geschichtserzählung im Interview. Der Zweite Weltkrieg aus der Sicht ehemaliger Mannschaftssoldaten*. Tübingen: Max Niemeyer, 1992.

Schulte, Theo J. *The German Army and Nazi Policies in Occupied Russia*. Oxford: Berg, 1989.

Schulte, Walter. "Cerebrale Defektsyndrome nach schwerer Hungerdystrophie und Möglichkeit ihrer Kompensierung mit einem Blick auf Heimkehrerdepression und forensische Komplikationen." *Der Nervenarzt* 24, no. 10 (1953): 415–19.

———. *Hirnorganische Dauerschäden nach schwerer Dystrophie*. Munich: Urban and Schwarzenberg, 1953.

Schultz, I. H. "Bemerkungen zu der Studie von Lang." In *Die Sexualität des Heimkehrers. Vorträge gehalten auf dem 4. Kongress der Deutschen Gesellschaft für Sexualforschung*, ed. Hans Bürger-Prinz and Hans Giese, 87–91. Stuttgart: Ferdinand Enke, 1957.

Schwan, Gesine. *Politik und Schuld. Die zerstörerische Macht des Schweigens*. Frankfurt am Main: Fischer, 1997.

Schwartz, Michael. "Apparate und Kurswechsel. Zur institutionellen und personellen Dynamik von 'Umsiedler'—Politik in der SBZ/DDR." In *Von der SBZ zur DDR. Studien zum Herrschaftssystem in der sowjetischen Besatzungszone und in der Deutschen Demokratischen Republik*, ed. Hartmut Mehringer, 105–35. Munich: Oldenbourg, 1995.

———. "Umsiedlerpolitik in der Krise? Das Vertriebenenproblem in der Gründungsphase der DDR, 1948–1953." In *Das letzte Jahr der SBZ. Politische*

Weichenstellungen und Kontinuitäten im Prozess der Gründung der DDR, ed. Dierk Hoffman and Hermann Wentker, 188–204. Munich: Oldenbourg, 2000.

———. "Vertreibung und Vergangenheitspolitik. Ein Versuch über geteilte deutsche Nachkriegsidentitäten." *Deutschland Archiv* 30 (1997): 177–95.

———. " 'Vom Umsiedler zum Staatsbürger.' Totalitäres und Subversives in der Sprachpolitik der SBZ/DDR." In *Vertriebene in Deutschland. Interdisziplinäre Ergebnisse und Forschungsperspektiven*, ed. Dierk Hoffmann, Marita Krauss and Michael Schwartz, 135–66. Munich: Oldenbourg, 2000.

———. "Zwischen Zusammenbruch und Stabilisierung: Zur Ortsbestimmung der Zentralverwaltung für deutsche Umsiedler im politisch-administrativen System der SBZ/DDR." In *Von der SBZ zur DDR. Studien zum Herrschaftssystem in der sowjetischen Besatzungszone und in der Deutschen Demokratischen Republik*, ed. Hartmut Mehringer, 43–96. Munich: Oldenbourg, 1995.

Schwarz, Hans-Peter. *Adenauer*. Vol. 2, *Der Staatsmann, 1952–1967*. Munich: dtv, 1994.

———. "Die ausgebliebene Katastrophe. Eine Probelmskizze zur Geschichte der Bundesrepublik." In *Den Staat denken. Theodor Eschenburg zum Fünfundachtzigsten*, ed. Hermann Rudolph, 151–74. Berlin: Siedler, 1993.

Scott, Joan. "The Evidence of Experience." *Critiqual Inquiry* 17 (1991): 773–97.

———. "Gender as a Category of Historical Analysis." In *Gender and the Politics of History*, ed. Joan Scott, 28–50. New York: Columbia Universtity Press, 1988.

Sedlmayer, Gerd. "Erfahrungen in der Behandlung kranker Heimkehrer." *Medizinische Klinik* 44 (1949): 257–59.

———. "Wandlungen im Krankheitsbild der Ostheimkehrer." *Medizinische Klinik* 44 (1949): 1223–25.

Seebald, W. G. *On the Natural History of Destruction*. Trans. Anthea Bell. New York: Random House, 2003.

Segev, Tom. *The Seventh Million: The Israelis and the Holocaust*. New York: Hill and Wang, 1993.

Shepard, Ben. *A War of Nerves: Soldiers and Psychiatrists in the Twentieth Century*. Cambridge: Harvard University Press, 2001.

Smith, Arthur. *Heimkehr aus dem Zweiten Weltkrieg. Die Entlassung der deutschen Kriegsgefangenen*. Stuttgart: Deutsche Verlagsanstalt, 1985.

———. *Die vermisste Million. Zum Schicksal deutscher Kriegsgefangener nach dem Zweiten Weltkrieg*. Munich: Oldenbourg, 1992.

———. *War for the German Mind: Reeducating Hitler's Soldiers*. Providence: Berghahn, 1996.

Solchany, Jean. "Konservative Interpretationen des Nationalsozialismus in Deutschland, 1945–1949." *Vierteljahreshefte für Zeitgeschichte* 44 (1996): 373–94.

Solga, Heike. *Auf dem Weg in eine klassenlose Gesellschaft? Klassenlagen und Mobilität zwischen den Generationen*. Berlin: Akademie, 1995.

Spahn, Carl Peter. "Heimkehrer ohne Heimat." *Zeitwende* 20 (1948–49): 905–10.

Springer, Phillip. *"Da konnt' ich mich dann so'n bisschen entfalten." Die Volkssolidarität in der SBZ/DDR 1945–1969*. Frankfurt am Main: Peter Lang, 1999.

Stadtland, Helke. *Herrschaft nach Plan und Macht der Gewohnheit. Sozial-geschichte der Gewerkschaften in der SBZ/DDR 1945–1953.* Essen: Klartext, 2001.

———. "Vergangenheitspolitik im Widerstreit. Ausgrenzung, Amnestie und Integration in der Gründungsphase der ostdeutschen Gewerkschaften." In *Vom kollektiven Gedächtnis zur Individualisierung der Erinnerung*, ed. Clemens Wischermann, 89–118. Stuttgart: Franz Steiner, 2002.

Stargadt, Nicolaus. "Opfer der Bomben und der Vergeltung." In *Ein Volk von Opfern? Die neue Debatte um den Bombenkrieg*, ed. Lothar Kettenacker, 56–71. Berlin: Rohwolt, 2003.

Staritz, Dietrich. "National-Demokratische Partei Deutschlands." In *SBZ Handbuch*, ed. Martin Broszat and Herrman Weber, 574–83. Munich: Oldenbourg, 1990.

Statistisches Bundesamt. *Volkszählung vom 6. Juni 1961.* Stuttgart: Kohlhammer, 1961.

Steen, K. "Ergebnisse aus 500 Sperma Untersuchungen (bei besonderer Berücksichtigung der Spätheimkehrer)." In *Methoden der Behandlung sexueller Störungen*. Vorträge gehalten auf dem 2. Kongress der Deurschen Gesellschaft für sexualforschung in Königstein, ed. Hans Bürger-Prinz and Hans Giese, 85–97. Stuttgart: Ferdinand Enke, 1952.

Steinbach, Peter. "Jenseits von Zeit und Raum. Kriegsgefangenschaft in der Frühgeschichte der Bundesrepublik." *Universitas* 7 (1990): 627–49.

———. *Nationalsozialistische Gewaltverbrechen. Die Diskussion in der westdeutschen Öffentlichkeit.* Berlin: Colloquium, 1997.

———. "Neuorientierung im Umbruch. Zum Wandel des Selbstversändnisses deutscher Kriegsgefangener in England und den USA." In *Doppelte Zeitgeschichte. Deutsch-deutsche Beziehungen*, ed. Arnd Bauernkämper, Martin Sabrow, and Bernd Stöver, 234–50. Berlin: J.H.W. Dietz, 1998.

———. "NS-Prozesse nach 1945. Auseinandersetzung mit der Vergangenheit-Konfrontation mit der Wirklichkeit." *Dachauer Hefte* 13 (1997): 3–26.

———. "Die sozialgeschichtliche Dimension der Kriegsheimkehr." In *Heimkehr 1948. Geschichte und Schicksal deutscher Kriegsgefangener*, ed. Annette Kaminsky, 325–40. Munich: C. H. Beck, 1998.

———. "Zur Sozialgeschichte der deutschen Kriegsgefangenen in der Sowjetunion und in der frühen Bundesrepublik. Ein Beitrag zum Problem der historischen Kontinuität." *Zeitgeschichte* 17 (1989): 1–18.

Steinert, Marlies. *Hitlers Krieg und die Deutschen. Stimmung und Haltung der deutschen Bevölkerung im Zweiten Weltkrieg.* Düsseldorf: Econ, 1993.

———. "Stalingrad und die deutsche Gesellschaft." In *Stalingrad: Ereignis-Wirkung-Symbol*, ed. Jürgen Förster, 171–85. Munich: Piper, 1993.

Steinhoff, Johannes, Peter Pechel, and Dennis Showalter, eds. *Deutsche im Zweiten Weltkrieg. Zeitzeugen sprechen.* Munich: Franz Schneekluth, 1989.

Stern, Frank. "Evangelische Kirche zwischen Antisemitismus und Philosemitismus." *Geschichte und Gesellschaft* 18 (1992): 22–50.

———. *The Whitewashing of the Yellow Badge.* Oxford: Pergamon Press, 1992.

Stolleis, Michael. *The Law under the Swastika. Studies on the Legal History in Nazi Germany.* Chicago: University of Chicago Press, 1998.

Stransky, Erwin. "Mehrfachdeterminationen der Sexualstörungen." In *Die Sexualität des Heimkehrers. Vorträge gehalten auf dem 4. Kongress der Deutschen Gesellschaft für Sexualforschung*, ed. Hans Bürger-Prinz and Hans Giese, 19–26. Stuttgart: Ferdinand Enke, 1957.

Straunzenberg, E. "Über das Hungerödem." *Das Deutsche Gesundheitswesen* 1 (1946): 261–63.

Strebel, Helmut. *Die Verschollenheit als Rechtsproblem. Eine rechtsanalytische und vergleichende Studie*. Frankfurt am Main: Alfred Metzler, 1954.

Streit, Christian. *Keine Kameraden. Die Wehrmacht und die sowjetischen Kriegsgefangenen, 1941–1945*. Stuttgart: DVA, 1978.

Strobel, Margund. "Der Fischerhof-die psycho-somatische-Krankenanstalt der Arbeiterwohlfahrt." *Neues Beginnen* 6, no. 8 (1952): 4–5.

Suhren, Otto. "Sexuelle Probleme in der Kriegsgefangenschaft." *Zeitschrift für Haut- und Geschlechtskrankheiten* 13 (1952): 216–17.

Tauber, Kurt. *Beyond Eagle and Swastika: German Nationalism since 1945*. Middletown, Conn.: Weysleyan University Press, 1967.

Tenbruck, Friedrich. "Alltagsnormen und Lebensgefühle in der Bundesrepublik Deutschland." In *Die zweite Republik: 25 Jahre Bundesrepublik—eine Bilanz.*, ed. Richard Löwenthal and Hans-Peter Schwarz, 289–310. Stuttgart: Seewald, 1974.

Teschner, Manfred. "Entwicklung eines Interessenverbandes. Ein empirischer Beitrag zum Problem der Verselbstständigung von Massenorganisationen." Dissertation, University of Frankfurt, 1961.

Ther, Philipp. *Deutsche und polnische Vertriebene. Gesellschaft und Vertriebenenpolitik in der SBZ/DDR und Polen, 1945–1956*. Göttingen: Vandenhoeck und Ruprecht, 2000.

———. "Vertriebenenpolitik in der SBZ/DDR und in Polen." In *Von der SBZ zur DDR. Studien zum Herrschaftssystem in der sowjetischen Besatzungszone und in der Deutschen Demokratischen Republik*, ed. Hartmut Mehringer, 137–59. Munich: Oldenbourg, 1995.

Thierfelder, Jörg. "Die Kirchenpolitik der vier Besatzungsmächte und die evangelische Kirche nach der Kapitulation 1945." *Geschichte und Gesellschaft* 18 (1992): 5–21.

Thoß, Bruno. "Die Zeit der Weltkriege—die Epoche als Erfahrungseinheit?" In *Erster Weltkrieg–Zweiter Weltkrieg. Ein Vergleich. Krieg, Kriegserlebnis, Kriegserfahrung in Deutschland*, ed. Bruno Thoß and Hans Erich Volkmann, 7–30. Paderborn: Ferdinand Schöningh, 2002.

———, ed. *Volksarmee schaffen—ohne Geschrei! Studien zu den Anfängen einer "verdeckten Aufrüstung"in der SBZ/DDR, 1947–1952*. Munich: Oldenbourg, 1994.

Thoß, Bruno, and Hans Erich Volkmann, eds. *Erster Weltkrieg–Zweiter Weltkrieg. Krieg, Kriegserlebnis, Kriegserfahrung in Deutschland*. Paderborn: Ferdinand Schöningh, 2002.

Thurnwald, Hilde. *Gegenwartsprobleme Berliner Familien. Eine soziologische Untersuchung*. Berlin: Weidmannsche Buchhandlung, 1948.

Tosh, John. "Hegemonic Masculinity and the History of Gender." In *Masculinities in Politics and War: Gendering Modern History*, ed. Stefan Dudink, Karen

Hagemann, and John Tosh, 41–58. Manchester: Manchester University Press, 2004.

Tulatz, Claus. "Exil hinter Stacheldraht. Die Vorbereitung politischer 999er in amerikanischer Kriegsgefangenschaft auf die Nachkriegszeit am Beispiel Fort Devens." In *Das "andere Deutschland" im Widerstand gegen den Nationalsozialismus. Beiträge zur politischen Überwindung der nationalsozialistischen Diktatur im Exil und im Dritten Reich*, ed. Helga Grebing and Christl Wickert, 173–99. Essen: Klartext, 1994.

Tumarkin, Nina. *The Living and the Dead: The Rise and Fall of the Cult of World War II in Russia*. New York: Basic Books, 1994.

Turner, Bryan. "Outline of a Theory of Citizenship." *Sociology* 24 (1990): 189–217.

Turner, Victor. "Betwixt and Between: The Liminal Period in Rites of Passage." In *The Forest of Symbols: Aspects of Ndembu Ritual*, 93–111. Ithaca: Cornell University Press, 1967.

Überschär, Gerd. "Das NKFD und der BDO im Kampf gegen Hitler." In *Das Nationalkomitee "Freies Deutschland und der Bund Deutscher Offiziere*," ed. Gerd Überschär, 31–51. Frankfurt am Main: Fischer, 1995.

———, ed. *Das Nationalkomitee "Freies Deutschland" und der Bund Deutscher Offiziere*. Frankfurt am Main: Fischer, 1995.

———, ed. *Der Nationalsozialismus vor Gericht. Die alliierten Prozesse gegen Kriegsverbrecher und Soldaten, 1943–1952*. Frankfurt am Main: Fischer, 1999.

Uliczka, Monika. *Berufsbiographie und Flüchtlingsschicksal: VW Arbeiter in der Nachkriegszeit*. Hannover: Verlag Hahnsche Buchhandlung, 1993.

Ulrich, Bernd, and Benjamin Zieman, eds. *Krieg im Frieden: Die umkämpfte Erinnerung an den ersten Weltkrieg: Quellen und Dokumente*. Frankfurt am Main: Fischer, 1997.

van Melis, Damian. " 'Strengthened and Purified through Ordeal by Fire': Ecclesiastical Triumphalism in the Ruins." In *Life after Death: Approaches to the Social and Cultural History of Europe in the 1940s and 1950s*, ed. Richard Bessel and Dirk Schumann, 231–41. Cambridge: Cambridge University Press, 2003.

Venzlaff, Ulrich. *Die psychoreaktiven Störungen nach entschädigungspflichtigen Ereignissen (Die sogenannten Unfallneurosen)*. Berlin: Springer, 1958.

Verband der Heimkehrer, ed. *Kriegsgefangenenkrankheiten. Tonband-Protokoll der Referate des ersten Ärztekongresses der Kriegsgefangenenkrankeiten am 17.10.1953*. N.p., 1953.

Verhandlungen des Deutschen Bundestags (VDBT). Stenographische Berichte, 1. und 2. Wahlperiode. Bonn, 1949–57.

Vogt, Timothy. *Denazification in Soviet-Occupied Germany: Brandenburg, 1945–1948*. Cambridge: Harvard University Press, 2000.

Volkmann, Hans-Erich, ed. *Das Russlandbild im Dritten Reich*. Cologne: Böhlau, 1994.

Vollnhals, Clemens. *Entnazifizierung. Politische Säuberung und Rehabilitation in der vier Besatzungszonen 1945–1949*. Munich: dtv, 1991.

———. *Evangelische Kirche und Entnazifizierung 1945–1949. Die Last der nationalsozialistischen Vergangenheit.* Munich: Oldenbourg, 1989.

———. "Die Evangelische Kirsche zwischen Traditionswahrung und Neuorientierung." In *Von Stalingrad zur Währungsreform*, ed. Martin Broszat, Klaus-Dietmar Henke, and Hans Woller, 113–67. Munich: Oldenbourg, 1990.

von Henting, Hans. *Die Kriminalität des homophilen Mannes.* Stuttgart: Ferdinand Enke, 1960.

von Hodenberg, Christina. "Die Journalisten und der Aufbruch zur kritischen Öffentlichkeit." In Ulrich Herbert, ed., *Wandlungsprozesse in Westdeutschland: Belastung, Integration, Liberalisierung 1945–1980*, ed. Ulrich Herbert, 278–311, Göttingen: Wallstein, 2002.

von Olenhusen, Irmtraud Götz. "Die Feminisierung von Religion und Kirche im 19. und 20. Jahrhundert. Forschungsstand und Forschungsperspektiven." In *Frauen unter dem Patriarchat der Kirchen. Katholikinnen und Protestantinnen im 19. und 20. Jahrhundert*, ed. Irmtraud Götz von Olenhusen, 9–21. Stuttgart: Kohlhammer, 1995.

von Plato, Alexander. "The Hitler Youth Generation and Its Role in the Two Postwar German States." In *Generations in Conflict: Youth Revolt and Generation Formation in Germany, 1770–1968*, ed. Mark Roseman, 210–26. Cambridge: Cambridge University Press, 1996.

von Plato, Alexander. "Zur Geschichte des sowjetischen Speziallagersystems in Deutschland. Eine Einführung." In *Sowjetische Speziallager in Deutschland 1945 bis 1950*, ed. Sergej Mironenko, Lutz Niethammer, and Alexander von Plato, with Volkhard Knigge und Günter Morsch. Vol. 1, *Studien und Berichte*, ed. Alexander von Plato, 19–75. Berlin: Akademie, 1998.

von Plato, Alexander, and Wolfgang Meinicke. *Alte Heimat, neue Zeit: Flüchtlinge, Umgesiedelte, Vertriebene in der Sowjetischen Besatzungszone und in der DDR.* Berlin: Verlags-Anstalt Union, 1991.

Stackelberg, Maria von. *Familie und Ehe. Probleme in den deutschen Familien der Gegenwart.* Bielefeld: Ernst Gieseking, 1956.

Voss, Albert. "Erfassung und Arbeitslenkung der arbeitsfähigen Bevölkerung." *Arbeit und Sozialfürsorge*, Jahrbuch 1945–47 (1947): 29–45.

Wagenlehner, Günter. *Stalins Wilkürjustiz gegen die deutsche Kriegsgefangenen.* Bonn: Verlag der Heimkehrer, 1993.

Weber, Herrmann, and Ulrich Mählert, eds. *Terror. Stalinistische Parteisäuberungen, 1936–1953.* Paderborn: Schöningh, 1998.

Weckel, Ulrike. "Spielarten der Vergangenheitsbewältigung—Wolfgang Borcherts Heimkehrer und sein langer Weg durch die westdeutschen Medien." *Tel Aviver Jahrbuch für deusche Geschichte* 31 (2003): 125–61.

Weckel, Ulrike, and Edgar Wolfrum, eds. *"Bestien" und "Befehlsempfänger": Frauen und Männer in NS-Prozessen nach 1945.* Göttingen: Vandenhoek, 2003.

Wegner, Bernd. "Hitler, der Zweite Weltkrieg und die Choreographie des Untergangs." *Geschichte und Gesellschaft* 26 (2000): 493–518.

———. "Der Krieg gegen die Sowjetunion 1942/43." In *Das Deutsche Reich und die Zweite Weltkrieg*, vol. 6, *Der Globale Krieg: Die Ausweitung zum Weltkrieg und der Wechsel der Initiative, 1941–1943*, ed. Militärisches Forschungsamt, 761–1102. Stuttgart: Deutsche Verlags Anstalt, 1990.

Wehler, Hans-Ulrich. "Deutsches Bürgertum nach 1945: Exitus oder Phönix aus der Asche?" *Geschichte und Gesellschaft* 27 (2001): 617–34.

———. *Deutsche Gesellschaftsgeschichte*. Vol. 4, *Vom Beginn des Ersten Weltkriegs bis zu der Gründung beider deutscher Staaten*. Munich: C. H. Beck, 2003.

Weigel, Sigried. "Pathologisierung und Normalisierung im deutschen Gedächtnisdiskurs. Zur Dialektik von Erinnern und Vergessen." In *Vom Nutzen des Vergessens*, ed. Gary Smith and Hendrik M. Emrich, 241–63. Berlin: Akademie, 1996.

Weinberg, Gerald. *A World at Arms: A Global History of World War II*. Cambridge: Cambridge University Press, 1994.

Weindling, Paul. *Health, Race and German Politics between National Unification and Nazism, 1870–1945*. Cambridge: Cambridge University Press, 1987.

Weiner, Amir. *Making Sense of War: The Second World War and the Fate of the Bolshevik Revolution*. Princeton: Princeton University Press, 2001.

Weisbrod, Bernd. "The Moratorium of the Mandarins and the Self-Denazification of the German Academe: A View from Göttingen." *Contemporary European History* 12 (2003): 47–69.

Weiss, H. "Ernährungsstörungen, ihre Begleit- und Folgeerscheinungen bei Heimkehrern." *Hippokrates* 20 (1949): 48–52.

Weitz, Eric. *Creating German Communism: From Popular Protest to Socialist State*. Princeton: Princeton University Press, 1997.

———. "The Ever-Present Other: Communism and the Making of West Germany, 1945–1956." In *The Miracle Years: A Cultural History of West Germany*, ed. Hanna Schissler, 219–32. Princeton: Princeton University Press, 2001.

Welch, David. *The Third Reich: Politics and Propaganda*. London: Routledge, 1993.

Welsh, Helga A. " 'Antifaschistisch-Demokratische Umwälzung' und politische Säuberung in der sowjetischen Besatzungszone Deutschlands." In *Politische Säuberung in Europa. Die Abrechnung mit Faschismus und Kollaboration nach dem Zweiten Weltkrieg*, ed. Klaus-Dietmar Henke and Hans Woller, 84–107. Munich: dtv, 1991.

Welzer, Harald, Sabine Moeller, and Karoline Tschugall. *"Opa war kein Nazi." Nationalsozialismus und Holocaust im Familiengedächtnis*. Frankfurt am Main: Fischer, 2002.

Welzer, Harald, Robert Monteau, and Christine Plass, eds. *"Was wir für böse Menschen sind!" Der Nationalsozialismus im Gespräch zwischen den Generationen*. Tübingen: Edition Diskord, 1997.

Wentker, Hermann. "Die gesamtdeutsche Systemkonkurrenz und die durchlässige innerdeutsche Grenze. Herausforderung und Aktionsrahmen für die DDR in den fünziger Jahren." In *Vor dem Mauerbau. Politik und Gesellschaft in der DDR der fünziger Jahre*, ed. Dierk Hoffmann, Michael Schwartz and Hermann Wentker, 59–75. Munich: Oldenbourg, 2003.

———. *Justiz in der SBZ/DDR, 1945–1953. Transformation und Rolle ihrer zentralen Institutionen*. Munich: Oldenbourg, 2001.

Wenzke, Rüdiger. "Auf dem Weg zur Kaderarmee. Aspekte der Rekrutierung, Sozialstruktur und personellen Entwicklung des entstehenden Militärs in der SBZ/DDR bis 1952/53." In *Volksarmee schaffen—ohne Geschrei! Studien zu den Anfängen einer "verdeckten Aufrüstung" in der SBZ/DDR, 1947–1952*, ed. Bruno Thoß, 205–72. Munich: Oldenbourg, 1994.

————. "Wehrmachtsoffiziere in DDR Streitkräften." In *Nationale Volksarmee— Armee für den Frieden. Beiträge zu Selbstverständnis und Geschichte des deutschen Militärs*, ed. Detlef Bald, Reinhard Brühl, and Andreas Prüfert, 143– 56. Baden-Baden: Nomos, 1995.

Werkentin, Falco. *Politische Strafjustiz in der Ära Ulbricht. Vom bekennenden Terror zur verdeckten Repression.* Berlin: Links, 1995.

————. "Der politische und juristische Umgang mit Systemgegnern in der DDR und in der Bundesrepublik in den Fünfziger Jahren." In *Deutsche Vergangenheiten—eine gemeinsame Herausforderung. Der schwierige Umgang mit der Nachkriegsgeschichte*, ed. Hans Misselwitz Christoph Kleßmann, and Günter Wichert, 253–70. Berlin: Links, 1999.

Wette, Wolfram. *Retter in Uniform. Handlungsspielräume im Vernichtungskrieg der Wehrmacht.* Frankfurt am Main: Fischer, 2002.

————. *Die Wehrmacht. Feindbilder, Vernichtungskrieg, Legenden.* Frankfurt am Main: Fischer, 2002.

————. "Zwischen Untergangspathos und Überlebenswillen. Die Deutschen im letzten Kriegshalbjahr 1944/45." In *Das letzte halbe Jahr. Stimmungsberichte der Wehrmachtpropaganda 1944/45*, ed. Wolfram Wette, Ricarda Bremer, and Detlef Volgel, 9–37. Essen: Klartext, 2001.

Wette, Wolfram, Ricarda Bremer, and Detlef Volgel, eds. *Das letzte halbe Jahr. Stimmungsberichte der Wehrmachtpropaganda 1944/45.* Essen: Klartext, 2001.

Wetzel, Ulrich. "Die Tuburkulose bei Heimkehrern." *Beiträge zur Klinik der Tuberkulose* 102 (1950): 519–24.

Wierling, Dorothee. *Geboren im Jahr Eins. Der Jahrgang 1949 in der DDR. Versuch einer Kollektivbiographie.* Berlin: Links, 2002.

————. "The Hitler-Youth Generation in the DDR. Insecurities, Ambitions, and Dilemmas." In *Dictatorship as Experience: Towards a Socio-Cultural History of the GDR*, ed. Konrad Jarausch, trans. Eve Duffy, 307–24. New York: Berghahn, 1999.

————. "Mission to Happiness: The Cohort of 1949 and the Making of East and West Germans." In *The Miracle Years: A Cultural History of West Germany, 1949–1968*, ed. Hanna Schissler, 110–25. Princeton: Princeton University Press, 2001.

Wiesen, Jonathan. *West German Industry and the Challenge of the Nazi Past.* Chapel Hill: University of North Carolina Press, 1997.

Wiethold, F. "Kriminalbiologische Behandlung von Sittlichkeitsverbrechern." In *Beiträge zur Sexualforschung 2 (1952): Methoden der Behandlung sexueller Störungen*, ed. Hans-Bürger Prinz and Hans Giese, 37–45. Stuttgart: Ferdinand Enke Verlag, 1952.

Wiggershaus, Norbert. *Die Frankfurter Schule. Geschichte, theoretische Entwicklung, politische Bedeutung.* Munich: C. Hanser, 1986.

Wildt, Michael. "Differierende Wahrheiten. Historiker and Staatsanwälte als Er-
mittler von NS-Verbrechen." In *Geschichte vor Gericht. Historiker, Richter und
die Suche nach Gerechtigkeit*, ed. Norbert Frei, Dirk von Laak, and Michael
Stolleis, 46–59. Munich: C. H. Beck, 2000.

Wille, Manfred. "SED und 'Umsiedler'—Vertriebenenpolitik der Einheitspartei
im ersten Nachkriegsjahrzehnt." In *Geglückte Integration? Spezifika und Ver-
gleichbarkeit der Vertriebenen–Eingliederung in der SBZ/DDR*, ed. Dierk Hoffmann and Michael Schwartz, 91–104. Munich: Oldenbourg, 1999.

———. "Die Vertriebenen und das politische System der SBZ/DDR." In *Von der
SBZ zur DDR. Studien zum Herrschaftssystem in der sowjetischen Besatzungszone und in der Deutschen Demokratischen Republik*, ed. Hartmut Mehringer,
203–17. Munich: Oldenbourg, 1995.

Wilm, Gottfried. "Die herrschende Ehekrise als Problem und Aufgabe." *Juristische Rundschau* 1 (1951): 17–18.

Winkler, Heinrich August. *Der lange Weg nach Westen*. Vol. 2, *Deutsche Geschichte vom "Dritten Reich" zur Wiedervereinigung*. 5th ed. Munich: C. H.
Beck, 2002.

Winter, Jay, and Emmanuel Sivan. "Setting the Framework." In *War and Remembrance in the Twentieth Century*, ed. Jay Winter and Emmanuel Sivan, 6–39.
Cambridge: Cambridge University Press, 1999.

Wischermann, Clemens, ed. *Vom kollektiven Gedächtnis zur Individualisierung
der Erinnerung*. Stuttgart: Franz Steiner, 2002.

Wischnath, Johannes Michael. *Kirche in Aktion. Das Evangelische Hilfswerk und
sein Verhältnis zu Kirche und Innerer Mission*. Göttingen: Vandenhoek, 1986.

Wolfrum, Edgar. *Geschichtspolitik in der Bundesrepublik Deutschland. Der Weg
zur bundesrepublikanischen Erinnerung*. Darmstadt: Wiss. Buchgesellschaft,
1999.

Wolgast, Elke. *Die Wahrnehmung des Dritten Reiches in der unmittelbaren Nachkriegszeit*. Heidelberg: Universitätsverlag C. Winter, 2001.

Wood, N. *Vectors of Memory: Legacies of Trauma in Postwar Europe*. New York:
Oxford University Press, 1999.

Wrobel, Heinz. *Verurteilt zur Demokratie. Justiz und Justizpolitik in Deutschland, 1945–1949*. Heidelberg: Decker und Müller, 1989.

Wulfhorst, Traugott. "Der 'Dank des Vaterlandes'—Sozialpolitik und Verwaltung
zur Integration ehemaliger Wehrmachtssoldaten und ihrer Hinterbliebenen." In
Die Wehrmacht. Mythos und Realität, ed. Rolf-Dieter Müller and Hans-Erich
Volkmann, 1035–57. Munich: Oldenbourg, 1999.

Wurm, Franz. "Schuld und Niederlage der Antifa." *Neues Abendland* 7 (1952):
404–14.

Wurzbacher, Gerhard. *Leitbilder gegenwärtigen Familienlebens*. Stuttgart: Ferdinand Enke, 1954.

Young, Allan. *The Harmony of Illusions: Inventing Post-traumatic Stress Disorder*. Princeton: Princeton University Press, 1995.

Zank, Wolfgang. *Wirtschaft und Arbeit in Ostdeutschland: Probleme des Wieder-
aufbaus in der Sowjetischen Besatzungszone*. Munich: Oldenbourg, 1987.

Zatlin, Jonathan E. "Ausgaben und Eingaben. Das Petitionsrecht und der Untergang der DDR." *Zeitschrift für Geschichtswissenschaft* 45 (1997): 902–17.

Zeidler, Manfred. *Kriegsende im Osten. Die Rote Armee und die Besetzung Deutschlands östlich von Oder und Neisse 1944/45.* Munich: Oldenbourg, 1996.

———. *Stalinjustiz contra NS-Verbrechen. Die Kriegsverbrecherprozesse gegen deutsche Kriegsgefangene in der UdSSR in den Jahren 1943–1955. Kenntnisstand und Forschungsprobleme.* Dresden: Hannah Arendt Institut für Totalitarismusforschung, 1996.

Zentner, Kurt, ed. *Aufstieg aus dem Nichts. Deutschland von 1945 bis 1953. Eine Soziographie in zwei Bänden.* Cologne: Kiepenheuer and Witsch, 1954.

Ziemann, Benjamin. "Fluchten aus dem Konsens zum Durchhalten. Ergebnisse, Probleme und Perspektiven der Erforschung soldatischer Verweigerungsformen in der Wehrmacht 1939–1945." In *Die Wehrmacht. Mythos und Realität*, ed. Rolf-Dieter Müller and Hans-Erich Volkmann, 589–613. Munich: Oldenbourg, 1999.

zur Nieden, Susanne. "Chronistinnen des Krieges. Frauentagebücher im Zweiten Weltkrieg." In *Ende des Dritten Reiches—Ende des Zweiten Weltkrieges. Eine perspektivische Rückschau*, ed. Hans-Erich Volkmann, 833–60. Munich: Piper, 1995.

———. "Erotic Fraternization: The Legend of German Women's Quick Surrender." In *Home/Front: The Military, War, and Gender in Twentieth-Century Germany*, ed. Karen Hagemann and Stefanie Schüler-Springorum, 297–310. Oxford: Berg, 2002.

Index

Adenauer, Konrad, 180, 182, 187, 247n33; and issue of missing POWs, 193–96; and Moscow agreement, 204, 209
aftermath, history of, 227–31
Allemann, Rene, 8
Allies, repatriation policies, 44–46, 306n25. *See also* war crime trials
Americanization, 125, 207, 210–11
American Psychiatric Association, 78
amnesties, Soviet, 203–4, 215, 218
amnesty laws (FRG, 1949, 1954), 167, 287n100, 301n77
anti-Bolshevism, 38–39, 51, 57–58, 100, 102, 113, 115, 210
anti-Communism, 59, 162–63, 166, 181
antifascism, 23–24, 113, 116, 126, 150, 169–75, 274n36, 274n37, 276n59, 279n114
antifascist activists, 153, 156, 162–64
antifascist conversion, 126, 128, 143, 170
antifascist reeducation program, East German, 50–51, 91–94, 130, 135–42; returnees' responses to, 142–45
antimilitarism, postwar, 47, 50
anti-Semitism, 39, 57–58, 172. *See also* Holocaust; Jewish experience
Applegate, Celia, 66
Arbeiterwohlfahrt, 108, 257n101
Arendt, Hannah, 31
Armed SS (Waffen SS), 114, 160, 214
army, Nazi. *See* Wehrmacht
Asmussen, Hans, 56
"Association of Former POWs for the Struggle against War" (proposed), 137–39
atrocities, Soviet, allegations of, 34–35
Aue, mines at, 148, 281n139
Auschwitz, 254n25
authoritarianism: of East German antifascism, 134; within family, 125
autobiographies of returnees, 53, 64, 144

Bansi, Hans W., 77, 255n38
"barbed wire disease," 71–73
Bartov, Omer, 164

Baumkötter, Heinz, 215
Bautzen internment camp, 183
BdO (League of German Officers), 23, 36, 164
Beckerle, Adolf, 215
Belarus, 3
Beria, Lavrenty Pavlovich, 203–4
Berning, Heinrich, 74
Bessel, Richard, 7
Best, Werner, 192
Bible, 57
Bodemann, Michael, 69
"bodily injury," in POW trials, 154
Bohn, Helmut, 53
Böll, Heinrich, 105
Bonhoeffer, Karl, 77
Bonn University, 79
Borchert, Wolfgang, 53
Bormann, Martin, 239n27, 241n64
bourgeois reconstruction, 99, 118–19
Brochhagen, Ulrich, 217
Broszat, Martin, 159–60
"brutal peacemaking," 19
Buchenwald, 183, 255n38, 288n106
Bundesgerichtshof (BGH), 158, 160–61
Bundessozialgericht, 214
Bürger-Prinz, Hans, 213
BVG (Federal War Victim's Law of 1950), 76

captivity, 33–34, 57, 71–76, 99, 101. *See also* POWs; returnees
captivity narratives, 75–76, 128
Caritas Kriegsgefangenhilfe, 106, 108, 141
casualties, World War II, 233n1; German, 19, 21–22, 35, 237n4 (*see also* suffering, German)
Catholic bishops, 48, 57. *See also* Christian churches
CDU/CSU (Christian Democratic Union/ Christian Social Union), 58, 109
Central Agency for the Prosecution of Nazi Crimes (Ludwigsburg), 217
charitable donations, 106, 141
children of POWs, 124–25, 152, 198

Christian churches, 21, 38–42, 48–49, 108, 122, 141, 224; and acts of commemoration, 187–93; and postwar redemption narratives, 98–105; and re-Christianization of returnees, 106–9; and victimization narratives, 56–58
Christian Democratic Union/Christian Social Union (CDU/CSU), 58, 109
citizen, use of term, 13
citizenship, 11, 13–14
citizenship, East German, 94, 130, 135, 145–46, 221; and exclusion, 167, 174–75; and family life, 151–52; and rearmament, 146–48; and war criminals, 196, 199; and workplace, 149. *See also* East Germany
citizenship, West German, 98, 106, 109, 210; and dystrophy, 76; and exclusion, 173–74; and family, 120–21; and homosexuality, 91; and rearmament, 114–15, 165–66, 211–12; and religion, 106–9; and VdH, 112–13; and workplace, 116, 119. *See also* West Germany
civilians: German, 5 (*see also* Germans, ordinary); Soviet, 3
civil society, West German, 106, 109–16. *See also* West Germany
Clauberg, Carl, 215, 217
Cold War, 10, 43–44, 81, 84, 97–98, 114–16, 153–54, 162–63, 181–82, 187–88; and East German purges, 168–75
collaboration, 153, 160, 163–65, 173, 286n80
collective guilt, 50, 173, 216
collective innocence, 216
collective memory, 11–12
commemoration, acts of, 100–102, 179, 186–93; day of faith, 187; day of loyalty, 189; week of prayer, 191; weeks of remembrance, 187, 189
commemorative culture, 100–102, 105, 228–29
commissar orders, 3
Committee for POW Issues (Stuttgart), 110
communal reconstruction, in East Germany, 151
compensation of returnees, 110–12, 159, 192, 212–13, 224, 267n95, 267n99
comradeship, ideal of, 165
concentration camps, 74, 171, 215, 254n25, 255n38, 288n106; equated with POW camps, 74, 98, 155, 214,

288n106. *See also* Holocaust; medical experiments, Nazi; *names of camps*
Confino, Alon, 11, 66
constitution, West German, 120
consumer society, postwar, 120
Conway, Martin, 162
courts, West German, 158, 160–61, 214, 286n63; and POW trials, 157–67
"crimes against humanity," in POW trials, 155–56, 283n9
cultural values, German, 99, 101–2, 105
culture of defeat, 99, 235n40

Dachau, 215–17
death certificates, issuance of, 185–86, 292n44, 292n49
decontamination, of former soldiers, 13–14, 102
defeat, German, 5, 7–10, 19, 43–44. *See also* redemption narratives; suffering, German; victimization narratives
Democratic Women's Union (DFD), 141–42
denazification, 56, 63, 157, 215–17
denial of war losses, 19, 237n4; as response to end of POW repatriation, 186
denunciation: in party purges, 173; of POWs by fellow POWs, 154, 159–62, 207 (*see also* POW trials)
depoliticization, of West German legal system, 162–63, 166
"deprivation of liberty," in POW trials, 154
desertion, 35–36
DFD (Democratic Women's Union), 141–42
disability. *See* compensation of returnees; employment issues of returnees; health issues of returnees
divorce rates, 121–23
Dönhoff, Marion Gräfin, 209
Dower, John, 97, 235n40
dystrophy, 71–76, 82–89, 92, 214, 259n124

East Germany, 7–10, 203; and acts of commemoration, 189–91; citizen-making in, 126–52; and last returnees, 218–25; and missing POWs, 196–202; purges in, 153, 167–75, 215; response to end of POW repatriations, 182–86. *See also* SED

EHIK (Evangelisches Hilfswerk für Kriegsgefangene und Internierte), 38–42, 106,
141, 244n124
EKD (Evangelical church in Germany),
56–57
employment issues of returnees, 116–20,
148–51. See also unemployment
Enzensberger, Hans Magnus, 231
Equalization of Burdens Law (FRG,
1952), 111
eugenics, 75–76
Europe, postwar, 10, 227–31
euthanasia program, Nazi, 79, 256n54
Evangelische Hilfswerk. See EHIK
exchange of POWs: for German Communists, 247n33; for Nazi activists, 48
exclusion. See POW trials; purges,
East German
exhibitions, commemorative: "Prisoners of
War Speak," 100–102; "We Admonish,"
100–102
expellee organizations, 266n90
"experience-induced personality
disorder," 213
externalization of fascist past, 128

families of MIAs/POWs, 24, 35–36, 41–
42, 223, 242n74, 244n105; and missing
POWs, 179–82, 194–201; and search for
MIAs/POWs, 25–33. See also children of
POWs; wives
family: East German, 151–52; West German, 88, 91, 102, 120–25
family reunions, 209
Faulhaber, Cardinal, 56
FDJ (Free German Youth), 132
fear, POWs' feelings of, 77–78
films: "movies of the rubble," 53; Nazi,
84; VdH documentary, 207; West German, 102–5
Fischer, August, 102
Fischerhof clinic, 257n101, 258n105
flight to West: by middle-class professionals, 150; by returnees, 143–44
food shortages and rationing, 118, 135
forced labor, Soviet system of, 5
Frankfurter Allgemeine Zeitung, 182
Frankfurt Institute for Social Research: Archive, 256n68; interviews with returnees, 80–81, 113, 115, 120, 267n105
fraternization, women and, 65
Free German Youth (FDJ), 132

Frei, Norbert, 167, 193
Fremde Heere Ost (Wehrmacht counterespi-
onage division), 34
Friedland transition camp, 45–46,
155, 204
Frings, Archbishop, 204
Fritzsche, Peter, 11
Fühmann, Franz, 144
Fulbrook, Mary, 139
Funk, Erich, 75
Fürstenwalde transition camp, 219

Gauger, Kurt, 84–85, 87, 257n92,
257n101, 258n105, 258n124
GDSF (Society for German-Soviet Friendship), 127, 132, 143
Gellately, Robert, 22, 240n46
gender issues, 12–13; in East Germany,
142, 149. See also masculinity
gender relations, 89, 121–24
generational relations, 124–25; in SED,
133–34
genocide, 34, 229–30; role of Wehrmacht
in, 3–4. See also concentration camps;
Holocaust
Gerlach, Christian, 3
German Communist Party (KPD), 49, 181.
See also SED
German Criminal Code (StGB), 154
German Economic Commission
(GDR), 148
Germans, ordinary: and Christian
churches, 39–42; and empathy with Ger-
many's victims, 31–33; and lack of empa-
thy with Germany's victims, 31, 52; re-
sponse of to defeat, 19–22. See also
families of MIAs/POWs
German Society for Sexual Research, 88
Germany, divided, 7–10, 206–9. See also
East Germany; West Germany
Gestapo, and search for MIAs/POWs,
27, 31
Geyer, Michael, 14, 73, 115
Goebbels, Joseph, 23, 26
Goethe, Johann Wolfgang von: Faust, 99
Gollwitzer, Helmut, 64
Goltermann, Svenja, 253n4
Göring, Hermann, 33
Gottschick, Johannes, 77
government, West German: civil service,
120; Federal Ministry of Expellees, Divi-
sion for POW and Returnee Issues, 110

Gronenfelde transition camp, 45–46, 61, 94, 131, 136, 139–40, 246n12, 291n26
Grossmann, Atina, 130
Grotewohl, Otto, 204
Grüber, Propst, 47, 247n29
guilt, POWs' feelings of, 77–78
guilt and responsibility, discourse of, 46–52, 128. See also collective guilt
Günsche, Otto, 215
GUPVI (Soviet Administration for Prisoners of War and Internee Camps), 131

Halbwachs, Maurice, 11–12
Hallstein, Walter, 194
health issues of returnees, 118, 212–14; in East Germany, 91–94; in West Germany, 70–91, 163–65, 212–14
Heckel, Bishop Theodor, 38–39, 57
Heidegger, Martin, 101
Heimat, concept of, 16, 65–67
Heimkehrer conferences, 127–30, 170, 272n5
Heinemann, Gustav, 209
Heitz, Gen. Walter, 27–28, 241n57
Hemsing, Walter, 99
Hermann, Judith, 73
heroic death, Nazi cult of, 20–22, 24, 28–29, 40
Herzog, Dagmar, 88
Herzog, Paul, 75
Heuss, Theodor, 187, 192, 204
"history burdened by the past" (Belastungsgeschichte), 9
Hitler myth, collapse of, 22
Hitler Youth, 133–34, 144–45
Höding, Edith, 94
Höfler, Heinrich, 38–39, 106, 245n132
Höhn, August, 215
Hollander, Walter von, 121
Hollunder, Erika, 241n55
Holocaust, 3–4, 21, 74, 130
Holocaust memory, 231
Holocaust survivors, 214
homeland (Heimat), concept of, 16, 65–67
home visits, by SED functionaries, 136
homosexuality, 90–91, 163, 259n150, 261n179
Hoth, Gen. Hermann, 191
housing shortage, West German, 117, 119

impotence, male, 88, 124
informal networks, among families of MIAs/POWs, 29–33, 37, 240n46. See also families of MIAs/POWs
Innere Mission, 141
international politics, and issue of missing POWs, 193–96

Jarausch, Konrad, 14
Jaspers, Karl, 46
Jensch, Nikolaus, 77
Jewish experience, 34, 229–30
Jews, killing of, 3–4, 32. See also genocide; Holocaust
jobs: blue-collar, 118; white-collar, 118–19
Jordan, Rudolf, 215, 225
judiciary, West German, 157–58
Judt, Tony, 63

Kaiser, Jakob, 216
Kameradenschinder trials, West German, 154–67, 173–75, 207, 217
Kapp, Karl, 215
Keitel, Wilhelm, 35
Kesselring, Gen. Albert, 191
Kienlesberg transition camp, 66
Kiessling, Werner, 192
Kirchheimer, Otto, 166
Kirchliche Kriegshilfe (Catholic Church War Aid), 38–42, 106, 245n132
Klessmann, Christoph, 9
Knoch, Habbo, 46
Koch, Ilse, 155
Königswinter, 216
Korean War, 193, 295n101
Korfes, Dr. Otto, 129
Koselleck, Reinhart, 63
KPD (German Communist Party), 49–52, 181. See also SED (Socialist Unity Party)
Kuczynski, Jürgen, 127
Kühne, Thomas, 123
KVP (Kasernierte Volkspolizei), 146–48

labor market, and reabsorption of returnees, 117–19
labor regulation, East German (Arbeitslenkung), 148–49
"labor society," East German (Arbeitsgesellschaft), 148–51
Lagrou, Pieter, 69, 97
League of German Officers. See BdO

legal responsibility, for actions under captivity, 158
Lerner, Paul, 77
Lewke, Karl, 50–51
liberalization, in West Germany, 227
Liebe 47 (film), 53
Liebeneiner, Wolfgang, 53
Limburg, 187
Lindenberger, Thomas, 151

Maier, Charles, 174
malnutrition, 73
Malten, Hans, 77
Manstein, Gen. Erich von, 191
Marshall, T. H., 13
masculinity, 11–13, 94, 102, 145, 165, 229–30; antifascist, 129–30; and *Heimat* concept, 66–67; and image of "heroic" POW, 206–7, 210; and returnee health issues, 87–91. *See also* remasculinization
massacres, committed by Wehrmacht, 3
Matern, Hermann, 167
medical experiments, Nazi, 74–75, 84, 215, 255n38
medical profession: diagnostic categories, 76–87, 163–65; and health issues of last returnees, 213–14; therapeutic strategies of, 80–83, 89
"Mehlem Conversation," 112–13
memorabilia, commemorating POWs, 187
memory, 11–12; politics of, 154–67, 214–17, 226–31
memory studies, 9
men, and transition from war to postwar, 37. *See also* masculinity
men's circles, 107
Merker, Paul, 126, 135–36
Merridale, Catherine, 230
Merten, Hans, 112, 180, 182
MIAs, 19–20, 23–24, 179, 235n34; search for, 24–33, 41, 56–57, 183–85, 239n32, 241n60 (*see also* families of MIAs/POWs). *See also* POWs
Michel, Max, 214
Mielke, Erich, 218, 222
militarism, and masculinity, 12
military: East German, 146–48; West German, 114–16
military justice, 35–36, 207
military service, in POW trials, 165–66
mines and mining, 148, 281n139
Mitscherlich, Alexander, 76

modernity, problems of, 58
Moeller, Robert, 6, 60, 100, 207
Müller-Gangloff, Erich, 99
Müller-Hegemann, Dietfried, 93

Naimark, Norman, 130
National Committee for a Free Germany (NKFD), 23, 33–34, 36, 50, 59, 164
National Democratic Party (NDPD), 139
nationalism, 99, 105, 210–11. *See also* cultural values, German; *Heimat*, concept of
National Socialism, returnees' views of. *See* antifascism
National Volksarmee (NVA), 146–47
NATO (North Atlantic Treaty Organization), 203
Naumann, Klaus, 9, 211
Nazi Party membership, 22
Nazi regime, 25, 35; and Christian church organizations, 38–42; popular collaboration with, 31; response of to casualties, 21–22; and search for MIAs/POWs, 24–26. *See also* Germans, ordinary; war crime trials; war criminals
NDPD (National Democratic Party), 139
Neues Deutschland, 219, 221
Neumann, Vera, 123
neutral countries, as potential intermediaries between Nazi Germany and Soviet Union, 29
"new cultural history," 10
Niemöller, Martin, 182, 195
Niethammer, Lutz, 144, 200
NKFD (National Committee for a Free Germany), 23, 33–34, 36, 50, 59, 164
North Rhine-Westphalia, 109, 117; archive of (Düsseldorf-Kalkum), 282n2, 283n9
NVA (National Volksarmee), 146–47

OKW (Army High Command), 23
Ollenhauer, Erich, 216
Operation Barbarossa, 2–3
optimism, of returnees, 67–68
oral history, 119–20, 123–24, 142–43, 151, 235n42, 279n105, 306n25. *See also* Frankfurt Institute for Social Research

Panse, Friedrich, 78–81, 83, 256n54
Panzinger, Friedrich, 215
paranoia, of SED, 139–42, 168–71
party purges, in SED, 134

party workers, returnees as, 130–34, 136, 275n41
patriarchy, 122–24
Pavlov, Ivan Petrovic, 93
Penal Battalion 999, 171–72, 289n127
pension claims of returnees, 76, 78–81, 83, 86–87, 257n85. *See also* compensation of returnees
pension neurosis, 78–81
personality, pathological, in POW trials, 163–65
Peukert, Detlev, 30
Pfleiderer, Karl Georg, 195
philo-Semitism, 273n15
philo-Sovietism, 128–29, 133, 273n15
physicians, and diagnoses of returnees' health problems, 71–93, 214. *See also names of doctors*
Pieck, Wilhelm, 49, 61–62, 167, 197
poetry, returnee, 145
politics of memory, 226–31; East German, 228; West German, 154–67, 214–17, 227
Politkultur officers, 147
population movements, postwar, 44
postfascism, 9
post-traumatic stress disorder (PTSD), 73–74
postwar, concept of, 1–2, 7–10, 180–83, 204–9, 227–31
POW aid program, of SPD, 59
POW camps, Soviet, 130–32, 142, 155–56, 288n106
POW compensation law (1954), 111–12, 192, 212
POW repatriation, end of, 179–86
POWs, 4–5, 19–20, 23–24, 33–34, 48, 146–47, 206–7, 235n34, 238n17; antifascism among, 23–24; correspondence from, 25, 27–28, 41, 64, 184, 197, 199; and end of repatriation, 179–86; families' response to (*see* families of MIAs/POWs); missing, 179–96; numbers of, 179–80, 182–83; returning (*see* returnees); Russification of, 75–76, 255n31; search for, 24–33, 41, 56–57, 239n32, 241n60
POWs, Jewish, 3
POWs, Soviet, 3
POW studies, 4
POW trials (*Kameradenschinder* trials), 154–67, 173–75, 207, 217

POW trials, Soviet, 179
private sphere, 98, 120–25. *See also* family
privatization of war, 37, 124–25
"privilege of emergency," 156–61
Probst, Maria, 112
Protestant Academy, Bad Boll, 107
Protestant church: and acts of commemoration, 189–91; and "confession of guilt" of October 1945, 48. *See also* Christian churches
psychiatrists, and diagnoses of returnees' mental health problems, 71–93, 212–14. *See also names of individuals*
psychic trauma, 81–87
psychotherapy and psychoanalysis, 84–87, 260n168
PTSD (post-traumatic stress disorder), 73–74
purges, East German, 153, 167–75, 215

radio broadcasts, Soviet, 26–27
Rajik, László, 168
Ramcke, Herman Bernhard, 114
rape, 60, 65, 89, 130, 235n32, 261n182
Rauschelbach, Heinz-Harro, 83, 258n110
readjustment, of late returnees, 212–13. *See also* employment issues of returnees; health issues of returnees
rearmament, West German, 114–16, 211
rebirth, returnees' feelings of, 67–68
re-Christianization, 98–102, 106–9
recovery, expectations of, 78
recruitment, coercive, of East German returnees, 148–49
"red capos," 288n106
Red Crescent, and search for MIAs/POWs, 29
Red Cross, German, 183
redemption, Christian concept of, 42, 98–102
redemption narratives, 97–105, 126–28, 144, 228–30
reeducation programs, 130–32, 169–70, 173
refugees, from East to West, 143–44
refusal to fight, 35
Reich Insurance Office, pension ruling of 1926, 78
Reichmann, Josef, 114
Reich Security Main Office (RSHA), 25, 28, 34
"religious conversion" model, 273n10
remasculinization, 12–13, 98, 107, 122–24, 129–30, 237n79

remembrance. *See* commemoration, acts of repatriation, 44–46

resettlers, 135

resexualization, of dysfunctional returnees, 89–90

resistance groups. *See* White Rose

resistance myth, 97

responsibility. *See* guilt and responsibility, discourse of

return, time of, 118, 246n11

returnee (*Heimkehrer*), use of term, 16

returnee camps, church-run, 107

returnee conferences, 127–30, 170, 272n5

returnee diseases. *See* dystrophy; health issues of returnees; medical profession

returnee homes, church-run, 107, 122

returnee hospitals, 85, 155

Returnee Law (Heimkehrergesetz, FRG, March 1950), 110–11, 117, 192

returnee marriages, 121–24, 142, 209–10. *See also* families of MIAs/POWs; wives

returnee organizations: East German, 137–39; West German (*see* VdH)

returnee pilgrimages, 263n31

returnees, 1–2, 5–6, 13–14, 44–46, 57–58, 113–16, 119, 143–44, 192, 253n5; accusations of against other returnees, 155–56, 166–67, 283n16 (*see also* denunciation); antifascist, 127–34, 150; employment issues of, 116–20, 148–51 (*see also* unemployment); health issues of, 70–94, 118, 163–65, 212–14; homecoming experiences of, 63–69; homeless, 46, 122, 148, 281n139; iconography of, 99–102; and *Kameradenschinder* trials, 154–67; last, 203–4, 213; numbers of, 45, 246n13, 281n142; response of to antifascist integration, 142–45; response of to re-Christianization efforts, 108–9; and SED purges, 167–75; and upward social mobility, 149–51

"return to normalcy," 121–22

reunification, 209

RSHA (Reich Security Main Office), 25, 28, 34

rumors concerning MIAs/POWs, 27–30

Russification, of German POWs, 75–76, 255n31

Sachsenhausen, 183, 215, 217

sacrifice, Christian concept of, 40, 42

Schelsky, Helmut, 91

Schenck, Ernst Günter, 74, 254n25, 255n38

Schissler, Hanna, 123

Schivelbusch, Wolfgang, 235n40

Schmitz, Wilhelm, 82

Schöne, Dr. Christian, 31–33

Schörner, General, 207

Schubert, Wilhelm ("Pistol Schubert"), 215, 217

Schulte, Walter, 82–83

Schumacher, Kurt, 58–59, 181

Schwartz, Michael, 137

Scott, Joan, 12

screening of returnees, for service in Bundeswehr, 211–12

SD (Sicherheitsdienst), and search for MIAs/POWs, 31

secret camps (*Schweigelager*), myth of, 181–82, 223

secret service: East German (*see* Stasi); West German (*Verfassungsschutz*), 212

SED (Socialist Unity Party), 49, 134, 136–37, 168, 251n106; and acts of commemoration, 189–91; and antifascist returnees, 130–34; and discourse on guilt and responsibility, 49–52; and end of POW repatriation, 182–83; and last returnees, 218–25; and missing POWs, 196–202; paranoia of, 139–42, 168–71; as "party of the new type," 126, 133–34, 167; recruitment of returnees, 131–33, 274n37, 275n41; and returnee health issues, 91–94; and victimization narratives, 61–62; and women's committees, 135, 141, 276n64

self-criticism, postwar German, 46–52

self-referentiality, of German people, 31

sentences, in POW trials, 159

sex offenses, committed by returnees, 89

sexuality, 13

sexual violence. *See* rape

Seydlitz, Gen. Walter von, 23, 36, 207

"shell shock," 76

silent camps, Soviet, 185, 196

Slánsky, Rudolf, 172

Socialist Unity Party. *See* SED

social mobility, in East German workplace, 149–51

social services, 109–10; Christian churches and, 106–9, 141

Society for German-Soviet Friendship (GDSF), 127, 132, 143

soldiers: fallen, 40 (*see also* heroic death, Nazi cult of); former, 107, 147–48, 184; frontline, 34–36. *See also* MIAs; POWs; returnees; Wehrmacht
Sorge, Gustav ("Iron Gustav"), 215, 217
Soviet Administration for Prisoners of War and Internee Camps (GUPVI), 131
Sovietization of Eastern Europe, 167
Soviet Military Government Order No. 234, 150
Soviet soldiers, captured, 33–34
Soviet Union, 1–5; and information on German MIAs/POWs, 26–27; and last returnees, 203–4; "secret" POW camps, 181–82, 223; silent camps, 185, 196; as source of redemption, 128–29; treatment of German POWs, 33–34. *See also* returnees
SPD (Social Democratic Party), 58–60, 111–12, 215–17
special camps, Soviet-run, 296n112
sponsorship campaign, for homeless returnees, 122
SS (Schutzstaffel), 2. *See also* Armed SS; SD
Stalingrad, defeat of Sixth Army at, 19–20, 23
starvation experiments, Nazi, 74
Stasi (East German security police), 218–22, 304n124
state, East German: collapse of, 279n105. *See also* East Germany; SED
state, West German: and acts of commemoration, 187–93; citizen-making efforts of, 109–16; returnees' perceptions of, 113–16. *See also* government, West German; West Germany
"state fathers," 152
Steinbach, Peter, 157, 233n7
Stephan, Hans, 58–59
Stern, 155
Stock, Jean, 215–16
Stransky, Erwin, 89
Streckenbach, Bruno, 215
Strecker, General, 28, 241n55
Strecker, Hedwig, 28
suffering, Christian concept of, 101
suffering, German, 6–7, 52–53, 74, 230
surrender, voluntary, 35
survival, focus on, 97–98

Tagesspiegel (West Berlin), 47
TASS (Soviet news agency), 179

Thayer, Charles, 193
Theilmann, Fritz, 101
torture, 243n92
"totalitarian other," 164
tracing services, for missing POWs, 183–85, 292n34, 292n44
transition camps, 45–46, 61, 66, 94, 106, 131, 136, 139–40, 155, 204, 219, 246n12, 291n26
trauma, concept of, 230. *See also* psychic trauma
Turkey, German embassy in, 29
Two-Year Plan (GDR), 148–49, 167

Ulbricht, Walter, 146–47, 167, 204, 218
Ulm, 181
unemployment, 118, 212, 281n145
United Nations, and issue of missing POWs, 193–94
United States, and issue of missing POWs, 193–94

Vatican, and search for MIAs/POWs, 29
VdH (Association of Returnees and Family Members of POWs and MIAs), 86–87, 100–102, 110–16, 192, 195, 207, 258n116, 263n31, 266n87; and acts of commemoration, 187–93; Mehlem Program of 1955, 112–13; and POW trials, 158–59
VEBs (People-Owned Companies), 132
vegetative dystony, 86, 213
veterans' organizations. *See* VdH
Vetzlaff, Ulrich, 213
victim, postwar concept of, 42, 68–69
victimization, German discourse of, 6, 37, 42
victimization narratives, 64–65, 69, 102, 110, 120, 305n16; East German, 60–63; West German, 52–60, 62–63, 74–76
violence, active *vs.* passive experience of, 1, 233n5
Vischer, Ernst T., 73
Volksgemeinschaft, Nazi, 151, 193, 197
Volkspolizei. *See* KVP
Volkssolidarität (People's Solidarity), 135, 141
Vorwärts, 216

Waldheim trials, East German, 183, 218
war crimes, in POW trials, 161–62, 179
war crimes, Nazi, 154, 159, 286n63

war crime trials, 192, 215, 219, 227. *See also* POW trials
war criminals, 45, 154–55, 159, 247n23, 295n87; convicted, 191–93; missing POWs as, 181, 183, 198–99; returnees as, 113–14, 218–25
Warsaw Pact, 203
"war sentenced," 218
WAST (Wehrmachtsauskunftsstelle für Kriegsverluste und Kriegsgefangene), 24–25, 28
Wehrmacht, 3–4, 19–20, 35–37, 47, 115, 160; myth of "clean," 102, 165, 174; and socialization of soldiers, 133–34, 145, 147
Wehrmachtsauskunftsstelle für Kriegsverluste und Kriegsgefangene (WAST), 24–25, 28
Weiner, Amir, 230
Weitz, Heinrich, 195
West Berlin, as site of commemorative acts, 187
West Germany, 7–10, 140, 203, 206; and acts of commemoration, 186–93; and convicted war criminals, 191–93; and end of POW repatriations, 180–86; and integration of returnees, 97–125; and issue of missing POWs, 193–96; and *Kameradenschinder* trials, 154–67, 173–75; and last returnees, 204–17; and rearmament, 114–16, 211. *See also* government, West German; state, West German

White Rose, 30
Wierling, Dorothee, 152
wives: of missing POWs, 198, 223; of returnees, 89, 123–24, 188–89, 209, 212
Wollenberg, Erich, 122
women, 37–38, 62, 65, 67, 120, 149, 242n71; and acts of commemoration, 188–89; East German, 141–42; as returnees (*Heimkehrerinnen*), 16, 45, 60, 88, 129–30, 253n146, 259n124. *See also* rape; wives
women's committees, in East Germany, 135, 141, 276n64
working class: East German, 223–24; West German, 216
World War I, 71–73; mental health issues, 76–77, 79, 92
Wurm, Bishop, 57

"year of the returnee" (1948), 272n2
Young, Alan, 73–74
youth, West German, 125
Yugoslavia, returnees from, 169

Zaitlin, Jonathan, 201
Zeit, Die, 180, 209
Ziegenhagen, Kurt, 91, 168
ZPKK (Central Party Control Commission), and purges, 167–70
zur Nieden, Susanne, 242n71
ZVU (Central Administration for German Resettlers), 135–36

Lightning Source UK Ltd.
Milton Keynes UK
05 December 2009

147085UK00001B/7/P